# THE MANCHU WAY

三等侍衛克什克巴圖魯伍克什爾圖

預軍門選聯鏑致
書纏頭幾萬翩如
入盧達阿克蘇跰
將及膝鉛彈在背
至今未出

乾隆庚辰春御題并識
勒恭銘

# THE MANCHU WAY

*The Eight Banners
and Ethnic Identity in
Late Imperial China*

*Mark C. Elliott*

STANFORD UNIVERSITY PRESS
STANFORD, CALIFORNIA

Stanford University Press
Stanford, California

© 2001 by the Board of Trustees of the
Leland Stanford Junior University

Printed in the United States of America on acid-free,
archival-quality paper.

*Frontispiece. Portrait of Imperial Guard Uksiltu
(see Note on the Frontispiece, page 373)*

Library of Congress Cataloging-in-Publication Data

Elliott, Mark C.
  The Manchu way ; the eight banners and ethnic identity
in late imperial China / Mark C. Elliott.
        p.   cm.
  Includes bibliographical references and index.
    ISBN 0-8047-3606-5 (alk. paper) : ISBN 0-8047-4684-2 (pbk: alk. paper)
    1. Manchus—Ethnic identity—History—17th century.
2. Manchus—Ethnic identity—History—18th century.
I. Title: Eight banners and ethnic identity in late imperial
China.   II. Title.
DS731.M35 E55    2001
951.004'941—dc21                                     00-064087

Original Printing 2001

Last figure below indicates year of this printing:
10    09

Designed by Janet Wood
Typeset by James P. Brommer in 10/14 Sabon

## FOR ANNA

Bo nad wszystkie ziem branki milsze Laszki kochanki,
    Wesolutkie jak młode koteczki
Lice bielsze od mleka, z czarną rzęsą powieka,
    Oczy błyszczą się jak dwie gwiazdeczki.

                    —*Mickiewicz, "Trzech Budrysów" (1829)*

# CONTENTS

LIST OF MAPS AND FIGURES

*Maps*

*Figures*

## TABLES

Open any book about China under the Qing and chances are good one will come upon mention of the dynasty's founders, the Manchus, a non-Han people who once dwelt in what is now China's northeastern frontier. The Manchus ruled China from 1644 to 1912, and figure in almost any discussion of Chinese history, especially political history, during this period. One of the most widely used textbooks of modern Chinese history—the one that provided me with my first introduction to the subject in college—speaks of Manchu rule as a "shaping force" that "generated a strong sense of nationalistic-racial consciousness among Chinese."[1] This textbook goes on to characterize the Manchus as being preoccupied with three things: securing legitimacy and support from the majority Han Chinese, preserving their own ethnic identity, and achieving military conquest. A more recent authoritative text confirms the same basic picture: the Manchus needed to win and retain the cooperation of Chinese soldiers and officials, to guard their ancestral institutions, and to consolidate the empire's ("China's") geographical limits.[2] The significance of the Qing as a period of "alien" rule is thus beyond dispute.

For all that is acknowledged to be important about them, however, the Manchus as a group remain relatively unstudied, at least in English.[3] By providing a historical description of the development of Manchu institutions and identity, I hope to address a major gap in our knowledge of this "shaping force" of modern Chinese history. My primary concern is to trace the development of the Eight Banners, the Manchus' trademark system of social and military organization, and the parallel evolution of Manchu identity in the seventeenth and eighteenth centuries, thereby providing a perspective on rule in late imperial China that is less "sinocentric," less predicated on an assumption of the all-encompassing centrality of Chinese civilization and less structured around a deterministic narrative of the rise of the Chinese na-

*less sinucentric*

xiii

tion. My other aim in this book is to demonstrate that ethnicity has an important role to play in historical analysis; that it is neither an exclusively modern concern nor a peripheral one, but leads, like gender history, from the margins right to the center of historical issues.

Three basic propositions lie at the heart of this study. The first is that Qing rule depended not only on the Manchu acceptance of Chinese political norms—sometimes thought of as "Confucian" legitimacy—and the recognition of that fact by Chinese literati, but also on the maintenance of lines of difference between the majority Han Chinese and the Manchu conquest group, including but not limited to the imperial house. I believe that processes both of acculturation (often called "sinicization" in the Chinese context) *and* of differentiation mattered in sustaining Manchu minority rule, and that, contrary to much written history, the Manchus, though highly acculturated, were never as a group assimilated into Chinese society in the Qing. Instead of framing Qing rule solely in terms of Manchu success in adopting Chinese methods of government—the most common approach to date—I look at the positive contribution to Manchu rule represented by their failure to completely break down the boundaries that separated them from the Han Chinese.

The second proposition is that certain advances made in anthropology since the 1970s regarding what has come to be called "ethnicity" can help explain the dynamics of group identity in complex societies, and, unlike the tired sinicization formula, do justice to the intricacies of the Manchus' place in Qing China. This new thinking permits us to talk not just about culture, but also about political, economic, psychological, and institutional factors that affect identity formation and boundary maintenance. A critical formulation of ethnicity, because it rejects group identities as being somehow essential or "primordial" and sees them instead as contingent and malleable, is helpful in conceptualizing the factors related to Manchus and "Manchuness"—categories which, as we shall see, were problematic and shifting. This approach puts us in a better position to appreciate how Manchu identity was constructed, how it was reinforced, and how it changed.

In taking this step, and particularly in linking Manchu identity to the institution of the Eight Banners, I attempt to restore a connection that has been obscured in modern historical accounts, but which, I believe, mattered greatly in the Qing. One difficulty in bringing this picture into focus is that ethnic difference under the Manchus, unlike ethnicity in the contemporary world, was not a topic for open discussion. Not that ethnic discourse was new in Qing China—it grew out of a tradition that dated from at least the Song, with roots that stretched back to the pre-Qin period. However, under Manchu rule, this issue was more politically charged than it had been in centuries. Neither the Manchus nor the Han Chinese could afford to invoke it too overtly or self-consciously without inviting serious consequences: exile or capital punishment (for the Han), delegitimation and rebellion (for the Manchus). Therefore, such discourse is revealed in the sources only indirectly. A second difficulty is that historians are uncomfortable dealing with ethnicity, a slippery category if ever there was one. Many see it as too unstable a concept for analysis or as too closely tied to explicitly modern social and political forms to be useful for thinking about the premodern era. Yet—and this is what led me to the study of the Manchus in the first place—if an explanation of the success of Manchu rule in China is to reflect the full complexity of the Qing situation, it must somehow account for *la différence Mandchoue.*

The third proposition underlying this book is that to gain a fuller understanding of the Qing imperial enterprise—why the Manchus took over, how they saw their empire, their people, and their fate—it is absolutely crucial that we examine what they wrote about themselves *in their own language.* Accordingly, the primary sources central to this study are Manchu-language documents, mainly palace memorials, housed in the First Historical Archives of China in Beijing. During the course of two research trips to the archives, for ten months in 1990 and for just under one month in 1995, I examined several thousand Manchu palace memorials from the first century and a half of Qing rule and in the end collected several hundred that have proved indispensable in reconstructing the story presented in these pages. Long neglected by scholars who (wrongly) assumed that they merely duplicated information more readily accessible in Chinese-language documents, many of these materials were still in the yellow paper wrappers in which Qing-period archivists had placed them. In some ways this very neglect was a blessing, as I was able to examine large numbers of materials before any modern archivist had a chance to "order" them. Documents I might not have looked at had they been separately categorized (notably greetings memorials) I was instead forced to read, often with real profit. As the reader will discover, the picture of the Qing that emerges when one has access to Manchu sources differs markedly from the one drawn from Chinese sources. Given the concerns of this study, Manchu-language documents are particularly important because they enable us to hear Manchu voices and to interrogate what has up to now been mostly an ethnic silence in Chinese-language materials.

While Manchu palace memorials are at the heart of the book, I have made use of other sorts of Manchu documents, too, including record books (*shishu*), genealogies, dictionaries, and miscellaneous archives such as draft inscriptions, results of archery contests, and so on. I have also relied on the Manchu versions of materials published during the Qing, such as the *Comprehensive History of the Eight Banners*, collections of memorials on banner affairs, the *Comprehensive Genealogy of Eight Banner Manchu Clans*, and the *Collected Institutes of the Qing*, although for the most part citations to these sources are to their Chinese versions. For the very early Qing, I have made use of key published Manchu sources such as the *Old Manchu Archives*, as well as the translated records from the Inner Historical Office published in Chinese as *Neiguoshiyuan Manwen dang'an yibian*. Of course, Manchu-language documents are vast in number—they are estimated to constitute about one-fifth of the total Qing archives (roughly ten million items), most of which are in Chinese—and this book makes use of only a tiny fraction of them.[4] The present work is thus but a first step toward reconciling the images presented by materials in these two very different languages. It is my hope that other students of the Qing will find inspiration here to take up the study of Manchu.

In my effort to include previously untouched Manchu sources I have not neglected, I hope, Chinese-language materials. Here again, I have concentrated on what was available in the palace memorial collections for the early Qing, the bulk of which have been published, though I also examined a small number of unpublished palace and routine memorials in Chinese. Probably the single most valuable Chinese source to me has been the Qing *Veritable Records,* but I have also found precious material in official compendia, local gazetteers, and in Chinese-language "random jottings" literature (*biji*). Other very useful materials have been Western-language accounts (mostly in English and French) from the seventeenth, eighteenth, and nineteenth centuries, as well as similar accounts left by Korean travelers, which I have read in their Chinese and Japanese translations. Fuller information on all these materials may be found in the bibliography.

This book consists of an introduction, eight chapters, and a conclusion. The Introduction sets out the reasons I believe that Manchu history is important and some problems that arise in the interpretation of that history, and details the ways in which the approach in this book departs from earlier analyses, especially in its use of the concepts of ethnicity and the connection it establishes between institutions and identity.

The main narrative is divided into three parts. Part I consists of three chapters that sketch the banner system's beginnings and its growth as a political and ethnic structure. Chapter 1 describes the origins of the Manchus, the foundation of the banner system, and the different hierarchies and populations within the banner system, looking particularly at the operation of ethnic categories. It shows how, apart from the place of the Eight Banners in Manchu military and political organization, this institution helped from the start to articulate a common Manchu ethnic identity, a role that grew in importance during the long Qing peace. Chapter 2 discusses the Manchu occupation of China and the establishment of so-called Manchu cities in Beijing and in garrisons around the country. This section focuses on the living arrangements of Manchus and others in the banners, modeled on the principle of separate residence, or "Manchu apartheid," and seeks to establish the background for the Manchu experience in China. I turn to consider the management of the Eight Banners and the place of the Manchu elite in Qing government in Chapter 3, where I elaborate on the ways in which the banner system functioned as an instrument for building the state and, simultaneously, reinforcing ethnic distinctions. By looking at the relationship between the emperor and his servants, I also suggest ways in which being a Manchu official differed from being a Han Chinese official.

Part II, also in three chapters, examines in more detail the various ways in which belonging to the Eight Banners entailed a mode of life that differed from the life of Han Chinese and that ultimately made "banner people" out of the Manchus. I lay out some of the fundamental aspects of banner life in Chapter 4, looking first at the bannerman's duties and burdens, and then at the significant economic, legal, and social privileges that people in the banners enjoyed as members of the conquest caste. Chapter 5 explores the relationship between the Manchus and the Han Chinese, elucidating the ideology of ethnic relations in the Qing and the way this played out in society and politics. I expand upon another crucial aspect of the place of Manchus in Chinese society in Chapter 6, examining their otherness from two angles: the distinctiveness of Manchu cultural practice and the distinctiveness of the concepts of "home" for those under the banners. I show how the court's eventual recognition that Manchu cities in the provinces were not just "temporary assignments" signaled a general reevaluation of the perception of the Manchu diaspora and marked a major turning point in the history of that diaspora, especially for bannermen in the provinces.

The two chapters of Part III examine the parallel transformation of Manchu identity and institutions that began under the Yongzheng emperor in the 1720s, and investigate key aspects of Manchu cultural and social history through the Yongzheng and Qianlong reigns. I examine the process of Manchu acculturation in Chapter 7, a discussion of the problems Manchus at court and in the provinces faced in coping with the deterioration of what were held to be the "old ways" of the Manchus: martial skills, frugal habits, and speaking Manchu. I pursue the theme of crisis to its conclusion in Chapter 8, first examining the staggering financial burden represented by the Eight Banners, then exploring the extent and cause of poverty within the banner system, which, like the crisis affecting traditional Manchu cultural practices, threatened to undermine traditional Manchu institutions. I then show how, by tying Manchu identity even more closely with banner status, new definitions of household status categories eased the institutional crisis in the banners. I frame this as the evolution of Manchus into banner people and of banner people as Manchus, a redefinition of Manchu identity that was less the product of elite political imperatives and more the result of distinctions upheld by institutional boundaries.

In the Conclusion, I summarize these developments to argue that practice ultimately mattered more than ideology, and that even with the waning of many of the obvious cultural markers of Manchuness, a coherent Manchu ethnic identity persisted, thanks largely to the survival of the banner system. Following a brief discussion of the interconnectedness of institutions and identity in a comparative context, I end the book with some thoughts on the larger significance of Manchu rule for the history of modern China.

In the many years of research, writing, and rewriting that went into this book, I have incurred a humbling share of debts, which it is my pleasure and privilege at long last to acknowledge. First thanks go to my teacher and mentor, Frederic Wakeman, Jr., who, having just completed one "great enterprise," provided me unfailing encouragement as I worked to complete my own. I am immeasurably indebted as well to Beatrice Bartlett, for sharing with me her knowledge of and enthusiasm for the Qing archives; to James

Bosson, who taught me Manchu and initiated me into the field of Altaic studies; and to David Keightley, whose model as a scholar and a teacher I keep always before me. My first attempt to wrangle with the issues raised in this book came in a graduate seminar taught by Jonathan Spence. I owe a special debt of gratitude to him as my first teacher of Chinese history, and to Vivien Lu, my first teacher of Chinese language, for planting in me the seeds of a lifelong interest. I would like to give special thanks also to Deborah Davis and Robert Geyer for their encouragement at an important time early in my career.

During the initial research for this book I spent an extended period in Japan, where I benefited immensely from the tutelage of Okada Hidehiro, whose unworthy *deshi* I am proud to call myself. Among other things, he introduced me to the riches of the Tōyō Bunko, where I was also extremely fortunate to be able to join the members of the Seminar on Manchu History in their meetings. To Kanda Nobuo, Matsumura Jun, Hosoya Yoshio, Nakami Tatsuo, Katō Naoto, Ishibashi Takao, and all the members of this group who welcomed me, provided every assistance, and invited me into their lives and homes, I remain profoundly grateful. My appreciation goes as well to Hamashita Takeshi, whose willingness to assist yet another American graduate student gave me full access to the wonderful collection at the Oriental Institute Library, Tokyo University.

In China, my gratitude goes first to two senior scholars, Wei Qingyuan of People's University and Wang Zhonghan of the Central Minorities Institute (now Central Minorities University), whose support in the early stages of this project was so crucial. Through them I was able to make the most of my limited time in the archives, and also to make the acquaintance of many wonderful people. Foremost among these is Ding Yizhuang, of the Chinese Academy of Social Sciences, with whom I have spent many enjoyable hours discussing the problems of the Manchus over the years; I consider myself extremely fortunate to have been able to share this interest with such an unselfish and patient *xuejie*. Many thanks also to Cheng Chongde, Guo Chengkang, Hua Li, Liu Xiaomeng, and especially Chuang Chi-fa of the National Palace Museum, Taipei, and Xie Zhaohua of the Liaoning Academy of Social Sciences, for their generous time and assistance.

James Lee and Ding Yizhuang read the entire manuscript in a penultimate draft; for their detailed and mercilessly honest comments and criticism, and those of anonymous referees, I am deeply grateful. Others who have commented on the manuscript at various stages include R. Bin Wong, Okada Hidehiro, Joanna Waley-Cohen, Beatrice Bartlett, Joseph Esherick, Joan Judge, and Gertraude Roth-Li. My thanks to them and to participants in forums at the University of California at Los Angeles, the University of Washington, and Dartmouth College, where parts of this work have been presented. This book is much, much better because of their contributions. Thanks also to Zhang Li, Shao Dan, and Nancy Oakes for very capable research assistance. Of course, I take full responsibility for the views expressed here, and for any errors or misattributions.

The research for this book was made possible by the generous support from the Joint Committee on Chinese Studies of the American Council of Learned Societies and the Social Science Research Council; the Ministry of Education of Japan; the Committee on Scholarly Communication with China; the Mabelle McLeod Lewis Foundation; and the Interdisciplinary Humanities Center at the University of California, Santa Barbara. My heartfelt thanks to them and to the dedicated people at the following libraries and institutions: the Institute for the Study of Languages and Cultures of Asia and Africa at Tokyo University of Foreign Studies; the Tōyō Bunko; the Oriental Institute Library, Tokyo University; Keiō University Library; Seikado Bunko; National Diet Library, Tokyo; National Central Library, Taipei; People's University of China; the libraries at the University of California campuses at Berkeley and Los Angeles; the University of Michigan Library; the Royal Ontario Museum; and the Library of Congress. Cathy Chiu and Peter Pang, East Asia librarians at the University of California, Santa Barbara, deserve particular recognition for going out of their way to help. For allowing me to use their priceless collections, I reserve special appreciation for the National Palace Museum Archives, Taipei; the Third Historical Archives of China, Shenyang; and most of all, the First Historical Archives of China, Beijing, where Qin Guojing, Liu Zhongying, Yin Shumei, and Zhu Shuyuan, along with Qu Liusheng, Wu Yuanfeng, and the other members of the Manchu department all extended invaluable assistance.

Finally, for their companionship and sustained interest in my work I want to say thank you to Timothy Brook, Joshua Fogel, Blaine Gaustad, James Hevia, Dorothy Ko, Fredrik Logevall, Melissa Macauley, James Millward, Donald Sutton, and Stephen West. In addition, my special gratitude goes to Bin Wong and James Lee for their many years of encouragement and friendship. John Finlay very kindly arranged a meeting with Mrs. Dora Wong of

New York City, who was most gracious in opening her collection of Qing paintings and in permitting me to use the image that appears on the dust jacket. I am also indebted to the infinitely patient Dottie McLaren, who created the maps and figures, and to the helpful people at Stanford University Press: Muriel Bell, Kate Washington, Elizabeth Berg, and Andrew Frisardi. Lastly, I am happy to acknowledge here the loving indulgence of Rena, my sisters, and above all, my mother. They can now see what I have been up to all this time.

For Anna and Thomas, my most faithful critics, who gave me the time, the patience, and the inspiration, thanks are not enough.

M.C.E.
Santa Barbara/Tokyo, May 1999–May 2000

Chinese words and names are transcribed according to the pinyin system of romanization. Chinese and Japanese names are given in the traditional order: surname first and given name last. Manchu words and names are transcribed according to the Möllendorff system, as explicated in *A Manchu Grammar* (Shanghai, 1892). Manchu genitive *i* is written together when the orthography justifies it (as when it modifies a word ending in a vowel); otherwise it is joined with a hyphen. For example, *gūsai niyalma* (banner person), but *meiren-i janggin* (lieutenant general). Manchu names have as a rule been transcribed from their original forms. Where the Manchu name is uncertain because it has been derived from its form in Chinese characters, or when someone is best known by that form of his name, the name is followed by the Chinese form in brackets, e.g., Hešeo [He-shou], Agūi [A-gui]. Certain Manchu names have been preserved in their Chinese forms. These names are written using pinyin and are hyphenated, e.g., Zhao-lian, A-li-ma.

Attention is called to the different pronunciations assigned the letter *c* in the pinyin system, where it is pronounced like *ts*, and in the Möllendorff system, where it is pronounced like *ch* (in pinyin the comparable sound is written with a *q*). Also, Manchu *š* is read *sh* (as is *s* before *i*) and *g* is always hard, as in the word *guitar*.

All ages are given in *sui*, according to the Chinese usage. The rule of thumb is to subtract one when calculating the age in the Western style.

# QING REIGN PERIODS

| | |
|---|---|
| Tianming 天命 /Abkai fulingga[5] | 1616–1626 |
| Tiancong 天聰 /Abkai sure[6] | 1627–1635 |
| Chongde 崇德 /Wesihun erdemungge[7] | 1636–1643 |
| Shunzhi 順治 /Ijishūn dasan | 1644–1661 |
| Kangxi 康熙 /Elhe taifin | 1662–1722 |
| Yongzheng 雍正 /Hūwaliyasun tob | 1723–1735 |
| Qianlong 乾隆 /Abkai wehiyehe | 1736–1795 |
| Jiaqing 嘉慶 /Saicungga fengšen | 1796–1820 |
| Daoguang 道光 /Doro eldengge | 1821–1850 |
| Xianfeng 咸豐 /Gubci elgiyengge | 1851–1861 |
| Tongzhi 同治 /Yooningga dasan | 1862–1874 |
| Guangxu 光緒 /Badarangga doro | 1875–1908 |
| Xuantong 宣統 /Gehungge yoso | 1909–1911 |

Strong from the cradle, of a sturdy brood,
We bear our newborn infants to the flood;
There bathed amid the streams our boys we hold,
With winter hardened and inured to cold.
They wake before the day to range the wood,
Kill ere they eat, nor taste unconquered food.
No sports but what belong to war they know:
To break the stubborn colt, to bend the bow
Our youth of labor patient earn their bread;
Hardly they work, with frugal diet fed.
From plows and harrows sent to seek renown,
They fight in fields and storm the shaken town.
No part of life from toils of war is free,
No change in age or difference in degree.

. . .

Even time, that changes all, yet changes us in vain—
The body, not the mind—nor can control
The immortal vigor, or abate the soul.
Our helms defend the young, disguise the gray;
We live by plunder and delight in prey.

—*Virgil,* The Aeneid, *Book 9, trans. John Dryden (1685)*

# The Problem with the Manchus

Friday, May 27, 1644, marked China's Hastings. On that day, one hundred and fifty miles east of Beijing, at the Shanhai Pass where the Great Wall meets the sea, three armies met. One was led by the rebel Li Zicheng, known to his followers as the Dashing King. Just the month before, Li had dethroned the Chinese Ming emperor (who then hanged himself), laid claim to the capital's magnificent palaces, and proclaimed himself head of a dynasty he named the Shun. Now at the height of his power, Li Zicheng knew as he rode to battle with his army of 60,000 men that they would be fighting 100,000 of the late emperor's soldiers, led by the redoubtable Wu Sangui. But the rebel did not know that the Ming general had two days earlier recruited outside help from the Manchus, founders of the upstart Qing dynasty. This new alliance between Wu and his erstwhile foes, 120,000 strong, would spell doom for the Dashing King, and also seal the fate of the unfortunate Ming, Wu's avowed cause. Manchu warriors, light of armor and true of aim, were feared like no others. The military prowess of their horsemen, combined with political and technological support from Chinese advisors, had enabled Qing leaders in just two generations to build a shaky confederation of border tribes into a powerful state with imperial pretensions. Already the Manchus had taken control of what once had been the northeastern territories of the Ming empire. At the end of the day on May 27 the field below Shanhaiguan, gateway to the Central Plain, would belong to them.

Having cut his hair to conform to Manchu style, on May 26 Wu issued instructions for each soldier to sew a piece of white cloth to the back of his armor.[1] Wu's men were to lead the attack, and these cloth patches would distinguish them from the other Chinese army (Li Zicheng's) once Qing troops, consisting of Manchus, Mongols, and "turncoat" Han Chinese, entered the battle. At sunrise the next day Wu ordered an advance on the rebel positions.

Li Zicheng's army stubbornly held its ground as wave after wave of Wu's best troops broke against the Shun lines. The slaughter continued for several hours, and by afternoon, Chinese troops on both sides were severely weakened. Then, from the west the wind began to blow fiercely across the battlefield, filling the sky with yellow sand and temporarily blinding men and horses alike. The Manchus seized the moment. Dorgon, the Qing commander and regent for the six-year-old khan, sent his vaunted cavalry into the fray, attacking the flank of Li's army. The scene bore an uncanny resemblance to the dramatic battle described at the opening of China's greatest historical novel, *Three Kingdoms*: "The next day, with banners waving and drums rolling, Zhang Bao arrived in force. Xuande rode out to face him. As the soldiers prepared to engage in battle, Bao used his powers and a storm sprang up as before. Sand and stones went flying, and a murky mist packed with men and horses began to descend from the sky."[2] The Shun soldiers, terrified by the unexpected appearance of hosts of mounted "Tartar" bowmen, panicked and fled, tripping over bodies as they scattered. The Manchu conquest of China had begun.

With his own forces decimated, Wu Sangui could only follow along as Dorgon led the victorious Qing army forward to Beijing, which they entered on June 5 without a fight. People expecting to see the triumphant Ming army no doubt stared in curious amazement at the shaved foreheads and dangling queues of the Manchu soldiers riding by, daggers at their waists and short recurve bows of horn and wood by their sides. The harsh, guttural sounds of their language somehow intensified the occupiers' fierce appearance. Still, they exhibited more restraint than had Li Zicheng and the tattered remains of his army when they returned in disarray from Shanhaiguan to Beijing. For five days the rebels had run amok, sacking the Ming capital and murdering its inhabitants before again fleeing west from the approaching Qing forces (they would be caught within a year). Fires set by Li Zicheng when he abandoned the palace he had so briefly possessed were still smoldering as amid the ruins Dorgon acclaimed his young nephew emperor of China.

ETHNIC SOVEREIGNTY AND 'PAX MANJURICA'

As unexpected as the Manchus' sudden appearance on the streets of Beijing was, their successful consolidation of power was in some ways even more surprising, not least to themselves. Who in 1644 would dare have predicted that Manchu emperors would continue to rule until 1912? That they did presents the historian with a number of interesting problems. One of the most basic of these is what might be called the "minority-rule question": the delicate matter of how the Manchus—who were outnumbered by the Chinese by about three hundred and fifty to one—managed to conquer China in the first place and then go on to rule for nearly three hundred years.[3] As Guo Moruo once commented, "That the Qing people entered China and ruled it for over two hundred years is truly a curious thing."[4] Related to this is another question, which asks what it mattered that Manchus, a Tungusic people distinct from the Han Chinese, ruled during this crucial phase of China's history, and *not* the Chinese themselves.

The usual answer to the first problem is that the Manchus maintained their position thanks to their sponsorship of neo-Confucian (read "civilized") norms of government, which won them the support of the wealthy, lettered Chinese elite that was essential to their political survival. As for the second problem—what I will call the "Manchu question"—the accommodation between the Manchu conquerors and their Chinese subjects, secured by the 1680s, has led in turn to the general conclusion that the Manchus became wholly assimilated into Chinese society and that it therefore did not matter much in the end that the Qing was a Manchu dynasty.

In explaining some of the reasons for Manchu success, this book attempts to weave together the heretofore largely separate strands of "Qing history" and "Manchu history." In so doing, it offers an alternative to the usual explanations of the significance of Manchu rule: I believe that the Qing dynastic enterprise depended both on Manchu ability to adapt to Chinese political traditions *and* on their ability to maintain a separate identity. That is to say, the Qing claim to rule, quite apart from its Confucianesque qualifications, rested upon Manchu domination as a separate people in a sense that transcended either the narrow interests of the ruling family or simple considerations of Manchu military dominance over the Chinese (though this was not unimportant, to be sure). Manchu difference carried significant political weight, and the tension characterizing Manchu-Han relations was an inherent, permanent feature of the Qing order. The old proverb thus had it only partly right: if it was true that the empire could be won, but not ruled, from horseback, it was just as true that the Manchus could never afford to stray very far from their horses once they dismounted. Maintaining the bal-

ance between these poles of legitimation was no easy matter; this book offers some new ways to think about how it was accomplished.

The idea of a dual foundation of Qing rule is not wholly new, nor is it
mine alone. In his 1990 study of the Qianlong era, Philip Kuhn captured the
problem this way:

> The rhetoric employed by the Manchu rulers displayed both the
> cosmopolitanism of the universal empire and the narrow defensiveness
> of the ethnic minority. As a minority people ruling a great empire, the
> Manchu monarchy had to have it both ways: they had to express their
> supremacy in both a cosmopolitan mode and an ethnic mode. Both were
> needed to solve the regime's basic problem: how to rule the universal
> empire as a legitimate dynastic house, and still preserve the coherence
> and élan of the conquest elite.[5]

The formulation here of "cosmopolitan" and "ethnic" modes of rule (or
"rhetorical arenas") is provocative: for Kuhn, cosmopolitanism revolved
around the sponsorship of "generally accepted norms of virtue and culture"
(i.e., neo-Confucian political and cultural ideals) while "militant ethnicity"
emphasized the preservation and celebration of special Manchu qualities.
We may assume that the former was required to win over the Chinese
scholar-elite, but it remains somewhat unclear what the "celebration of special Manchu qualities" provided the dynasty that cosmopolitanism did not,
and precisely why it was the Manchus needed to "preserve the coherence
and élan of the conquest elite."

I would like to propose that we think of this second mode of Qing rule as
objectifying a separate sort of legitimating (or empowering) authority, what
I will call "ethnic sovereignty,"[6] a term that refers to three interrelated dynamics. Most broadly, ethnic sovereignty refers to the special position of the
Manchu emperor at the apex of a universal empire composed of multiple hierarchies of lordship based on differing types of authority. This pattern of
emperorship was found throughout Central Asia and the Manchus found it
congenial in the creation of their own China-based regime.[7] In the Qing,
some of these hierarchies were Chinese, while others were Inner Asian (Manchu, Mongolian, Tibetan, Turkic). We thus find the early Manchu emperors
striking a number of poses, each equally "authentic" yet grounded in distinct
sources of authority, addressing different imperial constituencies. It is not my
wish to enter the debate over the nature of Qing imperial ideology—whether
the emperor "encompassed" the domains of other lords within his own,[8] or

whether the emperorship was an "integrating center,"[9] a set of "simultane-ities."[10] The point is that only in the person of a *Manchu* emperor could these multiple authorities be represented, for he straddled the differences be-tween hierarchies in a way that a Chinese emperor could not, at least not af-ter the appearance of protonationalist thinking in the Song.[11] Qing univer-salism—which comprehended Confucian cosmopolitanism—thus required the Manchus to continue to identify themselves as Manchus, and to be iden-tified as such by others. From this perspective, the empire of the Qing was truly a Manchu empire, not a Chinese one: *pax Manjurica*, not *pax Sinica*.

The second and third dynamics of ethnic sovereignty I understand in terms of Manchu domination over China proper, which, after all, was the economic foundation of the empire.[12] Here the argument put forward by Karl Wittfogel and Feng Chia-sheng regarding group cohesion of non-Han "conquest" regimes is instrumental. In their famous 1949 history of the Liao, Wittfogel and Feng—who were more interested in what they were care-ful to call the "acculturation process" than in agendas of putative assimila-tion—asked: *Did the Chinese ever absorb their conquerors as long as the conditions of conquest and political separation persisted?*[13] Their answer was in the negative. This led to a hypothesis of "limited assimilation" under the Liao (907–1125), Jin (1115–1234), Yuan (1215–1368), and Qing, which held that, to the degree these regimes maintained their ethnic integrity they could expect to retain power in their own hands. The idea here is that alien conquest produced a situation whereby greater distance and fear obtained between ruler and ruled than was the case with Han imperial families. On the one hand, non-Han groups who embraced warrior values and a martial culture relied not just on force, but on a climate of fear, to overwhelm rivals and to impose a new political order. Part of what made them masters of the realm was their assertion of the superiority of military (*wu*) over literary (*wen*) values and the arrogation to themselves of the right to rule on that ba-sis. On the other hand, these same groups feared being overwhelmed them-selves by the more advanced culture and superior numbers of the Han, and so sought ways to preserve their distinctiveness. Part of that effort was put into sustaining earlier cultural norms; another part went into maintaining lines of separation between conquest and conquered populations.

I am suggesting, then, that in the late imperial period (i.e., from the Song on), to the extent that the link between identity and power was explicitly or implicitly articulated through these three dynamics—maintaining the unity of the larger empire, instilling fear in the Han, and preserving the integrity of the conquest people—"ethnic sovereignty" mattered in the ability of non-Han groups like the Manchus to maintain control. To that degree also we must consider ethnicity in writing the histories of the dynasties established by those peoples. This proposition would seem to be supported by evidence from the Inner Asian historical context. As Joseph Fletcher once pointed out, interaction among groups on the steppes of Inner Asia "promoted the idea of a common ethnicity and social identity" which influenced the growth of "supratribal polities."[14] As much was borne out in Wittfogel and Feng's study of the Liao and is echoed in a perceptive essay by Herbert Franke on the conquest dynasties, in which he compares the development of Chinese-style structures with the tendency to retain "tribal" structures, "mechanisms . . . which worked . . . toward preserving the existing nationalities and toward organizing government according to ethnicity," particularly in the legal system.[15]

Maintaining differentiation between conqueror and conquered—which I will take as the primary sense of ethnic sovereignty—was thus essential to the vitality of all Inner Asian dynasties. This is supported, for instance, by Hok-lam Chan's work on legitimation during the Jin dynasty, when extensive debates were held on the nature of legitimacy. As Chan shows, while champions of Chinese-style legitimacy (Ch *zhengtong*)[16] won out in the end, they were vigorously opposed by "nativist" ministers and even by some emperors, whose concerns for the future of Jurchen rule were quite clearly tied to the decline of native traditions.[17] Also in connection with the Jin, Peter Bol has commented that because the Jurchens were a "conquering minority it was clearly in their political interest to remain distinct." Why? Bol explained, "In Chin, after all, power and privilege were distributed in the first place along ethnic lines. For the Jurchens to forsake a distinct political identity would have entailed accepting other criteria for the distribution of privileges and threatened the Jurchen elite."[18] I would argue that many of the same considerations applied also during the Qing: that shedding a distinct identity would have spelled disaster for the Manchus, and that Manchu rule was colored by an awareness of that fact. This argument picks up a theme developed most fully by prewar Japanese scholars, who interpreted the division between conqueror and conquered as a key strategy of the "other-nationality rule" (*iminzoku tōchi*) implemented by the Manchus. In their view, the three "conservative characteristics" of Qing rule all had to do with the prevention of assimilation and the concentration of power in Manchu hands. As Momose Hiromu wrote:

> 1. What sorts of efforts did the Qing make to obtain the cohesion of the Manchus among the Han ruling class?
> 2. Even though they did not change them fundamentally, what particular features emerged in Manchu implementation of control policies over the Han ruling class newly reconstituted by them?
> 3. How was the fusion of the Qing Eight Banners system with Han society prevented?[19]

Though such a stance was almost certainly influenced by contemporary political considerations (the Japanese themselves essaying an updated form of other-nationality rule), as we learn more about the Qing and the Manchus, it is an approach we cannot afford to exclude, especially for what it suggests about the importance of the Eight Banners.

In a comparative context, ethnic sovereignty can be seen as an important political factor in other cases of rule by a conquest group, particularly when that group is in the minority and the conquered are in the majority. Normans in England, Mongols in Russia, British in India, Turks in Byzantium, and Afrikaners in South Africa all relied on ethnic differentiation between themselves and their subject populations as a means of control. All endeavored, with varying success and through various means, to maintain those differences and thereby uphold the boundaries between ruler and ruled.[20] Of course, in virtually all monarchical systems the differentiation between ruler and ruled is an important one, since it helps to guarantee dynastic stability. Ethnic sovereignty, it may be ventured, is a special case in which that differentiation is made along ethnic lines.[21] In China, one might further argue, a non-Han ruling family which had come to power through conquest and was constantly on its guard in an alien, or at least not wholly native environment, might, because of this very vigilance, maintain its dedication longer and thus rule more effectively. John Fairbank raised this possibility twenty-five years ago in the following terms:

> The Chinese needed stable ruling dynasties, families that could hold power and preserve peace and order over a long period. This was a specialized function that depended for its steady continuation on the preservation of morale and on all-out commitment to the exacting task. This special quality might be preserved more readily in a small minority group of non-Chinese invaders, who were constantly on their mettle,

than in a Chinese ruling family that was more deeply embrangled in all the distractions of Chinese life.[22]

Though it has not received much attention, this hypothesis might provide some answers as to why China has been under non-Han rule for most of the last thousand years. At the very least, it underscores the often forgotten point that the rulers' notion of themselves was a fundamentally different proposition under Han regimes than under alien conquest regimes. In the former, the "in-group" was the imperial family (the Zhaos, the Zhus), while in the latter it was an ethnos.

## THE "MANCHU WAY"

To fully apprehend the operation of ethnic sovereignty in the Qing, we need to know more about who the Manchus were and what happened to them as a group—including the question of to what extent we can even speak of them as an ethnic group—before and after the conquest. We need to think in terms of the whole range of factors that conditioned Manchu lives and made them different from Chinese lives. We must, in other words, become more familiar with both the discourse of Manchu identity in the Qing—the discursive construction of the social and the social construction of the discourse[23]—and its practice. It was in this nexus that the "Manchu Way" arose.

The expression "Manchu Way" appears often in Qing-era discussions of venerable Manchu customs and practices, or, at least, of what were held to be venerable customs and practices. Most typically, these included archery, horse-riding, ability in the Manchu language, and frugality.[24] Especially in the eighteenth century, when acculturation was having a pronounced effect on the Manchu way of life, the court vigorously promoted the Manchu Way as a package of virtues expected of the compleat bannerman. By upholding the Manchu Way, a bannerman remained virile ("manly virtue" was sometimes also stressed as part of the package) and the Manchus remained distinct and vital as a group, since these were qualities that they supposedly possessed exclusively. The Manchu Way was thus an idealized identifying code for everyone in the banners, particularly males. There were expectations of Manchu and other women in the banners, too (which I explore in Chapter 6), but these were less frequently voiced. For the most part, the Manchu Way was for and about men.

People wrote about the Manchu Way using a variety of terms.[25] Sometimes it was "the old Manchu usages" (Ma *fe Manju-i an*),[26] "Manchu customs" (Ma *Manju tacin*),[27] or simply "the old customs" (Ma *fe tacin*).[28] The more abstract "way" (Ma *doro*) began to be used regularly in the 1720s and 1730s.[29] It appears, for instance, in such phrases as the "old way of the Manchus" (Ma *Manjusai fe doro*), famously invoked in 1727, when the Yongzheng emperor accused Sunu, a Manchu convert to Christianity, of having violated it.[30] Here the word *doro* implies something more than mere custom, akin rather to a way of life based on a specific approach to worldly affairs, so that for every *doro* was the implication of a distinct existential basis. There was, for instance, also a parallel Mongol Way, though it was nowhere near as common a refrain of imperial concern.[31]

While the Manchu Way is perhaps most closely linked with the Qianlong emperor, who fetishized it, the expression was as old as the Manchu fear of acculturation—which is to say as old as Manchu power itself. Even before the conquest of China, Manchu leaders were acutely aware of the fate of earlier Inner Asian dynasties which allowed their ethnic distinctiveness to fade. Not for nothing did they order that the translation of the dynastic histories begin with the accounts of the Liao, Jin, and Yuan periods. Manchu rulers were anxious to avoid the path of their Jurchen ancestors, who, four centuries before, faced a substantially similar position and, as the Manchus saw it, wavered in their commitment to maintaining Jurchen customs and practices, consequently falling from power.[32] In 1634, concern about the adoption of Chinese titles by some members of the Manchu elite prompted the khan, Hong Taiji, to issue the following warning: "I have heard that among the nations that have accepted Heaven's charge and founded an enterprise [i.e., established a dynasty for ruling China], none has abandoned their own language and turned instead to use the language of another nation. No nations that have abandoned their own language and taken up another nation's language have prospered."[33] In a famous speech two years later, Hong Taiji confided to a group of princes and close advisors his worries about the future of the "Old Way" (Ma *fe doro*): "What I fear is this: that the children and grandchildren of later generations will abandon the Old Way, neglect shooting and riding, and enter into the Chinese Way!"[34] Very early, then, Hong Taiji recognized that the maintenance of native ways was significant in cultivating a sense of difference with the majority Han Chinese, and furthermore equated the loss of that difference and the adoption of the "Chinese Way" with the surrender of Manchu dominance. Sustaining the Manchu Way was thus a task of immense political importance for the Manchu leadership.

The fear of "softening" or "declension" is a classic historical theme, of course, recognizable everywhere from the Roman and Ottoman empires to the American colonies. The fourteenth-century historian Ibn Khaldūn gave a memorable discussion of the problem among the Bedouins, whose primitive environment, he noted, inclined them toward greater virtue: "Superiority comes to nations through enterprise and courage. The more firmly rooted in desert habits and the wilder a group is, the closer does it come to achieving superiority over others."[35] When they settle in cities among sedentary people who "have become used to laziness [and] are sunk in well-being and luxury," however, he remarked that desert nomads "enter upon a life of ease."[36] As a result, their bravery decreases, they become less vigorous, and:

> The toughness of desert life is lost. Group feeling and courage weaken. Members of the tribe revel in the well-being that God has given them. Their children and offspring grow up too proud to look after themselves or to attend to their own needs. They have disdain also for all the other things that are necessary in connection with group feeling. This finally becomes a character trait and natural characteristic of theirs. Their group feeling and courage decrease in the next generations. Eventually, group feeling is altogether destroyed. They thus invite their own destruction . . . [for] when group feeling is destroyed, the tribe is no longer able to protect itself, let alone press any claims. It will be swallowed up by other nations.[37]

Arguing in effect for the importance of ethnic sovereignty, Ibn Khaldūn showed how a group's consciousness of itself was closely tied to its ability to dominate other groups, and that the loss of that consciousness meant a loss of power and the group's ultimate assimilation and disappearance.

By the 1720s and 1730s, about eighty years after the Qing conquest, it seemed that Hong Taiji's worst fears were being realized, as Bedouin-like "softening" set in. Many of the aspects of Manchu life that could authenticate their difference and martial preeminence began to fade. The hardened warrior was being supplanted by the effete pseudoliteratus who lacked the strength to draw his bow and took instead to more refined pastimes such as painting and poetry. These later Manchus *were* proud; they looked after their own needs poorly and neglected the cultivation of practices that linked them to other Manchus. Moreover, Manchus in the provinces were becoming estranged from the center of the Manchu world in Beijing, to which they were all supposed to return when their "temporary" sojourn in the outer Han world was over. Just as worrisome, the banner system which supported them and their entire way of life was overburdened by people with dubious claims on the right to support from the government. These developments, amounting to a crisis of Manchu consciousness, created considerable fear, not just at court, but among the Manchu elite generally, that the cohesion of the Manchus as a group and their separateness from the Han Chinese was in jeopardy. In response, the court energetically trumpeted the virtues of the Manchu Way as never before. In edict after edict, the Yongzheng and Qianlong emperors pushed the importance of studying Manchu, maintaining martial skills, and leading a Spartan lifestyle: "The old traditions of the Manchus, shooting, riding, and speaking Manchu, along with being able to handle a lance and a sword—all this is hollow decoration, with no benefit for practical affairs unless you train soldiers until they are skilled."[38] By 1752, the Qianlong emperor was so alarmed that he ordered Hong Taiji's warning of 1636 engraved onto stelae and displayed everywhere that bannermen trained, lest they forget the direct connection between individual practice and the distinct Manchu identity that guaranteed the dynasty's future.[39]

Despite these efforts, it is universally acknowledged that elite efforts to define and defend the Manchu Way were largely in vain. The Manchu language did not enjoy a renaissance, though it did not fall completely from use, either. Enthusiasm for hours and hours of riding and target practice did not rebound—though some bannermen made a doughty showing against the English in 1842 and even in 1860. Indebtedness and poverty among bannermen did not suddenly decline as the spirit of frugality swept through the ranks. On the contrary, the ways of life of Manchu bannermen not only failed to live up to, but diverged more and more widely from, the official ideal. Susan Naquin and Evelyn Rawski sum this up in their survey of eighteenth-century China:

> Qianlong was thus responsible for strengthening the foundations of Manchu identity at a time when Manchus were in danger of forgetting their roots. But the imperial payroll could not support the expanding banner population or screen out the attractions of Chinese culture. By the end of the century these all but fruitless attempts to prevent assimilation were abandoned.[40]

The Manchus, it seemed, were doomed.

This leads us back to the "Manchu question." If it is true—and I think it probably is—that, as Pamela Kyle Crossley notes, "there is no evidence that Hongli [i.e., Hungli, the personal name of the Qianlong emperor] was successful in any general sense in his campaign to hone the racial and cultural consistency of the Manchus,"[41] then how did Manchu identity manage to survive into the nineteenth century, when, according to Crossley, it evolved from a "racial" to an "ethnic" identity? Likewise, if, as Naquin and Rawski suggest, "Manchu culture became a memory,"[42] by what means was Manchu difference preserved beyond the end of the eighteenth century? For if we cannot explain how this happened, then we can only assume that the assimilation predicted by Ibn Khaldūn (and referred to by Naquin and Rawski) indeed took place. And if that is so, then it is nonsense to speak of Manchu difference or a Manchu empire in the nineteenth century, or even for much of the eighteenth, when acculturation was already proceeding at a very rapid pace. We should instead assume the bankruptcy of the Manchu Way, the meaninglessness of any category called "Manchu," and resign ourselves to agreement with those who have insisted all along that the Qing was essentially just another Chinese dynasty.

Yet we hesitate. For if we date the bankruptcy of the Manchu Way to, say, 1800, we might logically expect the Manchus, their ethnic sovereignty dissipated, to have fallen from power soon thereafter. But they did not. Moreover, thanks to the work of Crossley and others, we know that the Manchus did *not* in fact assimilate and disappear as a group in the nineteenth, or even in the twentieth centuries. We may still be justified in concluding that Manchu "group feeling" was preserved in some fashion, but the question remains, how was this accomplished?

The hypothesis raised in this book is that Manchu identity, and ethnic sovereignty together with it, survived mainly thanks to its imbrication in specifically Manchu institutions, most especially the Eight Banners (in Chinese, *baqi*, in Manchu, *jakūn gūsa*), created in about 1601. Manchu dominance was written in many forms, as in such bureaucracies as the Grand Council, but none was more explicitly Manchu than the Eight Banners. The Qing court was in the habit of calling the banners the "root [or foundation] of the nation" (*guojia zhi genben/gurun-i fulehe da*), and one goal of this book is to plumb the meanings of this expression. Even more than the emperorship, it was the Eight Banners, "the only definitive institution for historical identification of the Manchus,"[43] which became the preeminent emblem of Manchu hegemony. Ultimately unable to maintain the integrity of the cultural framework of Manchuness to its satisfaction, through its timely reform of the banner system the court nevertheless managed to save the institutional bulwark upon which Manchu identity had come increasingly to depend. These reforms, which lasted from the 1720s to the 1770s (the upper chronological limit of this study), gave the banner system, threatened with catastrophic financial overburdening, a new lease on life. In the end, although acculturation occurred, it was limited in its effects because the boundaries of Manchu identity—which I will argue were ethnic in nature—continued to be maintained by the Qing state via the Eight Banners.

MANCHU OR BANNERMAN?

To recapitulate, if our goal is an understanding of the Qing polity that factors in the alien presence of Manchus at the top of the imperial order, then it is useful to think of Qing authority as having two foundations, neo-Confucian legitimacy (required to successfully rule the Chinese state) and ethnic sovereignty (required to build and maintain a universal empire of a conquering minority ruling over many domains centered upon China). Neo-Confucian legitimacy arose largely from the Manchu embrace of Chinese literary culture and political norms, ethnic sovereignty from the Manchu embrace of the difference signified by their quasi-steppe origins and those political and social norms. In both instances, the sponsorship of institutions was of signal importance. Just as the examination system and the grooming of the bureaucracy afforded the Qing an opportunity to demonstrate their commitment to Confucian kingship and the general welfare, so the banner system afforded the chance to demonstrate the court's commitment to the values of the conquest elite and the welfare of Manchus and others in the Eight Banners. In the dynamic pull between cosmopolitan and ethnic modes of rule, it was the banners, a virtual "state within a state,"[44] that enabled the Manchus to maintain their cohesion in spite of acculturation.

The argument, then, is that the eighteenth-century transformation of Manchu institutions produced a transvaluation of Manchu identity by which it was membership in the banners that became definitive. One sign of this metamorphosis is that Manchus in the Qing were increasingly identified as "people of the banners" (*qiren/gūsai niyalma*). This leads us to the difficult task of untangling the ethnic web within the Eight Banner system itself. Because registration in the banners was an ethnic-specific practice, banner affiliation was for all intents and purposes an immanent indicator of ethnic identity. Yet not everyone registered within the banners was, genealogically speaking, Manchu. Many people in the banners were Mongols (itself a broad category) or frontier-dwelling Chinese, and there was even a sprinkling of Koreans and Russians. If by the eighteenth century Manchus had become "people of the banners," what was there to distinguish them from other people in the banners? Instead of the Manchu Way, shouldn't it be the "Banner Way"?

Strictly speaking, this might be correct. But just as Manchus became people of the banners, so the different people of the banners gradually became, for practical purposes, Manchu. In other words, that Manchus shared the same status with others in the banners did not lead to the disappearance of the ethnic component from the label "Manchu"; rather, it resulted in the melding of the terms "Manchu" and "bannerman."[45] There were, as we shall see, boundaries between the different groups of banner people, but these were not hermetic. Many of the cultural, economic, and, especially, institutional practices that shaped Manchu ethnicity thus seeped through to others in the banners and made "Manchus" of them all. The analysis of Manchu identity in this book attempts to explain how this was accomplished.

It may be objected that this approach to Manchu identity conflates all groups in the banners—Manchu, Mongol, bondservant, Chinese bannerman—into one category and neglects the distinctions within the Eight Banners that elsewhere I take pains to describe. I am sympathetic to this criticism, particularly in relation to Chinese banner people, whose identity was highly unstable and fits perhaps least well into the ethnic analysis attempted here. Nonetheless, I believe that my approach most accurately reflects the situation during the Qing, when the conflation of these categories was common—both among the Han population, which called these groups collectively "banner people" and tended to assume, correctly or not, that *qiren* were all Manchu, as well as among the court and those in the banners themselves, who often, though not always, considered banner people as a single group. Even the emperor addressed them as such on occasion. True, when it wished the court could and did make decisions that took into account the finer distinctions of ethnic and legal status within the banners, and for this reason I have felt it important to make clear what those gradations were and whence they arose. On other occasions, however, the court made policies that overlooked those same distinctions and dealt with people in the banner system in a more or less uniform way. This is precisely why the expressions "bannerman" and "Manchu" were able not just to coexist, but to overlap.[46]

It might be further objected that if Manchu identity in the eighteenth century increasingly reflected a hybrid "banner" identity, then we cannot really speak of "ethnicity," since *qiren* were, after all, of varying national origins. Again, my response is that this is how the labels worked during the Qing. While from a remote perspective the term *qiren* suggests a description of legal status alone, in practice it evinced a range of ethnic characteristics, functioned much like an ethnic category, and was widely perceived in arguably ethnic terms.[47]

That the category "banner people" came to signify "Manchus" and not the other way around was a consequence of two things: that the Eight Banners was essentially a Manchu institution and that court concern for the banners was dominated in the end by an emphasis on those in the banners classified as Manchu. From the outside, Han Chinese saw the advantages enjoyed by those in the banners as "Manchu" privileges unavailable to them; from the inside, Manchus, Mongols, and Han bannermen also tended to see such privileges as specifically "Manchu," with the difference that they shared in them to greater (in the Mongol case) or lesser (in the case of the Han bannermen) degrees. With the gradual strengthening of the banner system as a bulwark of Manchu identity in the eighteenth century, the perception of Manchus as "banner people" became more common; paradoxically, other distinctions within the banner system, such as gradations of privilege and pay, were simultaneously reinforced in order to guarantee the place of Manchus at the top of the heap.[48]

Perhaps the best proof of the growing congruence of "bannerman" and "Manchu" is in the evolution of these terms in the twentieth century. Soon after the 1911 revolution, Manchus sensitive to the racialized atmosphere created by Han nationalist revolutionaries invented a new name, calling themselves *qizu*, or the "banner ethnos."[49] The name did not become widespread—after the establishment of the People's Republic of China the modern name for the Manchus was stabilized as *Manzu* (Man[chu] ethnos)— yet, significantly, membership in this newly recognized minority nationality was open to anyone who could show that he or she had once been in any of the Eight Banners (Manchu, Mongol, Chinese, bondservant), or was descended from someone with such a pedigree.[50] For all these reasons, this book speaks of the "Manchu Way" rather than the "Banner Way."

THINKING AGAIN ABOUT ETHNICITY IN
LATE IMPERIAL CHINA

If Manchu identity in the Qing yet remains something of a puzzle today, I believe that part of the reason lies in an inadequate appreciation of the importance of ethnic sovereignty in Qing rule as sketched above. Another part of
the explanation has to do with the use of inappropriate assumptions about
identity formation and the relationship between identity, history, and culture.
In the past, the question "Were eighteenth- or nineteenth-century Manchus
still 'Manchu'?" has been answered by examining Manchu behavior. Since
most Manchus of the middle and later Qing behaved differently from those
of the early Qing, in that they obeyed different cultural norms, the conclusion was that the later Manchus were assimilated, that they had lost their
discrete identity. There are three major problems with this approach. One is
that it implies the existence of objective, unchanging standards of "Manchuness." How could an emperor who sacrificed to Confucius or a soldier
who feigned poor vision to avoid a simple archery test be called a "real"
Manchu? Another problem is that it makes an implicit equation between cultural performance and ethnic self-identification. Thus a Manchu who, say,
spoke Chinese instead of Manchu is assumed to have been no longer Manchu. This latter assumption raises a third problem, namely, the establishment
of a false dichotomy: Manchu *or* Chinese.

Over the last thirty years, scholarly work has come to show more and
more conclusively that identity does not operate so simply: that it is a process shaped and manifested in many ways, not just by or through "culture,"
and that people do not always conceive of themselves according to categories of either/or. There has been a gradual reconceptualization of identity
—in particular what has come to be called "ethnicity"—as a form of discourse arising from the social organization and political assertion of culture-
or descent-based difference, actual or perceived. This represents a fundamental rejection of the traditional idea that ethnicity is an immanent, immutable, "primordial" condition; the new interpretation views ethnicity, like
class and gender, as historically contingent. As one critic has recently written, "Ethnicity is ultimately a construction, like all other forms of social and
cultural life; within the range of action which history and 'tradition' provide,
there is considerable room for human inventiveness and the play of the pas-
sions and desires of the present."[51] Because it is constituted by social con-

tact, ethnicity is thus not something one has in one's pocket, like a passport, but something acquired through interaction with someone else; that is, it is inherently transactional, "an aspect of a relationship, not a property of a group."[52] For this reason, difference—cultural or genealogical, actual or "imagined"—in and of itself does not constitute ethnicity; rather, ethnicity is found in the signification assigned to such difference. What the difference is, or whether the difference is great or small, is therefore a matter of secondary importance; what is primary is the perception and freighting of that difference with social meaning. By this logic we can expect and indeed find instances where members of two or more groups may find it advantageous to ignore the existence of obvious differences between them and emphasize instead elements of commonality, or even descent, whether imagined or real. Under other circumstances, however, these same differences may be seized upon as a source of "essential" differentiation between groups to produce "ethnicity."

I find the concept of ethnicity useful in discussing the Manchus in Qing China for three main reasons. First, seeing ethnicity as dependent, not so much on real descent as on the symbols of descent and the individual's belief in them, allows a better understanding of the real processes of self-identification.[53] Because ethnicity is flexible and open to negotiation, it should be expected to change according to the needs of the group; such change may be influenced by other factors such as gender, politics, or economics. This permits an analysis of ethnic categories in terms of their political and practical utility, factors that frequently condition the choices people make over their own identity or identities. The strategies employed by Chinese bannermen and others in the banners show how such negotiations worked. The Chinese bannermen are a clear instance of a people who, according to a strict interpretation of descent lines, were not entitled to membership in an ethnic group but acquired ethnicity anyway by virtue of their adoption of the symbols of the system of persistent identity.[54]

Second, thinking about the Manchus in ethnic terms is helpful because it enables us to distinguish more easily between a "cultural" group and an "ethnic" group and to understand Manchu ethnic coherence in spite of apparent cultural incoherence. Ethnicity's transactional nature allows us to understand how, in a situation where extended contact between in- and out-groups causes cultural differences to become less apparent over time,[55] the communicated value assigned to those differences in the construction of identity increases. This mechanism is well-suited to pondering the paradox of Manchu identity, whereby the *cultural* distance between Manchus and Han Chinese was progressively reduced but the *ethnic* boundaries between Manchu and Han in most cases remained or were even strengthened. As Sow-theng Leong's discussion of these ideas makes clear, a cultural group, that is, a group that consciously or unconsciously shares a common culture and tradition, is held to "become 'ethnic' only when, in competition with another [group] these shared markers are consciously chosen to promote solidarity and mobilization, with a view to enhancing the group's share of societal resources or simply minimizing the threat to its survival."[56] As Chapter 1 shows, this sort of competition arose very early in the formation of the Qing state and it never went away entirely. Even after the cultural differences that initially produced ethnic interaction between Manchus and Han Chinese faded, interaction between these groups was always in this mode, or at least potentially so. Ethnicity also allows us to see how evident cultural differences between Manchus and others in the Eight Banners could be overlooked in the construction of a refurbished Manchu identity in the mid-1700s.

The third reason ethnicity is useful in talking about the Manchus is that it permits us to view ethnicity in China in a broader comparative historical context. The questions that surround the phenomenon of ethnicity—such as how ethnic identity is created, what purposes it is called on to serve, how it is transmitted and transformed—interest not only anthropologists, but historians as well. The former have dominated the discussion, leading to the serious charge (serious to historians, anyway) that work on ethnicity suffers from "historical shallowness."[57] The participation of historians is crucial if the processes of ethnic change and the creation of "invented pasts" and their place in ethnic (and national) formation are to be better understood.[58] For all of these reasons, using concepts of ethnicity to study the Manchu case appears not just useful, but appropriate and necessary.

I am aware that not everyone agrees that the analysis of ethnicity is an appropriate mode for premodern history, in China or anywhere else.[59] Some, for instance, believe that ethnicity is applicable "only within the context of the 'modern nation state.'"[60] Others see ethnic consciousness as a fundamentally modern phenomenon, "the product of imperial disintegration, and thus of the nineteenth and twentieth centuries,"[61] and specifically question its applicability to the Manchus before the late Qing. This view, which en-

joys wide support, is that ethnicity as a way of constructing identity is the result of alienation, peripheralization, and subordination, its essence tied to
qualities that are "local, particularist, minor, heterodox, [and] marginal."[62]
While I would certainly agree that ethnic thinking undergoes some important transformations in the late nineteenth century (when, in a new trans-
national discourse, identities were, to use Frank Dikötter's terms, "racialized"[63]), it will be obvious that my understanding of ethnicity in this study is
broader. I share the doubts of Prasenjit Duara regarding a distinctly "modern" mode of identity consciousness and individual self-awareness, and am
thus inclined to see ethnicity historically as a way of constructing identity
(i.e., "selfness") whenever and wherever human groups come into contact
and discover meaning in the differences between each other, which they may
then turn to various purposes.[64]

I do not mean to suggest that discussing ethnicity in a historical context
is unproblematic. Before the historian can explain why ethnic categories
were meaningful in the period he studies, he must first prove that the categories he observes were indeed ethnic, and not the stepchild of modern ethnic consciousness. The danger here of anachronism—what Eric Hobsbawm
has defined as "reading the desires of the present into the past"—is double.
Not only must one be careful to avoid accepting present claims of ethno-
historical "legitimacy," but also parallel *past* claims. Yet to surrender all
hope of objectivity seems unnecessarily pessimistic. In a different context,
Roger Chartier has put the problem this way: "What are the criteria by
which a historical discourse—always a knowledge based on traces and
signs—can be held to be a valid and explicative reconstruction (or at least
more valid and more explicative than others) of the past reality it has defined as its object?"[65] This is not an easy question to answer, and I make no
claim to do so fully. Nonetheless, my research leads me to believe that in its
principles the process of ethnicity did not operate all that differently two
hundred years ago than it does today. For instance, ethnic groups then, as
now (to take only one of the elements usually found in ethnic consciousness), employed conscious strategies of interpretation (or, less graciously,
manipulation) of the past in the process of self-construction. If present-day
Manchus reinvent an eighteenth-century past to serve present needs, this
does not necessarily mean that the ethnicity of eighteenth-century Manchus,
even if it was not what Manchus today claim it to have been, exists only as
the retrospective imaginings of today's historians. Likewise, if eighteenth-

century Manchus reinvented *their* seventeenth-century past to serve contemporary needs, this does not mean we can reject out of hand the ethnicity of conquest-era Manchus as the backward-projected fantasies of ideologues at the Qianlong court. As the narrative that follows shows, whatever the differences between them and the group that calls itself "Manchu" today, Manchus in the Qing participated in much the same sorts of self-definitional processes as people in ethnic groups anywhere, at any time.

Historian Yang Lien-sheng once famously wrote, "In studying the Chinese world order it is important to distinguish myth and reality wherever possible. Both can be influential."[66] Concerning ethnicity, the main task of the historian is not simply to distinguish fact from fantasy (though this is certainly of some importance), but to discover how myth and reality were used in the creation of ethnic identity, to trace the changes in ethnic identity and the uses of ethnicity, and to point out the tensions of boundary maintenance over time.[67] As an attempt to separate these narratives while preserving their historical interrelation, this book joins a growing body of work on identity and ethnicity to show how historical and anthropological approaches can illuminate pre-twentieth-century settings.[68]

## "BARBARIANS" AND "CHINESE": COMPETING VIEWS OF THE MANCHUS IN HISTORY

Apart from the difficulties already described, I wish to highlight two other impediments that have traditionally hampered studies of the Manchus and that demand negotiation by the conscientious historian. One is the relative neglect of Manchu-language sources, which scholars of the Qing period have almost totally ignored.[69] Without recourse to these materials, Manchu history and identity can only be reconstructed through their reflection in Chinese-language sources—not entirely a satisfactory method. While the use of Manchu materials obviously does not eliminate all the usual problems historians face when querying documents, it does at least minimize the unavoidable imprecision introduced when terms and ideas are transferred from one language to another. Admittedly, it does impose additional demands, such as learning another language. Nevertheless, as I hope the pages below show, the study of Manchu is not without reward.

Another, more intransigent difficulty lies in Chinese attitudes toward the Other, which have fundamentally shaped the historiography on the Manchus to date. Ninety years after the Chinese republican revolution, historians have by now found much to praise in Manchu stewardship of the Chinese state. The vast Qing realm outstripped every other country on earth in total wealth and witnessed a demographic expansion unprecedented in world history, as the population of the country grew from roughly 130 million in 1650 to 320 million by 1800, and then to 420 million by 1850.[70] This boom was accompanied by a substantial increase of cultivated land and a steady growth in the national economy, buoyed by a remarkably stable political order administering a realm perhaps twice as populous as all the states of Europe combined.[71] Moreover, during the "long eighteenth century" the Manchus conquered vast territories to the north and west of China proper,[72] forging an empire more than twice as large as the Ming and second only to Romanov Russia in size. Indeed, that China looks the way it does on the map today is very much a consequence of Qing rule. *This* legacy—the geographic constitution of the nation under the Manchus—may represent the single greatest impact of Manchu rule.[73] (More on this is said in the Conclusion.)

But splendid as the Qing golden age appears to us in hindsight, the appearance of Qing forces at China's front door in 1644 was hardly viewed as a splendid thing at the time by the Chinese. The successful grab for power by a foreign people whom they considered below themselves was a bitter pill to swallow. "Barbarians,"[74] popular wisdom went in the 1600s, patently lacked the virtue required to win the Mandate of Heaven: How could such a rough band as the Manchus govern China's civilized empire? Who would guard the welfare of the people? What would happen to ritual and propriety, to the nation's treasured customs and institutions? And what did it say about the Chinese themselves that they had again fallen into the thrall of northern invaders?

Questions such as these had swirled through literati circles for the first time when the Song dynasty (960–1279) allowed control of the northern quarter of the Central Plain, China's heartland, to pass to the Khitan Liao dynasty, founded by a seminomadic tribe descended from peoples who for centuries had raided the perimeter of the agricultural zone occupied by the sedentary Han Chinese.[75] The Song also lost the strategic Gansu corridor, portal to the west and the Silk Road, to the Tanguts, another pastoral non-Han people who founded the Xi Xia dynasty (ca. 982–1227). To secure peace between themselves and these foreign states, in the early eleventh century the Chinese rulers of the Song were reduced to paying both the Liao and the Xi Xia an annual danegeld of silver, silk, and tea.[76] In the early twelfth century, similar arrangements were made between the Chinese and the Jurchen Jin dynasty, which had defeated the Khitan and replaced them as the most powerful "barbarian" power in the north. By 1142, the Song position vis-à-vis the Jin weakened further, and even the heroics of the famous patriot Yue Fei (d. 1141) could not prevent the loss of the entire Central Plain to the Jurchens. Finally, as if all this were not enough to undermine the survival of the Chinese state, a century later, south China, too, slipped from Chinese hands as the final collapse of both the Jin and Song dynasties before the Mongol onslaught in 1279 meant that the whole empire was under the rule of an alien people. Only with the rise of the "native" Ming dynasty, which overthrew the Mongol Yuan dynasty in 1368, was "China" once more "Chinese."

To historically-minded Han Chinese, the rise of the Manchus in 1644 signaled the beginning of yet another cycle of foreign domination. Though the doctrines of modern nationalism were, of course, unknown at the time, belief in the universality of the Chinese cultural tradition was widespread enough that this epochal break provoked a national crisis. Ethnocentric assumptions of the superior values that defined the Chinese people and civilization itself, were rocked as once again the learned men of the empire debated the same basic question: "How should the superior person wishing to transmit the Way (Ch *dao*) behave toward the 'barbarian'?" The debate took place within a well-established framework. Chinese ideas toward outsiders (i.e., non-Hua, "Hua" being the Chinese term for all who participated in the same politico-cultural ecumene) predate the creation of the first Chinese empire in the third century B.C.E. They fall generally into two schools, which there is only room to summarize briefly here. One school, the "exclusivists," saw the non-Hua as essentially different, less than fully human, and incapable of self-improvement. A famous passage in the *Zuo zhuan* (ca. 300 B.C.E.) reads, "If he be not of our kind, he is sure to have a different mind."[77] "Relativists" (or "culturalists") on the other hand, admitted the possibility of transforming "barbarians" into civilized beings—but this transformation was assumed to occur in one direction only. As Mencius (372–289 B.C.E.) wrote, "I have heard of men using the doctrines of our great land to change barbarians, but I have never yet heard of any being changed by barbarians."[78] To a great degree, these positions governed most thinking about people outside the Chinese cultural ecumene for the entire imperial period.[79]

In the early Qing, as during the Song and under the Yuan, some took a relativist view, arguing that so long as Chinese ways were adopted, the new regime could legitimately claim to possess virtue and, consequently, the loyalty of the scholar-elite. That is, one did not have to be Chinese to hold the "Mandate of Heaven." It was enough to accept the philosophical basis of emperorship.[80] Others, such as the great seventeenth-century scholar and philosopher Wang Fuzhi (1619–92), took a more hard-line approach, insisting that a non-Chinese ruler could hardly be legitimate:

> There are two great barriers in the empire: [the first is the barrier between] Chinese (*hua-xia*) and barbarians (*yi-di*), [and the second is that between] superior people (*junzi*) and petty-minded people (*xiaoren*). . . . The barbarians, with respect to the Chinese, are born in alien lands. As their lands are alien, their customs are alien, and as their customs are alien, so their behavior is entirely alien.[81]

Innately alien, the Manchus (and other peoples we would recognize, using modern terms, as "non-Han") as such were obviously unfit to assume charge of the celestial empire.[82] They were to be resisted at all costs and did not merit the loyalty of the upright Confucian scholar, who, if he went over to the Qing side, would certainly be thought by some to have betrayed not just his former master (the Ming emperor), but his very culture and the Way itself. This theme is found again and again in politics, literature, and painting of the later 1600s.

The shock of the Manchu conquest did not die with Wang Fuzhi and his generation. The otherness of China's Manchu rulers was a constant, if often masked, theme throughout the eighteenth and nineteenth centuries, emerging at liminal moments such as the Opium War and the Taiping Rebellion.[83] The latter in particular is notable for its virulent ethnic sloganeering, as exemplified in the following 1852 rebel proclamation:

> O you masses, listen to our words. It is our belief that the empire is China's empire, not the Manchu barbarians' empire. . . . Alas! since the Ming's misrule, the Manchus availed themselves of the opportunity to throw China into confusion; they stole China's empire, appropriated China's food and clothing, and ravished China's sons and daughters.

This was blatant heterodoxy, of course, and confirmed the very worst fears of the Qing rulers that their place as legitimate "Sons of Heaven" was regarded with hostility. This and a following passage also confirm our suspi-

cion that differences between Chinese and Manchus were viewed in essen-
tialized ethnic terms, at least by some:

> The Chinese have Chinese characteristics; but now the Manchus have
> ordered us to shave our hair around the head, leaving a long tail behind,
> thus making the Chinese appear to be brute animals. The Chinese have
> Chinese dress; but now the Manchus have . . . discarded the robes . . . of
> former dynasties, in order to make the Chinese forget their origins. . . .
> The Chinese have the Chinese language; but now the Manchus have
> introduced slang of the capital and changed the Chinese tones, desiring
> to delude China with barbarian speech and barbarian expressions.

Especially noteworthy is the emphasis placed by the Taiping not just on the
Manchus' different cultural practices or their distortion of Chinese traits
(such as language), but also on their origins:

> We have carefully investigated the Manchus' Tartar origins and have
> found that their first ancestor was a crossbreed of a white fox and a red
> dog, from whom sprang this race of demons. . . . They established their
> own imperial throne and the wild fox ascended to occupy it [while] . . .
> we Chinese . . . fell into their treacherous plots, bore their insults, and
> obeyed their commands.[84]

That both cultural orientation and descent were perceived as elements that
made the Manchus different from—and inferior to—the Chinese strongly
suggests not only that the Qing was right to regard the Han with a wary eye,
but also that evaluating the Manchu case from an ethnic angle makes sense;
that it does not do violence to contemporary categories, but in fact helps us
to see them more distinctly.

When the Qing dynasty fell in 1912—revolutionaries like Zhang Binglin
having employed the same type of racist propaganda as the Taiping[85]—a
sense of urgency set in anew as once again Han Chinese grappled with the
significance of Manchu rule. This time, the question was not so much the political one of whether the scholar could serve an alien regime, but the historical one of how that regime managed to stay in power for so long and what
its place should be in Chinese annals. For intellectuals struggling with the
matter of China's identity and, indeed, its very survival in a postimperial,
post-Confucian world dominated by Britain and the powerful nations of the
West, explaining how a handful of supposedly benighted Manchus ruled an
empire of four hundred million Chinese for 268 years was a pressing and difficult matter, not to say an embarrassing one. (Imagine the task European

historians would face if all of Europe had been ruled from 1650 to 1900 as a reconstituted Roman Empire led by an "alien" conquest elite roughly equal in size to the Manchus—say, the Hungarians.)

As in 1644, debate on the minority-rule question and the Manchu question after 1912 (by which time a nationalist discourse was firmly in place) revealed a simmering crisis of political definition and cultural confidence. One view popular among Han-chauvinist historians (and now somewhat passé) is that the Manchus exercised a crude sovereignty over China and that the "barbarians" on the throne stunted the "natural" growth of Chinese society through the carrying out of literary inquisitions and other sorts of repressive campaigns,[86] a view broadly similar to traditional interpretations of Mongol rule over China, and over Russia, too, for that matter.[87] A more serious charge, one which is occasionally still pressed, is that the Manchus were to blame for failing to defend the country from Western imperialism, of "selling the country to save the dynasty,"[88] as capitulatory Qing policies led to national disgrace before finally (and deservedly) bringing down the dynasty itself. The Marxist variation on this theme is that the Manchus were evil because they were "feudal" and "backward."[89]

Another narrative stressed the assimilation (or "sinicization"; Ch *Hanhua*) of the Manchus in explaining how they held power for so long. According to this evolutionary perspective, though the Manchus were a rude and warlike people when they took over, the refinements of Chinese culture gradually sapped this raw vitality, so that at the latest by the turn of the eighteenth century, there ceased to be anything "Manchu" about the Manchus anymore. Explaining that by the late 1800s most Manchus had abandoned their ancestral language and customs for Chinese ways, the Chinese authors of the first authoritative history of the Manchus wrote,

> After the 1912 Revolution, the Manchu and Chinese cultures had basically melded into one. The few, minute differences preserved in their customs did not carry much social significance. This was the result of the exchange of Manchu and Han cultures. . . . It favored friendly relations between the Manchu and Han people, and fostered mutual learning and assistance as well as common development and progress.[90]

While acknowledging that the Han did adopt some Manchu ways (such as styles of clothing and hair), the dominant theme of acculturation to Chinese norms is plainly evident here, as is the superiority of those norms, which stand for the culmination of generations of development and "progress."

Twentieth-century western narratives, mainly shorn of the assumption of Chinese superiority, nonetheless concurred with the verdict that when the Qing fell in 1912, "the ancient Manchu conquerors had long been absorbed, drowned in the Chinese mass."[91] Related to this approach was the axiom that the Manchus ruled in essentially Chinese fashion. Indeed, this was key, as "the Manchu rulers stayed in power only by becoming as Chinese as their subjects."[92] The Qing emperor himself, though a Manchu, was "really" Chinese, after all; his Confucian demeanor was his "authentic" pose and other personae—Manchu and Mongol khan, patron of Tibetan Buddhism—merely guises assumed for specific political purposes. In both these ways, some scraps of Chinese pride could still be salvaged.

We do well to note the contradictions between these different narratives. On the one hand, the Manchus qua Manchus are said to have harmed China, while on the other hand they are said to have ruled as Chinese and even to have become "Chinese" themselves. The paradox is that this harm was ostensibly greatest in the nineteenth century, by which time, by the logic of sinicization, we can only suppose that the Manchus were most thoroughly acculturated. Moreover, both narratives acknowledge authentic cultural and political differences between Manchus and Han only for the early Qing, thus suggesting that Manchu-Chinese conflict in the eighteenth century and later was absent or nearly so. This leaves no explanation for the "reemergence" (if that is what it was) of anti-Manchu sentiment into the nineteenth century in the heterodox propaganda of various secret societies and the Taiping movement, not to mention its place in the revolutionary rhetoric of the 1890s and 1900s. The urgency of these nationalist narratives of Manchu rule notwithstanding, one cannot help but agree that they tell us much more about historians and revolutionaries than they tell us about the Manchus.[93]

## SINICIZATION AND THE MANCHUS

The insistence that the Manchus succeeded because they became essentially "Chinese" bears a striking resemblance to the reaction of seventeenth-century Chinese to the Manchu conquest. On these grounds, literati who sought official careers in the early Qing could (and did) insist that the Manchus possessed the Mandate of Heaven because they adopted tried-and-true neo-Confucian practices from their Ming predecessors. On the same grounds, politicians and historians of the early 1900s could point to signs of Manchu acculturation to argue that the Manchus, from the emperor down to the most lowly soldier, had in fact become Chinese during their long period of rule and that their dynasty was therefore not really an "alien" regime. The leader of the revolution himself, Sun Yat-sen, once declared, "When the Manchus conquered China, and ruled us for more than 260 years, they did not destroy the Chinese, but on the contrary accepted their civilization, and they became in fact Chinese."[94] The shameful fact of China's long domination by so-called foreigners was thereby resolved, and the Manchu conquest of China neatly reinterpreted as the Chinese conquest of the Manchus.[95]

As indicated earlier, this answer to the minority-rule question has dominated both popular and scholarly views for a very long time. Even today, it is the most common explanation one hears for Manchu success: how else could such a small group have managed to rule China for nearly three centuries except by becoming "Chinese" in the process?[96] One reason for the persistence of this view—what I will call the Sinicization School of opinion—is that it fits snugly with very old, ethnocentric notions of the relationship between China and the Other, outlined above. The hoary notion that the Chinese "absorb" their conquerors, founded on a belief that the Chinese urge to "civilize" (*wen-hua*) or, somewhat more neutrally, to assimilate (*tonghua*), is nigh irresistible and is not to be underestimated in interpretations of the Qing or any "alien" interlude in Chinese history.[97] Even Meng Sen, one of the few Chinese scholars in the early twentieth century to carefully study Manchu institutions, subscribed to the notion of the complete assimilation and eventual disappearance of the Manchus.[98] At the end of the century, another eminent historian, Ping-ti Ho, has zestfully advanced the sinicization argument yet again, writing, "in the latter half of the nineteenth century, the Manchus and the Han Chinese shared more and more a larger sense of identity—being all 'Chinese' in the same boat."[99]

Indeed, there is more than a grain of truth to the Sinicization School's arguments. Chinese civilization *has* exerted an enormous attraction and fascination upon all who have encountered it, virtually from the beginning of recorded time. All the major cultures of East Asia show the deep influence of Chinese beliefs and practices. In China itself, any dynastic house that aimed to rule the empire inevitably employed "Chinese" modes of government to some degree (including the employment of Han Chinese scholar-elites), or quickly fell. This was no less true for the Qing. The Manchus relied heavily on Chinese precedents and the political and moral vocabulary of neo-Confucian political values to consolidate and legitimate their rule. They also borrowed the essential framework for the government of China from their predecessors, the Ming. Moreover, within three generations of the conquest, many Manchus spoke and wrote Chinese better than they spoke and wrote Manchu, and their devotion to the pursuit of the arts of refined (and not so refined) Chinese gentlemen exceeded that of the Chinese themselves. Because many Qing imperial institutions *were* modeled directly on Ming precedents, and because Manchu acculturation *was* widespread by the nineteenth century, it is hard to deny the importance of Chinese influence on the Manchus and Manchu rule.[100]

Despite the many and varied signs of Manchu acculturation, it must be said, however, that using the word "sinicization" to describe this process is rather misleading. For one thing, adopting Chinese institutions did not mean becoming Chinese except in the most abstract sense: as Bol has argued for the Jin, "Jurchens could be *wen* without becoming Hans."[101] That is, "civilization" (to use Bol's term) must be seen separately from assimilation: a shift in cultural practices does not necessarily mean a shift in one's self-perception or in how one is perceived by others. Furthermore, a term like sinicization masks diachronicity and process; it obscures the fact that what is held to be "Chinese" has changed over time by essentializing the political or cultural forms of any given moment as somehow integrally, immutably Chinese. Beyond this, it must be said that another problem with the sinicization hypothesis is not that it explains nothing about how the minority Manchus ruled China so long and so well, but rather that it cannot explain everything. Advocates of a competing view, what I will call here the Altaic School, emphasize the point that "Manchuness" was as important a characteristic of the Qing as was "Chineseness." These scholars insist on the need to pay greater attention to the non-Chinese aspects of Manchu rule to gain a more complete picture of the Qing period; some have lately spoken of the development of a new "Qing-" or "Manchu-centered" perspective on late imperial Chinese history.[102]

This debate—a debate over what it means to say that the Qing was a "Manchu" dynasty—is not really new. Among Western scholars, it has been going on for almost two generations, ever since Franz Michael's influential 1942 study of the early Qing (for years the only English-language book on the period). Michael built on Owen Lattimore's thesis of the frontier's "ebb and flow" to argue that the organization and ideology of the early Manchu state was "of the Chinese empire" and that "it was the Chinese system, Chinese officials and Chinese ideas that enabled the Manchus to conquer China."[103] This is pure "sinicizationist" thinking. Yet Michael disagreed with the conclusions of the Sinicization School, perceptively noting that

> The Manchus never became completely absorbed into the Chinese culture. They remained the privileged group of conquerors; the group which retained part of the military and feudal past all through its history. A Manchu would always have his bowl of rice, a small pension at least, paid to the member of the conquering group by the conquered people.[104]

This element of Michael's view accorded more or less with the position expressed by Wittfogel and Feng in the introduction to *History of Chinese Society: Liao*. As noted, in that study they took issue with what they called the "Absorption Theory" of Chinese history, that is, the assumption held by the Sinicization School that the Chinese have always assimilated their Inner Asian conquerors, criticizing it on the grounds that it tends to "obscure rather than clarify the complex character of acculturation under conditions of conquest."[105] Instead of sinicization or cultural "fusion," Wittfogel and Feng called for a model of "social and cultural symbiosis" paralleling the ecological and economic symbiosis found along the frontier, a perspective that also owed much to Lattimore.[106] In its insistence that assimilation be specifically demonstrated, their challenge amounted to a rejection of the prevailing view that the Manchus, or any other group of northern conquerors, had been assimilated simply by virtue of extended residence in China proper. Scholars were faced with a clear choice: either identity and power were not linked, or, if (as the concept of ethnic sovereignty would suggest) they were, then the assumption of sinicization and loss of identity had to be questioned.

The clearest response to this challenge was put forward by Mary Clabaugh Wright in *The Last Stand of Chinese Conservatism* (1957), an enormously important interpretation of late-nineteenth-century politics. Wittfogel had argued that "absorption" could occur only when the social and cultural divisions between conqueror and conquered were eradicated, an event he placed after the fall of a dynasty.[107] Wright countered that in the Qing case these divisions ceased to exist in the 1860s, when many of the formal restrictions separating Manchus and Han Chinese were lifted. For this reason, she said, it was better to speak not of symbiosis, but of "a Sino-Manchu synthesis, a genuinely harmonious coalition that marked a new stage in the development of the non-national Confucian monarchy as the symbol of traditional culturalism."[108] According to Wright, the labels "Han" and "Manchu" had by the late Qing become coterminous—that it didn't matter to Han literati *who* the Manchus were—and she pointed to their support of the Tongzhi Restoration as evidence of this. Wright thus questioned not just the idea of persistent ethnic difference, but the very idea that Manchu identity and Qing power were in any way linked, even though this left her with no good explanation for virulent anti-Manchu hostility in the late Qing.[109]

Despite this weakness, Wright's view of the Manchu-Han synthesis dominated through the 1960s, 1970s, and early 1980s, being adopted perhaps most famously by Joseph Levenson. Levenson based his arguments concerning culturalism and nationalism on the belief that "by the twentieth century, the Manchus . . . had become the champions of the Chinese way of life" and asserted that any attack on them based on ethnic differences was at once ludicrous and specious. He very elegantly showed that the re-emergence of anti-Manchuism was the reflection of a new nationalism that took as its inspiration the Western nation-state and not the traditionally culturally-defined Chinese ecumene. Late-Qing racism thus had nothing to do with traditional Chinese views of the "barbarian," insisted Levenson, but was rather a "Nietzschean 'transvaluation of values' in Chinese culture."[110] Wright's influence can be seen also in Albert Feuerwerker's 1976 survey, *State and Society in Eighteenth-Century China: The Ch'ing Empire in Its Glory*. Stressing the universal nature of the emperorship, Feuerwerker argued that the Qing "was not just a closed Manchu holding company" and that "by becoming emperors of China the Manchu leaders in effect had already abandoned any simple commitment to serving Manchu parochial interests." Noting that the emperor's ultimate goal was nothing more and nothing less than the preservation of his power, Feuerwerker concluded that any differences arising from the Manchus' ethnic distinctiveness were in the long run inconsequential:

> In sum, I am not convinced that in the eighteenth and most of the nine-teenth centuries it made any great difference that the ruling house was not Han Chinese. There is little reason to believe that the great rebellions would not have occurred or that the foreigners' demands would have been withstood any more strongly if the dynasty had been established by domestic rebels—as in the case of the Ming—rather than by semi-acculturated "barbarian" conquerors.[111]

By the particular standards Feuerwerker sets, it may be true that it made no "great difference" that Manchus (who he allows were only *semi*acculturated) were on the throne. By other standards the difference may not have been so slight: Was the extent of Qing geographic expansion not related in some significant way to the Manchus' origins as conquerors? Were the governing institutions put into place by the Qing not connected to their Inner Asian political heritage?

Whatever issues the Sinicization School may have left unresolved, the resolution of the minority-rule question and the Manchu question in a way that downplays the dynasty's "otherness" has until recently prevailed among Qing historians almost everywhere, which is why the recent resurgence of an Altaic-centered approach appears so novel. Few have taken advantage of the groundwork laid in the 1960s and 1970s by scholars such as Jonathan Spence, Lawrence Kessler, and Robert Oxnam, who attempted to come to grips with Manchu sensibility and the hybrid nature of (elite) Qing society predicted by Wittfogel.[112] Two important Altaicists of this generation, David Farquhar and Joseph Fletcher, though endowed with enormous linguistic and historical talent, both died tragically in their prime, before their intellectual projects could be fully realized. In China, the pre-1949 work of Meng Sen (previously mentioned) and Zheng Tianting revealed a deep interest in the Manchu past as an independent tradition. But the ideologically charged nature of scholarship in the People's Republic of China and Taiwan has limited the freedom of most scholars to explore alternatives to mechanical Marxist or chauvinist narratives of Manchu history.[113]

The principal exception, as I have already suggested, is to be found in twentieth-century Japanese scholarship on the Qing. The tradition established by scholars such as Inaba Iwakichi, Wada Sei, Ura Ren'ichi, Imanishi Shunju, Mitamura Taisuke, Miyazaki Ichisada, and others, stressed the distinctiveness of the Manchu ruling elite as well as the separate historical and geographical background of Manchuria.[114] It cannot be denied that a primary aim of some of this work was to demonstrate that Manchuria was not part of China, and thereby to provide a cover for Japanese imperialist expansion on the Asian mainland, establishing in the process a precedent for the rule of China by an "alien race." Yet these scholars' sense of Qing rule had another source, too, which was their familiarity with the history and languages of Inner Asia, one reason that their descriptions and analyses of Qing institutions continue to ring true today, even after one accounts for the politics of the day. This tradition continues still. Japanese manjuristic expertise is rivaled only by European centers of Altaic studies in Germany, Russia, Italy, Finland, and elsewhere, such that a nonsinocentric view of Qing history has until recently found its home primarily outside the North American field of vision.[115]

NEW NARRATIVES

The renascence of interest in Manchu studies among United States historians since the mid-1980s has been shaped, it seems, less by the inspiration of foreign scholarship than by late-twentieth-century intellectual trends encouraging the questioning of heretofore privileged histories. As one such "hegemonizing" history, sinicization has come to be suspected (rightly so, in my view) of masking other narratives. Although not an explicit theme in this book, it is easy to see how studying the Manchus, the quintessential Chinese "Other," extends the possibilities of deconstructing "China," Chinese nationalism, and Chinese identity/identities, prominent concerns in much recent scholarship.[116] The tendency to see the Qing as something more than a virtual Chinese dynasty and to go beyond the sinicization debate has been boosted by this intellectual climate. These trends have been further enhanced by the availability since the early 1980s of vast new archival materials on the Qing.[117] The Manchu-Han relationship has figured prominently in this work, notably in research on the Qing communications systems, the imperial household, attitudes toward ritual, the relationship of intellectuals to the state, mysterious queue-cutting cases with sinister anti-Manchu undertones, and factional politics from the early eighteenth through the mid-nineteenth centuries.[118] Broader consideration of the military dimension as a defining quality of Qing rule also fits into this new "third wave."[119] A consensus is growing among some scholars that even if the Manchus were acculturated and ruled in part as Chinese, there always remained something palpably "different" about them, or at least the perception of something different. The problem is, of course, how to define that "something."[120]

The most significant contribution in this area undoubtedly has been the new research into Manchu history by Pamela Kyle Crossley. In her pioneering 1990 book, *Orphan Warriors*, Crossley questioned the prevailing interpretations on the Manchus. In a strong challenge to the conclusions of Mary Wright, Crossley argued that "knowledge of life at the court sheds no light upon the life of the Manchu people in China." Seeking to dissociate the interests and actions of elite Manchus from those of ordinary Manchu bannermen, Crossley's goal was to show how "ordinary" Manchus remained distinct from the Han Chinese as their identity was reshaped in the course of the late nineteenth century.[121] Furthermore, taking on Wittfogel, Crossley demonstrated that Manchu identity—what she eloquently called "an inner difference that [had] no outward sign"—in fact survived beyond the fall of the dynasty, well into the twentieth century.[122]

In her book and a number of important articles, Crossley has demolished traditional ideas of Manchu assimilation and sinicization and has constructed an altogether different model of the evolution of Manchu identity. Instead of a strong Manchu identity in the early seventeenth century weakening over time due to the effects of acculturation, Crossley portrays Manchu identity as having been originally quite weak but strengthening over time *in spite* of acculturation. Though she acknowledges the existence of descent groups as quasi-racial constructs in the Ming, for the Qing, Crossley perceives "an internal diachronicity" wherein identity progressed from "cultural to racial to ethnic arenas of negotiation."[123] Before the conquest, she argues, being Manchu was essentially a kind of cultural self-reference. Elsewhere, she calls it a political identity based on evident cultural orientation; entirely within the purview of state control, Crossley asserts that "identities could be and frequently were metamorphosed by edict."[124] By the mid-eighteenth century, however, court insecurity arising in part from the "dissipating cultural criteria of Manchuness" led, in Crossley's revisionist interpretation, to the creation of new "racialized" identities through the retroactive invoking of genealogy as a category for deciding who was and was not Manchu. This "ahistorical" use of genealogy owed to the political and ideological preoccupations of the Qianlong court, preoccupations which also stimulated the "documentary institutionalization" of Manchu history and culture. In this way, Crossley argues, "a sense of definitive culture receded before a rising concensus [*sic*] of definitive race—that is, of immutable identity based on ancestral descent."[125] An identity which, according to Crossley's definition, was truly "ethnic" emerged only in the mid- to late nineteenth century, after the devastation of the Taiping Rebellion (when Manchu communities in Nanjing and Hangzhou were slaughtered) meant the alienation of banner garrison communities scattered around China and the construction of a common identity for these newly marginalized groups.

It will be obvious that there are several points of disagreement between the narrative Crossley has offered and the story told in this book. In some ways, what I present here is a "neotraditional" version of Manchu history in the Qing. That is to say, like Crossley's view, it insists that the notion of Manchu difference mattered throughout the dynasty and that the Manchus were not in fact ever really absorbed or assimilated. At the same time, like older views (and unlike Crossley), the present study argues that this difference was always ethnic in nature—in other words, that with the creation of the Eight Banners in the early seventeenth century the fundamental outlines of Manchu identity were already falling into place, and that ethnicity did not suddenly appear in the second half of the nineteenth century. The differences in our arguments arise as much from our reliance on different sources as from our divergent interpretations of ethnicity. But however they differ, both the revisionist and neotraditional views agree on two key points: that Manchu identity was constantly in flux, and that without the Manchus a complete picture of the Qing world is impossible.

The new narratives of the Qing that have been written over the last fifteen years or so stressing the importance of including Manchus (and Chinese) as "ethnic" actors have enriched our knowledge of contemporary society and politics greatly and have breathed new life into the debate over the Manchus. They share a common weakness, however, which is that they do not offer a ready way to reconcile the acknowledged fact of Manchu acculturation, which the Sinicizationists stress, with the supposed continuity of Manchu difference, which the Altaicists stress. If ethnic sovereignty was maintained throughout the Qing, the obvious question is to ask how this was accomplished if the cultural "stuff" of Manchu identity was so quickly vitiated. Even though we know that Manchu otherness mattered to the Han Chinese we must demonstrate that being Manchu mattered to Manchus, too, and that Manchu ethnicity was somehow maintained after the late-eighteenth-century waning of the norms of an earlier age, embodied in what the court called the Manchu Way. Otherwise, it will be hard to avoid the charge that when it comes to the Manchus there was not really an ethnic discourse in the Qing at all, that their identity faded and its link to political power (if it ever existed) was cut, and that talk of a Manchu-centered approach is pure fancy.

My response to this challenge has been to reexamine Manchu lives and institutions in the new light of Manchu-language sources. By exploring various dimensions of the Manchu world, most notably the Eight Banner system, the chapters that follow show that Manchu ethnic identity emerged with the creation of the Eight Banners in the early seventeenth century, and that it was able to survive the dramatic effects of eighteenth-century acculturation because it was expressed through and reinforced by this vital, durable Manchu institution. They provide, I hope, a broader basis for evaluating the fate of the Manchus and the nature of Qing rule in one of the basic narratives of modern Chinese history.

PART ONE

# Structures of Eight Banner Society

# CHAPTER ONE

# The Eight Banners and the Origins of the Manchus

The Eight Banners, "the most famous of all Manchu institutions,"[1] began as an umbrella organization overseeing the mobilization of Qing military forces and the management of the many different populations associated with those forces in the forty-odd years leading up to the 1644 Qing conquest. Included within it were soldiers, officers, servants, and slaves; Manchus, Mongols, acculturated frontier Chinese, and Koreans; men and women, young and old, able and infirm. After the conquest, the Eight Banners was retained as part of the administrative structure of Qing government, its ranks restricted to the original Qing populations and their descendants, exclusive of Han Chinese civilians.[2] The banners were thus a closed corporation, although there were a few additions of new warrior groups later in the seventeenth century.

Among the early-seventeenth-century Manchus—then called Jurchens—as among the Mongols four centuries earlier, "the army was society."[3] Membership in the banners was acquired at birth, making them the institutional home of a martial caste—an exclusive hereditary social group distinguished by a common occupation, soldiering. Membership in this caste played a vital role in the maintenance of Manchu ethnic identity and the perpetuation of Qing rule. This role effectively ensured the political importance of the banners into the middle and later Qing periods and secured the perpetuation of the banner system until the dynasty's collapse in 1912, and even a bit beyond.[4]

## WHAT WAS THE EIGHT BANNERS?

The expression "banner system" (Ch *baqi zhidu*) is widely used by modern scholars, and the Eight Banners is commonly referred to as a single collective (and treated as such grammatically, too). But it is probably best to avoid thinking of the banners literally as an unchanging "system" or a unitary entity. The Eight Banners was a hybrid institution that combined a range of military, social, economic, and political functions; as the various dimensions of these changed over time, the banner system changed, too. As a military force, it was the engine of expansion and the mainstay of power during the Manchu takeover in the mid-seventeenth century, and retained an important military function through the eighteenth century and even, in a modified way, into the first half of the nineteenth. Individual banners also served as power bases for leading figures in the early Qing (not excepting the emperor, who held three banners under his personal command), making them politically significant. By the later 1700s, when the banners had ceased to be the home of the Qing "power elite," they continued to be the home of much of its "prestige elite," insofar as the Qing nobility managed to hold on to some of the cachet and wealth of earlier generations. As a social organization, the banners supervised the affairs of ordinary soldiers and their households, whose every member was registered in censuses taken at three-year intervals. Births, deaths, marriages, adoptions, changes in residence and employment—everything was reported to the banner, which was also responsible for the welfare of everyone on these registers and thus deeply involved in both national and local economies.

Like the Imperial Household Department (*Neiwufu/Dorgi baita be uheri kadalara yamun*) and the Court of Colonial Dependencies (*Lifanyuan/Tulergi golo be dasara jurgan*), the Eight Banners was a uniquely Manchu innovation in the government of Qing China and one of its most enigmatic institutions. Among native Chinese forms of military or civil organization, there was nothing like it; indeed, the hereditary principles underlying banner membership ran directly contrary to the idea of qualification according to individual merit which underlay the Chinese civil service since the Song. Perhaps its novelty or strangeness on the Chinese scene explains why it is so much less well understood than other parts of the imperial administration that boast of precedents in the Ming. As Meng Sen wrote in 1936:

> The Qing dynasty considered itself the Manchu nation, but the Manchus also called themselves "bannermen" (*qiren*). It is generally held that the Manchus were the original nation (*guo*) of the Qing. All Manchus were in the banners, so that within the [Manchu] nation were contained the Eight Banners and within China was contained the Manchu nation; not for one day were the two mixed together. But though the Qing ruled China for over 267 years, Chinese people are unable to say what the real nature of the Eight Banners was.[5]

While it is an exaggeration to say that Manchus and Chinese never mixed together, Meng's statement that "people are unable to say what the real nature of the Eight Banners was" contains a good measure of truth. Historians readily acknowledge the special niche of the banner system in Qing history, but its internal structure, its function in the governance of the empire, and its place in Manchu history during the Qing remain unclear at best. Much of this book is devoted to exploring different aspects of this hallmark Qing institution.

The Eight Banners was a fiercely complex institution (American readers might want to think in terms of a cross between the Marine Corps, the Civil Service, and the Veterans Administration, thickly overlaid with a combination of old-boy networks, political preferences, and partially articulated Affirmative Action policies) that evolved continually for over three hundred years. Moreover, for reasons of dynastic security, a lot about it remained hidden from public view. The present study thus does not pretend to be a complete institutional history of the Eight Banners, though I hope that it may serve as a useful introduction. There are a number of important areas of its workings, such as the role of the banners in Qing economic history, that I have been able to touch on only briefly. Throughout, my focus has been on the relationship of institutional structures and practices to Manchu ethnicity. Temporally, too, I have set the limits of my inquiry to the first half of the Qing period, which I see as the time when the connection between institution and identity was most crucially forged. This is not to say, of course, that changes do not occur during the later part of the Qing; but I would argue that, once established, the connection persisted with relative stability into the twentieth century.

Against the background of the rise of the fledgling Manchu polity I begin in this chapter by examining the early history of the Manchus as a people, their political organization, and initial registration into something called "banners." As will become apparent, these processes were concurrent, and linked closely with the initial formation of Manchu identity. I will show that institutional affiliation, along with interpretations of descent and culture, played an important role in the adumbration of ethnic categories and boundaries in the pre- and postconquest period. This assessment coincides with that of Jin Dechun, a Chinese bannerman-martial writing in the early eighteenth century:

> Each banner is divided into three sections. The tribes that were originally Nurhaci's . . . make up the Manchu [section]. The various bow-drawing

peoples from the Northern Desert . . . form the Mongol [section], while the descendants of people from Liao[dong], former Ming commanders and emissaries, those from the other dynasty who defected with multitudes [of soldiers], and captives are separately attached to the Chinese banners.[6]

It was also the understanding of the Qing historian Wei Yuan, writing in the 1840s:

> For the same group [*zulei*], language is the same, territory is the same, style of dress and habitation are the same, living in cities or hunting, the customs are the same. Thus civil officials were ordered to make a written national language based on the spoken language, and not use Mongolian or Chinese characters; thus Mongols and *Hanjun* were each accorded their own banner registration, and were not put into the Manchu Eight Banners.[7]

The goal of this chapter, then, is to build on these observations to see how ethnic identity and banner status were intertwined in the budding Qing state.

## MYTHS OF MANCHU ORIGINS

The ethnogenesis of the Manchus is not entirely clear. Much about it is hidden by a shroud of secrecy created by the Qing court in the mid-eighteenth century, when it was anxious to project a unified imperial image onto a fragmented and humble past and was in a position to edit some of the historical materials relating to that period. One approach to the question of Manchu origins is to briefly consider the circumstances surrounding the history of the Manchus as a minority group in China today. Once we know who the Manchus *are*, we will be in a better position to understand who the Manchus *were*.

A few years after the founding of the People's Republic of China in 1949, Manchus were officially recognized as a "minority nationality," in theory distinguished from the majority Han nationality on the basis of four defining characteristics set out by Stalin: territory, language, economy, and psychological nature.[8] One might expect that those who wished to declare themselves "Manchus" (Ch *Manzu*) had to produce some sort of evidence along these lines testifying to their non-Han ethnic status. Since, however, most Manchus left their native land for China in the 1600s, and since all but a tiny fraction had also long since lost the ability to speak the Manchu language and in many other ways had become highly acculturated, demonstrating one's "Manchuness" was not always easy. Nonetheless, in 1953, 2.4 million people nationwide were registered as Manchus, the majority in Beijing and in the Northeast (Ch *Dongbei*, i.e., Manchuria).[9] Twenty-five years later, a 1978 survey revealed that this number had grown by 10 percent to 2.65 million.[10] At the time of the first "modern" census in 1982, however, the Manchu population had risen to 4.3 million; in 1987, the number had increased again to 7 million, almost three times what it had been nine years before.[11] Astonishingly, in 1993 the figure rose further, to a total of 9.82 million—more than four times the number of Manchus reported forty years before—making the Manchus the second most numerous minority population in China today.[12]

The rocketing rate of Manchu population growth obviously cannot be explained by normal rates of reproduction. The fact is that, owing partly to liberal state policies toward official non-Han minorities, within the past two decades many people who formerly preferred to hide their Manchu identity have gradually decided to declare it openly. In addition, among these nearly ten million people are some who evidently never thought of themselves as Manchus before but have now chosen to do so. In other words, not everyone who claims Manchu ethnic status today can be considered Manchu in terms of actual descent from a Manchu clan (not that this means they need be regarded as any less "Manchu"). As Wang Zhonghan has made clear (and as mentioned in the Introduction), a great number of those people who in recent years have decided to identify themselves as Manchus are Han Chinese whose ancestors were registered somewhere within the banner system —in the Chinese banners, the Imperial Household Department, as servants in Manchu households, or as agricultural workers on banner-run manors.[13] Although by strict standards of descent such people could be considered Han, their historical association with the Eight Banners qualifies them under the minority nationality laws of the Chinese government to choose ethnic status as Manchus.[14]

That anyone who is able to prove descent from a banner person can claim to be Manchu signals two things, already touched on in the Introduction. First, it signals the constructedness of ethnic categories in contemporary China and cautions us against essentializing the category "Manchu" or assuming some constant of "Manchuness" over time. Second, it signals that Manchu identity and banner identity to some degree overlap. More important for our purposes in this book, these two observations about contemporary Manchu ethnicity raise important questions about Manchu ethnicity in the Qing. First, it is worth asking whether it is not probable that Manchu ethnicity in Qing China conforms to what we know about ethnicity just about everywhere and that, like the twentieth-century category, the seventeenth-century category "Manchu" was also "constructed." Second, if Manchus today are Manchus by virtue of having been in the banners (or related to someone who was), how can one be sure that the same was not true of Manchus in the Qing? All of which is to say that "Manchu" is and always has been a malleable classification. To find out who the Manchus were we must trace the ways in which the category "Manchu" was shaped historically, how the boundaries that delimited it from other ethnic categories were made, how they were guarded, and how they changed over time. The history we discover in this fashion will not be the same history that the group tells itself, though it will intersect it at certain points. For while we can probably assume that anyone who has ever thought of himself or herself as Manchu—whether today or in the Qing—has done so with ultimate reference to a notion of who this group was, what it did, and where it came from, such notions are themselves the contested interpretations of the past. Sometimes they are represented as myth, sometimes as history. We can easily find both in the Manchu case.

First, the myth. In the Qing, the story that Manchus liked to tell about their origins centered on the legend of three heavenly maidens, Enggulen, Jenggulen, and Fekulen. According to the legend, the three sisters descended one day from heaven to bathe in a lake at the foot of Mount Bukūri (later said to be in the Changbai Mountains, near the modern Chinese border with Korea). When they emerged from the water, the youngest of them, Fekulen, found a magical red fruit on top of her clothing. The fruit had been placed

*Fig. 1. (Opposite)*   Fekulen says farewell to her sisters. This illustration from the Qianlong edition of the *Manchu Veritable Records* shows the youngest heavenly maiden Fekulen bidding farewell to her sisters Enggulen and Jenggulen, who are returning to heaven. Lake Tamun is pictured below, and the peaks of the Changbaishan rise up on the right. At the top is seen the magpie, messenger from the Lord of Heaven, who placed the red fruit on top of Fekulen's clothes while the three maidens were bathing. The original legends in Manchu and Mongolian both read: "Having become pregnant, Fekulen is separated from her two elder sisters." The Chinese legend reads: "Having become pregnant, Fekulen is unable to jointly ascend." Reproduced courtesy of the Tōyō Bunko, Tokyo.

there by a magpie, a spirit-messenger from the Lord of Heaven. Having no-where to put the fruit while she dressed, and finding it very attractive, she placed it for a moment in her mouth. As soon as she had done this, however, it passed down her throat and her body suddenly became "heavy"—she had conceived a child. Her sisters returned to heaven, while she assumed a human form and later gave birth to a male child whom she named Bukūri Yongšon, the progenitor of the Manchu ruling house. As the oldest version of the legend (dated 1635) to come down to us tells it:

> Once the child became an adult, his mother instructed him: "You should go to the Jušen country to live. . . . When the Jušen people ask you who you are, who your parents are, and what your name is, say, 'I am from the shores of Lake Bulhūri at the foot of the Bukūri Mountains. My name is Bukūri Yongšon. My clan, descended from heaven, is the Aisin Gioro. I have no father. My mother was the third of heaven's daughters. . . . I was also a spirit of heaven above. My soul was made into a red fruit by the king of heaven, and was delivered by a spirit who had taken the form of a magpie. And so I was born.'"[15]

The story continues by explaining how Bukūri Yongšon became the leader of the Jušen (i.e., Jurchen) at a place called Odoli, and (in some versions) notes the settlement of his descendants later at Hetu Ala, which would become the first capital of the Qing founder, Nurhaci (1559–1626). The frequent re-telling of this myth in official chronicles, each time with slight modifications, bespeaks its importance as a legitimating account of Qing origins. Particularly revealing is the anachronistic substitution in later redactions of "Manchu nation" (Ma *Manju gurun*) for "Jurchen nation" (Ma *Jušen gurun*) and the link made between the kingdom ruled by Bukūri Yongšon during the Ming and the land of the Jin-dynasty Jurchens, changes which plainly sought to push back the horizon of Manchu continuity and establish the Manchus, and specifically the Aisin Gioro, as the inheritors of the imperial Jin legacy.

Incorporated into Qing chronicles by 1636 (the year after the name "Manchu" was officially promulgated), the foundation legend was only one way the past was put to use in the creation of Manchu identity.[16] Another way was as "history," that is, "the record or memory of actual (or supposedly actual) events which happened to the group."[17] One such history, written later in the Qing, was the *Researches of Manchu Origins* (*Manzhou yuanliu kao/Manju-sai da sekiyen-i kimcin*). This work makes detailed associations between the Manchus and the places, peoples, and rulers of the ancient Northeast; others tell of the rise of Nurhaci, his subduing of rival Jurchen leaders, and his right-eous grievances and campaigns against the Ming, which were carried on to fruition by his sons Hong Taiji and Dorgon, who finally realized the "great enterprise." As Crossley has shown in her study of this text, much of what is said is not historically verifiable, and some of it was plainly wrong. Its pur-pose, as she notes, "was not to bring science to Manchu origins, but author-ity."[18] For this reason, we might think of both the mythical and historical ac-counts as examples of what Anthony Smith calls "myths of restoration," which aim to "connect the present generation to a noble pedigree . . . to reg-ister a dynastic and territorial claim . . . and thereby to reinforce the often tenuous solidarity of their regna through an appeal to community of beliefs and customs founded on common ancestry."[19] In the creation of these "myths of restoration," accuracy was an entirely secondary consideration. Hence we can say that just as getting the facts wrong is an integral part of the process of creating "nations," so it is likewise an integral part of the process of creating ethnicity.[20] In proclaiming their timeless origins in the Changbai Mountains and stressing the antiquity of their imperial roots, the Manchus were only do-ing what ethnic groups have always done.

## WHO WERE THE JURCHENS?

In the search for Manchu origins, the most important point to note is that in the beginning, there was no Manchu nation, only many Jurchen tribes. The name "Manchu" and the creation of a unified state came about at vir-tually the same time, in the 1630s, prior to which time it is correct only to speak of Jurchen (*Nüzhen/Jušen*) peoples, Jurchen tribes, Jurchen leaders, and Jurchen institutions.[21]

Who, then, were the Jurchens? Judging only by the similarities between their languages (both part of the Tungusic branch of the Altaic family[22]), it seems quite likely that Ming-period Jurchens were the descendants of the people who founded the Jin dynasty in the twelfth century. These people originally lived in the forests and along the rivers of what is now the Rus-sian province of Primorskii krai and the Chinese province of Heilongjiang. Though many Qing and modern accounts stress a connection between them, the relationship between the Jurchens and other peoples known to have in-habited roughly the same region in earlier periods, beginning with the Su-shen (ca. 1100 B.C.E.), the Yi-lou (ca. 200 C.E.), the Wu-ji (ca. 500 C.E.), and the Mo-he (ca. 700 C.E.), remains uncertain.[23] By the turn of the fifteenth century, that is, not long after the fall of the Yuan and the founding of the Ming dynasty, Chinese and Korean records indicate that there were three main Jurchen groups: the Jianzhou, the Haixi, and the Yeren. These are called in Chinese *bu*, usually translated as "tribes," though how much each was possessed of "tribal" unity is open to question. All three Jurchen *bu* were under the nominal authority of the Chinese state, which administered Jurchen lands loosely through local commanderies, called *wei-suo*. Political ties to the court consisted principally of the patents that tribal leaders received—commanderies were commonly entrusted to them—confirming their positions and securing their subservience to Ming rule.[24] We also know that Jurchen leaders visited Beijing on occasion as part of tributary missions.

The Jianzhou Jurchens, named for one of the Ming commanderies, originally lived mainly in the eastern portions of the region, on the lower reaches of the Sungari River (see Map 1). Around the year 1400 some families—including that of the future Qing founder—led an out-migration of a few hundred households, first south to the Tumen River, near the Changbai Mountains where the Jianzhou commandery was located, and then, a few years later, somewhat to the west, on the eastern fringe of the Liao River basin. Two hundred years later, this area became a center of Jurchen political activity when the Jianzhou branch began to consolidate its power at the expense of its closest neighbors, the Haixi Jurchens and the Ming Chinese. The Haixi Jurchens were settled to the north and west of the Jianzhou, straddling the Sungari, Mudan, and Ussuri rivers south of the Amur. In addition to three main clans, the Hada, Ula, and Hoifa, among the Haixi was a group of western Mongol origin called the Yehe, who had taken over neighboring Jurchen lands and adopted a Jurchen surname, Nara, in the process.[25] The third Jurchen tribe, the Yeren (also called the Donghai Jurchen), inhabited the eastern and northern peripheries of the Jianzhou and Haixi territories. The core of what would become the "Manchu" people—that is, the people at the center of the banner system—were originally either Jianzhou or Haixi Jurchens, along with two of the Yeren tribes; the rest of the Yeren were never integrated, socially, politically, or economically, into what later became Manchu structures.

The traditional Jurchen way of life was a blend of the pastoral and sedentary, combining hunting and fishing with limited nomadism and agriculture, supplemented by the tributary trade to which they were entitled as

*Map 1.*   Manchuria in the early seventeenth century.

subjects of the ruling Chinese dynasty. Hunting was of primary importance among the Jianzhou and Haixi, while the Yeren relied more on fishing. Pasturing activities were seasonal; unlike the nomadic Mongols, the seminomadic Jurchens preferred to live in fixed settlements most of the year, and so dwelled in geographically distinct villages (Ma *gašan*).[26] The development of the village from a single-clan unit to a multiple-clan unit reflected the increasing complexity of Jurchen social organization in the fifteenth and sixteenth centuries and the shift from descent-based settlement patterns to geographically-based settlements. Early Jurchen villages appear to have consisted of families all belonging to the same "clan" or surname (*xing/hala*).[27] Since exogamy was practiced (one could not marry a person of the same surname), this eventually gave way to a situation in which families (*jia/uksun*) belonging to different clans inhabited the same village. Increasing geographic dispersion of its members meant that within each clan evolved different lineages (*shizu/mukūn*) sharing the same surname. The latter progressively lost its connotation as a marker of common descent (explaining why there were different branches of the Gioro, Gūwalgiya, and other clans), although it continued to serve this function symbolically.[28] At the same time, villages began to develop their own leadership structures. Both processes weakened the power of lineage ties and augured the introduction of vertical lines of social organization.

By the second half of the sixteenth century, Jurchen social organization was also greatly affected by burgeoning economic activity among the Haixi and Jianzhou. This included tributary trade with the Ming court (which required, among other things, ten thousand sable pelts annually), as well as regular supervised markets where Jurchens and Chinese could exchange horses, furs, honey, and ginseng for tea, silk, cotton, rice, salt, and agricultural implements. By the 1580s five such markets were convened monthly, each attracting several hundred to a few thousand people. The Jurchens supplemented this by engaging in unofficial trade with Chinese, as well as with Korean and Mongol merchants.[29] Artisanal industry was as yet quite limited. Their southward move put them much closer to Korean communities, as well as to Chinese communities inhabiting the Liaodong region, a fertile plain enclosed by the famous "Willow Palisade," and the one part of Manchuria that was fairly firmly under direct Ming control. At this point the Jianzhou evidently began to pursue agriculture more seriously. Not only could they obtain tools (including, for the first time, iron plowshares) and draft animals with greater ease, but they were also in a position to learn better farming techniques, such as the application of fertilizer to the soil. A report of 1492 points out, "The savage ones [i.e., the Jianzhou Jurchens] know only hunting, and did not originally till the land. [But] I have heard that recently [they have been] very active in agriculture."[30] Slightly later Korean observers were also struck by the rapid development of Jurchen agriculture, where "no field was left unplowed."[31] Still, hunting seems to have remained the backbone of Jurchen livelihood. This had very important implications for the Jurchens' later development into a military power on the Northeast frontier, since, unlike farming, hunting made use of quasi-military skills that were effectively practiced on a collective, not a household, basis.

Increasing economic development brought with it increasing social differentiation. Contemporary sources reveal three main types of population: those of elite status (Ma *irgen*), immediately beholden to the tribal leader (or, later, the khan); those of semi-free or dependent status, somewhat confusingly called *jušen*; and those of unfree status, called *aha, booi*, or *booi aha*, a term commonly translated as "slaves."[32]

At the lowest end of the social scale were the *aha*, who had long formed part of Jurchen households, where they performed menial tasks. *Aha* were chattel, freely bought and sold by their masters; many seem to have originally been Han Chinese or Koreans captured by Jurchen raiding parties, though it seems that they quickly assimilated into Jurchen society. As agriculture spread among the Jianzhou in the sixteenth century and the importance of *aha* as a source of labor rose, predation across the border also increased. In the late 1500s, with warfare between Jurchen groups becoming more common, a significant proportion of additions to the *aha* ranks were not Han or Koreans, but other Jurchens; still later, in the 1620s, would come more Han, captured during fighting with the Ming. Many *aha* were later incorporated into the banner system in so-called *booi* "bondservant" companies, by which time their social status had risen considerably, although they were still unfree. Ethnic divisions regarding these late-coming *aha* were, as will become clear, generally retained.

Above the *aha* were the *jušen*. The majority of the Jurchen population fell into this category, which formed the basis for the original constitution of regular banner companies around the turn of the seventeenth century. *Jušen*, it seems, were originally freeholders (though some had formerly been *aha*)[33] upon whom, in the course of the sixteenth century, were thrust an increasing number of obligations, most notably military service, garrison duty, and corvee. An important distinction between them and the *aha* was that *jušen* rendered service to the tribal or lineage head, not to any household master. They were also responsible for providing their own arms, indicating at least the expectation of economic self-reliance. As a phrase in the *Manzhou shilu* put it: "How would a master survive without *aha*? How would a chief live without *jušen*?"[34] We may think of *jušen* as essentially independent householders—many of whom owned *aha* themselves—who owed certain limited types of obligations to their social superiors. Not all *jušen* were Jurchens. Some were Koreans and Han Chinese who had come over to the Jianzhou territories, mostly in the late Ming when the frontier situation was already highly unsettled, and were welcomed there on a more-or-less equal basis as native Jurchens, although they usually tended to live in their own, separate settlements, referred to in Chinese records as *manzi cheng*.[35]

At the top of Jurchen society were the *irgen*, various types of elites to whom were due the services of ordinary *jušen* and who owned a disproportionate share of property and slaves. Most commonly these people were tribal chiefs (*buzhang* or *qiuzhang/beile*) allied with the Ming under the commandery system, lineage heads (*zuzhang/mukūn da*), or village leaders (*cunzhang/gašan-i da*), along with certain well-placed superintendents (*daren/amban*). All were in a good position to profit from tributary and trade arrangements or, in the case of booty, to claim the largest share of captured goods and people. The accumulation of assets and, gradually, military and political power, in the hands of a relative few was further accelerated by the general rule to keep chieftainships and headships within the same family. The hereditary nature of Jurchen leadership gradually intensified rivalry between the different groups, all struggling over the relatively limited pool of resources offered in the Manchurian frontier. This rivalry peaked in the decades just before and after 1600, producing sophisticated methods of social organization more conducive to the conduct of war. As it happened, these developments coincided with a marked weakening of Ming Chinese central authority, giving the victor in the Jurchen power game a golden opportunity to make a play for the biggest prize of all. This victor was Nurhaci, the "great progenitor" (Ch *taizu*) of the Qing imperial family, the House of Aisin Gioro.[36] The prize, of course, was China.

▸ THE JIANZHOU ASCENDANCY

Nurhaci succeeded to the leadership of the Jianzhou Left Branch in 1583, when he was twenty-four years old. This position had been in the same lineage, part of the Gioro (pronounced *ghee-ore-oh*) *hala* known as the Aisin, or "Gold" Gioro, for six generations, ever since Möngke Temür (later named a descendant of Bukūri Yongšon) led his people south from Odoli to the Changbai Mountain region in 1400 or so.[37] Möngke Temür was confirmed in around 1412 by the Ming emperor as head of a subdivision of the Jianzhou Jurchens, but was killed in tribal fighting in 1433, and leadership passed to his younger half-brother, Fanca. At this point the fate of the tribe, which numbered only about five hundred households (down by half from ten years before), was in peril. Fanca made the decision to move his people once again, this time farther west, away from the Korean border, which recurrent attacks by Korean forces had proved inhospitable. In 1440 the remnants of the Odoli group joined up with the main branch of the Jianzhou Jurchens, led by another chieftain, Li-man-zhu, at Hetu Ala (lit., "broad hill") on the Suksuhu River. After 1442, the Odoli leadership split into two factions, the Jianzhou Right Branch, led by Fanca, and the Left Branch, led by Möngke Temür's son (Fanca's nephew), Cungšan.

The main Jianzhou branch of Li-man-zhu at Hetu Ala was composed of Jurchen tribesmen who had also emigrated from a neighboring district in the north, and the three groups at this time joined forces and resumed their friendly relations. Their defensive capabilities thus renewed (Korean estimates were that the Jianzhou together could put as many as three to four thousand horsemen into the field), the Jianzhou population stabilized, and relations with the Chinese and Korean courts improved. Despite intensive intermarriage between their leading families, however, the alliance was a loose one; a request in 1472 by his son for aid to revenge the death of Li-man-zhu was spurned by the Left and Right Jianzhou.[38] Gradually, the descendants of Li-man-zhu faded from prominence, and by the early 1500s overall leadership of the Jianzhou Jurchens fell to the descendants of Fanca and Cungšan.[39] Intermarriage between leading clans of the two branches was common, but for most of the sixteenth century the Right Branch remained the stronger.[40] Gradually, a rift grew between it and the Left Branch, now led by Giocangga, the great-grandson of Fanca, and his five brothers, known collectively as the *ningguta beile* (the "six chieftains"). Twice, in 1574 and again in 1582, Giocangga and his son Taksi conspired with local Ming military officials to ambush the leader of the Right Jianzhou and secure the Left's ascendancy. They succeeded in their second attempt, but in the process Giocangga and Taksi were killed by Ming forces—perhaps by design—leaving both branches of the Jianzhou Jurchens in disarray.

This turmoil was worsened by the simultaneous decline of the Hada, the strongest of the four Haixi Jurchen tribes. The Jianzhou had maintained good relations with the Hada—again, frequently resorting to intermarriage—but were never on equal terms with them or any of the Haixi tribes. Power relations among the Haixi, who led the way in building walled fortifications, were more even, but the death of a prominent Hada chieftain in 1582 left the Haixi-Jianzhou alliance he had forged in a muddle and raised questions over the Jianzhou future.[41] This left an opening for someone who might wish to put the alliance back together and perhaps build something even larger—someone like Nurhaci, the eldest son of Taksi, to whom the chieftainship of the Left Jianzhou fell in 1582. Even if, as legend had it, he only had thirteen suits of armor to his name, Nurhaci found himself facing a uniquely favorable set of historical circumstances. It was in the manner of Chinggis Khan that, to avenge his father's death, Nurhaci chose to pursue a path of military expansion, which eventually led him to unify the Jurchen tribes, abandon his ancestors' policy of coexistence with the Ming, and establish his own competing imperial enterprise.

The details of Nurhaci's rise to power have been well told in other accounts, and do not require a full rehearsal here.[42] In 1587, he founded his first walled city, Fe Ala. Though close to the base of the "six chieftains," Nurhaci's decision to begin in a separate location likely indicates the existence of opposition to him among the Jianzhou themselves. In 1593 he successfully crushed an alliance of Haixi Jurchens and Mongols led against him by his brother-in-law, the Yehe chieftain Narimbulu, and in the same year he may have helped defend Korea against an invasion by Hideyoshi. These accomplishments bolstered his standing as the leader of the Jurchens and earned Nurhaci the gratitude of the Ming court, which granted him new titles and privileges. Backed by at least fifteen thousand men-at-arms, and with a sufficient economic basis now assured (he personally owned a herd of seven hundred horses),[43] Nurhaci pressed on with a successful attack on the Hada

*Fig. 2. (Opposite)*    Nurhaci attacking the Hada. Another illustration from the *Manchu Veritable Records*, showing Nurhaci in the saddle. The incident depicted here, involving Nurhaci in a skirmish with soldiers from the Hada tribe, took place in 1593. Outnumbered by the enemy, whom he hoped to draw into an ambush, Nurhaci—nearly thrown by his frightened horse—made a desperate crossing shot and felled the horse of the Hada chieftain Menggebulu, who then remounted the horse of his servant Daimbulu (seen running off at right center, covering his head). At the end of the day, Nurhaci and his men (three cavalry and twenty-odd infantry) had killed twelve men and captured six, along with eighteen horses. The *Manzhou shilu* is filled with such heroic tales. Reproduced courtesy of the Tōyō Bunko, Tokyo.

in 1599. A few years later, he relocated his base to nearby Hetu Ala, the old Jianzhou citadel, which became his first capital, named Yenden (Manchu for "ascent"). In 1606, he won recognition from Khalkha Mongol allies as the "wise and respected khan" (Ma *sure kundulen han*), and removed the last remaining internal threat to his authority by having his brother Šurhaci arrested in 1609. By then, he had extended his control over the Hoifa, and the Ula surrendered to him not long after, in 1613. In the meantime, the two main Yeren tribes, the Hūrha and Warka, were brought into the fold after a series of campaigns led by Eidu, one of Nurhaci's most trustworthy companions, culminated in their nominal subjugation in 1611.[44]

In 1616, Nurhaci openly declared his imperial ambitions by proclaiming himself the "bright khan" (Ma *genggiyen han*) of the "Latter Jin country" (*hou Jin guo/amaga Aisin gurun*). This was a major step. In so doing, he was deliberately suggesting that the political unity of the Jurchens was complete (or nearly so), and that he and his followers were the legitimate heirs to the imperial tradition left by the founders of the twelfth-century Jin dynasty. The simultaneous issuance of his "Seven Grievances" against the Ming, which explicitly blamed the Chinese for the treacherous murder of his father and grandfather, left no doubt that the Jurchens now openly rejected their former status as Ming subjects. The lines thus drawn, in 1619 Nurhaci delivered a major defeat to Ming forces at Sarhū, confirming his mandate as Jurchen khan and rival to the Ming emperor. Later the same year, the Yehe were finally persuaded to cease their resistance to Nurhaci, putting the finishing touches on the new Jianzhou-led pan-Jurchen confederation. Just two years later, in 1621, the waxing Jin state overran the Liaodong region and the Jin capital was transferred to Liaoyang (called *dergi hecen*, "upper capital," in Manchu). In 1625, the capital was transferred again to the former Ming city of Shenyang, later renamed Mukden ("florescence"), where Nurhaci died in 1626. It was from here that Nurhaci's grandson, Fulin, set off nineteen years later to assume his place on the Chinese throne in Beijing.

ROOTS OF POWER: THE FORMATION OF THE EIGHT BANNERS

As suggested earlier, the Jianzhou had never been the strongest of the Jurchen groups, and their rise as the supreme power in Manchuria must have seemed unexpectedly rapid to other Jurchens, as well as to Korean, Mongol, and Chinese observers. Many factors lie behind the Jianzhou success, most obviously perhaps Nurhaci's excellent political skills, his ability to win over former enemies, and his cautious accretion of personal power before proclaiming himself khan. Other factors include the dedication of the people he attracted to his side: like Chinggis (again), he relied more on the mechanism of the "companionhood" among his followers than on direct family ties to cement alliances and widen support.[45] Poor Chinese generalship and the erratic Ming response to the alarming developments on its northeastern border are also part of the story. But perhaps the most important explanation of Jurchen success is to be found in the development of the Eight Banners, which provided an efficient means of mobilizing an army and made the integrated Jurchen military virtually unbeatable; the banners also helped transform the disparate elements of the new Jin state into a unified, responsive whole by furnishing new, vertical organizational ties that decisively outstripped tribe and lineage in importance, and helped to compensate for the as-yet incomplete centralization of political power.

Unlike the origins of the Manchus as a people, there is no "foundation myth" for the Eight Banners—which does not mean, however, that its beginnings are very much clearer. It is generally believed that the banner system traced its origins to the methods used in conducting large-scale hunts, called *aba* in Manchu and commonly referred to in English by the French term *battue*.[46] Hunting culture was something the Manchus shared with most of the historic peoples of North Asia, including the Jurchens, the Khitans, and, of course, the Mongols.[47] The strategy of the *aba* called for many small hunting parties (probably no more than ten mounted archers each) to follow a pre-arranged schedule according to which they completely encircled a large swath of forest. Slowly and methodically, they then tightened the circle, driving the animals within into a clearing to be shot. All participants were guaranteed a share of the spoils (the proportion depending on their status), which provided their households with a crucial source of food.

This form of the chase lasted several days (it commonly took place in the fall) and required careful coordination and strict discipline, not to mention personal courage and a steady hand—a cornered tiger or bear, after all, was as dangerous as any human foe. So it is not surprising that the *aba* were thought of as quasi-military maneuvers. As the Liao emperor once said about the Khitan tribal hunt, "It is not simply a pleasure. It is a means of practicing warfare."[48] The compilers of the early Manchu chronicles considered Nurhaci's reliance on the hunt as a means of sharpening martial skills perfectly normal: "What needs to be said of [Nurhaci's] fondness for taking soldiers on the hunt," they asked, "when he would cultivate military discipline and establish laws and regulations?"[49] It is thus no accident that the small contingents into which Jurchen hunters were grouped, called *niru* (from the Manchu word for arrow), became the model for the basic military unit of the Eight Banners, also called *niru* (Ch *niu-lu*), usually translated as "company."

Scholars are still uncertain about the exact process by which the hunt-*niru* (disbanded at the conclusion of the battue)—were transformed into a formal military organization with permanent military-*niru* collected into larger divisions called *gūsa*, or "banners." Investigation of this problem is difficult since, as for much else in this early period, sources are scarce and references obscure. Difficulties are compounded because while it is possible to distinguish in the Manchu language between *gūsa*—a word signifying a large military division—and *tu* (or *turun*), a word meaning "flag, standard" —these two senses are conflated, not just in English, but, more critically, in the Chinese word used for both, *qi*, "banner." Chinese and Korean sources (which are written in Chinese) are therefore of limited use in trying to distinguish between the Jurchen military's use of banners, or flags, in battle, and the actual development of a military unit called the "banner."[50]

Regarding the military-*niru*, the best guess is that no later than 1601 (and quite possibly in the decade preceding), Nurhaci had begun implementing a blueprint for reconfiguring his ever-growing Jurchen army that called for armored soldiers (Ma *uksin*), both cavalry (Ma *aliha cooha*) and infantry (Ma *beki cooha*), to be formed into permanent companies of three hundred men each.[51] These companies borrowed the same name, *niru*, as the old hunting units, but were much larger; they themselves were subdivided into four groups of seventy-five, called *tatan*, though actual size—both of *niru* and of *tatan*—varied.[52] The new military-*niru* were also more comprehensive, in that each *uksin*, along with his entire household—other adult males (whatever their status or age), women, children, and servants—were enrolled as members of the company. Finally, the military-*niru* were permanent. The custom among Inner Asian peoples was that cooperative units (such as the *niru*), whether formed for hunting or for warfare, were temporary. When the hunt or battle was over, men expected to return to their families. The formal institutionalization of the military-*niru* made such organization permanent— essential if a state of military readiness was to be maintained indefinitely.

From the very outset, then, the new companies were more than simply military squads; they were units intended to support *uksin* directly and indirectly, taking responsibility for all functions essential to the maintenance of a professional hereditary military service.[53] Even after the elaboration of a larger superstructure, the companies retained these functions and discharged them, for better or worse, until the end of the dynasty. Their greater size and inclusiveness resulted in considerable authority accruing to the company captain (Ma *nirui ejen*, later *nirui janggin*), who was in charge of selecting and training soldiers as well as of the well-being of everyone registered in the company. Just as for most Han civilians the local magistrate "was" the government, for most people in the banners, the company captain "was" the banner system.

Like the creation of the military-*niru*, the next step in the development of the Jurchen military organization, the formation of *gūsa*, also eludes exact dating. Strictly speaking, the foundation of a system of *eight* banners occurred only in 1615, the year prior to the proclamation of the Latter Jin state.[54] But there is good reason to believe that banner units were already in existence before this time, since Korean sources mention them as early as 1607.[55] Indeed, it is likely that the military expansion and reorganization undertaken by Nurhaci that resulted in the creation of the military-*niru* in 1601 simultaneously resulted in the creation of the first *gūsa*.[56] Initially there appear to have been only four banners—yellow, white, red, and blue. In 1615 the number was expanded to eight with a red border added to the flags each unit carried in action (the flag of the red banner was bordered in white). Twenty years later, the banners, much expanded, were further subdivided on ethnic lines. Mongol companies were formally constituted as a separate establishment, called the Mongol Eight Banners (*baqi Menggu/Monggo gūsa*), in 1635, and between 1637 and 1642 companies of Han Chinese soldiers were organized into the Chinese Eight Banners (*baqi Hanjun/ujen cooha*).[57] The original banners at this point became known as the Manchu Eight Banners (*baqi Manzhou/Manju gūsa*). In a manner of speaking, then, the fully formed "Eight Banner" system, achieved in 1642, consisted of twenty-four banners: the original Manchu eight banners, plus eight each of the new Mongol and Chinese banners.[58] In addition, there were also bondservant companies, separate from, but attached to, the Manchu banners. (More on these divisions, and on the name Manchu, is found in succeeding sections.)

The company/banner system was an innovation of major importance, but it was not without precedent. In the twelfth century, the Jin dynasty formally instituted a very similar sort of socio-military establishment, called the *meng-an mou-ke*. Though the Qing system eschewed multiples of ten, both the *meng-an mou-ke* and the Eight Banners fit into the steppe practice of organizing the military on decimal principles to circumvent tribal authority and concentrate power in the hands of a single ruler.[59] The *meng-an mou-ke* originated as a way to rationalize management of the Jurchen population, but as the Jin state grew it also used the *meng-an mou-ke* system to attract and then integrate Chinese, Khitan, and other non-Jurchen groups into its military and social structure, much as the banners came to accommodate Mongols and Chinese. The two systems were similar also in structure. The smaller unit, the *mou-ke* (related to the Manchu word, *mukūn*, "clan, lineage"), nominally consisting of three hundred households, made it approximately comparable to the later *niru*; seven to ten *mou-ke* combined to form a *meng-an* (Ma *minggan*, "one thousand"), which was the equivalent of the *gūsa*. The *mou-ke* themselves were also subdivided into units of fifty households, called *pu-li-yan*, commensurate perhaps to *tatan*. As in the Eight Banners, military service was obligatory for all males in the *mou-ke*, and offices were held hereditarily. Finally, both the Eight Banners and the *meng-an mou-ke* were bedeviled by the twin evils of economic dislocation and martial declension.[60]

In their formation at this time, the banner companies (and, by extension, the banners) emerged as hybrid constructions bearing the imprint of earlier genealogical and geographical structures. *Niru* formation took place in various ways, but in the majority of cases it is clear that the company captain—whose position was usually hereditary, in recognition of his contribution by bringing men over to fight with Nurhaci—and the others in the company were all originally from the same place. Thus, in many instances, *niru* creation simply formalized the organization of preexisting units, whether these were extended families within the same lineage, or members of different lineages from the same village (who may, perhaps, have hunted together or shared pasture). Relations within the *niru* were thus not strictly bureaucratic; nor were they necessarily familistic, since below the company captain could usually be found from one to four lineage heads.

To a certain degree, the pattern of company formation depended on the circumstances of the people concerned. In founding the Donghai Jurchen companies, for instance, policy was fairly liberal: where it is possible to trace them today, the original chieftains were maintained in eighteen of twenty cases, minimally disturbing tribal organization. Jianzhou Jurchens were by and large also put at the head of Jianzhou-based companies, which formed the largest bloc. This was true both of Jianzhou who readily submitted to Nurhaci and of those who succumbed only after a fight, though the former clearly dominated numerically.[61] The distribution of Haixi Jurchens into companies, on the other hand, respected their original organization much less. Not only did Nurhaci enforce a policy of wholesale resettlement of Haixi populations once they fell under his control, but he was evidently wary of allowing them to form their own *niru*. Apart from those few Haixi who willingly joined Nurhaci (and who maintained some of their erstwhile fellowship), most were parceled out among various Jianzhou companies. Thus of a total 239 companies noted as having been founded at the "beginning of the dynasty" (Ch *guochu bianli*), 96 were captained by Jianzhou Jurchens, 67 by Donghai, and only 47 by Haixi (of the remaining 29, 16 were Mongol companies, and 13 are of uncertain origin).[62]

If it is true that in the formation of companies previous lineage and village structures were frequently left undisturbed, then it is obvious to question in what way the companies, and the banners into which they were organized, served as centralizing forces in the development of the early Qing state. First, as mentioned, it was frequently the case that those who switched their allegiance to Nurhaci only after defeat in battle suffered the further blow of being divvied up between various companies. Company size tended to vary, as groups who voluntarily submitted were usually allowed to form their own *niru* even if they fell short of providing the requisite three hundred soldiers, and dividing up recalcitrant foes was one way to even out company populations. This meant that, before long, a very large number of companies were mixed, composed of households drawn from different Jianzhou and Haixi lineages. Second, even in cases when internal genealogical or geographical ties were little disturbed, the distribution of companies across banners meant that larger tribal ties were seriously weakened. To take the case of the Donghai, who were put into their own "exclusive" companies, of the twenty cases we can track, seven were affiliated with the Bordered Yellow Banner, four with the Plain Yellow Banner, three with the Plain Red Banner, two each with the Bordered Red and Plain White banners, and one each with the Bordered White and Bordered Blue banners.[63] Even within the same banner, it was still possible to separate people by placing them in different regiments (*jia-la/jalan*).

A third way in which the company/banner system helped to streamline power relations was through its incorporation into the contemporary political structure. Each of the eight banners was headed by a banner commander (*dutong/gūsai ejen*, later *gūsa be kadalara amban*), who, along with the five state counselors (Ma *amban*) and numerous "princes" (Ma *beile*), ranked among the most powerful men in the state. In fact, one or the other status was required to win Nurhaci's trust in this militarily (and economically) powerful position: a 1621 listing of the eight *gūsai ejen* shows that three were *amban* and five were junior *beile* related to the khan.[64] All were members of the Deliberative Council founded by Nurhaci in 1615,[65] and all were also simultaneously hereditary commanders of several companies within the banners they headed.[66] Such ties lead most historians to conclude that the banners were a crucial power base for the khan, the princes, and the companions, who held them virtually as private property.[67]

The political importance of the companies was further underscored by their growing economic significance, as each soldier was assigned a tract of land once he was enrolled in a company. Though he was not required to farm it himself since he did not owe land tax (paid in kind), the other members of his household did, and either farmed themselves or made use of agricultural serfs. The use of serfs was especially common on the estates assigned to the Jurchen elite; but there is plenty of evidence to show that in the 1620s Jurchen farmers toiled under the same sun as Han Chinese farmers, many of whom were left on their own land in the immediate aftermath of the Jurchen conquest of Liaodong.[68] Rooting the company firmly in local soil had three notable consequences: it strengthened the centripetal tendencies in both the banner system and the state by further weakening older geographical ties; it provided a source of income that served to augment the wealth and overall standing of the Jurchen elite; and, perhaps most importantly, it constituted a stable economic foundation for the support of the Jurchen army. No doubt these were the same considerations that led the twelfth-century Jin to adopt a similar agricultural program for the *meng-an mou-ke*.[69] The relative success of the land system in Manchuria at this time may explain why, after they conquered China, the Manchus implemented a similar system of banner landholding there. This system never worked as well, however, and, as we shall see, the resulting problem of how to support the banner population as it became steadily impoverished was a great headache for the Qing court.

By the late 1610s articulation of the structural framework of the banner system was complete. Steady expansion of the Jurchen state to include new populations, however, meant a concomitant growth in the banner system. At first this was accommodated simply through the addition of more companies. *Niru* increased in number from 201 in 1616 to 234 in 1626, 292 in 1631, and 419 in 1635.[70] But not all of these companies were made up of Jurchens. It was becoming clear that further changes in the structure of the banner establishment were necessary if it was to keep pace with rising Jurchen ambitions. How to respond was one of the many challenges faced by the new Jin khan, Nurhaci's eighth son, Hong Taiji.

## ROOTS OF IDENTITY: THE BANNERS AND THE MANCHU NATION UNDER HONG TAIJI

Elected khan after Nurhaci's death in 1626, Hong Taiji (Qing Taizong, 1592–1643) devoted much attention during the first ten years of his reign to consolidating his father's gains.[71] This involved shoring up his own political position, strengthening alliances, securing borders, and devising ways to administer new territories and manage the large population now under Jurchen control, swelled dramatically by the addition of one million Liaodong Chinese in the early 1620s.[72] Toward this end, Hong Taiji, who alone among the sons of Nurhaci was literate,[73] instituted a rudimentary bureaucratic structure, including a chancellery and Six Boards patterned on the Chinese model, or at least superficially so.[74] He authored ethnic policies that were initially more moderate than his father's and brought about a crucial enlargement of the Chinese role in the Jin army.[75] He led campaigns against Korea, ordered the first direct raids on North China, and fought the Chakhar Mongols for control of the approach to Beijing leading from Manchuria over the Yanshan Mountains; he also exploited differences between his brothers and nephews that allowed him to gain greater personal authority and wealth. These efforts at consolidation came to a climax in the mid-1630s, a major watershed in the development of the Jurchen state. First, the name "Manchu" was officially adopted in 1635 as the name for all Jurchen people. Then, in 1636, an imperial seal of the Yuan emperors was presented to Hong Taiji by the widow of the defeated Chakhar leader, Ligdan khan.[76] With this new form of legitimation, Hong Taiji rechristened the Latter Jin the "Great Qing" and the Jin "khan" became the Qing "emperor."[77] Eight years later, having swept back into the littoral plain connecting Manchuria and North China, the Qing was poised to deliver the final blow to the beleaguered Ming dynasty.

Although he died before he saw Beijing, Hong Taiji is greatly credited for the success of the Qing conquest. His most important contribution is generally seen to have been the centralization of power in the person of the khan, which prevented the Jin state from splintering. But another important accomplishment was his shaping the Eight Banners into an instrument that could serve the often contradictory ends of national integration and ethnic segregation, a role the banners continued to play after the conquest. The expansion of the Mongol and Chinese divisions of the Eight Banners between 1635 and 1642 was crucial to this, as it permitted a high level of cooperation between different ethnic groups yet successfully maintained the supremacy of Jurchen political interests. Under Hong Taiji not only were the banners a crucible for the forging of a new pan-Jurchen "Manchu" identity, but they also played a decisive role in the creation of a new polyethnic "Qing" state by providing a home for Mongol, Han Chinese, Korean, and other adherents.

This is a good place to pause to ask on what grounds the differences between the Jurchens, Mongols, Chinese, and others were indeed "ethnic" and in what senses the organization of the Eight Banners followed ethnic principles. To be sure, the historical record for this period points to a concern with identifying people according to tribal or national provenance. But some recent scholarship has claimed that the structuring principles of the Eight Banners actually *ignored* considerations of descent and were purely cultural and political in scope.[78] If true, this would cast doubt on the apparent ethnic quality of such labels as "Jurchen," "Manchu," "Chinese" (Ma *Nikan*), "Mongol" (Ma *Monggo*), and "Korean" (Ma *Solho*). In order to fully understand their institutional expression in the Eight Banners and elsewhere, we need to determine how these categories were constructed and used at the time, how differences between various in-groups and their Others were interpreted, and how these mesh with the criteria for an ethnic group set out earlier.

Joseph Fletcher once observed of the steppe tribe that "it had its own traditions, institutions, customs, beliefs, and myths of common ancestry. These, if the tribe was of mixed linguistic or ethnological origin, promoted unity and the idea of a shared identity."[79] Fletcher's belief that interaction among groups on the deserts and steppes of Inner Asia led to an emphasis on elements of ethnicity such as history, descent, and culture in constructing difference—determining who "we" are and how "we" differ from "them"—is borne out by an examination of the early-seventeenth-century record, which suggests that at the time the Eight Banners was formed, people in the Manchurian frontier were indeed thinking and acting "ethnically." In addition to the above elements, in the Manchu case ethnicity also came to include the idea of a common territory. Let us look at these elements of early Manchu ethnic construction one by one.

### Myth/History

The question of history has already been addressed in part. As mentioned, the Jurchen origin myth was written into the very first account of the rise of Nurhaci written in the mid-1630s, and was aimed at legitimating the royal pedigree of the Aisin Gioro house. It also lent credibility to the claims of the Jianzhou and all Jurchens to an imperial past free of any negative association with the actual place of the Jurchens as a tributary people of the Ming. But the myth operated on a broader level, too, by asserting the ancient origins of all Manchus and the existence of a single Jurchen nation in the past. However inaccurate by academic standards, such notions fostered Jurchen solidarity, so crucial to Hong Taiji's efforts to hold together the Jurchen confederation and the Qing state along with it. By the early eighteenth century, these ideas were firmly entrenched, permitting the Yongzheng emperor to state confidently that: "The Manchus are all the descendants of the august ancestors Taizu [Nurhaci], Taizong [Hong Taiji], Shizu [the Shunzhi emperor], and Shengzu [the Kangxi emperor]."[80] In other words, all Manchus shared the same origins, which were folded into the noble myth of the origins of the Qing ruling house—a belief conforming to the general Inner Asian insistence that "All members of the tribe, including the common people, were, by tradition, considered descendants of a single ancestor."[81]

### Lineage/Genealogy

As the immediately preceding quotation suggests, lineage and myth were closely intertwined. In a broad sense, Manchu documents from before and after the founding of the Latter Jin state in 1616 show concern for genealogy in their unceasing attention to lineage-based tribal divisions even after the subjugation of these groups by the Jianzhou. For instance, a 1613 statement by

Nurhaci stressed that the Jurchen state combined the "Yehe, Hada, Ula, Hoifa, Mongol, Sibe, and Gūwalca of the nine surnames [*uyun hala*]."[82] References to Jurchen subdivisions are scarcer in the record for Hong Taiji's reign, probably in consequence of the emphasis on a unified Jurchen identity. But despite the existence of companies and banners—structures that weakened them considerably—older tribal and lineage lines, as well as the position of lineage leader, persisted throughout the Qing. More than one nineteenth-century writer wrote of the "eight great clans,"[83] and the rumor after 1911 was that the Qing downfall was the revenge of a woman of the Yehe lineage (the Empress Dowager Cixi) for the subjugation of her people by Nurhaci nearly three centuries before. The perception of such differences indicates that persistent descent-based divisions were commonly recognized among the Manchus.[84]

The importance of descent in the early Jurchen state is seen in a number of other ways, too. First, as described above, the creation of *niru* was very much, though never exclusively, guided by preexisting genealogical affiliations. More often than not, when people were brought into the Jurchen confederation, the groups in which they came were incorporated directly into companies, preserving earlier relationships. The importance of lineage and origin is apparent as well in the common habit of referring to people in terms of their biological relationship to others and in the detailed accounts given of certain families, such as the descendants of the Hada chieftain.[85] It is strikingly displayed in a systematic 1610 listing showing the disposition of hundreds of (mostly) Haixi Jurchens into servitude, giving their *mukūn* and *tatan* affiliation and identifying each by owner, name, place of origin, original position, and date of capture (some of which were already more than forty years in the past).[86] Finally, since company captaincies were as a rule passed down through the same family, attention to genealogy was imperative. Indeed, for many in the banners, this may have given the most concrete meaning to the facts of one's descent and lineage. Scrupulous attention to these matters is revealed in the *qifenzhi* sections of the *Comprehensive History of the Eight Banners*, compiled in the 1730s, which were based on lineage genealogies. That one can find confirmation in confidential, noncirculating seventeenth-century materials of the family histories that were recorded and published over a century later is good evidence that genealogy and family history had always mattered in the banners.[87] The continuing importance of lineage is reflected also in banner household registers from the eighteenth and nineteenth centuries, which depict lineage and family relationships in great detail over many decades, and allow scholars to see that status as a lineage head, for example, carried real social and economic meaning.[88]

*Geography*

The attachment of a geographical sense to labels connoting descent at the level of the "tribe" was not unusual in seventeenth-century Manchuria,[89] but territorial distinctions attached much more frequently to higher-level divisions between *gurun*. For instance, there was clearly the awareness of a border (Ma *jase*) between the Jurchens (not just the Jianzhou) and their Chinese, Korean, and Mongol neighbors.[90] The implication is that each *gurun*, that is, each "nation" or "people," occupied a finite territory that was understood to be its "place" (Ma *ba*), its proper country or homeland, as in a note from 1621 stating that "on the east is Korea [*Solho gurun*] . . . on the north is the Mongol country [*Monggo gurun*] [and] in the west is the great Chinese country [*amba Nikan gurun*]."[91] Another statement from 1619 expressed the same sort of geographical self-awareness in slightly different terms: "East from the Chinese *gurun* all the way to where the sun rises in the eastern waters; north from the Korean *gurun*, and south from the Mongol *gurun*—in this year, the pacification of the *gurun* of the Jurchen tongue was completed."[92] The Manchu word *gurun* appears to make a firm connection between a people (or "nation") and territory.[93] In this regard, it is also telling that in a long peroration to some of his men in 1622, urging them to stop thinking of the Chinese as "permanent" and the Jurchens as "temporary," Nurhaci felt it worth raising an additional item: "Also, Nanjing, Beijing, and Kaifeng have from the beginning never been the dwelling places of just one person. They are places that have been exchanged back and forth between the Jurchens and the Chinese."[94] The implication here was that the Jurchen "great enterprise" was justified in part because of a historic geographic claim not just to Manchuria, but to specific sites in China as well that had been the scene of interaction between the Jin (who made their capital at Kaifeng [Bianjing]) and the Song.

Territoriality is not necessarily always part of ethnicity, but it is often found as an element around which identity is built, whether or not the place in question is actually occupied or only virtually so (i.e., as a memory).[95] One can see that the official Qing ban on migration to Manchuria by Han Chinese, which lasted until the twentieth century, was one way of maintaining this Manchu "homeland" and upholding its place in the constitution of Manchu identity. That Manchus in the Qing occasionally referred to themselves as being from the Changbai Mountains, and that in 1677 the Kangxi emperor instituted formal sacrifices to these mountains as the site of Manchu origins, were two notable ways this aspect of identity manifested itself. The mapping of Manchuria ordered by the Kangxi emperor in the early eighteenth century fit in with this same set of concerns.[96]

### Culture

Different aspects of cultural behavior—for example, language, dress, lifestyle—are generally held to play an essential part in the construction of ethnicity, since they are among the most obvious manifestations of the differences in which "ethnic" significance can be read.[97] Language is widely recognized as one of the most important markers of membership in ethnic groups, because it so effectively defines who is "in" and who is "out." As the line referring to "the nation of the Jurchen tongue" cited above reveals, language filled a central role in defining Jurchen identity. Most Jurchens spoke the same language (what we now call Manchu), and the emphasis placed upon that point at the time makes it clear that this was seen as an important unifying element of the pan-Jurchen *gurun*. The importance of Jurchen linguistic unity emerged most clearly in Jurchen attempts to define their relationship with Mongol groups: "You Mongol people raise stock, eat meat, and wear leather," wrote Nurhaci to the Jarut Mongols in 1619, "[while] our people till the soil and eat grain. We two are not one people, but people of different languages."[98] Here Jurchen-Mongol difference was being mapped onto lifestyle and language: if the former was different, the latter should be, too. But the nature of the differences between Jurchens and Mongols was open to interpretation. In a letter written earlier the same year to the Khalkha Mongols, the emphasis was on the similarity of Jurchen and Mongol ways: "Only the speech of the two nations of Chinese and Koreans [*Nikan Solho juwe gurun*] is different; they are alike in the clothes they wear and in their way of life. Only the speech of our two nations, Mongol and Jurchen [*Monggo Jušen muse juwe gurun*], is different; in the clothes we wear and our way of life, we are alike."[99] Very similar phrasing is used twice again in other letters sent at about this time, both emphasizing that,

> Although the languages of China and Korea are different, because their coiffures and style of dress [*etukui ulhi*, lit., "garment sleeves"] are

identical, those two countries are as one. Our two nations, Mongol [and Jurchen], though originally [speaking] different languages, are as one in the clothing we wear and in all our various modes of living.[100]

While for political reasons the perception of overall similarity between Jurchen and Mongol ways varies in these passages, in both it is clear that language was central in the constitution of a *gurun*. The logic of this proposition was further strengthened by the parallel drawn between the Chinese and the Koreans, who were seen to share a fundamentally similar lifestyle, yet spoke different languages. The lesson that Nurhaci no doubt hoped his Mongol audience would draw from this is that there were degrees of ethnic difference; groups distinguished only by language were not as different as groups distinguished both by language and by lifestyle, dress, and other features. Thus while language divided the Jurchen and Mongol nations, clothing and livelihood united them.

This was something of a stretch, since the Jurchens were not really the same sort of nomads as the Mongols. But Nurhaci was not interested in expounding on the actual extent of shared characteristics between his people and the people whose cooperation he needed to realize his grandiose ambitions; and there was just enough truth in what he was saying, so that, as a pitch toward ethnic solidarity, his ruse worked. Just the next year (1620), the Jurchens approached their Khalkha Mongol allies with the line, "Our two countries are as one. Let our two families live as one. Let us attack the Ming as one."[101] Accenting Jurchen-Khalkha commonality was designed to secure the aid of the latter against the Chinese and to forestall the possibility of on attack by the Mongols on the Jurchen flank. The Jurchen-Mongol (later Manchu-Mongol) ethnic fraternity was made possible by their shared Altaic background, but this alone was not enough to realize it; ethnicity was conditioned by mutual political and strategic considerations, which continued to shape it over time.

The same can be seen in the case of the Yehe. The only Jurchen group specifically excluded from the main linguistic community, the Yehe spoke a language somewhere in between Manchu and Mongol. Yet this did not keep them from being considered Jurchen: "As for the Yehe and ourselves, our speech differs but are we not of the [same] Jurchen nation?"[102] Had it suited him, Nurhaci could just as easily have taken a position that excluded the Yehe from the Latter Jin state; as it happened, it better served his, and ultimately Yehe interests, to incorporate them.[103] However, he could not do this, as he had done with the Jianzhou, the Yeren, and the other Haixi, by stressing their shared language. The Yehe were not part of that *gurun*, "the nation of the Jurchen tongue." Only after 1619 was it possible to include them in the Jurchen nation on other grounds—namely, descent (intermarriage with other Jurchen lineages), geography (prolonged residence in Jurchen territory), and aspects of culture apart from language (e.g., hunting, dress, religion)—a good illustration of historical contingency in the configuration of ethnicity: if language cannot be called on to construct a common identity, and a common identity is mutually desirable, then something else will be found.

The written language, too, played an important role in the construction of identity. Much has been made of Nurhaci's inspiration to order the creation of a Jurchen writing system in 1599 (up to that time, Jurchens only wrote in Mongolian). Certainly it is correct to stress the new system's importance to Jurchen cultural and political development, as it made it much easier to borrow words, and hence concepts, from the Chinese. But the new alphabet was at the same time a tool of national unification. Jurchens already spoke the same language, and now they could write the same language, too. The invention of a suitable writing system, which made possible a "national literature," was a major step forward in the development of Jurchen/Manchu identity.

The contours of ethnic practice in early-seventeenth-century Manchuria thus emerge fairly clearly. Apart from three principal factors—descent, geography, and language—other cultural elements such as hairstyle,[104] religion,[105] treatment of women,[106] funeral customs, clothing, and food[107] further distinguished the Jurchens from the other groups with whom they had regular contact. Disease, too, furnished another type of ethnic marker.[108] One important thing was still missing from Jurchen identity, however, and that was a common name. As already mentioned, Jurchen tribal differences did not disappear overnight, and the continued use of the name "Jurchen" brought up potentially bitter and divisive memories, particularly where the Haixi were concerned.[109] There was the additional problem that "Jušen" had come to acquire specific social meanings as the name for the dependent class of Jurchen households.[110] Furthermore, even with the elaboration of a legitimating myth "proving" a noble genealogy, it was hard to overlook the historical fact that it was the Jurchens, and not some other group, who for centuries had been loyal subjects of the Ming. The exigencies of ethnicity and politics all converged on this point: a new name was required. Hence the "Manchus" were born.

The renaming of the Jurchens took place in November 1635. Hong Taiji's proclamation, issued two days before the submission of the Chakhar and the transfer of the Yuan imperial seal, ran as follows:

> Originally, the name for our people [*gurun*] was Manju, Hada, Ula, Yehe, and Hoifa. Ignorant people call these "Jurchens." [But] the Jurchens are those of the same clan of Coo Mergen Sibe. What relation are they to us? Henceforth, everyone shall call [us] by our people's original name, Manju. Uttering "Jurchen" will be a crime.[111]

After this time, use of the name Jurchen was officially proscribed: everywhere that *Jušen* once was used, *Manchu* took its place.[112] Hong Taiji was being disingenuous in asserting the hoary origins of the name "Manchu" and claiming that "Jurchen" applied only to the descendants of Coo Mergen Sibe, known from Mongolian chronicles as a companion of Chinggis Khan.[113] As the examples cited above attest, "Jurchen" was used countless times to refer to the Jianzhou, Haixi, and Yeren; especially after the defeat of the Yehe, the name was routinely applied to the collectivity, even if this was the result of habit rather than careful consideration. By 1635, however, the increasing prominence of the Latter Jin as a power to be contended with, and the new found authority of Hong Taiji as successor to Chinggis Khan created a need for a universal label for all Jurchens that would be formally on a par with "Mongol," "Korean," and "Chinese."[114] "Manchu" served precisely this purpose. Though it had occasionally been used before 1635,[115] its invocation by Hong Taiji at that time affirmed Jurchen identity in a way that unequivocally distinguished it from other groups, against which its own sense of identity was constructed in exactly the sort of "transactional" process characteristic of ethnicity. Much more than simply a political designation, then, this name was intended precisely to *hide* political differences by proclaiming—indeed, insisting on—the ethnic unity of the Jurchen *gurun*.

We may never have any answers as to what "Manchu" really meant before 1635 and it may not matter much if we ever do: like the Basque word *Euzkadi* for "Basque country," it was a plausible political invention that was accepted and became real.[116] Like "Jurchen," "Chinese," "Mongol," and "Korean," all of which operated as substantive social and political categories based on commonly-held perceptions of differences arising from descent, place of origin, language, and other cultural markers, "Manchu" conveyed both senses of *gurun*—a collective people as well as their geopolitical community—and was used on its own as an adjective and as a noun.[117] Its acceptance suggests that the Jurchen groups who came to constitute the Manchus *did* share enough of a common identity (including history, blood, geography, economy, language, religion, dress, and customs) for the name to stick. Acknowledging that political motives were at work in the promulgation of "Manchu" does not mean that the category lacked ethnic content, only that, like most other ethnic labels (African-American, Québecois, Bosnian, Kurd, Hutu), it was shaped by a range of political and social needs. If Hong Taiji's "trick" in declaring his people "Manchu" worked, this was not because "Manchu" was a name from the Jurchen past, but because it was a name from the Qing future.

The process of formally reconstituting the Jurchen state initiated by the switch to "Manchu" was followed the next year by the renaming of the Latter Jin to the Great Qing dynasty (*Da Qing/Daicing gurun*). Where "Jin" (*aisin*, "gold") had stood for the dynastic claims of the inchoate Jurchen *gurun*, "Great Qing" was the dynastic calling card for a state that incorporated not just Jurchens—now Manchus—but also Chinese, Mongols, and Koreans, and had become a serious rival to the "Great Ming" (*Da Ming/Daiming gurun*), whose name it closely imitated.[118] Indeed, one could argue that the creation of the *Manju gurun* was almost immediately overshadowed by the creation of the *Daicing gurun*, of which the former was but a part. But this did not mean the end of the Manchu nation. Rather, the Manchu nation lived on in the reorganized Eight Banners.[119]

THE MONGOL AND CHINESE BANNERS

While it is commonly argued that the importance of the Eight Banners in the Qing state-building project was primarily military (the banners as armed force) and political (the banners as power base), the ethnic angle (the banners as ethnic preserve) should not be overlooked. It is no coincidence that the separation of the Eight Banners into three ethnically distinct divisions occurred at the same time as the other changes going on in the nascent Qing state. The original registration of Jurchens into companies had weakened horizontal ties of kinship and native place, a process which the banners hastened by fostering a sense of unitary identity as an imperial people. The heightened articulation of ethnic identity in the Eight Banners under Hong Taiji meant the important addition of new institutional factors into the mix that generated Manchu identity. Things came full circle later in the Qing, when, as I will show, Manchu and banner identities flowed together once again.

I say "heightened articulation" because, as we have seen, ethnicity was immanent in the banners from the beginning. Though before 1635 the Eight Banners sometimes appears to have been seen essentially as a Jurchen organization (as in records speaking of "the banners, the Mongols, and the Han"[120]), membership in the banners had never been open to everyone who joined the Jurchen cause; nor were all those registered in the banners considered to be Jurchen. Apart from isolated individual cases, neither Mongols nor Han Chinese were *ever* wholly integrated into the Manchu banners; even when formally included within a Manchu banner, their organization into separate companies was consistently maintained.[121] The distinctions between different types of ethnic and legal status that existed from the very outset were consonant with the principle of ethnic segregation that characterized Jurchen policy toward nonbanner populations (this issue, and the experiments in Jurchen-Chinese cohabitation that departed from the policy, are described in the next chapter). These were more broadly institutionalized with the creation of the Mongol and Chinese banners, organizations that show very clearly the way in which the social organization and political assertion of communicated cultural differences was institutionalized in the banners.

### The Mongol Eight Banners

The 1635 organization of Mongol forces into banners on the Manchu model culminated a process that began in the early 1620s. Until that time, relations between the Jurchens and different Mongol groups took place outside the banner organization. This pattern was broken in 1622, when Kharachin Mongols who came over to Nurhaci seeking refuge from their common enemy, the Chakhar, were put into companies affiliated within the banners.[122] Gradually, the Kharachin came to form a significant force, and by 1626–27 there were enough Mongol companies to warrant their redistribution, five to a banner. These forty *niru* presented themselves separately at reviews and also fought separately as a unified force during battle (though this latter policy appears to have ceased by 1634).[123] In 1635 Hong Taiji decided to establish a separate Mongol banner hierarchy, at which time these forces numbered around ten thousand, in sixty to seventy companies. Enough additional *niru* were created to make an even eighty, which were then spread between eight banners identified by the same flag patterns as the original banners. The new Mongol banners were still not wholly independent, however, but remained subject to the Manchu head of the color-banner of which they were part.

Not all Mongols allied with the Latter Jin/Qing were included in the Mongol Eight Banners. Some Kharachin Mongols who, because they were brought over to the Jurchen side en masse, were left in groupings (also referred to as "banners," but differing in structure) under their original commanders. A second group consisted of about 650 Khalkha households who had submitted to the Latter Jin in 1621 and 3,000 Oirat households who came over in 1622.[124] After leaguing with the Jurchens, these troops were at first organized into two separate "banners" of their own, but in 1632 the Mongolian princes at the head of these banners were removed—probably for political reasons—and the banners dissolved, their companies placed for a time into the regular banner system.[125] At the time of the foundation of the eight Mongol banners in 1635, the two Khalkha companies were incorporated into the Manchu Bordered Yellow Banner, while the ten Oirat companies were divided between six of the remaining Manchu banners (no Mongol companies were included in the most elite of the Manchu banners, the Plain Yellow).

A third Mongol group that remained outside the regular banner system was the Chakhar, who finally surrendered to the Jurchens in 1635. The Chakhar ruler, Ligdan Khan (great-great-grandson of Dayan Khan and a lineal descendant of Chinggis Khan), had perished on the way to request help from Qinghai Mongols to aid him in fending off Manchu incursions. After his death, his followers saw little hope in holding out further, and ended their resistance. The Chakhar thereafter provided able service to the dynasty as a separate force. Though organized into eight "banners," these were distinct from the Eight Banners organizationally and structurally, as households were not divided into companies. Still, they were included under the umbrella of the banner system, as later census figures show, and were a crucial military auxiliary to the main banner forces.[126]

### The Chinese Eight Banners

The development of the Chinese Eight Banners was also a long and convoluted process, similar in some ways to the evolution of the Mongol Eight

Banners in that Han soldiers were at first organized either as companies within the Manchu banners or as separate forces led by their original Chinese commanders under close Manchu supervision. However, unlike the Mongol banners, created at a single stroke in 1635, the Chinese banners appear to have been expanded in stages, with two banners first formed in 1637, doubling to four in 1639, and again to eight in 1642. Only then did they achieve formal independence of the Manchu banners.[127]

Compared to the Mongol banners, the step-by-step creation of the Chinese banners reflects the caution and uncertainty characteristic of Manchu policy toward the Han generally before (and after) the conquest. We have already seen evidence of the Jurchens' sense of a shared identity with their Mongol allies, based, among other things, on the broad similarities in their cultures. The Mongols who came over to their side were accustomed to a military existence and so were easily and logically incorporable into the Jurchen military. As members of the Jurchen banners, albeit in segregated companies, they had plenty of experience living in the banner system and had become thoroughly familiar with the Jurchen way of organizing life and war. Moreover, because most Mongols joined the Jin cause individually or in small groups, and lacked any original internal cohesion (unlike other Mongol groups under Jurchen authority), they posed no political threat. This was not the case with the Han Chinese population, which was both far more numerous and varied in status. The Latter Jin leadership experimented with different approaches, so until 1637, when the first two Chinese banners were formed, policy toward Han Chinese was inconsistent. By that time, Han living under Manchu rule hailed generally from one of three backgrounds: "transfrontiersmen" and defectors prior to 1618; captives of the Liaodong and Liaoxi campaigns of 1618–22; and Ming defectors to Hong Taiji (in particular those surrendering under Zu Zerun and Zu Kefa at Dalinghe in 1631 and those surrendering under Geng Zhongming, Kong Youde, and Shang Kexi during the naval engagements of 1633). Members of the first group were generally so acculturated to the Jurchen lifestyle as to make their distinction as "Chinese" virtually meaningless except in strict genealogical terms (even then the picture was not always so clear).[128] Such people were relatively few in number, but many occupied prominent positions among the Latter Jin elite. At the other end of the spectrum were members of the third group. The least acculturated of all, these soldiers, though they fought for the Latter Jin and then the Qing, remained in their original divisions under their original commanders. Even their incorporation into the banner system in 1642 failed to break these ties, which endured until 1683.[129]

Members of the second group, depending on their original status as well as on the timing and circumstances of their capture, met the most diverse fates. For instance, all of those captured at Fushun in 1618 and at Mukden the following year were awarded as slaves or bondservants by the khan to his followers.[130] On the other hand, the garrison commander who surrendered Fushun to the Manchus, Li Yongfang, was extremely well treated (he married a granddaughter of Nurhaci), and the thousand troops he brought with him were all granted freeholder status.[131] Likewise, majors Bao Chengxian, who would in 1637 formally propose that banners on the Manchu model be established for Chinese banner troops, and Shi Tingzhu, one of the first Chinese banner commanders, both surrendered at the fall of Guangning in 1622 and went on to enjoy successful military careers.[132] The majority of the one million Chinese who came under Latter Jin rule after 1621, however, were neither enslaved nor elevated to positions of responsibility, but were permitted to live more or less as before, working their own land, outside the framework of the Eight Banners. The creation of the post of *dutang* at this time—an official completely outside the banner system specifically charged with managing the affairs of the Han population—was a sure sign that the Latter Jin state was aware that administering the Chinese called for distinctive measures.[133]

The year 1621 also marked the first attempt at a Han army under Jurchen command, as one out of every twenty adult Chinese males was conscripted.[134] This experiment can be seen as part of a policy adopted in 1622 calling for equal treatment of Jurchens and Han—an experiment that failed with that policy in 1625.[135] For even before the well-poisonings and other incidents of 1623, there is strong evidence of misgivings toward the Chinese, even those in service to the Jurchen state. In a speech to Han officials in 1622, Nurhaci upbraided them severely, saying, "You don't think of the beneficence extended by the khan who has nurtured you, and your failure to handle matters carefully—what [sort of attitude] is this, that getting booty is all there is? We don't trust you Chinese now."[136] With this sort of doubt so openly expressed, it was only a matter of time before a reaction against the "equal brotherhood" policy set in. The backlash came after a massacre of Jurchens by Chinese in 1625, at which time the Han troops were disbanded and the Chinese population reorganized to provide agricultural labor.

A Han army was regrouped, however, by 1631, under the name "Old Han Troops" (*jiu Han bing/fe Nikan-i cooha*), in part as a result of Hong Taiji's melioration of the treatment and status of Han Chinese in the Latter Jin khanate. Many who had been demoted to slave status in the mid-1620s were made independent households again, and newcomers, such as those who surrendered in 1630 after the capture of Yongping, were also rewarded with freeholder status. But strategic needs were at least as much the reason for the re-formation of a division of Han troops. The Chinese knew how to cast and use cannon and were already practiced with muskets, weapons without which further progress against the Ming would be difficult. Eight months after successfully casting its first artillery, the Han troops dragged it into battle at Dalinghe, the scene of a terrible siege which ended ultimately in a victory for the Latter Jin.[137] It was the hauling of this cannonry that by 1634 earned the Old Han Troops the designation *ujen cooha*, "heavy troops."[138]

The Han division created in 1631 was divided into six battalions and numbered perhaps as many as thirty thousand men. Like the "Old Mongol" troops, Han soldiers drilled and fought separately from the Manchu banners, although unlike the Old Mongols, they were not registered within Manchu banners. Some sources refer to them as the first Han "banner," but there is no evidence to show that anything like the *gūsa*-banner was instituted among the Han ranks, and the designation should be understood as referring rather to the flag under which these battalions were grouped.[139] Only in 1637, when the single division was divided into two, were soldiers and their dependents organized into companies. This properly marks the first step toward the creation of the Chinese banners. Even then, despite the use of the term "banner," companies were still attached to the Manchu banners and the flag patterns of the Manchu and Mongol banners were not yet adopted. These final steps toward parity were taken only in 1642, when ninety-nine companies of Han soldiers were culled from the Manchu banners and instituted as eight banners separate from and parallel to the other sixteen banners.[140] The creation of the Chinese banners thus occurred just in time for the conquest of China begun two years later.

Because they were relative latecomers *and* because they were Han, the Chinese bannermen never received equal treatment in the banners. From the outset they were "poor relations," assigned the disagreeable work of transporting heavy cannon; later, after the conquest, the privileges that all bannermen enjoyed—a guaranteed monthly salary, legal immunities, lightened punishments, special prisons, quotas in the examination system, easier advancement to office, participation in the imperial hunts—came to them in attenuated or diminished form, indicative of their second-class status. Whether or not it was a lack of confidence in Han allies that led Hong Taiji to hesitate before granting them organizational equality and autonomy,[141] prejudice against Chinese bannermen almost certainly reflected a Manchu bias against Han Chinese generally,[142] and remained deeply ingrained throughout the Qing. Only during the dynasty's first decades did they achieve any kind of equality. Because they could speak Chinese, they were natural intermediaries during the conquest process, and since they were bannermen, and not civilian Chinese who might have served the Ming, they were more trusted and, during these transitional years, more extensively employed in civil officialdom.[143] But this "honeymoon" period, when the Chineseness of Chinese bannermen was deemphasized and their chances of employment were relatively good, was of short duration. By 1680, the number of Chinese bannermen governors and governors-general had fallen sharply, never to recover.[144] The job prospects for Chinese bannermen were also hampered by increasing disparagement of their martial skills and their loyalty to the dynasty. In the late 1600s, before signs of deterioration appeared among Manchu soldiers, the Kangxi emperor was already lamenting the steep decline in the quality of the Chinese banner troops he inspected: "It used to be that the Chinese banner troops were brave and strong men. They were also very good at riding and shooting, only a little inferior to Manchus. Lately the Chinese bannermen have come gradually to be more like the Green Standard, ordinary and weak."[145] By the mid-1700s, their banner status had degraded to the point that the court came to view them as essentially "Chinese," and many Chinese banner households consequently lost out when status categories in the banner system underwent a comprehensive review and restructuring at this time. These developments are more fully explored in Chapter 8.

## HIERARCHIES OF ETHNICITY AND STATUS IN THE BANNERS

The Eight Banners proved a flexible tool of empire-building. The differentiated ethnic hierarchy described above, according to which Manchus generally outranked their Mongol cousins, and both outranked Chinese bannermen, was only one of a number of hierarchies and subhierarchies that spread under the spacious canopy of the Eight Banners.[146] These structures were the result of years of expansion during which first the Jurchens and later the Manchus needed to find ways to integrate many different types of non-Han people under the leadership of the khan, though some groups were inevitably left out, notably the vast majority of the Han population after 1644. Apart from interbanner distinctions based on ethnicity, other intrabanner divisions were based on birth, occupation, legal status at the time the banners were formed, and the manner of incorporation into the banners.

One of the broadest distinctions was that made between the "Upper Three Banners" (*shang san qi/dergi ilan gūsa*), code for the three banners that were the personal property of the emperor, which were more populous and in general enjoyed the lion's share of banner resources, and the "Lower Five Banners" (*xia wu qi/fejergi sunja gūsa*).[147] A second broad division was that between the left and right "wings" (*yi/gala*).[148] These designations referred to battle array, and were reflected also in the arrangement of banner pavilions before the main audience hall at Mukden and of banner neighborhoods in Beijing, where the left wing took over the eastern half of the city and the right wing the western half ("wing" organization also applied at some provincial garrisons). A third division, between the capital Eight Banners and the garrison Eight Banners, was arguably much more important; this is discussed at greater length in the following chapters.

In addition, there were other, more informal divisions, such as those based on economic standing, which share many similarities with the class structure of Chinese society at large (though there are some important differences). An understanding of these various hierarchies is necessary if the full complexity of banner organization—and the degree to which ethnic considerations ran right through it—is to be appreciated. These are briefly summed up in the following sections on the Qing nobility, the imperial guard, bondservants, "New Manchus," and on movement between hierarchies.

### The Qing Imperial Nobility

Recent work on the Qing nobility has done much to shed light on the social history of this important group, particularly its demographic behavior.[149] Here the discussion will be confined to a few basic generalities. The Qing nobility is understood to include members of the Aisin Gioro clan who were descendants through the patriline of the Qing founder, Nurhaci, traced as far back as his grandfather, Giocangga. This group was divided into two main groups: members of the "main line" (*zongshi/uksun*), who were direct descendants of Giocangga's son Taksi (i.e., Nurhaci and his brothers); and members of the collateral line (*jue-luo/gioro*), who were direct descendants of the rest of Giocangga's line (i.e., Taksi's brothers and uncles).[150] The former were popularly called "Yellow Sashes" and the latter "Red Sashes," from the distinctive apparel they were permitted to wear. By the end of the Qing, estimates are that more than eighty thousand people were included in the main and collateral lines.[151] Although considered part of the Eight Banners establishment and registered within banners, imperial nobles were not put into companies. They were thus not under the authority of company commanders but of the Imperial Clan Court (*zongrenfu/uksun be kadalara yamun*), which supervised their affairs and recorded their life events.

Apart from the main-/collateral-line distinction, the main-line nobility was more finely graded according to precise rank. There were twelve principal titles for males, and as many paired titles for females. The top eight included "princes of the blood" (*qinwang/cinwang*) of various ranks, followed by four titles for other nobles. Most of these ranks were further divided according to different degrees and classes (e.g., *duo-luo bei-le/doroi beile*, "prince of the blood of the third degree," *yideng zhenguo jiangjun*, "first class noble of the imperial lineage of the ninth rank").[152] Titles were hereditary, but usually dropped one or more ranks when passed to the next generation. Exceptions were made for a few titles that the emperor specifically allowed to be transmitted "with perpetual right of inheritance." The best known of such titles were those awarded to the so-called Princes of the Iron Cap (Ch *tiemaozi wang*), men who had rendered extraordinary service to Nurhaci and Hong Taiji. Held by Manchu families outside the imperial lineage, they were the only nobility who did not claim descent from Giocangga.

Both main-line and collateral nobles received regular subventions of silver and grain from the state. Amounts varied according to rank: a prince of the blood of the first degree received ten thousand ounces of silver and five thousand piculs (1 picul = 107 liters) of rice annually, while a "first class noble of the imperial lineage of the ninth rank" received a "mere" 410 ounces of silver and 205 piculs of rice.[153] (Collaterals received lesser amounts.) Nobles also received a broad array of entitlements and privileges that covered housing, education, marriage, and funerals; and they enjoyed distinct advantages in finding official positions in the civil and military administration, even if they did not usually perform very well in the examinations.[154] They were especially well represented in the ranks of the elite guards. These basic privileges were similar to, if considerably more generous than, those available to most "regular-household" bannermen (on the meaning of "regular household," see below; on the details of state support for such households, see Chapter 4). Even so, at the lower ranks many nobles became impoverished as their numbers grew, support thinned, and jobs grew scarce. In this, too, the fate of the nobility mirrored the fate of non-noble Manchus and others in the banners.

### The Imperial Guard

Another elite group within the Eight Banners was the imperial guard. There were three such corps: the Guard, the Vanguard, and the Imperial Bodyguard, in ascending order of exclusivity, pay, and prestige. All were Manchu institutions tracing their origins to before 1644. Soldiers from the regular Manchu and Mongol banners could aspire to join the Guard (*hujun ying/ bayara*), which was assigned to protect the palace. The Vanguard (*qianfeng ying/gabsihiyan*) was also made up of Manchus and Mongols, but with only about fifteen hundred men, it was just one-tenth the size of the Guard. When the emperor left the palace, the Vanguard led the way, as it did also in battle. The most elite guard unit was the Imperial Bodyguard (*lingshiwei* or *qinjun ying/hiya*), which followed the emperor everywhere.[155] Members of the Imperial Bodyguard were drawn only from the Manchu banners, and primarily from the Upper Three Banners (there was, however, a separate Chinese bodyguard). About the same in number as the Vanguard, to the Imperial Bodyguard fell the job of protecting the emperor's safety at all times, within and without the palace. Within both the Guard and the Vanguard were separate bondservant divisions (designated *nei/dorgi*, "inner"). Other special detachments within the banners included those detailed to the Beijing Gendarmerie (*bujun ying/yafahan coohai kūwaran*), the Artillery and Musketry Division (*huoqi ying/tuwa agūrai kūwaran*) (which also had a bondservant division), and the Light Division (Ch *jianrui ying*). The latter two, assigned squads to guard the palaces north of Beijing, were formed during the early eighteenth century in part to provide more employment opportunities for idle bannermen.

### Bondservants (booi)

It is hard to think of a set of people about whom there is greater confusion and conflicting information than the bondservants. What follows is only a short sketch of the meaning of bondservant status and the origin of the group in the early years of the dynasty, a subject which really deserves a separate study.

Confusion over the *booi* begins with the name. There is no proper Chinese name for the people we call in English "bondservants." They are called *bao-yi*, but this is nothing more than a phonetic rendering of the Manchu phrase *booi*, literally, "of the household."[156] As to the absence of a Chinese name, the short explanation is that there was no corresponding status in Chinese society for *booi*, people who were nominally "slaves"—that is, of unfree status—but who often served in powerful positions and were sometimes intimates of the emperor. Calling them "slaves" in Chinese (*nuli, nupu*) conveyed the wrong impression, so to distinguish them from actual slaves they were called *bao-yi*. This compromise, however, later produced further misunderstandings, as people have assumed that everyone described by the term *booi* was a bondservant, and that the Manchu word *booi* was just another word for a domestic slave. A careful reading of Manchu documents, however, shows that, *booi* in Manchu only *sometimes* means "bondservant"[157] and that it is not, as is commonly believed, an abbreviation for *booi aha* or *booi niyalma* ("household slave" or "household person"). These expressions sometimes refer to bondservants, but not always; they may also refer to actual slaves in a household, or simply to "the people in my house," translated variously in Chinese as *huxiaren, nupu, jiaren, jiashu,* and so on.[158] Strictly speaking, *booi* in the sense of bondservant is short for *booi nirui niyalma* (*urse*), "person (people) of a bondservant company."

Another source of confusion is the social and ethnic origin of the *bao-yi*. With the rise of the company/banner organization, the classifications of different types of population in early Jurchen society (elites, dependent households, and unfree households) gave way to a new system of statutory identity. There was comparatively little change in the status of elites (Ma *irgen*), many of whom were able to parlay their initially advantageous position into continued elite status in the Eight Banners. However, the other two groups experienced greater changes, especially after 1644. The dependent households (Ma *jušen*), who had provided the bulk of the population that constituted the early banner armies, saw the ties binding them to their masters gradually weaken as an independent banner administrative apparatus took on more and more responsibility for managing their lives: distributing grain and silver, filling vacant positions, awarding housing, settling disputes. This "bureaucratization" culminated in the 1720s with the complete curtailment of the privileges of the banner elite over them, about which more is said in later chapters. By this time they had long since ceased to be called *jušen*, a word which is already defined in Kangxi-era dictionaries as "Manchu slave" in Chinese (*Manzhou de nuli*) and clearly did not apply to ordinary people in the banners. Their formal designation was as "regular households" (*zhenghu/jingkini boigon*), or, more popularly, *zhengshen qiren*, "regular-body person of the banners."[159] In most cases, when one encounters the Chinese expression *qiren*, "person of the banners," the reference is to someone of this status. Often, though, the reference is to a *booi*. We can therefore say that *booi*, too, were *qiren*, but traced their roots to the remaining group, those of unfree status called *aha*.

As mentioned, prior to the foundation of the Latter Jin in 1616, the *aha* consisted of Koreans, Mongols, Chinese, and Jurchens who were held as chattel after being bought, taken captive, or condemned to servitude as a punishment.[160] When military companies and banners were formed, *booi* were put into their own *niru*, generally attached to the same banners as their masters. Depending on the banner, these bondservant companies (*bao-yi zuoling/booi niru*), formed part of the personal establishments of leading Manchu families (only Manchus could hold *booi*). The bondservant companies in what came to be the Lower Five Banners were distributed among different members of the nobility; those attached to the Upper Three Banners became part of the imperial household and were subject to the authority of the Imperial Household Department. The literal meaning of this name, "bureau supervising internal affairs" (Ma *dorgi baita be uheri kadalara yamun*), explains why imperial bondservant companies were spoken of as "inner companies" (*nei zuoling/dorgi niru*), as opposed to the "outer," or non-bondservant companies of the regular Eight Banners.[161] Because of their status as the emperor's personal property, Imperial Household Department bondservants were frequently called on to perform special tasks and fill important offices, as Jonathan Spence made clear in his classic study of one famous bondservant, Ts'ao Yin.[162]

It is a common misperception that *booi* ranks were composed mainly of Chinese captives from 1621.[163] In fact, this group was but one important source, and there is no indication either that they constituted a majority of the bondservant population or that the bondservant companies affiliated with the Imperial Household Department were made up exclusively of such people.[164] On the contrary, the bondservants were an ethnically diverse lot. It is all the more important to note, then, that even though grouped together in the same banners, *booi* were still differentiated by company according to their origin and ethnicity. Most obviously, Chinese who were put into bondservant companies during the Liaodong campaign were all put into the so-called standard-bearer and drummer companies (*qigu zuoling/ cigu niru*) attached to the Manchu banners.[165] In addition, there were two companies of Korean bondservants, three companies of Korean freeholders, and one company of Russians.[166] All other bondservant companies appear to have been captained by (and thus likely filled by) Manchus who formerly had been Jurchen *aha*. Typically, mention of the Eight Banner Manchus refers only to those Manchus registered in companies of regular households within the Manchu banners; but it is worth remembering that there were many, many more ethnic Manchus within the bondservant companies in those banners, too.

### "New Manchus" and Others

While Manchu, Mongol, *Hanjun*, *zongshi*, and *booi* were arguably the most visible and most important categories within the banners, there were numerous other special categories of populations within the banner system. Most of these special groups were found in the Manchu banners, but always, it appears, in separate companies, following the principle of institutional ethnic segregation. These include small, easily identifiable non-Manchu groups such as those identified above. Apart from Chinese in the *qigu* bondservant companies, there were also Han Chinese registered in other bondservant or regular household companies. Called Tai Nikan and Fusi Nikan (literally "watchpost Chinese" and "Fushun Chinese," respectively[167]), these groups were brought into the banners after the conquest of Liaodong. The number of individuals in both groups was small, only about 150. Well over half (ninety) were in bondservant companies; nearly all of these were Fusi Nikan. The remaining sixty, predominantly Tai Nikan, were in regular Manchu companies.[168]

After the conquest, the banners continued to expand. Under the Kangxi emperor, there was a major overhaul of the company structure of the banners, accounting for most of the growth that saw a doubling of the number of companies between 1644 and 1735.[169] Much of this expansion resulted from the "splitting" of companies in order to accommodate population increase and keep companies from becoming too unwieldy in size, but there was other growth, too. In 1683 a Russian *niru* was created and attached to the Manchu Bordered Yellow Banner. This company consisted of captives taken at Nerchinsk (Albazin) and brought to Beijing, together with two groups of people who had come over to the Qing earlier, in 1648 and 1668.[170] By the early 1700s, the captaincy of this company was in Manchu hands; its members were gradually "manjurified" through intermarriage and long residence.[171] The Kangxi reign also saw the incorporation of non-Jurchen Manchurian tribes not included in the original banner formation. Small groups on the northeastern frontier such as the Kuyala, Hurka, and Heje[172] were brought in as "New Manchus,"[173] while larger, more militarily significant groups such as the Sibe, Solon, Daur, and Butha were also formally constituted at this time into their own companies and banners, and posted to garrisons in Heilongjiang, near the Qing border with Russia. These tribal groups, whom geography, language, and way of life put somewhere in between the Jurchens and the Mongols, had managed to remain outside the formal confines of the Eight Banner system during the rise of Nurhaci and Hong Taiji, though the Sibe and Daur had nominally been affiliated with the Khorchin Mongols. In 1692, the Kangxi emperor transferred both groups to the Upper Three Banners, ordered them into *niru*, and placed them under the authority of Sabsu, the Manchu military governor of the Heilongjiang region.[174] In like fashion, the Solon and Butha were also put into companies and banners to serve the Qing court. Perhaps because they were never wholly integrated with the Manchu Eight Banners, and rarely served in provincial garrisons, they retained more of their "raw" martial spirit and were widely regarded as fearsome warriors.[175]

### Mobility Within the Eight Banners

While ethnicity was a basic organizing principle in the creation and structure of the Eight Banners, it was admittedly not the only one. Because ethnicity was very often not a cut-and-dried issue, the banners could take into account mitigating factors in classifying individuals or even entire populations. As we have seen, military or political considerations sometimes necessitated the enrollment of some Manchu families, such as that of Shi Tingzhu, in the Chinese banners, and of some groups of Mongols and Chinese in the Manchu banners.[176] However, these anomalies do not justify wholesale rejection of the proposition that ethnic principles were at work within the Eight Banner system. As already noted, even when put into the same ethnic banner, ethnically distinct groups continued in almost all cases to be registered in separate companies within the banner. By the same token, individuals of mixed ancestry—including the emperors themselves, whose genealogies reveal Manchu, Mongol, and Chinese parentage[177]—could be considered unproblematically as belonging to only one category. It is fair to conclude that while ethnic categories were followed in the internal structure of the Manchu, Mongol, and Chinese banners, ethnicity was certainly fungible when justifiable ends presented themselves. I would suggest that such manipulation does not void the general meaningfulness of Qing ethnic categories, but rather confirms it.

The ways in which banner *and* company affiliation could be consciously used as an avenue for expressing ethnicity, rank, and status can be seen in cases of movement between the different banner hierarchies. This movement could occur in any number of ways—official promotion, marriage, and adoption, for example—and not all movement had ethnic meaning. The transfer of companies between the color-banners within an ethnic division, for example, which happened all the time in the first decades of the Qing, might simply reflect bureaucratic need. The conversion of a bondservant company into a regular-household company reflected more a change in status than in ethnicity.[178] Another type of movement across hierarchies, called "banner elevation" (*tai qi/gūsa doobumbi*), often (though not always) involved a change of ethnic categories. Banner elevation was an honor reserved for a handful of the court's most loyal servants and the families of imperial concubines. In these cases, individual households in the Mongol or Chinese banners were re-registered within the Manchu banners, usually the Upper Three Banners. Those already in a Manchu banner company (regular or bondservant) also might be moved to a preferred spot in the Upper Three Banners. It is possible to think of banner elevation as a compromise of ethnic principles, but it was a conscious compromise, based precisely on the recognition of those principles and of the superior privilege attached to membership in the Manchu banners.[179] Hence I would argue that banner elevation is best understood, not as evidence of the nonexistence or total porosity of ethnic boundaries between banners, but, again, rather as evidence of the "instrumentality" that sometimes lay behind ethnic identification in the Qing.

One of the most famous cases of banner elevation involved the Tong family, a prominent banner lineage. The case arose from a 1688 petition submitted by Tong Guogang, a maternal uncle of the Kangxi emperor, who asked that he and his entire lineage (over eighty-four hundred people in fifteen *niru* spread between two banners) be moved from the Chinese to the Manchu banners. His reason for making this unusual request—and it *was* highly unusual—was the claim that the Tongs were descended originally from a Manchu (that is, a Jurchen) clan. After some deliberation, the emperor approved this petition and one other similar one submitted at the same time, but only in a limited way. He ordered that the Tong name be recognized as a Manchu name, but that the registration of the Tong lineage remain in the Chinese banners.[180] This gave the appearance of banner elevation without the reality. In the end, only Tong Guogang, his father, and grandfather were accorded the honor of being considered "Manchu" in official accounts (as evidenced by their inclusion in the *Comprehensive Genealogy of Eight Banner Manchu Clans* and in a list of hereditary honors of the Bordered Yellow Banner in the *Comprehensive History of the Eight Banners*). Their company alone was elevated into the Manchu banner; the rest of the Tong companies were still held in the Chinese banners.[181]

That Tong felt it necessary to couch his appeal in terms of original descent reveals the degree to which this element played a part in determining identity at the time. It is possible that his petition was approved because of the claim that his family was "originally Manchu." But it is more likely that it was approved because of Tong's status as an imperial in-law; throughout the Qing, nearly all immediate in-laws, regardless of their ethnicity, were elevated into the Manchu banners.[182] Just as in contemporary Chinese (or American) society, where declaring a particular ethnicity can sometimes bring prestige or concrete benefits, so it was in the seventeenth century. To be sure, identities were "ambiguous and negotiable,"[183] just as they are now, and people who saw an opportunity to improve their life chances by switching ethnicity might attempt to do so, but there were limits as to how far and in what ways this could be engineered.[184] That is to say, Manchu ethnicity necessarily meant invention, but it was not a case of "anything goes."

Up to now, the ethnic significance of the Eight Banners in the Qing has been much less well recognized than its military and political importance. This chapter has demonstrated that from the earliest period of Qing history the parameters of identity were set according to the typical criteria used in speaking of ethnicity, including shared myths, belief in common descent and geographical origin, and similar cultural markers, and that these criteria were reflected in the organization and internal divisions of the Eight Banners, at first by company and later by company and banner. Ideally these criteria were all supposed to line up. However, as the Tong case, and the larger case presented here of the Manchus as a whole also shows, a certain amount of historical license was permitted in the invention of ethnicity and "nationality" in early Qing China. While such categories were not immutable (particularly where it concerned Han Chinese who had lived for a long time among the Jurchens), by and large, distinctions of ancestry (real or assumed), language, and culture were respected: Manchus were enrolled in the Manchu banners, Mongols in the Mongol banners, and Ming-frontier Chinese in the Chinese banners. As the following chapters will show, by the middle of the eighteenth century, these distinctions faded somewhat in significance as the Manchus settled permanently in China and the peculiar tenor of life under the banners came to exercise a defining influence over what it meant to be "Manchu."

CHAPTER TWO

# Manchu Cities: Tigers on the Mountain

Accounts of the establishment of Qing rule generally emphasize the promises and compromises made by Chinese and Manchu elites as the "real story" of the conquest, and pay little attention to such mundane matters as the actual physical accommodation of the Manchus in China. Yet much as the Berlin Wall once stood as the symbol of the divide between socialist and capitalist camps during the Cold War, so the walls partitioning Beijing and other Chinese cities symbolized the basic fact of Manchu domination during the Qing period. By representing dynastic territorial rights in some of China's oldest conurbations (two hundred years later, another group of imperialists would similarly stake out their own sections of treaty port cities), separately delineated "Manchu cities" were, with the queue, one of the two most enduring and obvious manifestations of the conquest nature of Qing rule. Writing in 1856, Thomas Taylor Meadows remarked that "the mere sight of these garrisons has been a constant reminder to the Chinese of their being under the dominion of an alien, barbarian race; and as the latter have always borne themselves with much of the insolence of conquerors, their acts have been a constant excitement to disaffection."[1] Meadows's comments should be regarded with the caution properly reserved for a nineteenth-century British gentleman's writings about China, but it is hard to dismiss them entirely: when the dynasty fell in 1912, the end of Manchu domination was celebrated by the dissolution of the garrisons and the immediate destruction of the walls dividing Manchu and Han.[2]

As extensions of central power parallel to, yet separate from, the provincial government, the symbolic, political, and strategic importance of Manchu cities was such that the court lavished huge sums on their construction and upkeep. More important for our purposes, as the setting for the lives of banner people in the Qing, Manchu cities were sites both of integration and of alienation, places where traditional military virtues were practiced, where banner privileges were exercised, and where banner and Chinese societies met. As nodes of cultural and institutional difference, Manchu cities were sites of the re-formation of Manchu ethnicity in the Qing. For more than in the corridors of the palace, it was in the streets of Beijing and the garrison cities across China that the Manchu adaptation to Chinese realities took place and a new Manchu identity was forged. If we wish to learn something about the circumstances of Manchu lives in the Qing and how settlement in China shaped the identity of those in the Eight Banners, it is essential that we study the environment that shaped those lives. The picture that emerges will help us imagine the specific character of Manchu rule over China, highlight the link between Manchu institutions and identity, and show how this "disposition of bodies" was linked to the expression of Qing power as it operated "through the practices of everyday life."[3]

This chapter opens by sketching the historical background and overall structure of the Qing garrison system. It then takes up the matter of separate residential areas for banner people, beginning with the Manchu partition of Beijing in 1648 and the creation of walled Manchu cities in the provincial banner garrisons, to show that residence patterns and living arrangements in Beijing and other Manchu cities decisively shaped postconquest Manchu identity. The second part of the chapter is more concerned with the idea of occupation itself and with how Manchu cities fit in the larger framework of Qing rule. Here I wish to demonstrate that the Manchu occupation of the country was not simply a contingent response to unexpected circumstances, but a predetermined strategy seized on immediately after the conquest that offered a solution to the dilemma of minority rule. A concluding comparison of the Eight Banner garrison system with that established under the Green Standard Army illuminates the special place of the Manchus, and the banners generally, in the Qing state and the embeddedness of ethnicity, residence, and occupation.

## GARRISONS BEFORE THE CONQUEST

Wherever and whenever military force is required to acquire and hold territory, garrisons are bound to exist. We may think of garrisons as fixed, fortified military installations aiding in the extension or maintenance of control by a central authority, often as the consequence of invasion or occupation.

Thus imperial Rome was garrisoned by a force of ten thousand troops (about half of whom belonged to the famous Praetorian cohorts), while the expansion and defense of the empire depended upon permanent camps (*castra*) established in the frontier military zones, where the soldiers of the legions were based.[4] The garrison town (*kastron*) featured, too, in the landscape of the Byzantine empire, whose soldiers were to defend cities against external threats as well as to protect the local institutions and representatives of the state.[5] The Norman conquest of England in the late eleventh century hinged upon the placement of soldiers in garrisons—castles, actually, which were a Norman innovation. Strategically placed to form defensive networks, Norman castles served both as bases for sorties as well as havens for refuge from enemy attacks.[6] Closer to our own times, garrisons of Soviet troops were maintained in most of the countries of the Eastern Bloc during the Cold War, and garrisons of United States' troops may still be found today in various places around the world. In all these instances, tensions between the imperial (or quasi-imperial) center and the periphery were frequently focused upon garrisons as imperfect microcosms of the occupiers' native domains. As we will see, such tension was characteristic of Qing garrison cities.

Like Rome and Byzantium, Chinese empires routinely placed troops in defensive positions on the frontiers. The "long walls" of the Qin period (221–207 B.C.E.) represented a defensive strategy perhaps less common in the West, but it was the *garrisoning* of the walls that determined their effectiveness.[7] Beginning in the Han period, the establishment of self-supporting military colonies (Ch *tuntian*) on the empire's northern fringes became standard practice for Chinese governments. Although they were expensive, required considerable logistical support, and incurred potentially serious political risk (witness the rebellion of the Tang general An Lushan in 755 C.E.), this type of garrison system was instituted by many dynasties, including the Ming, which maintained a strong military presence in Liaodong, one of the "Nine Frontiers" border-defense zones along the empire's northern periphery.[8]

Garrisons figured as a means of defense under non-Chinese regimes, too. But because they generally relied more than did native regimes on the use of force (or threats of its use) to maintain control, alien dynasties like the Jin and the Yuan resorted to the placement of troops in the interior as well as on the frontier. The Jin, for example, placed garrisons of Jurchen military households all across north China. The Mongols also established several score garrisons (the exact number is unknown) over a wide area throughout the country. These were at first continually relocated according to military expediency, but a permanent empire-wide system was in place just two years after the fall of the Southern Song in 1279.[9] Urban centers, especially those on the Yangzi River, such as Hangzhou, were probably heavily garrisoned, which the testimony of Marco Polo confirms. Polo's telling comment that at Hangzhou "[the townsfolk] cannot bear the sight of a soldier or of the Great Khan's guards, believing that it is through them that they have been deprived of their own natural kings and lords" prefigures the sort of tension that existed in Manchu cities centuries later.[10] Most of these troops were not Mongol soldiers (as Polo was aware), who were rarely stationed south of the Huai River. Instead, two other Yuan forces, the "Northern Chinese Armies," which included Jurchen soldiers from the defeated Jin, and the "Newly-Adherent Armies," made up of former Song troops, garrisoned the south, where, all in all, the Yuan presence was somewhat limited.

Though these precedents may not have been known to them at first, the budding Jurchen state followed this pattern when it began establishing garrisons early in the seventeenth century.[11] Nurhaci is known to have stressed the importance of wall-building, as the ruins of the early Jurchen capitals demonstrate,[12] and by the late Ming defensive needs forced him to initiate a garrison network of his own. The first garrisons were small walled forts (called *tai* in Manchu, after the Chinese word, *tai*, for watchposts) which were probably simply well-supplied towns fortified with heavy gates and a small military force supported by a modest civilian population.[13] While some *tai* may have served, like Norman castles, as internal fortifications, most were frontier guard posts.[14] Before long, more impressive defenses were put in place. Between 1618 and 1621 the Jurchens assumed control of more than eighty garrisons belonging to the Ming *wei-suo* system (itself a legacy of Mongol rule). Five thousand banner troops were stationed at the most important of these (Gaizhou, Jinzhou, and Niuzhuang), where they were poised to defend the conquest of Liaodong against remnant Ming forces in the Liaodong Peninsula.[15] At this point, the frontier surrounding the new Jurchen capital at Liaoyang was divided up between banners, so that Gaizhou, for instance, was the responsibility of the Plain White Banner and Jinzhou the responsibility of the Bordered Blue Banner.[16] As yet there were no garrisons in the areas west or south of the Liao River (i.e., Liaoxi and the Shanhaiguan corridor), which remained a kind of no-man's land until 1626, when a Ming victory over the Jurchen at Ningyuan enabled the Chinese to reposition large garrisons at the main Liaoxi fortresses of Dalinghe, Chinchou, and Songshan.[17]

After his father's death and his own failure to dislodge the Ming from Liaoxi in 1627,[18] Hong Taiji turned to the consolidation of territory already under Latter Jin control, improving defenses by adding three garrisons along the frontier with China, four along the Korean frontier, and several on the Mongolian frontier, some in former Ming *wei-suo* locations.[19] After the capture of Dalinghe in 1631, when the Latter Jin borders for a while ceased their steady expansion, garrisons (heretofore relatively mobile) took on a more permanent character, as personnel were fixed and their number increased. This was particularly true after 1636, by which time Korea had been subdued and peace made with the Chakhar Mongols. Free to concentrate his attention southward, Hong Taiji now ordered major defensive fortifications built and expanded at Liaoyang, Pingcheng, and Kaicheng. This strategy appears to have been the inspiration of his Chinese advisors, who pushed for more favorable treatment of civilians in captured cities and who complained, in reference to the loss of the Bohai littoral, that "the problem with us is that everything is put into getting [a city], and then we let it go easily."[20] The Qing foothold at Dalinghe served as a springboard for the siege and capture in 1642 of the two remaining Ming garrison cities in the Shanhaiguan corridor, Songshan and Chinchou. These newly acquired garrisons in turn played a key strategic role as Qing forces moved farther and farther south, eventually into position for the seizure of Beijing in the spring of 1644.

Apart from holding down the frontiers of the expanding Jin state, garrisons in preconquest Liaodong also became involved in efforts to establish more effective control over the Han Chinese population, and were charged with quelling local unrest and preventing Chinese from escaping Latter Jin territory.[21] In their evolution from mere border stations to fortified links in a flexible network that could be relied on to reinforce Qing military maneuvers, define "national" borders, and suppress internal rebellion, the preconquest garrisons thus provided the Manchus some invaluable lessons and in many ways prefigured the system that developed after 1644.

OUTLINE OF THE QING OCCUPATION

With the conquest of China, the vast majority of original Qing subjects moved from Manchuria to the Chinese provinces. To accommodate them, walled enclaves called "Manchu cities" (*Man-cheng/Manju hoton*), were built in a number of cities, beginning with Xi'an, Nanjing, and Hangzhou.[22] Eventually Eight Banner garrisons (*baqi zhufang/jakūn gūsai seremšeme tehe ba*) were established at eighteen locations in China proper—nineteen, counting the capital. Part military bastion, part administrative center, and part ethnic ghetto, the Manchu city became the exclusive home of banner officers and soldiers, their families, and servants, giving the dynasty a high profile in major urban centers and functioning as anchors in the steady expansion of Qing control.

Schematically, the Qing occupation of China involved the main Beijing garrison, plus four garrison networks covering the metropolitan area around Beijing, Manchuria, the northwest frontier, and, of course, the Chinese provinces.[23] The situation in Beijing is described in the next section. The twenty-five banner garrisons in the metropolitan zone (Ch *jifu zhufang*), which provided a defensive cordon around the capital, constituted the most compact garrison network and represented the nucleus of the new postconquest Qing banner garrison structure. Manned exclusively by Manchu and Mongol bannermen, they served to hold down territory in the immediate vicinity of Beijing as well as to screen the capital from potential attacks from the north (before the conquest, the Manchus themselves had used the passes in the mountains directly north of the city to stage raids on the suburbs). Posted at such strategic passes as Gubeikou, Dushikou, and Xifengkou, bannermen here were also charged with monitoring traffic between Mongolia and the capital.

The second garrison network, extending across Manchuria, was the legacy of the preconquest struggle to establish and defend the frontiers of the Jurchen state. Originally, everything from the northern frontiers of Heilongjiang (Ma *Sahaliyan ula*) and Jilin (Ma *Girin-i ula*, "Ningguta") to the southerly reaches of Shengjing (Ma *Mukden*), sometimes Fengtian (Ma "Fungtiyan) was in the hands of the garrison general at Shengjing. In 1653 a garrison general was posted to Ningguta, and in 1683 to Heilongjiang, partly in response to Russian expansion in southern Siberia. These three positions were the mainstays of a dense network of garrisons that was home to about one-fifth of banner soldiers.

The third network was made up of garrisons in the Northwest, primarily Mongolia and Xinjiang, most of which were founded in the course of Qing expansion in the second half of the eighteenth century.[24] Though far less

*Map 2.* Eight Banner garrisons in the Qing empire. Locations of principal garrisons around the empire at its height in the second half of the eighteenth century.

densely planted, garrisons here bore greater resemblance to the arrangement in the Northeast, in that garrison commanders were responsible for all aspects of the administration of an area that was often very large and populated by non-Han ethnic groups, Han colonists, and exiles. For this reason, Eight Banner military posts here were sometimes not spoken of as garrisons but as "military prefectures" (Ch *junfu*).[25]

The fourth network, upon which we shall concentrate our attention, was made up of the provincial Eight Banner garrisons (Ch *zhisheng zhufang*), all located in or near cities of China proper.[26] Most of these were founded in two separate twenty-year periods, first in the beginning decades of Qing rule over China, with a later period of expansion coming at the very end of the Kangxi reign and extending through the early Qianlong era. The provincial garrisons were established along five overlapping "chains": the Great Wall chain (Beijing-Youwei-Suiyuan-Ningxia-Zhuanglang-Liangzhou); the Yellow River chain (Dezhou-Kaifeng-Taiyuan-Xi'an); the Yangzi chain (Jingkou-Nanjing-Jingzhou-Chengdu); the Grand Canal chain (Beijing-Dezhou-Jingkou-Hangzhou); and the Coastal chain (Tianjin-Qingzhou-Zhapu-Hangzhou-Fuzhou-Guangzhou).[27] As a force of permanent occupation, the Eight Banners were thus present in the coastal and northern provinces, but absent from Anhui, Jiangxi, Hunan, Guangxi, Guizhou, and Yunnan.[28]

Garrison bannermen were drawn from the three main ethnic corps of the Eight Banners, as the old practice of assigning entire areas to certain banners was abandoned (perhaps for fear that this would provide a toehold for ambitious banner leaders). Each company within the banner was in principle required to supply a certain number of soldiers for garrison duty, so that every color division of the banner (plain yellow, bordered blue, etc.) was represented in more or less equal numbers at a given garrison. However, the ethnic distribution of troops was not uniform at every location. For instance, while Xi'an was garrisoned by Manchu, Mongol, and Chinese banner soldiers, Kaifeng was garrisoned only by Manchu and Mongol soldiers, and Qingzhou only by Manchu and Chinese banner soldiers. Regardless of their original affiliation, soldiers serving in the provinces came to be labeled collectively the "garrison Eight Banners" (Ch *zhufang baqi*), in distinction to those serving in the "capital Eight Banners" (Ch *jinlü baqi*). As later chapters will show, the implications of this hierarchy acquired more significance by the eighteenth century, as the world of the garrisons diverged more and more from the world of the capital.

As the government continued to adjust the system, the size of garrisons also varied, both between different locations as well as over time at the same location. The largest garrisons had as many as ten thousand banner soldiers,[29] the smallest garrisons as few as fifty or even less. Garrison command structure corresponded to size. Major provincial garrisons, i.e., those with over fifteen hundred soldiers, were commanded by a garrison general (*jiangjun/jiyangggiyūn*), a garrison lieutenant general (*fudutong/meiren-i janggin*), or banner commander (*dutong/gūsa be kadalara amban*).[30] Secondary garrisons, manned by between three hundred and fifteen hundred soldiers, were headed by a senior commandant (*chengshouyu/hoton-i da*). Garrisons with fewer than three hundred soldiers were headed by a junior commandant

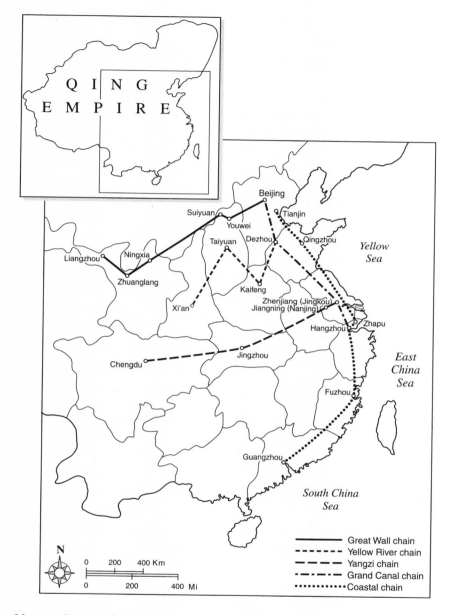

Map 3. Provincial Eight Banner garrisons. Garrisons in the Chinese provinces fell into one or more of the five networks ("chains") shown here.

(*fangshouyu/gūsai da*) or other officer of lesser rank. Despite considerable variation between them, discussions of the banner garrisons in later official compendia make it clear that they were seen as belonging to one unified system of extended defense.[31] At the same time, however, they played different parts in the occupation of China and the defense of the realm. Some were responsible for coastal defense, some the defense of external borders, and others for guarding internal land routes and maintaining local control.[32]

## MANCHU APARTHEID AND THE DIVISION OF BEIJING

Residence of the emperor and some one hundred thousand banner soldiers, Beijing was the largest Manchu city in the Qing empire.[33] As such, it was the capital of the Manchu world and, after 1644, the official home for Manchus and all others in the Eight Banners—a fact underscored by the dynasty's residency and repatriation policies for bannermen outside the capital (taken up in Chapter 6). During the Qing, of course, Beijing was not spoken of as a garrison, or even, for that matter, as "Beijing," but as "the capital" (*jingshi/ gemun-i hecen*). Yet, like all Manchu cities, it featured a strictly segregated residence pattern. The city's basic layout is well described by an Italian Jesuit who lived there in the early eighteenth century:

> Peking is composed of two distinct cities, one being called the Tartar city, the other the Chinese. The Tartar city is so named because it is inhabited by Tartars, and by those who, though not Tartars, are enrolled in the Ki-hiu-ti [*qixiade* = Eight Banners], or eight bands which constitute the Tartar troops. The Chinese city is inhabited by Chinese alone. . . . The Tartar city is square, and encircled by a yellow wall.[34]

The division of the city into two districts, one for those in the Eight Banners and the other for Han Chinese, was so basic that it is sometimes easy to overlook. This is especially so today, now that the massive walls that defined Beijing and gave the city its soul have been destroyed, and with them the last physical reminders of the barriers that once separated the Inner (or "Tartar") City from the Outer (or "Chinese") City. But this division was an essential feature of Manchu urban planning.

Segregation of Manchus and Han Chinese, what Frederic Wakeman has termed "Manchu apartheid,"[35] traced its origins to before the conquest. In 1621, when the expansion of the Latter Jin state into Liaodong brought large numbers of Han under the direct authority of the Jurchen khan, scarcity of land and housing forced Nurhaci to adopt a policy of co-residence.[36] This idealistic plan, part of an overall attempt to level differences between conqueror and conquered (rationed grain was distributed equally to all and taxes on agricultural production were the same for both groups), called upon Chinese to share their houses and fields equally with their new masters and literally criminalized household strife. Begun as a temporary economic measure, co-residency soon ran into serious problems. Not only did Chinese resent having to share housing and farmland with uninvited guests (with whom they probably could not even have communicated very well), but Jurchens assigned to live with Chinese felt that living on equal terms with a people whom they supposedly ruled was beneath their dignity. Incidents of exploitation, theft, poisoning, and murder grew frequent, with the spiral of violence ending in open rebellion of the Chinese population in 1623. Some attempted to escape south to Ming territory, while others sought revenge on their Jurchen masters by poisoning their water and food supplies.[37]

The simple solution to interethnic friction was to separate the two groups. The cohabitation policy was abandoned. Within a few months, far from living with them, Jurchens were forbidden to even visit Chinese. By July 1623 plans for resettling populations around Niuzhuang and Yaozhou specified that Jurchens were to be settled on one side of town and Han Chinese on another.[38] From that point on, there is no further evidence of joint residence; instead, separation came to be seen as the key to peaceful relations with the Chinese. This principle is fully evidenced in 1630, for example, when, in a letter to the forces occupying Luanzhou and three other cities beyond the Great Wall, Hong Taiji's cousin Amin instructed that "the Jurchens and Chinese shall be separated, each occupying their own sector (Ma *giyai*, lit. "street"). Do not go into the Chinese sector. Any Jurchen found to have gone into the Chinese sector will be apprehended."[39] (That this injunction was addressed to Jurchen soldiers, and not Chinese civilians, suggests that the Jurchens were still in the habit of harassing the Chinese.) The primary aim of segregation was to ease ethnic tension, with mutual isolation in effect a means of protecting the state's Chinese subjects.[40]

The assumption that unrestricted contact between the groups invited trouble—as well as the pose that the Manchus were the protectors of the Chinese population (this time against the Shun rebels of Li Zicheng)—was carried over into the immediate postconquest period. Concern, for instance, about future conflicts over landholding in the metropolitan area led a former Ming censor who went over to the Qing to propose a complete survey and redistribution of all land in the area so that entirely separate regions could be created for Manchus and Chinese. His memorial of early 1645 put it this way: "The borders between Manchu and Han must be made clear . . . Manchus are to all gather in one area. . . . Manchu and Han will each take care of his own territory; this way there will be no mutual depredation and no cause for disputes."[41] This proposal was approved two weeks later to become the basis for the Qing encirclement of land around the capital. The language of the edict makes it clear that Manchus and Han were to be separated: "However, if, on this type of [masterless] land, Manchus and Han were to live intermingled, there would be no end to disputes. In every prefecture, department, county, district, and village, let Manchus and Han live separately, each observing the boundary [between them]. This will prevent conflicts later on."[42] In Beijing itself, however, the occupation of the city in the summer of 1644 did not immediately result in the creation of separate districts for Manchus and Chinese. An "edict" issued by Dorgon in July 1644 states, in part, that those in the capital choosing to live together with the civilians whose houses they have occupied will be granted one year's tax amnesty, pointing to the absence of a distinct urban division between the two groups at this time.[43]

This anomalous situation lasted only four years. In October 1648, ostensibly in response to reports of increasing strife (robbery, murder) and mutual recrimination that were attributed directly to mixed residence of Manchus and Han Chinese, Dorgon ordered the segregation of Beijing's banner and nonbanner populations. The order decreed that in the interests of long-term peace and harmony, all Chinese living within the city walls would have until the end of the following year to move to the southern suburbs. The only exceptions were Han who served as guards at government offices, Buddhist and Daoist monks, or servants within banner households. People were free either to dismantle their houses and rebuild them in the suburbs or to sell them. Henceforth Chinese would be permitted in the city during the day only, and were officially forbidden to stay overnight in the Inner City.[44]

It is difficult to know how seriously to take the court's insistence that its action was prompted by rising interethnic conflict within Beijing. There is little in the documents to suggest this was the case; the majority of incidents involving Manchus and Chinese are cases of escaped captives and are concentrated geographically in the metropolitan suburbs, not in the capital itself.

On the other hand, archival records from before 1653 are extremely fragmentary. It is, of course, entirely possible, even probable, that the sorts of incidents the court was alluding to were common. But it seems at least as likely that the court all along had been planning to divide the city and simply waited until it had consolidated control somewhat before moving forward. Indeed, given the preconquest precedent and the decision to isolate the banner populations that by then had already moved into Xi'an (see below), it would have been quite surprising had no eviction order ever been handed down to Beijing's Chinese residents. Even if we cannot be sure whether they viewed the segregation policy as "an arrogant act of imperial despotism,"[45] it is not too much to suppose that they were extremely displeased and inconvenienced by it. The court's anticipation of such a reaction explains why the segregation order acknowledged the burden placed upon people but stressed that, while the inconvenience was temporary, the benefits for both groups were enduring.[46]

The expulsion of the Han changed the character of the city. The Manchu occupation of the Chinese capital made it a very diverse place—more, one imagines, like it had been under the Yuan. Qing Beijing was an unmistakably bicultural city, a Sino-Manchu hybrid, as reflected in the languages over the gates and in the streets (even Beijing's Mandarin showed signs of Altaicization[47]), the entertainment in teahouses and theaters,[48] its food (many of the sweets and delicate cakes for which Beijing was famous were Manchu innovations), its temples (which now also included Tibetan Buddhist foundations), and the dress of its people. Not without reason did the court insist this was the new Manchu home. As if to emphasize this, the old division of the city into thirty-one "neighborhoods" (Ch *fang*) was eclipsed by a new system of organization based on the Eight Banners, transforming Beijing into an enormous garrison.[49]

Administration of the Inner City thereafter became a private dynastic affair, with each banner occupying a carefully defined sector: the two yellow banners were located in the north, near the Andingmen and Deshengmen gates, which it was their responsibility to guard; the two white banners were stationed in the east by the Dongzhi and Chaoyang gates; the red banners defended Xizhimen and Fuchengmen on the west, while the blue banners were ensconced in the south near Chongwenmen and Xuanwumen. Zhengyangmen (informally known as Qianmen), the city's central southern gate, was manned in rotation by the gendarmerie, which included troops drawn

| Legend: | | NORTH<br>earth<br>*yellow*<br>YELLOW | |
|---|---|---|---|
| DIRECTION<br>Element<br>*Traditional color*<br>BANNER COLOR | WEST<br>fire<br>*crimson*<br>RED | CENTER<br>wood<br>*blue-green* | EAST<br>metal<br>*white*<br>WHITE |
| | | SOUTH<br>water<br>*black*<br>BLUE | |

*Fig. 3.*    Five-agents schema for the placement of the Eight Banners in Beijing. After the conquest, it was said that the Eight Banners were assigned positions in the city according to the place of a banner's color in the Chinese system of the five agents. This was certainly a myth; not only were the correspondences imperfect, but the similarity of the arrangement to the positions taken by the banners during the hunt (yellow in the north, red in the west, white in the east, blue in the south) is too striking to be ignored. Data from *Baqi tongzhi chuji* (1739).

from all eight banners as well as from the Green Standard Army.[50] The most common explanation for this arrangement derives from the traditional "five agents" (Ch *wu xing*) associations linking (among other things) colors and points of the compass (Fig. 3). Placing the yellow banners in the north, the white in the east, the red in the west, and the blue in the south was an auspicious arrangement that ensured the proper correspondence of extinguishing and generating elements. However, the correspondence was not perfect. While the substitution of red for crimson could be overlooked, blue for black was not so easily finessed.[51] The absence of the wood agent also spoiled the symmetry.[52]

Appealing as the five-agents rationale was, at the same time, it is hard to overlook the organizational advantages of making residence patterns conform to banner structure.[53] As the official history of the Eight Banners remarked: "For military mobilization, the significance of the complementary placement of the Eight Banners thus is [the creation] of order and discipline; for establishing the dynasty, it is to strengthen the screen."[54] The "screen"

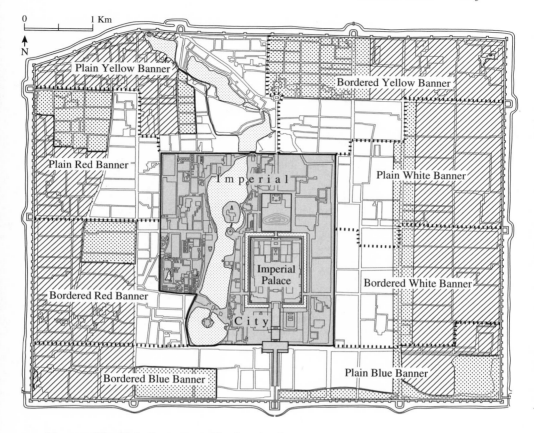

*Map 4.* The Eight Banner neighborhoods of Qing Beijing. Beijing under the Manchus was divided into eight sectors, each sector serving as the residential zone for one of the Eight Banners. Each zone was further divided into Manchu, Mongol, and Chinese banner neighborhoods. Unshaded areas were for the Manchu banners; shaded areas were for the Mongol banners; and diagonally barred areas were for the Chinese banners. Data from *Baqi tongzhi chuji.*

alluded to the defensive positions taken up by the banners around the imperial city: "When the Shizu emperor [Shunzhi] established the capital at Yanjing [Beijing], he divided the Eight Banners, arranging them so they surrounded the imperial palace."[55] In fact, close consideration suggests that Manchu hunting formations were the real inspiration for this arrangement, particularly field encampments, where soldiers' tents formed a protective circle around the imperial yurt, located in the center—a practice strongly re-

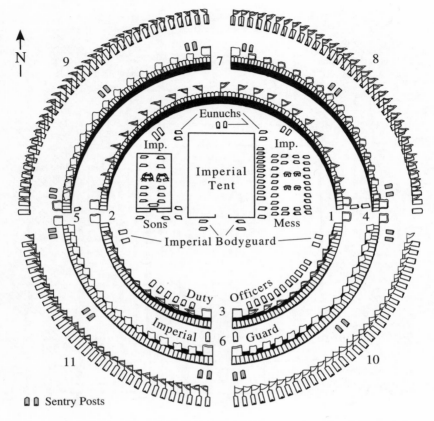

*Fig. 4.* Arrangement of tents on imperial expeditions. When the emperor left the capital and was forced to camp for the night, as on hunting expeditions, the encampment was arranged according to a fixed plan to achieve maximum security. In the center was the emperor's tent, protected by eunuchs and members of the imperial bodyguard, and flanked by the tents of his accompanying sons (Ch *age suo*) and by tents in which meals were prepared. Surrounding this central area were the tents of the rest of the imperial party, formed into three concentric circles. Reproduced from *Da Qing huidian tu* (1818), *juan* 104.

calling the Mongolian *ordo* (Fig. 4). That Manchu banners (not Mongol or Chinese banners) were situated closest on all sides of the imperial city underscores the degree to which Altaic traditions and security concerns, and not geomancy, determined the look of the capital.

The militarized character of the city was further heightened by tight security measures. Movement between and within each quarter was controlled through an extensive system of barricades, called *jalan*, which were closed at night. During his stay in Beijing in 1793, Lord Macartney, the British emissary to the Qianlong court, was strongly impressed by the constant state of alert:

> The police is singularly strict. It is indeed stretched to an extent unknown I believe in any other city, and strongly marks the jealousy of the Government, and their unceasing apprehension of danger. At night all the streets are shut up by barricadoes at each end and a guard is constantly patrolling between them so that no person can pass after a certain hour without assigning satisfactory reasons. . . . A number of watchmen are also stationed at short distances who carry a rattle and every two or three minutes proclaim their vigilance by the exercise of their instrument. One or two of these guardians of the peace had their stands so near to my house that I could not sleep a wink for the first three or four nights.[56]

There were also numerous sentry boxes (*duizi*/*juce*, *jucei boo*) and guard stations (Ch *guanting*) to keep watch, which were manned by the Beijing Gendarmerie.[57] A similar system of sentry boxes in the provincial garrisons was manned solely by bannermen,[58] whose function is described in this 1730 report: "Arriving in Zhapu, I placed one sentry box per banner inside the Manchu encampment, in the manner of Eight Banner sites. One corporal and nine soldiers are stationed at each guardhouse during the day, and at night they stand watch, apprehending malefactors and keeping on the lookout for fires. Also, two colonels are assigned to inspect the sentry boxes at irregular intervals."[59]

## MANCHU CITIES IN THE PROVINCES

As mentioned, the territorial extension of Qing control in the 1640s and 1650s necessitated the settlement of Eight Banner garrisons beyond the Northeast and the capital to China proper. Considered transient postings, the provincial garrisons, miniature Beijings that revolved like satellites around the main capital, constituted a "home away from home" for Manchus outside the capital—a role emphasized by the emperor's preference to stay within the garrison confines when on tour.[60] The first provincial garrison was at Xi'an, the former Tang capital and, after Beijing, the most important city in north China. On July 13, 1645, Holohoi, then nominally commander of the

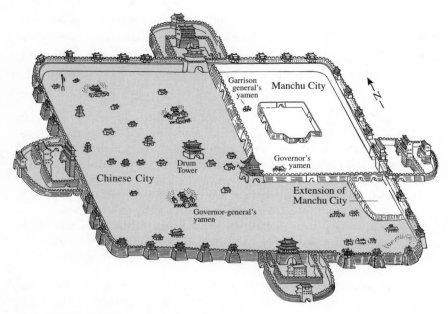

*Fig. 5.*    Xi'an garrison. Established in 1645, the garrison at Xi'an occupied the entire northeastern quarter of the city. It was later extended to the southeast to include more of the Chinese city. The banner population of Xi'an was the largest of any garrison, exceeded only by that of Beijing. Reproduced from *Shaanxi tongzhi* (1735).

Mukden garrison, was instructed to "take three men from every company" to garrison Xi'an.[61] He probably did not reach the city until late in 1645, but was certainly there by early 1646, when he led the garrison forces in a successful defense of the city against Ming loyalists in February 1646. Xi'an thereafter remained firmly in Qing hands and played an important role in the pacification of Shanxi, Shaanxi, and Sichuan.[62] More Manchus lived there than in any other city except Beijing, and it served a vital function as the hub of the garrison system in west China and a base of military operations during the campaigns in Qinghai and the far northwest in the eighteenth century.

The garrison at Nanjing[63] was founded at about the same time as that at Xi'an, just six months after the surrender of the city to Qing troops. Banner lieutenants Bašan and Kangkala were put in charge and, like Holohoi, were instructed to select three men from every company to form a garrison

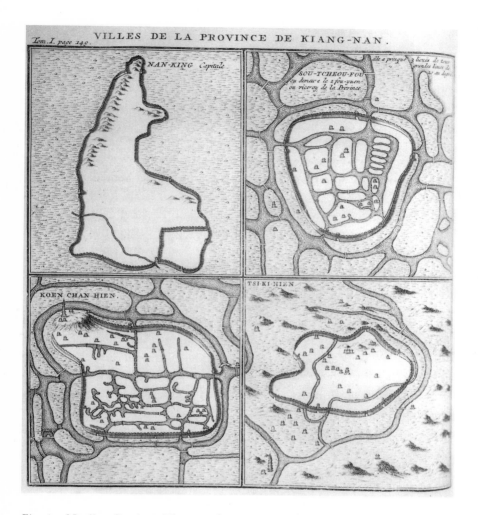

*Fig. 6.* Nanjing Garrison. The Manchu city at Nanjing, founded in 1646, was located in the southeast on the grounds of the former Ming palace. The wall around the garrison, clearly shown in the drawing, encircled an area of roughly two and two-thirds square miles, making it the largest Manchu city outside Beijing. Reproduced from Jean-Baptiste du Halde, *Description géographique, historique . . . de l'empire de la Chine et de la Tartarie Chinoise* (The Hague, 1736), vol. 1. Courtesy Special Collections Library, University of Michigan.

force.[64] By the middle of March 1646, the garrison had already been called on twice to defend the city against "bandit" attacks.[65] Ming loyalists advanced on the city again in the fall of 1646, and for the last time in the summer of 1659. The garrison held on both occasions, its strong showing an important factor in the quelling of unrest in the region generally.[66] The same December 1645 edict establishing the Nanjing garrison ordered the creation of a garrison at scenic Hangzhou, 150 miles (240 kilometers) to the east. The capture of Hangzhou had taken place in July 1645, very shortly after the surrender of Nanjing. At the end of the year, banner lieutenants Jumara and Hoto, part of the army led by Lekdehun against Ming loyalists, were told to select five men from every Manchu and Mongol company under their command (probably fewer than one thousand soldiers). Like Xi'an and Nanjing, the Hangzhou garrison soon faced its own challenges from forces loyal to the Ming, which it managed to put down.[67] The other permanent banner garrisons established during the Shunzhi reign were at Taiyuan (1649),[68] Dezhou (1654),[69] Jingkou (modern Zhenjiang) (1654), Fuzhou (1656), and Guangzhou (1661). The last three were originally manned entirely by troops drawn from the Chinese banners. Because of their ethnic background, the court had fewer reservations about sending them so far south. Moreover, they were supposedly more comfortable on the water than either Manchus or Mongols, and coped better with the hot, humid weather of south China.[70]

In the 1670s, the Rebellion of the Three Feudatories revealed weaknesses in the Qing garrison system that were remedied by enlarging some sites and placing new garrisons at strategic points such as Jingzhou (founded 1683)— an ancient city and a major axis of north-south communications located roughly at China's geographical center—and Kaifeng (1692). At the same time, garrisons were added along the northern frontier at Ningxia (1676), Guihua (1683), and Youwei (1693). Forty-odd years later, three more were added at Suiyuan, Liangzhou, and Zhuanglang (all 1737). The most southwesterly of the Eight Banner garrisons, Chengdu, in Sichuan province, was established in 1721 to serve as a base for campaigns in Tibet. But not all garrisons were founded, it seems, for strategic purposes. The naval installations at Tianjin (1726) and Zhapu (1728)[71] and the Qingzhou garrison (1729) were founded for reasons having more to do with the need to provide employment for bannermen than with military necessity.[72]

Following the principle of Manchu apartheid, separate banner compounds

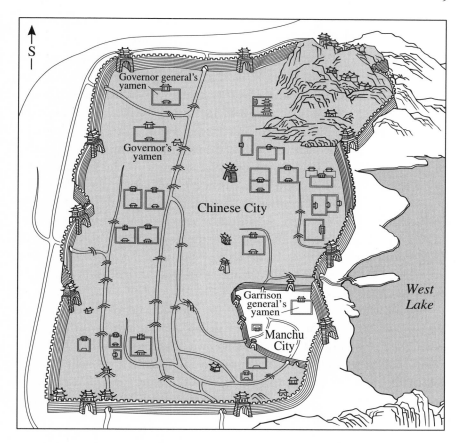

*Fig. 7.*   Hangzhou garrison. Though the smallest in area of the provincial banner garrisons, the Hangzhou garrison may have been the most picturesque, located as it was on the shores of West Lake. A significant proportion of bannermen here lived outside the garrison walls. Reproduced from *Zhejiang tongzhi* (1735).

were created at all of the provincial garrisons by building new walls within the old walls of the Chinese city. Indeed, populations were segregated at Xi'an and Nanjing even before Beijing. The banner quarter at Xi'an was marked off in 1645 by a wall going straight from the enceinted north gate south through the center of town to the bell tower, and from there east to the main Changle gate. In 1683, the walls were extended in the southeastern sector to enclose another part of Xi'an's main town, increasing the original area of 1.12 square miles (about 720 acres or 291 hectares) to 1.34 square miles, nearly 30 percent of the city's walled area (4.63 square miles)—larger than the average 20 percent of total city area for garrisons empire-wide.[73] (See Table 2.1 for a tabulation of Manchu city areas.) Though its banner population was never as numerous as Xi'an's, at 2.67 square miles (692 ha), the area of the Nanjing garrison was over twice the size of the Xi'an Manchu city, equaling 17 percent of Nanjing's walled area.[74] The city was first laid out in 1649; when construction was completed in 1660, a wall thirty feet high and over seven and one-half miles around encircled the banner district, where Manchu and Mongol bannermen lived alongside the former Ming imperial city precincts.[75] At Hangzhou, where residents enjoyed a splendid location near West Lake, walls thirty-five feet high and seven feet thick surrounded the garrison. The walls were enhanced by six gates and, in later years, by pavilions such as those commissioned by the Kangxi emperor, visible from the garrison gates.[76] Occupying an area of only 419 acres (170 hectares)— just over 13 percent of walled Hangzhou—this was the smallest in area of the major provincial garrisons.[77]

Not all Manchu cities were graced by such formidable brickwork. At Kaifeng, where the Manchu city was situated in the northwest corner of town, the garrison was surrounded only by a ten-foot earthen wall. The enclosure was very small, both in population and in area, with eight hundred soldiers confined to an area measuring about one-quarter mile square and occupying a mere 5.5 percent of the city's area.[78] At Taiyuan, a wooden palisade separated the garrison on its north and west sides from the rest of the town. Like Kaifeng, this was a lesser foundation of only five hundred men. At .21 square miles in size, Taiyuan was also somewhat smaller than the Kaifeng garrison, though it took up a roughly similar proportion of the Chinese city.[79] Another smallish garrison was that at Chengdu, which accounted for just 3 percent of the walled area of the city.[80] No wall surrounded either the Guangzhou or Fuzhou garrisons, but here, as elsewhere, Han Chinese dwelling in neighborhoods designated for banner residence were forced to relocate, ostensibly with compensation for their losses.[81]

Of the provincial garrisons founded in the Kangxi reign, all but Ningxia were built within the walls of the Chinese city. At Jingzhou, for instance, a kilometer-long wall right through the center of town divided the Manchu half of the city from the Chinese half (Fig. 8).[82] In contrast, with the exception of Chengdu, Tianjin, and Zhapu, all later provincial garrisons were like Qingzhou (in Shandong)—physically separate walled towns built from

TABLE 2.1
Approximate Area of Eight Banner Garrisons

| Garrison | Circumference of Wall | | Approximate Area | | Percent of City Area |
|---|---|---|---|---|---|
| | ZHANG* | MI/KM | SQ. MI | ACRES/HA | |
| Jiangning | 3412.5 | 6.54/10.52 | 2.67 | 1710/692 | 17% |
| Xi'an | 2222.1[1] | 4.25/6.84 | 1.34 | 857/347 | 40[2] |
| Jingzhou | 1258 | 3.70/5.95 | 0.79 | 507/205 | 50[3] |
| Hangzhou | 8 *li* | 2.76/4.44 | 0.65 | 419/170 | 13.25 |
| *Suiyuan* | 9 *li* 13 *bu* | 3.12/5.02 | 0.61 | 389/158 | — |
| *Ningxia* | 1360 | 3.03/4.87 | 0.57 | 366/148 | — |
| *Liangzhou* | 7.2 *li*[4] | 2.49/4.00 | 0.39 | 248/100 | — |
| Canton | 1270.5[5] | 2.83/4.55 | 0.33 | 212/86 | 17 |
| Fuzhou | 1130 | 2.16/3.48 | 0.29? | 186/76 | 15 |
| Kaifeng | 6 *li* | 2.07/3.33 | 0.27? | 171/69 | 5.5 |
| *Qingzhou* | 1049 | 2.01/3.23 | 0.25 | 161/65 | — |
| Tianjin | 960 | 1.84/2.96 | 0.22 | 138/56 | n.a. |
| Taiyuan | 843.4 | 1.62/2.60 | 0.16 | 99/40 | 5 |
| Chengdu | 811.7 | 1.55/2.50 | 0.15? | 96/38 | 3 |
| *Zhuanglang* | 4.4 *li*[6] | 1.52/2.44 | 0.14 | 92/37 | — |
| *Tongguan* | 492 | 0.94/1.52 | 0.06 | 35/14 | — |
| Jingkou | n.a. | | | | |
| Zhapu | n.a. | | | | |
| Dezhou | n.a.[7] | | | | |

N.B. Unless otherwise noted, all data for this table are taken from *juan* 24 of *Baqi tongzhi chuji.* Percentage of walled city area is calculated according to the figures given in Chang, "The Morphology of Walled Capitals," 91. Italic garrison names denote an extramural Manchu city. The garrisons at Youwei and Guihua are absent from the table because no exclusive banner compound existed at these sites.

\* The equivalents used in calculating the figures for this table are 1 *li* = 555 meters and 1 *zhang* = 3.08 meters.

? No dimensions are provided for any side of the compound, preventing accurate figuring of the area. Figures represent the largest possible size, calculated for a square-shaped city.

[1] The measurements at Xi'an are given in *bu* (paces): 1028 *bu* by 1200 *bu* in the main city, plus an additional area of 460 *bu* by 513 *bu* on the southwest corner. One *bu* is equal to 1.536 meters, making the circumference of the main city 6844 meters; for ease of comparison, I have converted this into *zhang*.

[2] According to the figures in Otagi, *Chūgoku no jōkaku toshi*, 186, the walls at Xi'an measured 2.6 kilometers from north to south and 3.35 kilometers from east to west (slightly longer in the south), for an area of 8.71 square kilometers or 3.44 square miles.

[3] Calculated according to figures in Otagi, *Chūgoku no jōkaku toshi*, 191–92.

[4] Figure from Ma, "Qingdai Mancheng kao," 31.

[5] There being no wall at Canton, these measurements describe simply the size of the banner quarter. Its smaller area is accounted for by its rectangular shape, of length equal to roughly twice its width.

[6] Figure from Ma, "Qingdai Mancheng kao," 31.

[7] Bannermen at Dezhou were confined to the northeast corner of the city, but there was no wall around them. The figure cited by Ma of 10 *li* and 13 *bu* for the wall at Dezhou probably refers to the wall around the entire Chinese city ("Qingdai Mancheng kao," 30).

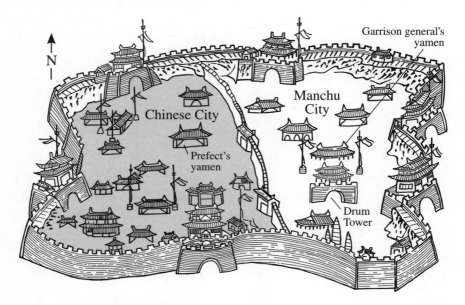

*Fig. 8.* Jingzhou garrison. The wall that created the banner garrison at Jingzhou (modern Shashi) divided the city into a Manchu half and a Chinese half. Communication between them was through the North Boundary and South Boundary gates, shown here. As at other garrisons, Chinese living in the "wrong" part of town were moved over to the western side in 1683 when thirty-six hundred bannermen from Beijing and the Xi'an and Nanjing garrisons were settled here permanently with their families, servants, and horses. Reproduced from *Jingzhoufu zhi* (1880).

scratch and located near the cities they were supposed to garrison. Two generations after the conquest, it was evidently neither practical nor politic to install thousands of Manchu and Mongol soldiers in the middle of Chinese civilian habitations. With expropriation and resettlement of urban Han populations no longer an option, the court had no choice but to construct wholly new banner enclaves. These "citadels" carried a high price tag, too: the construction of the Suiyuan garrison, for instance, cost 1.24 million taels; that at Ningxia, 1.2 million taels.[83]

The garrisons at Guangzhou and Fuzhou were exceptional in that, as mentioned, no walls separated the banner compound from the Chinese section of the city. This is perhaps explained by the early settlement of Chinese bannermen at these locations, which obviated the need for strict separation along ethnic lines.[84] Despite the absence of a wall, the Guangzhou garrison,

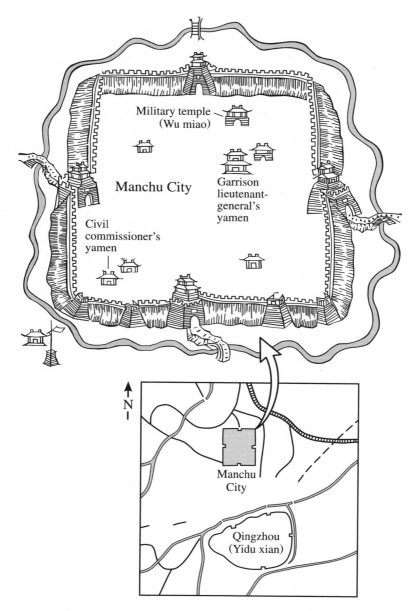

Fig. 9.   Qingzhou garrison. The separate Manchu city created at Qingzhou
in 1729–32 was typical of the extramural garrisons founded in the eighteenth
century. Like all the garrisons, Qingzhou was crowded. Though only about
one-quarter of a square mile in area, soon after its founding the population
was said to be fifteen thousand. Reproduced from *Qingzhoufu zhi* (1859).

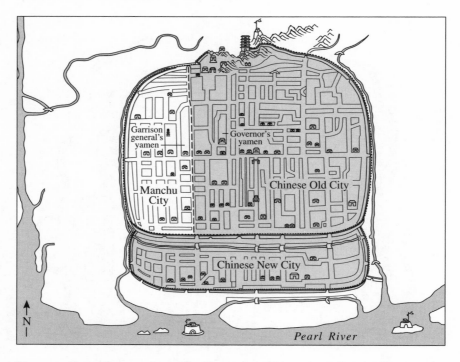

*Fig. 10.*    Guangzhou garrison. The Guangzhou (Canton) garrison, approximately one-third of a square mile in area, was one of the few not surrounded by a wall. After the mid eighteenth century, Guangzhou was the only garrison still staffed by Chinese bannermen. Reproduced from *Guangdong tongzhi* (1864).

about one-third of a square mile in size,[85] was easily distinguishable from the rest of the city. The French Jesuit Gaubil left this description of the city in 1722:

> On the north, the Tartar city has grand prospects and is sparsely inhabited; from its center as far as the Chinese city, the city is beautiful and well-constructed, with attractive, well-paved streets, and filled with handsome triumphal arches. As they are dispersed along a straight line so that the archways correspond, the effect is excellent. . . . There is nothing special in the Chinese city.[86]

Here, as in other Manchu cities, the impression made upon the visitor was grand, and entirely distinct from that left by the nondescript Chinese town. A century or more later, nineteenth-century descriptions by Westerners of

Guangzhou's "Tartar Quarter" (as they called it) also mention that the streets were wider there and that the buildings looked very different, all of them whitewashed and decorated with black designs, an effect caused by a building technique different from local norms: the bricks were sun-dried instead of kiln-dried.[87] The same was true of the buildings at Hangzhou, and at the Zhapu garrison, of which a nineteenth-century British visitor left this detailed description:

> The houses are generally of a very humble character, being small and low. If it may be said the abodes of the Tartar soldiers agree in being strait and confined, they differ widely in point of accommodation; some, though unpromising in outward show, are well stored with the necessaries, the comforts, and the elegancies of life. Each house is seated in a small enclosure, surrounded by a wall six or eight feet high. The courtyard is paved with stones, and earthen jars are placed here and there for holding fresh water. The walls of the house are constructed of brick plastered over and whitewashed. The doors consist of two folding leaves secured by a cross bar, and the windows are wrought in a kind of trellis work in Chinese fashion.

The mention here of whitewashed exteriors accords with the description above of the Guangzhou garrison, while the interior offered evidence of a lifestyle that, despite its characterization as being "altogether Chinese," in fact differed from the Chinese:

> The decoration of the rooms, so far as pictures are concerned, is altogether Chinese; scenes of courtship, of the pomp and pageantry of court levies, and of displays of military prowess figure in alternate succession upon the walls. As their business is fighting, bows and arrows, matchlocks and gingalls [a kind of heavy musket], powder and other warlike materials are blended with the furniture of the dwellings and meet the visitor at every turn.[88]

Streets in the garrisons were sometimes curbed, with wooden railings running along the sides at larger intersections.[89]

The basic physical requirements for Manchu cities would seem to be simple enough: houses (which for officers doubled as bureaux), storefronts, and training grounds. The latter, along with cemeteries (after the 1740s) and pastures for horses, were also found outside the city walls. It is striking, then, that of the four characteristics typifying Chinese administrative cities —city walls, city-god temple, school temple, and an open altar outside the walls[90]—all but the last were incorporated into Manchu cities, even the extramural foundations constructed *ab novo*. Indeed, an active temple life was one urban activity—along with buying provisions and eating out—that Qing bannermen shared with their Han neighbors. Temples located within the garrison precincts were taken over and shared in many cases (especially in Beijing), while in newly built Manchu cities such as Qingzhou, apart from official buildings, imperial authorization was issued for the construction of two brand-new temples for the exclusive use of banner people.[91] Within Suiyuan's walls were fifteen temples, eleven receiving annual subventions from the garrison general for incense and candles.

The large number of temples in Manchu cities points to an active and catholic religious life in the banners.[92] For the most part temples were part of Chinese popular or official cults, such as the "Long-Life Palace" (*Wan-shou gong*), where the emperors were sacrificed to, the city-god temple, and those dedicated to the god of wealth, the god of fire, Wen-chang, and Guan Di. The latter's military heroics made him far and away the most popular deity in the banners, and his temple was present in almost every garrison—he was even incorporated into some shamanic rituals.[93] Other religious foundations, such as the banner temple (*Qi miao*) and the horse-god temple (*Mashen miao*), show traces of native Manchu beliefs. The same is true of the temples found around the city gates, including a *Nai-nai miao* at the west gate and a *Niang-niang miao* at the east gate where Manchu women went to pray for sons. In addition, in some cities there was a "traveling-palace temple" (*Xing gong miao*) near the north gate where a paper image of the city god would be borne on the second day of the second lunar month, one of the major holidays in the garrison.[94]

CLOSE QUARTERS

The apartheid policy in China's Manchu cities seems to have been fairly effective for at least a century in Beijing, and longer in the provinces. As noted, by the middle 1700s some Manchus were moving into the Outer City, and by the early 1800s many Chinese had taken up residence in Beijing's Inner City. Though the physical separation of the banners from the civilian population thus deteriorated over time, it is striking that even in the late Qing, Han Chinese still did not feel free to roam the banner quarter of provincial garrisons. Reminiscences of former residents of garrison cities commonly remark on the fact of residential separation.[95] If the two communities mixed, it was more often the result of bannermen having left the garrison enclaves.

One reason that people may have left the Manchu cities is that they were overcrowded. The approximate number of adult males (excluding bondservants) in the Eight Banners at the time of the conquest was not much less than three hundred thousand, and perhaps as great as five hundred thousand (of whom roughly 43 percent were Manchu, 22 percent Mongol, and 35 percent Chinese) (see Appendix A). By the early eighteenth century, this figure had risen to somewhere between 850,000 and 1.6 million, indicating a total banner population (including bondservants and females) of anywhere from 2.6 to 4.9 million. Moreover, fairly reliable figures of soldiers serving in the garrison cities and Beijing show that roughly 50 percent of active bannermen were employed in Beijing, 20 percent in Manchuria, and 30 percent spread around the rest of the garrison system, including those in China proper and, later, in the northern and western frontiers. In the middle of the Qianlong reign, this translated to one hundred thousand banner soldiers and officers in Beijing, forty-two thousand in Manchuria, and about sixty thousand in provincial and other garrisons.[96] But these figures don't tell the whole story, since they do not indicate the populations or population densities of individual Manchu cities.

Until population registers surface for the capital and the garrisons, it will be impossible to determine the population of any Manchu city with precision. In Beijing, one of the two or three most peopled cities in the world at this time, if not indeed the most populous,[97] Dray-Novey estimates that between 1650 and 1850 there was a population of "certainly one million or more." This is probably a conservative estimate, given the various figures proposed by Western observers during this time, which range from 1.5 to as much as 3 million, the latter figure coming at the end of the eighteenth century, when the city was at its most populous (population apparently declined in the nineteenth century). One (admittedly imperfect) way to check this figure is to estimate total numbers by fixing as best we can a ratio of dependents per employed bannerman.[98] We know that about one hundred thousand bannermen were posted to the capital in the eighteenth century.[99] The ratio of dependents per salaried bannerman at some locations was 10:1 (see below), but this is almost certainly too high for Beijing, where employment opportunities for bannermen were about twice as great as in the provinces.[100]

Halving the estimate of dependents (including bondservants) per salaried bannerman to 5:1, I propose a figure for the middle eighteenth century of a total banner population in Beijing of five hundred thousand. Accepting a low-end estimate of one million for the population of Beijing at this time, this would mean that "people under the banners" constituted about one-half of the city's total population.

This very rough estimate fits reasonably well with other estimates of 567,000 (for 1711) and 541,000 (for 1781) in Beijing's Inner City.[101] It is also supported by extrapolations from archival figures. In 1723, 26,300 males in the Plain Yellow Banner lived in Beijing.[102] This represented 24 percent of all healthy adult males registered in the banner.[103] It is unlikely that this proportion was the same for all banners at all times, but it is reasonably certain that no other banner would have had a significantly *higher* proportion of people living in Beijing. (Members of the Plain Yellow Banner, one of the Upper Three Banners, would have had a better-than-average chance of winning and retaining assignments in the capital.) For lack of any better estimate, therefore, we shall assume that at any given time the same proportion—that is, approximately one-quarter—of banner males lived in Beijing.[104] Likewise, we shall also assume that the same percentage of bondservants as in the Plain Yellow Banner (35 percent of the total population) were attached to all Beijing banner households. Using archival figures for banner males ("Total *ding*") and calculating conservatively an average of three dependents per *ding* (able-bodied male), we find that the regular Eight Banner population in Beijing (excluding *booi*) rose from roughly 148,000 in 1657 to about 386,500 at the end of the Kangxi reign. If the total population of Beijing at this time was in the vicinity of one million (certainly possible), this means that members of regular banner households (Manchu, Mongol, Chinese banner) made up about 30 percent of the city's people. Adding to this the 230,000 bondservants attached to imperial, noble, and ordinary banner households, yields an approximate population of 616,500, showing again that more than one-half of the city's residents were either bannermen or people associated with banner households (Table 2.2).

The implications of population size and growth for living conditions are startling. Combining the conservative figure of five hundred thousand with the city's total area of a little over eleven square miles (excluding the relatively sparsely populated imperial city), we arrive at a population density of about forty-five thousand people per square mile. Since population in-

TABLE 2.2

Estimated Eight Banner Population in Beijing, 1657 and 1720

| Banner division | Total ding | Eight Banner males in Beijing (TOTAL DING X 24%) = M | Eight Banner population in Beijing M + (3M) |
|---|---|---|---|
| | | 1657 | |
| Manchu | 49,695 | 11,927 | 47,708 |
| Mongol | 26,053 | 6,253 | 25,012 |
| Chinese | 78,782 | 18,908 | 75,632 |
| Subtotal | 154,530 | 37,088 | 148,352 |
| Bondservants | 237,338 | 56,961 | 227,844 |
| TOTAL | 391,868 | 94,049 | 376,196 |
| | | 1720 | |
| Manchu | 154,117 | 36,988 | 147,952 |
| Mongol | 43,636 | 10,473 | 41,892 |
| Chinese | 204,870 | 49,169 | 196,676 |
| Sub-total | 402,623 | 96,630 | 386,520 |
| Bondservants | 239,494 | 57,479 | 229,916 |
| TOTAL | 642,117 | 154,109 | 616,436 |

SOURCES: 1657: An Shuangcheng, "Shunzhichao baqi nanding Manwen dang'an xuanyi," *Manxue yanjiu* 1 (1992), 415, citing memorial of Ceke (SZ14.10.8); 1720: An, "Shun-Kang-Yong sanchao baqi ding'e qianxi," 101, citing memorial of Yūnsiyang (YZ2.11.7).

creased rapidly throughout the eighteenth century, we can only imagine that population pressure mounted apace, too.[105] In fact, by the late nineteenth century, population density in parts of Beijing was reported to be about eighty thousand per square mile.[106]

Some of the provincial garrisons were even more crowded. Reports from late 1730s Xi'an regularly refer to between nine and ten thousand soldiers at the garrison, at the same time noting the total number of "banner-related mouths" at roughly one hundred thousand.[107] A contemporary estimate for Hangzhou was that "a soldier's household . . . was made up of one soldier [Ma *uksin*], a servant [Ma *baitangga*], and anywhere from five or six up to fifteen or more people to be supported."[108] This suggests an approximate average dependent-to-bannerman ratio of 10:1 in the provinces, that is, ten people relying on one actively employed soldier to provide them with food, shelter, and clothing. This ratio appears to have been lower in Beijing (where there were many postings available) and at newly established garrisons. When construction of the Qingzhou garrison was finished in 1732, two thousand Manchu bannermen were relocated from Beijing,[109] while the total population was reported to hover at around fifteen thousand people,[110] yielding a ratio of just 6.5:1.[111] Using these different proportions, I have estimated populations of the provincial garrisons and then calculated population densities using the figures of Manchu city size in Table 2.1 (see Table 2.3).

The picture is one of almost unbelievable crowding, as large populations were squeezed into relatively small areas, giving population densities that rival modern urban levels. At Qingzhou, for instance, fifteen thousand people lived in an area of one-quarter square mile, resulting in a density of sixty thousand people per square mile, roughly equal to that of present-day Manhattan. The population density of Hangzhou's Manchu city (using the 1740 figures cited above) comes out to about thirty-five thousand inhabitants per square mile, comparable to the Ningxia garrison. But residents had plenty of elbow room there compared with Xi'an and Jingzhou, where one hundred thousand people were packed at a rate of nearly seventy-five thousand per square mile, just less than the density of Beijing's Qianmen district in the early twentieth century (cited above). And the numbers for Jingzhou suggest an even higher population density: ninety-six thousand people per square mile! This makes it easy to understand why garrison general Unaha was concerned when an epidemic of influenza loomed over the Manchu city in 1728—with everyone living so close, the potentially rapid spread of the illness threatened catastrophe literally overnight.[112]

Facing this kind of demographic pressure, garrison populations could not avoid spreading outside the banner enclave's formal boundaries to ease overcrowding. Population densities were almost certainly not as high as a strict application of the numbers would indicate—the description above of the Guangzhou garrison as a place "sparsely inhabited" makes this clear.[113] From the court's point of view, however, dispersion was highly undesirable, as Manchu apartheid required everyone under the banners to live within the confines of the garrison. Their scattered residence among the Han threatened central control and raised the potential for interethnic conflict, or, worse, Manchu assimilation. Steps were thus taken to limit mixed residence. When it was discovered that Manchus in Beijing were relocating, not to rural spots on the outskirts of the city, but to the Chinese city, the emperor ordered an

TABLE 2.3
## Approximate Population Densities of Eight Banner Garrisons

| Garrison | Bannermen population | Dependents: bannermen | Total population | Area (PER MI²) | Density (MI²) |
|---|---|---|---|---|---|
| Jiangning | 5,100 | 9:1 | 51,000 | 2.67 | 21,000 |
| Xi'an* | 10,000 | 9:1 | 100,000 | 1.34 | 75,000 |
| Jingzhou | 4,700 | 9:1 | 47,000 | 0.79 | 60,000 |
| Hangzhou | 4,400 | 9:1 | 44,000 | 0.65 | 68,000 |
| *Suiyuan* | 3,900 | 5:1 | 23,400 | 0.61 | 38,000 |
| *Ningxia* | 2,800 | 5:1 | 16,800 | 0.57 | 29,000 |
| *Liangzhou** | 2,000 | 5:1 | 12,000 | 0.39 | 31,000 |
| Canton | 3,000 | 9:1 | 30,000 | 0.33 | 91,000 |
| Fuzhou | 2,100 | 9:1 | 21,000 | 0.29 | 72,000 |
| Kaifeng | 800 | 9:1 | 8,000 | 0.27 | 30,000 |
| *Qingzhou** | 2,000 | 6.5:1 | 15,000 | 0.25 | 60,000 |
| Tianjin | 2,000 | 5:1 | 12,000 | 0.22 | 55,000 |
| Taiyuan | 500 | 9:1 | 5,000 | 0.16 | 31,000 |
| Chengdu | 2,000 | 5:1 | 12,000 | 0.15 | 80,000 |
| *Zhuanglang** | 1,000 | 5:1 | 6,000 | 0.14 | 43,000 |

N O T E : An asterisk * signifies data on number of bannermen and/or total population from archives (consult text for specific references). Otherwise, data on number of bannermen from *juan* 28 of *Baqi tongzhi chuji*. Figures of garrison area from Table 2.1, above. Garrison names in italics denote an extramural Manchu city. All figures are rounded off to the nearest one hundred. Population density per square mile is rounded off to the nearest one thousand.

immediate stop to this "highly inappropriate" situation.[114] At Hangzhou, the situation was such that from the outset bannermen there were forced to seek residence outside the garrison. When in 1763 Chinese banner soldiers were removed from Hangzhou's banner rolls it became possible to resettle all of the 2,050 Manchu and Mongol soldiers who remained within the garrison walls.[115] Yet in many places, as garrison populations continued to grow through the eighteenth and nineteenth centuries, more and more people inevitably made their abode outside the garrison walls—though it is important to note that this did not necessarily mean that they ceased to identify themselves with the garrison.[116] In fact, it would seem that bannermen who lived outside the confines of the garrison still kept mostly to themselves, and did not necessarily assume a closer attachment to surrounding Chinese communities.[117]

## THE IDEA OF OCCUPATION

The preceding sections have outlined the general framework of Manchu residence in China. The following two sections attempt to put the matter of residence into a larger perspective, first by asking whether from the outset the Qing plan for the occupation of China included the establishment of the Manchu cities, and if so, then to ask why the court decided to put bannermen there when it had a much larger army of Chinese soldiers, the Green Standard, able to serve in this capacity.

By the early Qianlong reign, Manchu, Mongol, Chinese bannermen, and "New Manchu" bannermen had been settled at nearly one hundred different garrison locations outside Beijing: fifty-two in the Northeast, twenty-five in the metropolitan area, and eighteen in the Chinese provinces. Further expansion continued until the 1770s, when the addition of further outposts in Xinjiang raised the number of garrisons eventually to a peak of one hundred-eight. After this time, the system contracted slightly, but it remained in place until the last days of the dynasty. The vast extent of the system prompts the question, Did the Manchus mean to occupy China, or did it just end up that way?

Exigency arising from the military takeover of China is usually thought to be the predominant factor determining the establishment of banner garrisons in the provinces. This assumption, in turn, has led to the belief that the garrison system as it finally emerged was the more or less accidental product of the conquest years, and that until the 1680s all garrisons were maintained on an ad hoc basis. An oft-quoted statement from one of the few English-language studies of the Eight Banners puts this quite clearly: "There was no systematic and permanent Banner garrison [*sic*] aiming at repressing possible domestic insurrection before the Revolt of the Three Feudatories."[118] Following this, other scholars have also recently affirmed that "the establishment of Manchu garrison communities in China was in fact a tentative, gradual, regionally unsynchronized process that did not reach full development until the Qianlong period."[119]

This question is important. If we are curious about the terms of Manchu residence in China, especially in the provinces, in addition to establishing what those terms were and how they changed, we must also establish how the court viewed the terms it set. If walled garrisons were an accidental by-product of the conquest of China, an unintended consequence of Qing expansion, so to speak, then one can understand disarray and inconsistency in court policy toward people in the banners who lived outside Manchuria— the one place where there were no "Manchu cities." However, if they were the result of planned measures consciously adopted in order to consolidate and hold the gains made after 1644, then one might anticipate a different set of court policies and expectations. The interpretation one adopts directly affects one's understanding of the garrison system and of Manchu residence in China generally.

There is much to suggest that the banner garrison system indeed initially evolved as a temporary measure and then developed in response to changes in the military situation and the need for prolonged Qing military presence in areas brought under central control. For one thing, there is no direct evidence that before 1644 it was anticipated that Eight Banner forces would end up being permanently dispersed as garrison forces in China proper, no documentary proof of a systematic plan for an empire-wide garrison network. Many early garrisons—fourteen out of twenty-two founded during the Shunzhi reign—were in fact transitory, relocated or removed in response to shifting strategic priorities. Those that remained experienced frequent changes and fine-tunings. Furthermore, there are significant lags in the dates of garrison foundations, with new provincial garrisons created as late as the 1730s. Garrison histories written in the later Qing support this "evolutionist" view; Jingzhou's, for example, states that "although during the Shunzhi reign garrisons were sent, it was not an established system."[120] We also have court affirmations that duty at the garrisons was merely a "temporary assignment" and that everyone's real home was Beijing, suggesting that the whole arrangement was provisional.[121]

A second look turns up some dissonant signs, however. For instance, there is no evidence that the court ever considered withdrawing bannermen from the provinces and bringing everyone to live permanently in the capital. There are also signs that the *banners*, and not Beijing, were seen as the actual home for Manchus, a question I shall explore later.[122] This divergence between rhetoric and reality reveals a tension between the wish of the Manchu elite to avoid exposing bannermen to acculturating influences, and its recognition that, for both practical and political reasons, the banner population absolutely had to be dispersed around the country. The simple reality of minority rule meant that the Qing had to maintain as strong a presence as possible outside the capital; and logistically it was plain that the entire mass of banner households could not easily be supported if everyone were concentrated in and around Beijing. Under the circumstances, and recalling once again the precedents established by the Jin and Yuan dynasties, a policy of isolating Manchus and others in the banners from the Han population in the garrison cities was a reasonable compromise. I think it is unlikely that the Qing elite accidentally stumbled upon this solution.

Hence, in spite of some evidence to the contrary, the contention here is that the deployment of Eight Banner soldiers at provincial garrisons in China was not the unforeseen by-product of military contingency upon which later generations simply set their seal, but the result of a concerted strategy effected very early in the dynasty for the de facto occupation of China by the Eight Banners. Heeding the dictates of necessity, yet mindful of the risks of diaspora, and bearing in mind their own historical experience and that of other non-Han rulers before them, the Qing court quite sensibly concluded that a closed garrison system would serve the needs of the new state best. One must acknowledge that the number of garrisons gradually increased over time, and that true uniformity and stability in the garrisons (as in many other areas of Qing policy) became a conscious goal only in the Yongzheng reign. Yet the *idea* of occupation was there from the very start. The evidence for this argument comes from a close examination of the foundation dates and locations of the provincial Eight Banner garrisons and of policies regarding nomenclature and command structure, population transfer, and the disposition of land. All of these point to the conclusion that, from their inception in 1645, the provincial banner garrisons formed a coherent system of Manchu residence in China. This system enabled Qing rulers to dominate and intimidate the majority Han population while in theory insulating their own people from the ill effects of extended habitation among the Chinese. Let us look at these different factors one by one.

### Geographic Placement

The strategic placement of garrisons in the provinces along five "chains," already described above, is one of the strongest indications that the court consciously guided the evolution of the system to establish permanent lines of defense following different natural boundaries. The absence of banner garrisons in the southwest reminds us that even after the 1680s the provincial garrisons never formed a truly national network. If the Yongzheng emperor's plans to expand the garrison system had been fully realized, it is possible that provincial representation would have been more complete, but it does not seem that the system ever aimed for universal province-by-province coverage. Instead, as noted earlier, garrisons were placed at a number of key points within an overall scheme. The separate networks dedicated to the defense of the Northeast, Mongolia, and the far west show that while the Manchus were accustomed to thinking strategically in terms of the steppes and deserts of Inner Asia, they also had a clear awareness of the strategic importance of waterways in ruling China itself. Four out of the five provincial garrison chains were established along marine and riverine boundaries.

### Dates of Foundation

Analysis of the dates of garrison foundation shows that the system was essentially built during two twenty-year periods, 1645–65 and 1718–38, and that the basic structure of the garrison system was already in place before 1670. During the first twenty years of Qing rule, eight of the eighteen permanent provincial garrisons, the backbone of the system and home to the majority of garrison bannermen in China proper, were established.[123] From this it is evident that all but one of the five garrison networks existed in embryonic form by the beginning of the Kangxi reign. The exception was the Great Wall chain, which was largely the creation of the middle and later years of the Kangxi reign, in direct response to the threat posed to the Qing by the Dzungars.[124] If we exclude the garrisons along the frontier with Mongolia, then with the sole exception of the Jingzhou garrison (founded in 1683), there were no further foundations for over fifty years, when a second burst of institutional activity between 1718 and 1737 saw the addition of eight more garrisons.[125] This bunched pattern suggests that the growth of provincial garrisons was not so tentative, gradual, or unsynchronized as it might at first seem.

### Nomenclature and Command Structure

When we compare the title given to the commanding officers of garrisons that became permanent, we see that this differed from the title given to commanders of expeditionary garrisons, which were disbanded or relocated according to military needs, suggesting that when garrisons were established it was already known whether they would be permanent fixtures. Permanent provincial garrisons were all headed by an officer called, in Manchu, *amba janggin* (lit. "great general"), together with one or more officers titled *meiren-i janggin* (lieutenant generals).[126] Expeditionary garrisons, on the other hand, were headed by a *gūsai ejen*.[127] Thus, whereas at the Xi'an and Nanjing garrisons the title *amba janggin* appeared in 1646,[128] the commanders at Baoqing and Hanzhong in 1648 were all titled *gūsai ejen*.[129] Another case in point is the garrison established at Guizhou in 1658, also led by three officers with the title *gūsai ejen*, also temporary.[130] Especially revealing is a change the same year at the Hangzhou garrison, when the position of *gūsai ejen* was eliminated and the commander of the Hangzhou garrison was given the title *amba janggin*. This signified the final stage of the permanent occupation of Hangzhou, explaining why this year has frequently been taken as the garrison's founding date, even though garrison troops arrived here in 1645.[131] When Fuzhou and Guangzhou were refounded in 1680 the same pattern was repeated, with the appointment of an *amba janggin* at each place.

### Population Transfer

Family relocation was another factor affecting a garrison's permanence. Though never an explicitly stated policy, the practice of assigning families together with male heads of household appeared at some of the preconquest garrisons in the Northeast that became permanent.[132] After the conquest, evidence that families were to accompany soldiers to live permanently in the garrisons is largely indirect. The requirement was laid down in 1648, for example, that soldiers whose families had joined them were to formally return land they held in the Beijing area; if only half of the family had come, then only half the property needed to be returned. A related regulation from the same year stated that family members left behind in the capital were to receive grain rations from the capital, while those who had already moved to the garrison were to receive rations there.[133] While it is not clear from these rules whether relocating one's family at the garrison was voluntary or under what conditions family members could remain in Beijing, the stipulation that land be returned makes it amply clear that when a family moved, it moved for good.[134]

### Disposition of Land

The disposition of land really amounts to two separate issues, that of land grants and that of residential segregation. At garrisons destined to become permanent features of the Qing urban landscape, the principle was to grant land to banner soldiers at the garrison to provide a stable and lasting source of income that would support them and their households (land for pasture was also requisitioned).[135] In 1647, garrison bannermen at Xi'an and Nanjing were awarded tracts of land varying in size from ten to forty *xiang*. Where there was not enough land to spare, as at Hangzhou, direct salaries of money and rice were paid instead. Whether they received new grants of land or a supplemental stipend instead, new arrivals at garrison locations were required to forfeit any land they held in the capital area. In so doing, garrison bannermen cut probably the most important material tie binding them to Beijing, replacing it with a property tie to the garrison locality, a step that emphasized the permanence of their move to the provinces.[136]

The other aspect of the disposition of land involved the situation of the banner population in garrison cities. From the dates of initial building activity of the walls surrounding banner compounds in different Manchu cities— 1645 at Xi'an, 1648 at Hangzhou, 1649 at Nanjing, 1654 at Dezhou, and 1659 at Jingkou—it is apparent that at most garrisons, construction of the banner compound commenced very early and that in every instance when such building activity is observed, the garrison was a permanent foundation.[137] This was a costly operation for the court materially, in terms of expense (walls and buildings required frequent extension and repair[138]), as well as politically, in terms of the animosity it aroused among the Han populace. As Wakeman notes, the establishment of the garrisons frequently "incite[d] the very kinds of disturbances they were intended to dispel."[139]

The conclusion here is that the foundation of Eight Banner garrisons in the provinces was a conscious process as early as 1645, when the first Manchu city was built at Xi'an. The appointment of certain ranks of officers, the dispatching of family members, the bestowal of property, and the construction of walled banner compounds in garrison cities all indicate that, very early in the conquest, the court had already made up its mind to settle bannermen permanently in China. Even if it is true that "at the time of the conquest, Manchu rulers by no means clearly wanted to establish a garrison system, and had no unified plan to put into place a system of Eight Banner garrisons at key locations across the country,"[140] this does not seem to have stopped the court from doing just that. Individual banner garrisons generally did not grow to become more important, though in the Qianlong reign many became *less* important and suffered reductions in size. Rather, it was clear beforehand which were more and which less vital to dynastic security, and therefore which should have larger forces and which smaller. By this same logic, it does not make sense to say that the garrison system as a whole evolved from a temporary to a permanent system: the permanency of the occupation was obvious to everyone as soon as the walls enclosing the garrisons went up.

### GARRISON DYARCHY

So far, the Qing plan for the permanent occupation of China has been discussed solely in terms of the Eight Banner garrisons. But apart from the Eight Banners, the Qing state also maintained a second armed force, the Green Standard Army (*lüying bing/niowanggiyan turun-i cooha*). This army, made up of Han Chinese soldiers, was about three times larger than the banners and was commanded by a mixed staff of Eight Banner and Green Standard officers.[141] Green Standard soldiers were scattered in their own garrisons throughout the provinces, as well as in the frontier regions. At first glance, the placing of bannermen in garrisons around China seems redundant. One would think that, in their pursuit of Li Zicheng in the west, bandits in the east, various pretenders to the Ming throne in the south, and Mongol rebels in the north, Qing policy makers would have been loath to assign even one Manchu cavalryman to garrison duty when his skills were needed to bring the empire to heel. Surely Han Chinese soldiers were more suited to service in garrison posts than bannermen? So why, given that Green Standard soldiers were garrisoning the provinces, was it deemed necessary to station Eight Banner troops there, too?[142]

This question was debated even at the time. In 1657, a Censorate official suggested decreasing the number of bannermen in the provinces on general principles.[143] Two years later, another Han Chinese official advised against sending any more bannermen to garrison the provinces, complaining, among other things, that Manchu soldiers disrupted the lives of the people, "filling everyone with dread," and that, besides, the presence of Green Standard soldiers made the placement of bannermen in the same location superfluous.[144] But the court's insistence on a dual system of garrisons in spite of such arguments hints that, though there was some overlap in their duties (both suppressed domestic rebellion, performed naval duties, fought in frontier campaigns, and manned frontier garrisons), the two armies served different needs. As a supplemental force to the Eight Banners, the Green Standard fulfilled a

Qing wish to "use Han to rule Han" (Ch *yi Han zhi Han*) when possible—a neat turn on the Chinese strategy of "using barbarians to govern barbarians" (Ch *yi yi zhi yi*). "Since ancient times, when Chinese [Ch *Hanren*] have rebelled," the Kangxi emperor once said, "only Han troops have been used to suppress them. Why now should Manchu troops aid them?"[145] That the Green Standard Army provided the bulk of forces fielded against Wu Sangui reflected the emperor's wish to keep Manchu troops out of the fray and preserve dynastic military strength. Moreover, their greater number enabled Green Standard troops to maintain a substantial presence in rural areas, where they functioned more as a police or national guard force, quelling local unrest and supervising river conservancy and grain transport, activities in which bannermen were rarely involved.[146]

Banner troops, on the other hand, were there to provide an enduring dynastic presence, mainly in the cities.[147] "In establishing [Eight Banner] garrisons in the provinces," wrote the Yongzheng emperor, "our dynasty set for them the [role of] protection of the locale and the explicit expression of military readiness."[148] A slightly different emphasis was offered by the Qianlong emperor: "Sending Manchu soldiers to garrison provincial cities was originally intended to awe and pacify those areas."[149] In other words, unlike Green Standard Army troops, banner troops were there to inspire fear and submission in the Chinese population. In a memorable statement, the editors of the Jingzhou garrison history captured very well the role of the banner garrisons to discreetly maintain both order and fear: "When things are calm, [the garrisons are there to] provide protection and keep control, secretly, like a tiger or panther on the mountain. When things are stirred up, then they are to match the enemy's hostility and give everything in the defense of the city depending on them."[150] In marked contrast to the image they acquired later in the Qing dynasty—an almost comic image of sloth and ineptitude—bannermen in the early Qing, like their samurai contemporaries, were feared men. Swords at their sides and daggers at their belts, their mere presence impressed and intimidated local populations, as later chapters will show. The court took advantage of this resource to remind the Chinese that a watchful Manchu eye was always upon them.

In seeking to understand the distinctiveness of the banner garrison system, we find another clue in the structure of the Qing civil bureaucracy. It is generally known that in the Six Boards, the Grand Secretariat, and the Hanlin Academy, the Qing instituted a dyarchical system in which bannermen (usually Manchus) were paired with Han Chinese officials at a wide range of top official positions so as to maintain an ethnic balance in the central government and to secure the cooperation of the Han scholarly elite. As we now also know, the presence of a board "superintendent," who was always Manchu (and who outranked either president), and the creation of an imperial "privy cabinet" (later the Grand Council) that was at first a Manchus-only club, stacked the deck in the Manchus' favor, giving them an extra guarantee of security and a better purchase on decision-making power.[151] In similar fashion, concern for the preservation of ethnic sovereignty dictated the need for a separate system of garrison defense, and for this only bannermen, whose loyalty to the dynasty was unquestionable and who boasted a reputation for fearlessness and ferocity, could be trusted. That is, both Green Standard and Eight Banner troops could achieve local control, but only the latter were "awesome"—only they could fulfill the role of protecting Qing interests and projecting the proper image.[152] This point was effectively made by an official traveling through Nankou (on the way to Juyongguan, near the Great Wall), who complained that the pass—where there was no Eight Banner garrison—was manned by only a few Chinese soldiers of the Green Standard: "Nankou is close to the capital and every year Mongol embassies pass through it, making it an important pass. Stationing banner troops here would benefit the area and render it more imposing."[153]

Finally, it is useful to compare the Jin, Yuan, and Qing garrison systems to better understand the latter's distinctiveness, the most important element of which is that Qing garrison forces were physically segregated, enclosed in walled compounds. This practice was evidently unknown in the Jin or the Yuan, although it is not entirely clear what Jurchen settlements in north China were like (Jin soldiers lived in "fortresses and camps among Chinese villages" but engaged in agricultural work, a type of labor hardly encouraged among Qing bannermen). Besides, the routine control functions of the Jin garrisons made them more like the Green Standard Army.[154] Also, while both the Mongols and the Manchus used Han soldiers to maintain control in the south, the Qing reliance on Chinese auxiliary forces was not as lopsided as under the Yuan. Soldiers from the Manchu banners were extensively deployed in south China, along the Yangzi, for instance, as well as in Zhejiang and at Chengdu. Furthermore, compared to both the Jin and the Yuan, Qing garrison troops were much less dispersed. The wide dispersion of Jurchen troops, especially, was blamed for the "gradual disappearance of the Jurchen people's national characteristics."[155] As we have seen, the "keypoint" system favored by the Qing placed larger numbers of troops in a handful of carefully selected locations. Finally, while the Mongols preferred to keep the supervision of garrison affairs at the provincial level, during the Qing, garrison commanders were in effect national-level appointees. These men, whose official status equaled that of provincial governor-generals, were usually hand-picked by the emperor and in the early Qing frequently could boast of a personal relationship with him. Like other high officials, they reported directly to the throne. More on this subject is said in the next chapter.

Many of the problems afflicting the Jin and Yuan garrison arrangements, such as the impoverishment of soldiers and the flagging of martial spirit, were the same as those that later bedeviled the Qing garrison system. Nevertheless, the survival of the Qing banner garrison system to the early twentieth century despite such problems betokens not only its superior organization, but also the greater institutional support the system received from the government, which looked upon its continued existence as an essential element of dynastic rule.

Assuming control over the Chinese realm forced the Manchu elite to make difficult decisions that had direct and serious implications not just for them but for the majority of people within the Eight Banners. This chapter has tried to show what those implications were in terms of where people lived their lives. For the elite, the building of Manchu cities through the provincial banner garrison system was a solution to the problem of where to keep the dynasty's soldiers once the "dirty work" of the conquest was over and was perceived in this way as soon as the Qing took over. Sequestering banner people from the Han limited ethnic conflict and the potential for acculturation and softening of Manchu soldiers. Moreover, putting bannermen in the provinces also afforded the dynasty greater security as well as a heightened ethnic profile, filling a role that the Han soldiers of the Green Standard Army simply could not.

For ordinary banner soldiers and their households, life in China was a fundamentally different proposition from life in Manchuria. Over the course of two generations, people found themselves moved from a mainly village-based existence into a crowded and tightly controlled urban environment. To some Chinese bannermen these new surroundings might not have been so unfamiliar; yet for everyone under the banners the new life in China brought immense changes in their life choices and expectations. It is hardly surprising that this dislocation also meant major changes for the banners themselves, as their military and strategic functions were gradually, though never wholly, supplanted by their political, social, and economic roles. The Qing occupation brought changes to Chinese cities, too. In their layout and appearance, all cities in late imperial China reflected state power, but in the garrison cities this influence was more pronounced than elsewhere. Banner compounds pointedly symbolized not only the authority and wealth of the Qing state, but also the military prowess and institutional privilege of the dynasty's loyal servants. This was especially so in the far west, where the construction of separate Manchu cities was an enduring element of Qing imperialism. The dual city, bejeweled with the appropriate monumental architecture, came to be a hallmark of Qing expansion on the frontier.[156] Owen Lattimore described the Manchu "New City" at Urumchi, which he visited in 1927, as "one of the last monuments of the Manchu Imperial tradition. The clean lines of the solid walls, the wide streets, the temples built not by chance in the corners but planned with dignity in commanding sites, all show the mark that the Manchus were able to leave, here and there, in the very farthest of their dominions."[157] Clearly, the model of the segregated polyethnic city originating in the garrison cities of the seventeenth century provided the blueprint for the builders of the high Qing imperial order in the eighteenth.

# CHAPTER THREE

# The Emperor's Men

The initial evolution of the Eight Banners before the conquest, traced in the first chapter, was only the beginning of a long process of increasing formalization of Manchu political and social structures. With the settlement of the banner population in Beijing and other Manchu cities, the banner system came to be defined less by its capacity to wage war and more by its ability to administer the daily affairs of banner people, if for no other reason than that the regularization of Manchu life after 1644 required a standardized management to support it. One sign of this growing institutional identity was that, beginning in the eighteenth century, Manchus and others in the banners came to be known as "banner people" (Ch *qiren*, a translation of the Manchu expression *gūsai niyalma*), in distinction to "commoners" (*minren/irgen*) or, sometimes, "Han Chinese" (*Hanren/Nikan*).[1] This was true both in the popular mind, where the term *qiren* overlapped with the label "Manchu" ("One doesn't distinguish between 'Manchu' or 'Chinese,'" the old Beijing saying went, "but asks 'banner' or 'civilian'"), and within officialdom.[2] The description of "Eight Banner posts" in the *Comprehensive History of the Eight Banners* lists posts not only in the various Eight Banner hierarchies, but *all* posts throughout the government that were reserved for Manchus (Ch *Man-que*).[3] On the virtual equivalence of "banner" and "Manchu" in official life, one Qing memoirist commented to the effect that "it would seem that where bannermen were exclusively used the post was called a Manchu slot, but this did not mean a narrow use of Manchus only."[4] Legal statutes, too, applied mainly to "bannermen," not to "Manchus."[5] Even for the Qing ruler, "bannerman" and "Manchu" could be interchangeable: in a 1741 edict to Manchu soldiers, the Qianlong emperor referred to them as "all banner personnel youth."[6]

These various usages unmistakably show the enmeshment and mutual reinforcement of the banner system's institutional and ethnic aspects, the central issue taken up in this chapter. Focusing on the Eight Banners as an administrative structure, I examine the roles of banner officials, their mutual relations, and their relations with the civil bureaucracy and the emperor. Apart from demonstrating the ways in which banner administration (which is poorly understood in comparison with the civil administration) intertwined with Manchu ethnicity, this approach permits us to explore the hybrid nature of local control in the early and mid-Qing and the special place of the Eight Banners in it, revealing new dimensions of the banners' contributions to the building of the Qing state. As illustrated below, although the portfolio of local banner officials was formally confined to garrison affairs, in practice it ranged widely across the whole sphere of provincial affairs, civil as well as military.

Indeed, it seems that Manchu officials formed a separate network upon which the emperor relied for information and to which he looked for the maintenance of the "edge" of Manchu rule in China. The shorter "administrative distance"[7] that lay between the throne and the ethnic preserve that was the Eight Banners reminds us that, as in the regular administration as well, the putatively rational lines of organization within the Qing bureaucracy were everywhere overlaid, not just with Confucian assumptions of service and loyalty,[8] but, among Manchus and other bannermen, with ethnic assumptions of the same. This point could as well be made by studying groups of Manchu officials in other parts of the larger bureaucracy, as Beatrice Bartlett has done in her study of the Grand Council. In keeping with the focus of this book, I have restricted myself here mainly to an examination of Manchus in their service as officials in the banners.[9]

THE NATURE OF THE BANNER BUREAUCRACY

Though responsible for the welfare of less than 2 percent of the population of the empire, banner officialdom was one of the biggest subsections of the Qing bureaucracy. Its exact size in the seventeenth century is hard to know, but the archives permit us to make a good guess for the eighteenth. Taking as representative a 1723 figure of fifteen hundred as the total number of salaried officials (officers) in the Plain Yellow Banner permits an estimate of about forty-five hundred banner officials for the Upper Three Banners.[10] Since there were about three hundred fewer slots each in the Lower Five

Banners, an estimate of six thousand officials here (twelve hundred per banner) is probably realistic.[11] The total number of officials in the Eight Banners
thus approached ten and a half thousand—more even than in the entire
Qing civil administration, with its eight to nine thousand officials.[12]

The remarkable size of the banner bureaucracy points to a fundamental
difference in court management of banner and Han populations. While both
were subject to central rule, the latter were governed according to traditional Chinese methods—that is, at something of a distance, with a small official establishment (at the lowest level of the state bureaucracy, the county,
there were only fifteen hundred magistrates) ruling with the assistance of a
considerable unofficial establishment and the cooperation of the local gen-
try. In contrast, those in the banners were subject to micromanagement by
the court: births, deaths, marriages, employment, retirement, and residence
were all scrupulously tracked in triennial censuses of the banner population.[13] Minding the welfare of all the emperor's subjects was important, of
course, but the proper administration of affairs in the banners, the emperor's own people, was of special concern. This may explain why, of all imperial institutions, only the Eight Banners had its own, exclusive administrative monograph, the *Comprehensive History of the Eight Banners*, first
published in 1739 and later issued in a revised version in 1795.

What did this administrative structure look like? Command structure
within the Eight Banners called for a banner commander at the head of each
of the twenty-four ethnic banners, followed by two vice-commanders each,
five lieutenant colonels, and any number of captains and lieutenants (usually
between ten and twenty, according to the number of companies). Banner
commanders were the most senior officials in the banners, and reported directly to the emperor (later also the Grand Council). They were frequently
called on for opinions on banner-related (though not general military) matters, but their authority lessened as time wore on and was gradually limited
to supervising the correct registration and management of people and positions in the capital Eight Banners. Officers of the guard and vanguard units
within the Manchu and Mongol banners (there were no vanguard units in
the Chinese banners) were also subject to the authority of the banner commander. However, command of the Imperial Bodyguard, which was drawn
exclusively from the Manchu and Mongol divisions of the Upper Three Banners, rested with the two chamberlains, who equaled the banner commander
in rank.[14]

Furthermore, the banner commander had little reach over the Garrison Eight Banners. This was separately structured, with its own companies, and individually managed by the garrison general or other commanding officer. From his post in the provinces, the garrison general routinely reported not to the banner commanders, but to the Board of War, though on some matters he might go straight to the emperor. Garrison commanders thus enjoyed virtual independence from the Eight Banner command in Beijing and at the larger garrisons rivaled them in power and prestige (both ranked as military officials of grade 1a, later 1b). Indeed, as later sections show, the portfolio of the garrison general frequently exceeded the narrow bailiwick of banner affairs, making him not only a senior military figure but also a high-ranking provincial official.

Eight Banner commanders, garrison generals, and other banner officials were graded like civil officials according to the same system of ranks and steps, each distinguished by the badge and regalia proper to his rank.[15] Unlike civil officials, though, almost all banner officials obtained their posts without any sort of degree, as the military examination system was not an important mechanism for their selection—the exams are not even mentioned in the chapter on appointment of officials in the *Comprehensive History of the Eight Banners*. Selection of officials and officers was a prerogative of the emperor, who relied, as in the civil service, on officials' recommendations. Actual selection varied by position, but in general vacancies were filled either by transferring personnel of the same rank or by promoting personnel from the next lowest rank or ranks. For instance, commanders of Mongol banners were selected from among vanguard commandants, captains-general of the guard, and vice-commanders of Manchu and Mongol banners. The search could be further expanded to include garrison generals and lieutenant generals and hereditary nobles of the four highest ranks. Records of promotions of garrison lieutenant generals show that appointees there came from a wide range of backgrounds, including imperial bodyguards of the first rank, imperial manufactory superintendents, and Manchus assigned as regiment colonels in the Green Standard Army.[16]

Manchus were free to assume positions in any ethnic division of any banner hierarchy, as were Mongols; opportunities for talented Chinese bannermen were fewer, since they were by and large restricted to appointment within the Chinese banners. First eligibility for the post of vice-commander of a Manchu banner fell to vice-commanders of Mongol banners, suggesting that experience in both banners was deemed desirable for officers of each.[17] A significant difference between banner appointments and Chinese civil and military appointments is that there was no "law of avoidance" in the banners preventing people from taking posts in their own banners.

Until late in the Yongzheng reign, the selection process for banner positions remained surprisingly informal. When a vacancy opened, candidates' names and curricula vitae were written on wooden laths (probably similar to the green-tipped wooden *lütoupai* used in imperial audiences) and reviewed by officials making recommendations; after being used for this temporary purpose, the laths were destroyed. Nominations frequently depended on happenstance and suitable candidates were sometimes overlooked. In 1734 the selection process was made more formal; vacancies were to be announced to all relevant offices, which submitted the names of eligible candidates to the "left wing" office of the banner (which discharged the duties of the Board of Civil Appointments).[18] There, all names were compiled into a "names list" (*tang dan/gebu-i jedz*); officials then reviewed these lists and marked the names of those recommended for appointment, which the emperor could then approve.[19]

Like the selection process, the transaction of banner business in the pre-Yongzheng period was also done in a more or less haphazard fashion. The personal residences of banner officials in Beijing usually doubled as their offices, but in contrast to the garrisons, these residences were not yamens in the usual sense. A high official who lived in a large mansion might not have noticed the difference, but an official who happened to live in a smaller house would soon find the papers piling up in the corners. As bureaucratic demands increased, the maintenance and preservation of systematic records for the Eight Banners became a court concern. In response to fears that banner commanders were not addressing this problem (many were barely literate), in 1723 the emperor established the "Offices of the Eight Banner Commanders" (*baqi dutong yamen/jakūn gūsai kadalara ambasai yamun*) in Beijing.[20] There were eight such offices, each located in the part of the city assigned to that particular banner.

The bureaucratization of the banner system is one of the better-known aspects of its history. Some have identified this as the culmination of a larger process of centralized state-building in the Qing empire,[21] which reached a turning point during the Yongzheng reign, when the Eight Banners were transformed from a set of quasi-independent fiefs into a unified department of "eight government yamen."[22] In his desire to keep the banners from being used as a power base by imperial nobles (as they had been up to that point), the Yongzheng emperor—whose legitimate accession to the throne was seriously questioned by some of those very nobles—replaced top personnel in seventeen of the twenty-four banners with his own trusted followers, stripped princes and other nobles of traditional privileges they had enjoyed in the banners, and decreased the number of companies under their direct command. He also turned many *niru* into companies led by appointed instead of hereditary captains, strengthening imperial powers in deciding midlevel banner leadership.[23] In addition, he issued hundreds of edicts concerning banner affairs, the publication of which set uniform precedents in matters such as rank, pay, and administration.[24]

It should be pointed out, though, that while the trend was toward greater bureaucratization, at no time in the Qing did there arise a central office for the Eight Banners as a whole, no clearinghouse for all banner-related business. Thus the Eight Banner commanders handled the affairs of regular bannermen in the capital and the wider metropolitan area, the Imperial Clan Court the affairs of imperial clansmen (who were found in the Manchu divisions of all eight banners), and the garrison bureaucracy those of garrison bannermen in China and the frontiers. In addition, the boards of revenue and war were heavily involved in the financial and military aspects of banner affairs. The diffusion of responsibility among so many different institutions indicates the limits to the centralization process in the banners. If the court had pursued the rationalization of the banner system to its logical conclusion, one might have seen the creation of a single banner "board," or the formal dissolution of the ethnic or color divisions within the banners. This did not happen, although a Banner Inspectorate (*zhinian qilaniya aliha gūsa*), with oversight functions rotated annually between banners, was formed in 1752.[25] In this sense, the Eight Banners never entirely escaped its fragmented origins as a tribal organization, retaining a considerable diversity that belies its frequent description as a "system."

## THE GARRISON GENERAL

Lack of sources limits for now a more detailed investigation of the banner commanders or the Banner Inspectorate in Beijing, so a closer examination of banner administration must begin in the provinces, with the garrison general.[26] Sitting at the center of the garrison compound, with thousands of banner soldiers under his command, the garrison general was a powerful man, and not just within the Eight Banners. In terms of the provincial balance of power, the garrison general—there were between nine and eleven of them for most of the Qing—was in effect the military counterpart of the governor-general (or "viceroy," Ch *zongdu*), the highest civil official in the provinces (grade 1b, later 2a), whom he technically outranked.[27] The importance of the office was reflected in the architecture of the garrison general's compound, as seen in this description of the Guangzhou "Tartar General's yamun":

> The entrance to this building is rendered imposing by the large quadrangle kept clear of buildings and of traffic in front of it, occupied only by two lofty flag staffs and two small pavilions whence the official band discourses sweet (Chinese) music on occasion. The gateway is approached by a fine flight of granite steps, and consists of the usual three enormous double gates which indicate rank and importance. . . . These lead to a raised platform surrounded with a balustrade of time-worn marble, upon which is placed the range of buildings, the high-pitched roof of which rests upon massive columns of black hard-wood, constituting the offices and tribunal of the Tartar commander. . . . From the outer gateway to the end of the tribunal is a distance of one hundred yards, and the entire depth of the yamun is 300 yards by a breadth of one hundred.[28]

This description proves, of course, only that the British found the general's offices and quarters imposing—and helps explain why they walled off the rear portion after 1861 to form a residence for the British consul. But from other evidence we know at the very least that the two large stone lions that graced the front entrance to the yamen were considered by the Chinese, too, to have been particularly remarkable.[29]

In the later Qing, the post of garrison general became something of a sinecure, reserved for the aged and feeble. One nineteenth-century Western observer who had official dealings with them noted that, while some "excellent Tartar generals" could be found in some locales, the garrison general "is really often sneeringly regarded as an 'old frump,' or a 'drunken swab.'" He went on to reminisce, "When I was second at Canton, my consul used to say: 'Let's go and see the *maiden aunt* on the way to the Viceroy's,'"[30] a clear indication that in the later Qing real power lay with the governor-general, not the garrison general. Such anecdotal evidence is backed by Pamela Crossley's finding that nearly two-thirds of garrison generals at Hangzhou in the

1800s either died in office or very shortly after retiring.[31] But it is uncertain when this decline began. Comparing gross morbidity of garrison generals and other senior officials in the 1600s and 1700s, we find only minimal discrepancies: In cases where reasons are given for vacating a post, 23.4 percent of garrison generals, 22.1 percent of governors-general, and 21.4 percent of board presidents left because of retirement, illness, or death (Table 3.1). It would not seem fair to assume on this basis that, at least up to the end of the eighteenth century, the post of garrison general differed in this respect from other high administrative positions in the empire, or that appointees were being farmed out to the provinces in order to end their careers in tranquillity. Nor is there convincing evidence pointing to the post of garrison general as a reward for service; the dynasty had more impressive means for this, and few names of eighteenth-century garrison generals are those of returning war heroes.[32] Moreover, throughout the 1700s many governors-general had prior experience as garrison generals.[33]

For the first century and a half of Qing rule, then, we can say with some confidence that the garrison general was a personage to be reckoned with in the provinces and performed duties vital to national security. The importance of his position was made plain in an edict of June 1645 to the Xi'an and Nanjing generals, the earliest description of the garrison general's duties:

> You are specially commissioned to defend the land and calm the people. You are to promote wise and capable officials and drill the soldiers, making sure that weapons are kept in good condition. [Also], proclaim the rule of law, maintain ships and train [the men] in naval warfare. The disposition of all feed, grain, and funds in silver and copper [for the garrison] is to be decided in tandem with the governor and circuit officials. Military discipline is to be strictly observed, and no unauthorized aggression or wayward behavior should be tolerated. Practices that ruin civilian property, such as cutting down fields in order to pasture horses, shall not be permitted. You must soothe both the soldiers and the civilian population.

The emperor also warned his men about exceeding their authority:

> One more thing: civilian affairs are all under the jurisdiction of the local officials and you are not to concern yourself [with them]. By devoting all your loyalty and all your strength, proclaiming virtue and showing intimidation, you will thereby do away with villains and bring peace to the people. If you can do this, you will succeed in your duty.[34]

TABLE 3.1

## "Mortality" Among Garrison Generals, Governors-General, and Board Presidents, 1644–1795

### Garrison General

| LOCATION | NO. OF TENANTS | RETIRED/ILL/DIED IN OFFICE | PERCENT OF TOTAL |
|---|---|---|---|
| Guangzhou | 31 | 7 | 22.0% |
| Hangzhou | 36 | 13 | 36.1 |
| Jiangning | 39 | 12 | 30.8 |
| Jingzhou | 32 | 6 | 18.8 |
| Ningxia | 27 | 5 | 18.5 |
| Xi'an | 40 | 5 | 12.5 |
| Combined average | | | 23.1% |

### Governor-general

| TITLE | NO. OF TENANTS | RETIRED/ILL/DIED IN OFFICE | PERCENT OF TOTAL |
|---|---|---|---|
| Chuan-Shaan[1] | 48 | 10 | 20.8% |
| Huguang[2] | 56 | 11 | 19.6 |
| Liang-Jiang[3] | 40 | 10 | 25.0 |
| Min-Zhe[4] | 47 | 14 | 29. |
| Liang-Guang[5] | 39 | 6 | 15.4 |
| Combined average | | | 22.1% |

### Board president

| BOARD | NO. OF TENANTS | RETIRED/ILL/DIED IN OFFICE | PERCENT OF TOTAL |
|---|---|---|---|
| Civil appointments | 53 | 17 | 32.1% |
| Revenue | 45 | 10 | 22.2 |
| Rites | 55 | 21 | 38.2 |
| War | 60 | 7 | 11.7 |
| Punishments | 57 | 7 | 12.3 |
| Works | 58 | 7 | 12.1 |
| Combined average | | | 21.4% |

N.B. Officeholders appointed more than once to the same post are counted only once. Officeholders whose date of death fell less than two years after leaving office are counted as having retired; those who died by execution are excluded.

SOURCES: Qian Shifu, *Qingdai zhiguan nianbiao*, vols. 1, 2. Additional information on garrison generals is from "Huangchao wuzhi dachen nianbiao/Zhisheng zhufang jiangjun dutong dachen nianbiao," National Palace Museum Archives, Taipei. Specific breakdowns by individual tenure are found in Elliott, "Resident Aliens," tables 4.1.a–f.

[1] 1666–81 counted for Shan-Shaan; 1748–59 counted for Shaan-Gan.

[2] 1668–73 counted for Chuan-Hu.

[3] 1661–65 counted for Jiangnan.

[4] 1658–87, 1728–34, 1736–39 counted for Fujian.

[5] 1661–65 counted for Guangdong.

The charge to "defend and calm," to simultaneously intimidate and pacify, was as difficult as it was important. The garrison general needed to cooperate with civil officials on fiscal matters—and to stay out of others. It is not surprising, then, that as the section below demonstrates, relations with the civil bureaucracy long remained delicate.

Of what little has been written about the garrison general, most has been based on official prescriptions such as the above. Relying on Manchu- and Chinese-language archives, it is possible to go beyond this to reconstruct career patterns and discover more about the post and the men who held it. One initial observation that should come as no surprise is that the overwhelming majority (85 percent) of garrison generals were Manchu bannermen.[35] Only at garrisons where Chinese bannermen predominated, such as Guangzhou, did Chinese banner generals make up a significant proportion of the total.[36] Although Chinese bannermen were depended on at first in the provincial senior civil service and were often appointed commanders of provincial Green Standard forces, the provincial garrison hierarchy was unquestionably a Manchu domain.

A second observation is the wide variation in the length of time garrison generals were allowed to remain at the same post. Table 3.2 summarizes lengths of average and median tenure at six garrisons. Tenures of ten or even fifteen years were not uncommon, with the longest stays running to over twenty years (and it is significant that garrison generals who served in the same post for over ten years were nearly all members of the imperial clan, whose trustworthiness was usually above suspicion).[37] Extremely short tenures, on the other hand, were also very frequent: over one-third of all tenures were of a duration of one year or less,[38] and, as the median figure of 2.88 years shows, one-half of garrison generals were at their posts for less than three years. The trend toward shorter terms accelerated over time. Before 1740, average tenure was 5.51 years; by 1760, the average had dropped to 4.72 years, and by 1795, it fell further to 3.74 years,[39] though at certain key locations, such as Xi'an and Jingzhou, average tenure remained high (around six years). The shift to short tenures at most places was almost certainly the consequence of increased bureaucratization in the banner system as a whole. As already mentioned, the selection process for vacant positions was rationalized during the Yongzheng reign; the more rapid turnover of senior officials at that time shows that appointment to office was becoming part of a bureaucratic routine similar to that in operation in the Chinese

TABLE 3.2
Average and Median Tenure of Garrison Generals

| Location | Average tenure to 1740 | Average tenure to 1760 | Average tenure to 1795 | Median tenure to 1795 |
|---|---|---|---|---|
| Guangzhou | 5.83 | 5.38 | 3.97 | 3.0 |
| Hangzhou | 4.60 | 5.16 | 4.16 | 4.0 |
| Jiangning | 4.33 | 4.36 | 4.19 | 3.0 |
| Jingzhou | 6.61 | 4.62 | 3.61 | 2.5 |
| Ningxia | — | 3.35 | 2.70 | 2.0 |
| Xi'an | 6.16 | 5.43 | 3.83 | 2.75 |
| COMBINED | 5.51 | 4.72 | 3.74 | 2.88 |

SOURCES: Same as Table 3.1.

civil service and that the office was subject more and more to administrative, and not strategic, considerations.

Preference for experience also affected tenure. As in the civil realm, where appointees to governorships of financially important provinces were mainly experienced officials,[40] 82 percent of garrison generals were appointed from positions elsewhere in the Eight Banner hierarchy, more than half (55 percent) from other garrison posts; only 12.2 percent of appointees came from the civil or nonbanner military bureaucracy (Table 3.3). These men came in equal proportions from capital and provincial posts, and included many promoted from senior positions in the Board of War, or from posts as governors-general or commanders-in-chief. The distinct preference for tested bannermen-bureaucrats, especially those with experience in the garrisons, suggests that this area of the banner bureaucracy was staffed by a specialized cadre of garrison functionaries who spent their careers rotating between different garrison assignments. A few case examples illustrate this type of career.

*Fusen.* A collateral member of the imperial house, Fusen began his career in 1725 with an appointment as lieutenant general of the Chinese banners at Hangzhou. Within two years he was promoted to lieutenant general of Hangzhou's Manchu banners, where he remained until October 1729, when he was given command of the new Zhapu garrison. Five years later he was ordered back to Hangzhou, this time as garrison general. He served for nine years until being transferred in 1743 to Heilongjiang. After six years on the

TABLE 3.3
In-Posting of Garrison Generals

| Location | From garrison Eight Banners | From capital Eight Banners | From regular capital post | From regular provincial post | Unknown |
|---|---|---|---|---|---|
| Guangzhou | 14 | 6 | 3 | 7 | 1 |
| Hangzhou | 20 | 12 | 2 | 1 | 1 |
| Jiangning | 16 | 15 | 3 | 1 | 4 |
| Jingzhou | 18 | 10 | 2 | 1 | 1 |
| Ningxia | 17 | 3 | 1 | 2 | 4 |
| Xi'an | 27 | 10 | 1 | 1 | 1 |
| COMBINED | 112 | 56 | 12 | 13 | 12 |

SOURCES: Same as Table 3.1.

banks of the Amur (no doubt a shock after the mild Jiangnan climate), he was assigned to be commander at Xi'an, the most important of the provincial garrisons. The seven years spent there, from 1749 to 1756, were the pinnacle of his career. In 1756, after a career of thirty-one years, he apparently retired.[41]

*Jonai.* Jonai first appears in the records in 1727 as a lieutenant general at Xi'an. In 1729 he was lieutenant general at the Ningxia garrison and in 1732 advanced to garrison general there. Removed from this post in 1734, he resurfaced in 1745 (at a lower rank) as Chengdu lieutenant general. Removed in 1749 to Guihua, he served there scarcely one year before being promoted to garrison general at Ningguta. Again a year later he was transferred to the Hangzhou garrison, but by the winter of 1751 he had been demoted to Zhapu lieutenant general. He served there until the end of 1755, when he returned as lieutenant general of the Hangzhou Manchu banners, his final posting after a series of brief appointments at seven different garrisons.

*Salhadai.* In contrast to Jonai, the career of Salhadai was remarkably stable. In 1734 he was appointed lieutenant general at Zhapu (replacing Fusen), and after nine years at last won promotion to Hangzhou garrison general (again taking over Fusen's job). Salhadai's seventeen-year tenure at Hangzhou, broken only by a six-month stint as Jingkou garrison general in 1757, was the longest in the history of the garrison. He died in office in 1760.

*Sungcun.* Garrison stalwart Sungcun enjoyed one of the longest careers of the eighteenth century. A member of the imperial clan, Sungcun became garrison general at Jingzhou in 1757. His abilities in this post were evidently highly valued, as he served in the same position at five other garrisons (Xi'an, Suiyuan, Nanjing, Ningxia, and Mukden) before retiring thirty-four years later, in 1791.

It is worth remembering that the careers of these men were in fact longer than the extant record can show, since they started out, of course, at lower ranks than that of garrison general or lieutenant general. Salhadai, for instance, was appointed lieutenant general after serving for an unknown length of time as a regiment colonel at Hangzhou.[42] Unfortunately, middle- and low-level positions are generally untraceable, and it becomes possible to track careers only once individuals reached positions higher in the bureaucracy. Occasionally, however, officials revealed something of their background when they were promoted to this senior level, as Hangzhou garrison lieutenant general Bašinu did in a memorial of 1739:

> At first your servant was a very stupid unemployed official of the lowest class. Thanks to the gracious nurturing attention of emperor Shizong [Yongzheng], from being an official without a posting, I received appointments as company captain, regiment colonel, and inspector-general of banner affairs. My lord showed me great favor by selecting me ahead of precedence and appointing me banner vice-commander of the Chinese Bordered Red Banner in the capital . . . two months ago I was again chosen to be provincial garrison lieutenant general at Hangzhou.[43]

Jarhū, lieutenant general at the Jingzhou garrison, rose to his position in a different way:

> Originally your servant Jarhū was someone of the lower ranks. Thanks to the generous grace I received of the late emperor, as a military *jinshi* [the highest examination degree] I was selected to be an imperial guardsman at Qianqing Gate [in the Palace]. [Later] I was also advanced to be colonel at a Green Standard Army post in the provinces. From colonel, again extraordinary grace was shown me and I was appointed lieutenant general at Jingzhou.[44]

The latter account is interesting because it is one of the few times a banner official is seen to have advanced on the merit of an examination degree. In the majority of cases men at the top of the garrison bureaucracy lacked such distinguished backgrounds and simply worked their way up the ranks. This was the case with Nanjing garrison lieutenant general Unaha:

Your servant was at first a guard of ordinary rank. On campaign I did not distinguish myself by my hard work, yet without my even asking at the door the emperor, Shengzu, bestowed on me an honorary title of the eighth degree and appointed me [to posts] from imperial guardsman in the vanguard division on up to lieutenant general. Every time I think on the favor that has thus been shown me my flesh goes to water and my heart melts.[45]

Though he never achieved the same fame or power, Unaha's story is similar to the story of Hešen, the Qianlong emperor's favorite, who was also a guardsman plucked from obscurity, suggesting that promotion from the guards was a long-standing tradition and that routinization of the appointment process in the banner bureaucracy, as in the civil bureaucracy, was always subject to the emperor's power of special appointment.

Special appointment to office, which "emphasized closeness to the monarch,"[46] was fairly common in parts of the civil bureaucracy. R. Kent Guy has found that among provincial governors, special appointments accounted for 31.15 percent of appointments made between 1700 and 1900. Data are lacking for a comprehensive comparison of the special appointment rate for senior officials in the Eight Banners, but statistics from the last year of the Yongzheng reign show the rate for garrison positions to have been extraordinarily high (73.6 percent), and considerably lower for capital positions (24.4 percent).[47] This suggests that here, too, the Yongzheng emperor used the special appointments mechanism to respond to particular needs (especially of a military nature) and put his own stamp on provincial administration.[48] It should be anticipated that the emperor was comparatively very well informed on conditions in the banner garrisons and on close terms with its officials, many of whom he personally had placed in their positions. This expectation is confirmed by the intensely private nature of much of the communication between them, presented later in this chapter.

## THE GARRISON LIEUTENANT GENERAL AND OTHER STAFF

Among subordinate officers, the most important assistants to the garrison general were the garrison lieutenant generals. They ranked just behind garrison generals in the banner hierarchy and, as we have seen, often succeeded to that position later in their careers. The basic duties of the lieutenant general included supervision of military training, inspection of troops and weaponry, and solving disputes in the garrison. They were also deeply involved in the management of banner finances. As second-in-command in the garrison, when the garrison general was away, a lieutenant general would usually be nominated as his temporary stand-in, though sometimes a Manchu civil official, such as the governor-general or provincial commander-in-chief, was assigned this duty.[49] Beyond this, lieutenant generals often brought back imperial instructions for the garrison general when returning from Beijing, where both of them went periodically (in theory every year or two but in fact far less often).[50] Garrison lieutenant generals, who seem to have enjoyed slightly longer tenures in their posts than garrison generals, provided continuity between administrations, while garrison generals, for their part, contributed greater experience, often gained from military campaigns.

Relations between the top garrison officials have been characterized as a "partnership," with the two sharing all responsibilities, cosigning documents and nominating lower-rank officers for promotion.[51] As the garrison general's deputies, lieutenant generals were exhorted to "assist the garrison general in training and caring for the soldiers and keeping the local people at peace."[52] Xi'an lieutenant general Nimašan was instructed never to try to hide any information from the garrison general, but to make himself as "one body" with him.[53] The Yongzheng emperor in particular stressed symbiosis between garrison officers. When naming a new Ningxia lieutenant general in 1729, the emperor advised him, "If you meet up with a good garrison general, [things] will be fine. If you come up against a run-of-the-mill garrison general, [things] will be ordinary."[54] Moreover, since a lieutenant general could realistically hope for eventual promotion to garrison general, success in one's tenure as a junior officer was important for the future, and he was encouraged to take the garrison commander as an exemplar. Upon his transfer to the Ningxia garrison, Xi'an lieutenant general Jonai received this advice from the emperor:

> My thinking in moving you to Ningxia was especially to have you look closely at the thoughts and actions of General Sibe and to have you follow diligently his teaching and guidance. Strive as best you can! Imitate him! If you can really come to think like Sibe . . . then by forever repaying my favor you will certainly become an honored and famous official.[55]

A month later, Jonai was upbraided for lackadaisically responding only that he would do his best to assist Sibe in his duties according to the edicts that the garrison would be receiving: "What do you mean, saying that you will just align your thinking with the general's and do whatever he says? 'Striving' means first of all [taking] a model. Act according to Sibe's instructions and guidance."[56] The emperor's displeasure arose over Jonai's failure to understand that he had to do more than simply follow orders, that he should become something of a disciple of Sibe (one of the few garrison generals in whom the Yongzheng emperor seems to have had any confidence). Sumurji was encouraged to model himself on Sibe's example, too: "When you can do that, then [all will be] well."[57]

Thinking of the garrison general and lieutenant generals as "partners" is correct as far as it goes, but it misses a basic tension arising from the dual nature of the lieutenant general's role: on the one hand, he was the garrison general's senior aide; on the other hand, he was a top-level banner official with substantial authority and autonomy of his own. To be sure, open conflict between the two was rare. But the relative autonomy enjoyed by both officials meant that it was not uncommon to find each reporting on the other secretly to the emperor—which fits the general pattern of mutual surveillance that operated as a control mechanism elsewhere in the Qing bureaucracy.[58] For though junior to the garrison general, the lieutenant general was not under his immediate authority. He was appointed separately by the emperor, very frequently by special edict,[59] and was provided with his own office and staff, giving him a fair degree of independence in his activities. The most important factor contributing to the lieutenant general's autonomy was that, like the garrison general, he was privileged to memorialize the emperor directly through the palace memorial system. Unobstructed access to the throne conferred prestige, power, and opportunity; however the emperor may have cautioned the lieutenant general against hiding anything from the garrison general, on occasion he encouraged just this sort of secrecy, as his rescript to Xi'an lieutenant general Sumurji testifies: "When you have ideas of your own, whatever they may concern, and if the garrison general, friends, or officials put pressure [on you], just memorialize secretly."[60] Newly transferred to the Xi'an garrison, Sumurji may have welcomed this reassuring note, the more so when his efforts to follow imperial orders in proposing reforms of certain practices at Xi'an met with the resistance of the garrison general. Sumurji reported his difficulties straight to the emperor in a palace memorial, and the emperor told him to take matters up with Shaanxi's Manchu governor-general, Jalangga. Ignoring the ostensible division between civilian and banner affairs, the emperor gave instructions to "discreetly and secretly apprise him also of your [previous] memorials and my rescripts."[61]

Another key element in the lieutenant general's relative independence was that though a garrison general could accuse him of malfeasance or incompetence, he did not have the power to dismiss him. What is more, the lieutenant general held the same right of impeachment over the garrison general.[62] Thus senior garrison officials were expected to report on each other secretly, passing opinions on predecessors in office or people at other garrison locations.[63] In one case the Liangzhou garrison general accused a lieutenant general at another garrison of embezzlement, favoritism, and mishandling food supplies to soldiers.[64] In another instance, a Xi'an lieutenant general was criticized for approving certain expenditures without recording them properly, forcing the garrison general to undertake an investigation to find the misplaced funds. In his memorial to the Qianlong emperor he complained, "If even this kind of unauthorized use of funds can take place, imagine what [other] sorts of ways lieutenant generals can exceed their authority." The emperor responded sympathetically, remarking that this was not a problem unique to Xi'an.[65] But sometimes it was the garrison general who was the object of criticism. After being dismissed from office, Xi'an garrison general Cimbu was accused by his successor of intrigue and nepotism, as well as arbitrarily changing decisions at his own whim: "The next day after matters had been talked about and settled together with the lieutenant generals, he would associate it with something somebody said, change his mind, and unanimously decide to handle the matter in the opposite way."[66]

Still, despite examples of mistrust, these officials cooperated harmoniously most of the time; ultimate authority usually rested with the garrison general, as this response (to a proposal by lieutenant general Bašinu to restrict the selection of captains from among corporals at the garrisons) implies: "Reading what is written here, even if it were right, it seems that it would be a lot of work to get going and very difficult [to keep up]. Talk it over well with Fusen [the garrison general] and give it a try."[67] Another lieutenant general, reporting on his investigation into the alleged wrongful removal of bannermen from active status, was commended for bringing the case to light—and ordered to report it to the garrison general and proceed from there.[68] A 1761 rescript affirming that together they were in charge of banner affairs at the garrison, and that decisions should be taken jointly, sums up the Qianlong emperor's notions of garrison general–lieutenant general relations.[69]

The importance of other officers in the garrison, such as regiment colonels and company captains, has been hinted at in the preceding discussion. On these offices, published sources have almost nothing to say, so again we must look to the archives for what little information there is. Middle-ranking officers were often mentioned as the most crucial in maintaining martial respectability. As Jingzhou garrison general Guntai put it, "Although the posts of all the officers in the provinces are important, the post of regiment colonel is more important than any. The supervision and training of all the officers and soldiers depends on the colonel's abilities or lack thereof." In his view, it was better to have men in this position who were familiar with Manchu life in the provinces: "Men from the garrisons, after all, know the local situation and the way things are done; thus appointing them as regiment colonels to be local officials is very advantageous for the banner and the company."[70] This was one of the arguments in the plan by Bašinu to make promotion to this position a garrison affair, rather than for appointments to come from the center, and is also evidence that the garrisons were coming to own an increasingly separate identity from the capital. Not only were these distinct bureaucracies, but even the sort of work to be done in the garrison was special, requiring particular knowledge acquired through long residence at the garrison that a Manchu coming from the capital would lack.

Aside from pay and status, place of origin and residence was thus the most significant divide between senior and lower officers. The garrison general and lieutenant general, as already noted, rotated in and out of office fairly frequently (usually either between garrisons or between garrisons and the capital). Most seem to have retired to (or been buried in) Beijing, so the notion of the garrison as a "place of temporary assignment" was true only for them. Lower officers up to the rank of regiment colonel, unless they received promotion to the upper ranks, tended to remain at the same location all their lives, and were the backbone of garrison administration: when a new general arrived, he would just as likely talk to a colonel as to one of the lieutenant generals.[71] Permanent tenure for many at this level of the garrison bureaucracy provided stability and opportunities for advancement; not coincidentally, it seems that corruption in garrison administration also began at this level.

The only lower-level official about whom detailed information is available is the *bithesi* (Ch *bi-tie-shi*)—the clerk or scribe. Clerks were in theory employees of the yamen,[72] and could be appointed to this position whether they were ordinary soldiers or lower officers such as corporals or lieutenants.[73] Sometimes they were chosen directly by the garrison from among local candidates who had passed the translation exam (see next chapter), and some were also appointed from the Board of Rites in Beijing; such clerks were supposed to return to the capital after a year or two of service in the provinces. Otherwise, there does not seem to have been a strict limit on their tenure: one clerk at Jingzhou was noted as being in the same job for ten years.[74] Among their duties were the usual keeping of records and writing of memorials, as well as translation of documents in and out of Chinese, Manchu, and (in frontier locations) Mongolian.[75] The language requirements meant that *bithesi* were usually drawn from the Manchu and Mongol banners.

Good clerks were always in short supply,[76] so that despite their nominal attachment to a particular office in a particular location (in addition to staffing the yamen of the garrison general, they also were present in the offices of the lieutenant general and, at certain garrisons, of the captain-general), they seem frequently to have become fixtures in the personal entourage of the men for whom they worked. Apart from opportunities to be transferred to the capital (there were hundreds of positions for clerks in the boards and in banner headquarters), clerks also traveled between garrisons; garrison generals often wrote to ask permission to bring especially valued clerks with them to new posts.[77] Their services were especially prized by banner officials who lacked formal education. Xi'an garrison general Cimbu, who was literate neither in Manchu nor Chinese, claimed that his reliance on others to write palace memorials for him required him to appoint men he could trust completely to serve as *bithesi* in order to avoid security leaks. He asked that two corporals who had been his clerks at an earlier post be transferred with him to Xi'an, even though that would increase the total number of clerks at the Xi'an general's yamen from six to eight, twice the standard number. His rationale ran as follows: "If I have some people who have worked near me and whose minds and hearts I know, it will be even better for me."[78] Ningxia lieutenant general Jonai was less studied in explaining his reasons for taking a clerk with him on temporary assignment to Ganzhou: "Your servant is not able to write himself and still needs to employ someone who can manage things and write. My Ningxia clerk, Baigiyei, is familiar with Manchu and Chinese, and is also useful in [official] matters."[79] Further work is necessary to improve our understanding of this and other positions in the banner administration, but it seems that the position of *bithesi* was very often the stepping-stone to a successful official career: among Manchus whose biographies are included in the standard Qing histories, more than 20 percent of those who achieved the top ranks of 1a and 1b began their careers in this position.[80]

### RELATIONS WITH THE CIVIL BUREAUCRACY

At least as important as their relations with each other were relations between the garrison general and officials in the provincial government. For a long time it has been assumed that the civil and Eight Banner provincial bureaucracies were entirely separate domains. In his ground-breaking 1970 dissertation, Wu Wei-ping provided the following characterization: "In China Proper except for the capital, the responsibilities or the authorities [*sic*] of the garrison commanders were limited to commanding their own forces. These commanders were not at all involved in the provincial administration."[81] Eleven years later, Kaye Soon Im gave a more complete description of the duties of the garrison general, noting that he was to "keep an eye on Chinese authorities in the province," and that toward this end, "all important business of the province was communicated to him, and he in turn reported this business to the emperor," to whom he was directly responsible.[82] She concluded that the relationship between the garrison administration and the provincial government was "typical of its relationship with the surrounding Chinese," implying the essential separation of the two, an assessment fundamentally consonant with the most recent Chinese scholarship.[83]

It is certainly true that the two bureaucracies were in principle independent. One was a military hierarchy and the other was a branch of the civil administration. Top officials in both cases were imperial appointees with the right to secretly memorialize the emperor, and were answerable only to him. The province's responsibilities to the garrison were mainly fiscal—it channeled funds to meet the garrison's budget and supplied the garrison with grain—and (as has already been mentioned) banner officials were not to interfere in local affairs. In a stern edict to garrison officers early in his reign, the Qianlong emperor hammered the point that military and civil officials had separate responsibilities:

> After arriving at the post, [you] must act in accordance with the established usages and regulations of the garrison. If any should bully superior civil officials with the line, "I am a Manchu!" or if they should fail to enforce regulations, fail to train soldiers properly, or *try to meddle in the regulation of civilian matters*, then *I will bring serious charges against them*.[84]

From this statement, it is clear that court concern arose partly from a wish to maintain separation between what it saw as fundamentally different types of administration, and partly from the fear of worsened ethnic tension (a theme explored in more detail in Chapter 5).

Nevertheless, despite its official promotion of separate spheres, the court appears to have been in fact undecided on the proper degree of separation between the civil and banner administrations and the proper level of garrison participation in local affairs. In 1708, Ohai, governor of Shaanxi province, received the following communication from the Kangxi emperor: "There is now a new garrison general [at Xi'an]. He was made an official after his efforts in battle. He is a good man, blunt and straightforward. His household is very poor. Since you and the governor-general are both getting by all right, each of you give 2,000 taels to the general. Show this to the general, too, in explanation."[85] A 1726 memorial from the Nanjing garrison general reveals a similar confusion of institutional spheres:

> As I was coming from Sichuan, Governor Famin, Financial Commissioner Fuhi, and Judicial Commissioner Cen Žu Sy [Cheng Rusi] together sent me 240 taels in silver for traveling money. Because I [already] had money for traveling, I didn't take it but sent it back. The next day they sent someone again, and again and again, so I accepted the money. That I accepted [it] I respectfully make known by this memorial.[86]

Thus, while the formal parameters governing their relations might seem to preclude an active partnership, banner and civil officials frequently cooperated on a wide range of matters. The emperor sometimes encouraged this, urging garrison officers to work together with civil officials "to the benefit of the locale."[87] Cooperation could occur in simple ways, as, for example, the sharing of bondservants for the delivery of memorials and other items to the capital.[88] Only the most important palace memorials were to be sent by one's own messenger; palace memorials touching on non-urgent matters (e.g., greetings, thank-you's) could wait to be sent with other items, even if someone else's servant was carrying it.[89] Edicts and imperial gifts also came this way.[90] Siju (the above-mentioned "poor general") wrote to thank the emperor for a gift of hazelnuts that had been delivered by the bondservant of his benefactor, governor Ohai.[91] In 1739, the emperor presented Nanjing garrison general Ilibu with a Hami melon, sending it with the messenger of interim governor-general Fan Shiyi, a Chinese bannerman.[92]

The heads of both bureaucracies could submit memorials jointly, and came together also on ceremonial occasions.[93] At the Nanjing garrison, for instance, the governor-general made an annual official tour of both the Manchu and Chinese cities,[94] and the governor-general of Fujian and Zhejiang was also invited to inspect the troops at Zhapu.[95] To an audience of top provincial officials held during an imperial visit to Jiangnan were invited the governor-general, the river intendant and the director-general of grain transport, the Jiangsu and Anhui provincial governors, the Jiangnan commander-in-chief, and the garrison generals from Nanjing and Jingkou.[96] On the emperor's birthday, formal ceremonies in celebration were conducted by the garrison general and lieutenant generals together with the governor-general and governor, and when garrison general Siju returned from the celebrations of the Kangxi emperor's sixtieth birthday in Beijing, the governor-general and lieutenant general came to meet him ten *li* outside the gates of Xi'an, bringing with them a host of officials, both civil and military.[97] In 1714, the Sichuan-Shaanxi governor-general traveled to Huashan with the garrison general, one lieutenant general, and the governor to perform sacrifices at temples on the mountain, while the other lieutenant generals remained behind in Xi'an to carry out sacrifices at temples in the city in conjunction with lower-level civil officials.[98]

Civil officials were involved in garrison affairs, too, but, as indicated, mainly where these touched on routine matters of finance and grain supplies.[99] Erentei, governor-general of Huguang and posted to Xi'an temporarily as garrison general in 1716, was told to hurry straight to Xi'an and confer with governor-general Ohai on the question of handling provisions to the garrison.[100] Shortly after the founding of the Ningxia garrison, general Sibe wrote to governor-general Tulišen to ask if grain and feed supply at Ningxia should follow the same rules as at Xi'an, and was told to discuss the matter with the governor, Shi Wenzhuo (a Chinese bannerman) and the provincial financial commissioner. When the results of their joint deliberation were reported by Sibe and his lieutenants to the Yongzheng emperor, the monarch responded: "The garrison general knows only about the soldiers and the governor knows only about the people. With this kind of small-mindedness and with [both] you and he memorializing without thinking of the nation, how am I supposed to have managed?"[101] In other words, in spite of the formal separation between their jurisdictions, the garrison general and the governor-general were encouraged to a degree to share the responsibilities of provincial affairs. The involvement of civil officials was even greater in provinces where the head of the garrison was not a garrison general or lieutenant general. Thus in Shanxi and Henan the governor appears to have been the de facto head of the garrison and could freely administer garrison business. For example, Shanxi governor Nomin, concerned about the high level of skilled but unemployed bannermen at the Taiyuan garrison, received permission to dismiss forty bondservants assigned to his personal retinue by the board and replace them with forty regular Manchu and Mongol bannermen who "could shoot and ride, were sharp men, and carry themselves like Manchus." Final selection of these men he left to Taiyuan commandant Alin, assisted by two of his own clerks. The governor himself went in his free time to see how things were progressing.[102]

As these cases illustrate, the participation of civil officials in garrison business was not unheard of; but the participation of garrison officers in civil affairs was far more common and extensive. Indeed, it seems it was part of the job. For quite apart from their banner-related duties, garrison generals and lieutenant generals, like provincial governors and other top-ranking imperial appointees, acted as the emperor's eyes and ears.[103] This is the best explanation for the large number of reports made by garrison officers—not only on local banditry and military affairs, which one would expect,[104] but on the weather, local crop conditions, grain prices, water conservancy, silkworms, and foreign embassies. Countless memorials on these and other miscellaneous subjects unrelated to banner matters can be found from nearly all garrisons throughout the Kangxi, Yongzheng, and Qianlong reigns.[105] In other words, officers at Eight Banner garrisons were like ombudsmen, gathering information on everything and capable of filling in anywhere at a moment's notice (in 1753 a Jingkou garrison lieutenant general was even put in charge of the Liang-Huai salt yards[106]). Furthermore, they were also supposed to keep an eye on the doings of provincial Chinese officials, an expectation held by every ruler up to and including the Qianlong emperor, who could be indignant when garrison generals failed to fill him in as they were supposed to.[107]

## BANNERMEN TO THE RESCUE

Despite court insistence on the separation of spheres between the provincial civil and banner administrations, then, in practice the lines between them were not so clear-cut. Indeed, the inconsistent stance of the court on the separation of these administrations could create real confusion for both civil and garrison officials. For example, in 1736, when Ningxia garrison general Alu reported his dealings with the Chinese peasants who had come to him for assistance, he got this response from the Qianlong emperor: "The affairs of the common people are those of the local officials. So why are you bothering to go and report [on such things]? There is no precedent [for this]. Very foolishly done."[108] In truth, this was not very fair; precedents *did* exist for such actions. Alu himself, as we will see in a moment, would be congratulated by the emperor just a couple of years later for his decisive intervention in the "affairs of the common people." The question of when to jump in and when to defer to civil authorities was seemingly easier to handle in emergencies, when garrison officials were expected not just to report on local affairs, but to act on them. When situations arose that in modern America would require leaders to "call out the National Guard," bannermen were called on to save the day.

A single dramatic illustration will perhaps suffice. In the winter of 1739 Ningxia was hit by a disastrous earthquake, reported as follows by the garrison general, Alu:

> At your servant's post in Ningxia on the twenty-fourth day of the eleventh month at the hour of the dog [from 7:00 to 9:00 P.M.], an imperceptible noise came suddenly from the northwest, and then the earth began shaking. It lasted only for a moment or two. From my house and yamen in the Manchu city down to the houses where the soldiers live, everything was flattened. Relying on my lord's good fortune, I luckily rushed out and stood in the yard. At that very moment, as I was looking, fires broke out from beneath the houses that had collapsed, since it is winter. As for those that had not been leveled, one by one soldiers would barely hit them with pieces of wood or throw mud or bricks at them and they would fall. At several places inside the city two- to three-inch cracks split the earth, from which water gushed out. The water continued that way all night long without stopping.

Only the following morning did the extent of the destruction become clear:

Once it got light and I had a look at the city, [I saw that] several of the towers [on the city wall] have toppled over. Although not much of the wall itself has come down, it is impossible to get through the gates. The light from the fires has been burning through the night in the Chinese city [*irgen hoton*, lit., "civilian town"], but I don't know exactly what the situation is there. In the Manchu city, it is impossible right now to determine the number of adults and children or the number of horses and camels crushed by collapsed houses. Later, after I have gotten some clear numbers, I will memorialize again, along with [information on] the situation in the civilian city.[109]

Written the day after the earthquake, this report was followed five days later by more specific information noting that 1,256 people had been killed in the Manchu city. Bandi, president of the Board of War, was sent by the emperor to inspect the disaster area.[110] One month later, the estimate was that a total of fifteen thousand people had been killed in Ningxia's dual cities.[111]

Three days after the earthquake, Alu was finally able to get out of the Manchu city and investigate the situation in the Chinese city, where he found that it too was reduced to a desperate landscape of ruin and death.[112] The homes of all the city's residents, officials as well as commoners, had been destroyed; fires were still burning; everywhere lay the bodies of those who had been crushed to death. Men and women wandered about the streets, which were filled with the sound of unceasing wailing. Having lost their homes and possessions, survivors were reduced to living in tents or lean-tos and had only the clothes on their backs to survive the subfreezing temperatures.[113] As the prefect had been killed, the preservation of order was left in the hands of Circuit Intendant Niu Tingcai and Brigade General Yang Dakai of the Green Standard Army. Neither man, as it turned out, was up to the task. It was Niu, the intendant, who first reported to Alu that the city's grain stores were being raided. Ningxia's eleven granaries had been destroyed in the quake, and the grain—tons of it—had flowed out onto the surrounding streets. In view of the crisis, it had been decided that each person was to receive an emergency ration of one *hu* of grain (about sixty-five pounds), but as half the granary staff had been killed there were not enough people to do all the measuring. With every passing hour, thousands more hungry and shivering refugees, many coming from outside the city, gathered about the exposed grain mountains and began filling sacks on their own. Niu's attempts to convince Yang to send some of his Chinese Green Standard soldiers to the granaries were rebuffed, so he appealed to the garrison general.[114]

Alu's first move was to order General Yang to send five hundred Chinese troops (apparently all that had survived) to guard the granaries. He also promised that five hundred bannermen would be deployed in the Chinese city to keep order and that he personally would supervise operations. Patrolling the city with his men, the garrison general reassured people that they would not starve and warned them against stealing: "The grain in the granaries is the country's. Are you not all the country's good people? Will it do to just take the grain yourselves?" The night passed without incident. The next morning, however, Intendant Niu sent his deputy to report that all the soldiers guarding the granaries had left at dawn and that people had resumed their pilfering. Alu immediately ordered the Manchu soldiers in the Chinese city to take up positions around the granaries and brought over another five hundred bannermen from the Manchu city to replace them in the streets. In addition, he sent someone to spur the governor into taking some action at Ningxia and three surrounding counties where heavy damage was also being reported. Alu's account of these events closed with a request that the emperor consider ordering the governor and the governor-general to get involved in managing the crisis.[115] This was quickly followed by another memorial describing his subsequent meeting with Brigade General Yang, who "behaved as though nothing much at all was happening." Alu charged him with incompetence and asked that he be removed from his position.[116] Eleven days later, an edict came down ordering just that.[117]

A few days later, another edict arrived, this one full of praise for the quick action taken by Alu and lieutenant generals Kara and Tungšan. The emperor commended all officers and soldiers who participated in the rescue operation, men who, "like those in the Chinese city, had also been through the earthquake, had their homes destroyed and very many in their households killed or injured," but "without the least hesitation or thought of protecting [their own], [had] exerted themselves in their duties, and following the general's orders, went to their designated posts to protect the people." Special rewards were in order. When Bandi, the emperor's emissary, arrived to inspect the situation a month or so after the earthquake, he was presented with a roster of 1,180 "heroes," who shared a bonus of twenty-thousand taels, taken from the provincial treasury. The rewards were conferred jointly by Alu and Bandi.[118]

In emergencies, then, the emperor looked with favor on the involvement of garrison officials in matters that were strictly none of their business. In dire circumstances, banner officials and soldiers represented a ready, reliable, and competent force to provide aid when time was short and lives hung in the balance. Other instances of this include garrison officials' taking the lead in repairing broken dikes or in managing grain-relief operations.[119] One cannot resist the idea that these activities also helped polish the image of bannermen, who in some quarters were already gaining a reputation for laziness and uselessness. Surely the idea of Manchus riding to the rescue of beleaguered commoners, halting theft, dispensing grain, and working side by side with Chinese soldiers to rebuild fallen dikes was not without political value. But there were limits to such involvement. Alu's call to get the governor and governor-general involved points to his awareness that the affairs of Ningxia outside the garrison were more properly the sphere of civil officials (no doubt he recalled being upbraided for meddling in peasants' lives in 1736). His exclusion from an inspection, undertaken by Bandi and top civil officials, of neighboring counties affected by the earthquake underscores this, particularly as Alu had been included on a tour of the wreckage of the Chinese city when they debated what steps to take.[120]

In sum, garrison officials had to walk a careful line. They needed to follow local developments without being drawn into them—unless there was a disaster of some sort. Yet even in non–crisis situations there was a certain amount of room for banner involvement in local affairs: as shown above, garrison generals and lieutenant generals were expected to join in local rituals, inspect the fields, and monitor silkworm cultivation. They were to carefully watch not only each other, but the markets, the people, and Chinese civil and military officials. Banner officials were thus entangled in many aspects of provincial government, while civil officials were to a lesser degree occasionally drawn into banner matters. Imperial edicts continually emphasized the notion of separate portfolios and mutual noninterference, but at the same time often encouraged civil and banner officials to act as though they were part of one unified body, loyal to the emperor. As we have seen, they shared messengers, shared the limelight in ceremonies and celebrations, shared the imperial trust, shared everything down to the fruits of the imperial hunt.[121]

If one accepts that the rhetoric of separate spheres of civil and banner administration was a product of the notion that Manchus and other members of the conquest group should be isolated and governed separately from Chinese society, then one might argue that the incomplete division of these spheres is evidence of an almost equal treatment of Manchus and Han Chinese, even a disregard for the importance of ethnic differentiation. A closer look, however, reveals that in many of the cases cited above, especially those occurring in the northwest provinces, the civil officials involved were themselves Manchus, or at least bannermen. This makes it difficult to know to what degree the ties between banner and civil officials were the result of a shared identity as "local officials," and to what degree they were the result of a shared ethnic outlook. Was there, as Jonathan Spence suggested over thirty years ago, a hidden network of banner alliances binding people together?[122] This seems especially likely when the top civil and military officials in a province were all Manchu, a situation that happened in Shaanxi in 1705, leading even the emperor to comment on what an extraordinary coincidence it was. In such instances, administrative lines blurred completely to produce a "shadow" Manchu officialdom controlling all aspects of provincial affairs.[123] To discover how conscious these officials were of their common identity and how this consciousness was cultivated and expressed in their relations with the emperor, one only need read their "letters" to each other.

RAGE AND PRAISE: LETTERS TO THE EMPEROR

In their reports to the throne, senior garrison officials left a record not just of their duties and accomplishments, but also of their relationships with each other and, especially, with the emperor. Their transmission of urgent, confidential information to the center—a role Spence characterized as that of "secret informant"[124]—was a consequence of the privilege granted them to write palace memorials (*zouzhe/jedz bukdari*). The palace memorial system operated alongside the system of routine memorials, through which most of the empire's quotidian business was handled; but because it provided greater efficiency and greater confidentiality than the routine system, it was used for military and other urgent business requiring secrecy. Spence noted that the system began with Li Xu's 1693 report on the Jiangsu harvest, but materials that have become available in the last decade make it clear that in fact the palace memorial system began several years before this, at least by 1689, and quite probably even a decade or more earlier.[125] By 1700 palace memorials had become the most important type of communication between high officials and the emperor.[126] The Kangxi emperor, who initiated the palace memorial system, and the Yongzheng emperor, who developed it further, engaged in frank exchanges with memorialists in responses and asides they themselves wrote in red ink directly on the memorials before returning them to the sender. These rescripts, some of which read like personal letters, provide a substantial base of material upon which to draw in analyzing their relations and the overall place of the garrison Eight Banners bureaucracy in the Qing order.[127]

Garrison generals were among the first officials to submit palace memorials,[128] and one of the most frequent types of communication between them and the emperor was the greetings memorial, which had to be submitted periodically to wish the emperor good health (as, for instance, on his birthday and on the New Year). Such memorials tended to be highly formulaic, and after reading a few it is easy to understand why the emperor once scribbled in exasperation, "Stop the incessant sending of these greetings!"[129] Yet these scrawls often make for interesting, even amusing, reading. Casual replies such as that written to Jilin garrison general Monggoro—"I am fine. Don't worry yourself on my account"[130]—leave the impression that the emperor took a stack of these with him when he was tired and answered according to his mood, particularly when he was writing to someone he knew well. A sense of familiarity emerges particularly strongly in communications between the Kangxi emperor and Xi'an garrison general Boji. A Manchu of the Bordered White Banner, Boji's career was long and distinguished, and the emperor seems to have known him almost as a friend.[131] Though the emperor of course exchanged pleasantries with other generals, with Boji he became truly personal, perhaps as a result of having gotten to know him in the field during Boji's service in the 1696 campaign against Galdan. The following 1707 rescript is a good example of this relaxed manner: "I am fine. It is cool now outside the passes. There has been enough rain, so the food is very good. There is nothing to do. Because my mind is unoccupied, I am looking really rather well. You're an old man—are grandfather and grandmother both well?"[132] Noting that he had sent the memorial on to his wife in Xi'an (he was in Tongguan at the time), Boji responded in kind to this friendly inquiry: "With this rescript, I feel as though I myself were near my lord in some very cool place."

The Yongzheng emperor was even more forthcoming than his father, and did not limit himself to personal responses on greetings memorials; reports on any type of business could inspire the emperor's apparently random observations. Sometimes the emperor's frankness was pleasant, as to Jingzhou garrison general Unaha, "Your reputation is very good,"[133] or to Nanjing garrison general Ilibu, "I very well know your intentions to exert yourself totally [in your post]."[134] But to others the emperor wrote with brutal directness, as to his cousin, Xi'an garrison general Yansin: "You do not teach your soldiers or officers with care and compassion. When complaints are made to me it is frequently pointed out only that you are cruel and prejudiced. Look thoughtfully [at yourself]: Do you act patiently?"[135] To another Xi'an general, Cimbu, he wrote: "You are not the model of your generation. Settle yourself in your post this time!"[136] And to Hangzhou lieutenant general Fusen: "I hear tell you've been drinking. If after receiving my edict you are not able to refrain, and so turn your back on my generosity, I will no longer want to value you or use your services. Act in accordance with my fond and well-meant instructions."[137] In all of these cases, as Bartlett has argued, the emperor's aim was to cultivate not just fear, but an intimacy that would spur officials to work harder.[138]

Bartlett has also remarked on the generally caustic tone of many Yongzheng rescripts,[139] and those written to garrison officials were no exception. Some of the sharpest imperial bile was reserved for Cangseli, Xi'an garrison general from 1727 to 1730. Not long after taking up his post, Cangseli's thanks for an imperial directive met with this snide comment: "If I weren't to give *you* instructions, what kind of person *would* I give them to?"[140] This was but the beginning. In the spring of 1729 a greetings memorial the garrison's officers had jointly sent to the emperor was returned with the rescript: "I have heard that Cangseli still cannot shake senility," cautioning the general's assistants to pay special attention to their duties.[141] Cangseli's reply was a long, rambling missive expressing his shame at his condition and fears about being able to continue in his post because of his age (he was sixty-eight *sui*). To this the emperor penned a sarcastic riposte: "You are, after all, still only *one* year older than you were last year?"[142] (A memorial sent a week after this by a Xi'an lieutenant general was rescripted, "It has been said to me that Cangseli is getting very much worse"—a clear indication that the emperor was receiving news from a number of sources.[143])

Cangseli's advanced years and ill health won him little sympathy from his master, as acid marginalia from one memorial of autumn 1729 amply demonstrate. In response to a purely rote remark that his promotions in office owed to imperial favor, the emperor wrote, " If you are unable to repay my favor, then you won't even be able to get back to where you started!" Cangseli's comment that "Heaven brings misfortune to the base and unfilial" provoked this angry retort: "So many guilt-ridden doomed knaves pass before me saying that the crime was Heaven's and that it just 'happened' to them. What good is this stupid idea?" The imperial fury peaked in the concluding rescript: "From the sixth month of this year there has been a great drought at Xi'an. You cannot fulfill any of the duties of a local official! . . . For what reason did you not memorialize to inform me that there was a drought? Deceitful liar, monstrous wicked and shameless slave!"[144] Cangseli's death the following year may well have saved him from a worse fate.

Yet the Yongzheng emperor could also be very generous to garrison and other banner officials, presenting them with gifts of all sorts: samples of his Chinese calligraphy, clothing, Buddhist rosaries, knives, flint pouches used by him, fruit, meat, tea, medicine, and slaves.[145] In his rescripts he also freely dispensed counsel and wisdom, some related to work, and some of a very general nature. Note the following piece of advice to Cimbu:

> I see that you are frequently willing to exert yourself for the sake of others, but you would do better to work hard for your own sake. Get a place where you can stand and make your master trust you. If you do this, what will there be in the ways of people that you must put up with? As time permits, make a small name for yourself and make a reputation. This is more than enough.[146]

Conveying personal thoughts to provincial officials was a method both the Kangxi and Yongzheng emperors employed in cultivating their dedication and loyalty, part of an approach that promoted in them a kind of personal fealty to one's lord (Ma *ejen*), and not only Confucian loyalty to one's ruler (Ch *jun*). The following lines to Sengboo, Xi'an lieutenant general, reveal this attitude well: "Acknowledged. I am placing a lot of hope in you as one man. Work well."[147] The uniqueness of each man's relationship to the emperor was impressed on Sengboo's colleague Sumurji when he read the emperor's closing words to him in one rescript: "This edict of mine is very secret. Only you are to know. Do not tell even your wife or children. Persevere."[148]

The imperial audience system was another instrument by means of which the emperor was able to achieve similar goals. The practice of calling all high civil and military officials regularly from the provinces to the capital for a private meeting with the emperor began soon after the Rebellion of the Three Feudatories had been suppressed, and was designed in part to forestall the possibility of another such treasonous misfortune. In theory, garrison generals and lieutenant generals were supposed to make an annual visit to Beijing for an imperial audience;[149] in practice, however, these visits were very often subject to cancellation. More often than not, it seems, a request for permission to leave the garrison to come to the capital was returned with a rescript saying, "Don't bother." (On the other hand, when the response was *jikini*, "I want you to come," one wonders whether this was cause more for celebration or for anxiety.[150]) The memorial system, more than the audience system, served as the conduit for shaping and cementing emperor-official relations.

## BANNER ADMINISTRATION AND THE MANCHU NATION

Whether expressing rage or praise, the intimate, even paternal, tone taken by the Kangxi, Yongzheng, and, on occasion, the Qianlong emperors toward garrison bureaucrats reveals an effort to nurture a banner cadre that was both capable and unswervingly loyal. I suggest that this effort arose not simply from concern for the proper administration of national affairs, but from belief in a common *Manchu* interest as well. For if Manchus could not be made to dedicate themselves to hard work and self-sacrifice on behalf of the dynasty, how could Han Chinese be expected to do so? The dynasty's future rested in part on the good example that Manchu officials (and Manchus generally) were supposed to set. In their private correspondence with banner officials we can see how the emperors encouraged this sort of performance, which transcended the limits of Chinese bureaucratic practice by emphasizing their ties as master (*zhu/ejen*) and servant (*nucai/aha*) and their common fate as Manchus.[151] This emerged as one strategy for the preservation of the Manchu "nation" and as such underscores the institutional importance of the Eight Banners in fostering a sense of ethnic solidarity that was key to the maintenance of Qing rule.

It would be wide of the mark to imply that emperors put their trust in this group of officials alone. The emperor's men were numerous, and included Manchus, Mongols, and Chinese bannermen, as well as very many Han Chinese. Furthermore, *all* ranked officials were "representatives of the monarch"—their authority was vested in the dynasty's legitimacy, and vice versa.[152] But bannermen, especially Manchu bannermen, were treated a bit differently. This difference may be conceived as that embodied in an intimate Manchu style, which revealed itself in three kinds of rhetoric: one that emphasized the use of distinctly Manchu cultural idioms; a second that emphasized duty to family; and a third emphasizing essential Manchu unity.

The first element emerged in specifically Manchu concerns, such as advice on how to learn Chinese—"Once you have made up your mind to learn it, you will succeed. It's not difficult. If you learn two characters every day, in a year you will know six hundred and will be reaching [a] usable [level]"[153]— or in reference to "northern" scenes. Some of these have already appeared; another is this passage from a 1705 rescript of the Kangxi emperor to Xi'an garrison general Boji, written from Rehe in colloquial language:

> I am fine. Right now there is no business. At this cool place outside the passes all the soldiers, down to errand-runners, have set up their tents. We've been living here eating the game and fish from the mountains and rivers. At night I cover myself with a cotton blanket. The rainfall has been just right. . . . My mind and heart are tranquil. How is the heat at Xi'an? How are you?[154]

Another example is this response from the Qianlong emperor to Qingzhou garrison general Kimbai: "This time there are more than twice as many beasts as last year. Everyone is talking about it, very surprised. It's because heaven has again blessed us with a good year. Inside, my thoughts are very joyful."[155] The emperor expressed himself this way only to other Manchus, for only another Manchu who had been there himself would understand the sort of pleasures he was talking about. There was no need here, either, to pretend to literary allusions or linguistic sophistication. Similarly, the Kangxi emperor's inquiry as to Boji's health (and, as we have seen, on occasion his wife's) conveys a kind of solicitude and easy familiarity rarely seen in communications with Chinese officials.

The second rhetorical element of the intimate Manchu style dwelled on duty to family and to the *gurun*.[156] This sort of obligation differed from Chinese filial piety in at least two important ways: first, it did not seek to ground itself in the classic teachings of the Confucian tradition; second, in stressing one's duty to one's forefathers, it simultaneously emphasized one's responsibility to posterity. This latter point has already emerged in the emperor's encouraging remarks cited in the preceding section; it comes through also in the following admonition:

> I have found perhaps one thing to be true. Don't be weak. Work hard and perseveringly. The officials who manage the troops . . . have fallen behind

in official matters and [upholding] the ways and customs of the nation. Their having stolen hollow fame is a bad sign. Not only is it greatly to the detriment of the nation, but they assuredly bring sorrow to themselves. For their transgressions they leave to their sons and grandsons.[157]

Such a message reminded Manchu officials that their personal reputations as well as the fortunes of the dynasty—and, by extension, all Manchus—was in their hands. It was up to them to maintain the conquest legacy left by earlier generations and to leave a respectable military and administrative apparatus to the next generation. The Yongzheng emperor especially tried to get officials to see their duties in this sort of perspective, to think not only about the past but about the future as well. His goal was to inculcate in them a sense of obligation to both ancestors *and* descendants—to family in both a narrow and broad sense. No doubt influenced by the example of his own father, Yongzheng frequently reminded officials of the hard work of their predecessors:

> If you are incompetent, if you are not able to enforce the law among your [charges], this amounts to your inability to transmit the nation's laws and the imperial grace! Work hard, respect, fear, and pay heed. Woe to my grace! Woe to your generation! Is it proper that you give not the least thought to your forebears who for so many years dedicated themselves to the nation? Rushing toward old age, it would be fitting for you to leave some good fortune to your children and grandchildren, instead of misdeeds. At your age, what more shall you get?[158]

The *gurun*, in other words, was a Manchu *gurun*, and its fate rested on Manchu shoulders. The Qianlong emperor, too, embraced this basis of a common and proud heritage when he sought to encourage Manchu guardsmen by reminding them that they were the "descendants of meritorious statesman of yore" whose memory they "ought to reflect upon."[159] On another occasion, he noted that he had placed his trust in people because of who their fathers and grandfathers had been, and for little other reason.[160]

The emphasis on ancestors and posterity in these entreaties suggests the degree to which Manchus viewed imperial service as a family tradition. When his brother was named Heilongjiang garrison general, Xi'an garrison general Erentei sent thanks to the Kangxi emperor and expressed gratitude for the honor the emperor had done his father and his entire family by showing such favor, simultaneously recalling the history of his family's service to the court.[161] Individuals in the banners often achieved fame or shame because of the deeds of relatives, which was, of course, also true in Chinese society. An important difference, however, was that such information was written into a bannerman's official dossier.[162] Moreover, since appointment and advancement in the banner bureaucracy was largely decided without the objective criteria of examination degrees, to which a Chinese always had recourse, family connections were more influential in deciding one's life chances in the banners. For this reason, quite apart from whatever influence the Confucian cult of filiality may have exerted on them, Manchus had their own reasons to be extremely conscious of their family heritage. Accordingly, the emperor also showed unusual concern for the sons of Manchu officials, a concern not displayed in his correspondence with Chinese officials. The long-suffering Cangseli received the following homily regarding his son Cangyung, recently elevated to an imperial guard of the third rank:

> Your son is a person very changed, a boy who is maturing a great deal. Teach him well. Make him truly excel at everything. No matter what, he must not follow the disgusting, muddleheaded ways of those who congregate with their packs of low-life comrades, deceive their officers, hide things from their master, put themselves first and neglect their public duty. If you can [instruct him properly], he will one day enjoy even greater fame than you.[163]

Such concern for the individual development of one perfectly ordinary Manchu youth is surely exceptional, evidence of the monarch's perception that the dynasty's future could only be secured if the younger generation devoted itself to mastering the virtues and abilities proper to a Manchu bannerman. As later chapters will show, the link between the continuity of Qing rule and the preservation of good Manchu customs was a theme heavily stressed by both the Yongzheng and Qianlong emperors.

Related to the notion that the welfare of the *gurun* depended on individual dedication to a "family duty," the third element of the "intimate Manchu style" was a call to uphold the tribal unity of Manchus. In the main, this involved exhortations to be vigilant against the Han Chinese and to maintain Manchu dignity before them. The implications of Manchu superiority for Manchu-Han relations will be discussed in more detail later, but the emphasis on preserving a distinction between Manchu and Chinese—emergent, as we have seen, in Nurhaci's day—did much to remind people (if they needed reminding) that Manchu interests were separate from the interests of the Han Chinese. This is plain in the following 1727 rescript of the Yong-zheng emperor:

> Don't be wicked; appoint good men; enforce the law; eschew empty fame; act shrewdly. . . . If you do not plan or distinguish between right and wrong and cannot make clear and [properly] implement rewards and punishments, the results will be very grave. . . . These trivial, stupid lessons must be grasped by us Manchu officials. Just as if you would wake up a sleeping person or sober up a drunken man, you must apply yourselves and strive to do what is right. If this you cannot do, there will be no going back. Work hard![164]

The penultimate phrase, "there will be no going back," sounded a warning that dynastic fortunes would be endangered if Manchu officials failed to recognize the stakes involved in discharging their duties competently and energetically. Twenty-five years later, the Qianlong emperor made a similar point when he explained why he felt it was inappropriate for Manchu bannermen to serve as officers in the Green Standard Army in Guangdong. Not only would it damage morale among the Chinese soldiers, but if bannermen were to be stationed for extended periods in the south, where customs were degenerate (Ch *fengtu ruanruo*), they would become lazy. Even more worrisome, putting bannermen in the Green Standard system would inevitably result in their becoming servile:

> Imagine a junior bodyguard. Even before an imperial chamberlain of exalted rank he will scarcely bend a knee to show his respect. If you employ him as a major [in the Green Standard], before long he'll think nothing of getting down on his knees all the time. To tempt him with wealth and stir his desires will make him more willing to abase himself. This has major implications for Manchu esprit [Ch *fengqi*]. The governor [Arigūn, who made the proposal] did not think this far. How could he talk about Manchus being vigorous, quick, and of equable disposition, prone to be good managers, and not know that such a proposal could never be implemented?[165]

Of course, as has already been pointed out, bannermen did serve as Green Standard officers.[166] But if there were any doubt that Manchus and Chinese were believed to differ in their very natures, the above statement, with its assumption of innate Manchu qualities (pride, *gravitas*, efficiency) should be enough to dispel it.

The emperor naturally did his best to motivate his Han Chinese servants, but he could never invoke ethnic solidarity with them, or even with Mongol or Chinese banner officials, as he did with Manchus. He sometimes even went so far as to unify himself with the larger collective of "us Manchu officials" (Ma *muse Manju ambasa*), using the inclusive first-person plural pronoun. Such a rhetorical move was unthinkable in Chinese, where the emperor referred to himself exclusively using the word *zhen*, a first-person pronoun reserved for his use and his alone. Only in imperial confidences to Manchu banner officials *in Manchu*—which, significantly, lacks an imperial pronoun—could such exceptional collegiality be admitted. Here we have further evidence that a sphere of Manchu interests existed separately from Chinese interests, and that these interests related directly to the sensitive, and delitescent, issue of ethnic sovereignty. The partisan tone in these exchanges makes it plain that ethnicity in the Qing was, like ethnicity in many places, both the product and producer of prejudices that were manifestly shaped by a belief in essential difference between peoples. These biases were, in turn, sharpened by political concerns. Witness the comment made by the Kangxi emperor in confidence to his protégé Yentai: "On top of that there is the deceitful and crafty nature of the Chinese; though 'virtue' and 'filiality' are forever in their mouths, when [they] become famous or when it is to [their] advantage, [they] don't even recognize [their] own mothers and fathers."[167] In disparaging characterizations of "servile" or "hypocritical" Chinese it is not hard to spot the signs of simple ethnic prejudice. In the rescripts of the Yongzheng emperor we find a similar cut alluding to a Chinese proclivity to excitability:

> You mustn't go about equating a small rise in the price of grain with some kind of miniature disaster; this is like what those careless, insignificant Chinese do, getting their heads all in a bother over every little thing. All you officials must be more resolute and take minor things in stride. So don't be frightened at one small matter and let yourself be deceived by the talk of people who know nothing.[168]

This note is tied to the mistrust and contempt of the Chinese shared to a degree by all Qing emperors in the seventeenth and eighteenth centuries, a mistrust, as we will see in Chapter 5, that was generally shared by many Manchus. Nowhere is this more strikingly seen than in a 1707 rescript of the Kangxi emperor: "Pen and paper cannot accommodate all my thoughts. The idea of what I am saying here is very important: Learned Chinese officials do not want us Manchus to endure a long time—do not let yourself be deceived by the Chinese."[169] This extraordinary warning is a forceful reminder of the persistence of the enduring division between Manchu and Han that lay just below the surface of eighteenth-century politics, two generations and more after 1644. It fully explains the emperor's emphasis on Manchu pride before the Han: "As for [us on Earth] below, we glorify our fathers and forefathers; I very much hope I will remain in the history books as the 'general of the western regions.' No matter how I am mocked by the Chinese, they will not make me ashamed. Apart from diligence, surely everything [comes down to] what you have accomplished."[170] The emperor does not say here in what ways he was being "mocked" by the Chinese, or how he knew about their attitudes. Still, this statement cannot but lead one to believe that in their presence he may have felt uneasy and that he wanted the Han to be given no further evidence that might confirm what he feared was their low opinion of the Manchus.

A very similar attitude, tying respect for Manchu ancestors and the Manchu legacy with devotion to duty and pride before the Chinese, surfaced also in comments made by the Yongzheng emperor to Jingzhou garrison general Unaha in 1723: "I am counting on your accomplishments and diligence; you are brave, so don't be disrespectful by fearing to do something. Especially as you have returned from a campaign, teach everyone about things. Do not use violence in the locale. No getting ridiculed by the Chinese. The more [they] respect [us], the more [they will be] cautious."[171] Given what is already known about collective Manchu insecurity as rulers of China—from their insistence on the queue to the prosecution of cases involving suspected slander against the Manchus—such anti-Chinese sentiments have long been suspected, and their confirmation is perhaps not a great surprise. These tensions help explain the endless literary and political cases and account for the continued prevalence of Manchus in top posts in the central and provincial government for most of the late seventeenth and eighteenth centuries.[172] We see these sentiments expressed here only because these were people to whom the emperor could safely unburden himself on such matters, matters which had the potential to polarize tensions between Manchu and Chinese to an unsustainable degree. When considered in tandem with imperial concern for the proper education of the younger generation—and especially against the background of institutional crisis that loomed in the 1720s and 1730s (discussed in Chapter 8)—the expression of such thoughts suggests that concern was building among the Manchu elite that Qing ethnic sovereignty was weakening inexorably. This was perhaps the fear expressed by the Yongzheng emperor of the "drunken man," happy but deluded, who will not or cannot awaken to the danger that is around him.

In evaluating the role of Manchu banner officers it is clear that the good performance to which garrison officers were exhorted meant more than just good administration. Performance in office was important, of course, and Manchu officials, a great number (perhaps even a majority) of whom rose through the banner system, were a crucial cadre of loyal, competent talent. The throne valued them highly, just as it placed a high value on the role of the banners as a shadow provincial bureaucracy. On top of these institutional aspects, stress was placed on Manchu officials in the banners acting in a proper Manchu style and upholding Manchu solidarity: showing respect to the memorialist's and every bannerman's ancestors and the honor of his family; serving the *gurun* with pride and diligence; maintaining a good reputation as an official and, by extension, the reputation and fame of all Manchu officials; and, most of all, promoting the honor and reputation of the emperor. As the crucial "us Manchus" in the above-cited rescript indicates, the Kangxi emperor identified himself as one of the Manchus and the titular father of Manchu officialdom. This was true of the Yongzheng and Qianlong emperors as well. In a 1726 rescript to Xi'an garrison general Yansin, the Yongzheng emperor wrote about "the ways of us Manchu officials and soldiers."[173] And in a 1742 edict we see the Qianlong emperor speaking of "the old way of us Manchus."[174] In the emperor's emphasis on individual pride and family tradition one can see reflected his concern for the future of the *gurun*, that is to say, the future of the dynasty and of the Manchu people. As such, the fate of the banners, upon which the *gurun* depended, was one of the great issues of the first half of the Qing dynasty and provided a daunting challenge to the eighteenth-century emperors who wrangled with the changing nature of banner society and Manchu identity.

# PART TWO

# Patterns of Banner Life

# CHAPTER FOUR

# The Iron Rice Bowl of Banner Privilege

Within the ethnic hierarchy of the Eight Banners all males born to regular Manchu, Mongol, and Chinese banner households, whether or not they actually took up arms, were considered first and foremost military men. As suggested by such statements as "Manchu soldiers are the root of the nation," their potential as a military force was a key sense in which the banners, particularly the Manchu banners, were seen as the dynasty's foundation.[1] It was to prevent acculturation and maintain the force as a control mechanism that the court sequestered banner populations in Manchu cities in Beijing and around the empire, and it was to help maintain the difference between conqueror and conquered that the emperors strove to sustain an esprit de corps among "us Manchus." But apartheid and Manchu pride alone were not all that served to mark Manchu difference. There was also an array of substantial economic, legal, educational, and occupational privileges and restrictions that set the Qing *herrenvolk* apart from the Chinese.

This chapter examines the quotidian realities faced by ordinary banner households in the Manchu cities and highlights the ways such realities differed from those faced by the mass of the Chinese population. The first section explores the military tenor of banner existence and the demands made on men in the banners; the second section lays out the system of material support extended to banner families and discusses the implications of the bannerman's "iron rice bowl"; and the third section describes the legal and occupational privileges that distinguished banner people from the Han.

## AT THE TRAINING GROUND

Though the genesis of the Eight Banners was as a social institution geared expressly to war, scholars have paid relatively little attention to the military aspects of banner life. This is no doubt because impressions of banner life in the Qing tend to be colored by what people saw in the late nineteenth and early twentieth centuries, when the general opinion was that the banners were "practically obsolete for the effective purposes of war."[2] The privileged nature of banner life and the indolence it tended to invite were frequent objects of comment then, as was the lack of military spirit among bannermen. The novelist Lao She, born in 1898 to a banner family in the capital, drew this hilarious portrait of one uncle who was a captain in the banners:

> Although [he] was a military officer of the fourth rank, he rarely spoke of leading soldiers or fighting. When I asked him if he could ride a horse or shoot with a bow and arrow, his response was a fit of coughing, after which he steered the conversation back to bird-raising techniques. . . . Truly, he seemed to have forgotten that he was a military officer.

There was also the family cousin, Fuhai, who, though "a genuine Manchu bannerman in full possession of the riding and shooting skills which had been refined over the course of two hundred years," knew "only a smattering of Manchu." On the other hand, he was "adept at gambling, playing dominoes, guessing dice under cups, drawing lots, crapshooting, playing cards or kicking a ball around."[3] Fuhai was no doubt representative of his age—a point to which we shall return later—but it would be a mistake to accept this as an accurate description of banner life in Beijing or the banner garrisons in, say, 1750, or to assume, as some have, that after 1644 military service became "irrelevant" to the bannerman's life.[4] As this chapter shows, the real state of preparedness among bannermen varied widely geographically and chronologically, and imperial complaints on soldierly behavior cannot necessarily be taken to represent the actual state of affairs. During the first part of the Qing, the life of most bannermen was the hard life of the soldier and many in the eighteenth and nineteenth centuries continued to take their military duties quite seriously. For most of them, soldiering was not just an occupation, but a way of life.

In the years before and after the conquest when warfare was widespread, able-bodied bannermen did not lack for opportunities to exercise their professional skills. During the Kangxi reign, the Rebellion of the Three Feudatories in the south and campaigns against the Dzungars in the northern steppe continued to keep the professional soldier occupied. Garrison bannermen were frequently called on to participate in these military maneuvers. Soldiers from the Xi'an, Jingzhou, Hangzhou, and Nanjing garrisons took part in the campaigns in the south and southwest and two thousand men from the Xi'an garrison were included in marches against the Dzungars in the 1690s.[5] In 1716, Xi'an garrison general Erentei reported that thirty-three hundred of the seven thousand mounted banner corps under his command were away on campaign.[6] In the early eighteenth century, the formal expectations of the court concerning its elite forces still corresponded to a real need for trained archers and horsemen who, correspondingly, could expect that their bravery might earn them tangible reward and that their skill with a bow and arrow might mean the difference between life and death. Opportunities for experience in war grew more scarce later in the eighteenth century, yet they did not disappear altogether. Garrison bannermen from Nanjing, Hangzhou, and Jingzhou fought in Tibet in the 1720s, and men stationed in the Xi'an and Ningxia garrisons remained a regular source of soldiers for campaigns in the Northwest; even well into the 1770s, Jingzhou and Xi'an bannermen served in Xinjiang.[7] By this time the likelihood for most bannermen, especially those in the coastal garrisons, of fighting in a real battle was fairly remote and the kind of dissolute behavior noted by Lao She became more widespread. But since by profession bannermen were still soldiers and were forbidden from doing anything else, they were required to drill as though their chances of going to war were as great as ever. This may not have been as entirely useless as one might suppose. As late as the nineteenth century, when by most accounts martial skills had declined to abysmal levels, bannermen at the Jingkou garrison fought well enough against the British to earn praise for a "cool and determined resistance." Their main weakness was seen to be their outdated equipment.[8]

Indeed, the equipment used by bannermen changed very little over time. The main weapons used in training in the seventeenth century—bow and arrow, lance, musket, and cannon—were still the mainstays two hundred years later. Regular mounted soldiers were armed with one bow and a quiver holding anywhere from thirty to fifty arrows (the number changed from reign to reign), with officers and nobles entitled to more. Foot soldiers were divided into three groups: archers, lancers, and musketeers (some cavalry were also trained in the use of the lance). All soldiers were provided with uniforms and a short sword. Other, specialized equipment included cane shields, flails, cudgels, and different types of swords. Armor for cavalry consisted of a metal helmet and hauberk, while for infantry protective clothing was made of cloth. The uniforms of lieutenants and regular soldiers (cavalry and infantry alike) were colored according to their banner affiliation, while superior officers' armor was painted blue; there was no distinction in the red-tasseled helmets everyone wore.[9] An 1866 description of banner forces at Guangzhou (which at the time consisted of both Chinese and Manchu bannermen) gives some idea of how they looked in their traditional uniforms as they underwent training in the use of modern European artillery:

> The Tartar artillery at once attracted attention by their superior size and more soldierly bearing, no less than by the diversity of their uniforms, which consist of jackets either of white, yellow, blue, or red, according to the colour of the "Banner" beneath which each of these hereditary soldiers is born. White leggings tucked into boots reaching to the knee, and hats similar to those worn by mandarins in winter, but decorated with two fox-tails behind, complete the Tartar uniform.[10]

Apart from weaponry, a soldier (except of course for infantry) was responsible for the maintenance of three horses, including saddles, halters, and fetters for each mount. There was a wide array of other gear without which he was not properly outfitted: cooking pot, flotation belt, spade, scythe, iron handle, clamps, pegs, nails, rope, cloth sacks, flint, large knife, cleats, waterproof quiver and bow-case, round quiver, felt cape, and horsehide boots. Axes, saws, chisels, drills, awls, and pickaxes were packed separately in the company toolbox.[11]

Initially, a soldier was either outfitted directly by the Board of War (via the Board of Works)—most common for Beijing bannermen—or was given a silver supplement to cover the cost of having equipment made—at least thirty taels for an ordinary soldier, and as much as twenty times this amount for officers.[12] In the capital, once the boards got out of this business after 1758, equipment was ordered from blacksmiths, bowyers, and fletchers attached to the banner. At the garrisons, private craftsmen there made to the order of bannermen, who paid them directly. To check the inclination to pawn military gear, and to make sure that equipment was maintained in good order, periodic reviews were held at which soldiers had to present themselves in full battle array. If items were found to be lacking or in poor condition, replacements had to be ordered—but again, the government provided money for this.[13]

For all banner soldiers, formal collective drills were scheduled twice a year, three months in the spring (late February or early March to late May or early June) and three months in the autumn (mid–late August to mid–late

October).[14] Judging from the dates on memorials reporting their results, in the southern garrisons autumn exercises took place a month or two later, no doubt to avoid the summer heat. In their free time, bannermen were expected to drill on their own at the training grounds established for their use, and commanders were encouraged to keep soldiers in top form by springing unannounced exercises on them every so often.

Training concentrated above all on archery, toxophily figuring prominently, as will be seen, in the promotion of the ethnic ideal of the "Manchu Way." To nock an arrow and draw a bow well was the soldier's most fundamental skill and the source of his pride; the Kangxi emperor's talent at hitting the bull's-eye had passed into legend already during his time.[15] The small (four feet in length) but powerful compound bow used by the Manchus and Mongols, which had to be "cocked" before shooting by bending it backwards and refastening the silken bowstring (loosened when the bow was not in use), required years of practice to master. To encourage bannermen, prizes were sometimes offered for those who excelled at target practice.[16] In regularly held contests, expertness might be demonstrated by accuracy of aim, length of shot, or strength in drawing.[17]

It was the last of these that occasioned the most detailed comments by supervising officers. Bows were graded by "strength" (*li/hūsun*), from three to as high as eighteen, according to their stiffness. Ability at a strength of six (probably a pull of about 80 pounds) was considered minimal for a grown man, and a strength of ten (about 133 pounds) was required for participation in hunts.[18] A 1736 report found that of 3,200 troops at the Hangzhou garrison about 2,200 were able to draw bows of strengths six to ten, and 80 could handle bow strengths of eleven to thirteen. This, he noted, was a marked improvement over the previous year, when only 1,680 could manage bow-strengths of six to ten, and a mere 20 strengths of eleven to thirteen.[19] These results were confirmed a few months later by an officer who cautioned that among younger soldiers few were able "with ease" to use bows of strengths greater than seven or eight.[20] In comparison, the 500 troops at the small Dezhou garrison acquitted themselves with honor, all of them being able to take a five-strength bow, 203 a six-strength, 137 a seven-strength, and 85 a ten-strength bow.[21] By these standards, the military skills of garrison bannermen during the Yongzheng reign were for the most part still respectable.

Competition between them appears to have pressured bannermen to advance to the use of harder and harder bows. This prompted a statement from the emperor in 1727 to "let each decide what he is able to use." Discouraging excessive competition and warning against compulsion by superiors, he advised caution during training to avoid injury. In particular, the taking of drugs by those seeking to enhance their performance was forbidden:

> If there are those who wish to learn how to use a hard bow, they should practice naturally, gradually increasing the strength of the bow. How can one go to such extremes as to take medicine? Unless one knows the nature of the drug there is the chance that people will be hurt. Besides, using a hard bow on horseback is difficult, so what is the advantage? A bow that is of strength six or greater is enough.[22]

Those who were eager to master the use of hard bows were in the emperor's view all "ambitious" (Ch *xin shangjin zhi ren*), and for that reason the greater the pity that they were wrongly harming themselves. Hence the order: "Let the taking of drugs by those wanting to use hard bows be hereafter strictly forbidden." At the same time, the rich awards the emperor provided for powerful archers must have been a strong temptation for competitors to do whatever was necessary to gain an edge. The champion in a 1728 contest between the one hundred top bowmen in the empire won one hundred taels when he hit the bull's-eye using an eighteen-strength bow—an estimated drawing weight of almost 240 pounds![23]

Another area of basic training involved riding and shooting from horseback, usually considered together. Shooting while riding, for which the Manchu language has a separate verb, *niyamniyambi*, was considered a skill apart from shooting from a stance, called in Manchu *gabtambi*.[24] *Niyamniyambi* was probably the most difficult skill for bannermen, and achievement in this area earned high praise. To keep these skills honed, the court and some garrisons organized hunts (discussed below), in addition to regular training and contests. The Nanjing, Hangzhou, and Jingzhou bannermen who fought in Tibet were apparently reasonably proficient at shooting from a stance, but they appeared to be "very unpracticed" at shooting from horseback, and some were completely inept.[25] Equestrian skills were not limited to this, however: certain bannermen at Hangzhou were said to also be engaged in practicing stunts and tricks in the saddle—in their spare time, of course.[26]

Training with muskets was very often spoken of by officials at the same time as training in archery and riding, but ability in this area did not carry with it the same cachet or cultural significance.[27] Although an extra month

*Fig. 11.* Mongol horseman shooting. This late-nineteenth-century photograph shows a Buriat Mongol from the border area of Manchuria practicing what the Manchus called *niyamniyambi,* "shooting from horseback." Holding the reins up in his left hand, the soldier is free to pull the bowstring with his right arm. He could also grip the reins in his mouth and guide his horse using only the stirrups. The bow is of the short recurve (or reflex) type, typical of those used across Inner Asia. Extra bolts are in the quiver on his right side (the Manchu word for quiver, *jebele,* means "right-hand"). Photograph by Piotr Shimkevich, 1895. Reproduced courtesy of the Museum für Völkerkunde, Staatliche Museen zu Berlin/Preussischer Kulturbesitz.

of drills was demanded of musket divisions each season, a 1735 inspection of training at Qingzhou found techniques of loading and firing to be "not very good."[28] A detailed report from the Xi'an garrison in 1730 explained that there were fifty days of exercises for Xi'an's three thousand musketeers during each season. Each of the eight divisions trained separately, however, with only six days of joint exercises per season—hardly enough to do much good, as one lieutenant general acknowledged. Moreover, as the same officer pointed out, only two of these six sessions were conducted using live ammunition. He envisioned a shorter season with daily practice using live ammunition for every division to bring better results and petitioned the emperor to augment the garrison's supply of gunpowder and shot for this purpose.[29]

Bannermen at the naval detachments at Nanjing, Jingkou, Zhapu, Fuzhou, Guangzhou, and Tianjin had to master an entirely different set of skills, the most basic, obviously, being sailing. For Chinese banner soldiers this was perhaps not so traumatic, but for Manchu and Mongol soldiers, who were prone to seasickness, maneuvering on the water was quite a challenge. One training report read: "Thanks to the good fortune of the emperor's blessing, the Manchu officers and soldiers aboard the ship were standing and firing without dizziness. No one was in the least afraid or frightened. They even behaved [as though] they were having a good time."[30] Nanjing sailors took sand junks borrowed from the Jingkou garrison out on a branch of the Yangzi so as to stay out of the way of civilian craft—implying that crews could not be counted on to maneuver very expertly.[31] At Zhapu, exercises at sea were always carried out on calm days, and never farther than twenty or thirty *li* (less than ten statute miles) from the coast.[32] If the wind was strong or the waves high, training was canceled.[33] As a result, men had no experience with rough conditions on the open sea.[34] Apart from basic techniques of sailing and navigation (taught by Chinese sailors from the Green Standard Army), bannermen had to learn how to adjust the use of muskets and cannon to naval conditions. They practiced auxiliary skills, too, including boarding and disembarking, casting anchor, hoisting sails, climbing up the mast, punting, and so on.[35]

## FROM CHASE TO CAMPAIGN

Other activities in general military training included practice with swords, nimchuks, and spears, as well as sports, including wrestling, jumping, lifting heavy stones, and a kind of football called *mumuhu*.[36] To keep fit in the winter, soldiers in the capital assembled to play a version of ice hockey and compete for prizes in speed-skating competitions.[37] But perhaps the most important paramilitary exercise that garrison troops engaged in was hunting. The ability to hunt, like the ability to ride and to use a bow and arrow skillfully, was a hallmark of the Manchu Way. A legacy of their Inner Asian origins, hunting for the Manchus was much more than mere recreation: as pointed out in Chapter 1, it was a form of military training and an expression of tribal community, as it had been for the Khitans, Jurchens, and Mongols. It was, moreover, a chance to escape confining court rituals and to show off a different kind of prowess than could be demonstrated in palace courtyards, one that might win imperial notice. In this respect the Manchu hunt was not unlike the hunt among Norman kings as described by Simon Schama:

> [F]or a warrior state, the royal hunt was always more than a pastime, however compulsively pursued. Outside of war itself, it was the most important blood ritual through which the hierarchy of status and honor around the king was ordered. It may not be too much to characterize it as an alternative court where, free of the clerical domination of regular administration, clans of nobles could compete for proximity to the king.[38]

Though during the conquest of China hunting ceased to be a seasonal activity for the Manchus, the chase was not long forgotten. In 1684 the Kangxi emperor ordered the garrison generals at Xi'an, Suiyuan, Nanjing, Hangzhou, and Jingzhou to organize local hunts. The emperor's straightforward decree read: "If the officers and soldiers at the provincial garrisons are not made every year to go hunting to practice their martial skills, they will eventually become lazy."[39] The sudden revival of his interest in hunting was very possibly linked to a 1681 trip north of the Great Wall when, accompanied by a large number of banner troops, the emperor visited lands belonging to the Kharachin Mongols and joined them in a hunt. At its conclusion he hosted a feast and praised the bounty of the territory. In return, we are told, the Kharachin presented the area—known by the Chinese name of Rehe ("hot river") because of its thermal springs—to the emperor, who declared it an imperial hunting reserve. This preserve paralleled other hunting grounds already in existence in Manchuria, particularly an older hunting preserve east of Mukden set up by Hong Taiji in 1630.[40]

Rehe became one of the favorite destinations of both the Kangxi and Qianlong emperors. It was the site of the grand hunts (*qiu xian/muran-i aba*), which took place nearly every year, and served as the dynasty's unofficial summer capital, continuing the practice under the Liao, Jin, and Yuan dynasties of maintaining an estival retreat north of the Great Wall.[41] South of the hunting grounds grew a complex of buildings, modest at first, blossoming later under the Qianlong emperor to include Chinese gardens and an impressive array of Tibetan-style temples. A Chinese town, Chengde, developed just outside the imperial precincts. Apart from hosting the court and the bannermen and Mongol allies who arrived to join the hunt, Rehe also saw visitors from Central Asia, including Kazakh chieftains and Tibetan prelates, who came *here*, not to Beijing, to pay their respects to the emperor. The staging ground for the Manchu hunts thus became a microcosm of the Qing empire.[42]

At first, the hunts, which usually began in the fifth month and could last until the ninth,[43] included only soldiers from the capital banners. Starting in 1702, garrison soldiers from Xi'an, Nanjing, and Hangzhou were invited to take part, with men from Jingzhou added nine years later.[44] A limited number of the most outstanding archers and horsemen from each location—Manchus and Mongols only—had their way paid to the capital, where they joined the main force of capital bannermen before proceeding north to Rehe. Once encamped there, they faced a month or more of scheduled activities that included smaller-scale *muran* hunts (in which a whistle and decoy deer heads were used to lure prey into shooting range) and the more elaborate *aba*-hunts in which thousands of cavalry were deployed over a large area to drive game into one of the many clearings (Ma *hoihan*) that dotted the landscape. The grandeur of the Manchu battue is caught in a brief poem by Chen Zhilin, a seventeenth-century Chinese exile to Manchuria:

*Hunting Song*

The flags of the Eight Banners darken the frosty sky;
Ten thousand horses gallop, reveling in the adverse wind.
Startled ranks of geese break high above;
Thunder filling the sky arises from carved bows' release.

Though not expressly about the scene at Muran, the image conveyed in these lines aptly conveys the impression of banner huntsmen as an unstoppable force, powerful enough to overcome the elements and threaten the very order of nature.[45]

Temporarily discontinued by the Yongzheng emperor, who while on the

*Fig. 12.* *Mu-lan*, scroll 4, *Hunting Deer*. Detail from the fourth of a series of four paintings commemorating the annual imperial hunts, executed by the Italian Jesuit Giuseppe Castiglione (1688–1766). The series was commissioned by the Qianlong emperor, who is depicted on horseback (left center) about to shoot a stag. Serried troops of the Eight Banners stand behind him still in the semicircular *aba* ranks they formed to flush deer and other game from the forest (note the soldiers in the upper right shooting hares). Once shot, game was loaded onto camels (right center) for transport back to camp. © RMN—Arnaudet. Reproduced by permission of the Musée des arts asiatiques—Guimet, Paris.

throne never once went "outside the passes" to hunt (though he went often as a prince), the hunts were begun again in the Qianlong reign on a wider scale.[46] The emperor advertised this to the Qingzhou garrison general (who would be selecting men to participate for the first time): "In training officers and soldiers, it is imperative that the traditional ways of us Manchus not be allowed to disappear. From the third year [of my reign] the former institution of the regular training hunt will be begun. Only then will I know whether you have truly practiced as you have preached."[47] In this and other edicts the emperor signaled the inclusion of the hunt as part of the Manchu Way. In 1752 he wrote, "The battue hunt as a martial display originated as an old Manchu practice. Every year during the sixty years my grandfather was on the throne he would go north [Ch *chu kou*, lit., "exit the pass"] to hunt. This really was the best way to train Manchus." The emperor went on first to note an edict of the Yongzheng emperor stressing the importance of the hunt and then to state his own intention to follow in the path of his father and grandfather by employing the annual hunt to "cultivate the Manchu Way" (Ch *wei jiaoyang Manzhou zhi dao*).[48] Only the hunt could guarantee the maintenance of the art of shooting from horseback, so essential to the Manchu military repertoire. Only the hunt could bring men together around their "sacred lord" in a less formal setting where they would not be encumbered by Chinese court protocol. Outside actual battle, the hunt was the only way that banner warriors were reminded of how Manchu life used to be.

Thus by the second half of the eighteenth century, the hunt—elaborately staged to show off imperial prowess and provide occasion for imperial largesse—had became a part of the complex of sacred Qing institutions. As a cultural performance, it embodied a historical tradition with links not only to the Qing past and present, but also to precedents set by earlier conquerors that pricked Manchu historical consciousness in a decided way. Recalling as it did the rugged origins of the horse-riding Manchu *gurun*, which decorated its early palaces with the skins of tigers and bears and made the first royal throne out of stag antlers, reenacting the imperial hunt demonstrated the persistence of Manchu tradition, even as the custom of hunting grew rarer among ordinary Manchus. Court mindfulness of the element of ritual in the hunt (which by the end of the Qianlong reign was already tending toward the nostalgic) gave it a "magico-religious stamp; . . . by linking the emperor to his ancestors, the rite affirmed imperial legitimacy, supremacy, and power."[49] As such, the Qing hunt may be thought of as an instance of what Eric Hobsbawm has called "invented tradition," the result of "a process of formalization and ritualization, characterized by reference to the past, if only by imposing repetition."[50] This is plain in the lines from an 1804 essay on the hunt in which Qianlong's successor, the Jiaqing emperor, remarked, "Hunting in battue-style is the family training of our nation. . . . Can the son who is heir to the house betray the aims of his ancestors? Hunting at Muran in the autumn is the eternal way that must not be forgotten, but preserved for all time by generation after generation of sons and grandsons."[51] Like other invented traditions, the stylized late-eighteenth-century hunt represented an adaptation of an older practice for newer purposes, in this case the promotion of Manchu ethnic consciousness.

No matter how strenuous the training or how difficult the conditions of the hunt, the true test for bannermen surely came on military campaigns. From the pages of official accounts of these campaigns it is difficult to imagine the toil and misery soldiers faced marching and riding across the steppe in pursuit of an unseen enemy, hacking through high grass on the Tibetan plateau, or struggling with horses in the dampness and heat of the southwest jungle. A fragmentary memoir of the late 1600s gives us a soldier's perspective on these events. The author of this memoir, a capital bannerman named Dzengšeo, relates the progress of the Qing army from western Guangdong across Guangxi to Yunnanfu (modern Kunming), scene of the final defeat in December 1681 of the Rebellion of the Three Feudatories. The account closes with a description of the journey back to Beijing through Guizhou, Huguang, Henan, and Zhili in 1682.[52] Because it provides a unique window on the world of the Manchu soldier, it deserves special attention.

Dzengšeo (his Chinese name was Zeng-shou) belonged to the army led by Manggitu, a general sent in 1677 to fight Wu Sangui in Guangdong, Guangxi, and Yunnan.[53] Though Dzengšeo's rank is not clear, several clues point to his being a low-level officer, possibly an adjutant (*yin-wu zhang-jing/janggin*).[54] As adjutant, his duties would not have been limited to writing reports, but included field leadership as well. At some points during the march Dzengšeo notes that he was named to lead a squadron of soldiers, and he was involved as well in logistics, the procurement of rice, and overseeing everything from moat construction to the pitching of the general's tent. In addition, Dzengšeo acted as a regular soldier, standing night watch and taking part in fighting.[55] His account makes explicit many of the hardships borne by Qing soldiers on campaign, chief among which was a chronic shortage of food.[56] When polished rice ran out, unhusked rice had to be located and then pounded (usually, though not always, by servants) in pits dug in the earth.[57] At places where purchases could be made, prices were outrageously high, inciting some soldiers to theft, or even murder.[58] Progress in the mountainous terrain of south China was frustratingly slow, with marches on most days covering only twenty or thirty *li* (seven to ten miles), and sometimes as little as ten or even three *li*.[59] When it was feared that the enemy might appear, soldiers had to march wearing armor, which slowed and tired them even more.[60] They had to cross river after river, either on unsteady pontoon bridges, by fording, or by boat. On the way to Nanning, a boat with over thirty soldiers and attendants from the Plain Yellow Banner capsized, drowning all. Two days were spent looking for bodies.[61] Forward progress was limited also because of the inability of horses to adapt to the rugged terrain. Near Yuanzhou (in Huguang), the rocky way spelled doom for many of them, as the stones imbedded in their hooves caused infection and gangrene. On one treacherous mountain path, as the horses were being led carefully across slippery mud, the earth gave way. Dzengšeo could only watch as the animals plunged down the cliff, one after another, and were killed.[62] Night marches appear to have been not infrequent.[63] On nights when they did stop, the men slept in crude tents, sometimes not even of cloth or felt but of grass.[64] Heavy rain meant yet greater discomfort:

> On the third day of the fourth month we reached Pingyue fu [in Guizhou]. We saw the temple at Zhangsanfeng. On the fifth we set up camp in a valley in Qingping county. At night it suddenly began to rain cats and dogs, and the water pouring off from the mountain flooded into my tent up to my knees. My clothes, my rice, my blanket, my mattress— everything was dripping wet. Because of the damp, we rested for two days and dried [everything] by the fire.[65]

Other obstacles hurled at soldiers included blinding dust storms and floods. Two months after the above-mentioned rains, outside Jingzhou, Dzengšeo escaped from the house he was staying in just in time to see it get washed away by the overflowing Yangzi.[66]

With so many hardships over his ten years in the field, and thousands of *li* between him and home, it is hardly surprising that Dzengšeo's morale sometimes fell. In the eighth month of 1680, three of his attendants died, along with twenty of his horses: "I was very worried. How would I be able to go on with so few attendants and no horses? I sobbed unhappily under my blanket. Since I had nothing to do, I drank every day. I even sold some women [servants] and bought some horses."⁶⁷ Apparently, even midranking bannermen on campaign traveled with a sizable (and disposable) retinue. Dzengšeo himself fell seriously ill at one point and as his attendants were also sick, a Chinese banner officer took Dzengšeo into his own tent and nursed him back to health.⁶⁸ Later that year a special detachment of men was formed to guide back to the capital those men and officers too sick to go on. A gruesome caravan, they brought with them as well the bodies of those who had already died, corpses that had to be buried in the capital.⁶⁹

The New Year appears to have been especially hard. The extant fourth chapter of the narrative in fact begins on that day, January 31, 1680:

> General Manggitu, with the councillors, all staff officers, and local officials, gathered in Dongyue Temple inside the city walls of Nanning in Guangxi and performed the rituals. The officers, in two wings, and the officials kowtowed to each other. For the New Year, the banner soldiers and low-ranking officers all ate and drank, with the imperial guardsmen and cavalrymen themselves out on the street, dressed up like women, singing the "doo yang k'o" and cavorting. In my heart I thought unhappily about my parents.⁷⁰

Dzengšeo marked the following New Year by crossing the border from Guangxi into Guizhou. Again, he found little to celebrate:

> On the first day of the twentieth year of "Universal Peace" we started out from Xilongzhou and crossed [the river] on a pontoon bridge. We could see that the water in the Badu was green and turbulent. Since there was no place to camp, we [had to] camp on the sand at a bend of the river. The wind was blowing up the sand. We bought several catties of water and wine and one pig, and passed the New Year. Inside I was sad. I was thinking only of the old folks and missing them. I cried under the covers.⁷¹

Depression struck again during one especially dismal stage of the campaign in late 1680, which saw Dzengšeo's detachment spend three days advancing just five *li* through a mountain pass north of Nanning in Wuyuan county. He wrote in his diary: "Since I had few attendants and horses, I departed [Nanning] in a foul temper. 'The only thing to do is to die in battle,' I said to myself, 'and gain fame.'"⁷²

With so many trials on the march, danger in battle was almost more easily faced. Dzengšeo vividly describes this encounter with the enemy outside Yunnanfu:

We soldiers in the second division moved all together and advanced on the enemy in attack. Calling to our banner and the Bordered Red Banner, Councillor Hife pointed with his spear to several enemy squadrons occupying the bridge fortification, who up to then had not yet moved [from their position]. Our two banners attacked, raising a shout, but we could not withstand the cannon fire, fire-arrows, and musket fire. When the two banners became mixed together in one place under the cover of the destroyed wall, I was standing alone on the [far] bank of the river. I could see that our soldiers were continually getting wounded. Just at the moment when Hife sent someone with an arrow with the command to the infantry to attack, the bandits' rearguard fell apart in disarray.

At that point Dzengšeo sprang into action:

I then picked up a flag and, crossing the river, pursued their rear. At that, the bandits fled. As I gave chase and told them to surrender, they all knelt on the ground, threw down their weapons, and pleaded for their lives. [But] when [someone in] the vanguard shot one bandit, they all got up and ran off. Two bandits picked up swords that had been thrown down and, yelling "Kill!" they advanced, slashing. Quickly whipping my horse, I moved higher up on the bank. Looking back, [I saw that] bannerman Dengse was unable to climb up the bank. The bandits came to cut him down, but because Dengse was afraid and had leaned over to one side, they cut his quiver and the hindquarters of his horse. Dengse fell. I shot down one of the bandits. . . . When I saw that nothing had happened to Dengse, I hastily picked up my flag and pressing and killing [my way on], got to the base of the city wall. I saw that there the bandits were prepared, arrayed in doubly dense ranks. Cannon were being fired from the top of the wall. Upon hearing the sound of the conch-shell horn announcing retreat, our troops all withdrew.[73]

Dzengšeo was part of other battles as well, including one involving the enemy's use of elephants; Qing soldiers shot one elephant so full of arrows that they "looked like the quills on a hedgehog." The soldiers were amazed when the pachyderm still managed to run away into the mountains.[74]

Spirits were lighter on the way home. After leaving Yunnan, Dzengšeo spent several harrowing days on the rivers of western Hunan, sometimes covering as much as three hundred *li* per day, the boat "flashing by as though it were flying." When he reached Jingzhou, it was almost like coming home: "There were our soldiers' homes and our soldiers' camp, with doors and windows just like Manchu houses"—an indication that the distinctive architecture of Manchu cities was reproduced throughout the empire. Two servants from his Beijing household appeared to greet him, and he sent on one of his own attendants to inquire after his parents' health.[75] He was almost home. Incidents in which two soldiers were killed in a hunting accident and several horses shot, however, put him in an ironic mood: "In my heart I was afraid, and thought: 'I have spent more than ten years fighting on campaign, and my life was not taken in battle. Now I have to be careful of some soldier who doesn't know how to shoot from a horse!'" Surviving this last hazard, he rode with the army as it approached the capital on December 10, 1681. The emperor rode out to greet them. After a brief formal ceremony, Dzengšeo left and rode on to Lugouqiao, where his father was waiting for him. After a tearful reunion, they returned together to Beijing, where there were more tears as he greeted his mother. His brothers hugged him; the young ones in the family no longer recognized him.

## EATING THE EMPEROR'S RICE

The arrangement between the dynasty and its loyal minions was straightforward: in exchange for the loyalty of men like Dzengšeo, their willingness to endure endless training and extreme hardship, and even risk death, the state saw to the material needs of all banner soldiers and their families. Bannermen needed cash; the court paid them in silver (which they preferred to the copper used by most Chinese for everyday transactions) or loaned it to them from the state treasury. The housing and food needs of bannermen were met by the court's dispensing of a regular allowance of grain either from the granaries around Beijing or (for garrison bannermen) from the provincial grain tax quotas, and the court's building and maintaining quarters for bannermen in Beijing and the provincial Manchu cities. Bannermen were also supplied with weapons, each man outfitted, as already explained, at government expense. Some bannermen were required to keep horses; the court provided the appropriate number (to the Manchu and Mongol banners only) as well as an extra allowance for the purchase of fodder (hay and beans). Bannermen ran into unusual expenses for travel, weddings, and funerals, for which the court allowed special supplements. When bannermen fell deep into debt, despite the court's financial assistance, the court supplied them with the necessary funds to pay off their creditors. Since in these ways the dynasty supported them from cradle to grave, it can be said, using the figurative phrase to describe anyone on an official income in imperial China, that all in the Eight Banners "ate a salary"(*shi lu/funglu jembi*). Later in the Qing, bannermen identified themselves in just this way, as people who "ate the emperor's rice."[76]

Prior to the Qing conquest, of course, bannermen did not live on salaries and imperial largesse, but relied on booty and income from landholding to support their families and outfit themselves for battle.[77] Grain stipends, called "walking provisions" (Ch *xingliang*), were issued to soldiers only when they were on campaign, and many households supplemented their income through agricultural or artisanal work. The installation of the Qing on the Chinese throne and the consolidation of Manchu control meant that less disruptive means had to be found to support the army, since the continued plundering of villages and cities could obviously not be tolerated.[78] A regular system of salary support, called "sitting provisions" (Ch *zuoliang*), thus came into being during the first ten years of the Shunzhi reign.[79]

Financial support for Eight Banner households during the Qing in theory took two forms: silver and grain salaries on the one hand, and property grants on the other. Silver salaries (called in Chinese *fengyin* in the case of pay for officers, *bingxiang* in the case of soldiers) were paid monthly. The amount of silver a bannerman received depended on his rank and where he served; typically, a capital bannerman received four taels of silver per month, while garrison bannermen received three. Grain salaries also varied according to rank, and were usually paid twice a year in the spring and fall. In the capital, the standard annual ration for guardsmen, corporals, and cavalrymen was twenty-two *shi*, two *dou*.[80] Amounts for provincial garrison bannermen varied slightly from location to location, but were usually about thirty *shi* per year (two and a half *shi* per month). A portion of the grain salary was distributed as actual grain, while the remainder was commuted and paid in the silver equivalent calculated at current rates.

Why provincial bannermen received a smaller silver salary is unclear; perhaps it was imagined that their expenses would be less, or that their families were smaller than banner families in Beijing. But we can say that their larger grain salary, which helped offset this difference, probably owed to the unequal distribution of property among the banners. The fact is that land grants, not silver and grain stipends, were originally intended as the mainstay of support for the Eight Banners. Much of more than fourteen million *mu* of property (one *mu* = one-sixth of an acre) encircled in the course of the conquest around Beijing went to the Manchu nobility,[81] but large tracts also went to the banners for the support of ordinary banner families. In the first years of the dynasty, each male on the banner rolls arriving in Beijing received a tract of land of thirty *mu* or more, depending on rank. Banner land was tax-exempt and was supposed to provide a permanent source of income, since it was inalienable and could be sold only to other bannermen.[82] Farming was left to Chinese serfs or tenants, with estate supervision usually in the hands of an overseer (*zhuangtou/jangturi*), also Chinese.

For reasons that are not hard to discern, this element of the new Eight Banner economic order began to fall apart after only twenty years. One is that honesty and fairness do not seem to have been qualities sought after in overseers, which resulted in countless cases of cruel treatment of Chinese peasant-serfs, who, laboring under miserable conditions, fled the land.[83] Nor were overseers above cheating their Manchu masters. Therefore only bannermen with the time and energy to keep close tabs on the management of their estates were in a position to make it as landowners—but most bannermen were away fighting at this time. It was not long before rental income dried up and owners either lost track of the land or it was simply abandoned, eventually finding its way back into the market and Chinese hands. The periodic prohibitions the court announced on the buying and selling of banner land are the best evidence that it was unable to stop the alienation of that land. Even though some illegally sold land was later reclaimed,[84] for ordinary bannermen, banner land (in sharp contrast to the similar system instituted for samurai in Edo Japan) never became the permanent solution to the problem of income that Qing policy makers had hoped it would be and people in the banners became increasingly dependent on the court's steady supply of cash and grain. By the middle of the eighteenth century banner people were already building a reputation for an idle, parasitic existence, and for an extravagant lifestyle that was progressively more at odds with their growing poverty.

Bannermen at all garrisons were also supposed to receive land grants, at least in theory.[85] However, this seems to have happened at just a few locations where land was available for encirclement, among them Xi'an, Nanjing, Taiyuan, and Jingzhou, though it may well be that land was encircled at other garrisons, too. Materials describing the situation at Nanjing give the impression that the alienation of land from the banners was not as serious a problem at the garrisons as at the capital, and that the basic nature of landholding in the provinces was somewhat different. A 1728 memorial concerning the distribution of Nanjing banner-land rents dealt primarily with the necessity to split income more fairly between the left-wing banners (Bordered Yellow, Plain White, Bordered White, Plain Blue) and the right-wing banners. The left-wing banners, which arrived at Nanjing first, received property, whereas officers and men from the right-wing banners, arriving forty years afterward, found there was nothing left to be granted them. When in the 1720s appointments to midlevel rank (captain, regiment colonel) began to be made from within the garrison, the greater profitability of receiving an appointment to one of the left-wing banners was reported to engender considerable contention. This suggests that ownership of land, or at least the right to the income from the land, had migrated from being held by the person to being a perquisite of the post.[86] This may have been a result of long-standing policy (in effect until the 1760s) prohibiting bannermen from purchasing or owning land in the provinces.

The rents involved were not trifling—the garrison general's property generated over eight hundred taels annually—and income disparities could be large. At Nanjing, the left-wing lieutenant general's 120 *mu* brought two hundred taels, while the regiment colonel of the Bordered White Banner took in over six hundred taels on his smaller parcel. Other colonels and captains made anywhere from thirty to two hundred taels on their land.[87] Neither regular bannermen nor low-ranking officers (such as corporals) received any land, despite their having been forced to surrender their capital-area landholdings when they were sent to the garrisons. This suggests that dependency on stipend income for garrison bannermen was built into the system for their support and was not, as in Beijing, the result of the misfiring of a dual system relying on land ownership and stipendiary income.[88]

It was partly to address differences between capital and garrisons that garrison bannermen who did not receive land were awarded an additional supplement intended to compensate them for this lost income. This stipend was called *kouliang* or "family rations" (*jiakou miliang/booi anggalai bele*) and was fixed universally at one-quarter *hu* per household member per month. Bannermen receiving *kouliang* stipends included soldiers who established residence in the capital after 1647 and nearly all soldiers at garrison locations. With a typical household size of ten persons, the *kouliang* stipend was worth a handsome two and a half *shi* per month or thirty *shi* of rice a year, equivalent to another year's base grain stipend.[89] Thus in Beijing a typical soldier's income consisted of the income from landholdings (itself more than enough to comfortably support one household),[90] a salary in silver, plus a supplemental salary of *xiangmi* grain, awarded in proportion to the amount of his silver salary.[91] A capital bannerman without land received a silver salary, a grain salary, and a *kouliang* grain supplement. Landless garrison bannermen were perhaps less well-off, but still received salaries of silver and grain plus their *kouliang* supplements.

On top of these amounts came further benefits. Twice a year bannermen in the Manchu and Mongol banners were given an allotment (in kind or in silver) for feed for horses. Beginning in 1724 (1729 in the provinces) Manchu and Mongol bannermen were also eligible to receive special stipends for "red affairs" (*hongshi/fulgiyan-i baita*) and "white affairs" (*baishi/sanggiyan-i baita*), i.e., weddings and funerals. Chinese bannermen were made eligible for these payments (which varied according to rank—cavalrymen got about ten taels for a wedding and twenty for a funeral) in 1735. Amounts were typically greater in Beijing than elsewhere.[92] Supplements were also provided to soldiers having to outfit themselves for military campaigns. Amounts were not standardized until the 1780s, but here again, capital bannermen profited more, being awarded a single payment of forty taels, where bannermen from the Manchurian garrisons received thirty and provincial garrison bannermen twenty. Since their regular salaries continued to be paid to their families, bannermen on campaign usually also received a monthly maintenance of "salt and vegetable silver" plus an extra grain stipend, similar to the preconquest *xingliang* "walking provisions."[93] Bannermen sent on campaign were also supplied with additional mounts as well as supplements for horse and camel fodder.[94] This is not even to speak of the system of monetary rewards for bravery in battle, which could be in the hundreds or thousands of taels, or of the pensions paid to disabled soldiers or the families of deceased soldiers.

These highly favorable arrangements for bannermen were even more favorable for banner officers, whose salaries and other benefits were higher and who, as noted, could sometimes rake in hundreds of taels in rental income. The official salary of a garrison general varied, but was usually 180 taels, the same as for a grand secretary or a governor-general. Most also received a healthy chunk (up to 200 taels) of silver for seal ink and paper.[95] Officers also kept larger stables and were provided with larger stipends to maintain them. The "nourishing honest allowance" (*yanglian yin/hanja ujire menggun*) paid to civil officials beginning in the Yongzheng reign was also paid to banner officials, with garrison generals receiving from one thousand to twenty-five hundred taels and lieutenant generals six hundred to eight hundred.[96]

From the outside it no doubt seemed that life in the banners was very attractive, the proverbial bowl of cherries. The economic concerns of most banner families, people at once servants and wards of the state, were limited to the regular collection of their silver and rice stipends, which were theirs even if their lives seemed wholly unproductive.[97] Indeed, it seems safe to say that, at least for the first century or so of Qing rule, the standard of living in the banners was well above that in the average Han Chinese household, which may explain why so many Han civilians were eager to enter the banners during this period (an issue taken up in Chapter 8).[98] But the comparative security and affluence of banner life did not last very long. After monthly salaries were fixed in the 1680s, regular levels of banner support, like Qing tax quotas, were never revised again.[99] Since price levels were hardly so stable, stipends covered less and less of a family's actual living costs over time. Higher rates of inflation in the eighteenth century, along with the substitution of silver for grain in banner grain salaries ("commutation"), heightened financial difficulties.[100] Furthermore, as population grew, fewer and fewer males succeeded in finding paying posts, resulting in a large class of "idlers" (*xiansan/ sula*), as they were called, who relied on the income brought by other family members for their subsistence. By the mid-1700s, life in the banners was no longer so financially secure, and many banner families lived on the margin, even in want, giving rise to what Qing officials dubbed the "Eight Banners livelihood problem" (Ch *baqi shengji wenti*), one of the major statecraft dilemmas of the mid-Qing.

Moreover, as we have seen, the actual level of support for bannermen differed dramatically according to rank, ethnic status, and physical location. In the capital, the system combined income from land with a fixed salary paid in silver and grain. In the garrisons (with the apparent exception of Taiyuan, where land grants were permanent), the system provided only grain and silver salaries, plus the *kouliang* supplement. Officers were paid significantly more than regular troops, capital bannermen were paid more than garrison bannermen, and Manchus and Mongols were paid more than Chinese bannermen, who also experienced greater unemployment. Furthermore, the commutation of a significant portion of their grain stipends to silver exposed garrison bannermen to the fluctuations of the market in a way that capital bannermen were not. These factors could combine in devastating ways.[101]

In thinking about the economic privileges of banner life, it is important to remember that it was never the court's intention to provide a subvention sufficient to cover all living expenses for all banner families for all time. This may explain why salaries were not pegged to the cost of living: land ownership, the court had assumed, would provide many banner families with a natural hedge against inflation. The court may also have assumed that such protection would be passed on from Beijing bannermen through family connections to their relations in the garrisons, who (unrealistically, as it turned out) were expected to maintain family ties with the capital. The failure of the banner land system in the capital meant that the general trend in the system of support for all bannermen was one of increasing dependence on salaries and stipends.[102] Without a hedge for inflation, this put the court in an untenable position. In the end, though the size of Eight Banner forces (i.e., paying positions) remained about the same after 1735, the steady growth of the total banner population dependent on active bannermen—and ultimately the state—meant increased pressure on limited resources. The "free ride" for the banners could not go on forever. How to end it and who merited support were matters at the heart of the eighteenth-century reforms of banner household registration and finances discussed in the last chapter.

A PRIVILEGED PEOPLE

Banner life was distinctive not only economically; bannermen also enjoyed a raft of special legal and occupational privileges that further accentuated the separateness of the Han from the Manchu socio-military caste. Echoing Franke's observation on the persistence in conquest regimes of mechanisms of differentiation, one scholar has recently remarked, "Chinese and Manchus continued to belong to two different worlds, as imbricated as they were. They were institutionally, juridically, and economically separate, each group having its own statutes."[103] In this section, I outline the distinctive institutional, legal, and economic contours of the banner world.

*Legal Privileges*

Because they were conquerors and also military men, regular local officials (magistrates, prefects) lacked authority over bannermen, even though bannermen were theoretically subject to the same civil code.[104] For this reason, crimes and disputes involving bannermen as a rule were handled differently

than those involving only Han Chinese. This difference before the law manifested itself most commonly in that a bannerman caught breaking the law,
whether the infraction was theft from a market stall or premeditated murder,
could only be remanded to local banner authorities for trial and possible
punishment; magistrates' investigations were limited to discovery, and then
only in cooperation with banner officials or their representatives.[105] Bannermen, like degree-holding Chinese, could not be tortured during interrogation.
Moreover, although when bannermen waited to be tried they were held, like
other criminal suspects, in prison, they waited in prisons especially for them.
The following excerpt from a 1727 edict underscores the superior social position of bannermen: "Concerning putting all bannermen who have committed crimes in the prison of the Board of Punishments: the many people who
are in that prison smell foully. As far as imprisoning goes, is it all right to put
[bannermen] together with commoners, serious criminals who are all evil, rebellious, and mean?" Separate prisons were set up in that year for wayward
bannermen, but by 1735 these had filled up with other kinds of undesirables
(eunuchs, bondservants, and slaves convicted of crimes) so that the earlier
problem was repeating itself. The emperor was then asked to order these
types back to the Board of Punishments prison where they belonged, "lessening sickness and discomfort among those Manchus who have committed
crimes and also preventing their contamination by evil servants."[106] In the
provinces, special cells for bannermen were found in the offices of the civil
commissioner.[107] Clearly, Manchus were too good even to share prison cells
with other people.

Their immunity from normal prosecution made it difficult for Chinese
civilians to pursue grievances against Manchus who may have wronged them
and, not surprisingly, led to an attitude of arrogance among bannermen.[108]
One scholar has remarked that garrison compounds could become asylums
for criminals and ne'er-do-wells in the banners.[109] More work is needed to
determine to what extent they actually fulfilled this role. However, we do
find that in a 1737 case in which a Chinese was murdered in the Xi'an Manchu city, it was reported that civilians didn't dare to probe the case and soldiers didn't dare get involved, "so there is no way to enforce the law inside
the Manchu city."[110] A century later, Manchu lawlessness in Taiyuan was
such that the city's Chinese residents called the Manchu city a *Liangshan bo*,
in reference to the hideaway of the outlaw heroes of the novel *Shuihu zhuan*
who always remain beyond the reach of authority.[111]

The problem of conflict between bannermen and civilians was one the court could not and did not ignore. In Beijing, legal disputes between bannermen and Han Chinese (as well as those exclusively between bannermen) were the responsibility of the Gendarmerie or, for those under the authority of the Imperial Household Department, that body.[112] The situation outside the capital was more complicated. Beginning as early as the Shunzhi reign, a special official, the "civil commissioner" (*lishi tongzhi/tungjy*), was appointed to mediate disputes and legal issues between bannermen and Chinese in the provinces. The civil commissioner was technically a local official, not a banner official, and was supposed to work with the garrison commander and local Chinese authorities to resolve disputes. Yet the authority and discretion of the civil commissioner were limited. He was not always included in the investigation and settlement of cases that involved only bannermen, which appear often to have come under the sole jurisdiction of the garrison's senior officers. Also, whatever type of case (whether banner-civilian or intrabanner), when guilty verdicts were reached, the civil commissioner was required to leave enforcement of punishment of bannermen to the garrison commander, with capital cases referred directly to Beijing, not to the provincial governor or governor-general, as was the case with civilian capital offenses.[113]

A Manchu convicted of a crime could always hope that the garrison general or other senior banner official might find a way to protect him. If that did not happen, he could still take comfort in another special privilege—the mandatory lessening of punishments meted out to bannermen. Deference to lofty Manchu sensibilities is the single most persuasive explanation for the more lenient treatment Manchus sometimes received for offenses that brought severe punishments down on Chinese.[114] This bias can in fact be traced to before the conquest. In 1623, after the revolts of Chinese under Jurchen rule, the principle of Manchu-Han equality briefly adopted by Nurhaci was rejected by him for a policy that explicitly favored Manchus: "If one of us Jurchens commits some crime, inquire as to his merits and his service. If there is even the smallest reason, I want you to use that pretext to pardon him."[115] Thus if a punishment called for flogging with a bamboo stave—one hundred blows of which were enough to inflict fatal injuries—a bannerman would instead be whipped, which, in the Qing legal context, was hardly punishment at all.[116] For those in the banners, all sentences involving penal servitude (Ch *tu*) were to be commuted to the wearing of a cangue: one year's servitude translated into twenty days in a cangue, while three years' servitude was twice that. Like whipping, sentencing someone to wear a cangue was more a form of humiliation, though a very heavy cangue could transform it into a kind of punishment.[117] The cangue was also substituted for banishment (Ch *liu*), considered a form of punishment just short of a death sentence.[118] Since banishment (or exile) was a more severe punishment than servitude, a bannermen sentenced to exile would instead be forced to wear the cangue for longer periods, from fifty days (for an exile of two thousand *li*) up to sixty days (for the maximum exile of three thousand *li*). The penalty of military servitude (which made little sense for bannermen anyway) resulted in from seventy to ninety days in the cangue. The rationale for this separate standard of punishment for those in the banners was clearly spelled out:

> The original intent of this law was that from birth banner people are entered into a register and the strong ones serve as soldiers to strengthen and protect the foundation [of the *gurun*]. It is not suitable (Ch *bubian*) to [have them] at a great distance. [In the case of criminals who have] committed crimes [meriting the punishments of] servitude and exile, the cangue shall be directly substituted as punishment. The essence of right is the same.[119]

While only practical reasons are alluded to here, the exemption from flogging, as well as a general exemption from being tattooed,[120] indicates that Manchu pride, as well as national security, guided the development of banner legal privilege.[121] This clarifies why, when certain of the immunities enjoyed by Chinese bannermen were eliminated in 1726, those for Manchu and Mongol bannermen remained untouched.[122]

### Occupational Privileges

The occupational privileges of bannermen were like a two-edged sword. One edge cut in their favor, in that they received far more than their fair share of government posts (military and civil) and enjoyed much better odds than Han Chinese at landing prestigious and powerful appointments.[123] The other edge cut against them, in that they were prevented from seeking any employment outside the banner system or the state bureaucracy. For many years, though, the career benefits for bannermen far outweighed the disadvantages of being in the banners. The state didn't guarantee every male in the banners a job, but it did undertake to guarantee everyone—male and female, young and old, strong and weak—food, shelter, and clothing. After 1687, the state took steps to make it even easier for garrison posts to be inherited by sons, in the understanding that at least one paid position in a family was needed to keep a household going.[124] And since everyone was being supported, it was obviously in the best interest of the state to put as many of those people as possible to work. On more than one occasion positions for bannermen were added, new kinds of posts invented, and other slots expanded for them. In other words, work was *found* for bannermen, if only as a pretext for the payment of a salary. Joblessness was certainly still a problem, however, and not just for the individual. As I will show later, state concern over increasing unemployment among Manchus led in the mid-1700s to the dismissal of many in the banners deemed less deserving of employment in favor of those deemed more worthy, that is, "real" Manchus. The state did not distance itself from total responsibility for Manchu welfare until the 1860s, when it finally granted permission to Manchu bannermen to seek whatever employment they wished. That few took advantage of this opportunity reveals the degree to which the "parasitic" banner lifestyle was by then ingrained.

The ban on nonmilitary occupations for bannermen admitted one major loophole, which was the possibility open to some of entering the civil bureaucracy. In this regard, too, Manchus and others in the banners enjoyed a significant handicap, none more effective than the court's decree that certain posts could be filled only by Manchus. The number of Manchu-only slots in the government was very great, since ethnic dyarchy—a basic principle of central administrative structures—meant that at nearly every level in the Beijing bureaucracy, posts were doubled: for every board there was a Manchu president and a Han president, two Manchu vice-presidents and two Han vice-presidents, and so on. This was meant to make things "fair," but, of course, since there were far, far more Han Chinese in the pool for potential appointments, the quota system worked very much in the favor of Manchus. This was widely recognized during the Qing, one nineteenth-century commentator observing pithily: "The path of promotion for Manchu officials is quicker than for Han officials because they are few and posts reserved for them are many."[125] Further tipping the balance in the Manchus' direction were the large number of positions open to Manchus only that were outside the strict dyarchical system—posts in the Imperial Household Department, the Imperial Clan Court, the Lifanyuan, the secondary capital bureaucracy

in Mukden—and those positions for which the quota was split unequally between Manchu and Han (e.g. scribes, translators) or which for other reasons
(not always named) were set aside for Manchus and Mongols.[126]

As mentioned earlier, the designation of such positions as "Manchu
slots" (Ch *Man-que*) did not mean that they were reserved exclusively for
*Manchu* bannermen, but for Manchu and Mongol bannermen in general
(though in some instances there were separate quotas for the latter). While
there were some set-asides specifically for Chinese bannermen, usually they
had to compete with Han Chinese outside the banners for regular appointments. Furthermore, in the early and middle Qing, as is well known, many
important provincial posts (also outside the dyarchical system) were officially or unofficially reserved for bannermen. For instance, until 1667, Han
Chinese were explicitly forbidden from serving in the posts of provincial
governor and governor-general.[127] After the 1680s, when the appointment
of Chinese bannermen to provincial posts declined, such posts continued to
go mainly to Manchus, particularly in the Northwest, where governorships
(for Shaanxi, Gansu, and Shanxi) were officially Manchu-only posts after
1666, and in the salt administration, the imperial factories, and the customs,
where bannermen (notably bondservants) were frequently employed to the
exclusion of Han Chinese.[128]

The court's pro-Manchu bias in appointments was plainly stated by the
emperor in a 1725 edict to Nian Gengyao in which, after a requisite nod
in the direction of impartiality to all in the banners, the emperor abruptly
switched tone, writing as if in response to a criticism that he had shown undue favor to Chinese bannermen:

> Also, it has been the case up to now that Manchu, Mongol, and Chinese
> bannermen have all been treated as slaves without any distinction. Since
> coming to the throne, when making appointments to the vacancies left
> by the old officials from the times of my khan-father, and following his
> example, I have chosen Manchus. Not only that, what Chinese banner-
> men or Chinese have I put in the job of a Manchu or a Mongol? Besides
> which, in posts such as financial and judicial commissioner of provinces
> such as Shandong, Henan, and Zhejiang, as well as intendant and even
> prefect, which have up to now always been held by Chinese, I have placed
> many Manchus. As for Mongols, I have increased many times the number
> of different positions they may fill [titles omitted]. Originally there were
> no Mongols named to be regiment colonel at a provincial city, and I have
> named several from the Mongol banners. Where the general commander

of the Chakhar banners has always been a Manchu, I have changed this and named Mongols.[129]

In this distribution of privilege one can easily see the operation of ethnic categories which consistently favored Manchus and Mongols over the Han as well as over Chinese bannermen, too. While the above comments were made confidentially, many of these preferences were no secret at the time, since they were written into the dynasty's statutes and were the subject of contemporary commentary, as the notes to this section show.[130] While it appears to have moderated by 1800, the reliance on Manchu-only quotas for so many offices can only be regarded as a reflection of abiding insecurity among the Manchu elite regarding the loyalties and abilities of Han Chinese.

A second significant advantage that Manchu and Mongol bannermen, especially those in the capital, enjoyed over Han Chinese and Chinese bannermen lay in the special examination arrangements made on their behalf. The structure and operation of the examination system that conferred the degrees required to enter government service are in general quite well known and need not be repeated here.[131] In this area of endeavor, Han Chinese held the clear advantage in mastering the classics and writing the elegant essays the examinations required. The evidence on this point is quite stark. Only one of the 108 first-place palace examination honors given during the Qing ever went to a bannerman (a Mongol at that); no bannerman ever finished second, and only two Chinese bannermen managed to cop third-place honors.[132] Had absolutely impartial standards been adhered to, few, if any, bannermen (Manchus or Mongols) would ever have won a metropolitan (Ch *jinshi*) degree in the regular examination, which was the usual minimum for Han Chinese to qualify for service in the top bureaucracy. Yet the court could not abandon the examination standard when it came to the civil service. This presented a dilemma: how to encourage bannermen to acquire the requisite literary expertise to succeed in the examinations without risking the neglect of martial skills? The early Qing court grappled with this question for decades, first permitting, then forbidding bannermen to sit for the regular examinations, and later permitting it again.[133] After the 1730s policy stabilized, but the court never came out enthusiastically in support of bannerman participation in the examinations (even the military examinations), certainly not to the extent it encouraged ambitious Han Chinese to make the examinations their life's goal. Beijing bannermen sat with other candidates from Shuntian prefecture (the prefecture in which the capital was located); but until 1843, garrison bannermen, when they were permitted to take the examinations at all, could not take it locally. They had to travel to Beijing.[134]

If Manchus were to acquire degrees, then, the court was obliged to use other means to facilitate access by Manchus and other bannermen to powerful posts—although even then the results were not especially impressive.[135] One technique was to offer handicaps to bannermen for examinations, sometimes by imposing a quota of successful banner candidates, so that the examination standard was, so to speak, on a "curve," with a certain number of Manchu, Mongol, and Chinese banner winners guaranteed to be produced. These quotas varied considerably, but were never abandoned.[136] Second, early in the Qing, examinations on Chinese texts contained Manchu translations to help exam-takers cope with difficult passages. They were even allowed to write their responses in Manchu. Third, the essential anonymity of examination papers was often badly compromised in the case of bannermen who wrote in Manchu and was soon dropped altogether. After 1669, in order to assure a minimum number of passing examinations, a special notation was made on the examination booklet of candidates writing in Chinese that the candidate was in fact a Manchu or Mongol bannerman. At this time, quotas for Chinese bannermen were diminished, though still maintained.

Another innovation intended to provide bannermen an entree to the bureaucracy was the "translation examination" (*fanyi kaoshi/ubaliyambume simnen*), introduced in 1661. Loosely modeled on the regular examinations, the translation examination was open only to bannermen, and tested their ability to translate between Manchu and Chinese, usually passages from the Chinese classics (which were often simply memorized).[137] After 1722, this "translation examination" resulted in special *shengyuan, juren,* and *jinshi* degrees that qualified the recipient for appointment as a *bithesi*, translator, or secretary. Since, as noted in the previous chapter, a clerkship was an important entry to an official career for Manchus, the translation examinations provided a valuable alternate route to office that was not open to Han Chinese aspirants.[138] However, all bannerman test-takers, whether sitting the civil, military, or translation examinations, had one extra hurdle to clear that Han Chinese were spared—they had to prove their skill at archery, both from a stance and from horseback. As time went on, this initially token requirement became a more formidable obstacle, and strategies to avoid it (e.g., bad eyesight) became increasingly predictable. In 1775, of 125 Manchu bannermen who were to take the metropolitan examinations, 73 claimed to be nearsighted—but at least 20 of these were shown to be shamming.[139]

Of course, not every Manchu who served in a high civil post had a degree. Even Manchu sub-chancellors in the Hanlin academy did not have to have degrees.[140] Many Manchus rose through the Eight Banner hierarchy and bypassed the examination system altogether in forging successful careers. Others distinguished themselves in battle and were rewarded with high posts; in a 1752 edict, the Qianlong emperor made it clear that this was really the key to Manchu success:

> If we are speaking of our dynasty's military policies [Ch *wo guojia yong bing*], from the very beginning up to the present—in pacifying the Dzungars and quelling the Muslim tribes—this has all been accomplished by us Manchus and Solons. Our brave generals and strong soldiers have broken ten thousand *li* through the enemies' lines. The troops of the Green Standard have never been of the slightest use. And when have we ever relied on people who came up through the military examinations? Would we place our leadership and trust in them?[141]

Indeed, throughout the eighteenth century many leading Manchu statesmen (Agūi, Fuheng, Šuhede) built their careers on their military records.

Another advantageous path to office (mentioned earlier) was a position in the imperial vanguard, which gave the diligent and capable soldier opportunity to catch the attention of the emperor himself (as the well-known case of the imperial favorite Hešen proved, good looks didn't hurt, either). It goes without saying that such opportunities were denied Han Chinese.[142] In addition, a disproportionate number of important posts went to well-connected Manchus of high birth. For instance, Agūi, one of the most illustrious personages of the Qianlong era, got his start as a secretary thanks to his eminent father, Akdun, a noted official.[143] Han Chinese from elite families, like the Fang of Tongcheng County, Anhui,[144] enjoyed similar sorts of advantages, of course, but these were almost always overshadowed by those extended to members of the larger Manchu families, particularly those families blessed with inheritable positions, which were unknown among the Chinese. This aspect of their access to power was one important way in which Manchu social structures ran directly opposite to the dominant ideology of the later Chinese empire, and is a reminder of the sort of irreconcilable tensions that the grafting of the Eight Banners onto the imperial institution introduced in Qing society.

A third and final career advantage for bannermen was that the mourning period they were required to observe was considerably shorter than for Han Chinese. When a parent died, the filial duties demanded of a Han official required him to resign his post and return to his ancestral home for an extended period—nominally three years, but in reality twenty-seven months. A bannerman, in contrast, was enjoined to observe mourning by cutting off his queue, removing rings and tassels, and remaining sequestered at home one hundred days (at first this was only one month), during which time he was not to shave his face or head.[145] Significantly, bannermen were not required to officially resign their positions, but could simply entrust duties to someone else for a little while.[146] At the same time, in concession to the "universal norm" (Ch *tianxia wanshi fashi*) of twenty-seven months, bannermen officials were excused from court rituals for this length of time (not counting intercalary months), during which they were also not supposed to engage in the Manchu pastimes of shooting and riding, participate in the examinations, or be put up for promotion.[147] Marriages were also forbidden during this time. The rules were originally somewhat different for garrison bannermen, who, like Han officials, were relieved of their posts and ordered to report to Beijing (the official home for all bannermen) for a full twenty-seven months of mourning.[148] Because capital bannermen (and all bannermen from the second half of the eighteenth century) did not have to give up their posts, a death in the family did not necessarily result in a temporary derailing of a Beijing bannerman's career or in any serious loss of income. In terms of one's individual prospects (as opposed to the group balance between Manchus and Han, which would be maintained), this was a real advantage. Han officials frequently viewed the three-year mourning obligation as extremely burdensome and for this reason often sought to be excused from the full term of mourning and allowed to stay on in their posts (Ch *duo qing*). Some even tried to hide the fact of a parent's decease, an offense for which the dynasty instituted stiff penalties.[149]

The different standard for Manchu mourning was explained in various ways. Early in the dynasty, the rationale was the same as that for not exiling bannermen: it was simply inconvenient to require banner officials anywhere in the bureaucracy to leave their posts because of grief.[150] Later explanations claimed it was necessary to avoid undue delays in official business, "which, because bannermen are so few, would inevitably result if all kept a three-year mourning."[151] One guesses that the relatively short supply of literate and capable banner officials made it difficult to find replacements. A 1749 edict suggested as much, at the same time pointing out that their social status imposed different obligations upon Manchus and Mongols than it did upon the Chinese: "But Manchus and Mongols are not as numerous as Han; besides, banner officials should not be allowed to remain idle and not perform public business anyway."[152] Another recognized problem with forcing bannermen to observe extended mourning was that officials dependent upon government salaries to maintain their households would be put in difficult straits if forced to give those salaries up for such a long time. One cannot help but wonder whether this was less true for Han officials, who may or may not have had substantial property holdings in their provincial hometowns. In any case, the mourning policy for bannermen illustrates how a culture of dependency was fostered among Manchus. Filiality was fine, but the services of bannermen to the dynasty were more important. After all, bannermen lived for the dynasty: how could they not work? In recognition of this quid pro quo, the dynasty made extra allowances it did not make to Han that kept a bannerman's career moving along and the silver and grain coming.

### The Gulf of Privilege

As the preceding sections have shown, distinguishing factors of banner life in the first century or so of Qing rule included a marked military tenor and a considerable degree of state economic support. Until the nineteenth century, bannermen could always count on their silver salaries to be dispensed every month; if they managed their households sensibly, the amount of grain and silver they received was sufficient to provide food for the table. They had little to complain about, and few complaints were heard.[153] Even when their stipends covered so few expenses that it could no longer be said that bannermen were as a group economically ahead (many in fact living in poverty), their dependent status continued to define them as a group. To paraphrase Franz Michael, even if he couldn't shoot an arrow straight, the bannerman would always have his bowl of rice.[154] It would in time likely double as a begging bowl, but it identified him no less surely for that.

By the late Qing, in fulfillment of Ibn Khaldūn's ironic prophecy, the traits that came to denote the declension of the Manchus were precisely those that grew to identify them. Far from being envied for their easy life (though the Manchu elite remained very well off), the common view saw banner people as poor and proud. The arrogance and indolence induced by this culture of entitlement was memorably described by one late-nineteenth-century Western observer:

> Of the Manchus, as distinguished from the Chinese, I can only speak touching those who inhabit Peking, Canton, Foochow, Nanking, and Chinkiang [Zhenjiang]. Except in the case of Peking, where the Manchu and Chinese population is so mixed as to be indistinguishable to any but the most observant eye, the Manchus are all "bannermen"; that is, a privileged caste of soldiers, having their families with them, living in cantonments amongst a people speaking (except in the case of Nanking and Chinkiang) a totally different dialect. Their life is a haughty and exclusive one, and what natural characteristics they may have are inevitably colored by the nature of their surroundings, just as a Prussian garrison in Schleswig, or a Russian garrison in Poland, however well disciplined, would inevitably give itself the airs of a conqueror. Of all these Manchus I should say their chief characteristic was a combination of laziness and pride; but wherever placed with foreigners in the relation of pupil to teacher . . . their bearing is distinctly less priggish and more gentlemanly than that of Chinese.[155]

Here again we encounter an Englishman's view, and must consider whether Chinese might have seen things this way. One suspects that if this facet of banner life was so palpable to an outsider, it could hardly have eluded the notice of Han locals, particularly as banner garrisons were the object of brutal attacks in the Chinese civil war of the 1860s. On the other hand, there is also evidence that the British tended to see the Manchu situation in China as comparable to their own situation in India, raising difficult questions as to the nature of their commentary on the position of the Manchus as minority rulers and the attitude of the Chinese toward them.[156] Certainly, similar statements from Chinese accusing the Manchus of sloth and arrogance are almost impossible to find until the very end of the dynasty, since a Han Chinese who expressed such an opinion in writing would have simultaneously been penning his death sentence. Most sedition against the Manchus was conveyed indirectly; the only Chinese who dared commit such a crime openly were rebels like the Taiping, who were not afraid of being accused of heterodoxy.

Nevertheless, even if the resentment they stirred was of necessity muted, it does seem that the privileges of banner life were indeed well known. That the occupational privileges of bannermen gave them—and Manchu bannermen from Beijing above all—a huge edge over Han Chinese in securing offi-

cial posts was beyond dispute even in the Qing. There was no other explanation for the clear predominance of Manchus in virtually all the top ranks
of central and provincial government, a predominance that was most pronounced during the first two hundred years of the dynasty, but which, even
after averaging in the last seventy years of the Qing (when Han Chinese made
up for lost time), never faded completely.[157] Awareness of this advantage,
whether it was viewed as privilege rightly due the conquering race or benefits unjustly squandered on spendthrift idlers, went far in defining the gulf
that persisted between Manchu and Han.

The preceding discussion of banner status has concentrated primarily on
what it conferred, but it is well to keep in mind that the "special treatment"
awarded under the banner system had its negative side. Banner status imposed many limitations on people. It confined the choice of occupation to a
very narrow range; it limited choice of residence; it prohibited people from
buying and selling property if they wished; as shown in Chapter 5, it even
limited their freedom in choosing a spouse. Being in the banners set people
apart in a position of de jure superiority that was for many a constrained
position of de facto inferiority. This limitation, linked with the declining
value of court support for those without such jobs, has been justifiably cited
by historians who have condemned the banner system as restrictive, a gilded
cage from which most of the gilding had fallen by the later Qing; the collapse of the banner system at the end of the Qing has thus been likened to a
"liberation" of banner people who at last enjoyed the same freedoms as
other Chinese citizens.[158] As we shall see, the court recognized the negative
effects of banner restrictions by the early 1700s when reports of poverty in
the banners first became common. But this did little to loosen the hold of the
banner system on individual lives or to bring major improvements in the levels of support people could expect. This evidence suggests strongly that the
banner system was not just about privileges and preferences, or even mainly
about these, but about upholding the boundaries that separated the Manchus and their allies from the Han Chinese and maintaining a difference between conqueror and conquered. The contumely and rancor bred by the unequal distribution of economic, legal, and occupational benefits produced a
consistent, if muted, tension throughout the Qing period at both official and
popular levels, fundamentally influencing the nature of relations between
Manchus and Han during the Qing.

CHAPTER FIVE

# Among the Nikan

Answering the basic question of how well Manchus and Han Chinese—that is, the *Nikan*[1]—got along is not an easy task. But it is an unavoidable issue in the study of Manchu history because in significant measure Manchu ethnicity, and, for that matter, Han ethnicity—was constructed along the boundaries and in the relations between Manchus and Han.

At the outset, it should be said that Manchu-Han antagonism does not leap out of the historical record and that it does not seem that late imperial Chinese society was wholly riven by ethnic strife.[2] To the extent this is true, its ability to accommodate ethnic plurality within a single order must be accounted one of the successes of the Qing political system. But there is also plenty of evidence to suggest that a certain degree of ethnic tension, at least between Manchu and Han, persisted throughout the Qing. Given the obvious differences between the conquerors and the conquered—not just of social organization and legal status, but of language, dress, and religion[3]—difficulties were predictable, especially in the very early years of the Qing, when brutal depredations by Manchus (often referred to derogatorily as "Tartars" [*dazi/dase*] in contemporary documents) were frequent. After all, one reason that walls to separate bannermen from Chinese were built in the first place was to keep the differences between them and the Han from exacerbating social tension.

The conqueror/conquered dichotomy never faded away entirely: it never could, as long as the primary structure in which it was embedded—the Eight Banners—remained in place, and never would, so long as ethnic sovereignty figured in the calculus of Manchu power. Hence, even when the Manchus had already been living in China for two generations and more, and their many overt differences with the Han had gradually become muted, ethnic antagonism remained fairly common. Exactly how common is very hard to say, since assuredly not every incident of Manchu-Han conflict was reported, and finding such incidents in the documents is largely a matter of luck. As mentioned in the Introduction, recent studies of eighteenth- and nineteenth-century politics suggest that mistrust between Manchu and Han at elite levels continued to influence national affairs throughout the dynasty. Though the issues involved in such cases must sometimes be inferred, since open discussion of the ethnic question was extremely risky, a belief in Manchu hypersensitivity at the top is not entirely without foundation.[4]

A general picture of a steady but manageable degree of conflict in society generally is confirmed by a random sampling from the ten-year period between 1725 and 1735, eighty or so years after the conquest, where we find at least six incidents that were reported all the way to the imperial court. These included a case involving Jingzhou Manchu bannermen who regularly got drunk and then went to quarrel with the Chinese in the other half of town;[5] the Manchus at Ningxia who did both their drinking *and* their fighting in the Chinese city;[6] the brutal beating of a Chinese civilian at the Luowenyu garrison (just outside Beijing) by a couple of Manchu captains who found him dumping oil onto the street;[7] the murder of a Xi'an civilian by an unknown bannerman who escaped back to the safety of the garrison compound;[8] the Taiyuan Manchu bannermen who occasionally charged into people's courtyards, creating a stir as they exchanged insults with the women of the house;[9] and the Tianjin Manchu soldiers who, dissatisfied with matters relating to the management of garrison-owned property outside the city, massed outside the civil commissioner's office and attacked the county magistrate, wounding him with a knife.[10] The foregoing are mainly incidents reported on in palace memorials; a systematic search of Board of Punishments routine memorials would almost certainly turn up many more cases.

In arguing that Manchu-Han tension was a permanent undercurrent in Qing politics and society, I by no means wish to suggest that ethnicity is the only category of meaningful social analysis in the Qing. Rather, I see Manchu-Han difference, and ethnicity generally, as but one key to interpreting political and social conflict under the Manchus. Beginning with a survey of the Qing ideology of ethnic harmony, then, this chapter compares the notion of a single family of Manchu and Han with the realities of Manchu-Han relations in Beijing and the provinces. I show that the privileged nature of banner life and the structures upon which Manchu-Han interaction were based produced friction, both among the elite, where it principally took the form of political factionalism, and among the non-elite, where conflict was most common in economic contexts. Ordinary Han Chinese were often vulnerable to Manchu predation, though we find that Manchus as a group also ended up being preyed on by the Chinese, especially in Beijing.

## THE MANCHU-HAN "FAMILY"

Ethnic harmony generally, and equality between Manchu and Han especially, was a fundamental and oft-promoted postulate of Qing rule.[11] Manchu rulers required the loyalty and services of talented Han Chinese and stressed the opportunities open to them in the civil bureaucracy. Moreover, because the Manchu emperors consistently positioned themselves as universal monarchs, ruling impartially over *tianxia*, they could not openly pursue policies of ethnic favoritism. The emperor had to be seen as being nonpartisan; Nurhaci understood this when he promulgated policies of cohabitation and equal privilege in the 1620s. A 1635 pronouncement elucidating the official Qing position that ethnic strife could only be dealt with effectively by applying justice equally across the board shows that Hong Taiji had mastered this rhetoric, too:

> The khan spoke: "We do not distinguish between Jurchen, Mongol, and Han, or between old and new, but have treated all the same. When any person fights with another, both parties are judged according to the law. In times when Han Chinese fight with Jurchen and Mongols, everyone suffers the punishment of beating. In this way, the heavy [force of the] law is demonstrated upon their arrest to ignorant and confused people who do not obey the dynasty's way of governing."[12]

The same ideal was carried over after 1644 in the face of self-evident ethnic discord. Soon after the conquest (and not for the last time), Dorgon, regent for the Shunzhi emperor, stressed that, "The empire is a single whole. There are no distinctions between Manchus and Hans."[13]

Thereafter in its propaganda the court regularly emphasized the evenness of the playing field and appeared to take the ideal of nondiscrimination seriously, creating, as already seen, a system of "dyarchy," or joint rule, whereby parallel offices for Manchu and Han were found throughout the metropolitan bureaucracy (though not the provinces). A frequently heard refrain was that "Manchus and Han are as one family" (Ch *Man-Han yijia*), a mantra that, with different variations, came into use as early as May 1645:

"Our nation [Ch *guojia*—i.e., the Qing] has borne the Mandate of Heaven and brought order to the Central Plain. Manchu and Han officials and civilians are all as one family."[14] Two years later, the same phrase cropped up in a vehement denial of imperial favoritism: "We have brought the people out from flood and flame and unified all under heaven. Manchus and Han are as one family; both alike enjoy tranquillity. What is this nonsense about discrimination?"[15] In a question put to those sitting for the palace examination in 1649, the emperor at once insisted that there was no discrimination (Ch *yishi*) between Manchus and Han, while at the same time asking how to "join Manchu and Han into one body and cause their minds and energies to unite harmoniously and continuously."[16] When in 1655 the emperor again insisted that "all Manchu and Han people are our children," the slogan was modified to include the familiar Chinese trope of the people of the empire as his own offspring.[17]

The Kangxi emperor issued at least twenty such similar edicts contending that the court regarded Manchu and Han impartially.[18] In his study of a famous 1713 sedition case, Pierre-Henri Durand argued that the Kangxi emperor went out of his way to balance decisions, one time favoring Han, the next time favoring Manchus, so that neither side could accuse him of prejudice.[19] Of course, this is not the same thing as impartiality and only proves that ethnicity was indeed an important element in court politics. The question of bias stubbornly remained an issue at the Yongzheng court. The emperor was supposed once to have expressed doubts about the qualifications of a certain man for a high post in the censorate because he was Han, when one of his most trusted advisors, Ortai, challenged him, saying, "My scheme for attracting people to serve the court is to not tediously distinguish between Manchu and Han." The emperor, whose thinking on some matters could be surprisingly open, went along with this,[20] also authoring several edicts in which he professed to see Manchus, Chinese bannermen, and Han Chinese as a unified whole, "with no differences made between them."[21] His 1729 dismissal of charges of bias said simply, "If there were discrimination between Manchu and Han there would then be discord between them, mutual suspicion and contempt. What sort of way would that be to rule?"[22]

By pointing out the philosophical incompatibility of these two propositions—the Qing claim to rule harmoniously and the charge that the dynasty practiced ethnic discrimination—the emperor obviously felt he had answered his critics decisively. It goes without saying, however, that governments undertake actions all the time that are at odds with their stated ideals;[23] and imperial protests notwithstanding, Manchu-Han equality was largely a myth.[24] Manchu and Han, that is, were not "one family": Manchus lived in separate ghettos administered by the Eight Banners, enjoyed a special relationship with the emperor, were significantly privileged over Han in terms of entry and promotion in officialdom, systematically received all manner of financial and material bonuses, and enjoyed special legal preferences. All of these privileges contradicted the constant assertion that the emperor viewed everyone equally. The vaunted notion of dyarchy, too, was fraught with internal contradictions. Many scholars have pointed to the inequalities in the system at its creation, to the pivotal role played in the 1600s by Chinese bannermen and Chinese bondservants, and the general tendency of Manchus to occupy higher bureaucratic ground that was effectively institutionalized with the creation of the Grand Council.[25] Beyond this, however, we can see the contradiction at the very heart of the idea of dyarchy, which is that the emergence of such a structure in Qing politics was itself a tacit admission that Manchu and Han interests differed. For if there were *really* no difference between Manchu and Han, why would each require separate representation in government councils? Indeed, that dyarchy was a myth was abundantly clear even in the Qing. As shown in Chapter 4, everyone was aware that Manchus had a huge advantage in making an official career. Writing in the eighteenth century, historian Zhao Yi noted that power in the central bureaucracy always ended up concentrated in the hands of one person; he stopped just short of saying that these were usually Manchu hands, but Beatrice Bartlett has demonstrated that this was in fact the case for most, if not all, of the Qing.[26]

There was thus a tension between the two fundamental truths of the Qing political world, namely that (a) bannermen, and specifically Manchus, enjoyed a certain superiority over Han Chinese, and (b) one had to play along with the official denial of this superiority (at least most of the time) in the name of Manchu-Han unity. The ideal of "family unity" received a good degree of lip service, but in reality the Manchus were *primi inter pares*—not for nothing did the emperor always speak of "Manchu and Han officials" (*Man-Han guanyuan/Manju Nikan hafasa*) in that order and *only* that order. Those suspected of challenging the Manchu place at the top of the heap —people such as Chen Mingxia, Dai Mingshi, and others—were efficiently eliminated. These notorious cases show what could happen when the dynasty's insecurity trumped its usually circumspect politics. They stand out not because they were exceptions to Manchu-Han camaraderie but because they were exceptions to the usual policy of not airing the "family" laundry in public.[27] Nor were all such cases given a high profile. A 1743 complaint by a Chinese court official that Manchus monopolized the upper echelons of office earned him immediate demotion.[28]

It is thus all the more important to point out that the actual supremacy of Manchus was not trumpeted in the same way as the "Manchu-Han family." On the rare occasions when it came up for discussion, it was defended on the grounds that the Manchus had contributed more to the stabilization of the empire than anyone else and that their sacrifices deserved special compensation. This was the gist of a 1653 memorial by Hong Chengchou, a prominent Chinese bannerman and minister: "The emperor does not distinguish Manchu from Han, but treats both as one body. Yet some Han officials impatiently raise objections. If [one were to] speak of the logic [of things], the privileging (Ch *shouchong*) of Manchus would in fact be appropriate."[29] The emperor expanded on this same rationalization a couple of years later, when he defended the harsh punishment of escaped Chinese slaves from their Manchu masters and asked his Han ministers to look at things from the Manchu perspective: "Since the Manchus rescued the Han from their troubles [i.e., the peasant rebellions of the late Ming], the Han should understand the Manchus' mentality (Ch *xin*)."[30] Long after the conquest, similar rationalizations for the privileges enjoyed by Manchus were still in circulation: "Bannermen and Chinese are not the same. Chinese have no burdens. They can obstinately stick together. But bannermen, because their positions in the banners are so demanding, have many responsibilities among their own clans. Even when they finish serving in official posts they can't help but having to shoulder other business."[31] While the Yongzheng emperor cited this point of view in order to criticize it, his failure to essentially alter the privileged position of Manchu and other bannermen in Qing society shows that, like any good politician, he did not always believe his own rhetoric.

From the very beginning, then, the overt ideal of impartial universality was subverted by a covert recognition of ethnic singularity. The court was forced to negotiate between these two extremes, since it could not afford to alienate either Manchu bannermen or Han literati. In steering a course between the "Manchu *gurun*" and the "Manchu-Han family," the court was navigating the waters between the Scylla of Confucian cultural inclusivity and the Charybdis of Manchu ethnic exclusivity. To the extent that one can observe these competing ideals at work in relations between Manchu and Han, the "Manchu question" figures in any account of Qing politics and society.

## FAMILY QUARRELS

If the notion that "Manchus and Han are one family" was a myth of political convenience, what were relations between these groups really like? Looking first at elites in the capital, it seems fair to say that the ethnic divisiveness dyarchy was supposed to mask in fact manifested itself in many quotidian ways, such as who got to stand in front of whom in court ceremonies (Manchus, of course, got the front-row seats most of the time).[32] One type of daily tension concerned the use of language at court. Early in the Qing, the simple lack of a shared language was a major obstacle to communication. Many high Manchu officials were unable to speak Chinese and the number of Chinese officials fluent in Manchu was even more limited (more on this is said in Chapter 7). The appointment of Chinese bannermen and translators at different levels was supposed to solve this problem, yet at least some officials recognized that the language barrier could not be overcome so easily: "From the beginning the goal of Manchus and Han has been to join their strength and work with one mind. Manchus and Han are one family, and all think of repaying their lord['s favor]. Still, differences in language and writing make communication difficult, and differences of opinion are unavoidable."[33] In these situations, Manchus dominated to the obvious disadvantage of Han officials, who were essentially prevented from joining the debate. This problem was the subject of a 1660 exchange in which it was revealed that during important discussions of state policy the opinions of Han officials were not taken into consideration because those officials, who often were not even seated in the same room with princes, *beile*, and Manchu high officials, were reticent to interject their own views. As a compromise, Manchu officials proposed that each side prepare a written draft commenting on the issue at hand; but when it turned out that no Chinese draft was forthcoming, the Manchu draft was simply translated into Chinese and made the de facto Chinese draft. After a month the emperor closed the matter by denouncing the very idea of a "Manchu draft" and a "Chinese draft" (he used the terms *Qing gao* and *Han gao* in Chinese; in Manchu these were spoken of as a *Manju bithe g'ao* and *Nikan bithe g'ao*). Everyone should write his own views down and have them heard, he said, and Manchus and Han should discuss everything jointly.[34] Meanwhile, Chinese officials cut out of the decision-making process found ways to get revenge by writing lukewarm eulogies meant to honor meritorious Manchu officials who had passed away, reserving their most fulsome praise for departed Han officials.[35]

Linguistic difficulties and ethnic oppositionism persisted into the eighteenth century. The practice of "Manchu drafts" and "Chinese drafts," for example, continued into the eighteenth century. By then, however, as a 1729 report noted, bilingual deliberations at the ministerial level had again given way to monolingual debates, this time in Chinese. Now it was Manchu officials who were at a disadvantage at meetings of the Nine Ministers:[36] "Only the Chinese version is read, while the Manchu drafts are not read aloud. Among the Manchu officials are some who, though they can read a few Chinese characters, do not understand the meaning of the Chinese [draft]. Since they don't understand, it's hard for them to speak or put their own thoughts together."[37] Moreover, discussions over state policy were frequently carried on according to ethnic factions, with Han lined up on one side and Manchus on the other, each presenting separate recommendations to the throne. Ninety years earlier, the Shunzhi emperor had found this development quite alarming, but it was still going on.[38] A junior vice-president of the Board of Rites reported in 1723 on the uncomfortable tension at ministerial meetings:

> When the officials of the different boards and offices assemble before Your Majesty to present recommendations, they line up according to official rank, with Manchus and Han mixed together. There is no division of Manchus and Han into two separate groups. [However,] these days when the Nine Ministers gather in a meeting, Manchu and Chinese officials consistently line up on two different sides and oppose the other in discussions. On every single issue, if the Manchu officials' side is not pushing the Chinese officials, then it's the Chinese officials' side that is spying on the Manchu officials.

The official (a Manchu) urged that Manchu-Han distinctions should not be tolerated at this important level of government, reasoning that "the emperor's favor is shown each alike" and, predictably, because "all in the four seas are as one family."[39]

Other anecdotal evidence—such as the Qianlong emperor's 1738 complaint that partisanship dividing Manchus and Han Chinese would bring ruin to the country,[40] his 1740 criticism of a Manchu court faction centered on Ortai and a Han faction centered on Zhang Tingyu,[41] and his 1768 lament that administration was still plagued by lack of cooperation between Manchu and Han staff[42]—indicates that ethnic difference never ceased to matter among elites. Although in tracing the shift in Grand Council personnel over the eighteenth century, Beatrice Bartlett found that the early preponderance of Manchu officials gave way by the end of the eighteenth century to a better balance of Manchu and Chinese,[43] the comments of outside observers caution against assuming that ethnic factionalism was a thing of the past even in the 1790s. To quote once again the alert Lord Macartney: "Although the Emperor, as the father of his people, affects and professes impartiality, and wishes to have it understood that he makes no distinction between Tartars and Chinese, neither Tartars nor Chinese are imposed upon by the pretence."[44] Echoing Zhao Yi, Macartney claimed further that Qing dyarchy was really a fraud and ethnic harmony a sham:

> In all the tribunals of justice and finance, in all the courts of civil or military administration, an equal number of Tartar assessors is indispensably necessary to be present, in order to watch over and control the others. A Chinese may preside at the Board, and pronounce the opinion, but the prompter and manager is a Tartar who directs and governs the performers. . . . The predominance of the Tartars and the Emperor's partiality to them are the common subject of conversation among the Chinese whenever they meet together in private, and the constant theme of their discourse.

The general failure of Westerners to observe this feature of Qing government owed, in his opinion, to the "vulgar mistake that the Tartars had indiscriminately and sincerely adopted all the maxims, principles and customs of the Chinese, and that the two nations were now perfectly amalgamated and incorporated together."[45]

Since Macartney could hardly have known about the operation of court councils from his own first-hand observation, he must have gathered this information in conversations with Chinese officials. One incident he witnessed, however, on the way to Rehe, confirmed for him the tension that ran through Manchu-Han relations:

> The Embassy had now passed the Chinese wall when a Tartar, one of the attendants, was ordered to be punished by some of the Chinese mandarins for misbehavior. The man made a vigorous resistance, and exclaimed in a loud voice that no Chinese had a right to inflict punishment on a Tartar after having passed the Great Wall.

A second incident that took place later on the same journey was described by Macartney's companion in a way that demonstrates an awareness of the rivalry between Manchu and Han:

> An instance of claimed or affected superiority of Tartar chiefs over Chinese of equal rank occurred on his Excellency's [i.e., Macartney's] arrival at the next stage; where, receiving a complimentary visit from a Tartar military mandarin, Van-ta-zhin [i.e., Wang Wenxiong, a Chinese military official assigned to escort Macartney] scarcely ventured to sit down in his presence.[46]

These are all signs that tensions remained high between Han Chinese and Manchus at the Qing court throughout the eighteenth and into the nineteenth century.

The relationship between Manchu and Han elites in the provinces is much less well understood, and seems to have been less problematic, but this might simply be because provincial government itself has not been as carefully examined. Or the apparent, relative ease of their interactions might have been because there was no fixed arena of interchange between Manchu and Han officials on the provincial level, no single "court" which could serve to focus latent ethnic hostility. It should also be remembered that provincial government tended to be divided into two spheres, with Manchus frequently serving at the top level, as governors-general, governors, and financial commissioners, but only very rarely at the lower level, as prefects and magistrates, which were by and large the preserve of Han officials (Manchus were hardly ever appointed as magistrates).[47] This remained true in the Qianlong reign, when the proportion of Manchus in the upper provincial bureaucracy—where there was no dyarchy—actually increased over what it had been in the Yongzheng reign (mainly at the expense of Chinese bannermen), with Manchu officials occupying 38 percent of provincial posts, and 58 percent of governor-generalships and governorships.[48] As suggested earlier, senior provincial officials often found that in dealing with each other they were dealing with other bannermen, thus reducing opportunities for conflict here.

ETHNIC TRANSACTIONS

In non-elite Manchu-Han relations, it was not politics, but commerce, that engendered the greatest strife, both in Beijing and in the provincial garrisons. Despite the fairly strict separation of Manchu and Chinese cities, contact between bannermen and Chinese was never completely prohibited. When they did come together, most commonly it was in order to buy and sell. Banner households constituted a sizable market, particularly as they were forbidden from creating competition by going into business themselves. Even when, as during the implementation of the "interest-bearing silver" program (see Chapter 8), bannermen did open their own shops, Chinese-run establishments do not seem to have suffered very much. The existence of the banner market was often seen as a positive factor in the local economy. This was the opinion expressed by the Yongzheng emperor as he rebutted the objection of a key advisor, Li Wei, concerning the foundation of a banner garrison at Qingzhou: "If one says that the place is poverty-stricken and that there are not enough merchants, then by founding a large settlement and garrisoning many soldiers there, traders will naturally be attracted."[49] There were, it seems, at least some compensating factors for the dislocation brought about by the arrival of bannermen in the locale.

Economic exchange between Manchus and Han took several forms. In the capital, Chinese merchants rented space from bannermen landlords in the Inner City where they sold all manner of food and merchandise; at dusk they would close up their shops and return to their dwellings in the Outer City.[50] They purveyed goods to bannermen also at temple markets, where, for example, many of Beijing's Manchus bought their arrows.[51] At Nanjing, peasants came to the garrison gates to sell firewood. At Zhapu, Han merchants operated many kinds of businesses inside the Manchu city, and the Fuzhou garrison collected over one thousand taels of rent annually from Chinese merchants who took 690 storefronts in the Manchu city.[52] At Guangzhou, as in Beijing, the temples inside the garrison compound were frequently places where Chinese sold to bannermen. And Ningxia Manchus sank so low as to even rent their horses from enterprising Chinese.[53]

The most important economic dealing between Manchus and Chinese was the trade in surplus grain that bannermen sold to Chinese rice merchants. While technically illegal, this practice went on openly and was generally officially tolerated. According to an edict of 1710, banner households were free to sell their unneeded grain at market prices, and before long the rice trade between bannermen and Chinese merchants was recognized as instrumental in regulating the price and flow of grain in the capital.[54] The need for cash, however, meant that some of the grain being sold was not exactly "surplus" and that some households found themselves running out of food before the next distribution. The Yongzheng emperor was the first to criticize the shortsighted selling of rice by bannermen, but because a total ban on the sale of banner grain would have been both undesirable and unenforceable, he went only as far as "forbidding" them to sell so much that they ran out of food.[55] The emperor also tried another regulatory mechanism by instituting official Eight Banner grain-purchasing offices in 1728, which bought grain from bannermen at fixed prices and then resold it to them later in the year at a smaller mark-up than Chinese merchants. Astute business practices enabled the Chinese to survive even this challenge, and the offices were shut down in 1752. Other attempts were made in the late 1730s, with limited results, to restrict the amount of rice that could be bought up by merchants who sought to limit supply and inflate prices. In the end, banner grain in the capital became just another commodity, albeit one of unusual significance in Beijing's food-supply system.[56]

Much of the capital grain trade was in the hands of Shandong rice dealers, who had been authorized in 1735 to open eighty rice-polishing shops (Ch *duifang*) in the Inner City (ten per banner) to cater to the banner clientele.[57] These merchants were well known among Manchus for their ingenious ways of getting the better of bannermen. As recounted by an elderly Manchu around the year 1800:

> The people from Shandong who ran the rice-pounding shops in every *hutong* in the capital took the fine rice collected by bannermen every season to "refine" it, always giving [back] four quarts for every five they got. They really made a killing on that. They took advantage of the opportunity during the day when their long-suffering banner friends were away on business and there were few people at home [to deliver rice]. If a Shandong man came with the rice he deliberately gave just a little bit less. If you said to him that the amount wasn't enough and complained, not only would he tell you he wasn't giving you any more but he would get very pushy and start shouting, saying, "If you want to eat it, eat it. If you don't want it, pay me and I'll send someone over with your original [i.e., unpolished] rice." Since there was nothing we could do, we suffered through it.[58]

Because bannermen relied on these merchants to buy their surplus and to sell to them when they needed more, they were not in a position to risk offending them.

Shandong grain merchants were not the only ones who provided services to (and took advantage of) bannermen. Chinese proprietors of restaurants, theaters, and teahouses—which were legally allowed to operate only outside the confines of the Inner City—were already numerous in the early eighteenth century. Bannermen were their steady customers, and more than one capital official grumbled that, "among Manchu officers and soldiers are some disreputable types who take their salaries and with no planning [for the future] heedlessly go drinking and eating in the shops outside the city."[59] No manner of threat from the throne could make them desist, and though blame for the most part was put on lax supervision by officers and a growing love of luxury, some Manchus held the Chinese responsible for the worsening state of affairs:

> From all directions come Chinese drifting, looking to make a profit; they open all kinds of shops at the places where the soldiers gather daily, on streets both large and small; they entice naive bannermen into their shops, and give them wine and liquor to drink, meat and victuals to eat, all on credit. Even if they are too afraid to go to the brothels, they leave their children and women at home and go out with no-good servants looking to please their palates. Once they have found a place, they go in and eat and drink to their heart's content, again, on credit. . . . When the day comes to collect their salaries, if they are even a little bit short, "businessmen" go to their gates and doors, making them ashamed and embarrassed. Screaming and raging, they demand [their money]. The soldier has not the courage to resist, and doesn't make it home with his pay. If he has given it all and still doesn't have enough, then these "businessmen" wait for them in the street, strip them of their clothes and steal their weapons and gear. At this point, a soldier is no longer able to work.[60]

The blame put here on Chinese Shylocks for the economic and moral downfall of virtuous Manchus represented the realization of the worst fears of the Manchu elite concerning what Kuhn called the "theft of Manchu virtue"— with the difference that not just the indirect effects of Han decadence, but their direct economic exploitation, was responsible for it.[61]

Outside Beijing, bannermen and Chinese merchants at the Hangzhou and Jingzhou garrisons (and probably other garrisons as well) also engaged in the grain trade. Compared to Beijing, trade was of uncertain scale, since garrison bannermen received so much of their salaries in silver. Still, enough was changing hands at the Hangzhou garrison for lieutenant general Bašinu to propose establishing a banner granary there that would act in the same way as those in Beijing to protect bannermen from being taken advantage of by profiteering Chinese merchants.[62]

If bannermen were at times victimized in their commercial dealings with the Han, at other times it was the Han Chinese who suffered at the hands of unscrupulous bannermen. Indeed, many, if not most, of the disputes between bannermen and Chinese at the garrisons occurred at the marketplace or in the course of business transactions. Monitoring this interaction was a regular part of the duty of garrison officers. A Xi'an general in the late 1600s wrote, "When buying and selling various things to and from commoners I take strict care that there is no using of force [by bannermen]."[63] Reports of Manchus terrorizing the marketplace began early in the Qing: "The tyrannizing of local markets and trade by aggressive Manchus should be prohibited, as should the forcible purchase of goods by Manchu servants," read one proclamation of the Shunzhi court.[64] The same topic came up twenty years later during an imperial audience with a newly appointed Hangzhou lieutenant general: "It has come to my attention," began the emperor, "that the officers and soldiers at the Hangzhou garrison are extremely oppressive and harsh on the local merchants." The officer was instructed to rein in the soldiers at Hangzhou and to pass along similar instructions to the general at the Jingkou garrison, where the emperor had heard such troubles were even worse.[65] Whatever his efforts, they were of minimal avail. One unhappy Hangzhou resident was quoted as saying in 1689 that "ever since there have been garrison soldiers here, life for ordinary people has been turned upside down. There's just no peace anywhere!"[66]

In consequence, cautions to banner garrison officers to keep peace between bannermen and Han Chinese locals are seen time and again in edicts and rescripts.[67] Like their fellows at Hangzhou, soldiers at the Jingzhou garrison were ordered not to "disrupt and seize" at the markets and their officers cautioned not to let them invent pretexts to "disturb and oppress" the populace.[68] Scarcely a month after the meeting with the Hangzhou lieutenant general mentioned above, the Kangxi emperor sent an edict to the Fuzhou garrison general noting the long history of unrestrained misbehavior of Chinese bannermen, particularly with regard to their taking over markets, demanding things on credit, and buying an excessive number of slaves.[69] As if to underscore the emperor's point, the day after this edict was issued, a report was received from the governor-general of Zhejiang that people living in the north part of Hangzhou were refusing to open for business to protest the bullying tactics of neighboring bannermen: "The people are being forced by local toughs in collusion with bannermen to make

loans . . . and cannot live in peace. When they went to complain at the yamen the next day, bannerman Wang Heshang along with others led several
hundred people [against them], cursing and doing violence, breaking apart
the roof of the [intendant's] sedan chair." The massing of banner soldiers
and their attack on the intendant was condemned and the emperor was
asked to order the garrison general to hand over Wang Heshang and others
to the governor-general for interrogation.[70]

Such obstreperous behavior was in part the inevitable result of the dis-
ruption brought by the permanent installation of a large number of banner
soldiers at many locales, such as at Jingkou:

> Harm to the people of Zhenjiang should not be repeated. [But] when they
> hear that many troops will be stationed [there], they flee in panic. If
> soldiers are near then there is bound to be pillage and trouble. How can
> the people remain calm? Especially to be feared is that since Manchu
> troops are habitually fierce and cruel they will not obey orders.[71]

To a certain degree this fear never went away, and garrison soldiers seem to
have cultivated it, taking advantage of their superior status on a regular basis. It seems to have become part of being "Manchu." Of course, all bannermen, not just Manchus, engaged in this sort of activity. Nonetheless, it
was often seen as "Manchu" behavior, in the same way that the 1645 sack
of Yangzhou was seen as a "Manchu" crime even though most of the troops
responsible for the savagery there were Chinese bannermen. Nor does there
appear to have been much of an improvement after the Kangxi reign.[72] The
signs are that friction persisted between banner troops and Han civilians; arriving at the Xi'an garrison in 1729, Lieutenant General Cimbu found that
relations between bannermen and civilians were not at all good. He reported
continual friction between them at the markets, with bannermen always
grabbing more than they had paid for, cheating on the scales, squabbling
and making threats.[73] The previous year, Xi'an troops on the march to Liangzhou were reportedly responsible for seventy-five incidents of disturbing local Chinese.[74] Thus when Manchu soldiers were sent on their way to move
into the Qingzhou garrison in 1730, the Yongzheng emperor gave these orders to Shandong governor Yue Rui:

> After the officers and soldiers have entered the province, if anyone from
> the garrison general on down to the soldiers' servants should even slightly
> flout the law, insult the peasants, or disturb the locale, no matter whether
> the matter is major or minor, you should send all details to me in a palace

memorial. If you should try to cover something up and I hear about it from some other place, you will be held strictly to account.[75]

The same year, the Zhapu lieutenant general reported that quarrels sometimes broke out between "degenerate" bannermen and merchants at the south gate of the Manchu city where business was transacted.[76] Similar reports for the later eighteenth and the nineteenth centuries are not hard to find.[77] Writing in the mid-nineteenth century, Wang Qingyun documented many of these abuses in describing livelihood in the banners, although he was careful to say that it was their servants and slaves, and not banner people themselves, who were guilty of violent and arrogant behavior.[78]

## MEDIATING BETWEEN MANCHU AND HAN

One good indication that conflict between Manchus and Han Chinese was both common and serious is that its resolution came to depend on special legal structures developed specifically to address problems between bannermen and civilians. Given the special institutional status of bannermen and the potential for political trouble when Manchus stood accused of wrongdoing, such matters could obviously become very complex, and the tact required to handle them was highly valued. In 1724, for example, a Fujian prefect was recommended for metropolitan office by the Fuzhou garrison general on the basis of his record of "unemotional judgment" of cases involving garrison bannermen and Han locals.[79] A few years later much the same reasons were given for wanting to retain a certain Ningxia magistrate in his post, namely, that in a place where Manchu soldiers and Chinese commoners lived side by side, he managed to make them get along and treat each fairly.[80] Similar praise was posthumously awarded Hūwahiyan, governor-general of Sichuan and Shaanxi from 1701 to 1704, who was credited with making Manchus, Chinese bannermen, Chinese, and Mongols all get along well.[81] This was evidently considered something of an art, worthy of special commendation.

The official in most need of this art was the civil commissioner, mentioned briefly in Chapter 4, whose duty it was to mediate disputes between bannermen and civilians.[82] It will be recalled that, except for murder cases, Qing regulations stipulated that intrabanner disputes were the affair of banner or garrison officials while disputes between civilians were exclusively the responsibility of the regular civil bureaucracy. Settling disputes between these two groups thus presented a sticky jurisdictional dilemma. The post of civil commissioner was created in 1685 in response to the need for someone who could reasonably claim impartiality in investigating reports of Manchu-Han discord in the garrisons. While Ming precedents can be found for other sorts of commissioners, the civil commissioner was a Qing innovation intended to bridge the gap between the Chinese and Manchu institutional worlds. As an embodiment of the acknowledgment that these were, indeed, different worlds, the emergence of the civil commissioner further shook the "one family" facade of Manchu and Han.

The first civil commissioner seems to have been appointed at the Nanjing garrison sometime in the Shunzhi reign. The post was institutionalized in the mid-1680s, when the Kangxi emperor ordered one each at the Hangzhou, Guangzhou, Xi'an, Jingzhou, Zhenjiang, and Fuzhou garrisons.[83] Thereafter, a civil commissioner was posted to every banner garrison in the provinces, no matter how small. Under the Yongzheng emperor, the scope of the position was widened and civil commissioners were posted to the frontier areas as well (mainly Mongolia and Manchuria), where their duties were more broadly administrative, though they still included dispute resolution. Also under the Yongzheng emperor, civil commissioners were stationed in the metropolitan area around Beijing for the first time, where the presence of bannermen was great and they were needed to help relieve the bottleneck of cases in Baoding (up to that time the only garrison site in the region with a commissioner).[84]

It is important to point out that the civil commissioner was not an officer within the Eight Banner hierarchy, but a member of the civil bureaucracy.[85] However, this distinction may have been less meaningful than it initially appears. First of all, the post was always held by a bannerman, and nearly always a Manchu bannerman at that (making it unique in the lower bureaucracy, where Manchus were few).[86] Indeed, the position was sometimes used as a way to put qualified but otherwise unemployed Manchu degree-holders to work.[87] Another reason to question the actual independence of the civil commissioner comes from evidence that the garrison general may have had authority over the civil commissioner and could play a role in his appointment.[88] The civil commissioner post looked much like an extension of the banner bureaucracy not just in its administration, but also in its functions. While a big part of the civil commissioner's job was to keep Manchus in line —another reason it was good to have other Manchus as civil commissioners—more often than not it seems he ended up defending the interests of bannermen against the encroachment of Han Chinese, and not the other way around.[89] One incident, from 1838, vividly illustrates how the civil commissioner operated:

> The garrison soldiers at Taiyuan were wild, harboring thieves and other criminals completely without fear. Early in the ninth month, several Manchu soldiers tried to break through the street barrier [*jalan*] in the middle of the night, but the watchman refused to open it. The soldiers threw bricks and stones, injuring the watchman in the head and elsewhere. The next day, Li Tingyang, the Yangdian county magistrate, and Lin-yao, the civil commissioner, met to discuss things. Lin-yao feared the Manchu soldiers and gave no credence to the story that the watchman had been hurt by them; rather, he had the watchman beaten to appease the feelings in the Manchu garrison. The magistrate was unable to control [the situation] and dared not contest this. After this, the Manchu soldiers were even more reckless.[90]

In sum, the civil commissioner may have maintained one foot in the civil bureaucracy, but his heart was in the Eight Banners.

## MASTER AND SLAVE

In discussing relations between bannermen and Chinese, the matter of slave ownership among bannermen cannot be overlooked, even if this complicated and important issue can only be briefly treated here.[91]

Continuing a trend remarked in preconquest Jurchen society, the significance of slaves—a category encompassing agricultural slaves, household servants, and personal attendants—was great in the Manchu economy and lifestyle during the Qing.[92] All bannermen at all levels, in the capital and in the garrisons, were entitled to buy and own slaves, without whom their households would have ceased to function.[93] As it was phrased in one memorial, "In the homes of banner officers and soldiers, it will not do if there are no servants who can serve as *kutule* to accompany them on official business."[94] Along with bondservants, slaves managed the house, ran errands, paid bills, collected debts, managed daily finances, and supervised lesser slaves; women were made to work as personal maidservants in the house, and men were employed as grooms and taken on campaigns.[95] Even less well-to-do families had servants: When the Kangxi emperor ordered an investigation on homelessness in the capital, he excluded bannermen with servants from the count.[96]

In the early years of the Qing, millions of Han from all economic backgrounds became slaves after being captured by banner soldiers.[97] According to a practice called *touchong*, people from the country and the city alike offered themselves, their wives, their children, or their whole families for sale to escape bankruptcy, debts, taxes, or starvation. After the Shunzhi reign, slaves tended to be acquired in more businesslike fashion. Markets for the sale of people were legal and open and were found in Beijing and all garrison cities.[98] Contracts were of two types, "red" (officially sanctioned) and "white" (unofficial—so called because they lacked a red-ink government stamp), and tax had to be paid on the transaction. Following a pre-1644 practice, slaves could also be given by the emperor as gifts. This was another way that ordinary people and even bannermen could end up as slaves.[99] Records show that in 1740 some of the slaves belonging to bannermen at the Xi'an garrison were in fact exiled criminals who had been later transferred as slaves to soldiers who had distinguished themselves in battle.[100] In 1757, 360 Oirat captives were presented to bannermen at Baoding, Tianjin, and Qingzhou.[101] Another way that Chinese became slaves in banner households was by "adoption," as explained in this 1723 report by the censor Yangboo:

> [Formerly] when Manchu soldiers went on hunts or military campaigns they all would rely on grooms [*kutule*]. Owing to the blessings of the khan-lord, the Manchus have greatly multiplied, with father and son, brother and brother splitting into several households within one house. For this reason it became so that there were not nearly enough servants. As in former times, our sacred lord has again shown favor to the Manchus and made it possible to buy commoners using contracts. At that, not only are people too lazy or shiftless to work taking their children and wives and migrating from place to place begging, but when they come to Manchu houses, dreaming of a place to rest their bodies and not wanting to go hungry, they all ask to stay. In this way Manchus also take on slaves [Ma *aha*]. Over the years they will have their own children who will stay in the household as adopted ones [Ma *ujin*] and the number of servants per soldier is likely to increase.[102]

The memorial concluded with a request to the emperor to find some way to provide financial assistance to needy bannermen to help defray the costs of supporting so many slaves. The Manchu point of view emerges very clearly in this account: people who bought slaves were providing food and shelter to Chinese who might otherwise have nowhere to go. This patriarchal attitude is seen also in a note to the Yongzheng emperor that many of the servants at the Jingzhou garrison were poor peasants made homeless by flood who had come to the garrison general and sold themselves into slavery in the hope of getting clothing and something to eat.[103] Chinese slaves might also find refuge in banner households for other reasons. A 1756 report from Kaifeng found that many Manchu households were employing Han, noting suspiciously that in this fashion "troublemakers" sought to cover their tracks and hide from civil authorities.[104]

Not that the Manchu attitude toward slaves was always charitable. Indeed, it is easy to imagine the sorts of abuses and tragedies associated with trading and holding slaves. One odious incident uncovered in 1680 by a censor traveling in Shandong was a scheme for ensnaring free peasants and selling them into bondage. After first being promised work on the land, a whole family would be invited to spend a few days at the residence of a Dezhou garrison bannermen. Later they would be informed that they had been sold, though the possibility of becoming slaves had never been broached. They would then be tied up and forcibly taken to Beijing and sold at a Beijing slave market. Any who resisted would be savagely beaten, sometimes to death. The people running this particular scam allegedly captured and enslaved as many as eighty people in this way.[105] Though the court from time to time announced legal changes to make emancipation of slaves easier and to curb the excesses of cruel owners (the murder of slaves appears to have been not uncommon),[106] the lot of banner slaves was without question a miserable one.[107] In the mid seventeenth century there even remained the old Manchu practice of having servants accompany their master in death.[108] Perhaps the only slaves who saw an improvement in their lives were those attached to powerful banner households, who profited in various ways from the influence of their masters.[109]

Curiously, the number of slave uprisings recorded during the Qing appears to be small. Most slaves who wanted to protest their status chose the simpler, though no less risky, path of escape, and a large number of archival materials are tied precisely to this question. Though it is commonly viewed as a problem principally of the Shunzhi and Kangxi reigns, the banner fugitive issue was almost as troublesome in the eighteenth century. A 1730 memorial reported that ordinary Chinese (single men and married couples) from Zhili would sell themselves as slaves or indentured servants to Beijing banner households needing house servants and grooms, for which of course they received payment. After several months, they would flee back to the countryside, where they were protected by a new law of 1723 preventing the reporting of escaped slaves who had been bought on white contracts. Many bannermen complained that they lost their investments in just this fashion.[110]

This was a serious problem at the garrisons, too, leading the court to lay down penalties for failure to capture a quota of escaped slaves within a reasonable length of time. At the Xi'an garrison, for example, General Coldo complained that: "[Among household slaves are] scheming, rebellious types who, even if their masters treat them well, at the slightest provocation cannot be dissuaded from trying to escape."[111] He found after reviewing the garrison's records that every year anywhere between 170 to 200 slaves ran away, while only 20, and some years as few as 4, were recaptured. Disturbed by what he perceived as a growing trend, Coldo expressed doubt whether the quota system (which applied to civil officials as well) was not a disincentive to tracking down fugitives and suggested that each case be treated separately.[112] No action apparently was taken on this suggestion, and Coldo submitted a very similar memorial a few years later proposing that penalties for allowing slaves to escape should be levied on a basis proportionate to the size of the garrison, not simply according to the number of escapees. This was especially important for larger garrisons:

> Presently at Xi'an there are over ten thousand officers, soldiers, and idle bannermen and youth. With them are as many as eighty thousand slaves. . . . If the numbers of soldiers in every province were balanced out or the numbers [for fines] fixed according to the size [of garrisons] this would make penalizing by the docking of pay very fair.[113]

It is hard to know if Coldo was correct in assuming that the high number of slaves per banner male (an eight-to-one ratio) was the same at all garrisons. But one thing is certain: if service as the emperor's "slaves" was part of the Manchu Way, so was holding slaves oneself. Though the practice was rarely, if ever, questioned by Han officials, it undoubtedly rankled.

## ETHNIC TENSION AND COEXISTENCE

Returning to the question with which this chapter began—how well did Manchus and Han Chinese get along?—it is essential to ask whether conflicts between bannermen and Han were the result, not of ethnic tension, but of military-civilian tension. One way to address this is to control for the military variable by looking at relations between bannermen, Green Standard soldiers, and Han civilians. We find that while there was considerable tension between Manchu and Chinese military men, there seem to have been few incidents of off-duty conflict between Green Standard soldiers and ordinary Chinese. In other words, as between bannermen and civilians, the source of the tension between the different groups of soldiers appears to have been mostly ethnic, and mostly the fault of the bannermen. Why this should be so is apparent when we consider that though soldiers in the Green Standard Army participated in the military life, theirs was a far less prestigious place. The great majority were paid and fed less well than the lowest bannermen.[114] Their skills were often (though not always) inferior, and Manchu soldiers looked with contempt on them, which led to the occasional incident, as in Shandong in 1744 when banner soldiers and Chinese soldiers brawled during an opera performance at the city-god temple in Dezhou. The Shandong governor was given the usual exhortation to "keep the area quiet and protect the people," and told to investigate what was suspected by the court to be a situation of chronic abuse suffered by the Green Standard garrison at the hands of the Eight Banner garrison.[115]

Bearing this in mind, it appears that their status as conquerors and their qualitatively different lifestyle, and not simply their status as men-at-arms, was key in shaping conflict between Manchus and those outside the banners, whether civilians, soldiers, or officials. When consciousness of their superiority led Manchus to flaunt their status and abuse their privilege, they were taking advantage of the fact, not just of being soldiers, but of being Manchus. Insofar as throwing one's weight around was behavior that carried a distinct ethnic charge, one can say that ethnic strife was both the price and the proof of Manchu ethnic sovereignty.

True, one might be caught—but how many Han Chinese would have the nerve to bring charges against a Manchu? On the local level, a Chinese official who was aware of some sort of misbehavior by bannermen in his jurisdiction had to proceed very delicately, always couching his complaint in terms of "the soldiers" disturbing "the people." As we have seen in the case of the disgruntled Hangzhou resident who complained that "there's just no peace anymore," if ethnic labels were attached to these substantives, suspicions of anti-Manchu sentiment were instantly raised.[116] Under these circumstances, it is not so surprising that relatively few complaints were made. The general inability, for legal and political reasons, of local Chinese officials to effectively punish wrongdoing by bannermen probably led to still more incidents,[117] which Manchu officials naturally had no very strong incentive to report and which could be taken care of by an efficient civil commissioner.[118] One imagines that many, many disputes were left unsettled, or if dealt with, then informally so, saving Manchus a lot of face and everyone a lot of worry.

It would thus be an error to interpret the apparent silence of Han Chinese on matters relating to Manchu overlordship as indicating that things between Manchus and Han Chinese were otherwise problem-free. Among ordinary people, as the cases described above attest, conflict on ethnic lines seems to have been common enough. Among elites, the comments of Lord Macartney, who was struck during his 1794 visit to China by the Manchus' "superiority" vis-à-vis the "depression" of the Chinese, have already been cited. To him, the differences between the "Tartar" and the "Chinese" nations were immediate and significant. If some of these were the sorts of difference one would not expect to find mentioned by a Chinese author, we should not be too surprised. Since the dynasty belonged to the Manchus, they and their supporters were seen to be entitled, within limits, to write the rules—but only "within limits." By prosecuting only the very worst crimes and the most egregious abuses of privilege (this often worked at the same time as an excuse to get rid of political enemies), the court could be sure that the institutional framework of the banner way of life would remain fundamentally unchallenged. We might simply say that life was the way it was—with bannermen, especially Manchu bannermen, granted privileges and others not—because that was the way people expected the conquering elite to behave. In this regard, ethnicity was not merely a lightning rod for other, more "real" concerns; rather, it was itself a category of daily discourse. Indeed, the nature of the Manchu-Han relationship in the Qing reminds us that ethnicity then was much like ethnicity now, in that it was not easily divorced from economic, social, or political issues—nor was it merely reducible to those issues.

The intersection of two codes of behavior—for bannermen, the presumption of privilege, and for Chinese, the fear of challenging it—resulted in a murky zone of mutual reservation and doubt at all levels of Qing society. The existence of this mistrust is of course a well-known problem of Qing rule: Had people really accepted Manchu rule? Or were they just pretending to? That cases involving ethnic sensitivities worried the court because they were thought to reflect popular attitudes shows that the court was never entirely sure of itself, even at the local level.[119] And while the court was remarkably adept at keeping the undercurrent of ethnic tension within acceptable limits, at the same time, it could never hope to eliminate it completely.

If the fear of ethnic bias against them was a phobia that Manchus at the top never succeeded in overcoming, the pattern of Manchu-Han relations that emerges from our consideration of the regular existence of ordinary bannermen shows that this uneasiness persisted at lower levels, too, but primarily at the garrisons. As to why capital bannermen should have gotten along better with Chinese, one comes back to the different economic realities facing capital bannermen. Nearer the emperor, and with a whole city they could call their own, capital bannermen had a more secure place than garrison bannermen. They were less likely to be sent off to battle and more likely to remain in the capital where there were many more posts to be filled than at the garrisons. They were favored also with other privileges, chief among them being that they were paid more than garrison bannermen, and until the middle of the eighteenth century were better shielded from the effects of inflation and commercialization because they continued to receive steady amounts of grain (which became worth more and more) rather than silver (which bought less and less). Bannermen living in the garrisons, on the other hand, were more vulnerable on all these points. They were farther from the emperor and farther from his concerns; they were paid one-quarter less than capital bannermen for the same jobs, and received a major proportion of their salaries in silver, with which they were left to make do as inflation took its toll. Unlike capital bannermen, half of whom had lost their land, few garrison bannermen ever even received any. On top of all of this, they lived in impossibly crowded conditions, surrounded by people who not only outnumbered them but were either afraid of them or hated them or both. These factors may explain why one finds in general greater harmony in Beijing than in the provinces. They also take us one step further in sorting out the differences between banner life in the capital and life in the garrisons and help us understand why patterns of Manchu identity should have varied between these two halves of the Manchu world.

# CHAPTER SIX

# Resident Aliens

So far we have spoken of Manchu difference mainly in terms of its boundaries and their institutional manifestations: separate residence, economic privilege, and occupational preference. This has given us a good idea of how the structures and practices that characterized the special position of Manchus, Mongols, and Chinese bannermen contributed to a common banner identity and to the perception that those in the banners differed from those outside. It has also made it easy to understand the sorts of tensions that figured in their day-to-day relationships. But difference between banner people and Han was not constructed solely on the basis of institutions, nor did it emerge only at the points where the Manchu and Han worlds met. As the essentializing judgments of the Chinese cited earlier attest, Manchu-Han difference ran deeper and wider. Descent, expressed through membership in the banner military caste, together with a range of identifying cultural practices, also distinguished banner people, and especially Manchus, from Han civilians. Apart from the more ascriptive elements of Manchu identity wrapped up in legal and social status, such affective signs of ethnic identity are the sort that anthropologists like to see when they talk about "ethnic" situations.[1] I describe some of these practices below.

This chapter examines Manchu alienness from two broad angles. The first presents a few of the obvious cultural differences between Manchus and Han that accompanied and adumbrated the institutional gap between them. I exclude for the moment elements of the official ideology of the Manchu Way—language, martial spirit, frugal way of life—which will be discussed in the next chapter. Rather, I am interested here in other kinds of practices that denoted Manchuness, and have chosen three that were especially revealing of ethnic difference (and of the difficulty in limiting it neatly): religious practices, naming habits, and gender practices. The mere existence of these various practices, of course, does not make them ethnic; for by the definition of ethnicity adopted here, even when cultural performance of the Other differs significantly from one's own, it is only when it implies a socially or politically charged difference that such performance becomes ethnic. As will become clear, such was indeed the case in the Qing. Moreover, that many of the practices described below were tied not just to Manchus but to those in the banners generally, shows how banner status and all it implied socially and politically connoted ethnic norms. In this respect, one can see that cultural and institutional practice were never very far apart in the Qing, and often impinged directly on each other.

In addition, this chapter examines Manchu alienness in terms of the question of residence itself, especially the contradictions arising from the extended Manchu diaspora in China. In describing patterns of banner life not yet touched on, I show how residence policies originally shaped by the initial vision of the Manchu occupation gradually changed to accommodate the particular realities of the diaspora and in the process ended up altering some of the very cultural norms they were supposed to preserve. At the same time, these changes raised some very troubling questions about the dynasty's long-term prospects.

MANCHU SHAMANISM

Shamanism was not the only religion practiced by the Manchus, who were also interested in Buddhism (Chinese and Tibetan) and Daoism, but it was the most common and so the most representative. The subject is large, and can only be briefly treated here.[2]

Shamanic practices are found in many places in the world, but North Asia has historically been an especially fertile ground.[3] Shamanism among the Manchus traces its origins far, far back, well before the time of the formation of the Manchu state, and is still practiced today by some Tungusic peoples of Manchuria and Siberia, notably the Evenki, Orochon, and Even, as well as by Koreans and many of the Mongol and Turkish peoples of Inner and Central Asia. It is not possible to say when or where the first shaman arose, but it is worth noting that the word "shaman" is itself probably of Tungusic origin (the Manchu word is *saman*), and suggests that the Manchu connection with shamanism was very old indeed. Leaving aside the question of whether shamanism is "really" a religion, we can say that in general shamanic practices are founded on a belief in the omnipresence of sacred spirits (called *enduri* in Manchu, also translatable as "deities") in all of nature—sky, earth, water, animals, trees, and plants—worship of which may bring favor, health, and prosperity. Communication with *enduri* is possible only through a medium, that is, a shaman. The shaman must be a person of unusual ability, at once very strong and very sensitive, capable of unusual feats of perception and prediction.[4] Employing special techniques, music, dress, and language, the shaman is the one who makes sacrifices to the spirits and who approaches them with specific requests for intervention or protection. The shaman is also responsible for communication with the dead. Depending on the type of ritual, the shaman may fall into a trance or enter an altered state of consciousness often interpreted as "possession" by a spirit; others present at the ritual may also experience some sort of ecstatic state. The shaman's powers very often make him—or her, as a majority of North Asian shamans have traditionally been women—a person of considerable authority and prestige in the community.[5]

It is generally believed that the rise of shamanism is closely tied to the rise of clan organization. Each clan typically had its own shaman who would placate natural and ancestral spirits when necessary, ask them to bring a good harvest or a bountiful hunt, assure the success of a military raid, or heal the sick. It is also generally held that the rise of larger social organizations, political states especially, was inherently inimical to shamanism. When a more powerful clan absorbed another, the shaman of the weaker clan would be killed or exiled and her ritual implements destroyed;[6] eventually, the centralization of political power and jealousy or mistrust of shamanic authority would result in the disappearance of all shamans. Evidence of this trend was plain at the time the Manchu state was formed in the early seventeenth century. Shamanic practice did not disappear—in fact, it did not disappear until after the fall of the Qing—but it was already very much changed in the early seventeenth century from what it had been before the rise of Nurhaci.

In discussions of Manchu shamanism it is common to speak of two types of ritual, "domestic" and "primitive,"[7] and to further distinguish these rituals as practiced in two separate cults, "imperial" and "common."[8] Domestic ritual, which centered on liturgically based sacrifices made to heaven and to the ancestors, seems to correspond to the sort of ritual Caroline Humphrey has called "patriarchal" shamanism, which she identifies as that involved in the "symbolic reproduction of the patrilineal lineage, clan, or polity." Primitive ritual, with its sacrifices to various animal spirits for specific causes (e.g., exorcism and healing), appears close to what she calls "transformational shamanism," in which "wild shamans" directly engage spirits through possession, and even require the help of special assistants.[9] Domestic ritual was by far the most widespread type of shamanic observance among Manchus in the Qing. Its best-known manifestation was the rites that took place in the sacrificial shrine of the imperial clan, called the *tangse* (Ch *tangzi*; lit., "hall"), and in the main palace building reserved for the emperor's personal shamanic worship, the Kunning gong.[10] Such sacrifices were already observed in the preconquest period.[11] They occurred regularly throughout the year, with the main observance falling on the first day of the year.[12] Indeed, the first thing the Qing emperor did on New Year's Day was to visit the *tangse*, a smallish octagonal building to the southeast of the Forbidden City,[13] where he would participate in the sacrificial ritual to heaven, to the Manchu progenitor, to the horse deity, and various other spirits. Only members of the imperial lineage could witness the presentation of liquor, grain, and meat (a slaughtered pig), the burning of incense,[14] and prostration before ancestor portraits. On lesser occasions, the same ritual was held in the more convenient Kunning gong, while the emperor sent his representative to join in the ritual held at the same time in the *tangse*. In either location, the presence of Han or Mongol officials was forbidden.[15]

A nineteenth-century Manchu prince, Zhao-lian, left a description of the scene at the Kunning gong on the second day of the New Year. He relates that on the second day of the year, the emperor and princes, together with high Manchu civil and military officials, assembled to partake of the meat left over from the previous day's sacrifices. The emperor awaited their arrival in the room, sitting facing north instead of the usual south. The guests arrived in their finery, bowed once to the spirit hall on the west, then once in front of the emperor, before sitting down on mats on the floor facing south toward the emperor. Officers in charge of the sacrifice then brought in the offerings on silver plates, while the plates the emperor would use were brought in by officials on their knees. The emperor would then make cuts of the shoulder meat to be distributed to the present company; following Manchu custom, these would be eaten in slices. Tea (which the Manchus drank with milk) would be served once the meal was over, and the entire thing brought to a conclusion by a final bow to the emperor; the guests waited to depart until the emperor left for the palace.[16] The emperor did not lead the *tangse* rituals, however. That was the duty of the shaman. The *tangse* ritual was thus fundamentally different both in content and format from any Chinese ritual the emperor took part in, where he almost always had to be physically at the very center of things.[17] Even when he visited the *tangse* on such important ceremonial occasions as to formally inaugurate or close a military campaign, the emperor sat on the side while the shaman conducted the rite.

The imperial domestic ritual outlined above, already somewhat institutionalized, became increasingly formalized and liturgified after the conquest. In the mid-eighteenth century the imperial ritual was recorded in a well-known court publication called the *Manchu Rites for Sacrifices to the Spirits and to Heaven* (*Manzhou jishen jitian dianli/Manjusai wecere metere kooli bithe*), the Manchu version of which appeared early in the Qianlong reign, in 1747 (a Chinese translation followed thirty-three years later, in 1780). According to the preface, the imperial rite was supposed to serve as a model for all Manchu shamanic ritual, to iron out differences between the imperial and other cults, and to preserve "traditional" Manchu customs from further degradation,[18] since many of the prayers at this time were said in Chinese and those in Manchu were for the most part read in a Chinese phonetic transcription that probably made little sense to either the shaman or the other participants.[19] At around the same time, the *tangse* ritual was also inscribed in the dynasty's main compendium of institutional practice, the *Collected Institutes of the Qing*.[20]

While undeniably a part of the same eighteenth-century "documentary institutionalization" of Manchu culture that saw the publication of the *Comprehensive History of the Eight Banners*, the *Comprehensive Genealogy of Eight Banners Manchu Clans*, and the *Researches of Manchu Origins*, it is unclear what effect the promulgation of the imperial *Manchu Rites* actually had upon regular Manchu practice.[21] Accepted opinion has long been that by making the imperial cult the standard for all Manchus, the common cult adapted it as a new norm, and non–Aisin Gioro practices withered. Moreover, it is also argued that by the later 1700s the imperial cult was so formalized and stilted that it was no longer a religion but "an antique with form but no life."[22] But another view holds that, however syncretic and formalized, this was still shamanism, if only because those who were practicing it saw it that way. This view insists furthermore that the withering of the common cult was only a temporary retreat, and that the inability of the nineteenth-century court to effectively impose its will on ordinary banner families saw a revitalization of the common cult.[23] The fact that texts for many nonimperial clan rituals have been preserved is a good indication that the common cult probably survived better than has usually been thought.[24] There is also photographic evidence of the preservation of shamanic rites in ordinary banner households in early 1900s Beijing.[25]

The domestic ritual followed in the common cult was in the main the same as that in the imperial cult. Both were broken up into three main rites: dawn sacrifice (Ch *chao ji*), sunset sacrifice (Ch *xi ji*), and "light-extinguishing" sacrifice (Ch *beideng ji*, held at midnight). Both used the spirit-pole (*shen'gan/somo*) as a means of establishing a mystical connection with heaven; the offerings placed in the metal bowl fixed to the top of the pole would ideally be carried away by the chief Manchu totem, the *saksaha* (magpie), to his master, the Lord of Heaven.[26] The same sacrificial foods were used in both cults. But there were some important differences. First, ritual in the common cult was less lavish than in the imperial cult. Only the imperial cult had a building specially dedicated to shamanic worship; other clans had had *tangse* in the past, but at least by 1673, and possibly even before the conquest, they were formally prohibited.[27] Instead, households kept an "altar" on the western wall, called a *weceku*, on which a genealogy and ancestor portraits were kept and taken down when needed for the ritual. Second, in addition to the three principal rites, the common cult often added a morning and an afternoon sacrifice.[28] The common cult also included other deities not found in the imperial cult, and exhibited somewhat fewer signs of Chinese influence, as it lacked the Buddha and bodhisattvas which had been incorporated into the imperial pantheon.[29] However, the common cult was not immune to syncretism, as it seems that everyone from the emperor to the most ordinary bannerman sacrificed to "Lord Guan" (*Guan Di/Guwan mafa*), whose martial associations made him easily the most popular single deity among the Manchus. As we saw in Chapter 2, where there were bannermen, there were temples to him; in Beijing alone there were 116.[30] Another deity of the common cult popular among women in the banners was the "Niangniang" spirit, who could prevent illness and assure safe childbirth.[31]

The second type of ritual, primitive ritual, required different implements and sacrificial foods than its domestic variant, and also called for a knowledgeable assistant to aid the shaman during the ritual, which could last anywhere from two to nine days. In contrast to domestic ritual's bright atmosphere of harmony and sincerity, primitive ritual was "dark, scary, and mysterious." The deities involved were generally not those of the sky, earth, or ancestors, but animal spirits.[32] For a number of reasons, primitive ritual was less widespread among the Manchus in the Qing. For one thing, in primitive ritual far greater demands were made on the shaman, who was not just to recite a prepared text honoring a deity but really had to establish contact with a spirit and produce a specific result. One could hardly expect to find the requisite skills and familiarity with the sort of "wild" shamanic practices used in primitive ritual among the wives of the imperial clan, from among whose number were chosen the shamans to lead the domestic ritual. Those shamans were really more like priests. For another thing, the primitive ritual, with its reliance on techniques of ecstasy, had long been discouraged by the court (Hong Taiji proscribed it as early as 1636).[33] Because it was not at all liturgical it was undeniable proof of the Manchus' still-close ties to a "barbarian" culture and past. For this reason, the court did what it could to erase the primitive ritual, while at the same time maintaining a sanitized, dressed-up version of the domestic ritual as part of the bargain required by ethnic sovereignty. Thus it was excluded from the *Manchu Rites*.

For all that, primitive ritual does seem to have survived, though evidence for this is scant. A Qianlong collection of songs contains one called "Chenzao bianyang," which describes the singing and dancing of a shamaness trying to cure epilepsy and who is transformed into a sheep. A widely circulated late Qing anthology of ghost stories by the bannerman He-bang-e includes one about a shaman.[34] There is also the "Tale of the Nišan Shamaness," a valuable eighteenth-century text which preserves a number of rituals and songs from both domestic and primitive ritual.[35] One explanation as to why the primitive cult persisted virtually "underground" even into the early twentieth century is that these shamans fulfilled an important function in banner communities as healers.[36]

Shamanism was never formally enunciated as part of the Manchu Way,[37] but it contributed to Manchu ethnic identity in two ways. First, as others have noted, it provided the spiritual core of Manchu life that served to strengthen a common identity.[38] In his indictment of Sunu and other Manchu nobles who had converted to Christianity, the Yongzheng emperor reminded the rest of the Manchu elite that each people had its own way of honoring Heaven and that it was incumbent upon Manchus to observe Manchu practice in this regard:

The Lord of Heaven is Heaven itself. . . . In the empire we have a temple for honoring Heaven and sacrificing to Him. We Manchus have Tiao Tchin. The first day of every year we burn incense and paper to honor Heaven. We Manchus have our own particular rites for honoring Heaven; the Mongols, Chinese, Russians, and Europeans also have their own particular rites for honoring Heaven. I have never said that he [Urcen, a son of Sunu] could not honor Heaven but that everyone has his way of doing it. As a Manchu, Urcen should do it like us.[39]

A second way in which shamanism contributed to Manchu identity was by constructing a very obvious boundary between Manchu and Han. Despite the publication of the *Manchu Rites*, Manchu shamanic practices always were something of a mystery to the Chinese, no doubt because, as noted, they were never permitted to observe them. The accounts of shamanism that found their way into Qing-period occasional writings (*biji*) are fragmentary and often error-prone, while those that try to explain the language of the ritual are positively confounding.[40] Still, even if they did not understand much of what really went on in these "spirit-jumping" ceremonies (the literal sense of the Chinese term *tiaoshen*), one thing was certain: their departure from Chinese rituals aroused significant interest in this Manchu affair.[41] The several authors who mention them do so with the apparent goal of satisfying reader curiosity regarding this "exotic" practice, as if to suggest that one's otherwise seemingly normal Manchu neighbors in fact retained something different about themselves, after all, something secret and alien.

## MANCHU NAMES AND NAMING PRACTICES

Like shamanism, distinctive names were an important way that Manchu difference was marked. Chinese names consist typically of a single-character surname and a given name of one or two characters, the latter usually chosen for their auspicious meaning. Manchu names were different. For one thing, Manchus did not commonly employ surnames, identifying themselves usually by their banner affiliation rather than by their lineage. Even if they had customarily used both surname and given name, this would not have eliminated the difference with Han names, since Manchu names of any kind were very often longer than two characters—that is, two syllables—in length. Where a Han name (to pick at random two names from the eighteenth century) might read Zhang Tingyu or Dai Zhen, the full name of, say, Ebilun (a famous Manchu figure of the early Qing who belonged to the Niohuru clan) would have been the unwieldy "Niu-gu-lu E-bi-long" in Chinese. Moreover, the characters used in names were typically chosen to represent the sounds of Manchu, and not to carry any particular meaning in Chinese.[42] For educated Han Chinese accustomed to names composed of a familiar surname and one or two elegant characters drawn from a poem or a passage from the classics, Manchu names looked not just different, but absurd. What was one to make of a name like E-bi-long, written in Chinese characters meaning "repress-must-flourish," or Duo-er-gun, meaning "numerous-thou-roll"? Since neither *e* nor *duo* would have been recognizable as a surname-character (these are for the most part fixed in Chinese), such names were disorienting to the Han. To them they looked like nonsense (they still do to beginning students of Qing history). But they are not nonsense in Manchu: "E-bi-long" is the transcription of *ebilun*, meaning "a delicate or sickly child," and "Duo-er-gun" is the Chinese transcription of *dorgon*, the Manchu word for badger.

These names, in turn, point to further discrepancies between Manchu and Chinese naming practices that went beyond those reflected in conventions of representation and meaning. That is, not only did Manchus have different names, but they were named differently. No adult Chinese would have been saddled with a name like Sickly One or Badger. Such a name would have contravened the basic principles of Chinese beliefs about names, which are believed to govern one's fate in a most intimate way and are carefully chosen, often with professional help, to assure the child's health and protection. Manchus were much less fastidious in this regard, and Chinese in the Qing were surprised that Manchus did not make a point of remembering the sort of information that would have mattered to an astrologer.[43] Instead, Manchus frequently named their children—at least, males (there is little information on female names)—for their appearance, their personal characteristics (actual or hoped-for), for animals, plants, and objects. Thus we find names like Nikan (Chinese), Ajige (little), Asiha (young), Haha (male), Mampi (knot—a reference to the hair?), Kara (black), Fulata (red-eyed), Necin (peaceful), Kirsa (steppe fox), Unahan (colt), Jumara (squirrel), Nimašan (sea eagle), Nomin (lapis lazuli), and Gacuha (toy made of an animal's anklebone).[44] Names such as Jalafungga (long-lived), Fulingga (lucky one), Fulungga (majestic), and Hūturingga (fortunate), were not unknown, either, particularly after the seventeenth century. Although mightily foreign when written as Zha-la-feng-a, Fu-ling-a, Fu-long-ga, or Hu-tu-ling-ga, these names, their auspiciousness perhaps the result of Chinese influence, might have seemed less strange to the Chinese had they but known what they meant in Manchu.

As the above examples show, Manchu names often carried the grammatical markers of their origins; the suffix *-ngga* or *-ngge* means "having the quality of," and accounts for the many Manchu names we see that end in the characters *ge*, *ga*, *e*, and *a* when written in Chinese. Other common endings were *-ju* (Ingju, Siju, Maiju, Tangbooju, Fuju), *-boo* (Sengboo, Samboo, Laiboo, Mamboo, Foboo), and *-tai* (Bootai, Duruntai, Guntai, Jurantai, Yentai). The ending *-ju* was usually written in Chinese with any one of a number of characters with the sound "zhu"; *-boo* was represented by the sound "bao"; and *-tai* (probably from Mongolian, meaning "having") by Chinese characters all sounding "tai." While Chinese names, too, sometimes ended in characters with the sounds "zhu," "bao," and "tai," more often than not, such names in the Qing belonged to Manchus or other bannermen (Chinese bannermen and Mongols sometimes took Manchu-sounding names), even if the attached meaning is not clear (it is not certain that all names in fact had a specific meaning).

Giving "numeral names" was another unique Manchu habit. These were names that actually referred to numbers. Sometimes they were given using Manchu numbers—for example, Nadanju (seventy) or Susai (fifty). Other times number names used the Manchu transcription of Chinese numbers, as in the name Liošici (= *liushi qi*, "sixty-seven"), Bašinu (= *bashi wu*, "eighty-five").[45] Such names, unheard of among the Han, were quite common among the Manchus, and appeared from time to time among Chinese bannermen. Popular curiosity about this odd custom in the Qing was partly satisfied by the nineteenth-century bannerman-writer Fu-ge, who explained in his book of "jottings" that naming children for their grandparents' ages was a way of wishing longevity to the newly born.[46]

Other peculiar Manchu naming practices included naming individual dogs, horses, and even elephants, which the Chinese did not do.[47] Manchu naming practices also differed when it came to naming the children of the same generation. Chinese practice, at least among elites, typically called for all the children of the same lineage and same generation to share the same first character of the given name. All the brothers and cousins (or sisters and cousins) of the same generation would be identified by this character (sometimes called *beifen yongzi*), which greatly simplified the determination of relationships within the lineage. The Manchus were not so careful about this sort of thing. For instance, while there is some consistency in the names given to Nurhaci and his brothers Šurhaci, Murhaci, Yarhaci, and Bayara, it is not a consistency of the sort a Chinese would have recognized. Furthermore, it is hard to see any pattern in the names of Nurhaci's sixteen sons: Cuyen, Daišan, Abai, Tanggūdai, Manggūltai, Tabai, Abatai, Hong Taiji, Babutai, Degelei, Babuhai, Ajige, Laimbu, Dorgon, Dodo, and Fiyanggū; or in those of the sons of Hong Taiji, among whom were Fulin, Hooge, Gose, and Bombogor. This habit of "random" naming was soon abandoned by the imperial lineage. The children of the Kangxi emperor all sported the same prefix-character, *yin* (written "in" in Manchu), and every generation afterward was marked by the same initial character (or, in Manchu, the same initial sound) in the given name. While some Manchu families followed suit, many others did not, or did so inconsistently: for example, the brother of an early-eighteenth-century general, Erentei, was named Torio, while Xi'an general Cangseli named his son Cangyung, using the same sound, "cang" ("chang" in Chinese), for his *and* the following generation. The impression given by such anecdotal evidence is supported by a rough survey of names in the eighty-four Manchu companies of the Plain Blue Banner (chosen at random) as listed in the 1739 *Comprehensive History of the Eight Banners*. Of the approximately 106 instances where it is possible to compare the names of brothers and first cousins, 78 percent of the time common sounds or characters are absent. In the 22 percent of instances where characters are shared between brothers and cousins, half the time the sharing is inconsistent. That is, either the same character is used across generations (i.e., between fathers/uncles and sons/cousins), or the character is used for some names in a single generation, but not for all.[48] Thus through at least the middle of the eighteenth century naming practices for the majority of Manchus were fundamentally the same as they had always been, though the appearance of the same initial character across generations in some families (the family of the noted official Ortai being a conspicuous case) made it look suspiciously like a Chinese single-character surname, especially if the character used was in fact a surname character. This trend was the subject of more than one angry edict by the Qianlong emperor in the second half of his reign.[49]

While names were an obvious ethnic marker for the Manchus, it is important to note they were by no means an infallible indicator of ethnicity or status. That is, a Manchu might have a Chinese-sounding name, such as

Sioi-yuwanmeng (better known as Xu Yuanmeng or Xu-yuan-meng, 1655–1741), or a Mongol or Chinese bannerman might have a Manchu-sounding name. A glance through the names of captains of Chinese banner companies shows a number of such names, such as Ke-sheng-e, Fo-bao, Chang-shou, Hai-ning, Qi-fu, Ba-shi-liu, and Tun-dai.[50] In fact, where names were concerned, the blurring of ethnic boundaries seems more often to owe to the adoption of Manchu names by non-Manchu bannermen. Many non-Manchus who had infiltrated banner ranks were anxious to borrow some of the cachet and prestige associated with being thought a Manchu, and perhaps even hoped to pass themselves off as Manchus permanently, in which case having a Manchu name could help. At the upper levels of the banners, though, this was not so easy. This is seen in a curious incident of 1737 in which a Chinese banner officer named Arsai suddenly announced to the emperor that he wished to change his name back to his original name, the very Chinese-sounding Cui Zhilu. In an audience with the emperor earlier that year, Cui, a garrison bannerman at Fuzhou, was asked why, since he was a Chinese bannerman, he had a Manchu name. He explained that he had adopted the name Arsai when he was young because of his long study of the Manchu language. When an edict arrived from the emperor a few weeks later, Cui was sure it was a reprimand for having wrongfully assumed a Manchu name. Though the edict was in fact on an entirely separate matter, he was so unnerved that he still appealed for permission to change his name from Arsai back to Cui Zhilu.[51]

As the above episode suggests, names ideally were to be congruent with ethnicity: Manchus were expected to have Manchu names, Mongols Mongol names, and Chinese bannermen Chinese names. Because their identity was most crucial to the dynasty, it was among Manchus that this correspondence mattered most. If the emperor showed indifference when faced with a Chinese bannerman named Arsai, he did not hesitate to reprimand Manchu bannermen whose names veered too far from acceptable norms. For instance, Manchu names could bear syllables that, when written in Chinese, carried auspicious meanings; but when written in Manchu such names had to be written as if they were one word—they could not be written separately. The reason was simple: accepted practice was to write Chinese names separately in Manchu; thus to write a Manchu name separately was to imply that it was the name of a Chinese person, not a Manchu. This was going too far—so the emperor forbade it, and more than once at that.[52] The situation was roughly similar with lineage names. Most Manchus did not use lineage names in daily life, but they were expected just the same to know to which lineage they belonged. When the emperor discovered that some people did not know their own lineage, or that they were fabricating Chinese-sounding last names to substitute for their real lineage names, he declared an immediate end to the practice, noting, "the surname is the bannerman's root."[53] Names, in other words, were also part of the Manchu Way.

## THE PLACE OF MANCHU WOMEN

In their treatment of women, as in their religious and naming practices, Manchus followed significantly different norms than the Han. This was obvious not just to the Chinese, but to outsiders, too. When Westerners visited China in the Qing, what consistently caught their attention were the differences between Manchu and Han Chinese women. Accustomed to seeing Chinese women—when they saw them at all—tottering on bound feet, they could not help but be struck by the very different sight presented by Manchu women. The Spanish Dominican Navarrete, visiting Beijing in 1665, wrote: "The Tartar women wear boots and ride astride like men, and make a notable figure either afoot or a-horseback."[54] Korean visitors among the Manchus before the conquest pointed out that women rode as well as men, and that Manchu women sometimes even took part in the hunt.[55] The Manchu poet Singde (1655–85) left a couple of lines commenting on a winsome woman riding her horse down the street who, "though shy, still turned her head back to look" at him.[56] In the late 1700s, George Staunton, a member of the Macartney embassy, also commented on the equestrian habits of Manchu women, adding an additional observation on the absence of footbinding: "[There] were several women, natives of Tartary or of Tartar extraction, whose feet were not distorted like those of the Chinese. . . . Some of these ladies were in covered carriages, and others on horseback, riding astraddle like men."[57] In another passage Staunton remarked again that "the principal discrimination of the Tartar women consisted in the size of their feet."[58] This point was confirmed by Lord Macartney himself: "The Tartar ladies have hitherto kept their legs at liberty, and would never submit to the Chinese operation of crippling the feet." Macartney went on to say, however, that "it is said that many of their husbands were desirous of introducing it into their families."[59]

Indeed, though Macartney may not have been aware of it, the Manchus briefly tried to ban footbinding throughout the empire shortly after the conquest, abandoning the effort after four years in 1668.[60] Had they succeeded, this would have impressed upon the bodies of Han women a mark of their subjugation to the Manchus as noticeable as was the queue upon the bodies of Han men. Nevertheless, despite his hint that the custom might one day be taken up by the Manchus, it never was, nor was it ever adopted by Mongol women in the banners.[61] Chinese banner women did not bind their feet, either, although there is good evidence that by the early nineteenth century some of them were surreptitiously adopting the custom.[62] Even in the late Qing, the most a Manchu woman might do would be to wrap her feet tightly to give them a slender appearance,[63] or wear the peculiar "horse-hoof" shoes (Ch *mati xie*) developed to produce the uneven gait of the bound-footed woman without the physical discomfort of actual binding. This style consisted of a regular-sized shoe or slipper made to fit a natural foot set on top of a smaller platform, anywhere from two to six inches in height, fixed to the middle of the sole. The narrow-waisted platform, which was all that was visible beneath her garments, resembled a horse's hock, slender just above the wider hoof (though one might also say that the resulting shoe looked rather like an anvil).[64] Another innovation was the "boat shoe," which combined the upper slipper with a broad base that narrowed toward the bottom like the keel of a boat. Both the "horse-hoof" and "boat" shoe styles were favored by women of means; poorer banner women would have worn ordinary slippers with reinforced soles. According to one source, fancy shoe stores that catered to Manchu women advertised by hanging the special heel platforms for "horse-hoof" shoes outside the shop; the same source notes that while both Han and Manchu women might buy fabric for their shoes from the same shop, the Han woman, for whom creating her own footwear was a matter of great pride, would generally take the material home to make the shoe herself. The Manchu woman, in contrast, would take the necessary supplies to a shoemaker, perhaps after having embroidered the material first.[65]

Of course, not all Han women practiced footbinding in the Qing; and just as not every banner male with a Manchu name was a Manchu bannerman, not every woman with natural feet was necessarily Manchu. In the mid nineteenth century, one report was that 50 percent to 60 percent of nonbanner women in Beijing's Inner City did not bind their feet.[66] Still, odds

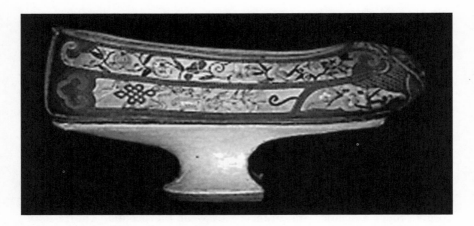

*Figs. 13a/b (above) and 14 (opposite).* Manchu women's footwear. Manchu women did not bind their feet as did many Han Chinese women, but were nonetheless influenced by Chinese aesthetic sensibilities. The platform "horse-hoof" shoe was intended to elevate the larger unbound foot above the hem of the gown, where it could not easily be seen. It also produced a tottering walk, perhaps not unlike that of a bound-footed woman. Both the high-heeled shoes and the keeled "boat" slippers worn by elite Manchu women show evidence of Chinese influence in their embroidery as well. Courtesy of the Beverly Jackson Collection, Santa Barbara, Calif.

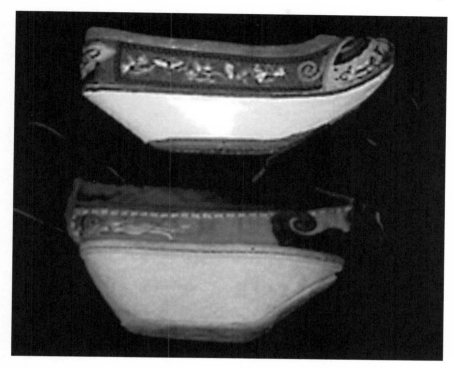

were that an urban woman with unbound feet was, if not Manchu, then a woman of other banner status.

Apart from her natural feet, the appearance of the Manchu woman differed from the Han woman's in a number of other ways. Her clothing, with its narrower sleeves,[67] and above all her hair, were also different. Especially in the banner garrisons, this set her clearly apart from local women:

> But in Foochow, there are a good many Tartars; they have a quarter to themselves, and their wives have all natural-sized feet. These women dress differently from the Chinese. The hair is all drawn back from the forehead and fastened in a knot behind, with a sort of skewer stuck through it, at the end of which there is a flower; their robe is a long affair, something like a man's dressing-gown. . . . There was a peculiarity in their faces which was very striking; they all had square, sensual-looking jowls—an appearance which I did not remark in the Tartar men.[68]

The hair gathered at the back of the head was a contrast to the coiffure worn by Han women, who are typically described as wearing their hair tied in a bun on top of the head (though the variation of headdress across China is well known and well documented).[69] Manchu women were actually better known for another trademark hairstyle, in which the hair (either real or artificial) was wrapped in an elaborate triangular pattern around a wooden, ivory, or metal fillet fastened behind the head. When complete, the coiffure extended dramatically above the head, as well as beyond it on both sides; tassels and flowers were often attached to the "bat wings" for an even more impressive display. This style captivated the nineteenth-century photographer John Thomson, who described it as a "trigonometrical chignon."[70] Thus, although hairstyle for males no longer denoted Manchuness—indeed, since all adult males had to wear their hair in Manchu fashion, it became for many a mark of "Chineseness," if anything[71]—hair continued to mark an ethnic difference among women.[72]

The Manchu woman also wore distinctive accessories and jewelry. Three earrings in each ear, for instance, was considered "traditional Manchu practice,"[73] and is mentioned in a popular late-eighteenth-century Beijing literary source, which provides a detailed description of the Manchu woman's toilette:

> With skilled hands, the aunt undid her jet-black hair,
> A tortoise-shell comb in her grasp.
> She combed and straightened, straightened and combed;
> When her hair was all combed, she put cassia oil in the tresses.
> Ribbons of shiny black artfully supported the now-dressed hair,
> Golden ear-picks of pure yellow pinned it sideways.
>
> . . .
>
> In the part of her hair, ever so narrow, she traced perfumed powder,
> The hair on her temples, cut ever so neatly, she daubed with light ink.
> Her fine and delicate eyebrows she lined with a silver hairpin,
> While glittering pearl earrings dangled down, three on a side;
> A modish, large flower she fastened in her hair,
> Along with many different hairpins all over her head.[74]

This passage, along with what has already been said about her natural feet, leads to the conclusion that a distinctive look marked the woman of the banners literally from head to toe.

Differences in appearance were but one way that Manchu and other bannerwomen were set apart from Han women. Manchu women, especially young women, had a range of legal rights that were generally denied to Han women, including inheritance of property.[75] They also enjoyed superior social standing and educational opportunities compared to their Han peers.[76]

*Fig. 15.* Manchu women's hairstyle. This nameless young Manchu woman, possibly a servant, posed for British photographer John Thomson in the early 1870s. The back and front photos provide a good record of the complex coiffure worn by Qing bannerwomen—called in Chinese by a number of names, *liangbatou* (two-fisted head), *jiazitou* (frame-head), *qitou* (banner-head), *yizitou* (the-character-one-head)—and its style of decoration. In particular, the unusual back view shows how the hair is twisted around a thin piece of wood; we can also see how the two long pins secure the entire hairpiece to the head. Note also that instead of three separate earrings, she is wearing a single "triple-decker" earring. Reproduced from John Thomson, *Illustrations of China and Its People* (London: Sampson Low, Marston, Low, and Searle, 1874), vol. 4, pl. 8, "Female Coiffure," nos. 16–17. Reproduced courtesy of the Tōyō Bunko, Tokyo.

Ultimately, these differences can be traced to the very different position of women in early Manchu society, where, as in Altaic societies generally, women enjoyed higher status and greater freedom than women in Chinese society.[77] Qing attitudes and expectations of Manchu women thus grew from different origins and continued to be influenced by distinct considerations, as not just the Qing court, but Qing commentators and their readers were well aware.

This is best seen in the case of Qing policy on the remarriage of banner widows. During the first century of Qing rule, Manchu widows had much greater freedom to remarry than Han women, as the dynasty did not pro-

*Fig. 16.* Manchu woman greeting a young girl. One of a series of paintings of everyday life commissioned by Emil Bretschneider, physician at the Russian embassy in Beijing, 1866–84. The original caption noted that Manchu customs differed from those of the Chinese: "Young Manchus, whether male or female, are required to fold their arms and make a low curtsey to an elder. Adults greet children with an outstretched hand. People of the same generation [and status?] simply shake hands." The image shows both the footwear and hairstyle (but not the earrings) typical of Manchu women. Note also the large sleeves. © 1995 K. Y. Solonin, ed., *The Bretschneider Albums: Nineteenth Century Paintings of Life in China.* Courtesy of Garnet Publishing, Reading, England.

mote the chaste-widow ideal among Manchu women under forty and in fact
encouraged childless younger widows to remarry.[78] At the provincial garrisons, widows of any age who wished to remarry in order to remain at the
garrison had the freedom to do so.[79] Certainly the Yongzheng emperor was
not convinced of the value of promoting widow chastity. In a gibing rescript
to a memorial praising some women from the Chinese banners, he wrote,
"You can't train the men to be good soldiers, but you are trying to turn all
the women of Xi'an into 'virtuous maidens and martyred wives.' What's the
good? . . . If every twenty or thirty years one virtuous woman happens to
turn up, but we cannot resist the enemy, this is shameful."[80] Widow remarriage at this time was common enough that rules were issued governing
when a woman who was remarrying was able to take servants from her husband's household with her, and when not.[81] The court justified its position
on widow remarriage on the grounds that forcing chastity on banner widows who had no children or immediate family was "unkind," and accused
those who stood in the way of remarriage (usually for reasons of pecuniary
gain) of "shaming Manchu face." When this policy is considered together
with banner marriage practices (see below), however, it seems clear that the
court's unspoken concern in encouraging widow remarriage was to maintain Manchu numbers by ensuring that all women of childbearing age were
married.[82] Only in the mid-1700s does there seem to have been a conver-
gence of Han and Manchu practices, with the same norm of chaste widow-
hood applying to both.[83]

Yet Eight Banner status did not always mean greater freedoms for Manchu women as compared with Han women. For example, all young women
in the banners were required to present themselves for selection for service
in the palace as "elegant females" (Ch *xiunü*). This ritual, called in Manchu
simply the selection of "the daughters" (*sargan jui*), took place every three
years. Banner officials, with the help of lineage heads, compiled a register
listing all females between the ages of thirteen and sixteen *sui* in the Manchu, Mongol, and Chinese banners. This register, which was forwarded to
the Board of Revenue, included girls in the capital and in the provincial
garrisons,[84] as well as the daughters of banner officials serving in nonbanner
provincial appointments. Only those with certified physical disability or dis-
figurement were exempt. (Girls in the imperial bondservant companies underwent a separate annual selection administered by the Imperial Household
Department.[85]) On the appointed day, young women were brought by their

parents (or an aunt, uncle, brother, or sister-in-law) to the Shenwu gate at the rear of the palace (after 1740, an ounce of silver was provided for "coach money").[86] There they were "inspected" by board officials, who matched those present against the list and chose as many as they required to serve in the palace for a term of five years. Those selected were paid one ounce of silver per month, and were given twenty ounces of silver when let go.[87] Most were released from their duties in their mid-twenties so that they could still get married, but a few were selected either as wives for members of the imperial lineage or even as imperial concubines, in which case they would remain in the palace forever.[88] This points to the most important function of the *xiunü* system, which was to guarantee marriage partners for the imperial clan and other nobles.

To judge from the numerous edicts detailing the punishment for failing to report an eligible daughter, the *xiunü* selection process was not popular. The court did its best, however, to ensure that all young women fulfilled this obligation by forbidding them to marry unless they could show they had been through it, and providing penalties for any who flouted this rule. In part this may have been to ensure that the most desirable wives went to the banner elite, which would explain why the daughters of ordinary garrison bannermen were exempt from the ordeal, and why later the exemption was broadened to include the daughters of all Manchu, Mongol, and Chinese bannermen who were not officers.[89] But more than this, the *xiunü* selection was representative of the generally tight control the Eight Banners held over Manchu nuptiality. Even after fulfilling her duties in the palace, a bannerwoman was not free to marry, as all matches had to be approved by the company captain. This system of banner-supervised marriage, called "directed marriage" (Ch *zhihun*), arose originally from Hong Taiji's desire to control marriage alliances among powerful Manchu lineages. It was eventually applied universally to marriages in the Eight Banners—yet one more way in which the parameters of banner life differed fundamentally from those governing life choices for Han Chinese.[90]

Men were also subject to the restrictions of the directed-marriage system, but control over female nuptiality in the banners was especially important also because it was an essential tool in upholding not just ethnic boundaries between Manchu and Han, but also fertility. While it seems that Manchu males frequently took Chinese banner or Han civilian women as secondary wives, or concubines (primary wives were almost always other Manchus or

Mongols), these women became part of the banners and their children were considered to be Manchus. Manchu females, however, were forbidden to marry Han civilian males and in practice almost never did. Moreover, as recent work on the imperial lineage has shown, the rate of concubinage in the banners was higher than the rate among Han males, implying that there was likely a chronic shortage of marriageable females in the banners. As with its original stance opposing widow chastity, by forbidding female exogamy, the court was in effect exercising supervision over Manchu fertility—a key element in the reproduction of Manchu power, particularly in the early years of the dynasty when the Manchu population was relatively small in size.[91]

## DIMENSIONS OF THE MANCHU DIASPORA

The way people construe their place in the world, the way they choose names for themselves, and the way they construct gender are all means of defining self and marking difference, and typically matter greatly in the construction of ethnicity. It was these sorts of differentiating practices, among others, that the Eight Banners was supposed to reinforce: as the institutional home of the Manchus, the banners were essential to Qing rule. However, as the changing styles of names and sleeves described above imply, and as the next chapter will make clear, the pace of acculturation grew rapidly in the eighteenth century. At bottom, the reason for this was that in addition to the banners Manchus and other bannermen had another home, and that was China. The remainder of this chapter is about the discovery of this "home."

The court was at first quite unwilling to recognize the permanency of the Manchu diaspora. With its echo of the Jin experience and all its implications of assimilation, permanent residence spelled potential disaster. If bannermen forgot who they were, if they lost sight of their special status as Manchus, shed their native ways and took up those of their Chinese neighbors, they would betray the trust of the ruling dynasty, which depended upon them to model the distinct and virtuous lifestyle that brought the Manchus to power in the first place. The court simply could not countenance such a reversal. In its desire to keep bannermen, particularly those in the garrisons, from putting down roots in the provinces, it for years simply ignored signs of the process of enracination. It could do this because even though the notion of an empire-wide system of Eight Banner garrisons was current from the first years of the Qing dynasty, it was never anticipated that people sent to the garrisons would actually live there permanently, generation upon generation. Rather, the garrisons were viewed as places where officers, soldiers, and their households would go on temporary assignment. This did not mean that the garrisons were temporary institutions, simply that bannermen deployed there were neither originally meant to be nor considered permanent residents of garrison cities. The Kangxi emperor made this quite plain when he wrote in 1687, "It was not originally meant to have officers and soldiers at Xi'an and other provincial garrisons live there a long time."[92]

Thinking of garrison duty as a temporary assignment may have reflected the situation early in the dynasty when soldiers were transferred back and forth between particular garrisons, while the garrisons themselves remained in place. But as a framework for managing garrison affairs, it was highly idealistic.[93] The fact is that court policy did not uphold the theoretically provisional nature of garrison service once a garrison was settled. As a rule, soldiers did *not* rotate in and out of the provincial garrisons; once sent to the provinces, most bannermen never returned to the families they left behind in the capital. In other words, the "tour of duty" for ordinary bannermen sent to the garrisons was exactly one lifetime. The only garrison personnel who regularly rotated assignments were officers, who, as we have seen, moved in and out from elsewhere in the military or the civil bureaucracy. This was pretty much the case by the middle of the Kangxi reign.

The court could not realistically argue that Beijing, the residence of the emperor, was just a "temporary place of work." Accordingly, one finds alongside the insistence that the banners were the proper home for Manchus an admission that *Beijing*—and ultimately Manchuria (one reason why the area was off limits to the Han)—was the home for all bannermen, and that everyone in the provinces would return to Beijing.[94] Yet the usual phrase in these discussions was that people should "return to the banner" (*gui qi/gūsa de bederembi*). This wording—that is, that people should go back to the *banner*, not the capital—is telling. The slippage here was one that the court managed to conceal for some time. By the 1740s, though, the gaps that emerged in the Manchu concept of "home" required the court to concede reality and change some of its long-standing policies. Slowly, the Qianlong emperor began to consider reversing court policy on the residency issue, admitting, in effect, that the "banner home" was not just in Beijing, but wherever bannermen lived.[95] This major reversal came only after the court had already tergiversated on a host of minor related issues. The gradual transformation of court views can be seen as the accumulation of particular responses to myriad unforeseen complications of extended residence in the Eight Banner garrisons. Together, these concessions amounted to a recognition that, whatever earlier rhetoric had maintained, the Manchus had settled in China for good, meaning that Beijing and the garrisons were lifetime assignments and had become the permanent homes of the banner families who lived there. At that point, the court needed something else to rely on to assure that Manchu (and Mongol) bannermen retained some sort of identification with the dynastic center. That something, as we shall see later, was a heightened emphasis on Manchu roots and a renewed attachment to the Eight Banner system.

## NO PLACE LIKE HOME

In considering the matter of residence, some fundamental questions are: What did bannermen feel to be home? Was "home" the banners? Beijing? The provincial garrison? Or was it someplace else altogether?

As just suggested, residency was an issue that in the beginning did not even occur to the court. The apparent absence of any long-term contingency plan is just one indication that no one in the Manchu leadership had carefully considered all the practical implications of extended residence in China proper. It was simply taken for granted that unless one were assigned to duty somewhere else, one belonged in one's original banner, ensconced in its own corner of Beijing. If one were assigned to duty in the provinces, one had to return to Beijing upon retirement; if one died "abroad," then one's body was to be "repatriated" to the capital for burial. This assumption was confirmed the first time the court took an explicit position on the matter in 1684. In evident response to a suggestion that retired bannermen and the families of deceased bannermen be allowed to remain in the locale, the emperor's second cousin Giyešu opined:

> Officers and soldiers garrisoned at Jiangning, Hangzhou, Jingzhou, Xi'an, and other locations are very important to those places, [which is why] companies have been deputed to stay there permanently for their defense. Nonetheless, *it is feared that if old, sick soldiers who have retired from duty or families of deceased officers and soldiers are not recalled to the capital, but allowed to remain in the outer provinces, then gradually they will be stained by Chinese habits and become inept at riding and shooting.* With the exception of [those at] Shengjing and Ningguta, retired soldiers and the families of deceased officers and soldiers at Jiangning and other

provincial garrisons are hereafter all ordered to return to the capital. . . .
Let this be made a precedent.[96]

The court's fear that prolonged residence among the Chinese would result in acculturation, and the negative light in which acculturation was held, are made plain here. By excepting those who lived in Manchuria from the "return to the banner" policy, this view also indicates that, apart from Beijing, Manchuria was theoretically "home," too.

The appearance of this decision forty years after the conquest is not coincidental. It was just at this time that the first full generation of bannermen serving after 1644 were entering old age or passing away. The generation before them had naturally maintained closer ties with the Northeast and the capital, where they were born and brought up and where many maintained property. There was no need for a regulation that would bring them back home.[97] In contrast, members of the post-1644 generation might have spent most of their adult lives either on campaign or at one of the garrisons, so for them retirement or burial in Beijing was not an immediate, obvious, or even convenient choice. However, it was the preference of the court, which had the requirement written into the books, adding to it the further stipulation that sons or other close male relatives in the household who had their own posts should be removed from them and sent "home" together with the rest of the family.[98]

Given the political risks of widespread acculturation and the practical difficulties of continually moving large numbers of troops, allowing bannermen to spend their careers at the garrison instead of moving them somewhere else every three years was a sensible compromise with the principle of garrisons as temporary assignments. The theory was that a soldier would serve at the garrison all his life; when he retired, he would take his family back to Beijing, and a younger member of the same banner and company would be sent in his place. If a bannerman died before retirement, then his family would return with the body and the vacancy would be filled by a young recruit from the capital who, with his family and servants, would occupy the quarters of those who had decamped.[99] In this way banner families would be prevented from putting down roots in the locality. Furthermore, because it was assumed (not without reason) that the upbringing received by young Manchus in the capital was stricter than in the provinces, the proper soldierly level of the garrison force would be maintained.

But before very long the practical problems of moving people around, and the need to provide a salary in every household, caused officials to search for easier ways to fill the job left vacant by the retirement or death of a garrison soldier (the selection of officers, as already explained, was more involved). In 1687 the emperor was asked to permit children of deceased garrison bannermen at Xi'an and other locations to assume their fathers' posts and take up garrison duty at those places, in effect authorizing a short-cut in the selection process for garrison openings. Somewhat surprisingly, in-stead of repeating the order to return to Beijing, the emperor announced that descendants were free to stay on at the garrison in the positions once occupied by senior males, provided they themselves were "skilled at horse-manship and archery, [and were] strong and brave."[100] In such cases a ban-nerman's retirement would not necessitate a "return to the banner." Upon his death the family would travel to Beijing to inter his body, and then af-terward resume residence in the garrison, supported by the son.[101]

Though this way of doing things greatly simplified the maintenance of steady strength at the garrisons, it compromised in a crucial way the 1684 edict affirming the capital as the bannerman's native place. Indeed, the 1687 decision implied nothing less than de facto continued residence in the prov-inces by successive generations of garrison Manchus. This development clearly contradicted the notion of Manchu temporary residence and eventu-ally subverted it. Nevertheless, by the Yongzheng reign the arrangement had become completely institutionalized. According to a 1726 decision, "If the widows of deceased officers and soldiers can be supported by their children in uniform, and if the garrison general or other supervising official can con-firm that there is no property in Beijing nor clan members there who can be relied on, then let them remain in the garrison."[102] From that time on, only in cases where there was no means of support at the garrison were families to return to Beijing.

With this precedent, the distance between the capital and the garrison be-gan to widen. It continued to widen throughout the 1700s as restrictions on returning to Beijing made it steadily more difficult for ordinary banner peo-ple outside the capital ever to come "home" again. Regulations for the Eight Banners issued in 1742 further specified that once a family had decided to stay on at the garrison with the son taking the father's post, no petitions to re-turn to the capital would be accepted later.[103] Ultimately, bannermen wishing to return to the capital (and certainly for many individuals there were ex-cellent reasons for wanting to do so) had to justify their wish on specific grounds, typically that they had elderly relatives in Beijing who had no one else to look after them.[104] By then, practical considerations had forced the court to radically alter the position once dictated to it by ideological concerns.

But these were eighteenth-century developments. For the first several generations of garrison banner families, the requirement to go back to Beijing and "return to the banner" was still a fact of life. Thanks to government assistance, getting back to Beijing usually did not pose too great a problem. Once a year all families from the garrison who were returning to the capital—that is, all families whose male head of household had retired or died within the previous year—assembled to form one group that would travel together. The garrison general provided each family with travel papers that specified the number in each household as well as the names of individuals. These documents were entrusted to an escort of garrison soldiers. Upon arrival the papers were given to representatives from the different banners, who made a check of names and numbers. After taking in the returnees, banner officials then issued return travel passes for the escort. If anyone had died or gone missing along the way, protocols signed by local officials had to be presented. Irregularities were to be investigated by the banner and reported to the throne, with possible punishment for the accompanying officers as well as the garrison general.[105]

Caravans of banner returnees, who usually traveled in the seventh or eight month, enjoyed a number of privileges. Their military escort took care of all arrangements and freed them from having to worry about possible attacks by bandits. Carts and boats were provided all along the way for the transport of women and children, household effects, and coffins. The travel permits authorizing the families to leave the garrison entitled them at the same time to use official military post roads and stations, which supplied them with fresh mounts and feed at no charge. A further, and very significant privilege, was free passage through all tax barriers.[106]

Despite these privileges, repatriation does not seem to have been a favored policy. For banner people in the garrisons, having to relocate to Beijing after several, or several tens, of years in the provinces, was very often not a welcome change. Not only ordinary garrison Manchus, but their commanders and banner officials in the capital who represented their interests to the court, felt they were much better off living out their lives in Hangzhou, Nanjing, or Qingzhou, rather than in Beijing.[107] Banner officials petitioned many times to have the "return-to-the-banner" policy changed. One memorial (from a senior Manchu in the Board of Revenue) suggested ending mandatory repatriation at least for those bannermen who had no property in the capital, arguing that this would save money "squandered" on travel expenses for families who came to the capital and then went right back to the provinces again.[108] The following 1732 edict was typical of the Yongzheng emperor's response to such petitions:

> How is one to treat today's prattling . . . that after garrison soldiers die their remains should be allowed to be buried there and their families permitted to continue living outside [the capital]? [People say this] only because they fail to realize that the places where soldiers are garrisoned are no more than sites for out-of-town errands. The capital is their native home. Is it reasonable that after their death, somebody's body not return with their family to their native home? If this were to be followed here, then eventually all garrison soldiers would become Han Chinese. The foundation of the dynasty's garrisons would end up having been the cause of the naturalization [Ch *ruji zhi you*] of its soldiers. Is this conceivable?[109]

Conceivable or no, this was precisely what was going on.

Though he memorably restated the dynasty's fears regarding permanent residence in the provinces and its reasons for insisting that bannermen return to Beijing upon the completion of their "out-of-town errands," the emperor addressed none of the concrete concerns about banner repatriation. Even the fiscal reformer in him was unmoved by reports of abuse of the tax-exempt status of returnee caravans from the south, loaded down so heavily with goods being smuggled to Beijing for sale that the craft—"widow boats" as they were sometimes called—could barely make it through the locks on the Grand Canal.[110] And while the emperor's unhesitating connection of burial and native place may have reflected Chinese sensibilities, his concern for the potentially disastrous results of changing the repatriation policy was all Manchu.[111]

A few years later, just months into the reign of the Qianlong emperor, another memorial arrived from Qingzhou garrison general Arigūn asking again that repatriation be made voluntary (as it apparently already was at the minor Taiyuan and Dezhou garrisons).[112] The Qianlong emperor responded in almost identical fashion as his father. After restating the court's objections to burial at the garrison, he went on to emphasize his main point:

> This is key: if the bodies of Manchus are buried here and there in the provinces, then with the passage of time I fear the disappearance of

Manchu ways. [Also], there is the fear that this will become a source of contention with the local people. . . . Furthermore, Beijing is where all Manchus belong. At the outset, stationing Manchu officers and soldiers in garrisons in the provinces was done particularly in order to keep a guard and keep the peace. If these are accidental places where people are sent to work, there is no cause that they be held there [forever]. Hence it is only advantageous if people are able to move quickly. If cemeteries are established in the garrisons, then when people are moved and transferred to other locations, the cemeteries will end up being permanently abandoned.[113]

The preceding makes it plain that, as before, apprehension over the permanent diaspora and assimilation of the Manchus remained the main reason for repatriation. Emphasizing Beijing as the only real and true home for all Manchus, wherever they might "temporarily" be, and insistence on the maintenance of family cemeteries *there* were important ways to assure that ordinary bannermen did not come to identify too closely with the Chinese provinces, that peace was kept, and that "Manchu ways" were upheld. The emperor professed shock that Arigūn seemed not to be aware of this:

> That Arigūn . . . should have memorialized in this way [concerning the "return-to-the-banner" policy], without giving thought to the old Manchu ways, is improper. . . . *If Arigūn as a garrison general is capable of this kind of report, what must those lower than he be saying? In protecting the local area, he has forgotten about such important matters as the old Manchu traditions and loving his lord. I think about this with great distress.*[114]

Forbidding garrison bannermen to own local property or to bury their dead anywhere but Beijing were thus vital planks in the platform of dynastic stability.

Another was the ban on garrison bannermen taking the examinations in the provinces, which the emperor linked specifically to the decay of military ability:

> The nation originally placed soldiers in the garrisons to carry arms to protect the cities, not to attack the literary arts and vie for fame with literati and scholars at the examination halls. Those soldiers without posts who were able in book-learning and conversant with literary meaning were invited to come to the capital to sit the examinations as a way of enlarging their career paths. There has never been a prohibition on pursuing scholarship. Now, however, if everyone is to be permitted to sit

the examinations in the provinces, each will do as he pleases and compete for hollow reputations, neglecting military affairs. They will become strangers to riding and shooting and forget to train and drill. Who will there be left in the future to staff the garrisons? . . . The whole intent of establishing the garrisons will be lost. There could be nothing more absurd than this. . . . Let there be no more of this ridiculous discussion.[115]

## MATTERS OF LIFE AND DEATH

In raising the issues of property, burial and the tending of graves, and examinations, the emperors touched on some fundamental difficulties of the "return-to-the-banner" policy and in the process suggested that these were the very things—very Chinese things, at that—which determined "home." Indeed, the Kangxi emperor had foreseen the importance of most of these elements fifty years before, in 1687, when he wrote, "If [bannermen] are allowed to acquire property and establish cemeteries, eventually they will end up the same as the natives. This is extremely undesirable. Let the garrison generals put an absolute stop to this."[116] In other words, if "home" was where one owned property, most bannermen could own property only in Beijing;[117] if "home" was where one was buried, bannermen must be buried in Beijing (unless they lived in the Northeast); and if home was where one sat for the examinations, then for bannermen this would have to be in Beijing.

It was surely the second of these points that the Qianlong emperor had in mind when he expressed concern over the establishment of cemeteries at the garrisons and their potential abandonment. The criterion of burial provoked no conflict for those who were born and raised in Beijing. By these standards, if the capital was anybody's home, it was theirs. Their own resistance to relocation out of the capital grew quite strong by the eighteenth century, as the court discovered when it attempted to resettle Beijing bannermen in positions specially created for them in the provinces or in the frontier.[118] But in attempting to apply this same standard to garrison bannermen, the court ran into practical and psychological obstacles. The reality was that unless they were officers, garrison bannermen would never leave the provinces. Burying the family in Beijing must have made little sense to them, and one finds it improbable that many were persuaded by the emperor's argument that those who buried their dead in local cemeteries would later be potentially guilty of abandoning their ancestors. People were abandoning grave sites, to be sure, but at the capital, not at the garrison.

Another logistical problem faced by garrison families was what to do with bodies that had to be kept several months before they could be sent back to the capital. At some garrisons, such as Qingzhou, the solution was to cremate them, since ashes were easier to store and transport than corpses. Furthermore, as garrison general Arigūn explained, cremation was advantageous because the ashes of as many as seven or eight bannermen could be loaded onto one large wagon, while unincinerated corpses in coffins required one wagon apiece. With wagons sometimes in short supply, and rates for transport to Beijing climbing to ten taels and more, cremation was a good means of economizing. Arigūn also justified the practice on the grounds that the road from Qingzhou to Beijing was rough and mountainous and that bumping and rattling about in wagons damaged coffins and their contents.[119] (This problem, he said, was even more serious for returnees from garrisons located further from the capital—suggesting that cremation was not limited to the Qingzhou garrison alone.[120]) The emperor was not impressed. He fired back an order forbidding cremation: the dead were to be properly buried, according to "ancient" custom. But the emperor was being disingenuous. Cremation was in fact a traditional practice among the Jurchens and later the Manchus.[121] Though Nurhaci himself was apparently not cremated, funeral records show that Hong Taiji as well as two of Shunzhi's empresses were.[122] The custom remained popular at least through the eighteenth century: in regulations from 1764 it is again proscribed and a memoir written as late as the mid-nineteenth century refers in passing to cremation as a "dynastic [*guo*, i.e., Manchu] usage found equally among the noble and base."[123]

In cremating their dead, garrison Manchus were thus rather maintaining, not violating, ancient practice. The most likely interpretation of the emperor's insistence otherwise is that he was concerned to conceal what he considered a distasteful, and possibly embarrassing Manchu practice, left over from the days when they had been "barbarians." But coming at a time when it was trying its best to hold the line on Manchu acculturation, it is striking how this position on cremation represents a court retreat from earlier Manchu practice. The one-time institutional habit and original Manchu practice overlapped, but the emperor, who ought to have been cheered by such a coincidence, instead tried to overturn it. This decision is comparable to the contemporaneous shift toward the support of Manchu widow chastity, and to the suppression of "primitive" shamanic ritual. In all these cases, the court showed itself capable of picking and choosing what it wanted to preserve of the Manchu past, fashioning new practices and discarding old ones with more "authentic" pedigrees, claiming all the while to be consistently supporting "traditional" Manchu customs. This engineering of identity through the manipulation of symbolically laden practice shows the Qing court squarely at its "ethnic" best.

Even after relocating to the capital, many garrison families faced uncertain futures. It was expected that banner veterans and widows with property or close relatives in Beijing would be taken in by the clan, which also took over responsibility for the funeral if there was one,[124] while the younger (male) members of the family waited for new assignments either in the capital or somewhere in the frontier garrisons. Those with no place to go and no relatives to turn to for help faced a more serious dilemma and could only hope for charity from the banner. According to regulations, the company was supposed to care for homeless widows and orphans.[125] It did so to the extent that the bodies they had traveled with were buried in charity plots belonging to the companies.[126] But indications are that other assistance was probably meager. This caused many to risk an illegal return to the garrison, where they might hope for help from relatives or friends who remained there, and where the surroundings were at least familiar.[127]

The court was well aware of the human cost that resulted from forcing garrison bannermen to bury their dead in the capital. Typical was the request by a lieutenant general at the Jingzhou garrison to retire to Hangzhou: "Since the days of my grandfather we have always lived in Hangzhou. All my sons and grandsons are now Hangzhou soldiers. I humbly beg for permission to live out my days there." What could the emperor do but accede?[128] In their protests to the emperor, banner officials in both the capital and the provinces were especially troubled by the dilemmas faced by grieving wives, husbands, daughters, and sons, and used this along with mundane logistical objections to argue for an end to repatriation. One explained that "returning to the banner" left wives and sons no way to carry out the proper uxorial and filial rites at the graves of their departed husbands and fathers if the son took the father's position and they returned to the garrison. Allowing burial of banner soldiers at the garrison would avoid this impropriety, he said, "making it possible for widows and orphaned children to fully display their filial thoughts according to the season."[129] In another request to change the repatriation policy, an official pointed out the tremendous bother everybody was put to—garrison officials, post-station employ-ees, civilians living near the post stations, the accompanying soldiers, and, of course, the families themselves—and then put a moral spin on things, commenting, "With no way for them [i.e., family members] to honor the re-lationship between father and son or that between brothers, then in spite of the incommodious use of my lord's post horses and wagons and the waste of my lord's money and grain, it does not seem that any good accrues to the deceased." He also spelled out quite plainly the problem for filial sons serv-ing in the provinces: "If they have someone in the capital on whom they can rely, then at the proper times [of the year] paper money is burned and the body does not dry out. If there is no such reliable person, the body and the grave end up withering."[130] Appealing on these grounds—to the emperor's sense of propriety, rather than his sense of expedience—was a more effective way to win concessions on the repatriation policy.

In his long 1736 memorial to the Qianlong emperor, cited earlier, Qing-zhou garrison general Arigūn argued that compulsory repatriation from the garrisons should be abandoned, not because families could not care for the graves of the husband or father, but because husbands were not buried to-gether with wives. This was because no provision existed for the transport of the bodies of wives, children, servants, or any member of a banner house-hold not presently or formerly on active service. If family members prede-ceased their husbands or fathers, their bodies were typically buried at the garrison in plots bought from peasants for this purpose, apparently illegally. Sometimes they were not even buried at all. Burying the husband's body back in Beijing later on meant that the resting places of the couple were apart: "How can their souls find peace?" Arigūn remarked. The Qianlong emperor's response, critical as it was, did contain one key concession, or-dering that not only husbands, but *all* family members should be brought back to Beijing for burial:

> From now on officers and soldiers stationed in the provinces shall bring *the bodies of their deceased* to be buried. If they are unwilling to bring them to the capital and have them buried at the garrison, then later, even if they are transferred elsewhere, *all will truly know that* they are willingly leaving *their ancestors* to be abandoned in these cemeteries. Let them do as they wish.[131]

This alteration of policy arguably sprang as much from the emperor's worry over the growing attachment of garrison Manchus to the locale as from his sincere feeling for their dilemma in wanting to show proper respect for their spouses and their parents. But it was not much of a solution. Instead of having to worry about getting one body back to Beijing, families now had to worry about getting many bodies there. In addition, there was still the problem that no one in the capital would be there to make the proper sacrifices and care for the graves once the family returned to the garrison. Just three years later, in 1739, the court introduced new exceptions recognizing that the welfare of childless, retired garrison bannermen might equally be entrusted to brothers, nephews, or even bondservants in the household if they were soldiers. In these cases permission for transfer to the garrison had to be obtained from the necessary officials and, in the case of those serving as officials, a dispensation obtained from the Board of War. However, retirees living in Beijing were not permitted to join children or relatives in the provinces for the purposes of spending their retirement there.[132] For this reason, bannermen in the garrisons were granted the right to apply for repatriation to Beijing in order to care for their parents.[133]

The court came partially to terms with the impracticalities of the increasingly Byzantine residency policy in 1742. In that year "returning to the banner" was made optional for families in the Chinese banners and retirement and burial in the locale permitted for them alone.[134] That decision noted that the fathers and grandfathers of serving Chinese bannermen had in many cases bought property or otherwise secretly established permanent ties to the garrison city, and that in view of this situation, those who wished to should be free to remain or, if now resident in the capital, return to the garrison city. The catch was that they would be required to leave the banner and become regular civilians.[135] This change, apart from revealing the enormous difference in attitudes among the Qing elite toward the Chinese banners, was proof that ownership of property was seen to constitute a real bond to the locale.

Only in 1756 did the court finally admit the failure of the repatriation policy for those in both the Manchu and Mongol banners. The emperor at last relented and permitted all bannermen to bury their dead in the provinces. At the same time, the court also granted them the privilege of buying and owning land in garrison cities:

> Considering that the nation has been at peace now for some time, and that those inside [the capital] and those outside [in the provinces] have all already formed stable groups, then to continue with the former precedent

would be a shortsighted plan bound to create worries for those on duty in the provinces wanting to turn the garrison into their permanent residence. And as far as continuing with sending [bodies], they feel this as an annoyance and the local officials are quite burdened by it. Henceforth let garrison officers and soldiers be free, by virtue of imperial grace, to acquire property in the provinces and to be buried there after death. Widows shall cease to be sent to the capital.[136]

This was a momentous decision: for provincial banner households, home was now the garrison. The same year, the court took the additional step of authorizing garrison officers to purchase land for public cemeteries, with the understanding that banner families with the necessary funds could establish their own private cemeteries, just as in Beijing.[137] Twenty-five years later, after having gone to so much trouble and expense for so long to assure the return of all bannermen, living or dead, to the capital, the court would actually forbid their return at all, unless they could demonstrate sufficient means.[138]

### RESIDENT ALIENS

The 1756 decision of the Qianlong emperor to permit Manchu bannermen to reside permanently in the provinces would seem to have at last answered the prayers of garrison officials anxious to be rid of the annual burden of arranging for the repatriation of several families, who were in most cases bound to return to the garrison anyway. But it also meant that garrison Manchus now formed minority communities of conquerors stranded forever in an otherwise Chinese world. No longer simply sojourners, they had become resident aliens.

This dramatic policy turnaround prompts a number of questions. One might well ask whether by officially acknowledging that for garrison bannermen "home" was henceforth the garrison, the court did not accept as a consequence the alienation of garrison Manchus from the center and, by extension, from the emperor and the "old Manchu traditions." If so, then wasn't the court in effect abandoning the garrisons and garrison bannermen to their own devices? Had the banner population outside the capital come to mean so little? And how could such an attitude be reconciled to the simultaneously renewed emphasis on the Manchu Way?

There can be little question that the policies adopted by the court from the very beginning of the garrison system were inescapably at odds with certain of its ideals. The Eight Banners was the "root" of the nation, the military and ethnic emblem of dynastic authority. The stationing of bannermen around China could hardly have been avoided if the Manchus expected to be able to maintain their hold on power. For strategic and political reasons, garrisons had to be built. So for decades, the court struggled mightily to reconcile the contradictions of the Manchu diaspora, to limit the effects of permanent residence and to preserve as much as possible the physical and psychological ties between the garrisons and the Manchu center. Bannermen were made to live with other bannermen in lesser Manchu cities that were imitations, even if rough ones, of the great Manchu city in Beijing; they were forced to send sons eighteen *sui* and older back to Beijing;[139] and they were limited to burying their loved ones in Beijing, and families "stranded" at the garrisons were ordered back to the capital, whether they had property and relatives there or not.

But the government lacked the financial and political means to make garrison duty in the Chinese provinces a truly temporary assignment. Once the court abandoned its position in 1756, other compromises that had already been made took on greater significance. Chief among these was the effective creation in 1730 of separate companies based in the garrisons (*zhufang zuoling/seremšeme tehe ba-i niru*). Where previously all companies were Beijing-based, after this time the triennial census of banner populations formally recognized the separation of companies between Beijing and the provincial garrisons.[140] In thus adapting to the new reality, we find evidence that the court continued to rely on the banner system, particularly at the company level, to maintain the integrity of Manchu communities in China. As the final chapter will show, this pattern—the shoring up of banner institutions to preserve Manchu identity—is consistent with the general approach adopted by the eighteenth-century court.

Of course, these changes did not lower the value to the dynasty of the banner garrisons. If these institutions had really come to be dispensable, it seems fair to assume that the court could have gone ahead and cut off support completely. But it did not do this. It would therefore be a mistake to read into the court's reluctant acknowledgment of Manchu permanent residence either the surrender of court interest in the garrisons or the surrender of the garrisons to local interests. One might rather see this as the evolution of interior and exterior spheres (sometimes even spoken of as such—*dorgi* and *tulergi*—in Manchu[141]), the formation of a system where Manchus living in the provinces, instead of being drawn regularly in and out of Beijing, remained instead at the garrisons in a more or less fixed orbit around the capital, still bound but at a greater distance than before.

In this and other aspects, the problems of "home" raised in this chapter are crucial to an understanding of how the Manchus saw their occupation of China and of how the occupation changed them. For the social problems arising from extended Manchu residence in the Chinese provinces—the repatriation of banner dependents, the separation of extended families, and the burial of deceased bannermen—constituted one more set of distinctive bannerman issues. Like the other peculiarities that came with being in the banners, diasporic issues shaped banner people's lives in unique ways and set them apart from the Han, though this happened independent of any court intention. They combined with distinctive religious, onomastic, and gender practices to accentuate the alien marginality of Manchus. Perhaps this is why most gazetteer editors in the Qing saw no need to include information on local bannermen or banner institutions in their histories: like minorities in so many places, they were invisible. The shifts in residence policy that came in the mid-1700s, though redefining "home" for provincial bannermen, seem not to have changed this.

Of course, the court could not have foreseen that this would be so; in between the lines of the memorials on residence issues, it read its own concerns of assimilation. In this connection, I would suggest that one immediate motive for the resurgent eighteenth-century emphasis by the Yongzheng and Qianlong emperors on preserving the Manchu Way in fact lay in the growing and undeniable realization that life in the garrisons had already come to be something not only very different from what the court thought it should be, but very different, too, from life in Beijing (where there was already plenty of cause for worry). True, garrison bannermen were now permanently in the provinces; true, they were separated both from local Han Chinese and from the main center of Manchu culture in Qing China, Beijing. But this did not mean that the court gave up the fight to maintain Manchu ways. On the contrary, it breathed new life into efforts to play up difference and raise ethnic consciousness.

Inasmuch as the shifts in residence policy represented a defeat in reconciling the Manchu presence in China with the danger of Manchu acculturation, they gave added urgency to finding other ways to address that threat. Acknowledging, as the Qianlong emperor finally had to do, that the garrisons were not "accidental places where people were sent to work," did nothing to lessen the undesirability and unpalatability of this development from the court's point of view. The many strains—strategic, logistic, financial, and psychological—on the capital-garrison axis brought about a loosening of ties and accelerated the creation of separate Manchu worlds, one centered in the capital and another in the provinces. Yet the importance of the garrisons remained unchanged. They were still supposed to be "tigers on the mountain." There was thus considerable anxiety over bannermen who no longer kept horses and didn't know how to ride or shoot from horseback: "Their children and grandchildren, unable to ride, will become useless people,"[142] lamented the emperor. What the court may not have realized was that, wherever they lived, wherever they died and were buried, their peculiar lifestyles and cultural habits meant that bannermen remained outsiders, safe from wholesale assimilation. The paradox was that it was now as much their life in China as people of the banners, as it was their warrior ways and maintenance of different practices from the Chinese, that made them Manchus.

PART THREE

# The Crises of the Eighteenth Century

# CHAPTER SEVEN

# Whither the Manchu Way?

When the Yongzheng emperor took power in 1722, he faced urgent problems on a number of fronts. There were simultaneous crises of legitimacy and factionalism stemming from the murky circumstances of his accession, a fiscal emergency linked to a whopping two-and-a-half-million-tael tax deficit, and immediate military concerns on the western frontier. The situation in the Eight Banners could offer him little consolation. Not only was the prolonged presence of bannermen in the Chinese provinces reducing the cherished ideal of temporary residence to a hollow fiction—provoking deep anxiety over the long-term effects of the diaspora with respect to Manchu identity—but there was also the rising threat posed by the sophisticated attractions of Chinese culture. Beyond this, the exorbitant costs of supporting banner personnel and infrastructure were beginning to raise questions about the very viability of this basic dynastic institution.

Sensing this danger, during the first half of the eighteenth century the Qing court stepped up rhetoric stressing "old Manchu ways," tried to find solutions to the chronic fiscal drain of the banners, and mounted a thorough housecleaning of banner ranks. The results were mixed. Though cultural practices tied to Manchu identity (language, for instance) continued to weaken despite fervent efforts to halt their decline, the court was relatively successful in its reforms of banner finance and registration, enabling the banners to survive another one hundred and fifty years. Thanks to these efforts, Manchu identity survived, too, part of a new Manchu Way bound up with the realities of banner life.

As earlier chapters have shown, the link between identity and institutions was coeval with the establishment of the Eight Banners, but it had never been so obvious as during the period between 1720 and 1780. Looking at the changes during those years, it seems the court saw quite plainly that to maintain the integrity of the Manchu ethnos it had not only to take a stand against the vitiation of what it deemed to be Manchu ancestral ways, but it also had to act decisively to shore up the chief institution behind Manchu ethnic solidarity. This chapter examines the first of these eighteenth-century crises by discussing the court-defined ideology of the Manchu Way and the nuances of the acculturation process among Manchus and other bannermen. The next chapter investigates the issues of finance and poverty in the banners, showing how policy considerations relating to banner finance forced a broad redefinition of legal banner identities that tied Manchu ethnicity even more firmly to the Eight Banners.

## ACCULTURATION AND THE MANCHU WAY

The origin of the phrases "Manchu Way" (Ma *Manjusai doro*) and "Old Way" (Ma *fe doro*) was presented in the Introduction. These and related expressions occur frequently in seventeenth- and eighteenth-century discussions of the professional and personal standards banner males were expected to meet. The principal elements of the Old Way included equestrianism, toxophilism, linguistic competence in Manchu, and frugality—essential characteristics, the court asserted, that made Manchus Manchu. Sometimes additional qualities, such as reverence for one's ancestors, devotion in service to the emperor, and what was called "manly virtue" (Ma *hahai erdemu*) were also included within the Way, along with naming practices and clothing; shamanism, as already mentioned, was never raised in this context. The emphasis on masculinity reveals this to have been primarily a male discourse of identity, but as the previous chapter has shown, women were expected to maintain certain standards, too.[1]

Fear for the future of the Manchu Way can be dated to the famous 1636 speech of Hong Taiji,[2] anxious after reading the history of the thirteenth-century Jin dynasty.[3] Evaluating the fate of his Jurchen predecessors, Hong Taiji remarked that the "Old Way" practiced by Agūda (Jin Taizu, 1115–22) and Ukimai (Jin Taizong, 1123–34) had been forsaken, as Xizong and his successor, Hai-ling Wang (1135–48 and 1149–60), followed the "Chinese Way" (Ma *Nikan-i doro*) of liquor, leisure, and riding in sedan chairs. "Under Shizong Ulu khan [1161–89]," he instructed his princely audience,

> . . . for the first time it was feared that [Jurchen] children and grandchildren would enter the Chinese Way. Over and over he [Shizong]

repeated: "Do not neglect the old ways of the ancestors. Wear Jurchen clothing. Learn the Jurchen language. Practice archery and horsemanship every day." Although he had thus spoken, the khans of later generations entered the Chinese Way, putting aside shooting and riding. By the time of Aizong [1224–33], the [Jurchen] Way was destroyed. The dynasty had been wiped out.

It is hard to imagine a clearer statement of Manchu fear of "sinicization" and what it would mean. Hong Taiji went on to defend his rejection of the proposals put forward by Dahai and Erdeni that the Manchus exchange their own clothing for wide-sleeved Chinese dress on the grounds that this would lessen martial preparedness. In a passage already cited, he concluded by expressing his grave worries over the future: "What I fear is this: that the children and grandchildren of later generations will abandon the Old Way, neglect shooting and riding, and enter into the Chinese Way!"[4]

By the first half of the eighteenth century, Hong Taiji's fears were beginning to come true. An official of the Kangxi era referred to the "old Manchu customs" in a 1704 call to preserve archetypal Manchu qualities, implying that even by the turn of the eighteenth century the hard life of the warrior was already viewed with some nostalgia.[5] Beginning under the Yongzheng emperor, the court regularly received reports on slipping standards among Manchus in the capital and garrisons, prompting imperial exhortations to banner officers to inspire their men to hold on to old standards and maintain Manchu self-respect. The following admonition, delivered in 1735 by a garrison commander to his men, is a typical example of the rhetoric used: "Study hard and learn well how to speak Manchu, how to shoot from a stance and from horseback, and how to handle a musket. Obey established customs and live frugally and economically. All of you have been raised and nurtured in due measure by our sacred lord [Ma *enduringge ejen*, i.e., the emperor]— you must work hard to repay his great favor!"[6] Of the skills mentioned here, prowess in the saddle, as described earlier, was the hallmark of Manchu authority and the bedrock of Qing military strength. The deterioration of this skill was therefore the most disturbing aspect of the decline of the Manchu Way, since it figured not only in terms of Manchu ethnicity but also, symbolically and practically, in terms of dynastic security.

It is impossible to date the beginning of this decline in any specific way. Hsiao I-shan put the horizon at the second quarter of the eighteenth century; by then, he said, the "traditional military skills of the Manchus . . .

were almost completely lost."[7] Inaba Iwakichi dated the decline to the end of the eighteenth century, timing it in with the decay of other institutions late in the Qianlong reign.[8] Yet another opinion holds that by 1820 "the lack of systematic practice and drill had already turned many Banner divisions into an army of 'paper warriors.'"[9] However one wishes to assess military preparedness among bannermen in the mid-Qing, four caveats are in order. First, it is essential to pay attention to ethnic stripe. Standards slid earliest and farthest among Chinese bannermen rather than among Manchus or Mongols, while troops like the Chakhar, Sibe, and Solon, important in the conquest of Xinjiang in the 1750s and 1760s, seem never to have lost their martial edge. A century later, even the Taiping seem to have feared them.[10] Second, skills differed according to location. Martial abilities at Beijing tell us little about abilities at the garrisons, and even between garrisons situations could differ substantially. Complaints about poor archery skills among one group of soldiers at one location cannot be taken to imply that skills were equally poor among all bannermen everywhere. Third, even at a single location, the situation could change over time. The arrival of a committed and energetic garrison general could mean the rapid transformation of a bunch of idlers into hard-working soldiers. Finally, because most evidence is anecdotal, one must be cautious. Opinions were often based only on brief observation or were hyperbolically calculated either to shock or win approval, and should be taken as only partial reflections of reality concerning a certain group of soldiers, rather than as blanket truths applicable to all bannermen.

Taking these factors into consideration, if one were to base a judgment on the frequency of calls for improvement in military performance, then one might date the decline in the Chinese banners as early as the 1680s, with noticeable deterioration in the Manchu and Mongol banners beginning in the 1730s. It should be noted, however, that military declension proceeded more quickly at the southeast and Jiangnan garrisons as compared to garrisons in the northwest, and that it seems to have proceeded most quickly in the capital. A better sense of the general situation emerges when we separately examine circumstances in different locations.

One of the very earliest comments on the problem of sloppy Manchu soldiering at the garrisons came in an edict to a Hangzhou lieutenant general after a visit by the Kangxi emperor to the south in 1683: "The Manchu soldiers at the Hangzhou garrison are absorbing vulgar customs. Many wear no belt and walk around in slippers. Since they are Manchus, they should respect the occupation of Manchus and diligently practice riding and shooting."[11] Sixteen years later, the emperor happily reported that the situation had improved: "Edict to the grand secretaries: Today I have reviewed the Manchu and Chinese banner officers and troops at Hangzhou. All of them excel at riding and shooting and speak Manchu fluently. This is all the work of the training under garrison general Jamyang. It is a great pity that he has passed away."[12] The assumptions revealed here, especially in the first quotation, linking Manchu identity and cultural performance, are "ethnic" in a very traditional sense; yet as the second quotation shows, categories were not neat, since links were also made between *banner* identity and *Manchu* performance. In either instance, expectations were often disappointed. The same year he praised the Hangzhou bannermen, the emperor registered his dissatisfaction with the Nanjing garrison: "Edict: If the Manchu soldiers garrisoned in the provinces idle away most of the time and do not engage in training, how will they be of any use? While touring the south, I have seen that the troops at Zhejiang [i.e., Hangzhou] are quite fine, but those at Jiangnan [i.e., Nanjing] are very poor."[13] Evidence for the latter claim was that "more than half" of young Nanjing bannermen were poor horsemen.[14] By 1702, concern for the situation at the garrisons finally prompted the emperor to include soldiers from Hangzhou, Nanjing, and Xi'an in the hunts at Rehe, which he no doubt hoped would prevent further decline and give garrison bannermen added incentive to keep their skills up.

The next we hear of troops in Jiangnan is in the 1720s, thirty years after the Kangxi emperor's last visit. In a 1725 rescript, the Yongzheng emperor complemented Jingzhou general Unaha on his work so far, adding, "No matter what, don't let the soldiers slip into ways of laziness and leisure. If they can't take hardship, what kind of soldiers are they?" Here is evidence of the fear of "softening" of once-tough men-at-arms; the use of "slip" (Ma *eyembi*) here and elsewhere conveys the unmistakable sense of slackening decline.[15] The same word appears in his 1724 missive to the newly appointed garrison general at Nanjing:

> Because for many years they have not gotten even one good general, the Jiangnan soldiers have been spoiled and their customs have very much slid into Chinese ways. Do your very best to teach them and put this right. Not making [them into] good, well-rounded men but [instead] favoring the soldiers because they are Manchu and having them oppress the people,

cause trouble in the locale, estranging them from military training, and permitting leisurely time-serving, while being oneself generous and nice are all suitably small ways of thinking.[16]

Significantly, blame for the "slide" into Chinese ways was placed not on the Chinese or even on the soldiers themselves, but on Manchu officers at the garrisons. Equally significant is the caution against giving preferential treatment to soldiers "because they are Manchus" and letting them abuse the Chinese locals, a confirmation that, as suggested in Chapter 5, such behavior was in fact typical. Reports from Hangzhou in the 1730s remained encouraging. There was steady improvement in archery skills with extra training for those who were unable to draw even a six-strength bow.[17] More candidly, Lieutenant General Bašinu, newly arrived at Hangzhou, found in 1736 that "in some companies the soldiers work with hard bows and are skilled at stationary and mounted archery . . . while in other companies the soldiers are less well trained at these things."[18] Still, bannermen at Hangzhou and its naval extension at Zhapu must have been holding the line, since Manchus at the Qingzhou garrison—"still not evenly practiced" at shooting, riding, and using a musket—were judged inferior to them in 1735. The proposal to revive Hangzhou's local hunts, described earlier, was floated at just this time. Horses were being added at both Hangzhou and Nanjing so that soldiers had the proper number of mounts (two per man). Furthermore, since equitation was important to preserving "soldierly virtue," more horses were to be bought for the Zhapu garrison, too.[19] Unless these reports were totally fabricated, the Qianlong emperor's declaration at this time that "the soldiers at Hangzhou and Nanjing all have entered into Chinese ways" seems melodramatic.[20]

Whatever the true state of the southeast garrisons, overall, the northwest garrisons, especially Xi'an, provided the court with more cause for optimism. After his 1703 visit to Xi'an, the Kangxi emperor wrote back to garrison general Boji, "Those who come from Xi'an are attentive and able to cope with difficulties. But at present it is still too soon to know whether or not this will not change over time. The customs at Xi'an are very good, so that it is as though the old Manchu etiquette from former days were still around. By no means must the ways at Xi'an be changed."[21] Imperial displeasure with standards at Xi'an in the early part of the Yongzheng reign appear to be linked to the emperor's uneasy relationship with the garrison general (Yansin, his cousin) than to serious deterioration of martial skills. In a 1726 rescript issued not long before Yansin's arrest, the emperor criticized Xi'an soldiers for their laziness, and accused Yansin of being tardy in arriving at military drills (how the emperor knew this is a mystery—perhaps from the report of a lieutenant general?).[22] But his replacement reported in 1730 that while the situation with the Chinese bannermen was lacking in some respects, most troops were up to standards.[23] Concrete information on Xi'an military skills in the early Qianlong reign is scarce, but there is good reason to suspect that they were quite superior to those at garrisons along the coast. Unlike most soldiers at Hangzhou, Nanjing, and elsewhere, many Xi'an bannermen had recent battle experience: for them, handling a bow and arrow on horseback was not an abstract exercise, and thus we find no precise counts of how many of them could take a six-strength bow, how many a ten-strength bow, and so on. Moreover, equestrianism remained very much part of the way of life of Manchu bannermen in the Northwest, since the problem of runaway *kutule* was felt keenly only here.[24] As garrison general Cimbu put it in a 1737 memorial, "for nearly twenty years the Manchu soldiers at Xi'an have continually been involved in military campaigns.[25]

In another memorial, Cimbu wrote,

> Although the customs are not the same as in bygone days, there is still attention to skill and diligence. . . . Each works hard at his official post, as well as at shooting from a stance and from horseback. As for setting off [on business], whether on foot or by horse, if word comes in the morning, departure is in the morning. If it comes in the evening, departure is in the evening. The men can still take it. Guided by the teachings of the nation, each looks after himself. Generally it seems that things are coming back to the simplicity and plainness set by custom and rule.[26]

The emphasis here on the soldiers' toughness and their Spartan habits implies that military standards were high at Xi'an; it also indicates that the Manchu Way was not just a court construct, but was an ideal internalized by the banner elite, too, and reflected in actual practice. Indeed, the biggest problems at Xi'an at the time seem to have concerned not military abilities but management difficulties such as fugitive slaves, housing, and unemployment. That the Manchu Way was alive at Xi'an is, very likely, one reason that bannermen there were chosen in the late 1730s to colonize new frontier garrisons at Tongguan, Liangzhou, and Zhuanglang. Although idle bannermen from the capital were sometimes transferred out to provincial garrisons (as they had been, for instance, to Ningxia), usually bannermen who retained in their customs and abilities something of the Manchu warrior ideal were preferred for frontier assignments. Later in the Qianlong reign this role would be assigned to Chakhar and Sibe,[27] so it is telling that in the late 1730s regular Xi'an Manchus (often younger men and their families) were still judged fit for this challenge.[28]

Really serious slippage in martial skills at the banner garrisons appears to have occurred in the second half of the eighteenth century; positive reports on the state of military preparedness at provincial garrisons virtually cease at this time. Even at Xi'an, the last bastion of Manchu military virtue in China proper, the evidence points to a steep decline by 1780. But this does not mean that all bannermen had completely forgotten how to ride or shoot—there were always enough soldiers to keep the imperial hunts going, and bannermen demonstrated their valor time and again in the warfare that continued through the 1760s, 1770s, and beyond. In the portraits made then to commemorate their exploits, one can still see the look of the steppe warrior.[29]

If the situation at some locations, particularly the coastal garrisons, was often lamentable, that in the capital was by all indications even worse. Indeed, most of the evidence documenting the pathetic state of Manchu military skills refers to Beijing, not garrison, bannermen. The statement quoted above, that by 1725–50 the "traditional military skills of the Manchus . . . were almost completely lost," relies almost solely on depictions of life in Beijing for this characterization.[30] A typical example drawn from the *Veritable Records* makes this clear. An edict of April 19, 1741, castigated members of the imperial clan and vanguard for "neglecting their basic duties" by failing to study Manchu and practice archery and horsemanship. Although "young Manchus" are also included in the charge, it is obvious from the context that the emperor had young Manchus living in Beijing in mind.[31] By one kind of logic, this is the opposite of what might be expected; Manchus living in and around Beijing formed the largest Manchu community in China. Their greater number, along with their proximity to the emperor and the center of Manchu power, should have meant greater confidence and cultural self-sufficiency for the community as a whole. Garrison bannermen, who had greater chances for contact with local Chinese, ought to have been the prime victims of "vulgar Han customs" and the first to lose their martial edge.[32] Yet the evidence I have seen suggests that this was not the case, and that rather it was Beijing Manchus who went soft first.

Perhaps because they were rarely sent on campaign and had not fought for some time, capital bannermen were not held as much to account for the decline in their martial abilities as were Manchus at the garrisons—although the Yongzheng emperor wasted no time in dismissing a captain-general in the guards who couldn't shoot an arrow.[33] Another explanation might be that capital bannermen did not feel themselves solely responsible for maintaining the local area in "awe," since the emperor was in Beijing and fulfilled that function himself.

One of the first complaints of poor skills among officers in the capital dates from 1684, just six months after the Kangxi emperor's negative review of the Hangzhou troops mentioned earlier. In 1723, when a flood of criticism of lax standards in the Eight Banners accompanied the change of emperors, most comments were directed at Manchus in the capital. Twenty years on, after restarting the imperial hunts in 1741, the Qianlong emperor complained most vociferously about the capital bannermen who had taken part in the hunt, not about the garrison soldiers.[34] The Suiyuan garrison general wrote that same year to complain about the sixteen hundred Beijing Manchus who were to be sent to him: "All of these men are [bound to be] mediocre horsemen who spend most of their time drinking," he wrote. "They are going to find it hard to get by if they come here." This pessimistic forecast went on to say that if the Dzungars made trouble, the transfers from Beijing would be of dubious value in battle.[35] One can easily imagine the emperor nodding his head sadly in agreement as he read this memorial. What is even more surprising about the decline of standards in the capital is that during these years the worst charges of incompetence in archery concerned—of all groups—the vanguard and guard divisions attached to the palace.[36]

Declining interest in archery had other ramifications as well. Consider this lament by vanguard captain-general Mantai:

> In our nation's olden times there was a blacksmith and a bowyer in every company, and every banner had its own craftsmen to do embossing, carving, silversmithing, saddlemaking, and so on, and not only fletchers. Looking into this further, it seems that because Manchus of yore used arrows that they had made themselves, fletchers came to be unnecessary. Today's Manchu soldiers use arrows they have bought from Chinese craftsmen at markets or temples; they no longer know how to make arrows. It has even gotten so that no one knows how to straighten arrows by filing and polishing them.[37]

That Manchus were no longer able to make and repair their own arrows was symptomatic of the loss of self-reliance that caused concern for the viability of the Manchu Way.

## LIVING THE GOOD LIFE

The Beijing bannerman's love of luxury—fine clothing, good food, gaming, entertainment, lavish wedding and funeral ceremonies—was another pattern of behavior frequently criticized by banner officials and the court as undermining the Manchu Way. Such behavior sapped martial vigor in a devious way and contravened another basic Manchu quality, referred to with words such as *gulu*, "plain, unadulterated," and *nomhon*, "pure, free of affectation." In Chinese it was sometimes spoken of as "the simple way of the Manchus" (*Manzhou jianpu zhi dao*).[38] Combining simplicity, frugality, and modest living with a native competence, this element of the Manchu Way was very close to the Bedouin or Spartan ideal. A sense of this comes from a story about the Qing founder that circulated at the time. Out hunting one day after a new snow, Nurhaci was observed to be lifting the hem of his garments as he walked. His companions wondered aloud why he cared so much about a simple item of clothing and were admonished by the khan, "It is not that I care overmuch about my clothing, for I often give you clothing as gifts. But how should it still look nice and clean if I let it get covered with snow? I am putting frugality into practice, and you would do well to follow."[39] This quality of economy was pointed to by Manchus as something separating them from Chinese, in particular southern Chinese, whose contemptible decadence was blamed for the Ming fall. Not that all Manchus were virtuous; but if they were not, they at least had to be capable.[40]

Nurhaci's concern to keep his robe clean sprang from a wish to extend its wearability, but similar concern among Beijing's Manchus more than likely owed to simple vanity. On an expedition to Rehe in 1694, the Kangxi emperor found fault with the finery worn by his hunting companions, many of them from the imperial guard: "Also, about your clothing and headgear. Although your fondness for expensive things made of sable and silk is a minor detail, it is related to economy. Don't you know how many fox-fur hats one sable hat could buy? Or how many sheepskin coats one silk garment is worth? Why do you wear such costly items?"[41] Such remonstrations evidently did little to curb Manchu material appetites. When the Yongzheng emperor took the throne, many officials seized the opportunity to inform the new monarch of the deplorable state of affairs:

> It would be good to set rules to control excess and extravagance. Since olden days, simplicity, moderation and economy have been exalted. [Yet] in the last several years, officers, soldiers, and commoners [in the banners] have steadily been competing in fine dressing at weddings and funerals, each trying to outdo the other in displaying their wealth and going well out of bounds in being extravagant. Not even the slightest distinctions are made [between groups], and each does what it pleases. This is certain to lead to the inability to sense shame or embarrassment.[42]

Another memorial a few months later complained that all officials, without regard for rank, were wearing Buddhist rosaries and leading their horses with fancily-decorated bridles. "And not only that," the official went on breathlessly, "but there are even some officials who sleep on spread-out silken cushions."[43] This in contrast to the Kangxi emperor who, as we have already seen, was happiest sleeping under a plain cotton blanket. Later the same year (1723) the chief of one of the Mongol banners wrote that "having encountered a period of peace, the children of some well-off officials, who are in the vanguard and guard divisions, pay no heed to rank and dress to excess. Over the years poorer soldiers have picked up on this and try to compete, and by now this has become a complete habit." He cited approvingly the emperor's edict outlawing fine silk clothing and boots among elite guardsmen and decreeing the use of thin silk (Ma *cuse*), linen, and felt.[44] This edict was followed shortly by another, sterner, warning (also addressed to guardsmen) to "cease competing with each other in clothing and accessories!"[45]

No less disturbing was the trend toward riding in sedan chairs, which explicitly linked court fears of extravagant living with worries of martial declension. An early proscription (though by no means the first), dating from 1750, noted that riding home in sedan chairs had become common among Manchu officials, particularly those working in civil administration, even though they lived very close to their offices. With the exception of those over sixty *sui*, the emperor ordered Manchus out of their chairs and back into the saddle: "What if some urgent business arises and you can't ride a horse? Ridiculous!"[46] A few months later word reached him that certain princes and ministers had found a way around the ban on sedan chairs by using horses and carriages instead. "What's the difference between riding in a sedan chair and riding in a carriage?" fumed the emperor, who once again cited the spread of laziness and neglect of "old Manchu customs" in extending the prohibition to carriages as well and promising stern punishment to scofflaws.[47]

In addition to well-appointed sedan chairs (for nuptials, some banner families in Beijing exceeded even this extravagance by hiring Western-style carriages to pick up new brides!),[48] urban China in the eighteenth century had many other pleasures to offer, not least food and wine. One of the earliest edicts of the Yongzheng reign was this one deploring drunkenness: "Among Eight Banner officers and soldiers are many who drink and drink and get so intoxicated that their appearance [permanently] changes. Taking life as a lark, they lose all their property and behave wildly and disgracefully. . . . I feel sorry and pity these people, and desire that they . . . be given a year or two to reform their ways."[49]

Reacting to the court's concern, the director of the Court of Sacrificial Worship proposed that squads be formed to patrol the suburban establishments haunted by Beijing bannermen and arrest those degenerates who were found there "blindly drinking and eating."[50] This was more feasible than a total ban on such patronage proposed by a captain-general in the Manchu Plain Red Banner who contrasted "law-abiding people" in the banners with "good-for-nothing types" who "meet their gang of friends and go off to teahouses outside the city walls," "making eating and drinking the only important things" in life, and spending many times their monthly salaries in the pursuit of sensual pleasure.[51] A report by Bootai (a grandson of the Shunzhi emperor), on the dissolute behavior of residents living in the housing built for impoverished bannermen just outside the walls of Beijing, described the circumstances there, deploring the neglect of "manly virtue":

> Because of the passage of time, habits have declined. Nowadays when the soldiers posted to the training ground return home from work they do not pursue proper manly virtue. Very many get in with bands of undesirable people, drink liquor and wine, and gamble. . . . The sons of the soldiers at the practice ground who live outside the city have nothing to do, so they hook up with these disreputable characters and learn evil [ways].[52]

Things would get worse. Later in the century, the unsavory establishments in the Chinese city would move within the very walls of the Inner City.

After numerous attempts to rein in overindulgence, in 1727 the emperor finally lost patience, sounding much like a fire-and-brimstone preacher as he vented his frustration at the intemperance of bannermen:

It is an established principle that the practice of frugality means not falling into poverty while extravagant spending always ends in cold and starvation. The ordinary disposition of us Manchus is to be pure and plain, . . . [but] lately the Manchus have not been doing well at making ends meet and their livelihoods have been sometimes meager or even miserable.

The tendency to essentialize difference between Manchus and others is one we have seen before. The emperor went on:

It looks as though the Manchus have forgotten frugality and are willing for the sake of their appetites to mortgage their houses and sell their property. Soldiers, for example, want to eat meat at every meal. With what they spend for one measure of meat they could pay for several days of vegetable dishes. The money they get for one month is not enough and after a few days of meat, the money is all gone. Plus their appetites are never satisfied. Those who eat meat every day get tired of pork all the time and must have a change of pace. No one keeps track of how much is spent every day. It's easy come, easy go, until the household is financially ruined. Moreover, these people do not think of storing up the rice provisions they get every season, but, for the sake of a few days of meat dishes, break the rules and sell them off cheaply [so that they can] have wine to drink and meat on the table.

The emphasis here on the place of meat in the diet suggests that Manchu dietary habits remained closer to what they had been before the conquest, when game was plentifully available, and that people were finding it difficult to switch to the largely vegetarian Chinese diet. Angry at this inability of banner people to acculturate when it might actually benefit them, the emperor let forth with his trademark irony:

They drink and eat until there is nothing left and the whole house is in want. At that point they want to eat something but there is no rice. They want to put something on but there aren't any clothes. Cold and hunger press in from both sides, but still they boast without regret, "I once ate fine food and wore beautiful clothing!"[53]

It is not hard to picture a clutch of bannermen, sitting at a table over wine and snacks, laconically musing over this latest malediction with a mixture of fear (of the emperor? of having enough money to pay the bill?) and disdain ("Maybe I'll make it to the training ground *next* week").

Of course, the good life of eating and drinking required entertainment to make it complete. The enthusiasm of Beijing bannermen for opera is well known, as is the court's uneasiness with this interest, since it saw theaters as corrupting pure Manchu morals as well as being "meeting-places for secret societies to plot disturbances and rebellion."[54] The official stance was pure hypocrisy, of course, since Manchu aristocrats, and the emperor himself, entertained the best opera troupes in the country, and were a profoundly important source of patronage in the development of what later came to be called "Beijing opera." But ordinary bannermen (women rarely could go[55]) who wanted to see the stage had to leave the Inner City for the squalid Qianmen district of the Chinese city where theaters, teahouses, and brothels were concentrated, as a 1671 edict had forbidden the construction of theaters (Ch *xiyuan*) in the Manchu city.[56] Even then they had to worry about being caught. As early as 1674 the Kangxi emperor noted with dismay the Manchu penchant for theater-going.[57] The first prohibition on theater-going by bannermen came in 1723 and another in 1738.[58] A fuller embargo was contained in the 1764 regulations for the Eight Banners:

> If officers, soldiers or unsalaried bannermen in the Eight Banners who have entered theaters to watch plays, listen to singing, or engage in mass drinking bouts are caught by the capital gendarmerie or are found out by their own banners, the officers will be impeached, the soldiers dismissed, and the unsalaried bannermen dealt with according to precedent.[59]

Similar prohibitions and sterner penalties were announced with growing frequency by the end of the Qianlong reign, a sure sign that opera was gaining in popularity. The court was particularly vexed by the moral decline signaled by the excessive attention lavished on young actors by Manchu officials.[60] It was powerless to do much about this, or about the participation of bannermen as writers and even performers.[61] By the nineteenth century a love of opera, more than a love of target practice, was a defining characteristic of Beijing's Manchus.

Other vices, such as gambling and betting, provided further objects of prohibition. One approach took account of the numerous previous bans that had come and gone and proposed instead outlawing the sale of cards and dice in the capital, with severe punishments for transgressors. Cockfights and quail fights were also prohibited.[62] Seeking the favors of prostitutes, which was not illegal before 1644,[63] was declared illegal by the mid-eighteenth century, with dismissal from one's post the punishment for patronizing brothels.[64] Of course, Qing bannermen were not the first soldiers to indulge in drinking, gambling, and whoring. But as testified to by the unending imprecations uttered against the profligacy and spreading "evil Chinese habits" among capital Manchus,[65] such behavior was interpreted precisely as evidence of the acculturation so feared by Hong Taiji, which undermined the Manchu Way.

Beijing definitely seems to have been the most fertile ground for the growth of extravagant tastes, but the Eight Banner garrisons were not without their own problems in this connection. The Xi'an general reported in 1708 that "day and night, from regiment colonels down to corporal and clan heads, all carefully watch out for those who are gambling, drinking, and creating mischief."[66] On the whole, however, the trend began later in the provinces, becoming widespread only in the Yongzheng reign. The garrison general of Ningxia was seriously embarrassed in 1726, when it turned out that his son was among those accused of taking part in endless drinking and gambling parties;[67] and there were other reports of debauchery at Xi'an insinuated in the redaction of new rules of behavior for the residents of the Manchu city that specifically forbade women to visit the hot springs: "Xi'an's [banner] women who go to the hot springs are very numerous, which greatly concerns their lives, since many of them now have bad reputations. It would be best to outlaw this, too."[68] But the first injunctions against luxurious habits directed specifically at garrison bannermen date only from 1728, when Jingzhou garrison general Unaha was instructed to prevent "gambling, the killing of cows, the wearing of too-fine clothing, and copper tools and weapons," and in general to "not let the soldiers become overindulgent," a trend the emperor somewhat over-optimistically claimed had been successfully suppressed in the capital.[69] Even during the second quarter of the eighteenth century, when admonitions to improve military readiness began arriving thick and fast at garrison generals' yamens, frugality came up rarely.[70] One is inclined to conclude that their remove from the court, along with the problem of poverty—a result in part of their lower salaries and greater vulnerability to inflation—limited the ability of garrison bannermen to indulge in luxurious lifestyles. It is perhaps not a coincidence that many of the reports of dissolute behavior at the garrisons, such as that at Ningxia, involved the sons of senior officers who had more money and presumably had spent time in Beijing and were accustomed to its rollicking ways. It was rather paradoxical, then, that in formally insisting on the repatriation of young men to the capital, the court cited the need to train them in proper Manchu virtues. If young Manchus looked forward to going back to Beijing, it was probably less because Beijing was the center of unsullied Manchu culture than it was because they would have the opportunity to sample some of the good life that marked that city's hybrid milieu. Less privileged bannermen in the provinces had no choice but to do as enjoined by the court, and to hew to "pure and simple" Manchu ways.

## THE "NATIONAL" LANGUAGE

Because of the emphasis laid upon it by Qing emperors from Hong Taiji on, perhaps no other aspect of the acculturation of the Manchus has attracted historians' attention as much as the decline of the Manchu language. Miyazaki Ichisada, for instance, spoke of the "complete overwhelming" of Manchu by Chinese, and of the "victory of the Han language, Han culture, and the Han people,"[71] while others have equated it with the loss of Manchu identity, making a direct connection between language and ethnicity.[72] What better symbol of the assimilation of the outnumbered Manchu than the abandonment of his native language for the literary richness of Chinese? How more aptly illustrated than by the feeble skills of the last Qing emperor, Puyi, whose knowledge of Manchu was limited to the command *Ili!* ("Arise!").[73]

Indeed, language has long been considered an essential part of both individual and group identity, and recent discussions of ethnicity continue to recognize it as one of the most important markers "gateposting" identity in ethnic groups.[74] A little reflection makes it clear, however, that language alone cannot be a reliable index of ethnicity. One need only consider the instance of members of minority groups in the United States, France, Germany, China, and elsewhere, who may speak, read, and write the language of the majority population but possess ethnic identities distinct from the majority. There is thus no reason to assume a neat parallel between language and ethnic identity. In the Manchu case, it is true that by the late eighteenth and nineteenth centuries relatively few Manchus were still fluent in their ancestral tongue. But it does not follow that they no longer thought of themselves as Manchu or that Han Chinese had forgotten the differences between themselves and bannermen. In other words, although the decline of spoken Manchu is impossible to deny, its importance and meaning for Manchu identity is open to interpretation. It would be better simply to say that the place of language in defining Manchuness was less conspicuous after 1750, even though the court stressed it unceasingly in official formulations of the Manchu Way.

To probe the significance of the decline of the Manchu language, we need to begin by exploring the history of Manchu language practices in the Qing, about which we know surprisingly little, even though Manchu was the first of the five languages of the empire (the others were Chinese, Mongolian, Tibetan, and Uighur).[75] It should be made clear, however, that Manchu never disappeared from use altogether. Even late in the dynasty when it was no longer being spoken, Manchu documents were still being produced in large quantities by the court.

During the Qing, Manchu was commonly referred to in Chinese as the "Qing language" (*Qingyu* or *Qingwen*) or the "national language" (*guoyu*); in Manchu such political labels were never used, and it was spoken of simply as the "Manchu language" (*Manju gisun*; *Manju hergen* described the written language only). While a substantial amount of government business was carried on in both languages (keeping translation offices busy day and night[76]), certain types of matters, most notably Eight Banner and military affairs, were handled almost exclusively in Manchu, leading some scholars to dub it a "security language," not without justification.[77] But quite apart from its official applications, Manchu was used in the creation of original stories, poems, and songs, much of it composed outside court auspices (and sometimes against court wishes). While it has only recently attracted scholarly interest, this popular literature is a valuable corrective to the assumption that Manchu was employed solely by bureaucrats and translators, and hardly even by them after 1800. Manchu translations of Chinese literature were also numerous and very widely read; while they obviously cannot be said to represent the vitality of a native literary tradition, they do attest to the language's popularity.[78]

Knowledge of Manchu was required of all bannermen. When appointed to office, people were expected to be able to say a few words in Manchu to the emperor, even if this was just a recitation of their records. Mongol bannermen, who were expected to know Mongolian, too, no doubt found Manchu very easy (although there were reports in the early eighteenth century that Chakhar soldiers understood commands only in Mongolian).[79] Chinese bannermen were also supposed to know Manchu, making them one of two groups capable of handling both languages in the immediate postconquest period, the other being bondservants, whose special skills and relationships to the emperor have been celebrated elsewhere.[80] Even Han Chinese officials needed to learn some Manchu; one requirement for entry into the Hanlin

Academy was to pass an examination in Manchu.[81] At the emperor's behest, Jesuits serving at the Qing court learned Manchu, too, which some found easier to learn and more precise than Chinese.[82]

The conquest generation of Manchus was basically monolingual. In the early Qing, official language policy regarding the Eight Banners was therefore far more concerned with ability at Chinese than at Manchu, which was taken for granted. As before 1644, proficiency at Chinese during the Shunzhi reign was considered the specialty of professionals, men like Dahai, Garin, and Kicungge who acted as bureaucrats, translators, and special advisors.[83] Among officers, not to mention ordinary Manchu bannermen, knowledge of Chinese, especially the written language, was very unusual indeed.[84] It was nearly thirty years before familiarity with at least the spoken language was widespread enough to eliminate the need for interpreters (*tongshi/tungse*) to assist Manchu officials in discharging their duties.[85] For most soldiers, ability in either language was mainly limited to oral skills. Only the minority who had the good fortune to receive some kind of formal schooling (see below), typically in anticipation of advancement to office, had knowledge of written Manchu; most of these were Manchus and other bannermen living in Beijing.

In the persistence of factionalism based on ethno-linguistic lines, we have already seen the extent to which, into the Qianlong reign, language was politics in the Qing.[86] The same kinds of tensions were mirrored in the court's inconsistent stance on language matters. On the one hand, the administrative need for Manchus who understood Chinese was obvious, and for this reason the study of Chinese was sometimes encouraged among the banner elite.[87] On the other hand, from a very early date the court was wary of the consequences this would bring and occasionally took a position discouraging the study of Chinese by Manchus, as when the emperor voiced his concern in a 1654 announcement:

> Edict to the Imperial Clan Court: Reflecting on the study of Chinese writing, I think that [it may lead to] entering into Chinese customs and the gradual loss of our old Manchu usages. Formerly, permission was granted to . . . send children in the imperial clan to study . . . Manchu writing, and those who wanted to were free to study Chinese. Thinking about it now, if [people] know Manchu they will be able to read for pleasure all kinds of Chinese books that have been translated. Let their study of Chinese permanently cease.[88]

The emperor here was not concerned that Chinese might replace Manchu as the language of the Manchus, but that knowing Chinese would contribute to acculturation and the loss of Manchu distinctiveness. Since there were many translations into Manchu already available for people to read, he argued, knowing Manchu was sufficient—and the presumed ability of the court to control what would be translated in the future gave the (false) hope that it would be able to circumscribe the cultural world of Manchu bannermen. Hence, the notion of setting up Chinese schools for bannermen long remained unpalatable.[89] Perhaps because of this discouragement, throughout the Kangxi and Yongzheng reigns it was not uncommon for Manchu office-holders to suffer some kind of linguistic handicap, usually an inability to read or write Chinese characters.[90] Around the turn of the eighteenth century, when one elite bannerman confessed during his tenure as Gansu provincial commander that he was ignorant of Chinese, the emperor upbraided him with the comment that "you should have a general knowledge of Manchu and Chinese writing,"[91] but this was evidently an ideal not always met, since the same problem continued during the Yongzheng reign. In 1723 a censor complained of the difficulties brought on by the absence of qualified personnel at the Six Boards:

> The affairs of the Six Boards are extremely important. Matters generated from the provinces are all in Chinese writing. After they arrive at the board, their substance is reviewed jointly by officials from the Manchu and Chinese departments. If the Manchu officials are unable to read Chinese, they will not be able to understand what the original matter was about. It is requested that hereafter when vacancies appear in the Manchu departments of the Six Boards that people be appointed who know Chinese and can investigate provincial affairs. Picking someone who at least knows Chinese, even if their career has been confined to using only Manchu materials . . . would also be beneficial.[92]

A few months later, knowledge of Chinese was made a requirement of all Manchus in the Grand Secretariat[93] and in 1725 the same expectation was voiced for Manchus chosen as top provincial officials.[94] But that ability in Chinese still could not be taken for granted was emphasized by another 1725 memorial, which reported that "among the Manchus there are many who can handle Manchu but few who can handle Chinese characters." The memorialist proposed that more translations of Chinese military and historical writings should be made and disseminated among capital and garrison officials down to the rank of regiment colonel, which, interestingly, he said would broaden their "masculine virtue."[95]

Things had changed little by the end of the Yongzheng reign, when banner company captain Fuming remarked, with evident dissatisfaction, the persistent dearth of linguistically qualified personnel in the sections of banner offices charged with dealing with the Six Boards:

> Although many internal banner affairs are being handled by [those] selected from among expectant officials, even today there are still few who understand written Chinese. What if during the night some urgent matter should come that is in Chinese? If there is no one there who can understand it, it is quite possible that a mistake will be made in dispatching it.[96]

From these indications, it is evident that not only military men, who could be forgiven for not knowing Chinese, but Manchus serving in top civil metropolitan and provincial posts, did not all know Chinese well enough to read it unassisted. In the 1730s Manchu was still their primary medium of communication and of understanding. Knowledge of Chinese among Manchus appointed to high office was probably not universal until after 1750. This occasionally produced some unusual logistical puzzles. Upon receipt of a rescript written to him in Chinese by the Yongzheng emperor, Xi'an general Yansin faced a serious problem: he was totally unable to read or write this "foreign" language. The memorial and rescript were of course secret, so he couldn't risk having it translated by someone else. He tried passing it on to his son, who, it turned out, was also illiterate in Chinese. Finally the two hit upon a method. As best they could, they copied all the characters contained in the emperor's message onto separate pieces of paper and distributed them among different people who knew both languages, who were then asked to translate the one or two characters they had been given into Manchu. Collecting all these slips of paper with their translated fragments, Yansin painstakingly reassembled them according to the original order of the characters and literally pieced together the meaning of the emperor's message.[97]

## SLIP OF THE TONGUE

By the middle of the eighteenth century, the chief preoccupation of official language policy had shifted from the ability of Manchus in Chinese to their ability in Manchu. At the capital, standards of Manchu first began to slip noticeably during the Yongzheng era (this trend began sooner in the garrisons, as will be seen). This provoked the emperor's fury, particularly when he heard imperial guardsmen lapsing into Chinese: "Edict: The Senior Bodyguard and Imperial Bodyguard always can count on sitting idly while on duty. Compared to that, studying Manchu is much preferable. Of late I have heard some of the newly selected guardsmen abandoning the study of Manchu and using Chinese, of all things, in their joking around. This is highly inappropriate."[98] Eight years later, in 1734, the emperor revisited the language issue:

> Edict: The study of Manchu by banner soldiers is of the utmost importance. Hereafter let the members of the senior bodyguard, the imperial guard and all those who guard palace gates and keep watch speak only in Manchu. No Chinese should be allowed. As far as training, when the soldiers are assembled and at the parade ground, they should also be made to use only Manchu.[99]

The same theme was hammered on in a similar edict issued one month later, after continuing use of Chinese around the palace quite literally reached the emperor's ear.[100] Such railing does not seem to have had a lasting effect: In 1750 the Qianlong emperor was still complaining about members of the vanguard speaking Chinese and had taken as well to scolding Manchus for wasting their time translating corrupt Chinese novels and trying to write poetry in Chinese.[101] For instance, in 1752 the emperor jeered at a Manchu official, Nailangga (Nai-lang-a) who had the temerity to approach him while hunting at Muran to present him with some poetry, "just like a Chinese." Even though at one point in his military career Nailangga had evidently acquitted himself well, his insistence on writing poetry (which the emperor suspected wasn't even his) suggested that he had forgotten the proper place of a Manchu and earned him dismissal. The emperor ordered that this case be publicized "throughout the Eight Banners so that afterward all bannermen will uphold the pure and simple ways of the Manchus, diligently study riding, shooting, and the Manchu language, and will not [let themselves] be imbued with the customs of the Han."[102]

Promoting Manchu for political reasons was not limited to narrow court circles. Recognition of the ideological importance of the "national language" arose in a memorial from Maitu, commandant of the vanguard left wing during the 1720s:

> Having gone with the army to Tibet, everywhere I traveled, on the way there and back, along the road, at borders, passes, and city gates there

were only signs in Chinese. There was no Manchu writing. I, your slave, respectfully submit that Manchu writing is that which perpetually promulgates the Manchu Way. My humble suggestion is that at the gates of all cities where a governor-general or governor lives it be done as it is at the gates of Beijing, where there is an inscription in both scripts, Manchu and Chinese.[103]

This statement shows that even midlevel banner officers were aware of the link between the Manchu language and the Manchu Way and were concerned to advance the language. A decade or so later, the commander of the small Kaifeng garrison gave a similar justification for establishing a Manchu school: "My humble thinking is that since the Manchu tongue is the root of the Manchus, if it is not now carefully taught, after the passage of time the old ways will gradually come to disappear."[104] Far from being a highly placed official on intimate terms with the emperor, Hesing was near the bottom rung of those who could directly memorialize the emperor. Nor was he responding to a specific inquiry from the court about the state of spoken Manchu in the provinces; rather, he was informing the court about what he saw as a disturbing decline in Manchu ability (more on his plans is said below). The terms here linking the prestige of the Manchu language, both written and spoken, to the preservation of the Manchu Way strongly echo phraseology that would become very familiar in the following decades.

Concern over the shift in primary language from Manchu to Chinese probably developed about one generation sooner in the provinces than at the capital. Before the 1720s signs of a problem in this regard are few, but clear enough. In 1708 Xi'an garrison general Siju reported to the emperor that teachers had been assigned to Manchu, Mongol, and Chinese banner soldiers as well as to unsalaried men. They were exhorted as follows: "You must every day teach and train the young people well. In the morning, make them read aloud. In the middle of the day, have them write. Toward evening, make them take up their bows and shoot. Make them speak Manchu. No speaking Chinese."[105] As this concerned Xi'an, the most purely Manchu of the provincial garrisons, one suspects that the status of spoken Manchu at places such as Hangzhou and Nanjing was more perilous. Indeed, a few years after taking power, when the Yongzheng emperor turned his energies to the garrisons, he found that Manchu-language abilities were already in serious decline.[106] He may have been prompted to investigate by clues dropped here and there, such as the admission of Nanjing garrison general Yonggina regarding his son, who, "although he is already seventeen, cannot really speak or read Manchu very well."[107] By 1726, alarm at court was growing and reports from the garrisons began regularly to carry remarks on the state of soldiers' language abilities. A memorial from Ningxia general Sibe noted that officers there made daily unannounced inspections of individual skills at archery and spoken Manchu,[108] and mention has already been made above of Xi'an general Yansin's 1727 report that soldiers were being taught written as well as spoken Manchu. The importance of this training was stressed again to Yansin's replacement three years later, who responded with the news that small, informal schools had been set up for Chinese banner soldiers at Xi'an, indicating that they may have been the only ones who needed practice in speaking.[109] An edict of 1734 distributed to the garrisons made the point quite plainly: "The soldiers have for generations been receiving the favor of dynastic support. Everyone must apply themselves to their work, be well-practiced at skills such as shooting and riding and speaking Manchu in order to repay [this favor]."[110]

It is hard to say how effective such measures were. One way to assess their impact would be to determine how many banner soldiers still could speak Manchu in 1735, when the Qianlong emperor took over. This cannot, of course, be known with any accuracy. One unusually concrete report from Hangzhou at this time stated, "As far as shooting from horseback and speaking Manchu, of the 1600 Manchu and Mongol troops, half are able to speak Manchu or at least say a few words extemporaneously in reply."[111] While it is hard to say how representative this situation was, a 1724 report hints at roughly similar linguistic circumstances at the Taiyuan garrison: "From among the 180 idle Manchu soldiers, 87 were picked who could shoot well from a stance as well as from horseback and who could speak Manchu."[112] It thus seems safe to assume that at least one-half of Manchu bannermen at provincial garrisons could not speak Manchu any more by the second third of the eighteenth century. The only bright spot was Xi'an, where the majority of Manchus could probably still speak the language then.

Why did the linguistic situation differ between the garrisons and the capital? One obvious reason is that, unlike the capital, for most of the Qing period (including the period we have been discussing so far), no official schools existed in the banner garrisons, whereas schools had been established in Beijing as early as the Shunzhi reign. This was the matter on which Hesing, banner commander at Kaifeng, wrote with some urgency in a remarkable 1734 proposal to teach Manchu and Chinese to young men in the banners:

> In the ten Manchu and Mongol companies garrisoning Henan are altogether over three hundred Manchu youths aged ten and over who have been born during the [present] enlightened age. I have long been teaching and encouraging them, and even though there are many among them who can speak Manchu, there are also many who cannot. This is all caused by the failure to build a regular Manchu school and teach there.

Here Hesing voiced his concern over the future of the "old ways of the Manchus," already cited above. He wished to establish two schools to teach Manchu, one for each wing, and to hire four qualified teachers. The next part of his proposal was somewhat surprising:

> I have observed that among young Manchus are some who also can read Chinese. But since they are the children of soldiers, they can engage no talented teachers. Even if they go to the Chinese city to study, besides the fact that it is a long way there, there are still no good teachers. No matter how much they are encouraged, they are only children and finally give up. . . . My idea is to establish within the Manchu city a Chinese school for each the right and left wings where young Manchus who couldn't hire teachers could go to study.[113]

Hesing went on to explain that if permission were granted for this project, he would ask the governor-general to pick a couple of expectant Henan *ju-ren* and *xiucai* to teach at the Chinese school. The emperor strongly approved of the idea to build a Manchu school, but scoffed at the suggestion of a Chinese school as "foolish talk." Whatever the arguments for teaching Chinese to bannermen in the capital, there was evidently no point in teaching it to Manchus in the provinces—perhaps because they would learn it soon enough, anyway. But it is clear evidence that knowing Chinese was by this time seen as essential for educated bannermen.

Another important point to be made in connection with this memorial is the explicit watershed marked by Hesing that Manchu children born at the garrison since 1723 could *not* all be assumed to know Manchu. Since the garrison had been established only in 1718, the children in question were the first Manchu generation born at Kaifeng. The families had lived there a relatively short time. It is therefore hard to attribute the failure to pass language skills on to the next generation simply to the passage of time. It is more likely that, in addition to a lack of education, the small size of the garrison and the correspondingly greater need for contact with the outside city meant that knowledge of Chinese was of more practical value. There may have been, one imagines, a correlation between garrison size and the preservation of Manchu. This would explain why, in general, skills persisted longer in Beijing than anywhere else and why Manchu could go on being spoken at Xi'an even after three or four generations when it began to disappear after only one at Kaifeng. As such, it warns against assuming a straightforward relationship between time and acculturation, and encourages a more nuanced view of the Manchu experience in general that takes into consideration geographical and sociological factors, and not only chronological factors.

Finally, the point raised by Hesing, that it was primarily young men in families with limited resources who suffered truncated educations, should remind us that economic divisions between bannermen did not fall neatly along capital/garrison lines. There were certainly well-to-do Manchu families in the garrisons, just as there were poor Manchu families in Beijing, who shared similar problems. This was clearly recognized by others at the time, too: "In the Eight Banners, apart from the children and grandchildren of propertied people who hire tutors to teach their children, the children of poorer people are not skilled at reading. Attaching themselves to idle, useless people, they may by degrees become worthless types themselves."[114] Yet the split was not simply between upper and lower classes. Manchus in the capital banners, no matter their background, were in a much better position to benefit from imperial concern, especially with the establishment of "public" banner schools in Beijing in 1727 that were open to all regular banner children and youth. In addition to Manchu, the whole gamut of traditional military skills was taught there. Similar schools were not established in the garrisons until the early nineteenth century.[115] By that time the old Manchu Way was already mostly a memory, supplanted by a new Manchu reality.

## LANGUAGE AND IDENTITY

As earlier sections have shown, emperors from Hong Taiji on all made the link between language and identity, but none perhaps as consistently as the Qianlong emperor. Because of his father's efforts in this area, the Qianlong emperor ascended the throne well aware of accelerating acculturation among bannermen, and determined to do something about it. He may have had inside information on the decline of language skills at Hangzhou and elsewhere, since just a few months after taking power, he initiated a blustering correspondence with the senior staff at the Hangzhou garrison:

> The old traditions of the Manchus, shooting, riding, and speaking Manchu, along with being able to handle a lance and a sword—all this is hollow decoration, with no benefit for practical affairs. You must train soldiers until they are skilled. You have a garrison general and lieutenant generals there [at Hangzhou]. So even [if one of you] drills [them] all day one day until the sun goes down, that still leaves you two days of leisure, does it not? I have already issued an edict on the matter of soldiers at Hangzhou and Jiangning entering into Chinese ways. In three years' time, soldiers from Hangzhou and Jiangning will be sent to take part in the training hunts [at Rehe], as used to be the case in the old days. At that time, if they shoot poorly and show themselves feebly on horseback, and if they can't speak and understand Manchu, I will be talking to you.[116]

The explicit association between "the old traditions of the Manchus" and "speaking Manchu," echoes the Yongzheng emperor's 1726 call for attention to the Manchu language and other of the "original ways of the Manchus." The above rescript provoked a number of memorials from desperate provincial banner officials emphasizing their understanding that garrison Manchus were still "men in stirrups" (Ma *tufun-i deleri niyalma*) and that they were being diligently trained to rid them of their Chinese ways and restore their martial and linguistic abilities.[117]

But these well-meaning efforts were in vain. In 1736, anxiety over the inability of Manchu Hanlin bachelors in their native language was expressed by Sioi-yuwan-meng, Manchu vice-president of the Board of Rites, who wrote:

> Later, after Manchu bachelors were tested only in being able to read Chinese, because they steadily began to favor Chinese writing they didn't use Manchu writing for very many things. Upon consideration, it seems that since Manchu bachelors, *juren* and *jinshi* alike, are being tested, there is no cause for worrying about [their ability at] Chinese writing. But if they cannot read Manchu, there is reason to fear this will lead to the gradual disappearance of the Manchu language. Wouldn't it be better if hereafter Manchu bachelors were divided up like the Chinese bachelors and made to study both Chinese and Manchu? That way it will not end up with the loss of Manchu.[118]

This memorial is evidence that at least by the first year of the Qianlong reign the future of Manchu as a living language was perceived to be threatened. The implication here is that while well-educated Manchus, most of them from the capital, could still speak Manchu, many were no longer so conversant with the written language as their fathers had been. Sioi-yuwan-meng blamed this on the lack of testing in Manchu, viewed as unnecessary under the Kangxi and Yongzheng emperors. An additional explanation for the deteriorating state of the Manchu language is the establishment of banner schools in Beijing during the Yongzheng reign (mentioned above), where the learning of Chinese was promoted, contrary to the warning of the Shunzhi emperor so many decades earlier. The institutionalization at the same time (1723) of the translation examinations, which further encouraged proficiency at written Chinese, leads to the conclusion that it was during the thirteen years of the Yongzheng reign—that is, the short time it took to educate an individual—that the linguistic balance between Manchu and Chinese among Beijing's Manchus was tipped the other way.

In light of the above evidence, the assertion that by the Yongzheng period "the great majority of bannermen could not speak the Manchu language" is surely not correct.[119] Rather, I would suggest that this was the state of affairs by the end of the Qianlong period, that is, the end of the eighteenth century. Indeed, the overwhelming evidence is that by 1800 the court had lost the fight to preserve Manchu as a spoken tongue among the majority of bannermen.[120] Where one Jesuit report from the 1720s noted that Manchu was still actively used at court, another report from the late eighteenth century declared that Chinese was the only language heard in the princes' mansions in Beijing.[121] The irony, of course, is that as Manchu became more and more an "official" language, attempts to promote it bore less and less fruit. The efforts of the Qianlong emperor to glorify Manchu and enhance its prestige—such as in the commission of false seal and other imaginary scripts for the printing of the *Ode to Mukden*—were for naught (Fig. 17a/b).[122] However, I would also emphasize that knowledge and use of Manchu never totally disappeared. Some Manchu officials from the middle or later eighteenth century were still illiterate in Chinese,[123] and Manchu continued to be very widely used in official communications even after it ceased to be spoken as widely as in earlier periods.[124] The "victory" of Chinese was perhaps not as complete and final as Miyazaki imagined. Memorials were routinely sent in Manchu until the end of the dynasty, and even among ordinary bannermen in the nineteenth century there is anecdotal evidence that Manchu books could still be found in banner households and that Manchu words remained a part of the bannerman's vocabulary well into the twentieth century. Moreover, as

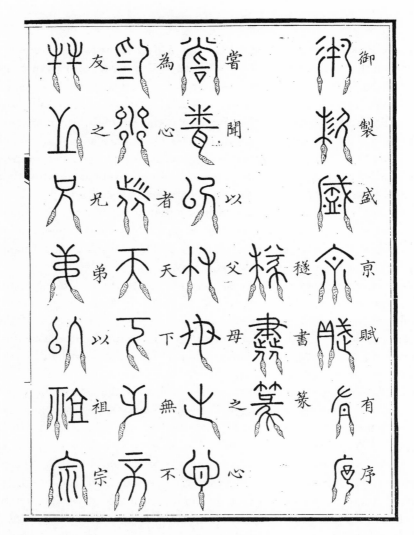

*Fig. 17a/b.* Decorative scripts for the Qianlong emperor's *Ode to Mukden* (1748). After his first visit to the Manchu homeland in 1743, the Qianlong emperor was moved to compose a long poem in praise of the wonderful places he had seen. The result was the bilingual *Ode to Mukden* (*Shengjing fu/Mukden-i fujurun bithe*), which was printed five years later in a special jubilee edition that used thirty-two decorative script styles. Some of the Chinese forms (17a, above) were authentic seal forms, but the Manchu forms (17b, opposite), many of which are almost illegible, all had to be invented for the occasion. Pictured are the first pages of the Chinese and Manchu texts in the same "tasseled-grain script" (*suishu zhuan/suihetu fukjingga hergen*). Each is glossed with standard script. Chinese text reproduced courtesy of the National Palace Museum, Taipei; Manchu text reproduced courtesy of the Tōyō Bunko, Tokyo.

ᠮᠠᠨᠵᠤ ᠦᠭᠡ ᠶᠢᠨ ᠵᠣᠬᠢᠶᠠᠯ

ᠮᠣᠩᠭᠣᠯ ᠦᠭᠡ ᠶᠢᠨ ᠵᠣᠬᠢᠶᠠᠯ ᠪᠢᠴᠢᠭ᠌

ᠬᠣᠯᠪᠣᠭᠠᠳᠤ ᠦᠭᠡ ᠶᠢᠨ ᠵᠣᠬᠢᠶᠠᠯ ᠪᠢᠴᠢᠭ᠌

just mentioned, even when Manchu bannermen did speak Chinese, they invariably spoke a particular Beijing dialect. That is, their speech, while not Manchu, nevertheless continued to mark a clear difference between them and the surrounding Han population.[125] This was true even in Beijing itself, where the Chinese of those in the banners was distinguished in various ways, including its vocabulary, and where a hybrid mix of Manchu and Chinese could be heard.[126]

The loss of Manchu, then, though undeniably evidence of acculturation, did not automatically result in the erasure of ethnic difference. We should not equate its decline, or martial enfeeblement, or growing epicureanism, or any other failure to conform to the court-defined Manchu Way, with the actual demise of Manchu identity. For even as the formal Manchu cultural edifice idealized by the court was crumbling, another set of structures was arising from within to define Manchu identity in its place, at the center of which was the banner system itself. Within this unofficial Manchu way, language and other practices continued to be important cultural markers of Manchuness, just as they had been before. The only difference was that it was no longer Manchu, but a particular way of speaking Chinese, which included both a distinctive accent and a vocabulary liberally spiced with Manchu words, that marked them. In like manner, Manchus became known more for bird raising and rice redemption than for virile pursuits and Spartan living.

There was little the court could do about these developments—appeals for the revitalization of the Manchu Way, like any typical call to preserve the (frequently imaginary) ideals of a past golden age, went largely unheeded for the simple reason that the cultural practices it encouraged and glorified were becoming less meaningful to more people. Yet they would never lose their significance altogether, remaining as memories: the brave grandfather who died in battle, the bow on the wall, and the Manchu books there on the shelf, no longer read.

# CHAPTER EIGHT

# Saving the Banner System

The critical situation relating to attempts to preserve the Manchu Way as the idealized articulation of quintessential Manchu identity was but one dimension of the dynastic predicament the court faced in the middle of the eighteenth century. The second crisis that threatened to undermine ethnic legitimacy was fiscal and institutional. Because the Eight Banners had grown to be a much larger institution than it had been a century earlier at the time of the conquest, the costs of keeping the system afloat—maintaining reasonable levels of support for banner populations, expanding the military infrastructure of the banners, and so on—had increased substantially by the 1740s. Despite the court's repeated efforts to address these rising costs, many banner families began to feel the pinch and slid slowly into poverty. Some of the reasons for their declining standard of living, such as extravagant living and dependence on fixed salaries that did not rise with inflation, have already been introduced. But it was not just that the resources provided by the center were shrinking; another explanation for the falling standards of living in the banners was that many people had surreptitiously joined the banner ranks, interlopers who had no right to be there.

The result was that by the Qianlong era the "Eight Banner livelihood problem" (Ch *baqi shengji wenti*) had become a common theme of Qing statecraft writing. Manchu and Chinese officials from both the civil and the banner bureaucracies actively discussed it, and many of their recommendations were included in a chapter of the *Imperial Collection of Statecraft Writings* (*Huangchao jingshi wenbian*), a famous collection first published in 1826.[1] Implicit in most proposals was the assumption that limits existed on the state's ability to support the expanding banner population, and that at some point difficult choices would have to be made about who would receive benefits and who would not. This was the practical import of suggestions (described below) urging that idle bannermen be put to productive work that would enable them to support themselves without relying on the government. In this roundabout way, a debate was carried on in the mid-1700s over the continued viability of the banner system. Few of the suggestions for altering the structure of state support for the Eight Banners were adopted, however, and those that were failed to really make much of a difference. Paradoxically, it was with respect to the infiltration of the banners by outsiders, not an aspect of the crisis featured in the *Imperial Collection*, that the court took its firmest stand and executed reforms that ultimately made the biggest difference to the future of the banner system.

This chapter investigates the institutional crisis within the banner system and the court's responses to it as it attempted to rescue Manchu privilege. It first presents the scale of expense involved in supporting the banner population and infrastructure, then examines the problem of poverty among banner households—its causes and the official reaction to the plight of immiserated Manchus—outlining the implications of these financial woes for the Manchu Way.[2] The second part of the chapter takes up the issue of Eight Banner "bloat," that is, the penetration of the military caste by people with no documentable proof of Manchu, Mongol, or Chinese banner ancestry. I look here at the reasons people wished to gain banner status, and the ways in which they did it, before turning to the process by which the court sought to identify these poseurs and impose a new system of household registration on the banner populations. For many people, and even for many Chinese bannermen, these reforms were bad news, since they meant their eventual expulsion from the banner rolls, but for the court the reforms were a relief. The elimination of people of secondary status from a mode of life that was meant above all to support Manchus saved the banner system—and Manchu ethnic identity, since the banner people who were left were by those standards now definitively "Manchu."

## THE COSTS OF THE BANNER SYSTEM

High military expenditures were a fact of life for the Qing. This was not a situation unique in Chinese history, since military costs often consumed a large part of the Chinese national product. But as a dynasty of conquest, the Qing, like the Yuan, had much more invested in the maintenance of its native military force than did a Chinese dynasty, since this force guaranteed the security and integrity not only of its geographical borders, but of its ethnic boundaries as well. The support of its soldiers and of all banner-household members—men and women, children and the elderly, servants, attendants, grooms, even horses—was a major investment. Ethnic sovereignty was not an inexpensive proposition.

From the very beginning of the dynasty, military spending remained far and away the state's single largest outlay, consuming anywhere from 50 percent to 60 or even 70 percent of the budget, depending on the estimates one accepts.[3] Most of this was for the country's two standing armies, the Eight Banners and the Green Standard. But the commitments here were not entirely commensurate, the biggest difference lying in the court's pledge to those in the banners to provide for their welfare from cradle to grave. That is, unlike the Green Standard, service in the Eight Banners was a hereditary privilege, and the number of people looking to it for a livelihood inevitably proliferated over time. Without a hedge against inflation—and the failure of the banner land system meant there was no such hedge—the welfare of the ever increasing banner population was a financial burden that fell wholly upon the state. The state bore this burden—which included silver salaries, grain stipends, feed supplements, housing subventions, matériel and weapons' purchases, retirement and widows' pensions, wedding and funeral subsidies, loan and debt amnesties, land buy-backs, plus the occasional salary bonus—with greater and greater difficulty. Its ability to meet these expenses directly affected the lives of the millions of people in the banners and, indirectly, the very future of the dynasty. By the mid-eighteenth century the support of the Eight Banners was threatening the dynasty's fiscal health. Yet to abolish the banner system, the "root" of the nation, was not an option. Other approaches had to be found.

The burdens of maintaining large numbers of troops were made plain early in the Qing. A 1660 report from the Board of Revenue read: "Also, the Eight Banner Manchu soldiers require very many provisions. [These] must be drained from every province, causing extreme hardship. In total, the empire's regular income comes to only 8,750,000 taels, while the amount of silver needed just for [military operations in] the one province of Yunnan is over 9,000,000 taels."[4] But it is difficult to say exactly how much the banner system cost the Qing state, because military expenditures, like population figures, were generally considered confidential information and precise numbers are hard to come by. Even when numbers do exist, they are problematic both because one cannot assume they are completely accurate and also because in most cases no separate breakdown is given for Eight Banners and Green Standard Army expenses. Furthermore, many figures date from the nineteenth century, forcing one to extrapolate back a century or more. One potentially useful set of figures, compiled by James Lee, relies on estimates found in nonarchival sources such as the *Draft History of the Qing*, the *Collected Institutes and Precedents of the Qing*, and administrative histories. Lee projects that in the eighteenth century an average of twenty-eight to thirty million taels went every year to support the military establishment. According to these figures, of the money spent by the court to maintain its two armies, roughly 40 percent (twelve million taels) went to the Eight Banners, while 60 percent (eighteen million taels) went to the Green Standard.[5] One must accept these estimates with caution, at least as far as they apply to the first half of the eighteenth century, since they are crude projections of the cost of regular salary support *only* to banner households in the capital and the garrisons. They are not based on archival evidence and do not include substantial appropriations from the treasury for the forgiveness of debts, the repurchase of banner land, or the establishment of the investment funds program, which ran into the millions of taels. Another set of figures is presented in a recent study of Qing military expenses by mainland scholar Chen Feng. Chen's summary of annual expenses for "military pay and horse feed" (Ch *bingxiang magan*), based in large part on archival sources, is presented in Table 8.1.[6]

These figures appear to confirm Lee's rough projections, and reveal an increase of more than four million taels in military expenses during the latter part of the Yongzheng reign. Chen attributes this above all to the expansion of the banner garrison system, though he acknowledges that augmentation of Green Standard ranks also played a role. He is also careful to note that his figures do not constitute the whole of Qing military expenses, since soldiers in the capital Eight Banners and the garrisons in Manchuria were paid from different sources and those funds were never included in routine estimates of military expenditures.[7] In the early eighteenth century, Chen estimates these additional expenditures at roughly six million taels, rising to nine million taels or more by the mid-1730s.[8] These figures are probably a bit low, as reports of actual expenses incurred in 1723 show that the cost of maintaining the capital Manchu, Mongol, and Chinese banner divisions of

TABLE 8.1
Permanent Military Expenditures, 1651–1849

| Year | Amount | Source |
|---|---|---|
| 1651 (SZ8) | 13,000,000 | Zhang Yushu, "Ji Shunzhi jian qianliang shumu," HJW 29 |
| 1685 (KX24) | 13,633,903 | *Huangchao bingzhi kaolue*, 1 |
| 1723 (YZ1) | 13,184,873 | memorial of Nacika, YZ1.12.5 |
| 1728 (YZ6) | 14,336,738 | *Ming-Qing dang'an* (Taipei: Academia Sinica), 41: 102 |
| 1730 (YZ8) | 14,483,790 | ibid., 43: 19 |
| 1731 (YZ9) | 15,076,469 | ibid., 47: 80 |
| 1732 (YZ10) | 17,003,294 | ibid., 52: 5 |
| 1733 (YZ11) | 16,644,443 | ibid., 55: 55 |
| 1735 (YZ13) | 17,881,066 | memorial of Zhang Tingyu, YZ12.12.21 |
| 1737 (QL2) | 17,714,161 | memorial of Shi-lin, QL2.9.10 |
| 1745 (QL10) | 17,092,038 | memorial of Necin, QL9.12.20 |
| 1750 (QL15) | 17,015,982 | memorial of Ai-bi-da, QL15.9.1 |
| 1812 (JQ17) | 17,245,018 | *Da Qing huidian* (1818), 12 |
| 1849 (DG29) | 16,821,061* | Wang Qingyun, *Shiqu yuji*, 2, "Ji lichao gesheng bingshu" |

* Chen inverts the last two digits to read 16,821,016.

NOTE: This table does not include the amounts spent on bannermen in the Capital Eight Banners or in the Northeast garrisons, which came to about six million taels annually before 1730 and about nine million taels after this date. Also, many of the figures reported above represent budgeted amounts rather than accounts of funds actually disbursed. It is difficult to know how great the differences were between these.

SOURCE: Chen Feng, *Qingdai junfei yanjiu*, 194–95 and 198–99.

the Plain Yellow Banner was approximately nine hundred thousand taels (Table 8.2). My extrapolations from these data indicate that seven million taels is a more realistic estimate for before 1730 (and, correspondingly, ten million taels for after 1730).[9]

The resulting totals for combined capital and provincial military expenditures are thus twenty million taels before 1730, rising to twenty-seven million taels after 1735. These still do not take into account the costs of housing, wedding and funeral subsidies, nourishing-honesty allowances, and so on, which Chen projects amounted to an additional five million or so taels.[10] Including these expenses raises the national total for the second two-thirds of the eighteenth century to thirty-two million taels, a figure that is consistent with Lee's high-end estimate of thirty million taels. Unfortunately, Chen

Accounts for the Capital Plain Yellow Banner, 1723 (in taels)

|  | Officers | Soldiers | Horse feed | Total |
|---|---|---|---|---|
| Manchu | 91,712 | 512,551 | 74,831 | 679,094 |
| Mongol | 16,912 | 66,840 | 18,731 | 102,483 |
| Chinese banner | 16,748 | 100,095 | 0 | 116,843 |
| TOTAL | 125,372 | 679,486 | 93,562 | 898,420 |

SOURCE: YZMaZPZZ 60, memorials of Marsa, Cimbu, and Lu Siyūn, dated YZ2.2.24.

does not attempt a separate analysis of Eight Banner and Green Standard expenses. However, the figure of ten million taels spent on the capital Eight Banners and the garrisons in the Northeast, which accounted for about 70 percent of banner households, allows us to extrapolate the cost for the banners as a whole. Assuming ten million taels to be equivalent to 70 percent of Eight Banner expenses leaves 30 percent, or about four million taels, for the provincial and northwestern garrisons. This yields an approximate total of fourteen million taels annually required for the permanent maintenance of the Eight Banner population as a whole. Subtracting this amount from the total thirty-two million taels of military expenditures leaves eighteen million taels for expenses relating to the Green Standard Army. Again, Chen's estimates—which, it should be stressed, derive from substantially different sources than those used by Lee—tend to confirm Lee's high-end estimates. If they are correct, this would mean that something on the order of 21 to 25 percent of the annual budget was devoted to the banner system. While this was not as large as the 27 to 32 percent spent on the Green Standard Army, proportionately it was a much greater investment of resources, since the numerical strength of the Green Standard Army was about three times that of the Eight Banners.[11]

Evaluating the overall internal cost structure of payments made to the banners reveals another startling fact: the majority of annual Eight Banner expenses went to the support, not of officers and soldiers, but of family dependents and horses. As Table 8.3 shows, in the mid-eighteenth century at the Xi'an garrison only 42 percent of silver disbursements, and a mere 7.4 percent of grain disbursements, were for the maintenance of men-at-arms. One-fifth of the silver and nine-tenths of the grain went to other household

TABLE 8.3
Structure of Expenses at the Xi'an Eight Banner Garrison

| Expense | Silver disbursed (taels) | Percentage of total | Grain disbursed (shi) | Percentage of total |
|---|---|---|---|---|
| Officers and soldiers | 225,582 | 42.0% | 9,064 | 7.4% |
| Household dependents | 110,349 | 20.5 | 110,349 | 90.5 |
| Horses | 201,242 | 37.5 | 2,527 | 2.1 |
| TOTAL | 537,173 | 100.0 | 121,940 | 100.0 |

SOURCE: Chen Feng, *Qingdai junfei yanjiu*, 47, citing *Shaanxi tongzhi*, juan 34.

members; while over one-third of the silver went to the purchase and feeding of horses. This pattern of resource distribution, and the investment of so much in an institution which, while claiming to support the deserving few, in fact sourced the welfare of the dependent many, reinforces the notion that political, and not only military, considerations were wrapped up in the maintenance of the Eight Banners. (It also raises questions about the notion of the welfare state as a modern development.) Had the court wished, more economical means for maintaining an army could no doubt have been devised—bannermen without military posts could have been put to work on the land, for instance, or allowed to enter other lines of work—but maintaining the Eight Banners as a closed, elite community of conquerors was a higher priority. By the time restrictions were lifted on banner occupations, in 1863 (even then finding other work was only voluntary), it was much too late to do any good.

That one-fourth to one-fifth of state revenues were set aside every year to pay the living expenses of a conquest military caste that was less than 2 percent of the population was certainly one of the more remarkable features of late imperial fiscal structure. It did not go unnoticed at the time. The general review of dynastic finances initiated by the Yongzheng emperor made it clear that many banner households were already living in want, and that it would be difficult to keep up support for them. From essays devoted to consideration of the situation in the Eight Banners written early in the Qianlong reign, we can see that the consensus was growing that some sort of fundamental change in the structure (Ch *biantong*) of banner support was demanded if the financial collapse of the Eight Banner system was to be averted. One essayist, the Manchu censor Šuhede, writing in 1737, put the problem this way: "If clothing and food are distributed on a person-by-person, house-by-house basis, there will not be enough for one department or one county, not to mention for the multitudes in the Eight Banners."[12] Another, noting that ordinary civilians had many ways of making a living, was even more direct:

> As for their livelihood, bannermen at the top can rely only on being officials, while those at the bottom can only be soldiers. In both cases they are provided for by public funds. Now, the country's budget is fixed, but there is no limit to population growth. Not even Yao and Shun [mythical emperors of Chinese antiquity] would have been able to provide broad support to so many if they had wanted to.[13]

The connection between rising payments to the banners and the country's fiscal strain was remarked, too, by Liang Shizheng, president of the Board of Revenue, who blamed the military directly for the deficit in payments in a 1741 essay:

> Reviewing the semiannual collections in spring and fall, the Board [notes that it] receives not more than seven or eight million taels and not less than four or five million. But the total of various debits for the capital comes to eleven or twelve million taels. What is taken in is not enough to cover what goes out. This is the case every year. Because the military expenses for the Eight Banners are so vast, expenses are increased. Because provincial expenditures on the Green Standard are continually rising, income is reduced.[14]

Complaints about the costs of the banner system had to be carefully couched so that it was clear the memorialist's concern was exclusively economic. The Manchu censor Hešeo noted that while "every year several million taels and more [are spent by the] country to graciously support the Eight Banners in utmost generosity and bounty, still there is not enough for the living expenses of those in the banners."[15] Similar concerns continued to be voiced even in 1770: "In the *ding* registers [of the Eight Banners] now are not fewer than several hundred thousand. Counting several mouths per *ding* means that there are several million [under the banners]. All expect to be fed at the public trough. How can there possibly be enough money for everyone?"[16] All of these officials acknowledged the importance of the Eight Banners as the "root" of the dynasty and emphasized the importance of keeping the root healthy in order for "branches and leaves" to thrive.

Of course, no one proposed the abolition of the banner system. But a number of essays proposed to fundamentally do away with some of the most important elements of banner privilege by resettling unemployed bannermen and their families in military colonies in the frontier, a received idea with a long history in Chinese military policy. Actually, this idea was floated very early in the Qing in a 1656 proposal by a Chinese official to whom the idea of a military caste perpetually supported by the state must have appeared quite strange. He wanted to transform the Eight Banners into eight military prefectures (Ch *fu*) on the Tang dynasty *fu-bing* model, which would have made Manchu and other banner soldiers self-supporting.[17] The proposal was not accepted, but similar ideas continued to come up periodically over the next two centuries, including in a number of the *Imperial Collection* essays.[18] Some efforts in this direction were made in the nineteenth century, but only one such colonized settlement of Beijing bannermen, that at Shuangchengpu in the Northeast, had any success.[19] Most bannermen tended to sell the land and drift back to the capital.

## THE WAYS OF POVERTY

In the end, the dynasty decided not to put the Manchus to work and resigned itself to providing support for the banners as it always had, at mid-eighteenth-century levels. But it did act to cut costs by decreasing the number of people eligible for that support and by restricting the support available to certain types of households. It also attempted to make work for as many bannermen as possible by expanding the number of posts available to them in the banners and banner garrisons. Limiting in this way the amount of silver spent on the Eight Banners appears to have eased the macroeconomic crisis in the banners. However, the microeconomic aspect of the crisis—that of increasing destitution among bannermen—was never really remedied, and poverty became one of the defining characteristics of life in the Eight Banners. Late Qing references to the problem make this clear: "Those who are still struggling over the Eight Banner livelihood problem hastily say that the country has virtuous groups of people [i.e., the traditional "estates" of *shi, nong, gong, shang* (scholars, peasants, artisans, merchants)]. Only banner people are not to pursue profit through commerce. Therefore they are as poor as they are." One might well agree with this assessment, that it was their powerlessness to take advantage of the enormous opportunities for the creation of wealth in the boom years of the Qing that prevented bannermen as a group from improving their standard of living, and that their misery owed directly to the fact that they had been left out of the thriving Qing commercial economy. The author of the above commentary, however, put the blame entirely on a lack of fiscal discipline among banner people, pointing out that emperors from Kangxi to Jiaqing had showered them with gifts of money and land.[20]

Indeed, given the assistance they received and the huge amounts of money transferred to their support, it is hard not to wonder why bannermen were so poor. One primary reason was demographic. Beginning as early as 1690, the phrase "the people are multiplying daily" (Ch *shengchi rifan*) was a constant refrain in discussions of Eight Banner problems, where comments about the "prolific numbers of children and grandchildren" and the "daily increase of households"[21] give the impression of ever growing numbers. As with the majority of the Chinese population, the number of people under the banners probably doubled within one hundred years after the conquest.[22] Demographic growth was a trend faced as well by Qing society generally, of course, but the difference for bannermen was that sources of additional income to feed and clothe family members were very limited. The number of openings for soldiers was finite, and becoming an official was more difficult still, so that population growth in the capital and garrison Eight Banners meant that there were more and more candidates for proportionately fewer and fewer salaried positions. The result was rising unemployment and an increase in the number of people dependent on a single salary. Households were overextended, with obvious results.

Faults in the general structure of economic support of bannermen were another basic reason for banner poverty. As explained in Chapter 4, the assignment of banner land to capital bannermen was intended to serve as a permanent guarantee of livelihood for those households. The large-scale alienation of capital bannermen from their land—half of which was estimated to be in Chinese hands by the 1740s[23]—meant that many banner families had lost an important source of income, one that, unlike silver and grain stipends, would have adjusted itself automatically to increases in the cost of living. Moreover, the many households (especially those in the garrisons) that had never received land grants had never enjoyed the benefit of this outside income. Their fixed incomes meant they were even more vulnerable to rising prices. The eventual triumph of market forces over government control of the trade in banner grain should be added to this as one of the factors contributing to the long-term impoverishment of capital bannermen.[24]

Third, extravagance and indebtedness were earmarked as a cause of banner poverty as early as 1674:

> The Manchus are the root of the nation. It is fitting to show them kindness. Recently I have seen that the number of poor and indebted Manchus is very great. Though gambling is forbidden, the practice continues, owing to inadequate supervision by banner leaders. The Manchu taste for theater and the excessive spending at Manchu betrothals, weddings, and funerals is simply beyond description. . . . These are the same Manchus as during the times of Nurhaci and Hong Taiji. How do today's banner commanders . . . and other officers compare to them? Their duties—fighting and hunting— were not fewer than [yours] today, yet there was no indebtedness and there was plenty to eat. This is because people [then] knew how to be frugal.[25]

As seen in Chapter 7, countless jeremiads emphasizing the importance of frugality to the Manchu Way appeared over the next one hundred years, to little apparent effect. Many banner households simply failed to take sensible steps to limit expenditures and live within their means, trusting instead that the court would bail them out.

A fourth cause of banner poverty was corruption among banner officers. One scheme run by lower officers was to buy grain from banner soldiers who had just been paid their rice stipends and were eager for cash. Borrowing capital from higher-placed officers, they would buy at a price of five to eight cash (*qian/jiha*) per quart, store the grain in banner granaries, and then sell the same amount several months later for 1.7 to 2 taels per quart, a business that brought handsome profits, but at the expense of the ordinary soldier.[26] Other opportunities for company officers to profit at the expense of ordinary bannermen lay in extortion, lending them money themselves, or in cooperating with Chinese lenders.[27] One Beijing operation obtained a guarantee for repayment directly from company corporals, who collected the soldiers' monthly silver stipends from the Board of Revenue.[28] On the day salaries were paid, corporals coming from the Board would go first to the shop to pay down the loan before proceeding to dispense any money to bannermen. One can be sure that they were compensated for their trouble—so that occasionally no money ever made it into the hands of the indebted bannerman, whose only option was then to borrow more in order to get by.[29]

Attempts to improve banner livelihood addressed each of these problems. Corruption was always fought, and we have already seen suggestions to remedy the structure of banner support by returning bannermen to the land. One experiment in this spirit was the Yongzheng emperor's attempt to implement the legendary "well-field" method in an agricultural venture designed to make farmers out of bannermen, which failed spectacularly.[30] Augmenting soldierly employment opportunities for bannermen was a more successful tack, especially under the Yongzheng emperor, when over twenty-two thousand jobs, including both regular and supernumerary (*yangyubing/hūwašabure cooha*) posts, were added between 1724 and 1738[31] (the 30 percent increase in military expenses noted during this time was above all else the result of such policies). In response to weaknesses in the basic system of banner support, and reacting specifically to the illegal sale of banner land to Han Chinese, the court also authorized redemptions of banner land. The first such buy-back occurred in 1730,[32] and this strategy was even more strongly pushed by the Qianlong emperor, who ordered redemption of banner land first in 1739, then again in 1746 and 1757. By 1760, one estimate is that four million taels had already been spent to buy over 226 million *mu* of land back from Han owners.[33] The land was then redistributed to deserving banner households, which in many cases turned right around and remortgaged or sold the land for cash. Still, the court pursued this policy doggedly, and land redemption efforts continued throughout the eighteenth into the nineteenth century, coming to an end sometime during the Jiaqing period.[34]

The other primary focus of court efforts to resolve poverty in the banners was to end insolvency, which suggests that the court felt that levels of support were sufficient (and that it could sustain the fiscal burden that support entailed) if bannermen would only watch their expenses more carefully. At first, the problem of debt was attributed to expenses incurred by soldiers on campaign, who had to replace at their own cost missing equipment and horses, and whose extended absence from home left households little to get by on, reducing them to living on credit.[35] One initiative was the creation of a special "public treasury" (*gongku/siden-i ku*) fund specifically targeted at providing low-interest loans to bannermen. After making a gift of five thousand taels for the repayment of loans in the Chinese banners, the emperor cautioned:

> Once the debts of Eight Banner soldiers have been fully repaid, there remains the possibility that some may be forced to take loans. Borrowing

from the Board would involve many complications, [so] a sum of silver should now be given to the Eight Banners. . . . In view of their [i.e., banner soldiers'] needs, this money should be lent and then every month an amount deducted from their pay. In this way soldiers will not be reduced to such straits and in the future will avoid the burdens of borrowing.[36]

This idealism was only rewarded, however, by ever-increasing debt and the rapid bankruptcy of the fund.

Another, simpler, solution was the straightforward forgiveness of banner debt. Qing emperors frequently presented bannermen with lump sums and loan amnesties. In principle one-time-only gifts, each time such bestowals were made people were cautioned that the money was intended to provide immediate debt relief and allow them to make a fresh start. By the first decade of the eighteenth century, not only had the emperor forgiven unpaid loans worth six million taels made from the public treasury, but he had made two grants worth a total of twelve million taels to help relieve all debts incurred by bannermen.[37] (Note that these eighteen million taels were nonroutine expenses not calculated into the regular budget for maintaining the banner system!) Though neither the Yongzheng nor the Qianlong emperor was as generous as the Kangxi emperor, both dispensed the occasional bonus to provide temporary debt relief among bannermen.[38] By then, for many in the banners accumulating debt had become a way of life.

Most commonly, bannermen acquired debt by taking ordinary credit, by mortgaging property, and by accepting direct loans. The granting of credit seems to have been a practice limited primarily to the capital and was typically an arrangement between Han merchants or proprietors and Manchu bannermen; the ethnic conflict brought on by these arrangements has already been described. The mortgaging of land was another way of raising cash, and played a key part in the downward spiral of banner livelihood since, as already explained, it contributed to the alienation of permanent assets that were supposed to provide a steady income. Borrowing against property, like credit, was a problem that received more attention in the capital than in the garrison. It was especially risky because it often resulted in the loss of domicile. Time and again the court tried to remedy the problem of homelessness, either by building housing projects for bannermen, outlawing property mortgaging, or regulating rents.[39] As explained by a banner officer, the problem was straightforward enough:

Thus not very much is left of the monthly silver salary of officers and soldiers, not enough to pay their travel expenses while traveling on their lord's business, to support, clothe, and feed their wives and children. They end up in distress. . . . But if rents for those homeless officers and soldiers were not permitted to exceed one *qian*, then [they] . . . would be able to make ends meet.[40]

One reason for reforming rents was not only because they were sometimes high, but also because they were unfair: Manchus and Mongols often paid less than Chinese bannermen, who were apparently discriminated against in housing.[41]

For bannermen in need of quick cash, direct loans were the most popular method of borrowing. Loans could be unsecured or secured. Unsecured loans were less popular as they involved extremely high interest—in the case of one Beijing moneylender, sometimes as high as 30 percent. So borrowing on security, that is, pawning, was the most usual way to get a loan. This involved the temporary surrender of some object of value, later to be redeemed, in exchange for a sum of cash. In Beijing there were many "well-off people" who opened small private pawnshops (*dangpu/dangpuli, damtun puseli*) where desperate soldiers would go with their bows, quivers, and swords. Charging high interest on loans, pawnbrokers restricted redemption to a period of ten or fifteen months, after which time the pawned item would no longer be claimable.[42] At some shops the terms could run as high as 10 percent per month, with six-month redemption limits.[43] The good money to be made here was one reason the Yongzheng emperor decided to get in on the act with the investment funds scheme (*shengxi yin/forgošome madabure menggun*). Not only did it augment sources of financing for the Eight Banners by allowing the organization a means of raising its own funds, but it also helped keep banner debt "in-house."

A characteristic innovation of the Yongzheng emperor, who advocated strong state intervention in economic matters, the investment funds program has been described, along with the "nourishing-honesty allowance" (*yanglian yin/hanja ujire menggun*) and meltage fee reforms as one of the three great finance reforms of the Yongzheng reign.[44] The program was targeted specifically at the Qing military, the Eight Banners receiving by far the greater share of the benefit. Its primary objectives were to reduce the amount by which banner expenses were subsidized by the state and also to reduce indebtedness among bannermen. Money put into the investment pool was to be used for business investments providing secure and stable returns. The income was then to provide a lasting source of extra support to bannermen. Under the guiding hand of garrison generals and lieutenant generals, who were jointly charged with the duty of "portfolio management," its successful development in the provinces realized—for a time, at least—the emperor's goal of providing a steady source of supplemental outside income that would cover the garrison's costs of funding the social welfare programs that existed for bannermen.[45]

The initial amount of money disbursed for investment in 1723 was huge—nine hundred thousand taels, or about one-ninth of the imperial treasury at the time.[46] The major recipients were the capital Manchu and Mongol Eight Banners and the Imperial Household Department. Money could be invested as recipients saw fit, either as loans to merchants, to buy land, or to operate pawnshops. In 1729, the scale of the program was expanded as yet more money was diverted, this time from the provincial treasuries, for investment by a wider range of recipients that included the provincial Eight Banner garrisons, the Chinese banners, and some Green Standard Army garrisons.[47] Between 1729 and 1746 an additional 1,700,000 taels were sunk into the investment funds initiative. These 1729 grants went to the garrisons in Xi'an, Nanjing, Hangzhou, Jingzhou, Ningxia, Youwei, Guangzhou, Fuzhou, Jingkou, Tianjin, Kaifeng, Tongguan, Zhapu, and Chengdu.[48] All received twenty thousand taels for investment, with the exception of the Kaifeng, Tongguan, Zhapu, and Chengdu garrisons, which received only ten thousand.[49] Fund administrators were warned against usury and other behavior that would, in the phrase so often found in orders to the garrisons, "disturb the locality." Reflecting a common concern of Confucian statecraft, this included unfair competition or encroachment on Chinese-run businesses. Provincial civil officials were to prevent any "incidents," while banner officials were to send yearly financial statements of fund activity.[50]

The capital received by the garrisons for investment was used in different ways. Pawnshops seem to have been the preferred option,[51] with regiment colonels put in charge of supervising day-to-day operations and keeping the books. Two pawnbroking shops were opened in each of the Manchu cities at Xi'an, Jingzhou, Tianjin, and Ningxia, with one each at Nanjing, Hangzhou, Qingzhou, Youwei, Kaifeng, and Liangzhou. These, it might be noted, were in addition to already existing pawnshops (at Tianjin, for example, the total rose to five). Despite the injunction not to interfere with Chinese-run shops, sometimes banner interests expanded beyond the confines of the garrison: at Jingzhou, because business in the Manchu city was said to be slow, an additional pawnshop was opened in the Chinese city. Pawnshop interest rates were not fixed, but were competitive, varying from 1 percent (Hangzhou) to 1.5 percent (Nanjing) or 2 percent (Jingzhou, Qingzhou), depending on location and sometimes on the amount.[52] Another very popular location of investment funds was with merchants, usually salt merchants, who received thirty thousand taels from the Tianjin garrison, twenty thousand taels from the Hangzhou and Zhapu garrisons (which pooled their resources), fourteen and a half thousand from the Guangzhou garrison, and eight thousand from the Nanjing garrison.[53] Investments here were considered safe and typically brought interest of 2 percent. Alternatively, the money was used to open up various retail shops inside the Manchu city. In their reports on the condition of the investment funds, some garrison generals describe these only as "trading shops," while others specify that there were stores selling rice and other grain, coal, wood, and cloth. At Nanjing the garrison administration ran a market selling reeds (presumably for use in starting cooking fires), while a money-changer's was opened at the Kaifeng and Zhuanglang garrisons. At Tianjin, where the enterprising spirit was especially strong, a shop selling bows and arrows was opened, as well as a used clothing store and a dyers'. A third type of venture was investment in land and property, which, since it returned only 0.7 percent to 1 percent interest, was the least popular form of investment.[54] At Qingzhou some buildings were rented out,[55] while at Tianjin land was bought in the countryside to bring in some rent. No other garrisons appear to have become involved in real-estate dealings.

Most of the garrison officers charged with handling the investment funds did fairly well. At Xi'an the total interest earned on 20,000 taels after eight years was reckoned at 11,608 taels; the Ningxia garrison recognized a net profit of almost 9,000 taels after nine years of investments. At Tianjin, which was unusually heavily endowed by two grants in 1729, one of 20,000 taels from the imperial treasury and an additional gift of 10,000 taels from the province, business was booming.[56] The garrison commander reported that as of early 1735, after subtracting the money given to bannermen in subsidy payments, over 35,000 taels in profit had been made. Seven years later, total earned interest approached 160,000 taels, of which the Tianjin garrison treasury still possessed 87,000 taels in goods and silver, the rest having gone for weddings, funerals, and overhead costs.

However, not everyone quite understood the importance of getting a good return on an investment, or even the basic principle that the seed capital was to remain untouched. At Jingzhou, the garrison general suggested that even if people had almost nothing to give as collateral, the investment-fund pawnshops should accept symbolic pledges from bannermen if they needed money "for something truly important."[57] Amazingly, this proposal, which amounted to giving out unsecured loans to bannermen, came just one week after an edict forgiving four hundred thousand taels in bannerman loans.[58] Kaifeng dry-goods stores opened using investment-funds capital were discovered in 1729 to be in fact operating as moneylenders. They had virtually no stock on the shelves, and almost three-fourths of their operating capital was loaned out to bannermen. The governor-general intervened and ordered the remaining money returned to the provincial treasury. A couple of years later, the same commandant was again accused of abusing the funds trusted to him by using both seed capital and interest to make loans.[59]

If thus a qualified success, nonetheless, at its height in the 1730s and early 1740s, the investment-fund program achieved its stated aims of financial relief to garrison bannermen. What is more, it promoted the greater integration of the provincial banner garrisons into the local economy. Banner-run pawnshops dealt not just with bannermen; banner-owned buildings were rented not only to bannermen; and the tens of thousands of taels that the garrisons put into the pockets of salt merchants were no doubt greatly appreciated. Indeed, one reason that the Qianlong emperor was unable or unwilling to dissolve the program all at once is that it had evolved into a large network with its own ties to local economies, providing money and business to a great many people, bannermen and Chinese, on many levels.[60] But eventually it was shut down, and the last shops were ordered closed in 1754.[61]

Two main factors explain its demise. One was increasing corruption. By 1748 it was reported that only 40 percent of earnings went to support bannermen, the rest going into administrators' purses, supposedly to pay for "tea and office supplies."[62] The other was discomfort at using state capital to participate in commerce in competition with Chinese merchants. This objection, based on a "conservative fiscal morality" that grew in strength during the Qianlong reign, had been raised as early as 1738 by a Manchu censor, Šuhede, who argued that it was unseemly for the court to be engaged in trade and wrong to pile "capital on top of capital, profit on top of profit."[63] Indeed, there is evidence of competition between banner and Chinese enterprises, but this was usually to the disadvantage of the former. The Tianjin garrison commander at one point reported that of late business was slow because Chinese merchants were selling at prices that undercut the banner shops.[64]

Despite an elaborate system for the subsidization of the conquest caste that put a tremendous financial burden on the state, bannermen were unable to get their finances under control. Memorials on the problem of banner livelihood and insolvency were still being received at court in the 1820s,[65] by which time poverty was endemic in many, if not most, banner households. By the turn of the twentieth century, payments of salaries and grain were becoming more and more erratic and bannermen were among Beijing's poorest classes.[66] If something may be said in their defense, it might be that borrowing was almost too easy for them, since, as wards of the state, their guaranteed incomes made them attractive credit risks. But just as the receipt of those incomes distinguished them as banner people, so did their chronic indebtedness. This aspect of banner life is well captured by Lao She: "When she [the narrator's aunt] had no money, she bought things on credit in her capacity as a viscount's daughter and captain's wife. She not only took great pleasure in buying on credit, she also looked down on friends and relatives who lacked the courage to do so or took no pleasure in it. Though she never said so, she probably thought, 'What good is it being a Manchu Bannerman if you don't buy on credit?'"[67]

### SECONDARY STATUS IN THE BANNERS

Like acculturation, poverty posed a serious threat to the Manchu Way. It directly affected everything from a soldier's capacity to maintain his military equipment to his ability to feed his family, leaving him demoralized and with no way to emulate the warrior ideal of earlier generations. As the eighteenth century wore on and immiseration in the banners worsened, the Qianlong emperor's fine words about not forgetting the ways of the ancestors must have sounded very hollow to the growing numbers of the down-and-out. Furthermore, the increasing disparity of wealth in the banners and the predations of an increasingly corrupt officer corps (also desperate to maintain its standard of living) introduced new tensions into Manchu life. Apart from the ways outlined above, then, the court also tried to alleviate poverty by limiting the size of the population entitled to banner status. A review of household registration begun in the 1720s laid the groundwork for a substantial restructuring of banner support that rejuvenated the institution, enabling it to continue as an ark of Manchu identity at a time when many of its more obvious cultural markers were fading fast.

The restructuring of the early 1700s targeted above all the growing number of people in paying posts who belonged to "secondary status" categories in the banners, that is, people who were not within the regular categories—Manchu, Mongol, and Chinese banner.[68] As explained in Chapter 1, during the early years of the banner system, statutory identity was determined according to one's classification either as a slave, a bondservant, or a "person of the banners." All independent and semi-independent households of non-servile status were known as "regular households," while household dependents of servile status were known individually as "household people." In the eighty years between the conquest and the beginning of the Yong-zheng reign two other categories gradually emerged to cover people of intermediate status. The first category included children of regular bannermen who had come of age and had set up independent households, but had no post that would qualify them for regular status. Such households were called "detached households" (*linghu/encu boigon*).[69] The other category, called "entailed households" (*kaihu/dangse araha boigon*), enjoyed rights somewhere between those of bondservants and regular bannermen.[70] Most entailed households belonged to former bondservants or slaves who, according to a precedent of 1674, were rewarded with semi-independent status for valor in battle or other distinction in service in the banners;[71] others were households that had been established by adopted children.

Though both of these new categories maintained dependency upon a regular household, the nature of this dependency was as different as its origin. Detached households were made up of descendants of regular Manchu (or other) bannermen, enjoying all the legal rights conferred by this primary status. Entailed households were still considered "mean" and had no such privileges. Punishment of a detached householder might mean exile to Hei-longjiang, where an entailed householder would be made the slave of a Jingzhou bannerman.[72] Confusion between these two intermediate categories grew during the seventeenth and early eighteenth centuries as population rose and the number of companies more than doubled. In some cases, entailed households were officially elevated to detached household status—an honor bestowed on a few soldiers who acquitted themselves with distinction on campaign.[73] In other circumstances, moving a servant (or his son) into a banner soldier's uniform through adoption was approved under certain conditions (such as when there was no male heir) to provide a livelihood to widows and to poorer detached and entailed households in companies where there was a shortage of regular Manchus.[74] Other cases of confusion, however, were out-and-out fraud. By falsely claiming regular (*zhenghu*) or detached (*linghu*) status, entailed (*kaihu*) households were able to circumvent the 1704 prohibition on their taking regular military posts.[75] They were often abetted in false registration by regular households eager to improve their general finances.

In carrying out the registration reforms, the detached-household *linghu* category presented a difficult problem, as it contained households of both "free" and "mean" statuses. In 1729 the court decided to distinguish between the different kinds of *linghu*: households found to originally have been of bondservant or slave status were given the new bureaucratic identity of "separate-register households" (*lingji dang'an hu/dangse faksalaha boigon*). (Detached households that were split off from regular banner households, however, were still permitted to be called *linghu* once the facts of their origin had been established.[76]) This stage of the reform was instigated by the 1729 discovery that many soldiers in the imperial guard and vanguard were not regular Manchus, but the Chinese adopted sons of bondservants who had been secretly entered as detached-household Manchus in company registers. The officials of Futai Company, who were held as an example of culpability, were ordered to "investigate and report the number of regular Manchus in the company." All other companies were to make similar registers showing how many of the adopted sons holding positions in the guard were actually Manchus and not Chinese. No one (for the moment) was to be dismissed; the clarification of records was stated to be for the purpose of avoiding later disputes regarding succession to these positions.[77]

Confirmed detached households were eligible for appointments and all the other privileges that were enjoyed by regular Manchus, whereas separate-register households were not. But because they were made semi-independent earlier, the status of separate-register bannermen was slightly superior to that of entailed bannermen.[78] Before the Yongzheng reign all were eligible for appointment to banner positions, although new decrees of 1726, 1727, 1738, and 1741 forbade men from any of these secondary-status categories (i.e., separate-register households [*lingji dangan hu*] and entailed households [*kaihu*]) to serve as regular soldiers. A major exception were households of foster sons (*yangzi/ujihe jui*) of regular bannermen. This was yet a third category, introduced in 1734.[79] Neither they nor other secondary bannermen could participate in the examination system, but they were allowed to take up banner postings.[80]

Secondary-status bannermen presented the court with a knotty problem. Though technically under the banners, they were virtually all originally Han Chinese, not Manchu. This might not have proved so awkward had they not become so numerous and come to occupy so many positions. But the number of "false Manchus" at some garrisons was very high. At the Liangzhou garrison, 380 out of 2,700 Manchu troops (about 14 percent) were separate-register Manchus.[81] At Ningxia, approximately 180 of 3,600 soldiers' households were of secondary status.[82] A 1747 report from Jingzhou said that among the over 1,600 unsalaried soldiers, 220 were from foster-son households and the rest a mixture of Manchu, Mongol, and separate-register bannermen.[83] Among the 800 bannermen sent to Zhapu from Hangzhou, 194, or nearly one-fourth, were from separate-register or foster-son households; of the 400 sent to Zhapu from Nanjing, 47 were secondary-status Manchus.[84] The higher proportion of secondary-status Manchus among the Hangzhou transferees to Zhapu piqued the curiosity of Zhapu's former lieutenant general, who found in 1740 that almost *half* of all Hangzhou garrison households were from the secondary-status ranks. Of 1,600 soldiers in the Hangzhou Manchu and Mongol banners, 800 were from separate-register and foster-son households; of the 1,600 Chinese banner soldiers, 900 were from those and entailed households.[85] With infiltration of the banners by Chinese on such a scale, it was small wonder that the court desired some more permanent means of sorting out who was who.

It is worth pointing out that the problem with secondary-status bannermen was not that they were poor soldiers. On the contrary, some of them were quite up to par, as the Zhapu lieutenant general noted: "All of them have been taught manly skills. Among the adopted sons and separate-register people are some who have a strong bow arm and are good at marching, so much like real Manchus that you can't tell them apart."[86] Rather, the problem was that these "Chinese Manchus" were usurping the economic and social privileges of deserving regular household bannermen, an untold number of whom, precisely because of the presence of so many grafters, were wrongfully being deprived of work and pay.

## GENEALOGY AND THE REFORMS OF BANNER
## HOUSEHOLD REGISTRATION

Seeing the necessity of some kind of reform if Manchus were to have access
to the positions that were their due, in 1727 the Yongzheng emperor initiated a major cleanup of the banner ranks, ordering the collection of comprehensive information on the original entry of families into the banners and
the compilation of new family registers based on the household (*hu/boigon*),
and not, as before, individual males of military age (*ding/haha*).[87] In addition, other information was collected such as whether men of service age
were at a post or unsalaried, and what posts their fathers and uncles might
have had. Registration was not the basis for dismissal (not yet, anyway), unless information were deliberately held back or status concealed, in which
case it was reserved as a form of punishment. But by making the different
subgroupings in the banner system more readily and surely identifiable, the
action unquestionably strengthened the rights of regular (*zhengshen*) and
bona fide detached household (*linghu*) Manchu, Mongol, and Chinese bannermen to positions as soldiers and officers. The court thus assured their priority over other household categories, all of whom were Han Chinese.

Historians have generally understood these reforms in economic terms, as
the court's attempt to halt the immiseration of Manchus by Chinese.[88] Yet
the usurpation of paid banner positions by secondary-status bannermen was
not only seen as a reason for the impoverishment of Manchus who might
otherwise be holding positions;[89] as I will show, it was also seen as potentially troublesome where hereditary captainships were concerned, and, even
more ominously, as a threat to the ethnic purity of the banners.

The household registration reforms were carried out largely on the basis of
written genealogies, used in investigating the history of individual claims to
be part of a certain lineage and company. Banner genealogies (*jiapu/giyapu*)
were of two general types, one centering on the lineage, the other on the company and the transfer of position and office. Information contained in one
was sometimes duplicated in the other, but since after the Yongzheng reign
company genealogies were stored in Beijing,[90] bannermen in the provincial or
frontier garrisons had no access to those materials, and many were motivated
to compile genealogies, if not of the whole company, at least of their own lineages. In contrast to the official registers kept in the capital banner office, informal clan genealogies were thus primarily for personal reference.[91]

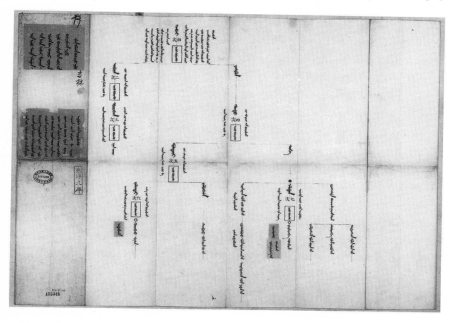

*Fig. 18.* Eight Banner Manchu genealogy. As part of its effort to more carefully regulate the status of Eight Banner households, the Yongzheng court initiated a general background check of all banner families, resulting in the collection of genealogies illustrating the origins of the family connection with its particular company (*niru*). The genealogy shown here was compiled to substantiate the claim of a certain Elden as the seventh holder of the captaincy of the company originally granted to his great-great-grandfather, Kabai (at the top of the chart). The label in the upper right corner explains that the hereditary captaincy was assigned to Kabai after he led the people of his lineage (*mukūn*) in submission; the label below it explains that succession to the captaincy should obey the rules of hereditary succession set down for banner companies. Elsewhere we learn that Kabai was the village head at a place called Gaijin, and that he brought eighty-six men with him, along with sable pelts, when he asked to join the Jianzhou forces at Ningguta. Reproduced courtesy of the Tōyō Bunko, Tokyo.

Court interest in the matter of individual origins stimulated the compilation of both kinds of genealogies, which became the basis of the 1744 *Comprehensive Genealogy of Eight Banner Manchu Clans* as well as parts of the 1739 *Comprehensive History of the Eight Banners*.[92] As explained above, Pamela Crossley has pointed to this emphasis on descent as evidence of a turning point in the evolution of Manchu identity, which she characterizes as its reinvention on "racial" lines in the Qianlong era. The evidence I have gathered indeed confirms this period as a turning point, but for other reasons. I would suggest that we might differently nuance our thinking about the Qing "genealogical turn" by recognizing that the process began, not in the Qianlong reign, but in the preceding Yongzheng era (or perhaps even earlier), and that an emphasis on descent as an element defining banner identity was not really novel at all. Quite apart from what has already been said on this question in Chapter 1, the *Comprehensive Genealogy of Eight Banner Manchu Clans* may not have been the first work of its kind: there appears to have been an earlier compilation, called the *Complete Book of Manchu Lineages* (Ch *Manzhou shizu daquan*), edited in 1713.[93] Second, while the earliest published Manchu genealogies date from the late 1730s,[94] the maintenance of genealogical materials was probably current among bannermen, especially Manchus, from well before this time.[95] There are references to the keeping of genealogies in edicts as early as 1723,[96] and the prefaces of two clan genealogies appearing in a modern published collection claim Kangxi pedigrees.[97] Moreover, new evidence confirms that the necessity to compile genealogies for hereditary company posts was recognized at least by the second decade of the eighteenth century, and perhaps as early as 1703.[98]

When we look more closely at particular genealogies, we find that some lineages maintained them through most of the seventeenth century. In a 1723 memorial on naming successors to the post of company captain in the Bordered Red Banner, Sunjaci, president of the Board of Revenue and temporary banner commander, was able to trace the inheritance of this position, which belonged to a Donggo lineage, six generations back.[99] The relevant company entry is found in the *Comprehensive History of the Eight Banners*, where the Fifteenth Company in the Fourth Regiment of the Bordered Red Banner corresponds to the company Sunjaci brought to the emperor's attention. Here are presented only the bare facts of who succeeded whom in the post of company captain.[100] A comparison of this entry with the entry for the Donggo lineage found in the *Comprehensive Genealogy of Eight Banner Manchu Clans*[101] shows the same company and the same people. However, the specific content is totally different, pointing unmistakably to separate origins for the two texts, that is, to the existence of separate genealogical traditions. The level of detail in the lineage genealogy, which even provides a supposed quotation of speech from the first clan member to have joined

Nurhaci, strongly suggests its being a very old text.[102] Moreover, the preservation of the title *jargūci* (a post held by the son of the first company captain), which disappeared after 1626, also points to the likely existence of very early written records that could be drawn upon later when formal genealogies were composed.[103] Such materials became instrumental in proving one's banner identity when these began to be scrutinized by authorities in the 1720s and 1730s. It is hard to imagine that the court was ignorant of the existence of these materials before that time. While the decision to call upon the criterion of descent in the reform of household registration may have been something of a departure in terms of the formalization of status categories, the idea that descent mattered was as old as the banner system itself.

Thus the Yongzheng banner registration reforms represent a turning point in the evolution of Manchu identity, not because Manchu identity was matched with descent for the first time, but rather because Manchu identity was more closely matched to banner status. By collecting this information, the court could determine who was really Manchu (or Mongol, or Chinese banner), who was originally a slave or a captive, and how many of the latter were illicitly serving as soldiers, fraudulently collecting salaries to which regular bannermen were properly entitled. The phrase sometimes used, *Manju beye* (lit., "Manchu bodies"), is telling. Because it could no longer be assumed that everyone in the banners belonged there by virtue of their descent, it was necessary to isolate Manchu impersonators so that the court could be confident that the banner people upon whom it lavished so much money were indeed the descendants of the original conquest population. Without this confidence, the dynasty's security was in jeopardy, since it was reasoned that Manchus—bodily Manchus—were vital to upholding the Manchu Way. A check of people's backgrounds requiring them to prove that their blood entitled them to be in the banners could provide that kind of confidence.

## MUTABLE IDENTITIES

In focusing solely on how Manchus lost the affective qualities that marked them ethnically, it is easy to assume that such change went in only one direction. It is thus important to remember that Chinese who infiltrated the banner system did so by affecting to be Manchu. As the Zhapu lieutenant general cited earlier remarked, these soldiers "were so much like real Manchus that you can't tell them apart." That they could and did become "Manchu" is a forceful reminder of the mutability of ethnic identities in the Qing, particularly as the institutional compromises made during the Kangxi reign gave many opportunities for secondary-status bannermen to parlay their positions into something more secure.

One incident from the Ningxia garrison illustrates how this could happen. The accusation that started this case was brought by one Fuju, an infantry captain in the Bordered Red Mongol banner stationed at Ningxia. In the genealogy sent to Beijing in 1735, Fuju was listed as the second son of a certain Liol, a separate-register dependent without a salaried position, originally from the household of a Mongol corporal, Soosar. Two years later, in 1737, Fuji took issue with this version of his family history, insisting that he was in fact the grandson of Soosar and that his father was a detached-household bannerman who had been a corporal as well. Boasting of three generations of service by his family, Fuju confidently testified to his and his brothers' status: "Quite clearly, these are independent households. There is not one here who is a separate-register household or adopted slave. Can it be that I am [expected to] quietly tolerate the present failure to present the true facts concerning my father?" However, when documents arrived from the main company in Beijing confirming that, as stated in the genealogy, Fuju's father was a separate-register householder, Fuju admitted that his story was all a concoction. Confessing the truth, he said that he didn't know the name of his real grandfather, where he was from, or from which company his father had originally been bought. "It is true," Fuju conceded in the end, "my father Liol was an entailed bannerman, raised [to that status] by his original master, Soosar."[104]

This case shows how much room there was for maneuver between primary and secondary household status. Despite his name, Fuju was not a Manchu or Mongol "in body," and his father, with the unlikely-sounding name "Liol" (possibly a rendering of Liu Er), was probably a Chinese servant or slave who had been rewarded with semi-independent status by his owner, the Mongol bannerman Soosar, for some act of bravery. Passing this status along to his children, who were given Altaic names, Liol enabled Fuju and his brothers, Duruntai and Bayandai, to qualify for military posts. Fuju was a noncommissioned officer, and the others were both garrison vanguardsmen, suggesting that they must all have attained reasonable martial skills. In addition, one suspects that, at a minimum, the brothers were either Mongol- or Manchu-speakers, or Fuju would never have dared assert that he was from a detached-household background.[105] By just about every standard but blood, Fuju and his sons were upstanding supporters of the Manchu Way.

Adoption, which was extremely common among bannermen, was another way in which ethnic categories in the banners were compromised. The court well understood the "fear of not having anyone to take care of them in the future," as one capital censor phrased it, and set only one condition for adoption: children adopted by Manchu bannermen should be Manchu. When it became known that Chinese children (many of them the children of bondservants) were being taken and falsely registered as Manchus by their adoptive parents, there was an outcry. The censor who blew the whistle on this practice, Batu, was a captain in the imperial guard and evidently knew what he was talking about. He described the process:

> Some shameless people take sons of well-to-do slaves and give them into other households to be raised, saying that they are their own children, and take payment for this. These people either make requests beforehand to the clan head, enter into secret agreements with unscrupulous corporals and deceive the company captains into entering the names into the Manchu registers, or the captain and corporal are themselves from the same clan and do not check, entering the names into the Manchu registers as a personal favor. All of them have this kind of explanation. Later, after things don't match with inside-the-clan [records], this leads to discussions and accusations arising.

In this way the boundaries between regular and detached household banner people were hopelessly muddied. The problem did not end there, however:

> The children of slaves and *booi* fraudulently entered into the Manchu registers all are soldiers in the guard. Since later on there is the possibility they will become officials . . . henceforth if bannermen without legitimate heirs are to be given children to raise as their own, these children should be children from within the clan. If there are no suitable children for adoption within the clan, then Manchu children from within the company or the banner should be adopted, this to be decided between the head of the child's original clan and the head of the clan of the proposed adoptive parents.[106]

Two messages were being sent here: one was that blood mattered; the other, that Manchu blood came first. In other words, Manchu hereditary rights ought to be passed to other Manchus, even if they were from other clans, companies, or even different banners. This fit in well with the court's general strategy that it was mainly interested in supporting Manchu and Mongol bannermen. At the same time, by assuring future posts for regular Manchus, it was also a means of securing the future of the dynasty. This was true even in a very immediate sense: the fear implicit in Batu's report was that unless careful attention were paid to the matter, the emperor's guard would consist entirely of manjurified Chinese. This was not only undignified and improper, it was positively dangerous.

The implications of the above picture are significant. First, the registration of non-Manchu households, legitimate or fraudulent, must be taken into consideration as one reason for rapid population increase in the banners. Second, the acculturation of the Manchus appears to have had its counterpart in the manjurification of the thousands of Chinese who, like Liol and his progeny, or the untold number of Han brides and foster children, found themselves in the banner system and made their lives there. In many cases this was a life that was markedly better than before; it was assuredly quite different. Third, it would seem that rather than speak only of its loss by prodigal sons unmindful of tradition, it would be better to speak of the gradual dilution of the Manchu Way through the surreptitious addition of so many Chinese into the banners. It is hard to know whether Chinese affecting Manchu, Mongol, or even Chinese banner identities would have been stirred by the court's calls to preserve the old ways, but it is easy to believe that the Manchu elite feared they would not. Economic reasons more than anything had drawn them into the banners; they were not the clansmen of the khan or the descendants of his servants. And while they may have acquired military skills, unless the environment provided them a strong incentive to hone them and to learn Manchu (as it probably did at a place like Ningxia), in the early eighteenth century the pressure to conform to another cultural milieu was unlikely to be strong enough to force a complete switch.[107]

From this vantage point, the banner registration reforms of the eighteenth century, most notably the comprehensive compilation and revision of lineage records, take on a very marked ethnic aspect. Through their implementation the court at first determined only to limit the number of those who would thereafter be entitled to support in the banner system. Criteria for deciding who was deserving were thus initially rather generous. Over time, however, the net was drawn tighter as the court's priorities shifted onto those who were most deserving. Thanks to the new registration procedures, it could now with some certainty locate its favorites, namely, regular and detached Manchu, Mongol, and Chinese banner households. As the next section will show, by the 1750s preferences would be narrowed yet further. Ever greater favor was given to Manchu and Mongol bannermen, since they, not the Chinese bannermen, and certainly not Han Chinese disguised as banner secondary households, were the people entrusted with the preservation of the Manchu Way (and the Mongol Way). They were the ultimate recipients of the emperor's trust, the court's own, so to speak. For that reason, it is fair to say that the restriction and defense of banner privilege was at bottom the defense of Manchu privilege, and the court's efforts to preserve the banner system were nothing less than an attempt to preserve Manchu identity itself, and Qing ethnic sovereignty along with it.

POOR RELATIONS: THE EIGHT BANNER CHINESE

In undertaking the reclassification of secondary-status households, the court was at pains to reassure people this did not mean their immediate expulsion from the banners. But this very step was predictably taken in 1756, when all of these groups were made to register as ordinary Chinese:

> Edict: The Eight Banner separate-register people were originally bond-servants in entailed households who pretended to be detached households. Afterward they made themselves known. Moreover, those commoners adopted as foster sons by bannermen and bondservants made [heads of] entailed households are all from the servile class in the banners. . . . Now in every banner and at the provincial garrisons it seems that there are very many of these people. All assignments for posts must first be made exclusively from regular bannermen in detached households before any appointments can be made from among them [i.e., the other groups]. They are all in search of a livelihood, but as they are tied to the banners they cannot act freely. And with so many people in the Eight Banners, . . . making a living is getting harder every day. . . . By imperial favor, let all separate-register, foster-son, and entailed households in the capital Eight Banners and in the outer garrisons be made forthwith to leave the banners and become commoners.[108]

For the first time, the economic and ethnic self-interest of the dynasty had led to the identification and exclusion of an entire group of people from the banners. This was a major watershed. Up to that time, the banners had experienced a century and a half of uninterrupted growth. The elimination of separate-register, entailed, and foster-son households signified the court's intent to salvage the banner system, if not by fiscal retrenchment then by demographic engineering.

Of course, reducing the size of the aggregated banner population had to be done carefully so that only people who were a drag on the system, who took advantage of it without contributing anything to dynastic stability, were removed. These hangers-on were precisely the secondary-status people identified during the household registration reforms: as the edict implied, they had only joined the banners because they were "in search of a livelihood." Since it was now "harder every day" to make a living in the banners, they were better off on their own in the world of Han Chinese—which is where they belonged, anyway. They stood to benefit, as did the dynasty and regular household bannermen, once banner registers were slimmed, costs cut, and jobs and space in the Manchu cities were turned over to the people who deserved them.

But the secondary-status households were not the only potential target for this kind of action. The later expulsion of many Chinese bannermen makes it even clearer that court thinking with respect to the future role of the Eight Banners saw it more and more as the preserve of Manchus and Mongols. Already in the course of the Yongzheng registration reforms, the Chinese bannermen suffered the greatest losses of any of the three ethnic banners. As the statistics cited earlier show, more than half of those removed from the detached-household category and deprived of primary banner status came from the Chinese banners.[109] Worse was yet to come.

The creation of the Chinese banners was explained in Chapter 1, and their importance in the early years of the Qing transition has also been mentioned. While more research on the role of this essential, yet strangely peripheral, group is still needed, it seems that their eventual fate was key in the resolution of the protracted crisis of identity in the banners, where they were regarded effectively as "poor relations." After all, only Manchu or Mongol bannermen, not Chinese, could be made princes and dukes, positions which throughout the Qing carried with them potentially great wealth and power. Only Manchu or Mongol bannermen could serve in the different elite guards divisions that protected the palace and accompanied the emperor wherever he went. Likewise, there were only Manchus and Mongols in the capital artillery division, even though artillery had originally been the forte of the Chinese bannermen. Membership in these divisions not only brought higher pay, but the opportunity for personal contact with the emperor that it afforded could mean easier promotion. Similar opportunities to impress the emperor arose also during the imperial hunts—in which only Manchu and Mongol bannermen were included.

Moreover, preferences within ostensibly identical banner-wide privileges were several, starting with a greater number of jobs for Manchu bannermen at all levels. The number of posts was of course limited within a company, just as the number of companies within a banner was also limited. In the eighteenth century, of a total 1,151 companies in the Eight Banners, 681 were in the Manchu banners, 204 were in the Mongol banners, and 266 in the Chinese banners. Since the total Chinese banner population is estimated to have been almost as great as the Manchu banner population, it is obvious that the Chinese banners had the fewest posts per capita of the three ethnic corps.[110] In addition, a higher proportion of the posts they did get were for infantry, who were paid one ounce of silver less than cavalrymen. A similar situation applied to low-level officer posts, since the greater number of companies meant that there were more openings of this kind in the Manchu banners than in the Chinese banners. Reports from early in the Yongzheng reign show 1,565 officials in the three ethnic corps of the Plain Yellow Banner: 1,211 (77 percent) came from the Manchu banner, 179 (12 percent) from the Mongol banner, and 175 (11 percent) from the Chinese banner.[111] In addition, promotion of Manchu over other bannermen was consistently practiced when it came to regular civil and military posts; Chinese bannermen were not even considered for jobs at the Board of Punishments.[112] Clearly, a talented and ambitious Manchu stood a much better chance of reaching his career goal than an equally talented and ambitious Chinese bannerman (not to mention an ordinary Chinese). With the various measures taken in the eighteenth century to improve the position of bannermen, such as the addition of posts, Manchu, and to a lesser extent, Mongol bannermen were again heavily favored.

Instrumental as they were in the first years of the conquest, just forty years into Qing rule, the Chinese bannermen had already earned an unsavory reputation as wastrels, and Manchu troops had to be encouraged to help them recover their military skills instead of mocking and intimidating them.[113] In 1684 the emperor addressed an assembly of the Chinese banner chiefs, vice-chiefs, and board vice-presidents:

> From the founding of the nation by the ancestors, the Chinese [bannermen] have been treated as one with the Manchus. There were many among them who worked hard and rendered great service to the country. . . . these days officials who are from the Chinese banners are no comparison to those from before. Whenever they leave the capital on assignment they bring many attendants, wasting a lot of money. They think only about getting bribes and burdening the people, are licentious and disorderly. . . . From today, you in the Chinese banners must all cleanse your hearts and sweep clean your minds, and extirpate these old habits.[114]

That the Chinese bannermen had been "treated as one with the Manchus" was as much a sop as the line about "Manchus and Han are one family." Just a couple of months before, the emperor had noted a shortage of qualified candidates among the Chinese bannermen, and ordered that vacancies at officer level in those banners should be given to qualified Manchu and Mongol bannermen, further worsening the already limited opportunities of Chinese bannermen for advancement.

The Kangxi emperor fulminated more than once at the degeneration among Chinese bannermen, especially those in the capital, who were the first to be accused of all manner of extravagant and "degenerate" habits that later spread among Manchus and Mongols:

> Of all the human virtues, none comes before filiality. Of late, when the Chinese bannermen have arranged funerals for their parents, these are social gatherings for relatives and friends, where plays are performed and wine is drunk, and people gamble with dice and cards. It's just like a banquet of swallows, with no respect for custom. . . . Staging plays at funerals is not something that Manchus or Han Chinese do. Only the Chinese bannermen are like this.

The same edict excoriated them for flashy dressing, gambling at dice, and having too many servants, concluding that "the evil habits of the Chinese bannermen are simply too far gone."[115]

Chinese bannermen were thus accused of all manner of sins, in particular of leading the way in the adoption of the soft life of the Chinese. By the 1720s calling someone a Chinese bannerman had even become a kind of insult, as when the Yongzheng emperor referred to his brother-in-law and former intimate, Nian Gengyao, as "nothing more than the son of a Chinese bannerman!"[116] All the problems that afflicted Manchus in the Yongzheng and early Qianlong reigns were magnified among the Chinese bannermen.

Chinese banner ability at the Manchu language, never the strongest, had faded to the point that many of them were unable to say even one word when brought before the throne for the requisite interview.[117] Sickened by their hopeless military abilities, in 1731, the Yongzheng emperor ordered the establishment of a special training camp just for the scions of famous Chinese banner families to improve skills to a point where they might be at least employable.[118] These developments bred a climate of opinion in which the Chinese bannermen were increasingly thought of as dispensable to the maintenance of the state and, hence, no longer worth keeping in the banners.

The situation at garrisons staffed only by Chinese bannermen offered no relief from the depressing state of affairs in the capital. Conditions at Fuzhou in particular seem to have been poor. In 1740, to restore standards, the Qianlong emperor placed Cereng (a member of the prominent Manchu line founded by Ebilun), at the head of the Fuzhou garrison.[119] After a few months in office, Cereng memorialized about the sad state of affairs he encountered, remarking that Fujian was well known for being a decadent place where things only got done by socializing and that this custom had spread to the garrison. Everyone, high and low, was said to be constantly engaged in organizing banquets, engaging acting troupes, and sending gifts of food and liquor. Soldiers were compelled to make presents of food and fruit to superior officers to curry favor. Cereng imposed a ban on all such practices, which he said had resulted in some improvement; gambling was also more under control. The biggest remaining problem was the killing of horses. Startled to learn after four months in office that 234 horses had died, Cereng ordered an investigation only to discover that the animals had not fallen to the climate but to the cleaver. Encouraged by the absence of control procedures when the death of a horse was reported, soldiers were slaughtering their mounts and selling the carcasses to one of the twenty restaurants in the garrison run by bannermen that specialized in horsemeat soup. Cereng promptly instituted inspections of dead horses and outlawed the restaurants.[120]

SACRIFICING THE CHINESE BANNERMEN

What emerges as frustration and indignation at the incorrigibility of many Chinese bannermen gave way in the course of the 1740s and 1750s to an attitude that moved beyond the merely negative. A fundamental shift in the perception of the members of the Chinese banners took place—they began again to be spoken of as Han Chinese. This is seen in a memorial submitted by a prominent Han official, Sun Jiagan, to the Qianlong emperor, probably around 1740. It read in part:

> Some Manchus who have been living in the provinces for a long time face difficulties, but the Chinese bannermen are different from the Manchus. They are originally Chinese [*Hanren*]. All the vocations—farming, manufacture, trading—they can learn, and that without trouble . . . henceforth let Chinese bannermen who have been assigned duty outside the capital to remain there if they wish after they retire and settle.[121]

According to Sun's plan, Chinese bannermen would be allowed to buy land and property in order to be able to make a real living to support their families, taking some pressure off the dynasty. Just in case of a call-up, their banner registrations would be maintained. This was both a revolutionary plan for the resolution of the economic difficulties in the capital Eight Banners as well as a radically different view of the Chinese bannermen. No longer were they "men of the banners," people of ostensibly distinct origin and part of a higher legal and social order; they were simply Chinese with peculiar backgrounds.

The view that the Chinese bannermen were essentially "Chinese" may not in fact have been really new. Zheng Tianting suggested the court never ceased thinking of them as Chinese, and their anti-Han prejudice explains why the Chinese banners ranked below the Manchu and Mongol banners in status.[122] The Chinese bannermen were seen this way by the Chinese, too. A memoir written at the end of the seventeenth century explained as follows: "The usage of the dynasty is to call the Eight Banner people from Liaodong 'Han soldiers' and the people from Zhili and the provinces 'Han Chinese.'" In other words, there were two kinds of Han: Han*jun* and Han*ren*; the former were in the banners, the latter were not.[123] In his short 1720 work on the Eight Banner system, *Qijun zhi* (already cited), Jin Dechun similarly defined the Chinese bannermen as being the "descendants of people from Liao[dong], former Ming commanders and emissaries, those from the other dynasty who defected with multitudes [of soldiers], and captives." According to Jin, the Chinese bannermen were simply in the middle on the spectrum between the Manchus and the Green Standard Army. Explaining the use of Manchu soldiers to control the Chinese bannermen, and the Chinese bannermen to control the Green Standard, he wrote: "It's just the same as the way that the body moves the arm and the arm moves the fingers."[124]

If this was the case, then it was their attachment to the khan and their adherence to the Manchu Way—plus their important strategic contribution to the Qing imperial project—that originally made the Chinese bannermen fit into the banner system in the mid-seventeenth century. By the mid-eighteenth century they were hardly the only Han Chinese who had pledged their loyalty to the emperor, and their place in the empire was far less important than that of Han scholar-officials. Few still upheld the old "Manchu" way of life, most having slipped—that is, having slipped *back*—into Chinese ways. Just as significant, intermarriage between the Chinese bannermen and Han Chinese was becoming more and more common, leading the Qianlong emperor to throw up his hands in desperation: "Marriage between Chinese bannermen and the Han has been going on for many years now. It is pointless to prohibit it."[125] The crucial distance between them and the *Nikan* was thus maintained only by the institution of the Eight Banners: the life in the garrison, the entitlements, and all the rest.

No doubt influenced by Sun's proposal, and looking for other ways to trim the banner ranks, the Qianlong emperor announced in 1742 that he considered all Chinese bannermen as "Chinese in origin":

> Edict: Since "following the dragon" [i.e., joining Nurhaci and Hong Taiji] and establishing the dynasty, the Chinese Eight Banners have been nurtured by the nation and prospered, their numbers increasing daily. Those who were engaged in military or civil service originally had a salary and stipend sufficient to support them. [Today], however, the number of unsalaried men is many and life is unavoidably hard for them. Furthermore, precedent has established that those on assignment outside the capital may not acquire property and keep a second residence there. Those unsalaried men who have relatives outside the capital on whom they might rely, or those who possess skills that would allow them to make a living who might have gone somewhere else [than the capital], have been prevented from doing so. The result is that they sit at home idly living on the dole. They are trapped in a corner, which causes me great concern.

The emperor's acknowledgment here of the economic difficulties faced by the Chinese bannermen shows that he had indeed been touched by the many reports of penury in the banners and was not unaware of the extent to which the banners had become a gilded cage, or the extent to which banner people were perceived as leading a lazy, even parasitic, life. Since at this time he had not yet changed his mind on the issue of the bannerman's "home," however, and continued to insist that banner people in the garrisons were on temporary "assignment outside the capital," his options were limited, especially where the Manchu and Mongol banners were concerned. But for the Chinese bannermen there was a way out:

> I consider the Chinese bannermen to be Chinese by origin. . . . [Some of them] joined the banners earlier, some later, and under different circumstances. Except for the descendants of those who "followed the dragon," who, in view of their generations of long service, do not need to be considered for any change, all other categories of Chinese bannermen, those who have ancestral homes at their [original] place of registration or who have clansmen or in-laws in other provinces . . . may return . . . and be enrolled in the *bao-jia* of those places together with the local people.[126]

This was a tentative first step. Only Beijing Chinese bannermen who entered the banner system after 1644 (such as households from the Three Feudatories) were affected, and even then they were only invited to leave. As a voluntary arrangement that provided no sort of material incentive—to use the modern term, no "golden parachute"—this policy produced mostly dissatisfaction. By 1743 only fourteen hundred Chinese bannermen had taken advantage of the opportunity for "freedom."[127] A clarifying edict the following year that the option was only intended for those who had no position and who wanted to set out on their own changed little[128]—the people who might have benefited most from leaving were poor families, but they also had the most to lose, since the banner at least provided an economic minimum, and still conferred some prestige and privilege. This was explained to the emperor in 1745: "These people, having been in the banners for over one hundred years, naturally find it difficult to leave empty-handed. If they are allowed to take their property with them and are given three or six years' stipend, then poor and rich alike would find a place to go." These measures were not adopted, however, and response remained negligible.[129] The next step came nine years later, in 1754. The entire body of Chinese banner soldiers at the Fuzhou garrison were simply excused from their duties and from the banners. They were allowed to go where they wanted and to take up whatever occupation they pleased; one option was for them to join the Green Standard Army.[130] In place of the Chinese bannermen excused from the Fuzhou garrison were put unsalaried Manchu and Mongol soldiers transferred from Beijing. "Truly both sides benefit," went the edict:

"Manchus from the capital get some relief, and Chinese bannermen from the garrison get the freedom to choose their way of life."[131]

This was not the first time that the replacement of Chinese bannermen by Manchu soldiers had been proposed. In 1702 Xi'an general Boji had asked for permission to remove three hundred Chinese banner soldiers from the ranks and replace them with Manchus in order to raise the number of Manchu soldiers at the garrison to an even six thousand. Boji's plan differed in that regular Chinese bannermen were not targeted; only what he called "household slave soldiers" (Ma *booi aha uksin*)—probably an early, unofficial reference to those who would be singled out later as separate-register households—would be removed.[132] This proposal prefigured not only the expulsion of the Chinese bannermen, but also the expulsion of secondary-status bannermen, which, as mentioned above, was directed in 1756, just two years after the expulsion of the Chinese bannermen began.

The process of the expulsion or, as some have termed it, the "repatriation,"[133] of Chinese bannermen lasted almost twenty-five years. Less than six months after demobilizing Fuzhou's Chinese bannermen, edicts came down for similar steps to be taken at the Jingkou, Hangzhou, and Guangzhou garrisons.[134] In 1761 Manchu soldiers from Beijing were sent to take the place of Chinese banner soldiers at Suiyuan. In 1763 Chinese banner soldiers at Liangzhou and Zhuanglang were ordered out. Finally, in 1778–79, it was the turn of the Chinese bannermen at the Xi'an garrison. By the time the "repatriation" ended in 1779, somewhere between ten thousand and fifteen thousand soldiers had lost both their jobs and their banner status.[135] Counting entire households, the population supported by the Chinese banners was probably reduced by well over one hundred thousand people, possibly as much as twice this figure. On top of this, in 1757 it was decreed that Chinese bannermen from the capital who were "aged or maimed, unable to engage in service, or whose service is mediocre and cannot be improved, are ordered to become civilians."[136]

Even regular and able Chinese bannermen in Beijing were eventually affected. A 1762 proclamation that all Chinese bannermen—not just those in the garrisons, but everyone, including the grandchildren and great-grandchildren of those Chinese who had been so useful in the early period of Qing rule in China—were free to leave.[137] In their case, quitting the banners was voluntary, as it had been originally for garrison Chinese bannermen. But in giving them options and life choices that were still denied Manchus and

Mongols, the court had confirmed suspicions that it did not see the Chinese bannermen as equal to the Manchus or as essential to the original dynastic mission which it was the place of the Eight Banners to fulfill. The only thing now separating these people from the Han Chinese was their choosing to stay in the banners.

## BANNERMAN AND MANCHU

Like the elimination of secondary-status bannermen, the purging of Chinese bannermen from the banners formed part of an emerging Qing policy aimed at the preservation of a unique Manchu status and identity through cutting costs and maintaining the banner system. By thinking of Chinese bannermen as "by origin Chinese," their affecting Chinese ways, though at first distressing and exasperating, became understandable, even forgivable. Indeed, to the extent that their (re)acculturation made it easier for the court to then excuse the highly fecund Chinese banner people from the increasingly crowded and costly banner ranks to make more room for Manchus, it was almost a welcome development. Less understandable, and totally unforgivable, was the disturbing process of acculturation among Manchu bannermen. By the middle of the eighteenth century the original repertoire of Manchu cultural practice—military skills, frugal and simple lifestyles, proficiency in the Manchu language—was well on the path to holding merely symbolic significance for a large number of bannermen (although even symbolic significance was worth something). They may have spoken somewhat better Manchu in the capital and ridden more professionally in certain garrisons, but there was no questioning the seriousness of the crisis.

Hence at the same time as it appealed to the progressively more idealized ethnicity embodied in the Manchu Way, the court wisely hedged its bets and consistently made certain that the institutional elements of banner existence were retained and expanded. Thus the privileges for Manchus and Mongols —the salaries and rice stipends, the extra legal cover, the fast track to office— were enhanced over time.[138] When the banners themselves showed signs of creaking under the weight not of acculturation, but of overpopulation and excessive expense, further action was required. Under the direction of its hands-on rulers, the Qing court did its best to make certain that the people in the banners really belonged there and were really entitled to the privileges that came with that status.

Using genealogical criteria to identify those who were "Manchu in body" eliminated many people from the banners, even those who by their performance alone "looked" Manchu. On the one hand, this demonstrated the court's determination to limit numbers and reduce the financial burden on the state. On the other hand, it also demonstrated the court's decision to reinforce Manchuness not according to the professed ideals of the Manchu Way, but at the boundaries of the institution that could best guarantee the survival of Manchu power. At this point, the banners went from being a Qing institution to being a more purely Manchu institution. Chinese bannermen who left became Han Chinese, while those who stayed became "Manchu." This is why, as already discussed, in the late eighteenth century Manchus often referred to themselves as "us banner people" (Ma *musei gūsai niyalma*), while continuing to distinguish, when such distinctions were important, between Manchus, Mongols, and Chinese within the banners and Chinese civilians (Ma *irgen*) and others on the outside.[139] Even in the heat of a fight, the banner/civilian difference could leap out: In 1795, two Beijing men involved in a street brawl with Hui residents had just come to blows when one said to other, "But we can't fight! You're a bannerman, too!"[140]—this just two years after the Qianlong emperor had announced that

> the language of the established precedent, "when a Manchu murders a Manchu," was never appropriate. The entry should be amended to say, "when a bannerman murders a bannerman," so that Mongol and Chinese bannermen are all thus included. For when one thinks of it, both Mongol and Chinese bannermen are in the banners, so how could it be that only they are not bannermen?[141]

Though cultural differences never fully vanished, by the later part of the eighteenth century, more than being able to shoot well or speak Manchu, it was above all the institution of the Eight Banners—the privileges it conferred, the limitations it imposed, and the particular way of life in Manchu cities—that defined the sense of election in being a Manchu.

The departure of the Chinese bannermen was the last major adjustment made to the structure of the Eight Banner system until the first decade of the twentieth century. That the system survived so long testifies to the success of the actions taken by the Yongzheng and Qianlong emperors to ensure its well-being. Moreover, the survival of the separate status and identity of Manchus to the end of the dynasty and beyond—indeed, the survival of the dynasty itself—testifies to the resolution of the Manchu identity crisis of the eighteenth century. Over and above the ideological campaigns to preserve an idealized Manchu Way, in the transformation of the Manchus from a people of conquest to a people of occupation, it was the institutional elements woven into their identity that created a new Manchu way.

# Manchu Identity and Manchu Rule in China

In *Xiaoting zalu*, his famous collection of stories, anecdotes, and factoids, the Qing nobleman Zhao-lian tells the story of a certain A-li-ma, a Manchu warrior who lived during the early conquest period. A-li-ma was reputed to be so strong that he could pick up the one-thousand-*jin* stone lions at the *Shisheng si* temple in Mukden. And not only that, he could even lift himself off the ground by pulling up on his own hair! Though his battle merits won him favor, it was not long after the Manchus settled in Beijing that A-li-ma ran into trouble, frequently landing foul of the law. The emperor eventually decided to have him arrested and, as punishment for his many crimes, executed. Upon hearing of the emperor's reasons for his arrest, A-li-ma took the news stoically, saying, "How should a good man fear death?" He was then bound and put in a cart to be taken to the execution ground southeast of Beijing. However, when the cart reached the Xuanwu Gate and was about to leave the Manchu city, A-li-ma stuck his foot into a hole in the brick wall, stopping the cart, and exclaimed, "If I have to die, I have to die. But I am a Manchu. Do not let the Han see my end. Please kill me inside the gates!"

Apocryphal or not, this tale, like the story of the heavenly maiden Feku-len and of Nurhaci trying to keep his clothes out of the snow, is another re-minder of the uses of history and legend in shaping Manchu identity during the Qing.[1] It is also a reminder that, however familiar their presence, the perception of the Manchus as being somehow "other" was a durable one. As remarked in Chapter 6, such a notion pervades the substantial number of references to them in the "jottings" literature that grew in popularity in the 1800's. *Xiaoting zalu*, written during the reign of the Jiaqing emperor in the early nineteenth century, was a well known work in this genre.[2] It appeared at a time when acculturation meant not only that such Paul Bunyan–like he-roes as A-li-ma had long vanished, but also that their stories were written, not in workaday Manchu, but in elegant literary Chinese. The story of A-li-ma and its retelling (by a Manchu prince, no less) testifies to the tenacity of Manchu pride despite the ravages of acculturation, and, with that pride, to a continuing sense of Manchu difference.

## HOW DID THEY DO IT?

I began this study of the Manchus with the conviction that knowing more about Manchu identity in the seventeenth and eighteenth centuries was important because it would help us answer the "minority-rule question" (How did the Qing manage to hold on to power for almost three hundred years?), as well as the "Manchu question" (What difference did it make to the history of late imperial China that the Qing rulers were Manchu, and not Han Chinese?). In addressing these questions, I have rejected accepted narratives of assimilation to paint a more complex picture that squares better with what Manchu-language documents tell us about Manchu history and with what we know today about ethnic formation, especially the by-no-means simple relationship between progressive acculturation and persistent identity systems.

Regarding the minority-rule question, I have sought first to establish the reasons that keeping the category "Manchu" alive mattered to the Qing dynasts. (That it did matter is plain even if one were only to count up the many thousands of occurrences of the word *Manzhou* in the *Veritable Records*.) My hypothesis has been that the legitimacy of the dynasty rested on, and was understood by Qing rulers themselves to rest on, two types of legitimating discourse: one based on orthodox Chinese ideas of kingship and the other on a narrower conception of the interests of the Manchus as an alien conquest group. Across these poles crackled the tension between broad majority claims and narrow minority interests, between universalism and particularism, between meritocracy and aristocracy, and between civil and military ideals. One of the major challenges the Qing court faced in ruling China lay in keeping these tensions in balance, since tilting too far in either direction risked disaster.[3] If the dynasty were to have abandoned the first of these types of discourse (what is commonly called neo-Confucian legitimacy)—for example, by abolishing the examination system—it would have lost the support of the Han literati, without whom governing would have been almost impossible. On the other hand, if the boundaries that set the Manchus as a group apart from the majority Han Chinese had been allowed to crumble and the Manchus had scattered among the general population, then ethnic sovereignty would have been vitiated and the dynasty's future imperiled.[4] The first path (to draw the sort of historical analogy that the Qing rulers would have grasped) was that of the Yuan dynasty, which lasted barely a century; the second was that of the Jin dynasty, which Hong Taiji saw as a warning of the dangers of acculturation.

To their credit, Manchu rulers (in notable contrast to a number of late-twentieth-century leaders) appear to have recognized that ethnicity was an unstable basis for politics. Hence it was their Confucian face that they most often preferred to wear in public among the Chinese, professing their impartiality toward Manchu and Han. Yet, as we have seen, their "private" thoughts—not to mention actual practice—told a very different story. Only rarely—as in the 1730 publication of the *Dayi juemi lu* (Record of great righteousness to dispel confusion), the Yongzheng emperor's defensive reply to his dead Chinese critic, Lü Liuliang—were the views of the anxious minority put on display. It is no accident that, in this case, the Qianlong emperor ordered the retraction of all copies of his father's manifesto less than two weeks after taking the throne: it was simply too revealing of the dynasty's preoccupation with its own image.[5]

If, then, tactfully preserving Manchu dominance and sustaining the coherence of the Manchus as a group were conditions for the success of Qing rule, and if we grant that Qing rule was, indeed, fairly successful (which it was, at least by the standard that it prevailed for almost three hundred years), the conclusion must be that, contrary to the sinicizationist view, Manchu ethnicity was somehow maintained. But every story we have about the Manchus, even those arguing for the persistence of Manchu identity into the nineteenth and early twentieth centuries, tells us that by the early eighteenth century Manchu identity was already in jeopardy and that court programs for saving it did not keep Manchus from forsaking their own customs and adopting Chinese ones. The court's demand—or was it a plea?—to uphold the "Old Manchu Way," a Spartan ideal that prized riding, shooting, frugality, and Manchu linguistic aptitude, fell on deaf ears. So how did Manchu identity endure?

The response essayed in this book has been structured around an investigation of the Eight Banners, the most fundamentally Manchu of all Qing institutions. A highly militarized form of social organization similar to those

employed by other Inner Asian groups in the past, the Manchus' banner system stood for all that was not Chinese about them. And since, with the sole
exception of the emperor, every Manchu man, woman, and child belonged
in the Eight Banners, its history is inseparable from the history of the Manchus. On these grounds, the preceding chapters have examined the nature of
Manchu identity as it evolved within the banner institution at both elite and
non-elite levels. What I have found is that as the Qing conquest of China
turned into the Qing occupation of China, the court ideal, a normative Manchu Way, was largely, though never entirely, eclipsed by a performative Manchu way.[6] The companies of the Eight Banners, as the "native place" of the
conquering people, ended up defining who those people were, making Manchus into bannermen and, conversely, making bannermen—some, anyway,
after a protracted weeding-out process—into Manchus. This process culminated in the ultimate recognition of all Qing banner people as members of
the "Manchu nationality" (Ch *Manzu*) by the Chinese state in the 1950s.[7]

As we have seen, Manchu identity was asserted and maintained through
the banners in two broad ways. On one level, the widespread presence of the
banner system in China proper asserted the Manchu identity of the dynasty
as a whole; on another level, the way of life imposed by the banner system
upon its people profoundly affected the evolution of the Manchu ethnos in
the seventeenth and eighteenth centuries. Let us review these briefly.

During the first eighty years or so of Qing rule, the court relied on bannermen in the capital and the provincial banner garrisons to assert and
maintain Manchu control in China in rather overt ways, not least by taking
possession of the entire city of Beijing and staking exclusive claim to sizable
portions of other major cities, beginning with Xi'an and Nanjing in 1645.
Eighteen "Manchu cities" were established altogether in the provinces,
twelve of them by 1700; at all of them, as at Beijing, the principle of segregated residence for bannermen was followed. Soldiers sent to the garrisons
brought their entire households and were allotted a place to live behind a
wall that separated them from local Han Chinese. Yet they were not allowed
to own property anywhere but in Beijing, and until the mid-eighteenth century, when bannermen died their bodies were returned to the capital for burial. This was all part of the idea that Qing occupation of the country was
provisional, that garrison duty was a temporary assignment, and that Beijing, and the banners that were based there, were still the real home of Manchus and all banner people. This fiction was central to the court's program

for maintaining inviolate the integrity of the Manchus as a conquest group and for preventing what the Yongzheng emperor called the "naturalization" of bannermen.

These policies worked quite well for the Qing. By dispersing troops of unquestionable tribal (or quasi-tribal) loyalty in most of the important provincial cities of China, and concentrating more than half of all banner forces in a protective cordon around the capital and its palaces, the dynasty won for itself a high degree of security. In the provinces, the Manchu cities provided the conquerors a permanent presence that constantly reminded Han Chinese there in whose hands supreme authority lay. The garrison network also afforded the court an additional surveillance apparatus. It became, as it were, part of a secondary bureaucracy staffed only by bannermen, mainly Manchus; no nod needed to be made here to ethnic parity. Provincial banner officials corresponded on a steady and intimate basis with the emperor: in addition to reporting on the performance of soldiers and other officers, they kept their "sacred lord" informed as well on the general situation outside the capital and on the activities of civil provincial officials. In some instances, garrison personnel acted in roles usually reserved for members of the civil bureaucracy, though the significance of this might not have been so great, since so many members of the top provincial bureaucracy were Manchus anyway.

At the same time, relying on the banners in these ways brought with it substantial economic and political costs. The importance of the banners to the dynasty was nowhere more evident than in the fortune invested by the court in the institutional support of bannermen. In the end, it is not possible to calculate what the cost came to, exactly how many hundred million ounces of silver were spent. Between the massive chunk of state income budgeted for annual banner salaries and the purchase of grain, the money for gifts, bonuses, loan amnesties and investment schemes, and the funds for extra positions and the construction of whole cities, it seems as though no expense was too great where the preservation of the banner system, the banner garrisons, and the banner way of life was concerned. A different type of economic cost was the enormous loss of labor potential that resulted from the tight restrictions on legal occupations for bannermen. These restrictions contributed directly to the steady impoverishment of many people in the banners, and worked ultimately to the detriment of the country as a whole. Other, more immediate, political costs owed to the deep mistrust that set Manchus and Han apart. Many Chinese (and not just in the early years of the dynasty) were skeptical of the Manchu claim to the Mandate of Heaven, and Manchu awareness of this doubt fueled their own mistrust of the Chinese and their own insecurity as rulers. For reasons of pride as much as of security, both sides had ample reason to hide their biases and fears, and were aided in doing so by the rhetoric of the single family of Manchu and Han. Nonetheless, as we have seen, Manchu-Han interaction was at all levels often quite strained.

The second way in which Manchu identity was imbricated in the banners was through the imparting of a set of practices in daily life that effectively divided banner people from the Han Chinese. The banner system separated people physically in the Manchu cities, with their walls, their military layout, and architectural distinctiveness; it marked them economically, granting them a status in Qing society that was both separate and privileged, especially where the Manchu and Mongol banners were concerned. Occupationally as well, the banner system specified what its constituents might do in life, forbidding them any profession other than soldier, clerk, or official (and, sometimes, agriculturalist), and in exchange extended them various considerations that worked very much to their advantage in the backbreaking competition to enter government service. Further, the banners conferred a separate legal status, as bannermen enjoyed general immunity from normal civil prosecution and automatically qualified for lenient treatment and lightening of penalties.

Taken individually and examined out of context there may not seem to be anything inherently "ethnic" in any of these incidental results of banner status. But the picture changes when we recall that banner status was itself hereditary. Not just characteristic privileges of an ever-mobile social elite, these institutionally established life patterns became the defining characteristics of a minority military caste whose membership was fixed and closely controlled from generation to generation. (The consistent, precise documentation of births, deaths, marriages, and adoptions among the people of the Eight Banners surely qualifies them as one of the most intensely inventoried and monitored populations in history.) Examined in historical context—the Eight Banners, as shown in Chapter 1, owed the particulars of its formation to the complicated ethnic makeup of the early Qing confederation—and in the political context of Qing ethnic sovereignty, the court's insistence upon the banner system and the Manchus both as the foundation of the *gurun* need not seem contradictory; in fact, they were virtually synonymous. The banners were an explicitly ethnic institution; together with various defining Manchu cultural practices, even though attenuated or altered, it was the Eight Banners that enabled the survival of the Manchu imperial ethnos as a distinct, coherent descent group bound by shared lifeways, shared institutions, and a belief in a shared past.

The "rescue mission" detailed in the final part of the book originated under the Yongzheng emperor, who was greatly alarmed by the acculturation of bannermen. In the disappearance of Manchu traditions and language, the court, together with the top and middle levels of the Manchu elite generally, perceived a threat to the dynasty's "root." The widening distance between the garrison and the capital Eight Banners was undeniable proof to the court that the terms of the Manchu occupation were changing. While making certain grudging compromises—namely that banner companies in the Manchu cities, like the *niru* in Beijing, could also function as "home"—the court was also determined to limit the process when and where it could. Perhaps anticipating that appeals to memory, historical consciousness, shame, and duty would work only to a limited degree, the Yongzheng emperor (always a practical man) soon decided that for the taxonomic integrity of the label "Manchu" to survive, reforms of the demographically and financially overburdened banner system had to be undertaken. As shown, these reforms hinged on a comprehensive review of the genealogies of everyone in the Eight Banners and the sharpening of the institutional and status divisions between Inner Asian and Chinese in the banner system. By 1779 Chinese bannermen had been eliminated from all Manchu cities save Beijing and Guangzhou, and virtually disappeared from view. This move made it painfully clear that, though a polyethnic institution, the raison d'être of the Eight Banners was nothing more and nothing less than the maintenance of the privileged position of Manchus (and Mongols) in the empire.

It was precisely here that the banner system played an important role in underpinning ethnic sovereignty. If preserving Manchu ethnicity meant protecting the system that granted the Manchus special status in China, this is what the court would do. In the process, whether or not the goal was expressed consciously, and even as the dynastic elite continued to insist on the ideals of the *fe doro*, the institutional and economic ties that had always characterized banner life took on even greater meaning. It was undeniably easier for the court to proceed in this way: at the cultural nexus it could not force people to speak Manchu, but at the institutional nexus it could withhold grain and silver. And even if it understood Manchuness differently for men than for women—stressing a nonacculturating "male virtue" within the sphere of a state-sponsored ideal while simultaneously encouraging a partially acculturated official ideal of female virtue—it was still assured control over marriage and reproduction through the banners.

Of course, it is impossible to say how successful these reforms were in any absolute sense: doubtless hundreds, even thousands, of cases of fraudulent identity escaped discovery, and many Manchus no doubt secretly quit the banners, setting up new lives outside the Manchu cities, where, if they tried, they could pass as Han civilians. But the reforms were successful enough in that the banner system survived, as did the Qing and the Manchus, into the twentieth century.

One might well ask, how "Manchu," after all, were these Manchus? By the official court ideal of the Manchu Way, not very. The view from the palace was bleak. All around, the emperor saw Manchus who didn't know how to ride, couldn't shoot, and who had forgotten how to speak their native language. About the only thing that remained of their original "Manchuness" was their hairstyle, the unbound feet of their women, and the memory of a glorious past. However, as cultural differences narrowed, membership in the banner system, along with all that this conferred in terms of genealogical authenticity (whether or not "genuine") and privilege, joined the other affective elements of Manchu ethnicity to become a crucial gatepost of Manchu identity. In this way, the organization originally only responsible for ordering Manchu life became also the repository of Manchu ethnicity. With everyone in the banners now "Manchu," banner status became at once a boundary-making and a constitutive element of ethnicity. Even if a man spoke Chinese, wrote poems in Chinese, and kept Han Chinese concubines at home, his status as a member of the banners conferred on him an inherent ethnic status. One could usually confirm various divergences from normative Hanness by finding out his name, glancing (discreetly, naturally) at his principal wife's feet and hair, inquiring whether he took milk in his tea, or hanging around to see how weddings, funerals, and festivals were observed in his household. And if he didn't really seem to do any work, well, that, too, was part of the bannerman's repertoire. In the words of one fed-up Han official, bannermen were "neither scholars, nor farmers, nor laborers, nor merchants, nor soldiers, nor commoners."[8] They would seem to have no place, then, in Chinese society; yet there they were.

In searching to establish what made the Manchus "Manchu," it is vital to bear in mind that the name never reflected an essential or true category of people who somehow were later polluted, even though the court sometimes liked to portray things this way. Rather, from the moment of its invention in 1635, "Manchu" was a highly politicized ethnic label, encompassing, but also transcending, the merely cultural and genealogical. At the same time, as indicated in many places in our story, even though the descendants of the original Manchu banners showed a high degree of acculturation (indeed, becoming famous for this across Inner Asia), more typical markers of ethnicity such as language, custom, dress, and religion never completely disappeared, and intermarriage for the most part remained uncommon. Banner communities appear to have been strong, strong enough to endure in many places until the present day. Hence, while we may find that the Manchus appear less "Manchu" in the later eighteenth and nineteenth centuries, if we agree that distinctive practice was what had made them Manchu in 1650, then they were as Manchu as they had ever been in 1750 or 1850, when different requirements for survival called forth different skills and adaptive strategies.

The Manchu case thus shows well not just the degree to which ethnicity is a "mere" political construct, but also the degree to which such constructs cannot do without the aura of cultural, historical, and genealogical legitimacy. It also suggests that attention to institutional status and structures—not normally directly associated with ethnicity—may be useful to historians and others who seek to explain how people come to be aware of a shared identity. As one scholar has commented, while much attention is placed upon ascriptive external operations (i.e., boundary maintenance) and affective internal operations (i.e., the constitution of ethnic platforms) as the two main areas of ethnic discourse, this leaves "unexamined the microprocesses by which collectivities of interest and sentiment come into existence."[9] This same scholar has suggested employing Pierre Bourdieu's notion of *habitus* to uncover the "preconscious patterns of practice" that in effect "authenticate" ethnic identities, whereby both the "objective grounding for perceptions and feelings of ethnic affinity and difference" and the "clear but irregular association between social structure and ethnic consciousness" are explained.[10] By offering a basis for understanding ethnicity in terms of the specific structures and institutions that shape it in complex, but frequently implicit and unvoiced ways through daily "practice," *habitus* may be helpful in coming to terms with the complicated evolution of Manchu ethnicity in the Qing.

This is particularly so if we think of ethnicity as representing possible constitutive "dispositions" within *habitus*, which Bourdieu argues "are so many marks of social position and hence of the social distance between objective positions, . . . and so many reminders of this distance."[11]

Thinking of the banner system in this way as a "structuring, transposable structure" generating the practices and representations that patterned Manchu lives suggests how we might conceive of the transformation of Manchu identity in the Qing. It allows that, even as the virtues of the courtly Manchu Way meant less and less to most Manchus, banner membership and the particular quality of life that characterized it came to define the real terms of Manchu existence in an increasingly comprehensive fashion, as guaranteed government stipends and residence in walled enclaves gradually superseded impressive military skills, ability in the Manchu language, and a Spartan lifestyle in defining Manchuness. While this approach is not without its own problems (in particular that of change within the *habitus*), it does seem to offer a more nuanced, complex view of ethnicity that integrates the many variables (social, cultural, psychological, political, economic) that go into its construction.

In thinking about the wider significance of the Manchu experience, it would be helpful to compare it to similar historical instances where identity and institutions are closely linked. But it is not easy to find historical parallels. One possibility that comes to mind is the role of the Protestant church in the construction of Britishness. But, as Linda Colley has shown, this did more to foster a sense of national, rather than ethnic, identity, and it would be difficult, moreover, to separate the importance of religious institutions from the importance of religious faith.[12] Another comparison, possibly more apt, is that of the Janissary corps, the elite military guard of the Ottomans. The relationship between these men and the sultan was not unlike that between bannermen (especially bondservants) and the emperor, in that they were awesome in battle and could be relied upon to serve with absolute loyalty. Janissaries were also ethnically distinct from the majority of the elite *askeri* class, since by origin they all came from non-Muslim households (most were Christian). Once they entered service as young men, their identities changed: they became Muslim and their life course was inextricably bound up with the military institution of which they were a part. This was not, however, an "ethnic" identity; moreover, Janissary status was not inherited, so that there was no sense of caste as there was with the Eight Banners.[13] A better, modern, parallel might be that of Native Americans, whose ethnicity is determined primarily by membership in an institution, that is, a recognized tribe, which is inherited. While individual claims to be a member of such-and-such tribe are often accepted at face value (sometimes documentation of descent may be demanded by the tribe), the legitimacy of the tribe itself—its right to claim an institutional existence—is determined by the United States government.[14] More careful comparative study in this regard would do much to enhance our understanding of ethnicity in history.

WHAT DID IT MATTER?

With respect to the "Manchu question," the second of the broad issues which this book has raised, answers must be more tentative. Nevertheless, I believe we can single out at least three areas in which it made a significant difference that the Qing rulers came from Inner Asia and were not Han Chinese. The first of these areas has to do with Manchu political style; the second with territoriality; and the third with ethnic plurality. All owe to the plain fact that Manchu empire—as predicted by the model of *iminzoku tōchi* and work on other conquest dynasties—was a very different proposition from Chinese empire. Indeed, the existence before 1644 of a Qing confederation that already spanned a good part of east-central Eurasia suggests a very different point of departure in the Qing imperial imagination. For behind the *Daicing gurun* lay the vision, not only of the first Qin emperor, but of Chinggis Khan as well. On the grand stage of history, the Manchus quite self-consciously assumed the place that had been vacated 250 years earlier when the Mongols departed the scene at the overthrow of the Yuan dynasty. Different parallels between the Qing and other conquest regimes, such as the maintenance of secondary capitals (at Chengde and Mukden), even though vestigial after 1800, have already been pointed out: the performance of songs at the Qianlong court celebrating the twelfth-century victories of the Jin dynasty over the Song is yet one more indication of the sense the Manchus had of following in the footsteps of the Mongols, the Jurchens, and the Khitans.[15] That this was in no way seen as incompatible with praise likening the Qing ruler with the legendary Chinese emperors Yao and Shun only shows how many-layered the Manchu imperial vision was, and how distinctive from the Chinese.[16]

The first area in which the Manchuness of Qing rule may have been most significant has to do with an aspect of Manchu political style that I will call solidary conservatism. By this I mean their tendency to close ranks and defend the status quo when threatened. Every ruling group is liable to this sort of behavior, of course, but ethnic sovereignty seems to have emphasized it among the Manchus. As remarked at many points in the preceding chapters—and as many other accounts of Qing rule also emphasize—the Manchu elite was quite insecure about its place atop the imperial hierarchy. Perceived challenges to their supremacy or legitimacy were met quickly and often brutally, accompanied usually by assertions that the emperor was a benevolent king in the tradition laid down over the centuries by previous Sons of Heaven. While such assertions sometimes have a "the-lady-doth-protest-too-much" quality to them, depending on one's perspective, the Manchus' energetic dedication to preserving their power and the superior position of banner people at large can indeed be seen in a positive light. For in fact, the Qing produced a proportionately greater share of capable monarchs than most other dynasties in Chinese history. This may simply have been good fortune, but there are at least two other possible explanations we should consider. One is that, because they were not Chinese, they were not bound by the tradition that required the eldest son to take the throne. Instead, in good Altaic fashion, they were free to choose the most capable heir, according to the rules of what Fletcher called "tanistry."[17] Thus the dilemma faced by regimes adhering to primogeniture, of what to do when the eldest son was an idiot or a rogue, was one the Manchus happily avoided, and by and large the Qing rulers appear to have been intelligent men who were truly conscientious in executing their duties. The other explanation for the general diligence observed among Qing rulers (and many Manchu officials, too, for that matter) was that, as suggested earlier, alien rulers found it necessary to be forever wary, on guard against threats to proprietary Manchu interests, and were thus always at the tiller. By the same token, they also seem to have felt it necessary to compensate for their "barbarian" origins and their otherness: to "try harder," as it were. As a consequence, in a pattern often observed among converts, they became even more fastidious Confucians than the Chinese.

These tendencies may help explain the impressive solidarity observed among the Manchu elite (as seen in Chapter 3), and the seriousness with which the Manchu elite devoted itself to the task of governing, but they also seem to have had negative consequences in the nineteenth century, when ferocious hypersensitivity was replaced by fearful conservatism. The changed circumstances of the post-1842 world—the near-total debility of the Manchu military machine, the rise of domestic instability, and the arrival of Western imperialism—demanded creative responses, of which the Manchu leadership had few. In the absence of other ideas, the Qing rulers appear to have all but abandoned their Altaic heritage, retreating instead into a survival mode that depended heavily on the rehearsal of gradually less meaningful Chinese rituals. At this point, having lost their formerly sure sense of the balance between Confucian cosmopolitanism and ethnic particularism, the Manchus' blind dedication to the preservation of the imperial house looked selfish; ultimately, it was self-destructive. After 1901, even when it embraced reform, conspicuous Manchu favoritism did little to assure Chinese subjects of Qing ability to manage national affairs, much less of any lofty impartiality, and hastened the dynasty's demise. Of course, even a native regime would have had its hands full trying to negotiate the transition from empire to nation, and there is no knowing whether a Chinese response to the challenges to imperial rule posed by demands for representative government would have been any more successful. The point is simply that the solidary conservatism that was the hallmark of Qing political style and which was in part responsible both for its success and its eventual failure, gave the Manchus' fall from power a peculiar coloring: historians still disagree whether the true gripe of republican revolutionaries was the imperial system or the *Manchu* imperial system. Meanwhile, the revolutionaries themselves moved quickly on to other issues, such as how to consolidate the vast territory that suddenly lay before them and how to govern its different peoples.

The geographical legacy of the Qing, the second of the three areas in which we can detect the distinctive imprint of Manchu rule, was referred to in the Introduction. In its most straightforward sense, this legacy refers to the Qing incorporation of much of Inner Asia—Manchuria, Mongolia, Tibet, Eastern Turkestan, and part of the Altai region—into the territory (the contemporary term was *bantu/nirugan dangse*; lit., "chart-record") of the empire and the inheritance of that territory by, first, the Republic of China and, second, the People's Republic of China. The case that this could only have been accomplished by the Manchus rests in part on the claim that it was their shared status as members of the traditional Chinese periphery that enabled the Manchus to win the confidence of other Inner Asian peoples and bring them into the fold, so to speak. While there is perhaps something to this—the inclusion of Manchuria, at least, was a direct consequence of Manchu rule[18]—in general the Manchu relationship with other Inner Asians was hardly so unproblematic. Ostensible Altaic fraternity seems to have been completely absent, for instance, from Manchu dealings with their hated enemy, the Dzungars, and even with the Eastern Mongols, arguably the Manchus' closest allies on the steppe, force was part of the equation that helped persuade different tribes to join the Qing. Until we know more about the perceptions of the Manchus that circulated in Inner Asia in the seventeenth and eighteenth centuries, the most one can say is that their own long history of dealing with the Mongols gave them a better understanding of the workings of steppe society that cautioned them against underestimating their opponents, and that (perhaps for this reason) the Manchus also had better intelligence on internal political developments across the sweep of the northern and western frontiers and were able to deal squarely and creatively with the threat posed by the expanding empire of Russia.

A better case for the exceptional nature of the Manchu achievement can probably be made first by acknowledging that the regimented martial lifestyle and love of battle they brought with them from the Inner Asian frontier made the Qing a fearsome military force—the most powerful army, as was demonstrated time and again in the seventeenth and eighteenth centuries, in contemporary Eurasia. Recognizing that the Manchu state and the Eight Banners were from the outset predicated on conquest makes the Qing march across Inner Asia more readily understandable, and no less remarkable. Not that a Chinese army was incapable of similar exploits; only that such feats were an integral part of how Manchus defined themselves and wanted to be seen by others—which was surely not true of Chinese in the late imperial period.

Second, it is important to look at the different conception the Manchus held of the proper limits of their empire. In the late imperial Chinese mind, "inner" and "outer" were divided, generally speaking, by the Great Wall: south of the wall was the *zhongyuan* (lit., "Central Plain"), the Chinese homeland; north of it was *saiwai* (lit., "beyond the pale"), a bleak no-man's-land of vast deserts and bitter cold. For the Manchus, the Great Wall held no such significance. Operating in a different historical continuum, the concept of the Manchu khan/emperor as universal ruler (the alternative sense of ethnic sovereignty discussed in the Introduction) raised their vision beyond such artificial boundaries. Though, as we have seen, the court did employ the conceit of internality versus externality, the line fell between Beijing and every place outside Beijing; the divide between *zhongyuan* as "China" and *saiwai* as "the frontier," in other words, was one the Manchus brought down. In this sense, their pronouncements on having "unified China" are legitimate enough, and extremely significant.[19] For by unifying "inner" and "outer" the Manchus redefined what "China" was and gave it what became its modern form. In both these regards, it is no exaggeration to say that, as in the making of Great Britain, war and empire were the means of the making of China.[20]

That said, the process by which this newly integrated territory became China is not so straightforward as a reading back from the perspective of twentieth-century nationalism might suggest.[21] The breakup of the Qing empire left the new Chinese nation-state with only part of Mongolia and, at different moments in the 1900s, with very uncertain authority over Inner Mongolia, Manchuria, Xinjiang, Tibet, and Taiwan. In some measure, this uncertainty derived from the usurpation of local control by outside colonial forces. But another source must also be that the political ideologies around which the modern Chinese republics have been built are very different from those of the Qing empire. It is therefore not entirely surprising that the proper place of these erstwhile frontiers in the Chinese state is a continuing source of conflict even today, despite the insistence of central governments on the perfect equality of all ethnic groups and the "great ethnic unity" (Ch *minzu da tuanjie*) of the "big national household" (Ch *minzu da jiating*).

This rhetoric, so similar to the Qing notion of the "single family of Manchu and Han," is the final area in which the implications of Manchu rule are great for the development of modern China. That the imagination of China as an ethnically plural polity should owe to the Manchus is somewhat ironic, given that their own ethnic difference was often held against them. But the initial appearance of such discourse coincided precisely with the fall of the Qing, when Sun Yat-sen, in a volte-face from his previous promotion of "monoracial unity,"[22] began in 1912 to argue instead for multiracial national unity: "The root of a nation is its people. National unity means unifying the areas where Han, Manchus, Mongols, Muslims, and Tibetans live as a single nation, and the union of these peoples as one people."[23] The division of the country along these lines and the introduction of such phrases as "the single family of the five races" strongly echoes the Qing formulation of empire— the correspondence to the five languages of the pentaglot *Wuti Qingwen jian*, compiled at the order of (who else?) the Qianlong emperor, is perfect.

Sun's position also foreshadowed the stance toward so-called "minority nationalities" that would be adopted later by the Communist Party. Indeed, it has been the government of the People's Republic that has most strenuously pushed the idea of a "unified polyethnic state" (Ch *tongyi duominzu guojia*) in maintaining its claim of sovereignty over the peoples of China. The formula that "the Chinese People's Republic is a state in which many nationalities are united" was first uttered in 1949 and has since become almost a cliché.[24] In expanding the number of ethnic groups it recognized to fifty-five and in promising equality between all of them, the PRC government has departed significantly from Qing precedent; but the Manchu hand is still felt. In a 1957 speech promoting the benefits of local autonomy for minority nationalities—in which he lauded the Manchus as a "capable people"—Zhou Enlai noted explicitly, "The extensive territory of our country today is a legacy of the Qing dynasty."[25] The notion of the People's Republic of China as the successor state of the Qing is obviously not limited to academic circles.

In this sense, one can say that the Manchus were indirectly responsible for the redefinition of the modern Chinese nation and, by extension, of what it has meant to be "Chinese" in the twentieth century. Were the Chinese the "Han" (Ch *Hanren*)? the "people of China"? (Ch *Zhongguo ren*)? the "Greater Chinese nation" (Ch *zhonghua minzu*)? To be sure, there are no definitive answers; yet the question itself remains urgent. One can see it emergent in Sun's struggle to somehow remap the much-expanded Chinese nation bequeathed by the Manchus onto the Han people, whose birthright, as he and other revolutionaries had long insisted, it was. Nevertheless, even with the Manchus as a foil, to make a nation-state out of empire (as the Russian case has shown) is not easy. As just seen, for Sun at one point the nation was the "five races"; later, he would insist that all races were (or should be) one, a line that was expanded on by Chiang Kai-shek, who denied that there were five races at all, only "five peoples," distinguished solely by religion, who were all of the same "clan." This clan, of course, was understood to be the "national family" dominated by the Han.[26] Such a position was influenced by a firm belief in sinicization and was no doubt aimed to lend support to the territorial claims of the Republic of China at a time of national crisis, as Chiang went on to say, "Thus, in the territory of China a hundred years ago . . . there was not a single district that was not essential to the survival of the Chinese nation, and none that was not permeated by our culture."[27]

This statement makes manifest the contradictions in claiming "China"— that is, the territorial expanse of the Qing empire—for the Han, while simultaneously claiming "Chinese" to mean "Han," since it was patently clear that neither the Han people nor Han culture in fact "permeated" all of this territory. The term *Zhongguo ren* partially satisfied the need for a looser, more capacious definition of "Chinese" that could resolve these contradictions, but the best solution has unquestionably been the term *zhonghua minzu*. Matching so well the names taken by the Chinese republics, this phrase had tremendous resonance in the twentieth century as a term meaning "the Chinese people" in its broadest sense, including Han, Manchu, Mongol, Tibetan, Uighur, and so on. Indeed, to say that *zhonghua minzu* is synonymous with "the former peoples of the Qing dominions," is not far from the mark.[28]

An essential component of the modern Chinese national myth has long been that "China" is a grand harmony of many lands and many peoples unified under the name *zhonghua*. As I have argued, the foundation of this myth rests in the specific territorial and ethnic legacy left by nearly three centuries of Manchu rule. This seems a bit of a paradox, since Manchu rule was, in the many ways shown above, so un-Chinese. Yet this very paradox ought to caution us against drawing too thick a line between the "Qing empire" and "China." It would be well first to ask how the Manchus saw their "Great Qing": Did it mean "China" to them? To the Han Chinese? To those on the periphery and beyond? If so, then "China" in which sense? The answers to these questions will furnish the stuff of future debates on the significance of the Manchus and their empire for China and Inner Asia in the modern world.

APPENDIX A

# Note on the Size of the Eight Banner Population

Estimates of the sizes of different populations under the Eight Banners—including those made in Chapter 2 of the present study—have usually tended to rely upon crude methods of extrapolation based on guesses of "average" household size. With the publication in recent years of archival data giving total numbers of able-bodied males (*ding/haha*), it has now become possible to apply standard demographic methods to estimate population size. Because this method (stable population theory) factors in such variables as life expectancy, disability, and population growth rates, it produces a range of possible outcomes rather than a single "definitive" figure. Applying this method to the archival figures now at our disposal[1] yields a population of between 1.3 and 2.44 million people in the Eight Banners in 1648 (including all regular and bondservant companies in the Manchu, Mongol, and Chinese banners). By ca. 1720, these estimates show a total population of between 2.6 and 4.9 million. The total Manchu population at the time of the conquest appears to have been between 206,000 and 390,000 (regular companies only, excluding bondservants); seventy years later it grew to between 577,000 and 1.08 million (see the table below). A fuller exposition of this problem, explaining the derivation of these estimates, is found in Mark Elliott, Cameron Campbell, and James Lee, "A Demographic Estimate of the Population of the Eight Banners" (article in preparation).

Range of Population Sizes for Eight Banners, 1648 and 1720

| | | *Manchu* | *Mongol* | *Chinese* | *Subtotal* | *Bondservants/other* | *Total* |
|---|---|---|---|---|---|---|---|
| 1648 | males | 111,871–210,506 | 58,232–109,574 | 92,752–174,530 | 263,319–495,485 | 438,920–825,912 | 702,239–1,321,397 |
| | females | 95,090–178,930 | 49,497–93,138 | 78,839–148,351 | 223,821–421,162 | 373,082–702,025 | 596,903–1,123,188 |
| | Total | 206,961–389,436 | 107,729–202,712 | 171,591–322,881 | 487,140–916,647 | 812,002–1,527,937 | 1,299,142–2,444,585 |
| 1720 | males | 311,876–586,665 | 124,599–234,458 | 414,448–779,863 | 850,763–1,600,872 | 554,163–1,042,764 | 1,404,926–2,643,635 |
| | females | 265,010–497,815 | 105,909–199,289 | 352,281–662,884 | 723,149–1,360,741 | 471,039–886,349 | 1,194,187–2,247,090 |
| | Total | 576,786–1,083,480 | 230,508–433,747 | 766,279–1,442,747 | 1,573,912–2,961,613 | 1,025,202–1,929,113 | 2,599,113–4,890,725 |

# Ranks in the Eight Banners

*Chart 1. Officer Ranks in the Capital Eight Banners*

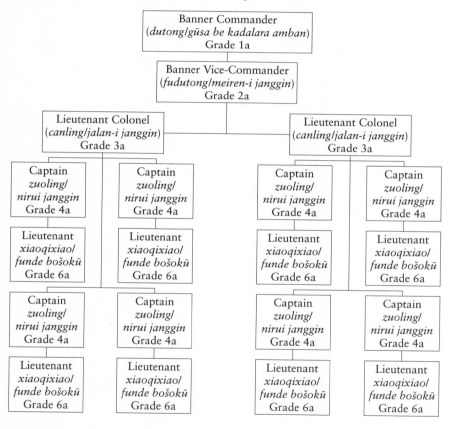

SOURCE: BQTZ 34, 42

NOTE: Structure simplified to show main ranks only. In the Manchu and Chinese banners, there were five *jalan*, hence five lieutenant colonels; in the Mongol banners, three. The number of captains and lieutenants per *jalan* varied according to the number of *niru*.

## Chart 2. Ranks in the Imperial Bodyguard, Vanguard, and Guard

*Imperial bodyguard.* Upper Three Banners (Bordered Yellow, Plain Yellow, Plain White) only.

> Chamberlain (2)
> *lingshiwei neidachen/hiya kadalara dorgi amban*
> Grade 1a

> Senior Assistant Chamberlain (no. varied)
> *neidachen/dorgi amban*
> Grade 1a

> Senior Bodyguard (3 grades, 200 total)
> *shiwei/hiya*
> Grades 3a–5a

*Vanguard.* Manchu and Mongol banners only

> Vanguard Commandant (1 per banner)
> *qianfeng tongling/galai amban*
> Grade 2a

> Vanguard Colonel (2 per banner)
> *qianfeng canling/gabsihiyan-i janggin*
> Grade 3a

> Vanguardsman (2 per banner)
> *qianfeng shiwei/gabsihiyan*
> Grade 5a

*Guard.* Manchu and Mongol banners only

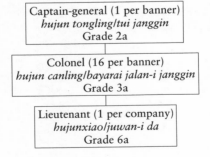

> Captain-general (1 per banner)
> *hujun tongling/tui janggin*
> Grade 2a

> Colonel (16 per banner)
> *hujun canling/bayarai jalan-i janggin*
> Grade 3a

> Lieutenant (1 per company)
> *hujunxiao/juwan-i da*
> Grade 6a

SOURCE: BQTZ 34, 42

## Chart 3. Officer Ranks in the Garrison Eight Banners

### 3.a. *Larger Garrisons* (Xi'an)

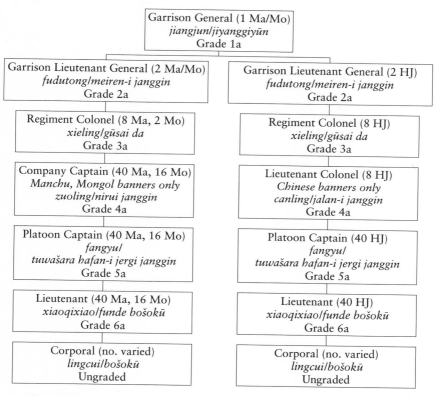

Garrison General (1 Ma/Mo)
*jiangjun/jiyanggiyūn*
Grade 1a

Garrison Lieutenant General (2 Ma/Mo)
*fudutong/meiren-i janggin*
Grade 2a

Garrison Lieutenant General (2 HJ)
*fudutong/meiren-i janggin*
Grade 2a

Regiment Colonel (8 Ma, 2 Mo)
*xieling/gūsai da*
Grade 3a

Regiment Colonel (8 HJ)
*xieling/gūsai da*
Grade 3a

Company Captain (40 Ma, 16 Mo)
*Manchu, Mongol banners only*
*zuoling/nirui janggin*
Grade 4a

Lieutenant Colonel (8 HJ)
*Chinese banners only*
*canling/jalan-i janggin*
Grade 4a

Platoon Captain (40 Ma, 16 Mo)
*fangyu/*
*tuwašara hafan-i jergi janggin*
Grade 5a

Platoon Captain (40 HJ)
*fangyu/*
*tuwašara hafan-i jergi janggin*
Grade 5a

Lieutenant (40 Ma, 16 Mo)
*xiaoqixiao/funde bošokū*
Grade 6a

Lieutenant (40 HJ)
*xiaoqixiao/funde bošokū*
Grade 6a

Corporal (no. varied)
*lingcui/bošokū*
Ungraded

Corporal (no. varied)
*lingcui/bošokū*
Ungraded

### 3.b. *Middle-sized garrisons* (Chengdu)

Garrison Lieutenant General (1 Ma)
*fudutong/meiren-i janggin*

Regiment Colonel (4 Ma, 2 Mo)
*xieling/gūsai da*

Company Captain (16 Ma, 8 Mo)
*zuoling/nirui janggin*

Platoon Captain (16 Ma, 8 Mo)
*fangyu/tuwasara hafan-i jergi janggin*

Lieutenant (16 Ma, 8 Mo)
*xiaoqixiao/funde bošokū*

3.c. *Smaller garrisons* (Kaifeng)

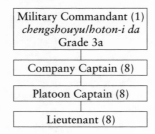

SOURCE: BQTZ 35, 42

APPENDIX C

# Foundation and Expansion of Provincial Garrisons

| Location | Date | Size at Foundation | 1662 | 1690 | 1739 | 1776 |
|---|---|---|---|---|---|---|
| **ZHILI** | | | | | | |
| Tianjin | 1726 | 3000 | — | — | 2000 | 3304 |
| **SHANDONG** | | | | | | |
| Dezhou | 1654 | 589 | 546 | 339 | 500 | 500 |
| Qingzhou | 1729 | 2000 | — | — | 2400 | 1740 |
| **SHANXI** | | | | | | |
| Taiyuan | 1649 | 860 | 353 | 413 | 500 | 540[1] |
| Youwei | 1692 | 5087 | — | — | 2883 | 3504 |
| Suiyuan | 1737 | 3935 | — | — | 3935 | 3830 |
| **HENAN** | | | | | | |
| Kaifeng | 1718 | 800 | — | — | 800 | 800 |
| **SHAANXI** | | | | | | |
| Xi'an | 1645 | 1800 | 4000 | 6700 | 8660 | 9160[2] |
| **GANSU** | | | | | | |
| Ningxia | 1676 | 3400 | — | 3600 | 2800[3] | 3400[4] |
| Liangzhou | 1737 | 2000 | — | — | 2000 | 2652 |
| Zhuanglang | 1737 | 1000 | — | — | 1000 | 1420 |
| **JIANGNAN** | | | | | | |
| Jiangning | 1645 | 1800 | 3100 | 4700 | 5093 | 6420[5] |
| Jingkou | 1654 | 3000 | 3000 | 2740 | 3000 | 1800[6] |
| **ZHEJIANG** | | | | | | |
| Hangzhou | 1645[7] | 1000 | 1000 | 3700 | 4505 | 3256 |
| Zhapu | 1728 | 1600 | — | — | 1600 | 1600 |
| **HUGUANG** | | | | | | |
| Jingzhou | 1683 | 3534 | — | 4700 | 4690 | 5180[8] |
| **SICHUAN** | | | | | | |
| Chengdu | 1721 | 2000 | — | — | 2000 | 1948 |
| **FUJIAN** | | | | | | |
| Fuzhou | 1656 | 2026 | — | 2000 | 2114 | 2482[9] |
| **GUANGDONG** | | | | | | |
| Guangzhou | 1661 | 1125 | — | 3000 | 3000 | 4500 |

SOURCES: HWT, *juan* 179, 183; BQTZ, *juan* 27; DQHD (1690), *juan* 82; DQHD (1733), *juan* 114; DQHD (1763), *juan* 96; STFZ, *juan* 63; *Shizu shilu*. Sources disagree in some instances on

369

exact dates of foundation and size of forces. When possible, I have tried to corroborate dates using archival sources. Figures include all soldiers as well as officers below the rank of lieutenant.

[1] Includes 40 supernumeraries.

[2] Includes 1000 supernumeraries.

[3] Figures in HWT indicate 4,200 soldiers at Ningxia in 1739, including 600 supernumeraries.

[4] Includes 600 supernumeraries.

[5] Includes 900 supernumeraries.

[6] Figures in the 1763 *Huidian* are obsolete.

[7] Formal date of establishment usually given as 1658, but actual existence from this time.

[8] Includes 400 supernumeraries.

[9] Includes 522 men at naval installation.

Reference Matter

## Note on the Frontispiece

The seventy-ninth of one hundred portraits commissioned by the Qianlong emperor in 1760 to mark the Qing victory over the Dzungars, this impressive scroll, measuring over six feet high, hung together with paintings of the other heroes of the campaign in the Ziguangge palace. The inscriptions, by three top ministers, are in Manchu (on the left) and Chinese (on the right), joined in the middle by the emperor's seal. The main text of the Manchu inscription reads as follows:

> Imperial guard of the third rank, "Cat Hero" Uksiltu was selected to go to the battle front. The reports he sent expressly arrived one after another: "Myriads of bandits remained, surrounding the army's camp. They behaved as though there was not a single outstanding man there." By the time he reached Aksu, the callouses [on his legs] reached almost up to his knees. Even today, the bullet that went into his back has still not been taken out.

The Chinese inscription is slightly different:

> Imperial guard of the third rank, *ke-shi-ke ba-tu-lu* U-shi-er-tu. He was selected to serve in the army and fight. [In the] letters [he] sent [he wrote]: "Of turbaned heads, there were myriads, who fluttered about as though entering a wasteland." Arriving in Aksu, the callouses [on his legs] reached almost to his knees. Even today, the bullet in his back has still not come out.

Different artists were likely responsible for the separate elements (face, hands, clothing, weaponry), resulting in a somewhat awkward stance. The single peacock feather and pearl on his cap were marks of imperial favor. Reproduced courtesy of the collection of Dame Dora Wong, OSJ.

## Abbreviations Used in the Notes

| | |
|---|---|
| BQMST | *Baqi Manzhou shizu tongpu* |
| BQTZ | *Baqi tongzhi chuji* |
| DHL | *Donghua lu* |
| DQHD | *Da Qing huidian* |
| DQHDSL | *Da Qing huidian shili* |
| ECCP | Hummel, *Eminent Chinese of the Ch'ing Period* |
| GZD/QL | *Gongzhongdang/Qianlong chao zouzhe* |
| GZMaZJ | *Gongzhong Manwen zajian\** |
| HJW | *Huangchao jingshi wenbian* |
| HWT | *Huangchao wenxian tongkao* |
| KXHaZZH | *Kangxi chao Hanwen zhupi zouzhe huibian* |
| KXMaZPZZ | *Kangxi chao Manwen zhupi zouzhe\** |
| MBRT | *Manbun rōtō* |
| n.m. | no memorialist |
| QLHaZPZZ | *Qianlong chao Hanwen zhupi zouzhe\** |
| QLMaZPZZ | *Qianlong chao Manwen zhupi zouzhe\** |
| QNMDY | *Qingchu neiguoshiyuan Manwen dang'an yibian* |
| QSG | *Qingshi gao* |
| QSLZ | *Qingshi liezhuan* |
| SJY | *Suijun jixing yizhu* |
| STFZ | *Shuntianfu zhi* |
| SYBQ | *Shangyu baqi* |
| YZHaZZH | *Yongzheng chao Hanwen zhupi zouzhe huibian* |
| YZMaZPZZ | *Yongzheng chao Manwen zhupi zouzhe\** |

\*Listed Under Archival Sources in References.

## Preface/Reigns

1. Immanuel C. Y. Hsü, *The Rise of Modern China*, 3rd ed. (New York: Oxford University Press, 1983), 4, 7–8.

2. Jonathan D. Spence, *The Search for Modern China* (New York: Norton, 1990), 3–5.

3. As this book was being revised, the first popular English-language history of the Manchus appeared, *The Manchus*, by Pamela Kyle Crossley (Oxford, and Cambridge, Mass.: Blackwell Publishers, 1997).

4. In the introduction to their holdings, the First Historical Archives' own publication indicates that these exceed ten million items (*jian*) in number

(*Zhongguo diyi lishi dang'anguan guancang dang'an gaishu*) [Beijing: Dang'an chubanshe, 1985], 3, 27). This figure is repeated in a 1994 article by Manchu archivist Wu Yuanfeng, who goes on to note that Manchu-language items number about 2 million *jian* (Wu Yuanfeng, "Qingdai neige Manwen dang'an shulue," *Manxue yanjiu* 2 [1994], 274). An estimate of 1.6 million Manchu archives appears in the afterword to the *Kangxichao Manwen zhupi zouzhe quanyi*, which is cited by Endymion Wilkinson in his immensely useful handbook, *Chinese History: A Manual* (Cambridge: Harvard University Asia Center, 1998), 890.

5. Name assigned retrospectively to denote the period during which Nurhaci ruled as khan of the Latter Jin dynasty.

6. Name assigned retrospectively to denote the period during which Hong Taiji ruled as Latter Jin khan.

7. Name assigned retrospectively to denote the period during which Hong Taiji ruled as first emperor of the Qing dynasty.

## Introduction. The Problem with the Manchus

1. The following account relies on the narrative in Frederic Wakeman, Jr., *The Great Enterprise: The Manchu Reconstruction of Imperial Order in Seventeenth-Century China* (Berkeley and Los Angeles: University of California Press, 1985), 290–318.

2. Luo Guanzhong, attr., *Three Kingdoms*, trans. Moss Roberts (Berkeley and Los Angeles: University of California Press, 1991), 14.

3. On the size of the Manchu population, see Appendix A.

4. Cited in Zhang Jinfan and Guo Chengkang, *Qing ruguanqian guojia falü zhidu shi* (Shenyang: Liaoning renmin chubanshe, 1988), ii.

5. Philip A. Kuhn, *Soulstealers: The Chinese Sorcery Scare of 1768* (Cambridge: Harvard University Press, 1990), 60.

6. For the Chinese term, I suggest *zuqun zhuquan*.

7. Joseph F. Fletcher, "Turco-Mongolian Monarchic Tradition in the Ottoman Empire," in Fletcher, *Studies on Chinese and Islamic Inner Asia*, ed. Beatrice Forbes Manz (Aldershot, England: Variorum Reprints, 1995), chap. 7.

8. James L. Hevia, "A Multitude of Lords: Qing Court Ritual and the Macartney Embassy of 1793," *Late Imperial China* 10.2 (December 1989), 81. This idea is more fully explored in Hevia's *Cherishing Men from Afar* (Durham, N.C.: Duke University Press, 1995), especially pp. 30–35.

9. Pamela Kyle Crossley, "*Manzhou yuanliu kao* and the Formalization of the Manchu Heritage," *Journal of Asian Studies* 46.4 (November 1987), 779.

10. Pamela Kyle Crossley, "The Rulerships of China," *American Historical Review* 97.5 (December 1992), 1483. David Farquhar was perhaps the first to point out the apparent discontinuities between the different images projected by the Qing emperor. See "Emperor as Bodhisattva in the Governance of the Ch'ing Empire," *Harvard Journal of Asiatic Studies* 38.1 (June 1978), 5–34.

11. See Hoyt Cleveland Tillman, "Proto-Nationalism in Twelfth-Century China? The Case of Ch'en Liang," *Harvard Journal of Asiatic Studies* 39.2 (December 1979), 403–28.

12. "China proper" refers to the territories of the Chinese heartland, i.e., those centered along the Yellow and Yangzi Rivers, as well as the southeast coast. This includes all of modern-day China except for Qinghai, the Tibet Autonomous Region, the Xinjiang Uighur Autonomous Region, the Inner Mongolia Autonomous Region, and the three provinces of the Northeast (Liaoning, Jilin, and Heilongjiang), and possibly also Yunnan and Guizhou provinces. To give some sense of geographic scale, the area of China proper is historically about 1.5 million square miles, while the total area of the Qing empire at its greatest extent, ca. 1800, was conservatively 4.6 million square miles. The present People's Republic of China (exclusive of Taiwan) covers an area of 3.67 million square miles. See Ho Ping-ti, "The Significance of the Ch'ing Period in Chinese History," *Journal of Asian Studies* 26.2 (February 1967), 189. To Ho's figure for the late-nineteenth-century empire I have added the roughly 400,000 square miles of territory lost to Russia after 1860, most of it in Manchuria.

13. Karl Wittfogel and Feng Chia-sheng, *History of Chinese Society: Liao, 907–1125* (Philadelphia: American Philosophical Society, 1949), 15; authors' emphasis.

14. Joseph Fletcher, "The Mongols: Ecological and Social Perspectives," *Harvard Journal of Asiatic Studies* 46.1 (June 1986), 19, 16.

15. Herbert Franke, "The Role of the State as a Structural Element in Polyethnic Societies," in Stuart N. Schram, ed., *Foundations and Limits of State Power in China* (London and Hong Kong: European Science Foundation, 1987), 87–112, esp. 99–102.

16. For ease of reference by specialist readers, an effort is made to provide original equivalents when important terms are first introduced. Chinese-language terms are denoted by "Ch" and Manchu-language terms by "Ma." When both are given, the Chinese term comes first.

17. Hok-lam Chan, *Legitimation in Imperial China: Discussions Under the Jurchen-Chin Dynasty (1115–1234)* (Seattle: University of Washington Press, 1984) 74–75, 85–86, 122–23.

18. Peter K. Bol, "Seeking Common Ground: Han Literati Under Jurchen Rule," *Harvard Journal of Asiatic Studies* 47.2 (December 1987), 485.

19. Momose Hiromu, "Shinchō no iminzoku tōchi ni okeru zaisei keizai seisaku," *Tōa kenkyūjo hō* 20 (February 1943), 27. For stimulating discussion of aspects of this problem in the Qing, see Ura Ren'ichi, "Shinchō no Kanjin tōchi no sho shūsō," in Ura, ed., *Tōyō kinseishi* (Tokyo: Heibonsha, 1939), 1: 5–112. Other relevant treatments that I have consulted include Aritaka Iwao, "Gen-Shin nichō no tai Kan seisaku sōi no yūrai," *Shichō* 4.1 (March 1943), 16–32; Inaba Iwakichi, "Manshū minzoku ni kansuru ryōhōmen no kansatsu," *Tōa keizai kenkyū* 13.4 (October 1929), 1–30, and 14.2 (April 1930), 15–37; and Oshibuchi Hajime, "Man-Mō minzoku no bunka keitai to Shina tōchi keitai," *Nihon shogaku shinkō i'inkai kenkyū hōkoku* 11 (March 1941), 166–77.

20. The British comparison is also raised by Franke ("The Role of the State," 102). This is not to say that ethnic sovereignty will always exist where rulership is concentrated in the hands of one group over another; only when ethnic meaning is attached to differences (of descent, culture, history) between those groups can we say that "ethnicity" exists. Thus in Hanoverian England, while George I was a "foreigner," refused to learn English, and visited Germany often, this did not affect his legitimacy as king.

21. One might also add here "racial lines," but I interpret so-called "race-based" attitudes and practices as one type of ethnic practice in which skin color and/or so-called phenotypal differences are the overriding signs used to demarcate (and often invidiously essentialize) ethnic difference. At the same time, I do not mean to deny that "ethnicity" is sometimes used by people or governments as nothing more than a euphemism for "race." A fuller discussion of my understanding of ethnicity follows below.

22. John K. Fairbank, "Varieties of the Chinese Military Experience," introduction to Frank A. Kierman and John K. Fairbank, *Chinese Ways in Warfare* (Cambridge: Harvard University Press, 1974), 14.

23. Paraphrasing Roger Chartier, *On the Edge of the Cliff* (Baltimore: Johns Hopkins University Press, 1996), 25.

24. In Chinese this Manchu cultural standard is commonly expressed by the slogan *guoyu qishe*, "national language, riding, and shooting." It will be apparent that this formulation omits mention of frugality and simplicity. Also, by collapsing "riding and shooting" into one phrase the specific skills that a Manchu was expected to master—namely, archery from a stance and mounted archery—are mingled.

25. In considering the problem of Manchu identity, Pamela Kyle Crossley has proposed another term, *manjurarengge*, said to be a "neologism of the

Qianlong era," which she translates as "Manchuness" ("The Qianlong Retrospect on the Chinese-Martial [*Hanjun*] Banners," *Late Imperial China* 10.1 [June 1989], 85n; and *Orphan Warriors: Three Manchu Generations and the End of the Qing World* [Princeton, N.J.: Princeton University Press, 1990], 21). Grammatically, *manjurarengge*—the proper form should be *manjurarangge* — is a nominalized form of the verb *manjurambi*, meaning either "to speak Manchu," "to learn to speak Manchu," or "to imitate Manchu ways," i.e., by a non-Manchu. See entries in *Da Qing quan shu/Daicing gurun-i yooni bithe* (1683), *Nikan hergen-i ubaliyambuha Manju gisun-i buleku bithe/Yin Han-Qing wenjian* (1735), and *Qingwen zonghui* (1897). Since Crossley provides no attestation of this term, it is difficult to determine if *"manjurarengge"* was ever really used to discuss Manchu identity. The only occurrence of *manjurarangge* I have found myself shows a meaning of "to speak Manchu" (QLMaZPZZ 249, edict of QL19.9.1). In a later article, Crossley refers not to *"manjurarengge"* but instead to the "Manchu Way." Like *"manjurarengge,"* however, she argues that the Manchu Way was an invention of the Qianlong reign. See her essay, "Manchu Education," in Benjamin Elman and Alexander Woodside, eds., *Education and Society in Late Imperial China, 1600–1900* (Berkeley and Los Angeles: University of California Press, 1994), 361.

26. KXMaZPZZ 351, Boji, KX43.10.10. See the Archival Sources section of the References for an explanation of this notation.

27. YZMaZPZZ 242, Fobiyoo, YZ12.9.10.

28. YZMaZPZZ 245, Mantai, YZ12.4.29; 252, Hesing, YZ12.6.25; QLMaZPZZ 50, Arigūn, QL1.3.15, where these are specified as the "old ways of us Manchus" ("musei Manjusai fe tacin").

29. YZMaZPZZ 265, Fusen, YZ13.12.7, imperial rescript; QLMaZPZZ 52, draft edict of QL1.5.25; GZMaZJ 5, Fusen, QL1.7.18; QLMaZPZZ 69, Fusen et al., QL2.12.1. *Doro* has various meanings in addition to "way," including "rule," "doctrine," "principle," "rite" and "ritual." The etymology of the word is unclear. Writing in the 1930s, Schmidt believed it was related to the Chinese word, *dao*, "way, path," but this hypothesis is questioned in the leading etymological dictionary of Manchu. See V. I. Tsintsius, *Sravnitel'nyi slovar' Tunguso-Man'chzhurskikh iazykov* (Leningrad: Nauka, 1975), 216–17. Tsintsius's skepticism is shared by leading Altaic linguists (James Bosson, personal communication). A more recent etymology has been proposed via Mongolian *dörö** (i.e., *törö*) from the Hebrew *torah* (Crossley, *The Manchus*, 33), but see the review by Juha Janhunen in *Studia Orientalia* 82 (1997), 288–89.

30. *Yongzhengchao qijuzhu ce* (Beijing: Zhonghua shuju, 1993), vol. 2, 1210, edict of YZ 5.4.19. My thanks to Eugenio Menegon for calling this edict to my attention. Sunu had died in 1725; for more on this very interesting

case, see chapter 3 of Miyazaki Ichisada, *Yōseitei, Chūgoku no dokusai kunshu* (Tokyo: Iwanami shoten, 1950), and the letters of Antoine Gaubil, S.J., in *Correspondance de Pékin, 1722–1759* (Geneva: Librairie Droz, 1970). The fate of Sunu's son, "Joseph" Urcen, is discussed in Chapter 6.

31. Information on the Mongol banners is always scarce, but materials in the archives, as well as those few items that can be found in published sources, point to a rising general concern during the same period (i.e., the first third of the eighteenth century) for deteriorating skills, especially Mongolian language ability, among Mongol bannermen. For instance, two memorials, one from 1723, the other from 1734, both express fear over the loss of this element of the Mongol Way (*Monggo doro*) (YZMaZPZZ 32, Bootai, YZ1.9.23, and YZMaZPZZ 252, Gendusehe, YZ12.11.5; see also SYBQ YZ7: 35a–b [YZ7.8.20] and other edicts from that collection).

32. See Chan, *Legitimation*, 75; also Jing-shen Tao, *The Jurchen in Twelfth-Century China: A Study in Sinicization* (Seattle: University of Washington Press, 1976), esp. chaps. 6–8, and Herbert Franke, "The Chin," in Herbert Franke and Denis Twitchett, eds., *The Cambridge History of China*, vol. 6, *Alien Regimes and Border States, 907–1368* (Cambridge: Cambridge University Press, 1994), 250.

33. QNMDY 1: 74–75 (Tiancong 8.4.9).

34. *Jiu Manzhou dang*, vol. 10, 5295 (Chongde 1.11.13). English translations of the Chinese version of this edict (found in the *Veritable Records*), each rather different, are found in Robert O. Oxnam, *Ruling from Horseback: Manchu Politics in the Oboi Regency, 1661–1669* (Chicago: University of Chicago Press, 1975), 36–37, and Wakeman, *The Great Enterprise*, 209. See also Chapter 7.

35. Ibn Khaldūn, *The Muqaddimah: An Introduction to History*, trans. Franz Rosenthal (Princeton, N.J.: Princeton University Press Bollingen Series, 1967), 107.

36. Ibid., 93–94.  37. Ibid., 109.

38. GZMaZJ 5, Fusen, QL1.7.18.  39. *Gaozong shilu*, 411: 5b–8a.

40. Susan Naquin and Evelyn S. Rawski, *Chinese Society in the Eighteenth Century* (New Haven, Conn.: Yale University Press, 1987), 18–19.

41. Crossley, *Orphan Warriors*, 6.

42. Naquin and Rawski, *Chinese Society in the Eighteenth Century*, 19.

43. Pamela Kyle Crossley, "Thinking About Ethnicity in Early Modern China," *Late Imperial China* 11.1 (June 1990), 11.

44. Franz Michael, *The Origin of Manchu Rule in China* (Baltimore: Johns Hopkins University Press, 1942), 118. See also the quotation from Meng Sen at the beginning of Chapter 1.

45. Crossley also remarks on the conflation of "bannerman" and "Manchu," but believes that this happened only by the turn of the twentieth century ("Thinking About Ethnicity," 9–11).

46. Among Jews in the state of Israel today we find a somewhat comparable situation between the two main groups, the Ashkenazim and the so-called Oriental Jews. Ashkenazi Jews are the descendants of those who settled in central and northern Europe after the Diaspora and "Oriental Jews" are those who settled in Islamic lands; included in both groups are the descendants of Sephardic Jews who migrated to other parts of Europe and to North Africa when they were expelled from Spain in the fifteenth century. All, of course, are Jews, and their faith unites all Jews as a "chosen people." But not all Jews in Israel are equal, just as not all bannermen were equal, even though all were integrated within the same caste that made them a "conquest people." Ethnic differences are reflected in various ways in society, politics, and the military, and sustain a hierarchy in which Ashkenazi Jews (like the Manchus) are at the top and Oriental Jews (like the Chinese bannermen) are at the bottom. See Avishai Margalit, "The Other Israel," *New York Review of Books* 45.9 (28 May 1998), 30–35. There is no intention here, of course, to imply an equivalence between the Jewish religion and the Eight Banners. The point is simply that the hierarchies existing within many ethnic groups are often obscured by the one-word labels applied to those groups, and that demonstrating the existence of such hierarchies does not invalidate their overall ethnic context.

47. Comments such as, "A Manchu brigade-general is a little higher than a Chinese brigade-general—what about general Manchu honor?" leave little doubt that status distinctions in the Qing were overlaid with ethnic distinctions as well (KXMaZPZZ 350, Boji, KX44.6.11). David Howell has found a similar overlapping between ethnicity and status in his article, "Ainu Ethnicity and the Boundaries of the Early Modern Japanese State," *Past and Present* 142 (February 1994), 69–93.

48. This is the thrust of the argument in Wu Zhijian, "Qingdai qianqi Manzhou benwei zhengce de niding yu tiaozheng," *Guoli Taiwan shifan daxue lishixuebao* 22 (June 1994), 85–117. Though he does not employ the concept of ethnicity, Wu's emphasis on the connection between the banners and Manchu identity is similar to my own.

49. Li Yanguang and Guan Jie, *Manzu tongshi* (Shenyang: Liaoning minzu chubanshe, 1991), 450.

50. Wang Zhonghan, "Qingdai baqizhong de Man-Han minzu chengfen wenti," in Wang Zhonghan, *Qingshi xukao* (Taipei: Huashi chubanshe, 1993), 67–68. See also Chapter 1.

51. Jack David Eller, "Ethnicity, Culture, and 'the Past'," *Michigan Quarterly Review* 36.4 (Fall 1997), 597–98. This essay offers a good summary of the main directions of work on ethnicity up to now. It is reprinted in Eller, *From Culture to Ethnicity to Conflict* (Ann Arbor: University of Michigan Press, 1999), 7–48.

52. Thomas Hylland Eriksen, *Ethnicity and Nationalism: Anthropological Perspectives* (London: Pluto Press, 1993), 12. This, I think, is the sense of Dru Gladney's term, "dialogic," in *Muslim Chinese* (Cambridge: Harvard Council on East Asian Studies, 1991), 76. In this regard, note also John Comaroff's point that apart from itself being a social fact worthy of analysis, ethnicity also refers to the set of concepts used to explain that fact ("Of Totemism and Ethnicity: Consciousness, Practice, and the Signs of Inequality," *Ethnos* 52.3–4 [1987], 301–23).

53. Frank Dikötter defines races as "population groups which are imagined to have boundaries based on immutable biological or other inherited characteristics," whereas ethnicities are "groups thought to be based on cultural acquired characteristics." See his introduction to *The Construction of Racial Identities in China and Japan* (Honolulu: University of Hawaii Press, 1997), 5. Most interpretations of ethnicity that I have come across, however, specifically include descent and genealogy together with cultural elements as part of the larger "ethnic package."

54. This term is Edward Spicer's. See "Persistent Cultural Systems," *Science* 19 (November 1971), 795–800.

55. Note that this outcome—acculturation—is a possible but not necessary result of extended contact.

56. Sow-theng Leong, *Migration and Ethnicity in Chinese History: Hakkas, Pengmin, and Their Neighbors*, ed. Tim Wright (Stanford, Calif.: Stanford University Press, 1997), 19–20.

57. Anthony D. Smith, "Nationalism and the Historians," in Anthony D. Smith, ed., *Ethnicity and Nationalism* (Leiden: E. J. Brill, 1992), 74.

58. More and more, scholars are calling upon ethnicity as a critical concept in their work on premodern periods. See, for instance, Terry F. Kleeman, *Great Perfection: Religion and Ethnicity in a Chinese Millennial Kingdom* (Honolulu: University of Hawaii Press, 1998), or a number of the papers presented at the conference, "Constructed Histories Along China's Western Frontiers," held at UCLA in February 1999. Some examples of such work in a non-Chinese context are Miriam Bodian, "'Men of the Nation': The Shaping of *Converso* Identity in Early Modern Europe," *Past and Present* 143 (May 1994), 48–76, and David Howell, "Ainu Ethnicity."

59. Cf. the cautionary views of Pamela Kyle Crossley: "It is not self-

evident that 'ethnicity' is an appropriate or exceptionally fruitful concept for the analysis of Chinese late imperial social history" ("Thinking About Ethnicity," 1).

60. Nicole Constable, *Christian Souls and Chinese Spirits: A Hakka Community in Hong Kong* (Berkeley and Los Angeles: University of California Press, 1994), 20. The basis for this judgment is her statement that only with the arrival of the "modern nation state" do individuals become "not just the subjects of history but active participants in its making," thus permitting "widely articulated identities." However, Constable's investigation of Hakka ethnicity, the origins of which she dates to the early nineteenth century, would seem to offer a contrary example.

61. Crossley, "Thinking About Ethnicity," 27.

62. Ibid., 13; Evelyn Rawski, *The Last Emperors: A Social History of Qing Imperial Institutions* (Berkeley and Los Angeles: University of California Press, 1998), 3–5. Scholars who have studied other non-Han groups in China also adopt the view that ethnicity by definition involves "peripheral" peoples under the modern state. See Gladney, *Muslim Chinese*, 79, and Jonathan Lipman, *Familiar Strangers: A History of Muslims in Northwest China* (Seattle: University of Washington Press, 1997), xxiv, n15. An exception is Stevan Harrell, whose position appears to be ambiguous. See "Civilizing Projects and the Reactions to Them," introduction to Harrell, ed., *Cultural Encounters on China's Ethnic Frontiers* (Seattle: University of Washington Press, 1995).

63. Dikötter, "Racial Discourse in China: Continuities and Permutations," in Dikötter, ed., *The Construction of Racial Identities*, 12–33.

64. Prasenjit Duara, *Rescuing History from the Nation: Questioning Narratives of Modern China* (Chicago: University of Chicago Press, 1995), 55–56, esp. n4.

65. Chartier, *On the Edge of the Cliff*, 9.

66. Lien-sheng Yang, "Historical Notes on the Chinese World Order," in John K. Fairbank, ed., *The Chinese World Order* (Cambridge: Harvard University Press, 1968), 22.

67. Bentley, arguing for an analysis of the "practice of ethnicity," also makes the point that a historical perspective is crucial to lend dimensionality to ethnicity and ethnic change ("Ethnicity and Practice," 49).

68. In addition to the Harrell volume already cited, see also Melissa J. Brown, ed., *Negotiating Ethnicities in China and Taiwan* (Berkeley: Institute of East Asian Studies, 1996), especially the essays by Patricia Ebrey, "Surnames and Han Chinese Identity," and Brown, "On Becoming Chinese." Also see Kleeman, *Great Perfection*.

69. In the United States, the importance of using Manchu sources has been stressed by Beatrice S. Bartlett and, most recently, by Pamela Kyle Crossley and Evelyn S. Rawski. On the importance of Manchu, see Bartlett, "Books of Revelations: The Importance of the Manchu Language Archival Record Books for Research on Ch'ing History," *Late Imperial China* 6.2 (December 1985), 25–36, and Crossley and Rawski, "A Profile of the Manchu Language in Ch'ing History," *Harvard Journal of Asiatic Studies* 53.1 (June 1993), 63–102. For work that actually incorporates archival Manchu materials, see Gertraude Roth[-Li], "The Manchu-Chinese Relationship, 1618–1636," in Jonathan D. Spence and John E. Wills, Jr., *From Ming to Ch'ing: Conquest, Region, and Continuity in Seventeenth-Century China* (New Haven, Conn.: Yale University Press, 1979), 1–38; Beatrice S. Bartlett, *Monarchs and Ministers: The Grand Council in Mid-Ch'ing China, 1723–1820* (Berkeley and Los Angeles: University of California Press, 1991); Rawski, *The Last Emperors*; and Nicola Di Cosmo, "Manchu Shamanic Ceremonies at the Qing Court," in Joseph McDermott, ed., *State and Court Ritual in China* (Cambridge: Cambridge University Press, 1999), 352–98.

70. Figures from William Lavely and R. Bin Wong, "Revising the Malthusian Narrative: The Comparative Study of Population Dynamics in Late Imperial China," *Journal of Asian Studies* 57.3 (August 1998), 719.

71. "The tripling of Chinese population is probably the most frequently noted feature of Chinese society in the eighteenth century. . . . Surely no single premodern government anywhere in the world ever attempted to rule a populace larger than the three hundred million (or more) under Qing rule in 1800" (Naquin and Rawski, *Chinese Society in the Eighteenth Century*, 106–7). Estimates of the contemporary population of Europe (including Russia) vary from 149 million to 180 million. See Jean-Pierre Bardet and Jacques Dupaquier, *Histoire des populations de l'Europe* (Paris: Fayard, 1997), 33; Lavely and Wong, "Revising the Malthusian Narrative," 719. My thanks to James Lee for the former reference.

72. Borrowing from Fernand Braudel, Naquin and Rawski define China's "long eighteenth century" as lasting from 1680 to 1820, encompassing the second two-thirds of the Kangxi reign, together with the Yongzheng, Qianlong, and Jiaqing reigns (*Chinese Society in the Eighteenth Century*, xi).

73. See the landmark essay by Ping-ti Ho, "The Significance of the Ch'ing Period in Chinese History."

74. I use this translation of the term *yi* advisedly, since objections to it are frequently voiced. But "barbarian" does seem to capture a good measure of the cultural superiority embodied in discussions of the non-Han.

75. "Han Chinese" is the modern ethnic label used to describe the

majority of people in China, as distinct from the approximately three-score "minority nationalities" as defined by the present Chinese state, which make up only about 6 percent of the population. Despite the somewhat problematic sense of "Han" (a reference to the imperial dynasty of this name, which ruled 206 B.C.E.–220 C.E.) as an ethnonym, this is the label that was used during the Qing to distinguish the Chinese culturally and ethnically from the non-Han Other. Non-Han may be thought of as those who were not subject to the emperor, did not engage in agriculture (or sericulture), did not use the Chinese language, did not adhere to the rituals and customs prescribed in the Chinese classics, and did not have ancestors who did any of these things. In general the non-Han were known by the existence of pronounced linguistic, cultural, and social differences with the people known by the classical name "Hua" (or "Hua-Xia"), i.e., the Chinese. See the discussion in Kleeman, *Great Perfection*, 3–4 and note.

76. The Liao and Song courts came to terms in the Treaty of Shanyuan, signed in 1004. The border agreed on in this treaty ran east from the sea to the Yellow River on a line just north of the 39th parallel (approximately the latitude of the modern city of Tianjin). A similar treaty was signed between the Song and the Xi Xia in 1044, except that no border was defined. See Denis Twitchett and Hans-Peter Tietze, "The Liao," in Franke and Twitchett, eds., *The Cambridge History of China*, vol. 6, *Alien Regimes and Border States, 907–1368*, 108–10, 122.

77. *The Chinese Classics*, trans. James Legge, 5: 354–55 (*Zuo zhuan*, bk. 8, yr. 5).

78. Ibid., 2: 253–54 (*Mencius*, bk. 3, pt. 1, ch. 4).

79. More on these ideas is found in chapter 1 of Frank Dikötter, *The Discourse of Race in Modern China* (Stanford, Calif.: Stanford University Press, 1992).

80. Richard L. Davis, "Historiography as Politics and Yang Wei-chen's 'Polemic on Legitimate Succession,'" *T'oung Pao* 59 (1983), 33–72.

81. Cited in John D. Langlois, Jr., "Chinese Culturalism and the Yüan Analogy: Seventeenth-Century Perspectives," *Harvard Journal of Asiatic Studies* 40 (1980), 364.

82. Rejection of the Manchus on exclusivist grounds may also have been tied to the different perceptions of the Other on China's northern, as opposed to its southern, frontier. Owen Lattimore has argued on the basis of geography and sociology for two distinct types of frontier, "dynamic" in the south and "static" in the north, producing respectively a "frontier of inclusion" and a "frontier of exclusion." See "The Frontier in History," in *Studies in Frontier History* (London: Oxford University Press, 1962), 377.

83. On ethnic tension during the Opium War, see Frederic Wakeman, *Strangers at the Gate* (Berkeley and Los Angeles University of California Press, 1966) and Mark C. Elliott, "Bannerman and Townsman: Ethnic Tension in Nineteenth-century Jiangnan," *Late Imperial China* 11.1 (June 1990), 36–74.

84. Franz Michael, ed., *The Taiping Rebellion: History and Documents* (Seattle: University of Washington Press, 1971), 2: 145–47.

85. See Kauko Laitinen, *Chinese Nationalism in the Late Qing Dynasty: Zhang Binglin as an Anti-Manchu Propagandist* (London: Curzon Press, 1990).

86. Note, for instance, Mo Dongyin's claim that "the backward social condition of the Manchus had an extremely destructive effect on China's social economy" (*Manzushi luncong* [Beijing: Renmin chubanshe, 1958], 164). A good summary of this historiography (a chief exponent of which was Sun Yat-sen) is found in R. Kent Guy, *The Emperor's Four Treasuries: Scholars and the State in the Late Ch'ien-lung Era* (Cambridge: Harvard Council on East Asian Studies, 1987), 197–200. The lasting influence of anti-Manchu sentiment upon Republican historiography on the Qing is also discussed in Harold Kahn, *Monarchy in the Emperor's Eyes: Image and Reality in the Ch'ien-lung Reign* (Cambridge: Harvard University Press, 1971), 57–59.

87. The notion that the Mongols desecrated Chinese culture may have originated with the founder of the Ming dynasty, Zhu Yuanzhang. See the discussion in John D. Langlois, Jr., introduction to his edited volume, *China Under Mongol Rule* (Princeton, N.J.: Princeton University Press, 1981), 12–20 ff., citing the scholarship of Wu Han and Qian Mu. Russian attitudes toward Mongol rule and its "brutalization" of native society and culture are summarized in Nicholas V. Riasanovsky, *A History of Russia*, 4th ed. (New York: Oxford University Press, 1984), 72–76.

88. The phrase is Mary Wright's, from *The Last Stand of Chinese Conservatism: The T'ung-chih Restoration, 1862–1874* (Stanford, Calif.: Stanford University Press, 1957), 51. Other, roughly parallel, accounts of this historiography may be found in Oxnam, *Ruling from Horseback*, pp. 3–8, and Crossley, *Orphan Warriors*, pp. 224–27. This was not only the verdict of historians, of course, but the feeling of many Chinese during the Qing (not all of them revolutionaries), and even of some Manchus. Sušun, a leading political figure of the 1850s, is reported to have confided in his Han colleagues, "Manchus are a dense lot, unable to exert themselves on behalf of the country. All they know is how to waste money. Once the country runs into trouble, it must rely on the Han!" Cited in Hsiao I-shan, *Qingdai tongshi* (Beijing: Zhonghua shuju, 1986), 3: 414.

89. This is the dominant tone, for instance, in the work of one of China's

most eminent Marxist historians, Fan Wenlan. See his *Zhongguo jindaishi* (Beijing: Renmin chubanshe, 1947).

90. *Manzu jianshi* (Beijing: Zhonghua shuju, 1979), 185–86. The evolutionary narrative of ethnic change in operation here, derived from Henry Lewis Morgan via Stalin, has long been the dominant paradigm in Chinese ethnic discourse. See Gladney, *Muslim Chinese*, 71–74, and Charles Mckhann, "The Nationalities Question," in Harrell, ed., *Cultural Encounters*, 40–46.

91. Thus fulfilling the prophecy of Abbé Huc, who wrote in the mid-1800s, "Let any revolution remove the present dynasty, and the Mantchou will be compelled to complete fusion with the empire" (Huc and Gabet, *Travels in Tartary, Thibet, and China, 1844–1846* [New York: Harper and Brothers, 1928], trans. William Hazlitt, 131). The quotation in the text is from René Grousset, *Empire of the Steppes* (New Brunswick, N.J.: Rutgers University Press, 1970), 519. Reflecting its high place in the popular wisdom, the myth of Manchu disappearance is enshrined in all but late-twentieth-century editions of the *Encyclopædia Britannica*.

92. John K. Fairbank and Edwin O. Reischauer, *China: Tradition and Transformation* (Boston: Houghton Mifflin, 1978), 225. Ping-ti Ho also stresses this factor: "[T]he Ch'ing is without doubt the most successful dynasty of conquest in Chinese history, and the key to its success was the adoption by early Manchu rulers of a policy of systematic sinicization." He goes on to observe that the Qing became a "strictly conformist 'orthodox' Confucian state . . . in fact, more Confucian than previous Chinese dynasties" ("The Significance of the Ch'ing Period," 191–93). There is a need here, I believe, to distinguish between "sinification" (sinicization) and "Confucianization." Though both arguably constitute acculturation, they were by no means one and the same process.

93. Oxnam, *Ruling from Horseback*, 8.

94. Sun Yat-sen, *The Three Principles* (Shanghai: North China Daily News and Herald, 1927), 7.

95. Chinese belief in Manchu sinicization is common enough to have been lampooned by the Taiwanese critic Bo Yang in *The Ugly Chinaman and the Crisis of Chinese Culture*, trans. Don J. Cohn and Jing Qing (Sydney: Allen and Unwin, 1992), 87–88.

96. John Fairbank once described this "Chinese achievement" as "a variation on the theme, 'If you can't lick 'em, join 'em,'" linking it to the not-wholly-unfounded notion that the Manchus succeeded because "a sufficient number of Chinese wanted it that way" (Fairbank, "Varieties of the Chinese Military Experience," 14–15). The standard view was perhaps put most clearly by Wolfram Eberhard: "[W]e do not find a Manchu minority in China

today. The Manchus are the only colonial rulers of China who were not killed or exterminated when their rule ended, but who also did not return to their old home country and did not try to reform unto a new unity under their own rulers. They simply became Chinese." *China's Minorities: Yesterday and Today* (Belmont, Calif.: Wadsworth Publishing, 1982), 34.

97. One finds it in the very first history of the Qing written after the fall of the dynasty, Inaba Iwakichi's *Shinchō zenshi*, first published in 1914. Inaba wrote, "The customs and practices of the Han were very strong, so that even though the Han had to submit to the military authority of the Manchus, as time went by, the Manchus all practiced culture and their thinking could not avoid following that of the Han [ . . . and became] assimilated (*tonghua*) to the Han." Cited from the Chinese translation in *Qingchao quanshi* (Taipei: Zhonghua shuju, 1960), 6–7.

98. Meng Sen, *Qingdai shi* (Taipei: Zhengzhong shuju, 1960), 7. In a 1996 history of the banners, Liu Xiaomeng perpetuates this myth when he describes the fate of the Manchus after the fall of the Qing: "Suddenly it was as though the existence of the various Manchu garrison cities had been a fantasy. The bannermen who had lived together for two and three hundred years dispersed quickly to live among the Han. Their distinctive clothing and their queue vanished without a trace." *Baqi zidi* (Fuzhou: Fujian renmin chubanshe, 1996), 207.

99. Ping-ti Ho, "In Defense of Sinicization: A Rebuttal of Evelyn Rawski's 'Reenvisioning the Qing,'" *Journal of Asian Studies* 57.1 (February 1998), 149.

100. These various factors are summarized in Ho, "In Defense of Sinicization." It is important to note that in places Ho acknowledges that sinicization does not have to be a zero-sum game. He writes, "I must also make clear that the growth of Manchu identification with Chinese norms of behavior and patterns of thought need not exclude other forms of identity. To pose such binary choices . . . distorts what individuals experience" (ibid., 125). Such a viewpoint is entirely consistent with the approach to ethnicity I adopt here.

101. Bol, "Seeking Common Ground," 492. Bol (correctly , I think) finds the term "sinicization" inadequate to describe the adaptation of Chinese institutional and cultural practices by the Jin dynasty, since it did not result in the loss of Jurchen identity. See the discussion in "Seeking Common Ground," 483–93. Franke has written, "At the latest in 1203 the Jurchen state of Chin had, in its own eyes, become fully Chinese and a legitimate link in the chain of successive dynasties," but this rather begs the question of how the Jurchens saw themselves as a people ("The Chin," 320). Elsewhere, Franke qualifies this view significantly, saying that "none of the dynasties of conquest developed into a state that can be regarded as fully Chinese in structure and content"

("The Role of the State," 97). In the Qing case, certainly, Manchu emperors saw theirs as a legitimate dynasty, but the Qing never became fully Chinese "in its own eyes."

102. Evelyn Rawski, "Reenvisioning the Qing: The Significance of the Qing Period in Chinese History," *Journal of Asian Studies* 55.4 (November 1996), 833; James Millward, *Beyond the Pass: Economy, Ethnicity, and Empire in Qing Xinjiang* (Stanford, Calif.: Stanford University Press, 1998), 13–15. The phrases "Qing-centered" and "Manchu-centered" clearly paraphrase Paul Cohen's call for a "China-centered" history of China, found in *Discovering History in China: American Historical Writings on the Recent Chinese Past* (New York: Columbia University Press, 1984).

103. Michael, *The Origin of Manchu Rule*, 79, 107.

104. Ibid., 119.                    105. Wittfogel and Feng, *Liao*, 15.

106. Ibid., 7.                      107. Ibid., 15.

108. Wright, *The Last Stand of Chinese Conservatism*, 56.

109. It is ironic (and revealing of the mutual inconsistencies in the standard exegeses of the "Manchu question") that Wright's rebuttal of Wittfogel's revisionist symbiosis hypothesis was itself revisionist history, in that she tried to dispel the Han nationalist notion that the Manchus were guilty *as a race* of wrecking the Chinese ship of state.

110. Joseph R. Levenson, *Confucian China and Its Modern Fate: A Trilogy* (Berkeley and Los Angeles: University of California Press, 1968), 95–98. Of course, not everyone agreed with this interpretation. As briefly mentioned in the Preface, Immanuel Hsü (paraphrasing Hsiao I-shan) pointed in his widely used textbook to the continuity of anti-Manchu sentiment from the early Qing as an example of "nationalistic-racial protest against foreign elements in Chinese life," which he argued (unfortunately without further elaboration) represented a "distinct theme of history" in modern China (*The Rise of Modern China*, 9).

111. Albert Feuerwerker, *State and Society in Eighteenth-Century China: The Ch'ing Empire in Its Glory* (Ann Arbor: The University of Michigan Center for Chinese Studies, 1976), 71.

112. Jonathan D. Spence, *Ts'ao Yin and the K'ang-hsi Emperor: Bondservant and Master* (New Haven, Conn.: Yale University Press, 1966); Oxnam, *Ruling from Horseback*; Lawrence D. Kessler, *K'ang-hsi and the Consolidation of Ch'ing Rule, 1661–1684* (Chicago: University of Chicago Press, 1976). One can see further steps in this direction in the essays contained in the volume edited by Spence and John E. Wills, *From Ming to Ch'ing: Conquest, Region, and Continuity in Seventeenth-Century China* (New Haven, Conn.: Yale University Press, 1979).

113. Some important exceptions include the Harvard-trained Wang Zhonghan and, in Taiwan, historians such as Li Hsüeh-chih, Ch'en Chieh-hsien and Chuang Chi-fa, who have produced valuable studies that highlight the unique Manchu contribution to the Qing polity.

114. For references see individual entries in the bibliography. An exhaustive listing of Japanese scholarship on Manchuria and other regions of Inner Asia is *Nihon ni okeru Chūō Ajia kankei kenkyū bunken mokuroku* (Tokyo: Centre for East Asian Cultural Studies, 1988).

115. This is confirmed when one scans the entries in Giovanni Stary's three-volume *Manchu Studies: An International Bibliography* (Wiesbaden: Kommissionsverlag Otto Harrassowitz, 1990), an essential starting point for all work on the Manchus.

116. For two outstanding examples, see Duara, *Rescuing History from the Nation*, and John Fitzgerald, *Awakening China: Politics, Culture, and Class in the Nationalist Revolution* (Stanford, Calif.: Stanford University Press, 1996).

117. A sampling of these new trends is presented in Gail Hershatter et al., eds., *Remapping China: Fissures in Historical Terrain* (Stanford, Calif.: Stanford University Press, 1996). Japanese and European scholars are less engaged in this enterprise than Chinese scholars, who since the 1980s have produced important new work on Manchu history in the Qing. Some of this research is still confined to a Marxist framework in which class differences a priori outrank ethnic differences, but one can see in attempts to reevaluate the nature of Manchu ethnic identity some tentative signs that alternative analytical models are rising in importance. The work of Ding Yizhuang and Liu Xiaomeng is notable in this regard.

118. See Bartlett, *Monarchs and Ministers*; Evelyn S. Rawski, *The Last Emperors* and "Ch'ing Imperial Marriage and Problems of Rulership," in Rubie S. Watson and Patricia B. Ebrey, eds., *Marriage and Inequality in Chinese Society* (Berkeley and Los Angeles: University of California Press, 1991), 173–203; R. Kent Guy, *The Emperor's Four Treasuries*; Pierre-Henri Durand, *Lettrés et pouvoirs: Un procès littéraire dans la Chine impériale* (Paris: Ecole des hautes études des sciences sociales, 1992); Kai-wing Chow, *The Rise of Confucian Ritualism in Late Imperial China: Ethics, Classics, and Lineage Discourse* (Stanford, Calif.: Stanford University Press, 1994); and James Polachek, *The Inner Opium War* (Cambridge: Harvard Council on East Asian Studies, 1992). Unfortunately, Rawski's *The Last Emperors* and Norman Kutcher's *Mourning in Late Imperial China: Filial Piety and the State* (Cambridge: Cambridge University Press, 1999) appeared too late for me to fully incorporate their insights into the present study.

119. In *The Great Enterprise*, Frederic Wakeman analyzes the military and political aspects of the transition to Manchu rule, and refers briefly to the establishment of the first garrisons on p. 480. A very detailed account of the military campaigns of the conquest is also found in Sun Wenliang, Li Zhiting, and Qiu Lianmei, *Ming-Qing zhanzheng shilue* (Shenyang: Liaoning renmin chubanshe, 1986), but they make no reference to the Qing garrison system. On the military profile projected by the Qing during the Qianlong reign see Sabine Dabringhaus, *Das Qing-Imperium als Vision und Wirklichkeit: Tibet in Laufbahn und Schriften des Song Yun (1752–1835)* (Stuttgart: Franz Steiner Verlag, 1994); also Joanna Waley-Cohen, "Commemorating War in Eighteenth-Century China," and Peter Perdue, "Military Mobilization in Seventeenth- and Eighteenth-century China," both in *Modern Asian Studies* 30.4 (October 1996). The portrait of the eighteenth-century war hero Uksiltu which appears on the cover and frontispiece of this book is another very powerful piece of evidence that throughout the 1700s the Qing imperial image—and the Manchu self-image—remained heavily influenced by martial motifs. See also Chapter 7, note 29.

120. A variety of different approaches is found in Rawski, "Reenvisioning the Qing."

121. Crossley, *Orphan Warriors*, 225.

122. Ibid., 228.

123. Crossley, "Thinking About Ethnicity," 8.

124. Crossley, "The Qianlong Retrospect," 65, 80. Cf. a similar statement from *Orphan Warriors*: "It should not be forgotten that the identification policies of the seventeenth century were arbitrary" (221).

125. Crossley, "*Manzhou yuanliu kao,*" 762.

*Chapter 1. The Eight Banners and the Origins of the Manchus*

1. Farquhar, "Emperor as Bodhisattva," 204.

2. Exceptions to this were those Chinese who affiliated on an individual basis (willingly or under duress) with the banner establishment as, for example, unfree labor in households or agriculture (so-called *touchong*); also the Chinese troops of the "feudatories" established in southern China, which were incorporated into the banners for a time beginning in 1681.

3. Fletcher, "The Mongols: Ecological and Social Perspectives," 23.

4. Though reduced in amount, payments of Eight Banner stipends continued until 1924, when the deposed emperor was ejected from the palace. Li and Guan, *Manzu tongshi*, 638–39.

5. Meng Sen, "Baqi zhidu kaoshi," in Meng Sen, *Ming-Qingshi lunzhu jikan* (Beijing: Zhonghua shuju, 1959), 218.

6. Jin Dechun, *Qijun zhi* (ca. 1720), 1a–b; in Jin Yufu, ed., *Liaohai congshu* (Fengtian: 1933–36; Shenyang: Liaoshen shushe, 1985), 4: 2603.

7. Wei Yuan, *Shengwu ji* (1846; reprint, Beijing: Zhonghua shuju, 1984), 9. On the *Hanjun*, see below.

8. This process is well laid out in Harrell, "Civilizing Projects and the Reactions to Them," 22–23. The evolution of minority nationality policy is usefully traced in Gladney, *Muslim Chinese*, 87–93. See also Colin Mackerras, *China's Minorities: Integration and Modernization in the Twentieth Century* (Hong Kong: Oxford University Press, 1994); and June Teufel Dreyer, *China's Forty Millions: Minority Nationalities and National Integration in the People's Republic of China* (Cambridge: Harvard University Press, 1976).

9. Although "Manchuria" is admittedly a problematic term, for the sake of convenience I will use it to describe the entire region covered by the Qing military districts of Shengjing, Jilin, and Heilongjiang, which includes areas not part of Northeast China today. On the origins of "Manchuria" as a place name, see Mark C. Elliott, "The Limits of Tartary: Manchuria in Imperial and National Geographies," *Journal of Asian Studies* 59.3, 603–46.

10. Wang Zhonghan, "Guanyu Manzu xingchengzhong de jige wenti," in Wang Zhonghan, ed., *Manzushi yanjiu ji* (Beijing: Zhongguo shehuikexue chubanshe, 1988), 1; Li and Guan, *Manzu tongshi*, 707. The Wang article is also collected in his *Qingshi xinkao* (Shenyang: Liaoning daxue chubanshe, 1990), 44–58.

11. Wang Zhonghan, "Qingdai baqizhong," 44.

12. Guan Jixin, ed., *Zhongguo Manzu* (Beijing: Zhongyang minzu xueyuan chubanshe, 1993), 8–9; there is a useful chart of the main "minority nationalities" in Piper Rae Gaubatz, *Beyond the Great Wall: Urban Form and Transformation on the Chinese Frontier* (Stanford, Calif.: Stanford University Press, 1996), 31.

13. Wang, "Qingdai baqizhong," 67–68. See also the careful analysis of the present Manchu population of Beizhen, Liaoning Province, in Hosoya, "Manju gurun to 'Manshūkoku,'" in Hamashita Takeshi, ed., *Rekishi no naka no chiiki*, vol. 8 of Shibata Michio, ed., *Sekaishi e no toi* (Tokyo: Iwanami shoten, 1990), 110–14.

14. Li and Guan, *Manzu tongshi*, 450–51.

15. Matsumura Jun, "The Founding Legend of the Qing Reconsidered," *Memoirs of the Research Department of the Tōyō Bunko* 55 (1997), 49. This myth continued to be passed down for almost three centuries, at least among the imperial clan. In his memoirs, Puyi, the last Qing emperor, reveals that as a child he was familiar with the story of Fekulen. Aisen-Gioro Puyi, *From Emperor to Citizen* (Beijing: Foreign Languages Press, 1964), 1: 54.

16. On the legend, see the previous note and Matsumura Jun, "On the Founding Legend of the Ch'ing Dynasty," *Acta Asiatica* 53 (1988), 1–23 (originally published in Japanese in 1972). Pamela Kyle Crossley, "An Introduction to the Qing Foundation Myth," *Late Imperial China* 6.2 (December 1985), 13–24, is also helpful.

17. Eller, "Ethnicity, Culture, and 'the Past,'" 578.

18. Crossley, "*Manzhou yuanliu kao*," 781. In addition to the *Manzhou yuanliu kao*, similar accounts are found in parts of the *Manzhou shilu, Baqi tongzhi*, and in Wei Yuan's *Shengwu ji*.

19. Anthony D. Smith, "Ethnic Myths and Ethnic Revivals," *Archives Européennes de Sociologie* 25.2 (1984), 294.

20. The locus classicus for this view is an 1882 address before the Sorbonne, "Qu'est-ce qu'une nation," delivered by the French academician Ernest Renan in which he said: "Forgetting, I would even go so far as to say historical error, is a crucial factor in the creation of a nation." See "What Is a Nation?" translated by Martin Thom, in Homi Bhabha, *Nation and Narration* (London: Routledge, 1990), 11. For more recent statements, see the final chapter, "Memory and Forgetting," of Benedict Anderson, *Imagined Communities*, 2nd ed. (New York: Verso Books, 1991); Eric Hobsbawm and Terence Ranger, *The Invention of Tradition* (Cambridge: Cambridge University Press, 1992). Cf. also Sow-theng Leong, writing in *Migration and Ethnicity in Chinese History* (75): "The culture of an ethnic group tends to be myth-making," citing Orlando Patterson; Anthony D. Smith, "Ethnic Election and Cultural Identity," *Ethnic Studies* 10 (1993), 1–25; and Eriksen, *Ethnicity and Nationalism*, chap. 4.

21. On the proclamation of the name "Manchu" (*Manzhou/Manju*), see below.

22. On the relationship between Manchu and other Tungusic and Altaic languages, see Denis Sinor, *Introduction to Manchu Studies* (American Council of Learned Societies, 1963), 7–13.

23. For the "Su-shen connection" as represented in Qing accounts see Crossley, "*Manzhou yuanliu kao*"; in recent histories, see *Manzu jianshi*, 1–7; Li and Guan, *Manzu tongshi*, 1–5; Guan, *Zhongguo Manzu*, 8–9. A useful review of these theories is found in Pei Huang, "New Light on the Origins of the Manchus," *Harvard Journal of Asiatic Studies* 50.1 (1990), esp. 240–53. Huang accepts their Su-shen origins.

24. See Hok-lam Chan, "The Chien-wen, Yung-lo, Hung-hsi, and Hsüan-te reigns, 1399–1435" and Frederick Mote, "The Ch'eng-hua and Hung-chih reigns, 1465–1505," both in the *Cambridge History of China*, vol. 7, *The Ming Dynasty, 1368–1644, Part I* (Cambridge: Cambridge University Press,

1988), 267 and 398, respectively; Liu, *Manzu de buluo yu guojia* (Changchun: Jilin wenshi chubanshe, 1995), 5–6. I have relied heavily on Liu's excellent history (based on careful use of Manchu-language materials) for much of this and the following sections.

25. Liu, *Manzu de buluo yu guojia*, 12–13.

26. Ibid., 46–53.

27. Liu (24) offers this as the reason why Manchus in the Qing were not in the habit of using surnames to identify themselves, since there was no need to do so for self-identification in the *gašan*.

28. Ibid., 29–35.

29. Ibid., 79–83.

30. Ibid., 39, citing *Yanshan junri ji, juan* 16.

31. Ibid., 89.

32. See Ishibashi Hideo, "Jušen shokō," in *Mikami Tsugio hakushi kijū kinen ronbunshū: rekishi hen* (Tokyo: Heibonsha, 1985), 163–75.

33. Liu, *Manzu de buluo yu guojia*, 103.

34. Cited in ibid., 107–8.

35. Ibid., 105–9. A derogatory referent for Han Chinese, *manzi* comes from the Chinese word *man*, meaning "southern barbarian."

36. Reflecting its spelling in some early sources, Nurhaci's name is sometimes romanized as "Nurgaci." While Nurhaci is more traditional, both are acceptable. The pronunciation of Manchu *h* was distinctly guttural; in a note to his *Carte générale de la Tartarie Chinoise*, D'Anville wrote that "In such words as Hotun and Hiamen, the *h* should be pronounced a little like a *k*." Thus *h* was not infrequently rendered orthographically in Manchu as *g* (e.g., *cooga* for *cooha*).

37. Basing himself on evidence from Korean records, Liu claims that the migration of the Odoli tribe took place before 1395 (*Manzu de buluo yu guojia*, 1). The exact location of Odoli is still unclear. Note that the Mongols also called their royal house the "golden" lineage (*altan urugh*) (Fletcher, "The Mongols: Ecological and Social Perspectives," 19).

38. Liu, *Manzu de buluo yu guojia*, 8–11. Much of this history can also be found in ECCP 594–96, a superlative account written by Fang Chao-ying.

39. Liu, *Manzu de buluo yu guojia*, 118; Li Xun and Xue Hong, eds., *Qingdai quanshi* (Shenyang: Liaoning renmin chubanshe, 1991), 1: 47.

40. Li and Xue, eds., *Qingdai quanshi*, 50–51, 59.

41. Liu, *Manzu de buluo yu guojia*, 112–15.

42. See Wakeman, *The Great Enterprise*; ECCP 594–99.

43. Liu, *Manzu de buluo yu guojia*, 132.

44. Ibid., 166–69. See the biography in ECCP 221–22. Campaigns continued sporadically for another thirty years.

45. Ibid., 123. On the importance of companions (Manchu *gucu*, Mongolian *anda*) to Chinggis, see Fletcher, "The Mongols: Ecological and Social Perspectives," 21–22; Franke, "The Role of the State," 97; and Thomas Allsen, "The Rise of the Mongolian Empire and Mongolian Rule in North China," in Twitchett and Franke, eds., *The Cambridge History of China*, vol. 6, *Alien Regimes and Border States, 907–1368*, 335–37.

46. It is not clear that the European battue (from the French, *battre*, to hit) and the Manchu *aba* have anything more in common than the idea of beating brush and trees in order to flush game out from cover into the open.

47. Sechin Jagchid and Charles Bawden, "Notes on Hunting of Some Nomadic Peoples of Central Asia," in *Die Jagd bei den Altaischen Volken*, *Asiatische Forschungen* 26 (Wiesbaden: Otto Harrassowitz, 1968), 90.

48. Wittfogel and Feng, *Liao*, 526.

49. MBRT 1, Taizu 4, 53.

50. In other words, while English "banner" and Chinese *qi* are synonymous, Manchu *gūsa* means something entirely different. Assuming that early-seventeenth-century Jurchens thought and worked using native terms, the notion—based purely on terminological similarity—that the banner organization owed its origins to the Ming practice of using flags to distinguish military units (Crossley, *The Manchus*, 207) is problematic. Manchu *tu* derives from the Mongolian *tugh*, meaning "flag." The origin of the word *gūsa* is less clear; see the discussion in Elliott, "Resident Aliens: The Manchu Experience in China, 1644–1760" (Ph.D. diss., University of California, Berkeley, 1993), 13–14, and in Mitamura (cf. following note).

51. This view was first put forward by Mitamura Taisuke, "Shoki Manshū hakki no seiritsu katei," in *Shinchō zenshi no kenkyū* (Kyoto: Tōyōshi kenkyūkai, 1965), 283–322; similar conclusions have been reached by Zhang Jinfan and Guo Chengkang (*Qing ruguanqian*, chap. 3), who appear not to be aware of Mitamura's work, and by Liu, *Manzu de buluo yu guojia*, 151–57, who cites Mitamura. Another scholar has recently argued that the first military- *niru* were established by at least 1593, and that 1601 in fact represented a fundamental reorganization of the *niru*. See Yao Nianci, "Manzu baqizhi guojia chutan," Ph.D. diss., Central Minorities Institute, Beijing, 1991, 10–13. This view is echoed in Li and Xue, eds. *Qingdai quanshi*, 86. Hosoya Yoshio posits an even earlier date, citing 1587–88 for the introduction of the military-*niru*; see "Manju gurun," 128. The impression that the military-*niru* were supposed to consist of three hundred *households* is given in Gertraude

Roth-Li, "The Rise of the Early Manchu State: A Portrait Drawn from Manchu Sources to 1636" (Ph.D. diss., Harvard University, 1976), 24–27, and is repeated in Frederic Wakeman, *The Great Enterprise*, 53.

52. The use of the word *tatan* here raises the question of how the development of the banner system paralleled and intersected with the development of another type of organization, more explicitly political, called the *mukūn-tatan* system. Like the banners, the *mukūn-tatan* system borrowed from an older vocabulary (in this case, that of lineage organization), but bears no resemblance to earlier *mukūn* organization. *Tatan* originally referred to a small group of people within the same village and/or lineage who engaged in collective gathering or small-scale hunting. See Liu, *Manzu de buluo yu guojia*, 61–64, 135–39.

53. The concept seems not so very far from that behind the extensive support provided to United States servicemen in the areas of housing, commissaries, schooling, home mortgages, and so on, though obligation of military service is obviously not hereditary—at any rate, not formally so.

54. *Manzhou shilu/Manju-i yargiyan kooli*, 181. "Regiments" (Ma *jalan*) also appeared for the first time in 1615 (Yao, "Manzu baqizhi," 15). It is tempting to conclude that the announcement of the imperial ambitions (and pretensions) of the Jurchen to the Ming court was attendant on the complete articulation of a military bureaucracy.

55. Mitamura, "Shoki Manshū," 310–11, in *Shinjō zenshi no kenkyū*.

56. Ibid., 311; that 1601 was the year for the first *gūsa* is also the view in Yao, "Manzu baqizhi," 37, and Liu, *Manzu de buluo yu guojia*, 174–77. Not all scholars are in agreement (see Zhang and Guo, *Qing ruguanqian*, 146–59); the details of the debate are found in Mark C. Elliott, "Resident Aliens," 13–18.

57. Zhang and Guo, *Qing ruguanqian*, 302–18. In the past I have used the term "Han-martial" as a translation of the Chinese name *Hanjun*. Crossley prefers "Chinese-martial" (see her explanation in *The Manchus*, 203–5). Because it identifies them no less accurately and does so much more conveniently, I have adopted here the simpler term "Chinese bannermen" to refer to the *Hanjun*. The Manchu name, *ujen cooha*, means "heavy troops." The origin of this name is explained below.

58. It was usual practice in the Qing to speak only of eight banners, but one finds occasional references to "twenty-four banners" (*Gaozong shilu*, 438: 4a). While on the basis of the Manchu terminology it seems accurate to speak of "Manchu banners" and "Mongol banners," Chinese-language usage would appear to justify expressions such as "Eight-Banner Manchus" and "Eight-Banner Mongols." That is, these banners were most

commonly called *baqi Manzhou* and *baqi Menggu*, not *Manzhou baqi* or *Menggu baqi*.

59. Fletcher, "The Mongols: Ecological and Social Perspectives," 29.

60. A detailed comparison of the *meng-an mou-ke* and the Eight Banners is found in chapter 5 of Zhang Boquan et al., *Jinshi lungao* (Changchun: Jilin wenshi chubanshe, 1986). See also his essay, "Lun Jindai meng-an mo-ke zhidu de xingcheng, fazhan ji qi pohuai de yuanyin," in *Liao-Jin shi lunwen ji* (Shenyang: Liaoning renmin chubanshe, 1985), 343–71. The considerable literature on the *meng-an mou-ke* system is summarized in Franke, "The Chin," 273–77.

61. The first were classified a few decades later as *laigui* or *laitou* (Ma *baime jihe*); the second as *zhengfu* (Ma *dailame dahabuha*). Liu, *Manzu de buluo yu guojia*, 160.

62. Ibid., 160–69; see also the tables, pp. 184–203. Liu bases his information, including the figure of 239 companies, on BQTZ.

63. Ibid., 167. By the early eighteenth century, over half had been transferred to different banners.

64. Roth-Li, "Early Manchu State," 23; Liu, *Manzu de buluo yu guojia*, 223–25. The list is found in MBRT 1, Taizu 18, 274–75.

65. Liu, *Manzu de buluo yu guojia*, 217–18.

66. Zhang and Guo, *Qing ruguanqian*, 202. Though it is hard to say why certain companies were assigned to be part of specific banners, it seems likely that their uneven distribution (some banners were comprised of as many as sixty-one companies and some as few as fifteen) owed to these particularistic allegiances.

67. Meng, "Baqi zhidu kaoshi," 80; Liu, *Manzu de buluo yu guojia*, 228–31.

68. Liu, *Manzu de buluo yu guojia*, 211–15.

69. Franke, "The Chin," 275.

70. Estimates of the number of companies during this period vary; I follow those in Fang Chaoying, "A Technique for Estimating the Numerical Strength of the Early Manchu Military Forces," *Harvard Journal of Asiatic Studies* 13.1–2 (June 1950): 208–9. For comparison, see, for instance, Zhang and Guo, *Qing ruguanqian*, 199–210. Both are in rough agreement on the figure of five hundred *niru* on the eve of the conquest.

71. Hong Taiji is the same person referred to mistakenly in older historiography as "Abahai." For the source of this error (most likely deriving from a Russian corruption of the Manchu reign name he adopted in 1626, *abkai sure*), see Giovanni Stary, "The Manchu Emperor 'Abahai': Analysis of an Historiographic Mistake," *Central Asiatic Journal* 28.3–4 (1984), 296–99.

His name in Chinese is often given as Huang Taiji, giving the (again) mistaken impression that he was a crown prince. Though indeed it derives ultimately from the Chinese *huang taizi*, as *Khung tayiji* (and other variants), this name, meaning loosely "Respected Son," was quite common among Mongols, from whom the Jurchens borrowed it. That Hong (not Hung) Taiji was indeed his given name, and not a title, is persuasively established on the basis of new documentary evidence in Tatiana A. Pang and Giovanni Stary, *New Light on Manchu Historiography and Literature* (Wiesbaden: Harrassowitz Verlag, 1998), 13.

72. This history is detailed in Wakeman, *The Great Enterprise*, 59–74.

73. Tie Yuqin and Wang Peihuan, eds., *Shengjing huanggong* (Beijing: Zijincheng chubanshe, 1987), 170, citing the Korean record, *Jianzhou wenjian lu* (*Konchu mun'gyon rok*), by Yi Minwhan.

74. As Liu Xiaomeng has recently argued, board autonomy was severely hampered by the presence of *qixinlang* translators who doubled as spies, and the ethnic division that obtained within the boards was an unmistakable reflection of Eight Banner organization (though placing officials of different banners in the same board also tended to break down intrabanner differences). Liu, *Manzu de buluo yu guojia*, 317–22.

75. Between 1631 and 1633, several noted Ming generals defected to the Jurchen side, bringing with them not only large numbers of experienced soldiers, but also intimate knowledge of the use of artillery, which the Jin lacked, and which proved decisive in later campaigns. See Wakeman, *The Great Enterprise*, 160–224.

76. Tie and Wang, *Shengjing huanggong*, 211–12; Okada Hidehiro, "The Yüan Seal in Manchu Hands: The Source of the Ch'ing Legitimacy" (paper presented at the 33rd Permanent International Altaistic Conference, Budapest, 1990).

77. On the name "Qing," see note 118, below. In Manchu the shift to empire did not involve a significant change in the address of the emperor comparable, say, to the introduction of a term such as *huangdi*, "emperor" (the Manchu loan word, *hūwangdi*, was generally reserved for deceased rulers). The Jurchen/Manchu leader, who was first awarded the title of *han* ("khan") in 1606, continued to be called this, though after 1636 this was usually "Sacred Khan" (Ma *enduringge han*). Imperial status was evident in the formal enthronement rituals and implied in references to heaven's having conferred the title, to occasional use of the phrase "heavenly khan" (Ma *abkai han*), and to "heaven's decrees" (Ma *abkai hese*, i.e., imperial edicts). See MBRT 6, Taizong 8, 993–94. On the borrowing of this terminology from Mongolian see David Farquhar, "Emperor as Bodhisattva."

78. Crossley, "Manzhou yuanliu kao," 779–80; *Orphan Warriors*, 5. Crossley's position, summarized in the Introduction, is that banner classification was originally devoid of genealogical significance, and that it was only because of the growing need of the eighteenth-century Qing state for "racial" definitions of identity that an attempt was made to retroactively interpret the creation of the banners as bearing relation to descent. This is clear from her statement, with respect to the request by members of the Tong family to be reclassified from the Chinese banners to the Manchu banners:

> The banners were creatures of the state itself, and all criteria related to banner identity were necessarily functions of state fiat; from the time of Nurgaci to the time of this petition [1688], identities could be and frequently were metamorphosed by edict. . . . In fact, the arguments made by Hūwašan and the Tong brothers rested on precisely one foundation, that of genealogy. Their premise was that genealogies had been the original criteria upon which Manchus had been distinguished from the Chinese-martial. This was manifestly not so. ("The Qianlong Retrospect," 80)

Shelley Rigger's essay "Voices of Manchu Identity" adheres closely to Crossley's interpretation. My reading of the Tong case, emphasizing that genealogy was as much a concern in the seventeenth as in the eighteenth century, is presented near the end of this chapter.

79. Fletcher, "The Mongols: Ecological and Social Perspectives," 16.

80. SYBQ YZ6: 2a–b (YZ6.1.29). This was uttered in the context of urging members of the imperial bodyguard to stop "joking around in Chinese" and apply themselves seriously to speaking Manchu.

81. Fletcher, "The Mongols: Ecological and Social Perspectives," 16.

82. MBRT 1, Taizu 3, 37–38; also MBRT 1, Taizu 16, 252; *Kyū Manshū tō Tensō kyū-nen*, trans. and ed. Kanda Nobuo et al. (Tokyo: Tōyō Bunko, 1975), 2: 296–98. This source is the transcribed and annotated *Jiu Manzhou dang* for 1636.

83. The eight great clans were the Gūwalgiya, Niohuru, Šumuru, Yehe Nara, Donggo, Magiya, Irgen Gioro, and Hoifa. See Chen Kangqi, *Langqian jiwen chubi/erbi/sanbi* (1880; reprint, Beijing: Zhonghua shuju, 1984), and Zhao-lian, *Xiaoting zalu* (1814–26; reprint, Taipei: Hongwenguan chubanshe, 1986).

84. Crossley's study of the different generations of the Gūwalgiya clan in *Orphan Warriors* clearly bears this out for the nineteenth century. Banner registers from late-Qing Beijing continue to identify which individuals were *zuzhang* (*Guangxu-Xuantong-Minguo hukouce*, "Xianghongqi Manzhou er jia-la, Bin-liang zuoling" archives in the Chinese Academy of Social Sciences Library, Beijing).

85. MBRT 1, Taizu 16, 252.

86. MBRT 3, Taizu 79–81, 1173–1220.

87. One easy way to do this is to look in the indices to MBRT contained in volume 3 (for Taizu) and volume 7 (for Taizong); individuals with listings in BQTZ and BQMST are so noted. For example, Gibkada, head of the eleventh company of the first regiment of the Bordered White Banner, is noted in BQTZ as having led his village from the Warka region across the Changbai Mountains to join Nurhaci, probably stopping on the way first to join the Ula (BQTZ 7, 108; 159, 3987–88). He appears also under the listings of the Warka Usu lineage in BQMST 37, 1b–2a. Entries for him consistent with the information in the preceding eighteenth-century sources are found in MBRT 1, Taizu 17, 266; 2, Taizu 57, 843–44; 3, Taizu 67, 1001, and Taizu 79, 1185. More will be said about the compilation of these genealogies in Chapter 8. While the MBRT, which was recopied in the middle of the Qianlong reign, is unreliable for certain specific matters of terminology, scholars agree that differences between it and the early-seventeenth-century originals upon which it was based, known under the name *Jiu Manzhou dang*, are for the most part terminological. More on the compilation of the *qifenzhi* is found in Hosoya Yoshio, "Hakki tsūshi shokyū 'kibunshi' hensan to sono haikei—Yōseichō sakuryō kaikaku no ittan," *Tōhōgaku* 36 (September 1968), 102–18.

88. For the richness of these registers, see James Lee and Cameron Campbell, *Fate and Fortune* (Cambridge: Cambridge University Press, 1997).

89. As in *yehe-i ba*, "the place of the Yehe" (MBRT 1, Taizu 13, 201).

90. See, for instance, MBRT 1, Taizu 15, 225 (for a Jurchen-Chinese border); MBRT 1, Taizu 1, 9; *Kyū Manshū tō*, 2: 277–78 (for a Jurchen-Korean border); and MBRT 1, Taizu 21, 318, and MBRT 2, Taizu 43, 627 (for a Jurchen-Mongol border).

91. MBRT 1, Taizu 26, 384. For *monggo-i ba* see MBRT 2, Taizu 45, 657 and Taizu 46, 678. Note that *gurun* sometimes also applied to tribes; for instance, "šun dekdere ergi hūrha gurun" (MBRT 1, Taizu 9, 147).

92. MBRT 1, Taizu 13, 189.

93. A preliminary analysis is found in Mark C. Elliott, "Manchu (Re)Definitions of the Nation in the Early Qing," *Indiana East Asian Working Papers Series on Language and Politics in Modern China* 7 (January 1996), 46–78.

94. MBRT 2, Taizu 41, 599–602.

95. Smith, for instance, writes, "We can now define an ethnic community, or ethnie, as a named human group claiming a homeland and sharing myths of common ancestry, historical memories, and a distinct culture." Anthony D. Smith, "Chosen Peoples: Why Ethnic Groups Survive," *Ethnic and Racial Studies* 15.3 (July 1992), 438. In another article, however, his definition omits

the territorial element, which, he says, is "often absent from *ethnie*," though it may still be present in symbolic references to "distinctive communities in their ancient homelands." "Ethnic Election and Cultural Identity," 10.

96. These issues are more fully treated in Elliott, "The Limits of Tartary."

97. Some scholars prefer to include descent here, since very often interpretations of descent are culturally determined. I have chosen to isolate descent as an element of ethnic identity because it seems to me that in the Manchu case belief in the inherited quality of identity—that who one is depends on who one's ancestors were—was separate from the other cultural elements listed here.

98. The last line runs, "Muse juwe, emu gurun geli waka, encu gisun-i gurun kai." MBRT 1, Taizu 13, 202.

99. MBRT 1, Taizu 10, 160.

100. MBRT 1, Taizu 13, 192; MBRT 1, Taizu 14, 211. In the second letter, emphasis is also laid on the similarity of Jurchen and Mongol hairstyles.

101. MBRT 1, Taizu 15, 237–38.

102. The original reads: "yehe, muse oci, encu gisun-i jušen gurun kai" (MBRT 1, Taizu 4, 47). On the nature of the Yehe language, see MBRT 3, Taizu 25 supp., 1222.

103. This claim was sometimes made defiantly; see the 1635 letter of the Jin khan to Ming officials in *Kyū Manshū tō* 2, 307.

104. The Jurchen hairstyle called for the forehead to be shaved high with the remaining hair gathered at the back of the head in a queue (Ma *soncoho*). This distinctive coiffure was imposed upon non-Jurchen subject populations as a mark of their loyalty to the Qing at least by 1621 (MBRT 1, Taizu 20, 295), and was one of the most controversial policies enforced in the immediate post-conquest era. See Wakeman, *The Great Enterprise*, 60, 646–50.

105. The Jurchens, like many Northern Asian peoples, practiced a shamanic religion, which they brought with them when they conquered China. See Chapter 6.

106. The Jurchen woman's single most obvious distinguishing feature was that her feet were not bound. Apart from this, Jurchen/Manchu women had specific coiffures, wore distinctive jewelry, and enjoyed significantly greater liberties and legal privileges than Han women. See Chapter 6.

107. Tan Qian, a former Ming official who lived in Beijing for three years in the 1650s, commented on various aspects of Manchu culture, including clothing, food (milk tea), and funerals (cremation), in his memoir, *Beiyou lu* (ca. 1660; reprint, Beijing: Zhonghua shuju, 1960).

108. For instance, Manchus were extremely vulnerable to smallpox, as observers noted at the time (ibid., 355), lacking immunity to it or any of the techniques developed by Chinese for preventing it. Hong Taiji, for example,

forbade soldiers who had not had the disease from going on raids into north China that crossed into Mongolian territory, as Mongols were notorious carriers of the disease. See ECCP 898, "Yangguri"; Wakeman, *The Great Enterprise*, 465–66n124, on smallpox and "racial segregation" in Beijing; Du Jiaji, "Qingdai tianhuabing zhi liuchuan, fangzhi ji qi dui huangzu renkou zhi yingxiang chutan," in Li Zhongqing [James Lee] and Guo Songyi, eds., *Qing-dai huangzu renkou xingwei he shehui huanjing* (Beijing: Beijing University Press, 1994), 155.

109. Hosoya, "Manju gurun," 125. For this reason, Hosoya finds that after the proclamation of the "Latter Jin" in 1616, *Jušen gurun* ("Jurchen nation") was much more commonly used than *Aisin gurun* to describe Nur-haci's budding state to the outside world, while *Aisin gurun* ("Jin nation") was used to describe it to other Jurchens (*Aisin gurun* could also refer to the twelfth-century Jin). But as the citation above shows, it was not unheard of for Jurchens to speak of the "Jurchen nation" to other Jurchens.

110. Ishibashi, "Jušen shokō."

111. *Kyū Manshū tō*, 2, 318 (Tiancong 9.10.13); QNMDY 205. The same edict, translated from the Chinese (and therefore differently worded) is found in Rawski, *The Last Emperors*, 36. This was followed up ten days later by an injunction that "The name of the country [*gurun*] is called 'Manchu.' The dependent people over whom the banner chiefs have control are to be called the Jušen of those banner chiefs" (*Kyū Manshū tō*, 2, 324).

112. Thus, where in the *Jiu Manzhou dang* one finds "Jurchen," in the MBRT (the Qianlong redaction of these original archives) one often (but not always) finds "Manchu" instead.

113. See Okada Hidehiro, "The Mongolian Literary Tradition in Early Manchu Culture," in Ch'en Chieh-hsien, ed., *Proceedings of the 35th Permanent International Altaistic Conference* (Taipei: Center for Chinese Studies Materials and United Daily News Cultural Foundation, 1993), 380–85.

114. Hosoya, "Manju gurun," 127, citing the scholarship of Mitamura Taisuke and Kanda Nobuo. Roth-Li says that "Manchu" appears "sometime after 1628" ("The Early Manchu State," 10).

115. Hosoya, "Manju gurun," 126–27; Giovanni Stary observes that in the *Manbun rōtō* it appears seven times between 1607 and 1626, and seventy times between 1627 and 1636 (some, but not all, of these occurrences replicate the wording of the older *Jiu Manzhou dang*). The oldest mention (in a Korean source) is from 1605; its first appearance in the *Jiu Manzhou dang* is from 1613. See Stary, "The Meaning of the Word 'Manchu': A New Solution to an Old Problem," *Central Asiatic Journal* 34.1–2 (1990), 113; Kanda Nobuo, "Manzhou guohao kao," *Gugong wenxian* 3.1 (1971), 43–49.

116. Marianne Heiberg, *The Making of the Basque Nation* (Cambridge: Cambridge University Press, 1989), 60. The official etymology advanced by the Qing court in the first chapter of the *Manzhou yuanliu kao* is that *manju* came from the name of the Buddhist deity Manjusri, who was associated with the Qing khan, but this is certainly not true. See Agūi et al., eds., *Manzhou yuanliu kao* (1783; reprint, Shenyang: Liaoning minzu chubanshe, 1988), 2. In 1777, the Qianlong emperor supposedly offered another derivation, this one from the name of the ancient Sushen people. Both etymologies are collected in Chen, *Langqian jiwen chubi*, 5: 94–95. The first modern discussions of the problem are Erich Hauer, "Das Mandschurische Kaiserhaus, sein Name, seine Herkunft und sein Stammbaum," *Mitteilungen des Seminars Für Orientalische Sprachen (Ostasiatische Studien)* 29 (1926), 1–39, and Feng Jiasheng, "Manzhou mingcheng zhi zhongzhong tuice," *Dongfang zazhi* 30.17 (1 September 1933), 61–74. In a recent review of hypotheses on the source and meaning of "Manchu," Pei Huang concludes that "it is futile to try to find the origin and true meaning of the term" ("New Light on the Origins of the Manchus," 272–80). A possible etymology, endorsed by some linguists, may lie in Tungus names for the Amur River (*Heilongjiang/Sahaliyan ula*). Another etymology has the Tungus stem *man-* (strong, great) joined with the optative suffix *-ju* (may you be) (Stary, "The Meaning of the Word 'Manchu,'" 113–15). Rather less likely is the link between *manju* and the Mongolian *baatur* ("hero"). See Aisin-Gioro Ulasicun [Wu-la-xi-chun], "Cong yuyan lunzheng Nüzhen Manzhou zhi zucheng," in *Aixinjueluo shi sandai Manxue lunji* (Beijing: Yuanfang chubanshe, 1996), 381–88 (mentioned in Wilkinson, *Chinese History*, 701–2).

117. The use of ethnonyms as substantives (i.e., free-standing nouns connoting a Chinese, Mongol, Jurchen *person*) is ubiquitous. For some examples, see MBRT 1, Taizu 13, 191 (*nikan* and *monggo*); MBRT 1, Taizu 8, 135 (*solho*); *Kyū Manshū tō* 2, 251–59 (*manju*). As nouns, each also gained a plural form (*monggoso, nikasa, solhosa, manjusa*). Tribal names (Yehe, Ula) also could be substantives, but lost this ability after the tribe was incorporated into the Jin state. Its changed meaning after 1635 may explain why "Jušen," though it originally worked as a noun, has no plural. Ishibashi's objection, that "Manju" at this time could not have any ethnic meaning because it referred only to a *Manju gurun*, seems to beg the question. See Ishibashi Hideo, "Shinchō nyūkango Manju no koshō o megutte," in Ishibashi, ed., *Shindai Chūgoku no sho mondai* (Tokyo: Yamakawa shuppansha, 1996), 34.

118. "Da Qing" means "great pure" in Chinese, but the Manchu name *daicing* (from Mongolian *daicin*) means "warrior." *Daicing gurun*—literally, "warrior nation"—may well have been a pun understandable only to Manchu

and Mongol speakers, though to my knowledge no firm link between this word, common in personal names at the time, and the new name of the Manchu state was ever made. Stary also points to this meaning of *Daicing gurun* ("The Meaning of the Word 'Manchu'," 114). A Buddhist origin for *daicing* is offered in Samuel M. Grupper, "Manchu Patronage and Tibetan Buddhism During the First Half of the Ch'ing Dynasty," *Journal of the Tibet Society* 4 (1989), 68–71. Some of the conventional explanations for the choice of "Qing" (referring to five-agent theory) are found in Wilkinson, *Chinese History*, 892.

119. Hosoya, "Manju gurun," 127, makes much the same point.

120. MBRT 2, Taizu 45, 651 and Taizu 50, 734.

121. The same practice governed the inclusion of a small number of Koreans and Russians into the Manchu banners. See below.

122. This account relies on Zhang and Guo, *Qing ruguanqian*, 263–99.

123. Yao, "Manzu baqizhi," 111.

124. This excludes the Bayud Khalkha led to Nurhaci in 1606. Their prince, Enggeder, is the first to have addressed Nurhaci as khan, calling him "Respected Khan" (*kundulen han*).

125. The princes concerned were subordinated to the Manchu nobles at the head of the banner system, but they retained control over their forces (Zhang and Guo, *Qingdai ruguanqian*, 285–90; Yao, "Manzu baqizhi," 111).

126. See An Shuangcheng, "Shun-Kang-Yong sanchao baqi ding'e qianxi," *Lishi dang'an* (1983.2), 100–3. The figures for the Chakhar, Oirat, and other Mongol groups are found together with those for the Eight Banner Mongols, but are not aggregated.

127. This is persuasively argued by Yao Nianci on the basis of the flags used by these troops in battle. See Yao, "Manzu baqizhi," 113–14.

128. Wakeman describes "transfrontiersmen" as Han Chinese who had migrated to Jurchen territory and went through a process of acculturation, "taking Manchu names and adopting tribal customs [so] . . . that they eventually lost their identity as Chinese, seeming in manner dialect, custom, and physique to be more akin to the Manchus than to their former countrymen" (Wakeman, *The Great Enterprise*, 43–44).

129. Chao Ch'i-na [Zhao Qina], "Qingchu baqi hanjun yanjiu," *Gugong wenxian* 4.2 (March 1973), 59; Hosoya Yoshio, "The Han Chinese Generals Who Collaborated with Hou-Chin Kuo," *Acta Asiatica* 53 (1988), 39–61.

130. Zhang and Guo, *Qing ruguanqian*, 299; Spence, *Ts'ao Yin and the K'ang-hsi Emperor*, 1, 9.

131. Wakeman, *The Great Enterprise*, 61; Zhang and Guo, *Qing ruguanqian*, 299–300.

132. Zhang and Guo, *Qing ruguanqian*, 300, 311–12; Kanda Nobuo, "Shinsho no kangun bushō Seki Teishū ni tsuite," *Sundai shigaku* 66 (1986), 4–5.

133. Yao, "Manzu baqizhi," 68–72.

134. Zhang and Guo, *Qing ruguanqian*, 301. It is incorrect to view this as an early imitation of Manchu-style organization, however, since no companies were formed.

135. See Roth, "The Manchu-Chinese Relationship, 1618–1636."

136. MBRT 2, Taizu 33, 467.

137. The population of thirty thousand had been trapped inside the city walls for nearly three months. Less than twelve thousand survived. Wakeman, *The Great Enterprise*, 189.

138. Ura Ren'ichi, "Kangun (ujen cooha) ni tsuite," in *Kuwabara hakushi kanreki kinen tōyōshi ronsō* (Kyoto, 1931), 815. Even during the existence of the first Han troops, responsibility for cannon appears to have been theirs; the later name, "heavy troops," is certainly more elegant than the earlier label of "Chinese troops who carried the cannon" (*poo jafaha Nikan-i cooha*) (MBRT 2, Taizu 50, 734).

139. See Hosoya Yoshio, "Qingchao baqi zhidu de 'gūsa' he 'qi,'" *Manxue yanjiu* 2 (1994), 47–51. This flag was a dark blue-green (Ch *xuan qing*), a color outside the scheme used in the Eight Banners—further evidence that they were not yet part of the system.

140. Yao, "Manzu baqizhi," 112–14.

141. Ibid., 113.

142. Zheng Tianting, "Qingdai huangshi zhi shizhu yu xiexi," in *Tanweiji* (Beijing: Zhonghua shuju, 1980), 58.

143. This question has been extensively investigated by many historians. For a good summary, see Wakeman, *The Great Enterprise*, 1016–36. Note, however, that even under Hong Taiji Chinese bannermen were not completely trusted. Chao, "Qingchu baqi hanjun yanjiu," 60–61.

144. This is graphically shown in tables compiled by Narakino Shimesu, reproduced in Wakeman, *The Great Enterprise*, 1022–24 and 1029.

145. *Shengzu shilu*, 116: 13b–14a. On the Green Standard Army, a separate military force composed of ethnic Chinese soldiers, see the discussion at the end of Chapter 2.

146. Whenever these three branches of the Eight Banners are mentioned in Qing-period writings, this order (Manchu-Mongol-Chinese banner) is invariably observed.

147. The Upper Three Banners were the Plain Yellow, Bordered Yellow, and Plain White, including all three ethnic divisions of each banner. On this

point, see Du Jiaji, "Qingdai baqi lingshu wenti kaocha," *Minzu yanjiu* (1987.5), 83–92. The Plain Yellow Banner was the original banner of which Nurhaci was banner commander; when Hong Taiji became khan, he brought the Bordered Yellow Banner under his authority; the Plain White Banner was added when the Shunzhi emperor consolidated power after the fall of Dorgon, whose banner it had been. For a detailed account, see ECCP 218, "Dorgon"; Yao Nianci, "Huang Taiji dujia lianghuangqi kaobian," in Wang Zhonghan, ed., *Manxue Chaoxianxue lunji* (Beijing: Zhongguo chengshi chubanshe, 1995), 75–98.

148. The left wing was comprised of the Bordered Yellow, Plain White, Bordered White, and Plain Blue banners; the right wing was comprised of the Plain Yellow, Plain Red, Bordered Red, and Bordered Blue banners.

149. See the works by James Lee, Guo Songyi, Lai Huimin, and Evelyn Rawski in the bibliography; another useful work is Yang Xuechen and Zhou Yuanlian, *Qingdai baqi wanggong guizu xingshuai shi* (Shenyang: Liaoning renmin chubanshe, 1986). This definition of nobility specifically excludes the native Mongol nobility, as well as those awarded honorary or posthumous titles in recognition of their service to the dynasty. Though sometimes inheritable (even if for only one generation), such ranks were fundamentally separate from those awarded to members of the imperial lineage, who were subject to the authority of the Imperial Clan Court (see below). One might thus think of someone like Li Hongzhang, awarded the hereditary title of "duke" (Ch *gong*), as a "peer," but not a noble.

150. Zhang and Guo, *Qing ruguanqian*, 446–47; Guo Songyi, "Qing zongshi de dengji jiegou ji jingji diwei," in Li and Guo, eds., *Qingdai huangzu renkou*, 116. The formal constitution of the lineage took place in 1635.

151. Lai Huimin, "Qingdai huangzu de fengjue yu renguan yanjiu," in Li and Guo, eds., *Qingdai huangzu renkou*, 135.

152. For specifics, see Guo, "Qing zongshi de dengji jiegou," table 1, 117; Lai, "Qingdai huangzu de fengjue," table 1, 135, and table 2, 137; also Brunnert and Hagelstrom, *Present-Day Political Organization of China*, trans. A. Beltchenko and E. E. Moran (Shanghai: Kelly and Walsh, 1911), entries 16 through 50, whose terms I adopt.

153. Guo, "Qingdai huangzu de dengji," 121.

154. Lai, "Qingdai huangzu de fengjue," 150. Lai estimates that only about 5 percent of nobles advanced to office via the examination route.

155. See Appendix B for a chart of these positions and their Chinese and Manchu names.

156. Manchu *boo* means "house" or "household," and *i* is a genitive particle.

157. The correctness of the definition found in Hauer, *Handwörterbuch der Mandschusprache* (and, following him, of Norman, *A Manchu-English Lexicon*) can be seen from such expressions as "booi mulu-i ton be bodome," (counting the number of ridgepoles in a house), and "harangga gūsai baci benjihe alban-i booi turigen-i menggun be gaire dangse be kimcime baicaci" (investigating the records of silver collected in public housing rent from the said banner) (YZMaZPZZ 239, Boošan, YZ12.10.5). Even when *booi* describes people, it is not always clear if the person referred to is a bond-servant or not. From the command, "jai Cangšeo be tob cin wang de. afabufi. booi aisilakū hafan de baitala" (also, let Cangšeo be given to the Zhuang prince and employed as *booi* assistant department director [an office in the Imperial Household Department]) (YZMaZPZZ 4, Bootai, YZ1.9.23), it would appear that Cangšeo is a bondservant; but in the phrase, "bi Lan Jeo de tehede. mini booi niyalma Namjal. ging hecen ci minde etuku benjire" ("when I lived in Lanzhou, a person from my household, Namjal, delivered my clothing from the capital") (YZMaZPZZ 97, Nian Gengyao, YZ3.3.24), it is impossible to say from the context whether Namjal is a *bao-yi*, i.e., a person enrolled in a bondservant company, or just a household servant or attendant. Similarly, from the following, it is hard to know if a bondservant is being referred to or, more likely, a household slave: "kubuhe lamun-i Manju gūsai. Futai nirui ilhi funde bošokū Cartai. emu nirui gocika bayara Surtai sebe. niyalmai booi aha seme habšaha emu baita be. wesimbuhede" ("when Cartai, a sub-lieutenant of Futai company of the Bordered Blue Manchu banner memorialized regarding the matter of a personal household slave [?] who accused the imperial bodyguard Surtai and others") (YZMaZPZZ 262, Dalhasu, YZ13.4.6). See Mark C. Elliott, "Vocabulary Notes from the Manchu Archives 2: On the *Booi*," *Saksaha* 3 (1998), 18–21.

158. See the examples in a brief discussion of this problem by Ishibashi Takao, "Booi in the Ch'ing Dynasty," *Bulletin of the Institute of China Border Area Studies* 18 (October 1987), 197–208. The distinction is also made in Li and Guan, *Manzu tongshi*, 398–406.

159. Note the similarity between *zhengshen* and the term for regular Yuan military households, called *zhengjunhu*. See Ch'i-ch'ing Hsiao, *The Military Establishment of the Yuan Dynasty* (Cambridge: Harvard Council on East Asian Studies, 1978), 19.

160. An accurate, if brief, account is in Spence, *Ts'ao Yin*, 7–9. For more detail, see Mo Dongyin, "Baqi zhidu," in *Manzushi luncong*, 136–48; Zheng Tianting, "Qingdai baoyi zhidu yu huangguan," in *Tanweiji*, 88–109.

161. The bondservant companies of the princely households fell in between, being neither "inner" nor "outer."

162. Spence, *Ts'ao Yin*, 1966.

163. "Most of the bondservants who later served the Manchus were members of Chinese families captured at Fushun and Shenyang" (Wakeman, *The Great Enterprise*, 70n126, citing Preston Torbert, *The Ch'ing Imperial Household Department: A Study of Its Organization and Principal Functions* [Cambridge: Harvard University Press, 1976]). "This institution [i.e., the Imperial Household Department] was staffed by men from bondservant companies that had been formed of Han Chinese captured by the Manchus in the Liao River basin of Manchuria before 1644" (Naquin and Rawski, *Chinese Society in the Eighteenth Century*, 7). More accurately, Charles Hucker writes of the Imperial Household Department that it was "staffed almost entirely by Imperial Bondservants, overwhelmingly Manchu" (*A Dictionary of Official Titles in Imperial China* [Stanford, Calif.: Stanford University Press, 1985], 4291).

164. The starting point for research on the bondservant companies are the pertinent sections of the BQTZ (*juan* 1–17) describing banner composition (Ch *qifenzhi*). Thus in the description of the bondservant companies attached to the Bordered Yellow Banner, we find five Manchu companies (*Manzhou zuoling/Manju niru*), ten half-companies (*guanling/hontoho*) and six "standard-bearer and drummer" companies (BQTZ 3, 41–45). The latter two were found only in the bondservant organization. See the following note.

165. The Qianlong-period dictionary *Yuzhi zengding Qingwen jian* defined the *qigu* as the companies into which bondservant Chinese were formed ("booi Nikasa be niru banjibuhangge be cigu niru sembi"), confirming Jonathan Spence's note that "the phrase *ch'i-ku* in fact seems to have been coterminous with the Chinese nationality of the officeholders, for a check through the names of the *ch'i-ku* captains shows that nearly every one has an ordinary Chinese name, whereas nearly all the *pao-i tso-ling* have Manchu names" (*Ts'ao Yin*, 35 and n158). The distinction between *qigu* and other bondservant companies appears to have remained strong in the middle eighteenth century. A banner guardsman (and imperial clan member) who had elevated a member of a *qigu* company into a regular Manchu bondservant company under his control was roundly castigated for having done so by the emperor (*Gaozong shilu*, 145: 6b–7a).

166. There was originally only one Korean bondservant company (identified as *Gao-li bao-yi*), but it was split into two in 1695. These were in the Manchu Plain Yellow Banner (BQTZ 4, 66). The other Korean companies, in the Manchu Plain Yellow and Plain Red Banners, were made up of people (identified as *Chaoxian laigui rending*) who had voluntarily joined the Manchus (BQTZ 4, 58; 6, 93; see also BQMST 73). On the Russian company, see below.

167. *Fusi* incorporates a contemporary error in rendering the place name "Fushun."

168. BQMST 79–80. Even though listed here, they remained identifiable as Chinese.

169. Manchu companies rose from 278 to 678, Mongol companies from 120 to 207, and Chinese banner companies from 165 to 270 (Fang, "A Technique," 208–9).

170. BQTZ 3, 38, listing for the Seventeenth Company, Fourth Regiment. This company probably did not exceed one hundred people altogether in original size.

171. See Tatiana Pang, "Russian and Manchu Sources on Russian-Chinese Relations" (paper delivered at the International Symposium on Non-Chinese Sources for Late Imperial Chinese History, Santa Barbara, California, March 1998).

172. Robert H. G. Lee, *The Manchurian Frontier in Ch'ing History* (Cambridge: Harvard University Press, 1970), 34–35.

173. Before 1644, "New Manchus" (*xin Manzhou/ice Manju*) referred to those brought into the Jurchen confederation after Nurhaci's death. Its meaning changed after the conquest, when it applied to those being put into banners in the Shunzhi reign and later; at this point, Manchus who were already in companies became effectively known as "Old Manchus" (*jiu Manzhou/fe Manju*).

174. *Xibozu dang'an shiliao* (First Historical Archives, Shenyang: Liaoning minzu chubanshe, 1989), 1: 30–32. This transfer did not mean the incorporation of Sibe and Daur companies into Manchu Banners, only that they came under the direct control of the emperor. They are not listed in BQTZ.

175. The Sibe and Solon, in particular, distinguished themselves in the Xinjiang campaigns of the eighteenth century. To consolidate that frontier when the fighting was over, several thousand were sent with their families to take up permanent garrison duties. They remain there to this day. The forty thousand or so Sibe (Ch *Xibo zu*)—who never did (and still don't) consider themselves or their language to be Manchu—constitute the last substantial Manchu-speaking population in the world today.

176. In a careful study of the problem of the ethnic composition of the different wings of the banner structure, Fu Kedong and Chen Jiahua concluded that in the Manchu banners were a total of 446 Mongols and 883 Chinese; all but 71 of the Chinese were bondservants. My own check of *juan* 74–80 of *Baqi Manzhou shizu tongpu* shows that all of these 71 were long-time residents in the Northeast, and that 63 were enrolled in separately created companies, *not* Manchu companies. In the Mongol banners there were 13

Manchus and no Chinese. In the Chinese banners were 17 Manchus and an unknown number of captured Mongols. See Fu Kedong and Chen Jiahua, "Baqi zhiduzhong de Man-Meng-Han guanxi," *Minzu yanjiu* 1980.6, 30–32.

177. Zheng, "Qingdai huangshi," 51.

178. For examples of regular Manchu companies formed on the basis of bondservant companies, see BQTZ 3, 28 (First Company, Second Regiment, Bordered Yellow Banner); 4, 55 (Fourteenth Company, Third Regiment, Plain Yellow Banner).

179. For instance, in 1741, Laiboo [Lai-bao], a Manchu who belonged to a bondservant company in the Imperial Household Department, was elevated to regular status in the Plain White Banner. The wording of the edict (*teming*, "by special order") made it clear that this was a special favor. Laiboo later went on to become a grand councillor (*Gaozong shilu*, 135: 11a; [*Qinding*] *Baqi tongzhi*, 161: 11b–18a). On *taiqi* generally, see Wang, "Manzu baqi-zhong," 63.

180. See Zheng, "Qingdai huangshi," 58; *Shengzu shilu*, 135: 2a–b. As Pamela Crossley has shown, the Tong claim was false; indeed, it was not even consistent with known history at the time. See "The Tong in Two Worlds: Cultural Identities in Liaodong and Nurgan During the 13th–17th centuries," *Ch'ing-shih wen-t'i* 4.9 (June 1983), 21–46.

181. BQMST 20: 1a–2b; BQTZ 15: 278–79; 16: 282–87; and 83: 1721–22. This case is altogether odd. According to the *Comprehensive History of the Eight Banners*, the reason that the Tong lineage was left in the Chinese banners was because it would too drastically alter the proportion of people in the Chinese banners if eight thousand people were suddenly re-registered elsewhere. Instead, they were simply entered as "Manchus" in the Chinese banner registers (BQTZ 143: 3726–27). I have been unable to trace the original company in *either* the Manchu or Chinese Bordered Yellow Banner listings in the *Comprehensive History*, but a 1738 entry in the *Veritable Records* makes it clear that Tong Guogang's company was indeed moved to the Manchu banners (*Gaozong shilu*, 81: 21a).

182. Zheng, "Qingdai huangshi," 58.

183. Crossley, "The Tong in Two Worlds," 41.

184. Cf. Eriksen: "It is true that ethnicity is a social creation and not a fact of nature, and ethnic variation does not correspond to cultural variation. But ethnic identities must seem convincing to their members in order to function—and they must also be acknowledged as legitimate by non-members of the group" (*Ethnicity and Nationalism*, 69). This touches on the general issue of "passing," discussed in Chapter 8, which often hinges on extremely subtle distinctions.

*Chapter 2. Manchu Cities: Tigers on the Mountain*

1. Thomas Taylor Meadows, *The Chinese and Their Rebellions* (London, 1856; reprint, Stanford, Calif.: Academic Reprints, n.d.), 31.

2. Ma Xiedi, "Qingdai Mancheng kao," *Manzu yanjiu* 1990.1, 33. Interestingly, however, the destruction of the walls did not mean the immediate end of these communities. For instance, Manchus at the Taiyuan garrison remained living in the Manchu city until 1928, when they were chased out by the warlord Feng Yuxiang. See Hosoya Yoshio and Wang Yulang, "Kaifū hakki chūbō no kōei—shingai kakumeigo no kijin seikatsu no hitokoma," *Tōhō* 143 (February 1993), 8–9. Even today, descendants of Qing bannermen remain in many former garrison cities and have managed to hold on to their identities through the turmoil of the last several decades. In some locations there have now formed local Manchu associations such as the *Manzu tongbao lianyi hui* in Fuzhou, Canton, and many cities in the Northeast, not to mention, of course, Beijing. On Canton's Manchus see Ma, "Guangzhou Manzu fangwen ji," *Manzu yanjiu* (1988.2), 36–41. In 1990 a newspaper, the *Manchu Gazette* (*Manzu bao/Manju uksura serkin*), was being published with news from around the nation (including Taiwan and Hongkong) on Manchu affairs. See *Manzu shehui lishi diaocha* (Shenyang: Liaoning renmin chubanshe, 1985) for an incomplete survey of the fate of these populations in the twentieth century; also Crossley, *Orphan Warriors*, 218–20.

3. Angela Zito and Tani E. Barlow, introduction to *Body, Subject, and Power in China* (Chicago: University of Chicago Press, 1994), 4.

4. Yann Le Bohec, *The Imperial Roman Army* (New York: Hippocrene Books, 1995), 20–25, 155–63; Thomas S. Burns, *Barbarians Within the Gates of Rome* (Bloomington: Indiana University Press, 1994), 118–29. After the second century C.E., the main frontiers were those with German tribes in the north and with Persia in the east.

5. Mark C. Batusis, *The Late Byzantine Army* (Philadelphia: University of Pennsylvania Press, 1992), 286–302.

6. In *The Normans in Britain* (Oxford: Blackwell, 1995), David Walker notes, "Castles were essential to Norman success and at times to their survival" (14); see also R. H. C. Davis, *The Normans and Their Myth* (London: Thames and Hudson, 1976), 110–11; and D. J. A. Matthew, *The Norman Conquest* (New York: Schocken Books, 1966), 137–40.

7. See the discussion in Waldron, *The Great Wall of China*, 42.

8. Charles O. Hucker, *The Ming Dynasty: Its Origins and Evolving Institutions* (Ann Arbor: The University of Michigan Press, 1978), 64–65.

Scholars still debate whether, following earlier arguments of Franz Michael, the *wei-suo* were not a model for the Qing banner system.

9. Permanent garrisons in northern China had been founded fifty years earlier (Hsiao, *The Military Establishment of the Yuan Dynasty*, 53). The following account relies on Hsiao's description of the Yuan garrison system.

10. Marco Polo, *The Travels*, trans. Ronald Latham (Harmondsworth, England: Penguin, 1958), 219–20. He claims that there were "huge forces of infantry and cavalry in the city and its environs" and cites a figure of thirty thousand soldiers for the garrison (221, 223).

11. This point was first made by Abe Takeo, "Hakki Manshū niru no kenkyū," *Tōhō gakuhō* 20 (March 1951); see also Ishibashi Hideo, "Shinsho no shakai—sono jōkyū mondai o megutte," in *Orui Noboru hakushi kijū kinen shigaku ronbunshū* (Tokyo: Yamakawa shuppansha, 1962), 247–62. Ding convincingly reiterates this point; for much of this account of the pre-conquest garrison system, I have relied on her excellent study, *Qingdai baqi zhufang zhidu yanjiu* (Tianjin: Tianjin guji chubanshe, 1992), 11–16.

12. On early Qing ruins see Toda Shigeki, "Kakuto ara jō kōsei no sobyō," in *Yamashita sensei kanreki kinen tōyōshi ronbunshū* (Tokyo: 1938), 655–95, esp. 678–80. Photographs of many early sites, along with a useful bibliography, is found in Giovanni Stary et al., *On the Tracks of Manchu Culture* (Wiesbaden: Otto Harrassowitz, 1995), 1–15. See also Naitō Torajirō, *Zōho Manshū shashinchō* (Kyoto: Kobayashi shashin seibansho, 1935).

13. Wakeman, *The Great Enterprise*, 170.

14. MBRT 1, Taizu 48, 54. In the first reference, Nurhaci affirms his determination to resist should the Ming attack, declaring that the Jurchen will "defend their land and erect gates at the frontier." Both types of garrisons appear as early as 1615.

15. MBRT 1, Taizu 18, 279.

16. Ding, *Qingdai baqi zhufang*, 13, citing MBRT 2, Taizu 41, 602–4. The term used here, *bargiyambi*, "to protect," differs slightly from the later word used for garrisons, *seremšembi*, "to defend."

17. The alternative romanization of "Chinchou" is used here to distinguish this city (written with the character for "gold") from the other, "Jinzhou," mentioned above (written with the character for brocade), located further to the north.

18. Sun, Li, and Qiu, *Ming-Qing zhanzheng shilue*, 24–55.

19. Ding, *Qingdai baqi zhufang*, 14.

20. Ibid., citing *Tiancongchao chengong zouyi*, "Ding Wensheng deng qing chengshou Lüshun zou"; "Ding Wensheng," in *Qingdai renwu zhuangao*, ser. 1, 3: 162–66.

21. Roth, "The Manchu-Chinese Relationship," 14.

22. Many contemporary maps of garrison cities clearly show the placement of the Manchu city. Vid. *Xi'an fuzhi* (1779), 6: 2b–3a, 4b–5a, and 74b–75a; *Sichuan tongzhi* (1736), 1: 13b–14a; *Jingzhou zhufang baqi zhi* (1879), *shou*, n.p.; *Dantuxian zhi* (1877), *shou*: 6b–7a. Some of these are reproduced below. Ding (*Qingdai baqi zhufang*, 163) distinguishes between *Man-ying*, banner "encampments" within a city's walls, and *Man-cheng*, separate banner towns such as were built at Qingzhou and Suiyuan. If such a distinction did exist, these terms were conflated no later than 1739, when *Man-cheng* described both arrangements (BQTZ 24). The usual Manchu term was simply *Manju hoton*, also meaning "Manchu city" (e.g., YZMaZPZZ *bao* 210, 240, 509, 511, 530, 1068, 1114). The use of *kūwaran* ("encampment") was rare; one example reads, "hoton-i dorgi Manjusa tehe kūwaran," "the encampment inside the city occupied by Manchus" (YZMaZPZZ *bao* 190). I have also come upon one instance of a garrison referred to as the "banner village" (Ma *gūsai falga*) (QLMaZPZZ 304, Tukšan, QL24.5.13). The non-occupied part of a garrison city was called either *Nikan hoton*, "Chinese city," or *irgen hoton*, "civilian city" (YZMaZPZZ *bao* 210, 240, 1068). The use of the word *hoton* in these expressions presumably refers to the existence of walls dividing the different quarters.

23. More detailed histories of the garrisons may be found in Kaye Soon Im, "The Rise and Decline of the Eight Banner Garrisons in the Ch'ing Period (1644–1911): A Study of the Kuang-chou, Hang-chou, and Ching-chou Garrisons," Ph.D. diss., University of Illinois, 1981; Ding, *Qingdai baqi zhufang*, 18–90; and Elliott, "Resident Aliens," 49–116.

24. Though there were imperial Manchu residents (Ma *amban*) in Lhasa after 1727, there were no Eight Banner garrisons there or anywhere in Tibet proper (Böd). The permanent garrison at Lhasa (established in 1728 and moved to the suburbs of the city in 1733) was made up of soldiers from the Green Standard Army, mostly Sichuanese, who served in three-year rotations. See Luciano Petech, *China and Tibet in the Early Eighteenth Century*, 2nd ed. (Leiden: E. J. Brill, 1972), 257.

25. Zhao Yuntian, *Qingdai Menggu zhengjiao zhidu* (Beijing: Zhonghua shuju, 1989), 105.

26. The garrisons that formed the "Great Wall chain" are understood to have been on the northern periphery of China proper.

27. The notion of five chains was proposed by Mo Dongyin (*Manzushi luncong*, 113). His formulation, however, omitted several garrisons, a flaw which I have endeavored to remedy by changing his "Southeast Coast" to cover the entire coast and by adding some locations, such as Zhuanglang, into

the chains to which they clearly belong (e.g., the Great Wall). It is understood that the Great Wall was, of course, not a natural boundary per se. A very similar model to the one described here (discovered in the course of revising this manuscript) is presented in Numata Tomoo et al., eds., *Iminzoku no Shina tōchi shi* (Tokyo: Kodansha, 1944), 241–42. See also Lin Enxian, *Qingchao zai Xinjiang de Han-Hui geli zhengce* (Taipei: Taiwan Commercial Press, 1988), 152, where the same model is discussed. Ding offers another model, which puts Beijing as the central node of a north-south and east-west axis (*Qingdai baqi zhufang*, 88).

28. A detailed description of the nonprovincial garrison networks is found in Elliott, "Resident Aliens," 49–73. See also Ding, *Qingdai baqi zhufang*, 58–85.

29. This is the figure reported for the Xi'an garrison in early 1737, exceeding the official figure for this time by fourteen hundred men (QLMaZPZZ 69, Cimbu, QL2.12.17).

30. The garrison general is the official frequently referred to in English otherwise as "Tartar General." To avoid some of the confusion regarding Eight Banner hierarchy found in such standard references such as Brunnert and Hagelstrom's *Present-Day Political Organization of China* (hereafter B&H) and Charles O. Hucker's *A Dictionary of Official Titles in Imperial China* (hereafter Hucker), I introduce some new English terminology here for this and a number of other positions. The main differences are the following: for *jiangjun*, "Manchu General-in-Chief or Tartar General" (B&H 744), I prefer "garrison general"; for *fudutong*, "Manchu Brigade-General" (B&H 745; Hucker 2107), I prefer "garrison lieutenant general"; for *dutong*, "lieutenant general" (B&H 719; Hucker 7321.3), I prefer "banner commander"; for *fudutong*, "deputy lieutenant-general" (B&H 720; Hucker 2107) I prefer "deputy banner commander." A chart of ranks in the Eight Banners, the banner vanguard, and the banner garrisons with their Chinese, Manchu, and English names is provided in Appendix B.

31. See the appropriate sections of the *Collected Institutes of the Qing* (*Da Qing huidian*) and the *Comprehensive History of the Eight Banners* (*Baqi tongzhi*).

32. A detailed description of the development of the entire system may be found in Elliott, "Resident Aliens," 49–73. See also Ding, *Qingdai baqi zhufang*, 18–90.

33. In 1757 an estimated ninety-five thousand banner soldiers, most of them in the Manchu banners, lived in the provincial garrisons. See Ding, *Qingdai baqi zhufang*, 179n2, citing First Historical Archives, *Manwen yuezhe dang*, Fuheng, QL22.8.26.

34. Matteo Ripa, *Memoirs of Father Ripa*, trans. Fortunato Prandi (London: John Murray, 1844), 51–52.

35. Wakeman, *The Great Enterprise*, 476.

36. The following account relies on Roth, "Manchu-Chinese Relationship," 16–25.

37. Roth-Li, "The Early Manchu State," 66, 76–77. This problem is also discussed in Kitamura Hironao, "Shinchō ni okeru seiji to shakai (1)—nyūkan mae ni okeru hakki no kanjin mondai," *Tōyōshi kenkyū* 10.4 (January 1949), 60–69; and Ishibashi Hideo, "Shinsho no tai kanjin seisaku—toku ni Taiso no Ryōtō shinshutsu jidai o chūshin toshite," *Shisō* 2 (October 1961), 1–17.

38. Roth, "Manchu-Chinese Relationship," 18; MBRT 2, Taizu 2, 819.

39. MBRT 3, Taizu 73, 1094.

40. Roth, "Manchu-Chinese Relationship," 25; Im, "Rise and Decline," 15; Wakeman, *The Great Enterprise*, 480; Ma Xiedi, "Qingdai Mancheng kao," 30.

41. *Shizu shilu*, 12: 3a; DHL 1: 31a.

42. Ibid.: 12b–13b; DHL 1: 32a; DQHDSL 1117: 3a–b. Of course, it did not prevent conflicts at all. In fact, the area around Beijing was notorious for bad relations between bannermen (and those who worked for them) and the local Han population. See below.

43. *Shizu shilu*, 5: 15a–b; DHL 1: 13a.

44. Ibid., 40: 9a–10a; DHL 3: 8b–9a. For those who chose to sell their houses, the going price was four taels (1 tael = 1.3 oz. of silver) per bay (Ch *jian*).

45. Wakeman, *The Great Enterprise*, 478.

46. *Shizu shilu*, 40: 9a–b. Couching controversial policies in positive terms was a tactic the court would employ again thirteen years later when it ordered the evacuation of coastal villages and a ban on coastal trade in the south and southeast in a successful effort to weaken the Zheng Chenggong resistance movement, a strategy that has gone down as another infamous example of Manchu disregard for the welfare of ordinary Han Chinese (*Shengzu shilu*, 4: 10a). See Xie Guozhen, *Mingqing zhi ji dangshe yundong kao* (Beijing: Zhonghua shuju, 1982), 237; see also Zhu Delan, "Qingchu qianjielingshi Zhongguo chuan haishang maoyi zhi yanjiu," in *Zhongguo haiyang fazhan shi* (Taipei: Academia Sinica, 1986), 2: 105–60.

47. Mantarō Hashimoto, "The Altaicization of Northern Chinese," in J. McCoy and T. Light, eds., *Contributions to Sino-Tibetan Studies* (Leiden: E. J. Brill, 1986); see also the views of Okada Hidehiro, who argues that "the Mandarin dialect of Beijing in Qing times . . . was a strongly Altaicized form

of Chinese" ("Mandarin, a Language of the Manchus: How Altaic?" *Aetas Manjurica* 3 (1992), 165–87.

48. On Peking opera, see Chapter 7. On *zidishu*, see Guan Dedong and Zhou Zhongming, *Zidishu congchao* (Shanghai: Shanghai guji chubanshe, 1984); and Stephen Wadley, "The Mixed-Language Verses from the Manchu Dynasty in China," Indiana University Research Institute for Inner Asian Studies, *Papers on Inner Asia* 16 (1991), 60–112.

49. However, the new division of the city was strongly influenced by the old neighborhoods, whose boundaries guided the delineation of banner quarters. See the maps and commentary in Hou Renzhi, *Beijing lishi dituji* (Beijing: Beijing chubanshe, 1985), 31–32 and 41–42.

50. BQTZ 2: 17–22, 26; DQHDSL 1112: 1a–3a; Yu Minzhong, ed., *Rixia jiuwen kao* (1788; reprint, Beijing: Beijing guji chubanshe, 1958), 72: 1208; Alison Dray-Novey, "Spatial Order and Police in Imperial Beijing," *Journal of Asian Studies* 52.4 (November 1993), 905–7. Note that the arrangement of the Eight Banners around Mukden was different. See Li Fengmin, *Shengjing baqi fangwei zhi mi* (Shenyang: Dongbei daxue chubanshe, 1998).

51. The pretext for this change was that because flags were used for practical military ends, black was undesirable since it could not be seen at night (BQTZ 2: 17a). The correspondence between colors, directions, and agents seems to have changed since their early codification in the Han dynasty; the arrangement shown here was that current in the Qing, as best as I can determine. Comparing this arrangement with the preconquest array of troops around Liaoyang (see above), it is clear that *wu-xing* principles were not obeyed in the 1620s.

52. The official explanation was that this agent had already been "exhausted" during the dynasty's eastern expansion, but that the "unification of the four seas" permitted nonbanner Chinese soldiers, conveniently enrolled under a green standard, to stand in. See BQTZ 2: 17; cf. also Wu Changyuan, *Chenyuan shilue* (1788; reprint, Beijing: Beijing guji chubanshe, 1981), 1: 20.

53. Politics, too, may have played a part, since the emperor's own Yellow Banners were granted the right to occupy many of the most desirable locations in the northern part of the city around Shisha hai.

54. BQTZ 2: 17; cf. also Yu, *Rixia jiuwen kao*, 37: 578.

55. BQTZ 2: 17. The precise locations for each regiment of each banner were spelled out in 1725. See DQHDSL 1112: 3a–12b.

56. J. L. Cranmer-Byng, *An Embassy to China: Being the Journal Kept by Lord Macartney During His Embassy to the Emperor Ch'ien-lung, 1793–94* (Hamden, Conn.: Archon Books, 1963), 158. Similar remarks are made by Staunton (who accompanied Macartney), except that they are found in his

description of Guangzhou: "At the end of each street is a barrier, which is shut every evening soon after the gates of the city; so that everybody is obliged to be at home by the time it grows dark. This regulation prevents many disorders in China, where the greatest cities are as quiet in the nighttime as if they consisted but of single families." George Staunton, *An Historical Account of the Embassy to the Emperor of China* (London, 1797), 449.

57. See Dray-Novey, "Spatial Order and Police," 894. My guess is that the word cited by Dray-Novey for sentry box, *duibo*, is a hybrid word that combines an element from the Chinese term *duizi* (or *zuodui*) and the Manchu name, *jucei boo*. See below.

58. Apart from Guangzhou and Fuzhou, garrison *duizi* are mentioned also for Qingzhou, Zhapu, Tianjin, and Suiyuan (BQTZ, 24: 460, 464, 465, 463, 447). Ma's interpretation of Guangzhou's *zuodui* as markers between the banner and nonbanner sections of the city (Ma, "Qingdai Mancheng kao," 30) is open to question, as the Manchu version of BQTZ explicitly calls them *jucei boo*, "guardhouses."

59. YZMaZPZZ 190, Fusen, YZ7.11.20.

60. The Kangxi emperor was quartered at the yamen of the Jiangning garrison general during the first Southern Tour in 1684 (Spence, *Ts'ao Yin*, 128) and with the Xi'an garrison general during his visit to the city in the Western Tour of 1703. *Shaanxi tongzhi* (1735), 14: 1a–b.

61. QNMDY 2: 92 (SZ2.6.20); using the best estimate of the number of companies at this time (579) and multiplying by three gives a force of approximately eighteen hundred men, including officers. On the number of companies, see Fang Chaoying, "A Technique," 192–215.

62. More details may be found Elliott, "Resident Aliens," 74–76; also Ding, *Qingdai baqi zhufang*, 27. Ding estimates the original size of the Xi'an garrison at one thousand.

63. Although it was formally renamed Jiangning ("tranquil river"; "Giyangning" in Manchu), the city was still commonly referred to as Nanjing ("southern capital") during the Qing (Wakeman, *The Great Enterprise*, 592n).

64. QNMDY 2: 189 (SZ2.11.7).

65. *Shizu shilu*, 24: 3a–b.

66. Wakeman, *The Great Enterprise*, 739–40; Elliott, "Resident Aliens," 77–81. Anticipating the loyalist threat, Manchu and Chinese banner troops stationed in temporary garrisons in Shandong and Henan provinces had been transferred to Nanjing in mid-1646, increasing the number of soldiers there to four thousand. Temporary housing for many was found in the northern and eastern parts of the city—one guesses without too much trouble, as 90 percent of houses were vacant. Pasture was more of a problem, however, and before

long, all the fields within sixty *li* of Nanjing had been decimated by the grazing herds of banner horses (Wakeman, *The Great Enterprise*, 591–92).

67. Elliott, "Resident Aliens," 82–84.

68. Taiyuan, initially a refuge for forces loyal to Li Zicheng, was stormed and taken by Qing armies in November 1644. The year 1649 twice saw Taiyuan gravely threatened by large rebel armies; in both instances Manchu troops saved the day for the Qing (Wakeman, *The Great Enterprise*, 805–15). A small force of Mongol bannermen appears to have been placed at Taiyuan early in 1649, with a regular garrison in place after the final defeat of the rebel armies in June of that year. This force, composed of Manchu, Mongol, and Chakhar bannermen, was one of the smallest of Eight Banner provincial garrisons, with fewer than nine hundred soldiers when it was founded in 1649, and later stabilizing at five hundred men (QSLZ 78, "Zhu Shichang"; *Shizu shilu*, 45: 10a; HWT 184: 6455).

69. Dezhou was one of the 1645 foundings consolidated into the Jiangning garrison in 1646. Perhaps because of its key location on the Grand Canal at the border of Shandong and Zhili, a garrison of about five hundred soldiers was refounded here in 1654.

70. The 1654 foundation of Jingkou is described in Elliott, "Bannerman and Townsman." As Ding notes, the garrisons at Fuzhou and Guangzhou also absorbed Chinese soldiers from the armies of Geng Jingzhong and Shang Zhixin, two of the defeated generals in the Rebellion of the Three Feudatories. These men were kept in separate companies from the "regular" Chinese banners, however, and received discriminatory treatment for at least a generation (Ding, *Qingdai baqi zhufang*, 34–36). A complete list of founding dates for provincial garrisons is found in Appendix C.

71. Zhapu was the naval extension of the Hangzhou garrison. See Crossley, *Orphan Warriors*, 69–70.

72. Ding, *Qingdai baqi zhufang*, 45.

73. BQTZ 24: 456–57; calculated at 1 *bu* = 1.536 meters. These figures would appear to accord with the map of the Manchu city in *Shaanxi tongzhi*, 6: 2b–3a. This and the following calculations are based on the figures given for total walled city areas in the table in Sen-dou Chang, "The Morphology of Walled Capitals," in G. William Skinner, ed., *The City in Late Imperial China* (Stanford, Calif.: Stanford University Press, 1977), 91.

74. BQTZ 24: 460; calculated at 1 *zhang* = 3.08 meters, and assuming (from maps of the Nanjing garrison) a roughly square shape. Nanjing's total walled area was 15.66 square miles, or 10,019 acres (4,055 ha). One possible explanation of the large size of the Nanjing Manchu city was that the looms of the imperial manufactory were located here (Spence, *Ts'ao Yin*, 90).

75. Ma, "Qingdai Mancheng kao," 30. See the maps in Im, "Rise and Decline", 164 and Frederick W. Mote, "The Transformation of Nanking, 1350–1400," in Skinner, *The City in Late Imperial China*, 135, 140.

76. Crossley, *Orphan Warriors*, 63.

77. Estimations of the size of the Hangzhou Manchu city vary. Crossley says it was 240 acres in size, with walls two miles in circumference (*Orphan Warriors*, 65), while Im, citing the *Hangzhou baqi zhufangying zhilue* (1894), says that the garrison was "roughly rectangular," and had walls approximately eight miles in length ("Rise and Decline," 16). Assuming the largest possible rectangular shape (a square), Crossley's estimate of the length of the walls would mean sides of one-half mile by one-half mile. Such a shape would yield a maximum actual area of one-quarter square mile or about 160 acres (65 ha), equal to 5 percent of the total 4.94 square miles (1,280 ha) within Hangzhou's walls, a proportion that must be regarded as too low, though it is close to the area given in BQTZ (124: 463) of 1,104 *mu* (182 acres). On the other hand, converting Im's eight miles of walls to its area equivalent would mean that 3.43 square miles, or 70 percent of walled Hangzhou was taken up by the Manchu garrison, making this estimate also impossible to accept. I have chosen to use Im's figures, but am assuming that by "miles" she means *li*. The result is an area for the garrison of about .65 square miles (419 acres), equal to a plausible 13.25 percent of the area within the walls of Hangzhou.

78. BQTZ 24: 465 says the walls were six *li* around; Ma claims it was four *li* (Ma, "Qingdai Mancheng kao," 31). Using Ma's dimensions the compound would have been a maximum .12 square miles in size. I have opted for the larger figure, with a resulting area of .27 square miles, 5.5 percent of the walled city. In terms of its walled area, Kaifeng was the fourth largest provincial capital of the empire.

79. BQTZ 24: 456. The dimensions of the garrison compound are clearly specified here: 260 *zhang* (.58 miles) on the north and south, 161.7 *zhang* (.36 miles) on the east and west. This corresponds to an area of 133 acres, just smaller than the Mall in Washington, D.C. (146 acres).

80. BQTZ 24: 459; *Sichuan tongzhi* (1736), 4: 1a–2b. The map in the latter reference (1: 13b–14a) would seem to confirm this estimate.

81. An early edict mandated only that compensation for civilian property occupied by Manchus be made "swiftly and fairly" (*Shizu shilu*, 14: 6a–b; DHL (Shunzhi reign) 2: 3a).

82. BQTZ 24: 460; *Hubei tongzhi*, ed. Wu Xiongguang, Bai-ling, Tong-xing, Tai-fei-in et al., 12: 21a–b; Otagi Hajime, *Chūgoku no jōkaku toshi* (Tokyo: Chūō kōronsha, 1991), 191–92. The map in *Jingzhoufu zhi, shou*, 2b–3a, shows this division clearly.

83. See Elliott, "Resident Aliens," 164–75. I adopt the term "citadel" from Millward, *Beyond the Pass*. On these "dual cities," see also the last note to this chapter.

84. Im, "Rise and Decline," 19, discussing the Guangzhou garrison. However, note that disputes between bannermen and civilians were remarked to still be very common at these locations. On the Fuzhou garrison, see Ma, "Qingdai Mancheng kao," 32. Guangzhou and Fuzhou bannermen also adopted a high profile in civilian neighborhoods by maintaining sentry boxes there, too.

85. BQTZ (24: 459) gives the total circumference of the garrison as 1,270.5 *zhang*, or about 3.91 kilometers. However, it is not possible to calculate the exact area since we lack dimensions for any side. Maps show the garrison to have been roughly rectangular in shape; a rectangle of proportions 1:2 would yield an area of about one-third square mile.

86. "Du côté du Nord, la ville Tartare a de grands vuides, et est mal habitée; du centre jusqu'à la ville des Chinois la ville est belle, bien bâtie, avec de belles rues, bien pavées, et remplie de beaux arcs de triomphe. Comme ils sont dispersés en ligne droite et que les portes se répondent, cela fait un bel effet. . . . La ville des Chinois n'a rien de considérable" (Gaubil, *Correspondance de Pékin*, 42).

87. Im, "Rise and Decline," 20, citing N. B. Dennys, comp., *The Treaty Ports of China and Japan* (London: Trübner, 1867; reprint, San Francisco: Chinese Materials Center, 1977), 153.

88. G. Tradescant Lay, "A Brief Account of the Mantchou Tartars at Chapu," *Chinese Repository* 11.8 (August 1842), 426–27.

89. Details mentioned in a description of the Qingzhou garrison (QLMaZPZZ 69, Ashai, QL2.12.20).

90. Cf. Stephan Feuchtwang, "School-Temple and City God," in Skinner, ed., *The City in Late Imperial China, passim*.

91. Two "built-by-edict" (*chi jian/hesei ilibuha*) temples were part of the original plan at Qingzhou (QLMaZPZZ 69, Ashai, QL2.12.20); five more were added over the years. The map in Ma ("Qingdai Mancheng kao," 34) shows seven, two of which are labeled *chi jian*. On temples in Beijing, see the forthcoming work by Susan Naquin, *Peking Temples and City Life, 1400–1900* (Berkeley and Los Angeles: University of California Press, 2000). I am grateful to her for the opportunity of examining parts of her manuscript as I revised these pages.

92. One exception to this picture was the Zhapu garrison, which, according to a report of 1759, apparently lacked any temples (QLMaZPZZ 304, Tukšan, QL24.5.13).

93. The Qing adoption of the Guan Di cult found nearly universal expression in Manchu cities, the cult's emphasis on Confucian loyalty dovetailing nicely with the hero's warrior image. On the history of the Guandi cult, see Prasenjit Duara, *Culture, Power, and the State* (Stanford, Calif.: Stanford University Press, 1988), 139–48. On shamanism see Chapter 6.

94. Tong Jingren, *Huhehaote Manzu jianshi* (Hohhot: Huhehaote shi minzu shiwu weiyuanhui, 1987), 83. Reminiscences of the religious activities of later Manchus is found in Jin Qizong, *Beijing jiaoqu de Manzu* (Hohhot: Nei Menggu daxue, 1989), 45–48.

95. See Ding, *Qingdai baqi zhufang,* 166–67.

96. Calculated from figures in DQHD (1763), *juan* 96; see also Sutō Yoshiyuki, "Shinchō ni okeru Manshū chūbō no tokushūsei ni kansuru ichi kōsatsu," *Tōhō gakuhō* 11.1 (March 1940), 176–203.

97. Dray-Novey, "Spatial Order and Police," 889 and note.

98. Unfortunately, lack of data prevents use of the demographically more sound method explained in Appendix A to estimate the population of Beijing.

99. See note 96, above. This figure does not count the relatively insignificant number of bannermen who had paying posts in the civil bureaucracy but held no post in the banners.

100. See note 104.

101. Han Guanghui, *Beijing lishi renkou dili* (Beijing: Beijing University Press, 1996), 126, table 3.20. Han's calculations appear to be based on average numbers of people per company.

102. YZMaZPZZ 60, memorials of Marsa, Cimbu, and Lu Siyun, YZ2.2.24.

103. Figured from the total of 100,745 *ding* recorded for the Plain Yellow Banner in 1720. See An Shuangcheng, "Shun-Kang-Yong sanchao baqi ding'e qianxi," 101.

104. Accepting that this percentage (24 percent) is approximately true, and taking the known proportion of salaried banner posts that were available to bannermen in Beijing (one hundred thousand, or about 50 percent of all such posts), permits us to say that one's chances at a job in the capital were twice those anywhere else.

105. By how much is hard to say. It may conceivably have doubled, reaching one million by 1800. Recent research has shown that fertility rates among the Qing imperial clan did not differ significantly from those of the general Han population. See James Lee [Li Zhongqing], "Zhongguo lishi renkou zhidu: Qingdai renkou xingwei ji qi yiyi," in Li and Guo, eds., *Qingdai huangzu renkou,* 4.

106. G. William Skinner, "Urban Social Structure in Ch'ing China," in

Skinner, ed., *The City in Late Imperial China,* 529. This figure was for the Qianmen district.

   107. QLMaZPZZ 69, Cimbu, QL2.12.17; Coldo, QL5.R6.16.

   108. QLMaZPZZ 85, Fusen, QL4.2.18.

   109. BQTZ 24: 464–65.

   110. Ding, *Qingdai baqi zhufang,* 55, citing *Zhupi yuzhi,* Yue Rui, 49: 33–34.

   111. In 1736, garrison general Ilibu wrote that the Liangzhou and Zhuang-lang garrisons would not be able to accept an additional three thousand soldiers, because together with their households this would mean a population increase in excess of ten thousand people, too large to be supported (GZMaZJ 6, Gioro Ilibu, QL1.7.24). At a ratio of only 2.33:1, this estimate seems suspiciously conservative, but it nonetheless does confirm that the 6.5:1 ratio for Qingzhou falls well within the normal range. One may suppose that only young families with simple households were sent to the two frontier posts.

   112. In his memorial thanking the emperor for the medicine sent to the garrison, he notes the benefit it brought to "the Manchus *within* Jingzhou city" (*Ging jeo-i hoton dorgi Manjusa*) (my emphasis) (YZMaZPZZ 509, Unaha, YZ6.7.2).

   113. Even if actual population densities were not as high as the crude numbers suggest, it is still hard to correlate these figures with reports of the spaciousness of Manchu cities that filter back from the nineteenth century.

   114. *Gaozong shilu,* 441: 15b–16a. Four hundred households, mostly of retired or out-of-work Manchus, were reported to be living in the vicinity of Qianmen. They were all resettled (ibid., 442: 6a–7a). If it was deemed inappropriate to have bannermen living outside the Manchu city, one would also assume that the court would frown on Han Chinese living within the garrison. But reports from Fuzhou and Zhapu in the mid-eighteenth century on Han households dwelling permanently within the garrison enclave provoked no angry demand that they be immediately expelled—perhaps because the households concerned were running businesses essential to the garrison's functioning? See ibid., 575: 14b; QLMaZPZZ 304, Tukšan, QL24.5.13.

   115. Im, "Rise and Decline," 16; Crossley, *Orphan Warriors,* 65–66. When soldiers were transferred to Chengdu in 1742, they could not be accommodated in the Manchu city, and special housing had to be built for them nearby (QLMaZPZZ 105, Yungning, QL7.1.20).

   116. Early in the Qianlong reign retired banner folk were encouraged to move out of the city to ease crowding (*Gaozong shilu,* 41: 27a–b). Cf. also the case of Fengrui at the Hangzhou garrison, as noted in Crossley, *Orphan Warriors,* 153.

117. Jin, *Beijing jiaoqu de Manzu*, 40–45.

118. Wu Wei-p'ing, "The Development and Decline of the Eight Banners," Ph.D. diss., University of Pennsylvania, 1970, 63, cited in Im, "Rise and Decline," 12, and Wakeman, *The Great Enterprise*, 1037n.

119. Crossley, *Orphan Warriors*, 48; Ma, "Qingdai Mancheng kao," 29. Ding Yizhuang also appears to agree with this position, stating that "the establishment [of the Eight Banner garrison system] followed a distinct randomness (*suiyi xing*). . . . [It] arose gradually, basically in response to the needs of specific locales at specific times and the steady expansion of the territory controlled by the Qing" (*Qingdai baqi zhufang*, 88). But cf. her earlier comment, "The Manchu rulers most certainly did not act carelessly when it came to the establishment of each garrison site" (38), which suggests that there was a method, and some kind of plan, after all.

120. *Jingzhou zhufang baqi zhi*, "Xiang-heng xu," 1b.

121. SYBQ YZ10: 15b (YZ10.7.1).

122. See Chapter 6.

123. Dezhou (1654), Taiyuan (1649), and Xi'an (1645) of the Yellow River chain; Nanjing (1645) and Jingkou (1654) of the Yangzi chain; Beijing, Dezhou, Jingkou, and Hangzhou (1645) of the Grand Canal chain; and Hangzhou, Fuzhou (1656), and Guangzhou (1661) of the coastal chain. Calculating using figures for 1739, 27,500 troops lived in the "Shunzhi Eight" garrisons, and 11,500 in the other five.

124. This agrees with the assessment in Ding, *Qingdai baqi zhufang*, 39–45.

125. Kaifeng (1718), Chengdu (1721), Tianjin (1726), Zhapu (1728), Qingzhou (1729), Liangzhou (1736), Zhuanglang (1737), and Suiyuan (1737).

126. There were two Manchu words for general, *janggin* (an older form) and *jiyanggiyūn* (an early Qing neologism; a variant form, *jiyangjiyūn*, is sometimes seen). Both derive from the Chinese word for general, *jiangjun*. *Janggin* (meaning not only "general" but the head of any grouping, civil or military), came into use under Hong Taiji, when it replaced the word *ejen*, "master," in military titles. Thus *nirui ejen* became *nirui janggin* and *meiren-i ejen* became *meiren-i janggin* (*meiren* in Manchu means "shoulder," and was used in the same way as English "vice-"); *ejen* was deemed fit only for banner commanders (*gūsai ejen*) and after 1734 was reserved for the emperor alone. *Janggin* in such titles was rendered phonetically into Chinese as *zhang-jing*, e.g., *mei-le zhang-jing*, until the early 1660s, when a general revision of nomenclature took place, and more meaningful Chinese equivalents put into use: *gu-shan e-zhen* was changed to *dutong*, an old Tang military title (Fu-ge, *Tingyu congtan* [ca. 1860; reprint, Beijing: Zhonghua shuju, 1959; 2nd ed.,

1984], 5: 128); *mei-le zhang-jing* was dropped in favor of *fudutong* (*meiren-i janggin* remaining unchanged in Manchu); *ang-bang zhang-jing* (which had been changed in 1660 to *zongguan* in Chinese [*Shizu shilu*, 133: 18b]) became simply *jiangjun*; and *amba janggin* was changed in Manchu to *jiyanggiyūn*. Note also the very early use of *amba janggin* for the commander of the "Old Han Troops" before the creation of the first Chinese banners in 1637 (Zhang and Guo, *Qing ruguanqian*, 309).

127. The one exception I have been able to find is at Jingkou, where the first garrison general, Guan Xiaozhong, was listed as an *amba janggin*, but whose immediate successors, Shi Tingzhu and Liu Zhiyuan, were *gūsai ejen*. In this case, the title did not correspond to "banner commander."

128. QNMDY 2: 302–3.

129. The garrison at Baoqing lasted barely one year, dispersed after its leaders were sent on campaign further east. The Hanzhong garrison functioned as the major base of operations for campaigns in Huguang and Guizhou. It endured until 1659, when its commander, Wu Sangui, left to lead the Qing campaign in Yunnan, at which time it was promptly eliminated (*Shizu shilu*, 38: 7b–8a; 124: 14b–15a; Qian Shifu, *Qingdai zhiguan nianbiao* [Beijing: Zhonghua shuju, 1980], 2220–2227).

130. *Shizu shilu*, 122: 14b–15b.

131. Ibid., 119: 12a–b.

132. As at Juliuhe (Ding, *Qingdai baqi zhufang*, 14).

133. BQTZ 18: 330–31.

134. The nonestablishment of a garrison at Wuchang sheds some light on this problem. The original decision to garrison bannermen at Wuchang directed that family members were to accompany them, but in December 1655 this decision was reversed. Two reasons were given: first, it was felt that the proposed relocation would lay too great a burden on civilians living along the route from the capital; second, it was feared that an unacceptable strain would be placed on Wuchang's Chinese population, a large number of whom would have to be dispossessed in order to make room for Manchu soldiers and their households. Instead, it was decided that families would stay in the capital and soldiers were to be sent in rotation from the capital to garrison Wuchang (QNMDY 3: 343; the same edict is in *Shizu shilu*, 89: 2b–3a). As Wuchang never became a permanent banner garrison, one may conclude that families were sent only to those locations where a garrison was deemed to be permanent, and that, conversely, where families were not sent, garrisons were not permanent.

135. DQHDSL 1119: 10a–11a.

136. BQTZ 18: 330–31; the right to land was confirmed again in 1693.

See also Im, "Rise and Decline," 99–102, and Liu Chia-chü, *Qingchao chuqi de baqi quandi* (Taipei: Wenshizhe chubanshe, 1964), *passim*. During the first year or two of the dynasty, it is sometimes hard to tell if a grant of land was an actual indication of permanence. One problematic case is that of the eight garrisons founded in Zhili, Shanxi, and Shandong in 1645. These areas corresponded with three of the four main regions of early military deployment, and numerous garrisons were founded here, only to be moved the following year. If these garrisons were meant simply as temporary field headquarters, it remains to be explained why it was stipulated that Manchu bannermen stationed here be given property, a decision which would seem to indicate the intent to settle soldiers permanently. I would suggest that in the absence of any other indications of permanent intent, property grants in the case of these garrisons were simply in keeping with the practice of granting land to soldiers as was so common in the first three years of the conquest. Soldiers would hold the land but not live on it, and receive (tax-free) any income the land might bring. They were not therefore tied to the vicinity.

137. BQTZ 24: 456, 460–465 ff. On the Hangzhou garrison see Crossley, *Orphan Warriors*, 62–67. The founding of the Jingkou garrison is detailed in Elliott, "Bannerman and Townsman," 41–45. Ding's conclusion that there was no original plan to create separate Manchu compounds in garrisoned cities cannot, I think, be taken to represent the situation everywhere (*Qingdai baqi zhufang*, 162).

138. For example, the walls of the Nanjing garrison were extensively renovated in 1660 (Lu Yanzhao, ed., *Jiangningfu zhi* [1880], 12: 1b).

139. Wakeman, *The Great Enterprise*, 480.

140. Ding, *Qingdai baqi zhufang*, 88.

141. The earliest estimate Luo Ergang gives for the size of Green Standard forces is 578,000 in 1686. See *Lüyingbing zhi*, 2nd. ed. (Beijing: Zhonghua shuju, 1984), 6–12. But we lack contemporary numbers for the Eight Banners. From later figures (e.g., those of 1811 showing 631,000 in the Green Standard Army and 277,000 in the Eight Banners), it is probably safe to assume that the Green Standard army was at least three times as large as the Eight Banners in the early Qing. Figures from 1811 are cited from James Lee, *The Political Economy of China's Southwestern Frontier, 1350 to 1850* (Cambridge: Harvard University Asia Center, forthcoming), table 1.8. Data from the middle Qianlong reign show that, on average, 44 percent of officers in the Green Standard Army were bannermen (primarily from the Manchu banners). The figures show a high of 73 percent in Zhili and a low of 22 percent in Jiangnan (*Da Qing zhongshu beilan* [1774]). See table 2.5 in Elliott, "Resident Aliens," 110.

142. This in effect reverses the question asked by Luo Ergang in his landmark study of the Green Standard Army: "Why, given that they already had the Eight Banner armies, did the Qing dynasty establish the Green Standard army system, too?" Luo's answer was essentially that the banners were too few in number and too rapidly lost their edge to be relied upon (*Lüyingbing zhi*, 1–3).

143. *Shizu shilu*, 109: 1a.

144. Not surprisingly, the memorialist's tactless remark on "dread" Manchu soldiers touched a nerve and earned him a sharp rebuke, though the opinions he expressed were surely not his alone (*Shizu shilu*, 129: 5a–6b; 132: 10a–b).

145. Luo, *Lüyingbing zhi*, 2–3. A similar analysis is given in Ōtani Toshio, "Shinchō gunsei no oboegaki—hakki, rokueisei no keizaiteki kihan o chūshin toshite," *Tōyōshi kenkyū* 33.1 (January 1974), 115.

146. Luo, *Lüyingbing zhi*, 4–5. Luo erroneously mentions the guarding of imperial mausolea as a duty of the Green Standard Army. Soldiers assigned to guard the Qing tombs were drawn only from the Eight Banners. Specific assignments are detailed in HWT 181: 6422–23; BQTZ 26: 509; and DQHD (1763) 96.

147. As one scholar has observed, "As foreigners who seized power by military conquest, the Manchus were in no position to identify with rural Chinese society. Instead they allied themselves with the literate and urban classes, extended their power through garrison cities, and attempted to bring rural society under centralized control." See John R. Watt, "The Yamen and Urban Administration," in Skinner, ed., *The City in Late Imperial China*, 357.

148. SYBQ YZ10: 14b (YZ10.7.1).

149. *Huangchao bingzhi*, 3, "xunlianmen, junling" (National Palace Museum Archives, Taipei).

150. *Jingzhou zhufang baqi zhi*, "Xiang-heng xu."

151. See Bartlett, *Monarchs and Ministers*, 25, 35–37.

152. Numata et al. describe their role as that of "feudal overseers." *Iminzoku no Shina tōchi shi*, 240.

153. YZMaZPZZ 222, Alin, YZ11.4.9. The suggestion was apparently not followed, since there is no record of any garrison at Nankou. There were two banner garrisons on the same road, however, at Changping and Zhang-jiakou. A similar comment was made a century later after the pacification of Eastern Turkestan, when it was deemed appropriate to place a Manchu in charge of the area: "The Muslim tribes of Ili cannot be compared to those of Barkul, Hami, or the interior, so it will be necessary to station troops in *tuntian* colonies. And a senior Manchu general must still be posted there.

[These tribes] are not [people] that a Green Standard brigade can keep under control" (*Gaozong shilu*, 610: 18a).

154. Tao, *The Jurchen in Twelfth-Century China*, 47 ff.

155. Herbert Franke, "The Chin," 281; see also Tao, *The Jurchen in Twelfth-Century China*, 25, 47 ff., and Hoyt Cleveland Tillman, "An Overview of Chin History and Institutions," in Tillman and Stephen West, eds., *China Under Jurchen Rule* (Binghamton: State University of New York Press, 1995), 28.

156. The first garrisons in this westward expansion were at Suiyuan and Ningxia; later followed those at Urumchi, where the Chinese city, established in 1765, was called Dihua, and a separate Manchu city, called Gongning, to its northwest, was built in 1771; at Ili (Kuldja), where a cluster of eight cities was built beginning in 1760, all surrounding the main Manchu city at Huiyuan; and at Kashgar (1762); as well as lesser ones at Hami, Turfan, Barkol, Gucheng, Tarbagatai, Kucha, and Yangi Hisar (Millward, *Beyond the Pass*, 160–86). More background on the planning and development of Hohhot, Suiyuan, and Urumchi is in Gaubatz, *Beyond the Great Wall*, 62–75, 174–75. Qingzhou was the only citadel built within China proper.

157. Owen Lattimore, *High Tartary* (New York: Little, Brown, 1930; reprint, New York: Kodansha America, 1994), 209.

*Chapter 3. The Emperor's Men*

1. Both types of distinction are made in official documents of the Yongzheng reign. I have not found any examples of the term *gūsai niyalma* in earlier documents but cannot rule out that some may exist. *Irgen* as applied to Chinese commoners must be distinguished from its meaning in early Jurchen society.

2. Wang, "Guanyu Manzu xingchengzhong," 10–11. The expression "bu fen Man Han, dan wen qi min" is found in Liu, *Baqi zidi*, 1.

3. See note in BQTZ 39: 721.

4. Fu-ge, *Tingyu congtan*, 3: 76.

5. Zheng Qin, *Qingdai sifa shenpan zhidu yanjiu* (Changsha: Hunan jiaoyu chubanshe, 1988), 59.

6. The phrase in Chinese was *ge qiyuan zidi* (*Gaozong shilu*, 143: 13b).

7. In the case of Qing provincial governors, Guy explains "administrative distance" as "defined by the nature of the governor's authority and the levels of official hierarchy between him and the center." See R. Kent Guy, "Imperial Powers and the Appointment of Provincial Governors in Ch'ing China, 1700–1900," in Frederick P. Brandauer and Chun-chieh Huang, eds., *Imperial Rulership and Cultural Change in Traditional China* (Seattle: University of Washington Press, 1994), 252.

8. "The civil appointee was bound not only to perform a function but also, and perhaps more fundamentally, to uphold the legitimacy of the dynasty" (Guy, "Appointment of Provincial Governors," 250).

9. For a study in which the focus is on Manchus in the regular civil bureaucracy, see Polachek, *The Inner Opium War*.

10. YZMaZPZZ 60, Marsa, Cimbu, Lu Siyūn, YZ2.2.24. "Officials and officers" (*guan/hafasa*) includes all those not classed as "soldiers" (*bing/cooha*), i.e., those of rank of lieutenant (*xiaoqixiao/funde bošokū*) or higher.

11. BQTZ 34, 618.

12. According to one estimate, three thousand officials were based in the capital and five thousand in the provinces (Guy, "Appointment of Provincial Governors," 250). Another estimate gives 8,950 civil officials in the Kangxi reign. See Guo Songyi, Li Xinda, and Li Shangying, eds., *Qingchao dianzhi* (Changchun: Jilin wenshi chubanshe, 1993), 261. The nonbanner military bureaucracy in the provinces numbered only 2,650 officials (Guo et al., *Qingchao dianzhi*, 261).

13. The registers produced by these censuses are extant for many subordinate banner populations in the Qing Northeast. These provide the basis for Lee and Campbell, *Fate and Fortune*. See also the works by Lee, Campbell, and Wang Feng in the Bibliography.

14. Guard units parallel to those in Beijing existed at the major garrisons, and in the eighteenth century vanguard units were also created, the first in Xi'an in 1718. The other garrison vanguards were at Jiangning, Hangzhou, and Jingzhou (YZMaZPZZ 820, Cangseli, YZ7.R7.18).

15. These ranks are listed in BQTZ 42.

16. Higher posts could in theory be filled by candidates from any banner, while middle- and lower-level posts (lieutenant colonel and below) were usually filled by candidates from within the banner (YZMaZPZZ 263, n.m., YZ13.8.20).

17. BQTZ 36: 658; full details on promotions are given in BQTZ 36 and 37.

18. The "left wing" offices paralleled those of the boards of civil appointments, revenue, and rites; "right wing" offices those of war, punishments, and works.

19. YZMaZPZZ 234, Buyantu, YZ12.10.17. Information on what appears to be one such list included the candidate's name, age, family background (e.g., so-and-so's grandson), years of service and age at first appointment, personal qualities, military experience, number of imperial hunts participated in, and whether he could write Manchu (GZMaZJ 4, n.m., n.d.).

20. The original proposal is contained in a memorial of Hada, a banner vice-commander, dated YZ1.9.17 (YZMaZPZZ 1).

21. Pei Huang, *Autocracy at Work: A Study of the Yung-cheng Period, 1723–1735* (Bloomington: Indiana University Press, 1974), 183.

22. First advanced in Meng Sen's seminal 1936 article, "Baqi zhidu kaoshi," this argument is convincingly elaborated on by Hosoya Yoshio in an important 1968 article, "Shinchō ni okeru hakki seido no suii," *Tōyō gakuhō* 51.1 (June 1968), 1–43. Similar views may be found in Huang, *Autocracy at Work*, 168–84 ff.

23. Huang, *Autocracy at Work*, 168–71. Other changes made during the Yongzheng reign are explained below.

24. These include *Shangyu baqi/Dergi hese jakūn gūsade wasimbuhangge* (10 *ce*, 1735); *Shangyu qiwu yifu/Dergi hesei wasimbuha gūsai baita be dahūme gisurefi wesimbuhengge* (1735; 2-vol. reprint, Taipei: Xuesheng shuju, 1976); *Yuxing qiwu zouyi/Hesei yabubuha hacilame wesimbuhe gūsai baita* (1735; 2-vol. reprint, Taipei: Xuesheng shuju, 1976); and *Baqi zeli/Jakūn gūsai kooli hacin* (Manchu editions of 1742 [ed. Ortai et al.], 12 *juan*, and 1764 [ed. Laiboo et al.]; Chinese editions of 1754 [ed. Laiboo et al.], 1764 ["*qinding*"] [ed. Laiboo et al.], and 1776 [ed. Fulungga et al.]). The earliest such regulations for the Eight Banners are those contained in the 1672 edition of *Zhongshu zhengkao*.

25. *Gaozong shilu*, 404: 1a. Prior to this, the office of "monthly recorder" (Ma *biya alire amban*) had been established in 1723, which rotated between banner commanders on a monthly basis.

26. Archival information on Beijing banner affairs in the eighteenth century is disappointingly scarce. The *Baqi dutong yamen dang*, for instance, contains a random assortment of documents, mostly from the nineteenth century. Partly for this reason, I have chosen here to focus on the provincial bureaucracy, inserting information on the capital when possible. Further research may well turn up more documentation.

27. On one occasion, when the bondservant Cao Yin (who held the not unimportant position of Liang-Huai salt censor) was received by the emperor in the company of the Xi'an, Hangzhou, Mukden, and Heilongjiang garrison generals, he remarked it a great honor (Spence, *Ts'ao Yin*, 258).

28. Dennys, *The Treaty Ports of China and Japan*, 154–55.

29. The lions were made of Zhaoqing stone, the same type used for the finest ink slabs, and were commissioned by Geng Jingzhong in the seventeenth century. See Xu Ke, *Qingbai leichao*, 1: 121 ("Guangzhou cheng").

30. E. H. Parker, *China, Her History, Diplomacy, and Commerce* (London, 1901), 247. Italics in the original.

31. Crossley, *Orphan Warriors*, 67–68.

32. As measured by the small number of those receiving posthumous titles (Ch *shi*) at the locations examined—5 out of 170 eighteenth-century generals.

33. Raymond Chu and William Saywell, *Career Patterns in the Ch'ing Dynasty* (Ann Arbor: University of Michigan Center for Chinese Studies, 1984), 37.

34. QNMDY 2: 312–13 (SZ3.4.22).

35. Between 1644 and 1795, of 205 garrison generals at six representative locations (Xi'an, Jiangning, Hangzhou, Canton, Jingzhou, and Ningxia), only 22 (10.7 percent) appear to have been from the Chinese banners and a mere 5 (4.4 percent) were Mongol bannermen. The findings presented in this section are based on tabulations of data obtained from Qian, *Qingdai zhiguan nianbiao*, and the archives of the Qing National History Bureau (*guoshiguan*) preserved in the National Palace Museum in Taipei. Complete data are presented in Elliott, "Resident Aliens."

36. Chinese bannermen were for the same reason also frequently appointed garrison generals at the Fuzhou and Jingkou garrisons, though increasing competition worked to the advantage of Manchu officials. The last Chinese banner garrison general at Fuzhou ended his term in 1728; at Canton in 1759. The data also confirm the generalization that "only rarely did Chinese brigadier-generals [i.e., lieutenant generals] become the general-in-chief of ethnically mixed garrisons" (Im, "Rise and Decline," 82).

37. Ding, *Qingdai baqi zhufang*, 134.

38. Average tenure at individual garrisons ranged from a low of 2.7 years at Ningxia to a high of 4.19 years at Jiangning, with a collective average of 3.74 years for the period before 1795. One study of the Hangzhou garrison has found an average tenure of 2.25 years for the garrison general, claiming this to be "on the long side compared to the dynastic average of tenure for that rank" (Crossley, *Orphan Warriors*, 68). Unfortunately, no figure is provided for the dynastic average. My own calculations for the Hangzhou garrison show an average tenure for the Qing period as a whole of 3.25 years, in fact shorter than the dynastic average up to 1795.

39. This trend is also reflected in the decreasing percentage of garrison generals who remained in the same post for more than five years. In the Shunzhi reign, this percentage was 66.6 percent and in the Kangxi reign, 59.8 percent; under the Yongzheng emperor, however, this figure was only 19.3 percent, falling in the Qianlong era to 17.4 percent. The number of garrison generals tenured for less than two years rose in the meantime from 7.7 percent and 14.1 percent in the Shunzhi and Kangxi reigns to 49.1 percent and 49.3

percent under the Yongzheng and Qianlong emperors (Ding, *Qingdai baqi zhufang*, 127, table 10.2). Ding's table is based on calculations for all garrison locations in the provinces *and* in the Northeast.

40. Guy, "Appointment of Provincial Governors," 255–60.

41. There is some confusion whether, as shown in the National Palace Museum archives, Fusen was transferred in 1751 to Ningguta. I have chosen to follow Qian, who shows two men with the same name active at the same time, one of the Gioro clan and the other—the one named to Ningguta in 1751 and later made president of the Board of War—a non-noble Manchu bannerman.

42. YZMaZPZZ 263, n.m., YZ13.8.20.

43. QLMaZPZZ 82, Bašinu, QL4.8.26. It is not clear which position is referred to by *gūsai baita be baicara janggin*; "inspector-general of banner affairs" is simply my translation of this Manchu title, for which no Chinese equivalent appears in Brunnert and Hagelstrom.

44. YZMaZPZZ 263, Jarhū, YZ13.10.11.

45. YZMaZPZZ 509, Unaha, YZ1.9.25.

46. Guy, "Appointment of Provincial Governors," 252.

47. YZMaZPZZ 263, anonymous items dated YZ13.8.20, one titled "gūsa be kadalara amban galai amban tui janggin meiren-i janggin-i gebu jedz," the other "geren goloi hoton-i jiyanggiyūn gūsa be kadalara amban meiren-i janggin."

48. Cf. Guy, "Appointment of Provincial Governors," 271–75.

49. Im, "Rise and Decline," 85. It would not seem, however, that, as Im states, the lieutenant general who had been at the garrison the longest would necessarily become the chief administrator. Before leaving Hangzhou for a visit to Beijing (his first in four years) garrison general Fusen asked the emperor to which of the lieutenant generals he should give the seals of office. He was instructed to give them to Bašinu, whose tenure at Hangzhou was at that point in fact the shortest (QLMaZPZZ 82, Fusen, QL4.8.26). Bašinu served once before as temporary garrison general just after arriving in Hangzhou in 1736 (QLMaZPZZ 52, Bašinu, QL1.10.3).

50. YZMaZPZZ 480, Yansin, YZ4.2.15; GZMaZJ 5, Fusen, QL1.7.18.

51. Im, "Rise and Decline," 82.

52. YZMaZPZZ 509, Unaha, YZ1.9.25.

53. YZMaZPZZ 377, Nimašan, YZ5.5.9. The original reads "jiyanggiyūn be emu beye obu."

54. YZMaZPZZ 1221, Sumurji, YZ7.5.15.

55. YZMaZPZZ 583, Jonai, YZ7.12.22.

56. YZMaZPZZ 583, Jonai, YZ8.2.8.

57. YZMaZPZZ 1222, Sumurji, YZ7.9.10.

58. Ding has also commented on this aspect of the garrison general–lieutenant general relationship and provides other examples that confirm the picture drawn here. See *Qingdai baqi zhufang*, 117–18.

59. For instance, thirty out of thirty-seven lieutenant generals serving in 1735 were appointed by special edict (YZMaZPZZ 263).

60. YZMaZPZZ 1221, Sumurji, YZ7.5.15.

61. YZMaZPZZ 1221, Sumurji, YZ7.3.13, YZ7.R7.24.

62. This is confirmed in a Qianlong edict: "The garrison general and lieutenant generals are both administrators at the same location. If the garrison general has faults, the lieutenant general should report these himself" (*Gaozong shilu*, 525: 10a).

63. Cf. Coldo's criticism of Cimbu, below. Other instances involved Xi'an garrison general Erentei, who was ordered to investigate the performances of his predecessor, Siju, and provincial commander-in-chief Šide (KXMaZPZZ 480, Erentei, KX55.4.14) and Jingkou generals Ma Sanqi and He Tianpei (KXHaZZH 5: 839–44, memorial of He Tianpei, KX53.1.6).

64. QLMaZPZZ 81, Ulhetu, QL4.7.21.

65. QLHaZPZZ, *yingzhi* no. 26, Jungyin, QL26.3.26.

66. GZMaZJ 6, Coldo, QL5.R6.16.

67. QLMaZPZZ 52, Bašinu, QL1.10.3.

68. YZMaZPZZ 434, Ilibu, YZ3.7.21.

69. QLHaZPZZ 26, Jungyin, QL26.3.26.

70. YZMaZPZZ 206, Guntai, YZ10.10.7.

71. Cf. YZMaZPZZ 822, Cangseli, YZ7.6.26, where the new garrison general questions regiment colonel Oyo on horse policy at Xi'an, and Oyo provides information going back as far as 1710.

72. Phrases such as "the clerks of the garrison general's yamen" and "the two clerks of the Tongguan commandant's yamen" make this clear (QLMaZPZZ 61, Cimbu, YL2.4.7). The same memorial speaks of making someone the "clerk at the Liangzhou garrison general's yamen."

73. Thus *bithesi* could be classified as "ranked" (*jergi bisire bithesi*) and "unranked" (*jergi akū bithesi*) (YZMaZPZZ 54, Yūnsiyang, YZ2.11.15).

74. QLMaZPZZ 85, Guntai, QL4.12.2. The clerk in question, Ingju, had been turned down for a promotion to be clerk at the banner in the capital.

75. YZMaZPZZ 240, Dingjeo, YZ12.6.10.

76. YZMaZPZZ 239, Fuming, YZ12.6.1.

77. Reasons varied: when Hangzhou garrison general Arigūn was transferred to the Qingzhou garrison, he petitioned to bring with him three of his Hangzhou-based clerks. Though clerks had been appointed to Qingzhou,

they were untried, and Arigūn successfully pushed for the temporary re-assignment of his own clerks, who returned to Hangzhou three years later—all apparently to care for their aging parents (QLMaZPZZ 61, Fusen et al., QL2.4.12).

78. YZMaZPZZ 1066, Cimbu, YZ8.3.20. Cimbu was later criticized by his successor, Coldo, for having discharged all but one of the clerks present on his arrival at Xi'an so that his favorites ended up receiving double salaries. He was also alleged to have appointed to soldier's posts many members of the clerks' households, including both regular Manchus and bondservants (GZMaZJ 6, Coldo, QL5.R6.16).

79. YZMaZPZZ 583, Jonai, YZ9.1.22.

80. Chu and Saywell, *Career Patterns in the Ch'ing Dynasty*, 52–53, citing Chen Wenshi, "Qingdai de bi-tie-shi," *Shihuo*, n.s., 4.3 (June 1974), 65–76. Cf. the comment of Chen Kangqi, writing in the mid nineteenth century, that the post of *bithesi* was a path to promotion for Manchus ("Manzhou jinshen zhi yi tu"), and that there was no shortage of aspirants (*Langqian jiwen chubi*, 5: 98).

81. Wu, "Development and Decline," 70. In his footnote, Wu rightly points out that the duties of the garrison general are not spelled out in the *Huidian* or other similar works, and that it is necessary to infer them from imperial instructions such as those appearing in the *Shilu*. In their study of the Qing provincial bureaucracy, Chu and Saywell also found that few garrison officials "were involved in local government at any level," by which they meant that bannermen were rarely appointed to office as prefects or magistrates (*Career Patterns in the Ch'ing Dynasty*, 37).

82. Im, "Rise and Decline," 86.

83. Ibid., 110–11; Ding, *Qingdai baqi zhufang*, 101–3. Pamela Crossley has since questioned this picture by suggesting that the garrison general was in reality "directly responsible to the governor-general" of the province, which would mean that the banner bureaucracy was subordinate to the civil authorities of the province in which the garrison was located (*Orphan Warriors*, 67). However, I have not found any evidence to suggest that as a rule garrison generals ever were expected to report to governors-general.

84. QLMaZPZZ 57, edict of 1.12.14. The Chinese translation of this edict appears in *Gaozong shilu*, 312: 23b–24a. Words in italics were added by the emperor to the draft of the edict. See also the edicts collected in Ding, *Qingdai baqi zhufang*, 102–3.

85. KXMaZPZZ 300, Ohai, KX47.5.1.

86. YZMaZPZZ 434, Ilibu, YZ4.6.15. The emperor didn't take it so seriously: "Accepting it was right. But how could they have been so stingy and

small?" This is one of many memorials rescripted by the emperor in a mixture of Manchu and Chinese. In this case the imperial response is in Manchu, but with one Chinese character (that for "stingy," *lin*, introduced after *ai uttu*, "how so."

87. *Shengzu shilu*, 163: 12b.

88. Memorialists often mentioned in passing that they gave the memorial to a bondservant to deliver, and sometimes even supply his name. One example from a 1730 memorial: "wesimbure jedz be aha mini booi niyalma Furtai de tukiyeme jafabufi," "this memorial has been entrusted to your slave's bond-servant Furtai" (YZMaZPZZ 583, Jonai, YZ7.12.22). Other examples are YZMaZPZZ 434, Ilibu, YZ4.4.8 and YZ4.10.4; YZMaZPZZ 812, Cangšeo, YZ4.12.8; YZMaZPZZ 189, Fusen, YZ8.4.3; YZMaZPZZ 1004, Sengboo, YZ8.12.8.

89. One Xi'an lieutenant general was upbraided for sending his bond-servant all the way to the capital with only a gratitude memorial, and instructed that in the future such items should be given to the garrison general—or, signifi-cantly, the governor-general or governor—for transmission together with their memorials to Beijing (YZMaZPZZ 426, Nimašan, YZ5.6.27). See also the memorial of Boji dated KX44.6.28, quoting a rescript encouraging cooperation between him, the governor-general, and the governor in the sending of memo-rials with one bondservant (KXMaZPZZ 351).

90. The son of Huguang governor-general Maiju is recorded as bearing an edict to Jingzhou garrison general Unaha (YZMaZPZZ 507, Unaha, YZ6.1.11).

91. KXMaZPZZ 468, Siju, KX48.10.24. The nuts were shared equally with the lieutenant generals and other officers.

92. YZMaZPZZ 434, Ilibu, YZ4.10.4.

93. Liu Ziyang, *Qingdai difang guanzhi kao* (Beijing: Zijincheng chuban-she, 1988), 163. Im notes that conscious efforts were made to emphasize their parity—both were permitted to wear a peacock feather and to be borne by eight bearers ("Rise and Decline," 86).

94. KXMaZPZZ 317, Okson, KX54.10.29.

95. YZMaZPZZ 859, Fusen, YZ13.R4.15.

96. *Shengzu shilu*, 139: 10a.

97. KXMaZPZZ 468, Siju, KX52.5.2.

98. KXMaZPZZ 300, Ohai, KX53.3.14. Jiangning garrison general Okson celebrated in the same way this year, though he appears to have made the rounds of the temples by himself (KXMaZPZZ 317, Okson, KX53.2.20).

99. See, for instance, YZMaZPZZ 189, Fusen, YZ8.4.3; YZMaZPZZ 527, Arigūn, YZ13.4.2; and QLMaZPZZ 81, Uhetu, QL4.7.21. More on provisioning the garrisons is found in Chapter 4.

100. KXMaZPZZ 478, Erentei, KX55.2.28.

101. "Jiyanggiyūn damu cooha be sara. siyūn fu damu irgese be sara. uttu buyaršame gurun booi sinde-i inde gūnirakū wesimbuci. bi adarame icihiyakabi" (YZMaZPZZ 114, Sibe, YZ4.3.10). The word *buyaršame*, from the verb *buyaršambi*, does not appear in any Manchu dictionary. I have tentatively interpolated its meaning from its most likely root, *buya*, "small."

102. YZMaZPZZ 1113 and 1114, Nomin, YZ2.R4.9 and YZ2.5.22. A parade around the Manchu enclave followed after the final selection of twenty-six Manchu and fourteen Mongol bannermen.

103. Cf. Guy's comment: "Provincial governors represented the central court's eyes and ears, outposts of central authority in a sea of local interests" ("Appointment of Provincial Governors," 248).

104. E.g., KXMaZPZZ 352, Boji, all memorials; KXMaZPZZ 355, Boji, KX41.5.21, KX45.2.2, KX47.2.19; KXMaZPZZ 469, Siju, KX51.4.6; KXMaZPZZ 482, Erentei, KX55.11.1; KXHaZZH 6: 873–77, He Tianpei, KX55.3.1.

105. See, e.g., KXHaZZH 2: 883–84, Guan Yuanzhong, KX49.5.26; KXHaZZH 3: 227–31, Zu Liangbi, KX50.1.8; KXHaZZH 3: 738–40, Ma Sanqi, KX50.9.2; KXHaZZH 4: 284–86, Guan Yuanzhong, KX51.6.27; KXHaZZH 5: 752–54, He Tianpei, KX53.9.8; KXHaZZH 8: 165–66, Huang Bingyue, KX57.6.13; YZMaZPZZ 513, Unaha, YZ5.9.28; YZMaZPZZ 512, Unaha, YZ7.10.1; YZMaZPZZ 527, Arigūn, YZ11.4.7; YZMaZPZZ 228, Guntai, YZ11.6.27; YZMaZPZZ 859, Fusen, YZ13.R4.15; YZMaZPZZ 275, Arigūn, YZ13.12.17; QLMaZPZZ 74, Fusen, QL3.9.15. For a memorial on silkworms (in Chinese), see that by Canton garrison general Guan Yuanzhong in KXHaZZH 3: 765–66, KX50.9.21; on the Fuzhou garrison general's involvement in handling a mission from "Sulu guo," see *Gaozong shilu*, 422: 20b–21b.

106. *Gaozong shilu*, 450: 22a–b.

107. Ibid., 360: 9a–b. The officer called on the carpet, Zhao Hong'en, was named garrison general at Zhenjiang in 1750. Zhao was one of the very few nonbannermen ever to have served as a garrison officer. As the son of the distinguished Chinese general Zhao Liangdong (1621–97), however, his credentials were virtually as good as those of a Chinese bannerman.

108. GZMaZJ 5, Alu, QL1.7.7. Alu had submitted a memorial in 1736 on the condition of farmland north of Ningxia. At that time, a group of three hundred Chinese farmers had come to him to complain of the poor condition of the land, which, after canals had been dug in an attempt to improve irrigation, was covered with a powder of alkali. The banner officers he sent out to inspect reported that "the land is nothing but a dull white as far as the

eye can see." Though he acknowledged in his report that this kind of matter was "not originally one of the things I was sent to manage," as an official on the border, he felt it was part of his duty to inform the emperor of the situation (GZMaZJ 5, Alu, QL1.7.7).

109. QLMaZPZZ 76, Alu and Kara, QL3.11.25. This report was received at court two weeks later, on January 18 (*Gaozong shilu*, 82: 20b–21a). It so happened that Ningxia's other lieutenant general, Tungšan, had left on the morning of January 3 to make an official visit to Beijing and had just set up camp (at Hongshan pu, by the Great Wall, twenty-two miles southeast of Ningxia) when the earthquake hit:

> Just before the watch was struck the ground suddenly moved. When it got to be the fourth watch [from 1:00 to 3:00 A.M.] the earth had trembled three or four times, though never very strongly. I got the local sergeant and asked him some questions, and he told me that none of the people had been seriously hurt, that a few rooms in some houses had collapsed and that was all. Thinking that it was the same in Ningxia, I traveled on to the next stop at Xingwu camp. When I got there, Captain Mengtu . . . caught up with me and told me that at our place at Ningxia . . . the houses of all the officers and soldiers had been destroyed and laid to the ground. He couldn't even say how many people had been crushed to death. Frozen with fear, I thought that since a disaster had befallen the place where I was appointed, how could I continue on to the capital?

He returned immediately to Ningxia. In his rescript the emperor reassured Tungšan that he had acted properly (QLMaZPZZ 76, Tungšan, QL3.11.30).

110. Bandi reported that many people had perished in fires that blazed in the city for days before the snow finally doused them or they at last burned themselves out. Water that welled up from underground and burst forth during the quake everywhere turned to ice (QLMaZPZZ 78, Bandi, QL4.1.2). The urgency of Bandi's mission is underscored by the speed of his journey. He departed Beijing on January 23; exactly two weeks later, on February 6, he arrived at Ningxia, 2,600 *li* (about 900 miles) away, thus averaging 185 *li* per day, nearly twice the standard daily minimum of 100 *li* for bannermen traveling on military post routes (YZMaZPZZ 54, Yūnsiyang, YZ2.11.15). Garrison officers who made the journey regularly every other year reported typical travel times of one month or even longer (YZMaZPZZ 583, Jonai, YZ8.2.8; 264, Kara, YZ13.12.1).

111. *Gaozong shilu*, 82: 28b–29a.

112. QLMaZPZZ 76, Alu, QL3.11.30.

113. QLMaZPZZ 77, Alu, QL3.12.9. The emperor's response to the disaster included emergency loans and distribution of free food, clothing, and

money to those in greatest need, forgiveness for bannerman debt, and a tax amnesty for residents of the five counties most devastated by the quake, many of whom were recent settlers (*Gaozong shilu*, 85: 8a–9a, 10b–11a; 87: 7b–8a). Three counties had the amnesty extended for a second year (ibid., 105: 16b).

114. QLMaZPZZ 78, Bandi, QL4.1.2.

115. QLMaZPZZ 76, Alu, QL3.11.30.

116. QLMaZPZZ 77, Alu, QL3.12.2.

117. *Gaozong shilu*, 86: 7b.

118. QLMaZPZZ 78, Bandi, QL4.1.2; Alu, QL4.1.26.

119. See Elliott, "Resident Aliens," 275–77.

120. QLMaZPZZ 78, Bandi, QL4.1.2.

121. As when the Kangxi emperor presented Xi'an garrison general Boji a gift of deer meat (including the tongue and tail) from a deer he had killed himself, and it was divvied up between all Manchu and Chinese civil and military officials (KXMaZPZZ 351, Boji, KX43.10.10).

122. "[I]t is quite possible that a whole network of personal allegiances subsisted among members of the Banner elite who were untouched by the laws of avoidance and the other checks that the Chinese had built into their bureaucracy" (Spence, *Ts'ao Yin*, 76 and note).

123. At that time Boji was both Xi'an garrison general and Sichuan-Shaanxi governor-general; Ohai was Shaanxi governor; Olo was provincial financial commissioner; and Hegu was provincial judicial commissioner. The emperor wrote to them as a group, and himself observed that it was unprecedented that all of these officials should be Manchus (KXMaZPZZ 350, Boji, KX44.6.11).

124. Spence, *Ts'ao Yin*, 226.

125. The earliest palace memorials I found in the course of my research (in the first half of the 1990s) were from 1689. In *Kangxi chao Manwen zhupi zouzhe quanyi* (Complete translation of the Manchu palace memorials of the Kangxi reign), published by the First Historical Archives in 1996 (Guan Xiaolian, Qu Liusheng, chief eds; Beijing: Zhongguo shehui kexue chubanshe), are found translations of a number of documents dating from as early as 1664. Whether the earliest documents translated here were truly palace memorials is debatable. For more on this question, see Guan Xiaolian, "Zai lun zouzhe qiyuan ji qi tedian" (paper delivered at the Second Conference on the Ming-Qing Archives and Historical Research, Beijing, October 1995), and Mark C. Elliott, "The Manchu-Language Archives of the Qing Dynasty and the Origins of the Palace Memorial System," forthcoming, *Late Imperial China*.

126. For an introduction to the palace memorial system, see Bartlett, *Monarchs and Ministers*, 49–64, and Spence, *Ts'ao-yin*, chap. 6. Also see

Bartlett, "Ch'ing Palace Memorials in the Archives of the National Palace Museum," *National Palace Museum Bulletin* 13.6 (January–February 1979).

127. The Qianlong emperor, on the other hand, was taciturn in his rescripts, particularly in the first years of his reign, when seemingly every memorial was signed either "acknowledged" or "let the board [or Interim Council] deliberate and memorialize." For this reason, it is difficult to interpret the position of the garrison general in relation to the throne during this later period. The lack of such intimate communication with the Qianlong emperor would seem to point to a more distant relationship (as well as to a routinization of the system), while the few longer rescripts that have been preserved show a tendency to threaten, perhaps arising from his desire to begin his reign with a strong hand. See, for example, QLMaZPZZ 50, Arigūn, QL1.3.15; GZMaZJ 5, Fusen, QL1.7.28.

128. Among the 1,657 Manchu-language memorials from between 1689 and 1710 held in the First Historical Archives, 348 (21 percent) are memorials from garrison generals Boji, Siju, Erentei, Okson, Yonggina, Tangbooju, Monggoro, Torio, and Centai. An additional 70, in Chinese, are from Chinese banner garrison generals Guan Yuanzhong, Zu Liangbi, Huang Bingyue, Ma Sanqi, and He Tianpei. Approximately 57 percent of the roughly 9,300 Kangxi-period palace memorials are in Manchu. Elliott, "The Manchu-Language Archives of the Qing Dynasty." For a description of some of these materials, see also Elliott, "Chūgoku no dai'ichi rekishi tōankanzō naikaku to kyūchū Manbun tōan no gaijutsu," *Tōhōgaku* 85 (January 1993), 147–57.

129. The original reads: "ere jergi elhe baire baita be ton akū wesimbure be naka" (KXMaZPZZ 149, Foron, KX28.12.9).

130. KXMaZPZZ 347, Monggoro, n.d.

131. Boji's career began in the Imperial Guard. In 1680 he was made commissioner of the imperial equipage, and three years later banner commander in the Bordered White Banner. He quickly moved up the ethnic ladder from the Chinese to the Mongol and eventually to the Manchu banner. In 1685 he was appointed Jiangning garrison general and was transferred to Xi'an in 1692, where he served for sixteen years. In 1704 he was given a joint appointment as Shaanxi-Sichuan governor-general. He died in 1708 (QSLZ 11: 802–4).

132. KXMaZPZZ 351, Boji, KX46.8.26. By "grandfather and grandmother" the emperor was referring to Boji and his wife, both evidently his elders.

133. YZMaZPZZ 506, Unaha, YZ3.10.3.

134. YZMaZPZZ 434, Ilibu, YZ4.10.4.

135. YZMaZPZZ 111, Yansin, YZ4.7.9.

136. YZMaZPZZ 1067, Cimbu, YZ7.10.28.

137. YZMaZPZZ 189, Fusen, YZ8.4.3.

138. Bartlett, *Monarchs and Ministers*, 56–64.

139. Ibid., 52–53.

140. YZMaZPZZ 820, Cangseli, YZ5.12.1.

141. YZMaZPZZ 820, Cangseli, YZ7.5.15. The phrase I have translated as "senility" reads "sakda mama uhukedere nimeku," literally "old-man-and-old-woman's weakening disease."

142. YZMaZPZZ 820, Cangseli, YZ7.R7.18.

143. YZMaZPZZ 1221, Sumurji, YZ7.R7.24.

144. All from YZMaZPZZ 820, Cangseli, YZ7.R7.18. Note that the emperor also lets drop here the notion that garrison officials were indeed thought of as *local* officials, as suggested above.

145. Cf. the long list of presents received by Xi'an lieutenant general Cangšeo (YZMaZPZZ 812, Cangšeo, YZ4.12.8). The Kangxi emperor also presented gifts to garrison officials; see *Shengzu shilu*, 117: 15b–16a.

146. YZMaZPZZ 1066, Cimbu, YZ8.10.29.

147. YZMaZPZZ 1004, Sengboo, YZ8.12.8. These sentiments are similar to those addressed a few months before to Yue Zhongqi: "I have no other people but you to take responsibility" (Bartlett, *Monarchs and Ministers*, 63).

148. YZMaZPZZ 820, Sumurji, YZ7.9.10.

149. Ding, *Qingdai baqi zhufang*, 117.

150. This was the Qianlong emperor's rescript to the Qingzhou garrison general's request to visit the capital at the New Year in 1760 (QLMaZPZZ 311, Erdemungge, QL24.11.11).

151. The use of the self-deprecating *nucai* (or *aha*), meaning literally "slave," was customarily confined to officials of the Eight Banners in their communications with the throne. Han Chinese officials were not to use this expression, and were liable to severe criticism if they broke this rule. When banner and Han officials submitted joint memorials, all used the same self-reference, *chen*, "official" (Wu, *Yangjizhai conglu*, 23: 256).

152. Guy, "Appointment of Provincial Governors," 250–51.

153. YZMaZPZZ 477, Yansin, YZ5.7.16.

154. KXMaZPZZ 353, Boji, KX44.5.26. My assessment of the language here as colloquial is based on the unusually high number of words written in variant forms not found in dictionaries. For assistance in reading this document I am grateful to Wu Yuanfeng and Zhao Zhiqiang.

155. Kimbai had been invited to take part in the revived hunts, but had to decline because of old age. "I cannot even kneel to accept the imperial edict," he confessed before going on to reminisce about his days hunting by the side of the Kangxi emperor (QLMaZPZZ 100, Kimbai, QL6.8.22).

156. The Manchu word *gurun*, which carried a variety of meanings, from "country," "nation," or "people," to "dynasty" and "court," was discussed in Chapter 1.

157. YZMaZPZZ 1221, Sumurji, YZ7.5.15.

158. YZMaZPZZ 820, Unaha, YZ7.12.1. There is also this comment: "Fine. It is proper that, thinking of the ancestors of the nation, you exert yourself diligently" (YZMaZPZZ 1096, Sibe, YZ7.5.10).

159. *Gaozong shilu*, 143: 14a.

160. Ibid., 446: 13a–14a.

161. KXMaZPZZ 480, Erentei, KX55.11.1.

162. SYBQ YZ12: 6a–b.

163. YZMaZPZZ 820, Cangseli, YZ5.6.6.

164. YZMaZPZZ 820, Cangseli, YZ5.R3.26.

165. *Gaozong shilu*, 415: 13b–15a. In 1760, the emperor found his worst expectations confirmed by the sloppy performance of two guardsmen charged with Green Standard positions. In admonishing other bannermen who had posts in the Green Standard Army, he again called up the refrain of upholding the purity of the "old Manchu ways" (*Gaozong shilu*, 616: 25a–26a).

166. Cf. Chapter 2, note 141. A 1738 proposal recommended that Mongol bannermen also be eligible for appointment to Green Standard posts, like Manchu bannermen (*Gaozong shilu*, 68: 6b–7a.

167. KXMaZPZZ 240, Yentai, KX49.R7.16.

168. YZMaZPZZ 513, Unaha, YZ5.9.28.

169. The original reads: "fi hooxan de mini gūnin wajirakū. mini ere gisun gūnin ambula oyonggo. bithe taciha Nikan amban hafan musei Manju be goidakini sere ba akū. si Nikan urse de hūlimburahū" (KXMaZPZZ 240, Yentai, KX49.R7.16). This memorial is missing from *Kangxi chao Manwen zhupi zouzhe quanyi*.

170. The original reads: "fejergi de oci ama mafa be eldembume. wargi ba-i gebungge jiyanggiyūn ofi suduri bithe de tutabure be bi ambula erembi. ainaha seme Nikasa de basubume mimbe ume girubure. kice ereci tulgiyen gemu toktofi yabure baita" (KXMaZPZZ 241, Yentai, KX46.7.26). This memorial is also not translated in *Kangxi chao Manwen zhupi zouzhe quanyi*.

171. YZMaZPZZ 509, Unaha, YZ1.9.25. My translation differs from that in *Kangxi chao Manwen zhupi zouzhe quanyi*; see Elliott, "The Manchu-Language Archives of the Qing Dynasty."

172. Cf. Bartlett, *Monarchs and Ministers*, 25–31. One might note that although, as Bartlett observes, the preponderance of Manchus in influential posts at court created many problems for the Yongzheng emperor, these

were "family" troubles, factions *within* the Manchu *gurun*. Ministers such as Zhang Tingyu, who was quite comfortable in Manchu culture, were very exceptional.

173. The original wording was, "muse Manju hafan cooha-i tacin" (YZMaZPZZ 110, Yansin, YZ4.5.11).

174. "Musei Manjusai fe doro" (QLMaZPZZ QL6.1, Šošofi, QL6.3.1). This edict appears in *Gaozong shilu*, 138: 7b–8b, but the Chinese translation reads only "the original (or established) Manchu customs" (*Manzhou suxi*), dropping altogether the sense of inclusiveness found in the Manchu text. In another hortatory edict issued later the same year, however, the emperor's words in Chinese (*wo Manzhou chunpu zhi feng*, "the unaffected ways of we Manchus") do reflect this sense of shared identity (ibid., 143: 13b).

## Chapter 4. The Iron Rice Bowl of Banner Privilege

1. BQTZ 29: 550.

2. Parker, *China, Her History*, 261.

3. Lao She, *Beneath the Red Banner*, trans. Don Cohn (Beijing: Panda Books, 1982; original ed.: *Zhenghongqi xia*, in *Lao She wenji* [Beijing: Renmin chubanshe, 1984], 7: 179–306), 17–18, 49–50.

4. Wu, "Development and Decline," 83. The evidence for this judgment is a quotation from the 1899 *Da Qing huidian shili*: "To pursue amusements, most of the bannermen spent days and nights on such pleasures as drinking, gambling, going to theaters and teahouses, and engaging in the fighting of cock, quail, and cricket."

5. *Shengzu shilu*, 179: 2b.

6. KXMaZPZZ 482, Erentei, KX55.11.1.

7. QLHaZPZZ 41, Wen-yuan, QL41.10.

8. Elliott, "Bannerman and Townsman," 38. One Qing observer, who dated the decline in martial ability among garrison bannermen from the first half of the nineteenth century, also noted the brave performance at the Nanjing and Hangzhou garrisons during the Taiping Rebellion (Chen, *Langqian jiwen chubi*, 1: 8–9, "Baqi zhufang jiangshuai gongji").

9. BQTZ 30: 565–67. Further elaboration of uniforms could be achieved through the attachment of patches on the back, such as the four-clawed dragon design devised (and paid for) by Nian Gengyao for Xi'an garrison bannermen in 1723 (YZMaZPZZ 823, Cangseli, YZ7.8.7).

10. Dennys, *The Treaty Ports of China and Japan*, 143–44, citing a report in the Hong Kong *Evening Mail*, which went on to describe the Chinese soldiers: "The Chinese troops, on the other hand, might at a distance be mistaken for sepoys, their dress consisting of red jackets turned up with white,

with light leggings worn knickerbocker fashion. Their head-dress is the ordinary conical bamboo hat."

11. KXMaZPZZ 482, Erentei, KX55.11.1. The *tulume* flotation belt, called in Chinese a *shui-dai*, was a hollow belt made of lacquered rattan. When filled with air it was useful in fording rivers and streams.

12. In 1740, garrison soldiers at Hangzhou who were new to the ranks were paying thirty taels to retiring soldiers for their accouterments (QLMaZPZZ 93, Bašinu, QL5.12.27). Elsewhere the price was higher: "For a saddle and bridle, bow, arrow, quiver, sword, and the repair of his armor, bannerman Cartu paid sixty taels" (Li Qiao, "Baqi shengji wenti shulue," *Lishi dang'an*, 1985.1, 91, citing a routine memorial of the Board of Punishments of unspecified date). Officers, of course, had even larger bills, ranging up to six hundred taels for members of the Imperial Bodyguard. For more on this issue, see Hu Jianzhong, "Qingdai wuqi zhuangbei yu zhizao," in Zhu Jiajin, ed., *Qingdai gongshi qiushi* (Beijing: Zijincheng chubanshe, 1992), 255–81.

13. BQTZ 30: 566–67; DQHDSL 1122: 1a–6b. Soldiers moving into positions were sometimes able to purchase equipment from retirees. Muskets were provided by the board, at first only to Chinese bannermen, and after 1690 to Manchu bannermen as well (*Shengzu shilu*, 148: 17b). The use of cannon, which was also originally limited to the Chinese banners, was expanded to include Manchus only much later, in 1725 (BQTZ 30: 569).

14. BQTZ 30: 569.

15. The emperor shot well from either side of his body (*Shengzu shilu*, 117: 16a–b, and 192: 30a–b; the latter incident is related in Spence, *Ts'ao Yin*, 130–31); see also Chen, *Langqian jiwen sanbi*, 9: 815, "Shengzu shan she."

16. BQTZ 31: 582.

17. Despite their scale, the results of contests were carefully recorded. Archival records of a competition held in Beijing in 1735 note over twenty thousand contestants from the Manchu and Mongol Eight Banners, including guard units, and Imperial Household bondservant companies (divided by wing). Each man shot five arrows. A score of at least four earned one a "top ranking" (Ma *uju jergingge*). Special comments were reserved for those who "looked good" (Ma *giru sain*), rode well, used tough bows or special arrows. Those who were especially bad were also singled out. See *Gongzhong Manwen zadang*, 64, "Zhongba dang" (original title: *Manju Monggo gūsai nadan jalan-i aigan gabtara de begu ejehe dangse*).

18. Estimates here of pounds of pull are conjectural and are based on an assumption that each degree of bow strength equaled a unit of 10 catties (13.33 pounds) of pull. A 6 bow thus would require a pull of 60 catties or 80 pounds, and a 10 bow a pull of 100 catties or 133 pounds (most modern bows

have drawing weights of 60 to 80 pounds). These figures would seem to square with statements that the "standard" bow had a pull of 100 catties, but that "ordinary" Chinese bows ranged between 40 to 80 catties. See Rudolf P. Hommel, *China at Work* (New York: John Day, 1937), 127. They also accord roughly with descriptions by other members of the Macartney mission: "Their bows are of elastic wood, covered on the outside with a layer of horn, and require the power of from seventy to one hundred pounds in drawing them; the string is composed of silk threads closely wounded, and the arrows are well made and pointed with steel." See William Alexander and George Henry Mason, *Views of Eighteenth Century China: Costumes, History, Customs* (1804–5; reprint, London: Studio Editions, 1988), 132.

19. YZMaZPZZ 265, Fusen, YZ13.12.7/1736.1.19. Interestingly, the difference between the skills of Manchus and Mongols on the one hand and Chinese bannermen on the other was not so great, each making up half the number of those twenty-two hundred who could handle a bow strength of 10. Of the eighty men able to handle tougher bow-strengths of 11 to 13, fifty were Manchus and Mongols, while thirty were Chinese bannermen.

20. QLMaZPZZ 52, Bašinu, QL1.10.3.

21. QLMaZPZZ 50, Arigūn, QL1.3.15.

22. SYBQ YZ5: 6b–7b (YZ5.3.11, YZ5.3.25).

23. SYBQ YZ5: 51a–b (YZ5.11.25).

24. Manchu *niyamniyambi* involved the same skills as those in Japanese *yabusame*, which developed during the Kamakura period (1185–1392) and is still practiced in contests and demonstrations in Japan today.

25. YZMaZPZZ 16, Necin, YZ1.8.13.

26. YZMaZPZZ 265, Fusen, YZ13.12.7.

27. Scholars have recently noted an abiding resistance to substantial military reform in the Qing. They adduce many reasons for this, but certainly one worth considering was the intimate link between the traditional instruments of war and the Manchu Way. As its frequent repetition in court pronouncements reveals, whatever other skills bannermen were supposed to have, the ability to shoot an arrow (from a stance and from horseback) and hit a target was fundamental. To have replaced the bow and arrow with more up-to-date weapons would have threatened a practice that was an axiomatic element of Manchuness. Second, the maintenance of horses, like archery, was a matter of cultural as well as military significance, and the Qing (like the Yuan) faced a real challenge in sustaining this aspect of their traditional way of life. The level of attention paid to this problem by garrison officers and court officials is striking when one considers the enormous difficulty of getting ponies to south China, the costs of keeping them healthy,

and their apparent uselessness other than as a symbol of a distant past. It seems that court conservatism on military technology owed much to political considerations that weighed more heavily than strategic ones. See Waley-Cohen, "Commemorating War in Eighteenth-Century China," and Perdue, "Military Mobilization in Seventeenth- and Eighteenth-Century China."

28. YZMaZPZZ 527, Arigūn, YZ13.4.2.

29. For the increased amount of matériel it would demand, such a proposal required the consideration of garrison general Jalangga. Each "blank" used up six *fen* (.06 ounces) of powder; a live shot took 2 *qian*, 4 *fen* (.24 ounces) of powder and 3 *qian*, 4 *fen* (.34 ounces) of lead shot, or about ten pellets. Soldiers were required to recover from the field 70 percent of pellets used, however, making the actual amount used only .012 ounces of shot per firing. Jalangga calculated that intensifying training would call for an additional 4,035 catties of gunpowder (about 23 percent more than the current allowance) and an extra 765 catties of lead shot (37 percent more) (YZMaZPZZ 328, Jalangga, YZ8.4.13). The catty (*jin/ginggen, gin*) was equal to 597 grams, or 1.31 pounds; 4,305 catties was therefore about 2,410 kilograms or 5,311 pounds—not quite three tons. These were not expensive items. The standard price for lead shot used by the court for calculating expenses was 3.5 taels for one hundred catties, though the market price in the Hangzhou area was quoted at 4.38 taels per one hundred catties in 1736 (QLMaZPZZ 51a, Fusen, QL1.4.10). Even at the higher price, the extra shot needed by the Xi'an garrison would have cost less than ten taels, and powder was even cheaper. One is led to wonder why it was necessary for soldiers to collect spent shot for reuse.

30. YZMaZPZZ 190, Fusen, YZ7.11.20.

31. YZMaZPZZ 18, Ilibu, YZ5.R3.18.

32. YZMaZPZZ 527, Arigūn, YZ10.2.19.

33. YZMaZPZZ 859, Fusen, YZ13.R4.15; GZMaZJ 5, Salhadai, QL1.7.24.

34. A 1732 proposal to sail for twenty days out and back across the bay to Dinghai (in the Zhoushan Islands) was gently quashed by the emperor: "Wait this year, and we'll see after another year or two of training" (YZMaZPZZ 527, Arigūn, YZ10.2.19).

35. DQHD (1763) 67: 46a. There were also different types of special weapons reserved for naval use, such as the "sickle lance" and the "flag spear." The former was curved and used for hooking as well as for cutting ropes; the latter was a straight throwing spear.

36. YZMaZPZZ 480, Yansin, YZ4.12.15; YZMaZPZZ 165, Jalangga, YZ7.11.22. My search for more information on how *mumuhu* was played has so far proved fruitless.

37. Wu Zhenyu, *Yangjizhai conglu* (preface dated 1896; reprint, Hangzhou: Zhejiang guji chubanshe, 1985), 14: 164–65.

38. Simon Schama, *Landscape and Memory* (New York: Vintage Books, 1995), 144–45.

39. BQTZ 31: 583. The edict quoted here is also quoted in Fusen's memorial, cited below, though the date of the original memorial from Wadai is given as the thirty-third year (1694), not the twenty-third (1684), of the Kangxi reign. Local hunts were also arranged at the Liangzhou garrison in western China, where men were taken out for twenty days in the wild once a year to keep their hunting and survival skills sharp (QLMaZPZZ 72, Uhetu, QL3.4.9). Achieving these goals was a little more difficult in the densely populated Jiangnan region, but a few determined officers were willing to give it a try. In 1736, Fusen proposed to reinstate hunts for Hangzhou bannermen. His plan called for three or four hundred soldiers to be taken out for a few days in the surrounding countryside where they would pitch tents and be taught the ways of the hunt. Fusen promised to notify the governor-general and alert the public to the upcoming exercise; revealingly, he was careful to stress that the people would be able to carry on with their usual business, and that there would be no formal sendings-off or welcomings by local officials, nor any supplies requested from them or the populace. Meals would be prepared by the men in simple tripod cooking pots. Moreover, the soldiers would be prohibited from bivouacking in any temples or in villagers' homes and any who used the hunting exercise as a pretext to disturb the locals would face punishment along with their superior officers. He went on in great detail to explain that because the planned route was narrow, filled with holes, and lined with mulberry forests, bringing along pack horses was not advisable (sacrificing some of the authenticity of the real Manchu hunt, to say the least). As had been done in the past, supplies would be delivered by boat to the field (the boats of local people sometimes being rented for the purpose). The reaction of the young Qianlong emperor to these exhaustive preparations was scornful: "Three years from now the soldiers will teach themselves at my training hunts [i.e., at Muran]. This hunting business [of yours] is superfluous, and the men don't even get very much out of it. Enough!" (GZMaZJ 5, Fusen, QL1.7.28).

40. Luo Yunzhi, *Qingdai Mulan weichang de tantao* (Taipei: Wenshizhe chubanshe, 1989), 1–2. Rehe is more familiarly romanized as "Jehol."

41. The imperial hunting reserve, about one hundred kilometers north of the city of Chengde, is today known as *Mulan weichang*, a compound of the Manchu word *muran* (phonetically rendered into Chinese as *mu-lan*), and the Chinese word *weichang*, "encircled place." While *qiu xian* means "fall hunt,"

*muran-i aba* means "the battue at Muran." As explained below, *muran* was also the name of another style of hunting.

42. See Philippe Fôret, *Mapping Chengde: The Qing Landscape Enterprise* (Honolulu: University of Hawaii Press, forthcoming); also the essays in James Millward et al., eds., *A Realm in Microcosm: The Manchu Palace at Chengde, Tibetan Buddhism, and the High Qing Empire* (manuscript in preparation).

43. Luo, *Qingdai mulan weichang*, 78. Note that participation in the hunt became part of one's official record.

44. See table in ibid., 139.

45. The poem, by Chen Zhilin (1605–66), is collected in Zhang Yuxing, ed., *Qingdai dongbei liuren shixuanzhu* (Shenyang: Liaoshen chubanshe, 1988), 131. Some of the language here in fact borders on the subversive. My thanks to Ronald Egan for assistance in decoding this poem.

46. QLMaZPZZ 69, Fusen et al., QL2.12.1.

47. QLMaZPZZ 50, Arigūn, QL1.3.15. The first such hunt under Qianlong is in fact recorded during 1741, the sixth year of the reign (Luo, *Qingdai Mulan weichang*, 79).

48. *Gaozong shilu*, 613: 5a–7a.

49. Hou Ching-lang and Michèle Pirazzoli, "Les chasses d'automne de l'empereur Qianlong à Mulan," *T'oung Pao* 55.1–3 (1979), 39.

50. Hobsbawm and Ranger, *The Invention of Tradition*, 4–5.

51. The stele on which this inscription, the *Mulan ji/Muran gi bithe*, still stands on the hunting grounds today. My thanks to Philippe Forêt and James Millward for yeoman assistance in recording the Manchu text. For the Chinese text, see Luo, *Qingdai Mulan weichang*, 212–13.

52. The text, *Beye-i cooha bade yabuha babe ejehe bithe* (A record of my personal military exploits), was discovered in the late 1970s in the collection of the Central Minorities Institute in Beijing. It was published in 1987 as *Suijun jixing yizhu*, edited and translated by Ji Yonghai (Beijing: Zhongyang minzu xueyuan chubanshe), in a three-part format with Chinese translation, romanization with word-for-word translation, and facsimile of the original ninety-eight-page Manchu text. The complete narrative of the text would appear to have begun in 1674. Unfortunately, of the original four chapters all but the last chapter has been lost, so that only the narrative from 1680 on remains. All translations below are my own and have been made from the Manchu. For ease of reference, however, page references are to the romanized text, as the facsimile text is not paginated. The notes here are based on Ji's preface. A complete translation of the text has been prepared by Nicola Di Cosmo for publication.

53. On Manggitu see ECCP 271 and BQTZ 192: 4518–21. He died on campaign of sickness at age forty-seven, and his command was taken over by Laita. Part of these forces were taken from the Nanjing garrison, with garrison general Ecu serving as a secondary commander.

54. Dzengšeo seems to have been well informed regarding the discussions and activities of the senior command staff, frequently noting who participated in meetings, when they took place, and the resulting decisions. In particular, he often notes the dates on which written messages between generals and Beijing were sent and received, as, for example, the date the order arrived from the Board of War naming Laita general in Manggitu's place (KX19.10.10) (SJY 42). Similar examples are found on pages 25, 29, 31, 41, 73, 74 and 84. Since the adjutant was in charge of correspondence, if this was Dzengšeo's position, such information would have come to him naturally in the course of his work. Moreover, the Manchu text is written in a neat, practiced hand, with almost no errors of orthography or grammar, showing the author to have been accustomed to writing. Finally, when listing officers receiving orders or proceeding with troops, Dzengšeo consistently places his name together with others of the rank of *janggin* (SJY 28, 70). At one point he also refers to his being appointed *janggin* in the Board of Punishments (SJY 67). It is hard, however, to be certain of the exact meaning of this, because in some cases Dzengšeo appears to use the term *janggin* to mean any kind of officer.

55. Leads squadron: SJY 44, 49, 56, 74; logistics: SJY 25, 26, 77; rice procurement: SJY 28–29, 31; moat construction: SJY 31, 59, 62, 69–70; general's tent: SJY 93; standing watch, fighting: SJY 32–33.

56. SJY 46–47, 68.

57. SJY 28–29, 46. This was the task performed for Beijing bannermen by Shandong rice dealers in their *duifang*. See Chapter 5.

58. SJY 75. The motive for Fusen's promise (see above) that Hangzhou soldiers on the hunt would not disturb regular economic activity thus becomes clearer.

59. SJY 49, 51. In contrast, once the army reached the North China plain, it easily managed sixty to eighty *li* per day or more (SJY 90–92).

60. SJY 52.  61. SJY 39.
62. SJY 51.  63. SJY 37, 47, 52, 56.
64. SJY 30.  65. SJY 81.
66. SJY 56, 85.  67. SJY 40.
68. SJY 64.  69. SJY 68.

70. SJY 24. "Doo yang k'o" probably refers to the Chinese *daoyang ge*, a folk song and dance to celebrate the New Year.

71. SJY 49. The correct name of the river is the Bada.

72. SJY 45.

73. SJY 60–62.

74. SJY 33.

75. SJY 84.

76. In Chinese, *chi huangxiang*. Documents from the Guangxu era measured a bannerman's career by the number of years he had been "eating a salary" (Ch *shixiang*).

77. Chen Jiahua, "Baqi bingxiang de shixi," *Minzu yanjiu* (1985.5), 63.

78. As noted in Chapter 2, the widespread expropriation of property (land, houses) from Chinese was, however, not only condoned but institutionalized in the first years after 1644.

79. Wu, "The Development and Decline," 49–54; Hosoya Yoshio, "Shinchō ni okeru hakki keizai no ichi danmen—hōkyō seido no seiritsu o megutte," *Ichikan kōgyō kōtō senmon gakkō kenkyū kiyō* 7 (1972), 44–49.

80. A *shi* (or picul), like a bushel, was a measure of volume, not weight, equivalent to 2 *hu* (about 107 liters). 10 *dou* made 1 *hu*.

81. Fu Lehuan, "Guanyu Qingdai Manzu de jige wenti," in Fu, *Liaoshi congkao* (Beijing: Zhonghua shuju, 1984), 417–418. This was an area roughly equal to 2.13 million acres or 3,330 square miles—about the size of Puerto Rico. These landholdings—modest, really, in comparison to the entire amount of cultivated land in China—were dwarfed by the huge imperial estates in southern Manchuria.

82. On the problem of banner land, see the many essays by Sutō Yoshi-yuki; the literature is nicely summarized in Ōtani Toshio, "Shinchō gunsei no oboegaki," 110–19. In Chinese, the main work is Liu, *Qingchao chuqi de baqi quandi*. See also the important collection of documents, *Qingdai de qidi* (comp. Institute for Qing History, Archives Department, Research Seminar on the Chinese Political System of People's University; chief ed. Wei Qingyuan; Beijing: Zhonghua shuju, 1989).

83. Resulting in the well-known early Qing problem of "escapee incidents" (Ch *taoren an*). A collection of documents on this topic was published in *Qingdai dang'an shiliao congbian*, vol. 10 (comp. and ed. First Historical Archives of China; Beijing: Zhonghua shuju, 1984).

84. The policy of buying back banner land was first announced in 1729, with new land registers completed by 1735. A second effort at reclaiming banner land began in 1739 and went on for another ten years. See Wang Qingyun, *Shiqu yuji* (1850; reprint, Beijing: Beijing guji chubanshe, 1985), 195–96, "Ji quandi." By then about one-half of all banner land belonged to Chinese civilians (Liu, *Baqi quandi*, 150).

85. BQTZ 18: 331.

86. I estimate that a total of about twenty-one hundred *mu* of land was encircled by the banners at Nanjing. This figure assumes a range of from ten to

thirty *xiang* (one *xiang* = six *mu*) for those in the officer ranks. Though the document does not specify who had how much, from other sources we know that the Nanjing garrison lieutenant generals received twenty *xiang* (*Shengzu shilu*, 3: 13b–14a)—half the amount received by lieutenant generals at the capital (Liu, *Qingchao chuqi*, 45). Assuming that the garrison general received thirty *xiang* and regiment colonels and captains probably fifteen and ten, respectively, and calculating for the four regiment colonels and twenty-four captains in the left-wing banners at the Nanjing garrison gives a total of twenty-one hundred *mu*. Though small compared to the amounts of land seized for the banners around Beijing, it seems to have been managed well and long enough to provide a healthy side income for garrison officers. Grants at Xi'an were slightly larger, ranging up to forty *xiang*. The passage in the *Veritable Records* specifies "twenty days" of land. The use of the word "day" (Ch *ri*) as an area measure (equal to a *xiang*) suggests that the Chinese text was translated from a Manchu original, since *ri* is probably based on the Manchu word *cimari*, meaning "morning, tomorrow" and "an area of six acres." One *cimari* was thus equivalent to one *xiang*. Note the similarity between Manchu *cimari* and German *morgen*, which also means "acre," i.e., the area of land that can be plowed by a single man with two oxen in the course of one day (hence, *morgen*, "morning" or "day"). I am unsure as to why the Manchus, who were not known as an agricultural people, used this particular measure.

87. YZMaZPZZ 152, Rasi, YZ6.3.3.

88. The only provincial garrison where banner soldiers as well as officers appear to have been assigned income-generating land (as opposed to pasture land for horses) was Taiyuan (BQTZ 18, 331). Perhaps this was because the amount of ownerless land in Shanxi was higher than in most other areas, owing to the greater devastation that occurred here before and after 1644 as well as to the presence of numerous Ming royal estates (First Historical Archives, *Huke shishu*, SZ10.1, entry for SZ10.1.23). Until well into the eighteenth century, garrison bannermen moving to Taiyuan continued to receive land in exchange for that which they forfeited in Beijing. In 1737 it was reported to the throne that a corporal and a regular cavalryman transferred from the capital to Taiyuan together were demanding 955 *mu* of land but had been told there was no more land to be given. From the size of this claim (several times the land grant of the top officers at Nanjing), it appears that an unusually high amount of land around Taiyuan came under banner ownership. When local officials investigated the situation at other garrisons and discovered that other provincial bannermen were receiving no land at all, they cried foul. The court decreed that Taiyuan bannermen would

be permitted no more exchanges and that bannermen transferred to the provinces should entrust property in the capital area to either a relative or to the banner (*Qingdai de qidi*, 1: 104–5).

89. Hosoya, "Shinchō ni okeru hakki keizai," 53. This amount, loosely equivalent to roughly 33.33 pounds of rice per person per month, was felt to be enough grain to feed a grown man. Hosoya was the first, I believe, to call attention to the difference between the special *xiangmi* (sometimes called *shangmi*) salaries, which only capital bannermen received, and *kouliang* stipends.

90. The same is confirmed in Wu, "Development and Decline," 96.

91. Hosoya, "Shinchō ni okeru hakki keizai," 55–57. The proportion between *xiangmi* grain and the silver stipend was initially set at three *hu* to two taels, but changed in 1653 to one *hu* to one tael. In 1685, *xiangmi* payments were made independent of silver salary, and for regular soldiers fixed at forty-six *hu* (ibid., 49, 51).

92. Chen Feng, *Qingdai junfei yanjiu* (Wuhan: Wuhan daxue chubanshe, 1992), 68–73. Another Manchu name for "red and white affairs" was "happiness and sadness affairs" (*urgun jobolon-i baita*).

93. The former was set at one and a half taels for a regular cavalryman (plus one-quarter tael for his groom or attendant), while there were conventional amounts of rice, millet, or noodles for the latter, which also included firewood and either beef or mutton.

94. Details are in Chen, *Qingdai junfei yanjiu*, 48–62.

95. Officers in the capital also received an annual *xiangmi* payment that matched their rank. Though garrison officers were paid no annual grain salary (unlike soldiers), they did merit a *kouliang* supplement calculated according to putative household size. For garrison generals this was forty people, which added up to over 117 *shi* of rice.

96. These amounts were considerably smaller than the amounts awarded to civil officials of equal rank; the governor-general, for instance, received a whopping sixteen thousand taels (Chen, *Qingdai junfei yanjiu*, 38–47). Salary and *yanglian* comparisons are made using tables 2.7 and 4.15 in Madeleine Zelin, *The Magistrate's Tael: Rationalizing Fiscal Reform in Eighteenth-Century Ch'ing China* (Berkeley and Los Angeles: University of California Press, 1984).

97. Note the description of the "useless lout" (and bannerman) Xue Pan in the eighteenth-century novel, *The Story of the Stone*: "Though an Imperial Purveyor, he was wholly innocent of business skill and savoir-faire; and though, for his father's and grandfather's sake, *he was allowed to register at the Ministry and receive regular payments of grain and money*, everything else

was looked after for him by the clerks and factors of the family business." See Cao Xueqin, *The Story of the Stone*, vol. 1, *The Golden Days*, trans. David Hawkes (Harmondsworth: Penguin, 1973), 118. Emphasis added.

98. This is also the judgment of Liu Xiaomeng. See *Baqi zidi*, 33.

99. BQTZ 29: 550, 556; DQHD (1776) 19: 26b. The cutoff date was 1686. Im's statement that "fixed salaries for bannermen in garrisons began about 1723" ("Rise and Decline," 103) is based on an edict of the Yongzheng emperor that almost certainly served only to confirm the status quo that had existed from the beginning of the Qing.

100. Im, "Rise and Decline," 144. Commutation of banner grain stipends, which was limited to the provincial banner garrisons, is pointed to as one effect of the commercialization of the Qing economy on the Manchu subeconomy. It appears to have been one way that provincial governments were able to insure against price fluctuations in providing grain to the garrisons, since the rate of commutation (set when the market price was low) typically was exceeded by the price of rice most of the rest of the year. See Wang Songling, "Lüelun Qingdai fengxiang zhidu de tedian," *Qingshi yanjiu tongxun* (1987.1), 2–3, and Elliott, "Resident Aliens," 341–44.

101. In 1741, the Hangzhou garrison general reported that six to seven of every ten Chinese banner households ran out of grain by the end of every month. Yet he also reported that the majority of Manchu and Mongol bannermen at the garrison were able to accumulate a rice surplus every month, selling off as much as three *shi*. Part of the explanation for this is that Manchu and Mongol households had within them more than one salary-earning soldier, while Chinese banner households were generally dependent on a single salary (QLMaZPZZ 93, Bašinu, QL5.12.27).

102. Hosoya, "Shinchō ni okeru hakki keizai," 57–61.

103. "Chinois et Mandchous continuaient d'appartenir à deux mondes différents, si imbriqués qu'ils fussent. Ils étaient institutionellement, juridiquement et économiquement séparés, chaque groupe ayant ses propres statuts" (Durand, *Lettrés et pouvoirs*, 243).

104. Military crimes (e.g., breaches of discipline, desertion, mutiny, etc.) were handled within the banners, while cases involving banner officers followed the same channels as those involving civil officials and were routed through the Board of Civil Appointments and the Board of Punishments.

105. Zheng, *Qingdai sifa shenpan zhidu yanjiu*, 63, citing the *Da Qing lüli*. For a late Qing case, see Kaye Soon Im, "On Manchu-Chinese Relations at the End of the Qing: A Legal Case of Manchu Soldiers Beating a Chinese District Magistrate at the Jingzhou Garrison in 1899" (unpublished paper, March 1999).

106. YZMaZPZZ 255, Šiju, YZ12.6.11.

107. Ura Ren'ichi, "Shoseidojō ni arawaretaru Shinchō no kanjin tōgyōsaku ni tsuite," *Shigaku zasshi* 2.1 (July 1930), 81.

108. This point is well made by Ura in ibid.

109. Zheng, *Qingdai sifa*, 63–64.

110. Ibid., 64, citing documents from the Board of Punishments.

111. Ding Yizhuang, "Qingdai lishi tongzhi kaolüe," in *Qingzhu Wang Zhonghan xiansheng bashi shouzhen xueshu lunwenji* (Shenyang: Liaoning daxue chubanshe, 1993), 267, citing Zhang Jixin, *Dao-Xian huanhai jianwen lu*. Incidentally, a Manchu translation of *Shuihu zhuan* was circulating by the mid-1700s, so Manchus would not have been ignorant of this literary allusion.

112. Ura, "Shinchō no kanjin tōgyōsaku," 79; see also the relevant sections of Zhang Jinfan, *Qingchao fazhi shi* (Beijing: Falü chubanshe, 1994).

113. Zheng, *Qingdai sifa shenpan*, 64. More on the civil commissioner is found in the next chapter.

114. *Gaozong shilu*, 73: 1a–2a. The matter was raised because the emperor thought it improper that for the offense in question (embezzlement) cases involving Manchus were evaluated individually while those involving Han Chinese automatically resulted in one hundred strokes of the bamboo. Evidently this had been the accepted practice up to that time (1738).

115. MBRT 2, Taizu 52, 771.

116. As Huang Liuhong's 1694 magistrate's manual notes, "Whipping is used today only during the process of interrogation, not as a form of punishment," and that the main point of whipping was to "instill a sense of shame." See *A Complete Book Concerning Happiness and Benevolence*, trans. Djang Chu (Tucson: University of Arizona Press, 1984), 283.

117. Ibid., 274, 277.

118. Ibid., 284.

119. QSG 143: 1496.

120. Joanna Waley-Cohen, *Exile in Mid-Qing China* (New Haven, Conn.: Yale University Press, 1991), 117. Ura says that even when Manchu criminals were tattooed, they were tattooed on the arm, unlike Han criminals, who were tattooed on the face ("Shinchō no kanjin tōgyōsaku," 83).

121. On the commutation of punishments for Manchus and others in the banners, Bodde and Morris comment, "the numerous references [ten] to Manchus and bannermen include only two in which commutation of bambooing and military exile to whipping and the cangue is mentioned" and note that in fact high-ranking imperial Manchu clansmen could be beaten with the bamboo (Derk Bodde and Clarence Morris, eds., *Law in Imperial China* [Philadelphia: University of Pennsylvania Press, 1967], 170). What this

overlooks is that commutation was a privilege, not a right, and therefore revocable. Further research into the relationship of bannermen and the law would do much to clarify the exact nature of this privilege. A start is Su Qin, "Qing lü zhong qiren 'fanzui mian faqian' kaoshi," *Qingshi luncong* (1992), 75–87, who argues that the Manchus were unable to reconcile their pre-conquest legal system with the Chinese legal system.

122.  *Gaozong shilu*, 73: 11b–12a. In this case, the immunity (from military exile) was restored in 1738.

123.  This is a well-established fact at the higher levels of the Qing bureaucracy. See, for instance, the conclusions of Chu and Saywell, *Career Patterns in the Ch'ing Dynasty*, or Bartlett, *Monarchs and Ministers*.

124.  *Shengzu shilu*, 127: 4a. This was to have important ramifications on the residence question. See Chapter 6.

125.  Chen, *Langqian jiwen sanbi*, 7, 776. More on dyarchy is said in Chapter 5.

126.  An example of some such set-asides may be found in *Gaozong shilu*, 139: 28a–b.

127.  *Shengzu shilu*, 22: 18b.

128.  Chu and Saywell, *Career Patterns in the Ch'ing Dynasty*, 46; see also Fu-ge, *Tingyu congtan*, 2: 51. For the early reliance on Chinese banner-men see Wakeman, *The Great Enterprise*, who relied on the work of Narakino Shimesu (see References); also Lawrence Kessler, "Ethnic Composition of Provincial Leadership During the Ch'ing Dynasty," *Journal of Asian Studies* 28 (May 1969), 489–511; and Chu and Saywell, *Career Patterns in the Ch'ing Dynasty*, 31–38.

129.  YZMaZPZZ 97, Niyan Geng Yoo [Nian Gengyao], YZ3.3.24.

130.  Fu-ge, *Tingyu congtan*, "Baqi zhisheng dufu dachen kao," "Baqi zhisheng xunfu kao," "Zhisheng Man-que xunfu kao," 57–76; Ura, "Shinchō no kanjin tōgyōsaku," 65. Quotas listed in the *Da Qing huidian* and the *Da Qing huidian shili* are nicely summarized in Guo et al., *Qingchao dianzhi*.

131.  The standard work is Miyazaki Ichisada, *China's Examination Hell: The Civil Service Examinations of Imperial China*, trans. Conrad Schirokauer (New Haven, Conn.: Yale University Press, 1981). See also the new work on this subject by Benjamin A. Elman, *A Cultural History of Civil Examinations in Late Imperial China* (Berkeley and Los Angeles: University of California Press, 1999).

132.  Ura, "Shinchō no kanjin tōgyōsaku," 68. Two of the three winners came in 1865, when the *primus* was the Mongol Chong-qi and the *tertius* the Chinese bannerman Yang Qi (Wu, *Yangjizhai conglu*, 9: 86). Chong-qi was no ordinary bannerman, but the son of Grand Councillor Saišangga and father-in

law to the Tongzhi emperor. He hanged himself in 1900 when foreign troops occupied Beijing (ECCP 208–9).

133. Wang Qingyun explains these fluctuations as corresponding to rising and falling military needs in the first decades of Qing rule (*Shiqu yuji*, "Ji Manzhou keju," 34).

134. Ibid.; Wu, *Yangjizhai conglu*, 9: 100; Crossley, "Manchu Education," 349 (the identification here of Shuntian as "Abkai imiyangga" is in error; Abkai imiyangga was Fengtian, i.e., the area around Mukden).

135. Chu and Saywell found that of the twenty-seven times the metropolitan examination was administered during the Qianlong reign, more than half the time fewer than three Manchus won the degree (*Career Patterns in the Ch'ing Dynasty*, 52).

136. Crossley, "Manchu Education," 350–51, 352.

137. This is one of a number of similarities between the Jin and Qing translation examinations. On the Jin examinations, see Bol, "Seeking Common Ground," 477–79.

138. See the detailed discussion in Ishibashi Takao, "Shinchō no 'honyaku kakyō' o megutte," *Rekishi to chiri* 393 (1988), 1–17.

139. Ibid., 10.

140. Fu-ge, *Tingyu congtan*, "Kemu," 78.

141. *Gaozong shilu*, 622: 3a.

142. Only in the nineteenth century would military service prove a fast track to political power for Han, and even then, most of the Chinese who achieved it had acquired the *jinshi* degree anyway.

143. ECCP 6. Later on, imperial respect for his father's age and stature spared his execution.

144. On this extraordinary family, which managed to keep producing degree-holders for five centuries, see Hilary Beattie, *Land and Lineage in China: A Study of T'ung-cheng County, Anhwei, in the Ming and Ch'ing Dynasties* (Cambridge: Cambridge University Press, 1979).

145. The period of mourning for all bannermen (Manchu, Mongol, Chinese banner) was decreed in 1653 at one month, but twenty years later was set at one hundred days. After the one hundred days was over, they could once again shave and return to work (*Shengzu shilu*, 4: 15b–16a, and 43: 7b–8a; DQHDSL 138: 2a–3b). Chinese bannermen who filled slots normally reserved for Han Chinese were required to observe twenty-seven months' mourning. On the removal of rings and tassels (from hats), see QLMaZPZZ 175, Kildan and Gandai, QL13.6.16. Many Manchus routinely wore thumb rings, which were intended to protect the finger when drawing a bow. These can often be seen in portraits. On the question of mourning under the Qing

generally, see Norman Kutcher, *Mourning in Late Imperial China*. A specific case is presented in "The Death of the Xiaoxian Empress: Bureaucratic Betrayals and the Crises of Eighteenth-Century Chinese Rule," *Journal of Asian Studies* 56.3 (August 1997), 708–25. The event described here became a well-known scandal of Manchus violating their own ritual taboos (Wu, *Yangjizhai conglu*, 4: 326). In venting his indignation and fury at the news, the emperor repeatedly called upon Manchus to remember the "old ways" (*Gaozong shilu*, 317: 3b–5b).

146. Wu, *Yangjizhai conglu*, 3: 34.

147. In 1737 censor Xue Yun incurred the young Qianlong emperor's wrath for having "wantonly" criticized him for frequently riding and shooting inside the palace grounds in violation of the conventions of grief (the Yongzheng emperor having passed away less than two years before). The emperor denied the charge as slander and outlandish rumor, yet excused Xue from punishment, allowing that he might have had a point had the emperor been guilty of hunting after having first removed his mourning garb—which one suspects may have been just the case (*Gaozong shilu*, 41: 26a–b).

148. This regulation was changed in 1749, when garrison Mongols and Manchus were required to come to Beijing to observe one hundred days of mourning, after which they would be given a new post. Chinese bannermen were not included here, so presumably the former twenty-seven-month requirement still applied to them. Bannermen in the Northeast were never required to return to Beijing for mourning.

149. Guo et al, *Qingchao dianzhi*, 296–98.

150. *Shizu shilu*, 76: 15a.

151. *Gaozong shilu*, 54: 2a–5a.

152. DQHDSL 138: 6a.

153. Isolated cases of genuine protest, such as that in Zhapu in 1730 (documented in Ding, *Qingdai baqi zhufang*, 215), did occur, but I have not found evidence to support the assertion that "unrest" in the garrisons was a chronic problem or that court policy responded consciously to its intensification (Crossley, *Orphan Warriors*, 56, citing *Manzu jianshi*, 113).

154. Michael, *The Origin of Manchu Rule in China*, 119. The context of this phrase was discussed in the Introduction.

155. Parker, *China, Her History*, 260–61.

156. Meadows says that he explicitly compared the position of the British in India to that of the Manchus in China in his discussions with Qing officials during the Taiping Rebellion, noting that the analogy made a deep impression (*The Chinese and Their Rebellions*, 293).

157. The numerous detailed studies of Narakino Shimesu in this con-

nection are especially revealing (some of these are used in Wakeman, *The Great Enterprise*, 1021–33). For specific references, see the bibliography. For the period up to 1735, see also the tables in Lawrence Kessler, *K'ang-hsi and the Consolidation of Ch'ing Rule*, 120–22.

158. This is a major theme, for instance, in *Manzu jianshi*. Cf. the comments on the "bindings" of the banner system being loosened (148, 153, 170).

## Chapter 5. Among the Nikan

1. The etymology of the Manchu word for the Chinese remains uncertain. It was frequently used as a given name in the early Qing, perhaps for children whose appearance was felt to be more Chinese than Manchu.

2. This point is sometimes forgotten by Chinese chauvinist historians celebrating "protonationalist" forces during the Qing conquest or the "revolutionary" anti-Manchuism of the Taiping rebels. See, for instance, the accounts of the conquest in Hsiao I-shan, *Qingdai tongshi*, vol. 1, or of the Taiping Rebellion in Fan Wenlan, *Zhongguo jindaishi*. The latter makes the claim that "The Chinese people had never ceased resisting the Manchu-Qing, and anti-Manchu societies spread throughout all provinces north and south in the years before and after the Opium War" (85). Outside the Yangzi delta open rejection of Manchu rule was actually uncommon in the conquest period. See Hilary Beattie, "The Alternative to Resistance: The Case of T'ung-cheng, Anhwei," in Spence and Wills, eds., *From Ming to Ch'ing*, 241–76.

3. These differences are taken up in the following chapters.

4. A classic discussion of Manchu sensitivity is found in Kahn, *Monarchy in the Emperor's Eyes*. To give just a few examples of what this could mean: in his study of the Dai Mingshi case of 1713, Pierre-Henri Durand refers to deep-set differences between Manchus and Chinese, as when he speaks of "Chinese morality versus a certain Manchu immorality" ("la moralité Chinoise contre une certaine immoralité mandchoue") (229); or in his evaluation of the emperor's decision in the case as his having to make Manchu and Chinese parties at court toe the line: "His policy was a twin hemming-in, first of the Manchus, who threatened his power, and second of the Chinese, who by their remarks tended to sap the dynasty's prestige, and hence its stability" (Sa politique était une double mise au pas, des Mandchous d'abord, qui menaçaient son pouvoir, des Chinois ensuite, qui tendaient par leurs propos à saper le prestige de la dynastie, donc sa stabilité) (Durand, *Lettrés et pouvoirs*, 265). Philip Kuhn's analysis of queue-clipping cases in 1768 makes it clear that this same dynamic persisted then: "Even as sinicized a Manchu ruler as Hungli [the Qianlong emperor] could not dissociate sedition from the ethnic factor" (*Soulstealers*, 226). And James Polachek's reinterpretation of mid-nineteenth-century

politics also emphasizes the ethnic factor: "There was, in short, a kind of unwritten agenda beneath the surface debates over foreign policy we have studied: an unspoken 'inner' agenda shaped, ultimately, by the insecurities to which all lettered-class Chinese were subject as they struggled with the problems of career-making in a still Manchu-dominated world" (*The Inner Opium War*, 287).

5. YZMaZPZZ 512, Unaha, YZ7.10.1, YZ7.12.1.

6. YZMaZPZZ 111, Sibe, YZ4.4.10.

7. YZMaZPZZ 241, Faršan, YZ12.2.2.

8. Zheng, *Qingdai sifa shenpan*, 64.

9. Ding, *Qingdai baqi zhufang*, 200, citing *Zhupi yuzhi*, Šilin, 58: 62.

10. *Shizong shilu*, 73: 15a–b. Other cases culled at random from the *Veritable Records* involve conflicts at Liangzhou (*Gaozong shilu*, 92: 11b–12a), Hangzhou (ibid., 453: 6b–7a), and Suiyuan (ibid., 614: 21b).

11. It ought to be noted, however, that Qing ethnic policy was not terribly consistent. Attitudes toward "northern" peoples, including most of the peoples it encountered in eastern Turkestan, were generally far more accommodating than attitudes toward "southern" peoples in Guangxi, Yunnan, and Guizhou, the chief exception in the Northwest being the Dzungars, who were mercilessly wiped out in the 1760s. The discussion of "ethnic harmony" in this chapter is restricted primarily to relations between the Han and the constituent groups of the Eight Banners, Manchus as well as Mongols and Chinese bannermen. It specifically excludes, however, the relationship between Manchu bannermen and Chinese bannermen, a complex subject taken up in Chapter 8. Although it is true that by the middle of the eighteenth century Chinese bannermen were thought of as being "originally" Chinese, as long as they held banner status they remained in a distinctly separate category from "Nikan."

12. *Kyū Manshūtō tensō kyūnen*, 2: 214–15.

13. Wakeman, *The Great Enterprise*, 873.

14. *Shizu shilu*, 15: 30b–31a. *Guojia* here is almost certainly a translation of the Manchu word *gurun*.

15. Ibid., 31: 21b. The context was the murder of a Han Chinese by a Manchu. The emperor went on to rebuke Manchus for oppressing Han civilians. He also castigated Han who had joined the banners as slaves and subsequently took advantage of their new, more powerful status to create trouble. Similar denials of favoritism may be found for 1654; see ibid., 86: 1b–2a.

16. Ibid., 43: 14b–15a.

17. Ibid., 90: 4a.

18. Li Hua, "Kangxi dui Hanzu shidaifu de zhengce," in Zuo Buqing, ed., *Kang-Yong-Qian sandi pingyi* (Beijing: Zijincheng chubanshe, 1986), 80.

19. Durand, *Lettrés et pouvoirs*, 264–65.

20. Chen, *Langqian jiwen chubi*, 10: 223. Regarding the Yongzheng emperor's "liberal" views, I have in mind his manumission of those of "mean" status (Ch *jianmin*), his exhortation of tolerance of different religious practices, particularly Islam, and his remonstration with banner nobles to be kinder to their servants: "They are people, too" (SYBQ YZ 2.6.12, 16a–b).

21. SYBQ 6.8.9: 36b.

22. SYBQ 6.10.6: 44a–b. The same edict is collected in BQTZ 68: 1316–17.

23. Cf. Albert Feuerwerker's comment in this connection: "The Yungcheng emperor should, I believe, be taken as expressing his true intentions if not always his practice when he claimed to 'make no distinction between Manchus and Chinese, but preserve only the most scrupulous impartiality toward all my subjects'" (*State and Society in Eighteenth-Century China*, 70). The trick here, of course, is to differentiate intent and practice.

24. At least one historian has dismissed the *Man-Han yijia* rhetoric as "a false propagandistic method" to deceive Han literati, a typical case of "hanging up a sheep's head and selling dog meat" (Li, "Kangxi dui Hanzu," 77–79).

25. Spence, *Ts'ao Yin*, 70–76; Kessler, *K'ang-hsi and the Consolidation of Ch'ing Rule*, 117 ff.; Oxnam, *Ruling from Horseback*, 77–79, 180; Chu and Saywell, *Career Patterns in the Ch'ing Dynasty*, 47; Wakeman, *The Great Enterprise*, 872 ff.; Bartlett, *Monarchs and Ministers*, 35.

26. Zhao Yi, *Yanpu zaji* (1829; reprint, Beijing: Zhonghua shuju, 1982), 34, "Jian guan buwu." Bartlett proves a decisive Manchu preponderance at the shadowy level of unofficial board "superintendencies," and concludes that "dyarchy eventually existed only among the clerks" (*Monarchs and Ministers*, 37, 224).

27. Details on these and other cases are available in ECCP; Wakeman, *The Great Enterprise*; Huang, *Autocracy at Work*; and Durand, *Lettrés et pouvoirs*.

28. Guy, *The Emperor's Four Treasuries*, 48. As he notes, this happened "with a speed which belied the Manchus' often proclaimed desire to rule without regard to ethnic distinctions." The offending official, Hang Shijun, supposedly advocated the appointment of more Han Chinese to provincial office. Once dismissed, he was never recalled to the civil service (ECCP 276).

29. *Shizu shilu*, 72: 3b–4a.

30. Ibid., 90: 4a–5a. Most of this edict is translated in Kessler, *K'ang-hsi and the Consolidation of Ch'ing Rule*, 16–17. See also the similar sentiments in a 1654 edict (*Shizu shilu*, 86: 1b–2b).

31. SYBQ YZ2: 1a–b (YZ2.2.2).

32. Chen, *Langqian jiwen chubi*, 13: 289.

33. *Shizu shilu*, 43: 16b–17a. Note the assumption just below the surface here that expression in different languages necessarily meant the expression of different "minds."

34. Ibid., 140: 3a–6a, 10a–13a; 141: 8b–10b.

35. *Shengzu shilu*, 149: 11–12.

36. "Nine Ministers" (*jiu qing/uyun king*) referred in fact to seventeen officials: the Manchu and Han presidents of the Six Boards, the Manchu and Han presidents of the censorate, the Manchu and Han directors of the Court of Judicature and Revision, and the president of the Court of Colonial Affairs (always a Manchu or a Mongol).

37. YZMaZPZZ 162, Yandene, YZ7.9.22. See also the undated memorial of the Yongzheng period complaining that while Chinese serving in the Six Boards were all degree-holders, their Manchu colleagues could not all be assumed even to be literate in Chinese (YZHaZZH, vol. 31, no. 3, memorial of Santai).

38. *Shizu shilu*, 74: 9a–10a.

39. YZMaZPZZ 1, Santai, YZ 1.8.10.

40. *Gaozong shilu*, 66: 4a.

41. Ibid., 114: 8a.

42. Ibid., 819: 15a–b.

43. Bartlett, *Monarchs and Ministers*, 266–67.

44. Cranmer-Byng, *An Embassy to China*, 227.

45. Ibid., 238–39. Macartney believed this mistake arose from the tendency of Westerners to assume, on the basis of the European model, that rulers everywhere were like the Habsburgs, who were Austrian in Austria but Spanish in Spain. Thus, he proclaimed, the present king (George III), was "as much an Englishman as King Alfred or King Edgar," whereas in Asia one's national origins ultimately mattered more than where a ruler happened to hold power (237). This points to fundamental differences in early modern ideas of royalty and sovereignty in Europe and China.

46. Staunton, *An Historical Account*, 330–31; punctuation and grammar slightly altered. The first incident, if true, testifies to the persistent place of the Manchurian "homeland" in the historical memory of mid-Qing Manchus.

47. Ura, "Shinchō no kanjin tōgyōsaku," 66.

48. The proportion of bannermen (including Chinese bannermen) filling governorships remained more or less the same in both reigns (58 percent under Yongzheng, 54 percent under Qianlong). Calculated from figures in Narakino Shimesu, "Shindai tokubu Man-Kan hiritsu no hendō ni tsuite," *Gunma*

*daigaku kyōikugakubu kiyō—jinbun shakaigaku* 14, 223–25; reprinted in
*Chūgoku kankei ronsetsu shiryō* 3.3 (1965), 551–60.

49. Ding, *Qingdai baqi zhufang*, 211, citing *Zhupi yuzhi* 31: 102.

50. As it turns out, Chinese often made better tenants than other banner-men. Whereas bannermen invented all kinds of excuses to avoid paying overdue rent, Han merchants tended to pay when pressed to because they were afraid to lose business—a sign not just that their leverage was limited, but that competition for commercial real estate was keen (YZMaZPZZ 239, Bašinu, YZ12.6.3).

51. YZMaZPZZ 245, Mantai, YZ12.4.29.

52. *Gaozong shilu*, 575: 14b; YZMaZPZZ 190, Fusen, YZ7.11.20; GZD/QL 12: 300, Sinju, QL20.8.10.

53. The memorialist called them *elemangga nikasa* ("crafty Chinese") and complained that Manchu honor (Ma *dere*, lit., "face") had been stained (QLMaZPZZ 305, Gioro Tunfuju, QL24.6.14).

54. Hosoya Yoshio, "Hakki beikyoku kō—Shinchō chūki no hakki keizai o megutte," *Shūkan tōyōgaku* 31 (June 1974), 184.

55. In response to a proposal to implement such a ban, it was noted that although some bannermen suffered when Chinese merchants who had bought their "extra" granary rice from them cheap sold it back to them at a higher price, outlawing the sale of banner rice would cause prices in the capital to rise even higher. The proposal was shelved (*Yuxing qiwu zouyi*, YZ1: YZ1.5.8, quoted in Hosoya, "Hakki beikyoku kō," 185). At the same time, supervising officers were instructed to pay closer attention to the amounts being sold by soldiers.

56. The banner grain trade and its relation to price stabilization is discussed in detail in Hosoya, "Hakki beikyoku kō." See also Helen Dunstan, "'Orders Go Forth in the Morning and are Changed by Nightfall': A Monetary Policy Cycle in Qing China, November 1744–June 1745," *T'oung Pao* 82 (1996); and Lillian Li and Alison Dray-Novey, "Protecting Beijing's Food Security in the Qing Dynasty: State, Market, and Police," *Journal of Asian Studies* 58.4 (November 1999), 992–1032.

57. YZHaZZH, vol. 28, no. 632, Li Xi, YZ13.6.25.

58. From the late eighteenth-century work by the Mongol bannerman Song-yun, *Records of Talks by One Hundred Twenty Elders*, cited in Hosoya, "Hakki beikyoku kō," 205n. The Chinese version of this passage is on page 186 of the article. I have retranslated from the Manchu text, found in *Emu tanggū orin sakda-i gisun sarkiyan*, *Asiatische Forschungen* 83, ed. and trans. Giovanni Stary (Wiesbaden: Otto Harrassowitz, 1983).

59. YZMaZPZZ 13, Sunju, YZ1.8.7. See also YZMaZPZZ 12, Ulibu, YZ1.9.20

60. YZMaZPZZ 235, Irantai, YZ12.5.29. The report went on to request a prohibition on any further sales of food and drink on credit to bannermen, particularly infantrymen. Compare the depiction of Shandong restaurateur Manager Wang in *Beneath the Red Banner*, who, though on good terms with his bannermen customers, was fond of repeating, "Business is business, friends are friends" (Lao She, *Beneath the Red Banner*, 85).

61. Kuhn, *Soulstealers*, 226.

62. QLMaZPZZ 93, Bašinu, QL5.12.27.

63. KXMaZPZZ 469, Siju, KX47.8.29.

64. *Shizu shilu*, 138: 24a. Manchus apparently were a terror in the Beijing markets, too, before the removal of the Chinese (ibid., 15: 17a–b).

65. *Shengzu shilu*, 104: 3a–b.

66. Ibid., 139: 26a. This complaint alarmed those who feared that such sentiments were widespread among commoners. When a search for its author turned up empty-handed, suspicion fell on Jin Quan, the provincial governor who had forwarded it to the center. He was exiled to Mukden.

67. For similar reports and pronouncements, see ibid., 123: 15a; 137: 26a.

68. Ibid., 111: 27b–28a.    69. Ibid., 104: 20a.

70. Ibid.: 20b–21a.    71. *Shizu shilu*, 129: 5a.

72. Ding notes that after the Rebellion of the Three Feudatories, relations between garrison bannermen and Chinese locals were "normalized," but that conflict remained common. She also cites political and economic inequalities as the main source of this conflict (*Qingdai baqi zhufang*, 198, 202–3).

73. YZMaZPZZ 1067, Cimbu, YZ7.10.28. Cimbu had already recommended several cases to local officials to handle and put up announcements warning against further such behavior.

74. YZMaZPZZ 820, Cangseli, YZ7.8.7.

75. Ding, *Qingdai baqi zhufang*, 113, citing *Zhupi yuzhi*, 49: 34–35.

76. YZMaZPZZ 190, Fusen, YZ7.11.20. Anxious to reassure the emperor, though, Fusen prefaced this by saying, "Since coming to Zhapu I have done things following custom, law, and discretion as required. Small affairs have come up but there have been no incidents of clashes with commoners."

77. E.g., *Gaozong shilu*, 393: 3b–4b; GZD/QL 1: 657, Kerjišan [Ke-er-ji-shan], QL16.9.14; 7: 32, Gioro Yarhašan [Jue-luo Ya-er-ha-shan], QL18.12.4. For the nineteenth century, see the incidents in Elliott, "Bannerman and Townsman," and Im, "On Manchu-Chinese Relations."

78. Wang, *Shiqu yuji*, 196–97, "Ji qiren shengji."

79. YZHaZZH, vol. 3, no. 530, Yi Zhaoxiong, YZ 2.9.25.

80. YZMaZPZZ 147, Sibe, YZ6.7.19.

81. KXMaZPZZ 296, Ohai, KX43.1.8.

82. This official was called a *lishi tongzhi* or *lishi tongpan* in Chinese, *weile beidere* ("crime-examining") or *baita beidere* ("matter-examining") *tungjy* or *tungpan* in Manchu.

83. *Shengzu shilu*, 125, cited in Ding, "Qingdai lishi tongzhi," 264. My account of this office and its functions draws on Ding's pioneering article, supplemented by my own findings.

84. YZMaZPZZ 5, Saksu, YZ2.10.21; and 75, Haišeo, YZ3.1.12.

85. The *lishi tongzhi* was ranked 5b, the *lishi tongpan* 6b.

86. Fu-ge, *Tingyu congtan*, 11: 220–21. In fact, when the position was first created, it was most commonly filled by Han Chinese because of a dearth of Chinese-speaking Manchus, becoming a Manchu-only slot in the 1690s. See Ding Yizhuang, "Qingdai lishi tongzhi," 265. By the early Qianlong reign, even the slot at the mainly Chinese banner Guangzhou garrison was reserved for Manchus (*Gaozong shilu*, 52: 5b–6a).

87. YZMaZPZZ 75, Haišeo, YZ3.1.12.

88. Cf. two cases from the 1730s, one in which the Hangzhou garrison general assumes responsibility for payment of a "nourishing-honest allowance" to the civil commissioner, and another in which the Jingzhou garrison general nominates Ingju, a long-serving scribe at the garrison, to fill the vacant post of civil commissioner (QLMaZPZZ 63, Bašinu, QL2.5.21; and 85, Guntai, QL4.17.2).

89. Ding, "Qingdai lishi tongzhi," 267–69. Ding argues that the civil commissioner's main duty was to "protect the interests of bannermen from encroachment in areas where bannermen and civilians lived in proximity," and that he was essentially a proxy for the garrison general, who might find it inexpedient to become involved in legal controversies. More work on the role of this anomalous post is needed.

90. Ibid., 267.

91. A fuller exposé is found in Wei Qingyuan, Wu Qiyan, and Lu Su, *Qingdai nubei zhidu* (Beijing: Zhongguo renmin daxue chubanshe, 1982), upon which much of the following is based.

92. Slaves also appear to have been of great economic importance in the Yuan military economy. See Elizabeth Endacott-West, "Yüan Government and Society," in Twitchett and Franke, eds., *The Cambridge History of China*, vol. 6, *Alien Regimes and Border States, 907–1368*, 614, for a summary.

93. Precedents governing the purchase, registration, and management of banner slaves are in DQHDSL 1116. Chinese bannermen could own slaves, too. A 1755 memorial from the Fuzhou governor-general asked that thirteen people condemned to slavery for their crimes who had earlier been awarded to

Fuzhou Chinese bannermen be remanded to newly arrived Manchu bannermen at Fuzhou (GZD/QL 11: 63, Kerjišan, QL20.3.24).

94. YZMaZPZZ 187, Bayartu, YZ8.1.25. *Kutule* were banner slaves
charged with caring for a soldier's horses. In the Manchu banners *kutule* were
always slaves, but this was not necessarily the case in the Chinese banners. In
the Yongzheng and Qianlong reigns, each soldier usually took with him one
such man. For more details, see Liu Xiaomeng, "Ku-tu-le kao," *Manyu yanjiu*
(1987.2), 121–28.

95. Though their duties appear to have overlapped to a degree, it is
important not to confuse these people with the other important group of
people of unfree status in the banners, the bondservants. As explained in the
first chapter, bondservants were enrolled in their own companies in the
banners and were attached either to the imperial household (if in the Upper
Three Banners) or to princely or other Manchu households (if in the Lower
Five Banners). Their presence as a hereditary caste in Manchu society dated
back to well before the conquest and they served in important official and
unofficial capacities. The majority were Manchu themselves. Regular slaves,
on the other hand, never belonged to companies. Their status in banner
households was incomparably inferior to that of bondservants. Almost all
were Han Chinese, most from poorer families.

96. *Shengzu shilu*, 167: 3a.

97. One might argue that the nearly universal ownership of slaves among
bannermen was one of the legacies of the preconquest period in Qing society.
See Wei et al., *Qingdai nubei*, 5; the authors estimate that by 1630 there were
two million slaves in the Latter Jin state (15).

98. Ibid., 49. One of the few restrictions on the slave trade was that high-
ranking provincial and garrison officials could not purchase slaves from
among the residents of areas under their jurisdiction. This restriction does
not seem to have been enforced, however (50). Slave ownership was not
limited to bannermen, of course; Chinese, too, could own slaves.

99. Bannermen who were condemned to slavery (typically for political
crimes) were stripped of all rights and became part of a special class of slaves
attached to the Imperial Household Department, called in Manchu *sin jeku
jetere aha*, meaning roughly "eighteen-quarts-of-millet-eating slaves." In
Chinese they were referred to as *xin-zhe-ku*. Chinese bannermen and bondservants, on the other hand, were usually sold as ordinary slaves—which was
not, however, always possible. When the household of Li Xu was confiscated
and its members put on the slave market in Suzhou, for more than a year
"nobody dared buy them because all in the south knew that they had been
bannermen" (ibid., 72).

100. GZMaZJ 6, Coldo, QL5.R6.16.

101. *Gaozong shilu*, 549: 19a–b, cited in Ding, *Qingdai baqi zhufang*, 206. After a 1784 Moslem uprising, the court gave more than twenty-six hundred people—the wives and children of those who had taken part in the rebellion—as slaves to bannermen at the Nanjing, Hangzhou, Fuzhou, and Guangzhou garrisons (*Gaozong shilu*, 1211: 27a, cited in Wei et al., *Qingdai nubei*, 60–61, and Ding, *Qingdai baqi zhufang*, 207).

102. YZMaZPZZ 24, Yangboo, YZ1.2.6. *Ujin* was the term used for children of household slaves. Derived from the verb *ujimbi*, "to raise, nourish," it was also the word to describe the colt of a family horse or calf of a family cow.

103. Ding, *Qingdai baqi zhufang*, 203, citing *Zhupi yuzhi*, Wang Shijun, 19: 79.

104. GZD/QL 14: 699, Turbingga [Tu-er-bing-a], QL21.6.22.

105. Wei et al., *Qingdai nubei*, 55–57.

106. *Shengzu shilu*, 191: 3a.

107. Some hair-raising cases are described in Wei et al., *Qingdai nubei*, 107–35. Commenting on the murder of a slave for drunkenness and trying to mellow the notoriously harsh Manchu treatment of slaves, the Yongzheng emperor was once moved to write, "Though slaves may be of mean origin, they are also people" (SYBQ YZ2: 16b [YZ2.6.12]).

108. Chen, *Langqian jiwen sanbi*, 2: 674, "Kangxi chunian baqi pubei zijin zhi duo." The figure there of two thousand servants must be an exaggeration.

109. One such "bully slave" (Ch *haonu*) belonging to Nian Gengyao was said to have amassed a fortune of several hundred thousand taels (Wei et al., *Qingdai nubei*, 87, citing *Shizong shilu*, 39).

110. YZMaZPZZ 187, Bayartu, YZ8.1.25.

111. GZMaZJ 6, Coldo, QL5.R6.16.

112. QLMaZPZZ 69, Coldo, QL2.12.17.

113. Ibid.

114. See the comparison in Peng Yuxin, "Qing wangchao pianchong Manqi de yiguan zhengce ji qi xiaoji houguo," *Qingshi luncong* (1992), 32–35.

115. After the initial fight, a sort of vendetta grew between the garrisons, with the Manchu soldiers surrounding the Green Standard headquarters at night and creating disturbances (QLHaZPZZ 9, Kerjišan, QL9.6.29, QL9.10.3 and QL n.d.).

116. See also the 1899 case at Jingzhou discussed in Im, "On Manchu-Chinese Relations."

117. Zheng, *Qingdai sifa shenpan*, 63–64, citing *Xing'an huilan*, chap. 1.

118. Provincial garrison officials were threatened with penalties for failure to investigate instances of harm to the populace or withholding of grain or salary payments, leading one to suspect that nonreporting was a widespread problem (*Zhongshu zhengkao* [1785], 15: 112).

119. See Kuhn, *Soulstealers.*

### Chapter 6. Resident Aliens

1. *Affective* (sometimes *emic*) typically refers to the power of internal markers of ethnic membership, in contrast to external *ascriptive* (or *etic*) markers of ethnicity.

2. A more detailed description of Manchu shamanism is found in S. M. Shirokogoroff, *Psychomental Complex of the Northern Tungus* (London: Routledge and Kegan Paul, 1935). See also the discussion in Margaret Nowak and Stephen Durrant, *The Tale of the Nišan Shamaness: A Manchu Folk Epic* (Seattle: University of Washington Press, 1977). A preliminary index of the Manchu pantheon is presented by Giovanni Stary, "Versuch eines Index des mandschurischen Pantheon," in Giovanni Stary, ed., *Shamanica Manchurica Collecta* 5 (Wiesbaden: Harrassowitz Verlag, 1998), 115–39. A fuller exploration of the political significance of Manchu shamanism is Di Cosmo, "Manchu Shamanic Ceremonies." See also the discussion in Rawski, *The Last Emperors*, chap. 7. A fascinating recent study of Mongolian shamanic practices similar to those of the Manchus is Caroline Humphrey, with Urgunge Onon, *Shamans and Elders: Experience, Knowledge, and Power Among the Daur Mongols* (Oxford: Oxford University Press, 1996). On Manchu interest in Chinese Buddhism, see Susan Naquin's forthcoming work on the temples of Beijing; in Tibetan Buddhism, see Samuel Grupper, "The Manchu Imperial Cult of the Early Ch'ing Dynasty: Texts and Studies on the Tantric Sanctuary of Mahakala at Mukden" (Ph.D. diss., Indiana University, 1979), Xiangyun Wang, "Tibetan Buddhism at the Court of Qing: The Life and Work of lCang-sKya Rol-pa'i-rdo-rje (1717–1786)," (Ph.D. diss., Harvard University, 1995), and Vladimir Uspensky, *Prince Yunli (1697–1738), Manchu Statesman and Tibetan Buddhist* (Tokyo: Institute for the Study of Languages and Cultures of Asia and Africa, 1997). Ben Wu, "Ritual Music in the Court and Rulership of the Qing Dynasty (1644–1911)" (Ph.D. diss., University of Pittsburgh, 1998), is a very thorough exploration of the place of music in Manchu shamanic (and other) court rituals.

3. "Shamanism in the strict sense is preeminently a religious phenomenon of Siberia and Central Asia." From Mircea Eliade, *Shamanism: Archaic Techniques of Ecstasy* (Princeton, N.J.: Princeton University Press, 1964), 4. Though outdated in some respects, this remains the classic work.

4. On the qualities expected of a shaman, see Vladimir N. Basilov, "Chosen by the Spirits," in Marjorie Mandelstam Balzer, ed., *Shamanic Worlds: Rituals and Lore of Siberia and Central Asia* (Armonk, N.Y.: M. E. Sharpe, 1997), 3–48. There is extensive discussion of this at various places also in Eliade, *Shamanism.*

5. In her fieldwork among the Daur Mongols in northern Manchuria, Caroline Humphrey observed the "confident bearing of Daur women and the many responsible positions they held," which her informants attributed to their role as shamans. She notes, however, that "by becoming a shaman one entered a quasi-androgynous state" (*Shamans and Elders*, 168, 171).

6. As happened during the unification of the Jurchen tribes under Nurhaci and Hong Taiji. See Fu Yuguang and Meng Huiying, *Manzu samanjiao yanjiu* (Beijing: Beijing daxue chubanshe, 1991), 67.

7. Chinese scholars call these *jiaji* and *yeji* (literally "family sacrifice" and "wild sacrifice"), respectively. See Fu and Meng, *Manzu samanjiao*, 66.

8. These are my terms. They correspond to the distinction made in almost all descriptions of Manchu shamanism between the rituals of the imperial house and the rituals of other Manchus.

9. Caroline Humphrey, "Shamanic Practices and the State in Northern Asia," in Nicholas Thomas and Caroline Humphrey, eds., *Shamanism, History, and the State* (Ann Arbor: University of Michigan Press, 1995), 198–200.

10. In the Ming, this part of the palace had been the residence of the empress. The Qing rebuilt it to serve as a place for shamanic ritual (changing, among other things, the style of windows and installing large cauldrons for use in preparing sacrificial foods). Its only other use was as a temporary wedding chamber for newlywed emperors. Other palace buildings used for shamanic rituals included the hall for sacrificing to the horse god (Ch *ji mashen shi*) located near the Shenwu men at the rear of the palace and the Ningshou gong, built in 1772. See Jiang Xiangshun, *Shenmi de qinggong saman jisi* (Shenyang: Liaoning renmin chubanshe, 1995), 7–15, 151. On the Ningshou gong, see Mo, "Qingchu Manzu de samanjiao," in *Manzushi luncong*, 195.

11. References to worship at the *tangse* in Mukden are plentiful and can be found, for example, in *Kyū Manshūtō*, 2, 259, 286.

12. That the emperor in fact did observe this rite was documented by Mo, *Manzushi luncong*, 190–91. Other major ritual occasions were the third day of the first month, the first day of every other month, the eighth day of the fourth month, the twenty-sixth day of the twelfth month, and two days each at the arrival of spring and autumn (Jiang, *Shenmi de qinggong*, 18–19).

13. Though the Manchu word *tangse* shows every sign of having come from the Chinese, the original Chinese translation of this word was *yemiao*,

"visitation temple." It acquired the more obvious name *tangzi* only after 1660 or so. The Beijing *tangse* was built in 1653 directly on the model of the Shenyang *tangse*. Its location was on the corner of what is now East Chang'an Boulevard and Taijichang Street, directly opposite the "modern" wing of the Beijing Hotel. It was destroyed during the Boxer Uprising. See Fu Tongqin, "Qingdai de tangzi," in *Ming-Qingshi guoji xueshu taolunhui lunwenji* (Tianjin: Tianjin renmin chubanshe, 1982), 271–75, 284.

14. The incense used was not Chinese stick-incense but an aromatic grass called "Tartar fragrance" (Ch *dazi xiang*) (Fu-ge, *Tingyu congtan* 6: 138).

15. Mo, "Qingchu Manzu de samanjiao," 194. Zhao-lian says that Mongol princes were permitted to attend, probably meaning those related by marriage to the imperial house.

16. Zhao-lian, *Xiaoting zalu/xulu*, 1: 377.

17. This raises questions about the relationship of Manchu ritual to other Qing ritual practices, in which the emperor was a "pivotal center." See Hevia, *Cherishing Men from Afar*,124.

18. Preface to *Manzhou jishen jitian dianli* (1781), in Jin, ed., *Liaohai congshu*, vol. 5.

19. Mitamura Taisuke, "Manshū shamanizumu no saishin to chokuji," in *Shinchō zenshi no kenkyū*, 386–87.

20. Liu Xiaomeng and Ding Yizhuang, *Samanjiao yu dongbei minzu* (Changchun: Jilin jiaoyu chubanshe, 1990), 137.

21. "Documentary institutionalization" is Crossley's term ("*Manzhou yuanliu kao*," 762). Yan, borrowing vocabulary from Fu and Meng, refers to this as a process of "codification" (*dianzhihua*) of shamanism, which went along with its "templarization" (*miaotanghua*) and "courtlification" (*gongtinghua*). See Yan Chongnian, "Manzhou guizu yu saman wenhua," *Manxue yanjiu* 2 (1995), 124.

22. Liu and Ding, *Samanjiao yu dongbei minzu*, 139; Shirokogoroff also was of the opinion that late-eighteenth-century court shamanism was not really shamanism at all. See Humphrey, "Shamanic Practices and the State," 212–13.

23. Fu and Meng, *Manzu samanjiao*, 60; Humphrey, "Shamanic Practices and the State," 213.

24. Mitamura, "Manshū shamanizumu"; Yan, "Manzhou guizu," 131; Li Lin, *Manzu zongpu yanjiu* (Shenyang: Liaoshen shushe, 1992), 126–30.

25. See Gösta Montell, *As Ethnographer in China and Mongolia, 1929–1932* (Stockholm: The Sino-Swedish Expedition, 1945).

26. Liu and Ding, *Samanjiao yu dongbei minzu*, 110–15; Li Hsüeh-chih [Li Xuezhi], " Manzhou minzu jisi tianshen bi ji shen'gan de shiliao yu qiyin,"

*Manzu wenhua* 2 (1982), 5–6. The spirit-pole was supposed to be nine Chinese feet in height, and made of clean wood. It was replaced every year. There is some uncertainty as to whether the *saksaha* represented the magpie (Ch *xique*) or the crow (Ch *wuya*), or both (Mo, "Qingchu Manzu de samanjiao," 178–79; Fu and Meng, *Manzu samanjiao*, 76–78).

27. Liu and Ding, *Samanjiao yu dongbei minzu*, 137; Jiang, *Shenmi de qinggong*, 146, says that Hong Taiji issued a decree forbidding any clan but the Aisin Gioro to maintain a *tangse*.

28. Fu and Meng, *Manzu samanjiao*, 58–59.

29. Ibid., 67–73; Li, "Manzhou minzu jisi tianshen," 5–6.

30. Liu, *Baqi zidi*, 154; Zhao Zhizhong, "*Ni-shan saman* yu zongjiao," in Wang, ed., *Manxue Chaoxianxue lunji*, 179.

31. Liu, *Baqi zidi*, 154.

32. Fu and Meng, *Manzu samanjiao*, 87–93.

33. Liu and Ding, *Samanjiao yu dongbei minzu*, 132–33.

34. Liu, *Baqi zidi*, 150. The Qianlong song collection is *Nishang xupu*, compiled by Wang Tingshao.

35. Zhao, "*Ni-shan saman*," 183. Different versions of this text have been preserved. The authoritative study in English is Nowak and Durrant, *The Tale of the Nišan Shamaness*.

36. Liu, *Baqi zidi*, 152. He points out that a good portion of the shamanic vocabulary recorded in Qing-era Manchu dictionaries is found in sections on medicine. This is a potentially promising area for further research.

37. Crossley includes it in her list of qualities the court expected of Manchus ("Manchu Education," 361), but I have not seen it listed as such in any Qing documents.

38. Liu and Ding, *Samanjiao yu dongbei minzu*, 133; Fu and Meng, *Manzu samanjiao*, 57; Yan, "Manzhou guizu," 133–34.

39. "Le Seigneur du Ciel est le Ciel même. . . . Dans l'empire, nous avons un temple pour honorer le Ciel, et lui sacrifier. Nous, Mantcheoux, nous avons le Tiao Tchin. Tous les premiers de l'An, nous brûlons des odeurs et du papier, et cela pour honorer le Ciel. Nous, Mantcheoux, avons nos rites particuliers pour honorer le Ciel; les Monkou, Chinois, Russien, Européans [*sic*], etc., ont aussi leurs rites particuliers pour honorer le Ciel. . . . Je n'ai pas dit qu'il [Ourtchen, i.e., Urcen, a son of Sunu] ne falloit pas qu'il honorât le Ciel, mais que chacun avoit sa manière de l'honorer. Luy étant Mantcheoux devoit le faire comme nous" (Gaubil, *Correspondance du Pékin*, 152–53). Gaubil was translating an imperial edict of April 17, 1727. I have been unable to trace the original of this edict in either *Shizong shilu* or SYBQ. On "Tiao Tchin" (*tiaoshen*), Gaubil adds the following note: "This is a ceremony unique to the

468    Notes to Pages 241–44

Tartars about which I am not informed" (Cérémonie propre aux Tartares sur laquelle je ne suis pas au fait) (161).

40. See Wu, *Yangjizhai conglu*, 7; other *biji* with information on shamanism are Yao Yuanzhi, *Zhuyeting zaji* (1893), Zhao-lian, *Xiaoting zalu*, and Chen, *Langqian jiwen sibi* (1880).

41. There does not appear to be sufficient evidence at this time to make the case for shamanism among Chinese bannermen. However, Chinese banner musical forms do show the distinct influence of Manchu shamanic music, suggesting there may have been some familiarity with at least parts of the shamanic ritual. See Liu Guiteng, "Samanjiao yu Manzhou tiaoshen yinyue de liubian," *Manxue yanjiu* 1 (1992), 245–47.

42. The use of characters in rendering numeral names in Chinese is an obvious exception. See below.

43. One seventeenth-century writer commented that, "Those under the banners do not record the hour of birth. . . . When someone asks [when a baby was born], they just figure by counting on their ten fingers" (Tan Qian, *Beiyou lu*, 386).

44. For more names, see the lists in Ch'en Chieh-hsien, "Qingshi xingming hanhua kao" and "Lun Yingwen zhushuzhong Manzhou renming zhi yinyi wenti," both in *Qingshi zabi*, vol. 1 (Taipei: Xuehai chubanshe, 1977), 147–98 and 199–217.

45. When written in Chinese characters, the latter names might be written using the obvious Chinese characters for those numbers (including the more complex *daxie* forms), or they might be written using homophones.

46. Fu-ge, *Tingyu congtan*, 11: 220. The range of numbers, from forty through ninety-eight, suggests that the numeral may have represented either the age of the father at the time of the child's birth, the age of the grandfather, or great-grandfather, or the combined age of the parents or grandparents. See Chuang Chi-fa, "Manzhou mingming kao—shuzi mingming de youlai," in *Qingshi shiyi* (Taipei: Xuesheng shuju, 1992), 140–41, and "Cong shumu mingzi kan Qingdai Manzu de Hanhua," in *Qingshi suibi* (Taipei: Boyang wenhua Enterprises, 1996), 73–85.

47. On naming dogs and horses, see Chuang Chi-fa, "Lang Shining 'shi jun quan' mingming youlai," in *Qingshi shiyi*, 144–148; on naming elephants, see Wu, *Yangjizhai conglu*, 290.

48. BQTZ 9: 149–64. The identification of brothers and cousins is only possible when the transfer of company captaincies was passed to them instead of to sons, grandsons, or unrelated people. For instance, in the Eleventh Company of the Third Regiment we find that the captaincy was held first by Chang-guo-zhu; then by his younger brother Chang-long; then by Chang-

long's son Chang-tai; then by Chang-tai's son Chang-yun; then by Chang-yun's cousin Chang-qing; then by Chang-qing's cousin Chang-guan. Here the use of the character "chang" spans two generations. In the Third Company of the Fifth Regiment, Su-lu-mai was succeeded by his younger brother Su-fei, who was succeeded by his nephew Su-er-ji. But then Su-er-ji was succeeded by three relatives of the same generation who did not bear the "su" element in their names: a cousin, Ku-ku-li, and two of Su-er-ji's own brothers, Sun-ta-ha and Weng-e-luo. In only one case (in the Thirteenth Company of the Fourth Regiment) did a family consistently use the same *beifen yongzi* character for all names of a single generation, and different characters for different generations. Much more common was a pattern like that in the Second Company of the Fourth Regiment, where four men of the same generation were named Da-er-han, Fu-bao, Mi-li-bu, and Shan-bu.

49. See Ch'en, "Qingshi xingming," 167–68 in *Qingshi zabi*. Ortai's "family name" was Silin Gioro. His given name was written in Chinese as E-er-tai. He had six sons, all with the same *e* character at the beginning: E-rong-an, E-shi, E-bi, E-ning, E-jin, and E-mou. Two of his nephews were named E-chang and E-min, and he had at least one brother, E-lin-tai. See E-rong-an, ed., *E-er-tai nianpu* (ca. 1748; reprint, Beijing: Zhonghua shuju, 1993). Using the *e* character (which is a Chinese surname-character) for everyone in the family suggests the influence of Han naming practice, but these were still not names that fit the Chinese pattern of *beifen yongzi*.

50. Chosen at random from the list of thirty Chinese Plain Blue Banner companies in the *Comprehensive History of the Eight Banners* (BQTZ 16: 281–87). Even here, consistency was not a concern. Fo-bao was the son of Tian-bao and the grandson of Li Yongfang. His brother was Li Yuanliang; his son was Li Shijing.

51. QLHaZPZZ, QL1, Arsai, QL1.11.26. The emperor took no action, and Arsai went on being known as Arsai, as far as the record shows. The emperor, of course, did have the power to rename people when he wished, as seen in the well-known cases of the Yongzheng emperor's brothers Insy and Intang, renamed Akina (*not* "Acina" [A-qi-na], as commonly written) and Seshe; other cases are those of Faššan and Manjišan. Faššan (1753–1813), a Mongol bondservant and *jinshi* of 1780, was originally named Yuncang. The Qianlong emperor renamed him Faššan ("diligent") to honor his prolific writing. On Manjišan (renamed Jišan), see Chen, "Qingshi xingming," 168.

52. *Gaozong shilu*, 115: 29b–30a; 614: 27b–28a.

53. Ibid., 614: 22b–23a. The example he gave was of people of the Niohuru lineage who were taking the Chinese surname Lang. But he did not explain the connection between these names (perhaps because it seemed

obvious at the time?). My guess is that the name Niohuru was linked to the word for wolf, *niohe* in Manchu, and *lang* in Chinese. A more decorous homonym *lang* ("young gentleman") was then substituted.

54. *The Travels and Controversies of Friar Domingo Navarrete, 1618–1686*, ed. J. S. Cummins, Hakluyt Society (Cambridge: Cambridge University Press, 1962), 2: 217. Orthography modernized.

55. Liu, *Baqi zidi*, 87, citing Yi, *Jianzhou wenjian lu*.

56. Cited in ibid.

57. Staunton, *An Historical Account*, 302.

58. Ibid., 320–21.

59. Cranmer-Byng, *An Embassy to China*, 228.

60. Dorothy Ko, *Teachers of the Inner Chambers: Women and Culture in Seventeenth-Century China* (Stanford, Calif.: Stanford University Press, 1994), 149 and note; also Susan Mann, *Precious Records: Women in China's Long Eighteenth Century* (Stanford, Calif.: Stanford University Press, 1997), 27 and note. An earlier proscription is said to have been issued in 1645. See Fu-ge, *Tingyu congtan*, 7: 160–61. The effort was taken up again at the very end of the dynasty, of course, when the Empress Dowager Cixi officially forbade footbinding in 1902.

61. Hong Taiji is said to have forbidden footbinding among Manchu women in 1638, but I have been unable to find the edict (Fu-ge, *Tingyu congtan* 7: 160).

62. In the 1804 selection of banner girls for service in the palace, the Jiaqing emperor was furious when he discovered nineteen young women in the Chinese Bordered Yellow Banner with bound feet: "This is a matter of great import. If [this practice] is not immediately rectified, before long [it] will end up like the evil habits of the Han" (DQHDSL 1114: 17b–18a).

63. This practice was called *daotiao* in Chinese. See Yao Lingxi, ed., *Caifei lu* (Tianjin: Tianjin shidai gongsi, 1936), 193–94. My thanks to Dorothy Ko for this reference; see her discussion in "The Emperor and His Women: Three Views of Footbinding, Ethnicity, and Empire," in Chuimei Ho and Cheri A. Jones, eds., *Life in the Imperial Court of Qing Dynasty China: Proceedings of the Denver Museum of Natural History* 3.15 (November 1998), 43–45. It has sometimes been called in English "loose binding." See Beverly Jackson, *Splendid Slippers* (Berkeley, Calif.: Ten Speed Press, 1998), 36–37. The modern novelist Feng Jicai gave the practice another name: "In the end, . . . the young Manchu women began, behind the backs of their parents, to bind their own [feet] in the less severe 'cucumber style.'" See *The Three-Inch Golden Lotus*, trans. David Wakefield (Honolulu: University of Hawaii Press, 1994), 2. Although I have not found any instances of it, one must admit

the possibility, of course, that some Manchu women may have violated the ban on footbinding.

64. Cf. this early twentieth-century description: "The shoes stand upon a sole of four or six inches in height, or even more. These soles, which consist of a wooden frame upon which white cotton cloth is stretched, are quite thin from the toe and heel to about the center of the foot, when they curve abruptly downwards, forming a base of two or three inches square. In use they are exceedingly inconvenient, but . . . they show the well-to-do position of the wearer. The Manchus are . . . a taller . . . race than the Chinese, and the artificial increase to the height afforded by these shoes gives them at times almost startling proportions." From Valery M. Garrett, *Chinese Clothing: An Illustrated Guide* (Oxford: Oxford University Press, 1994), 61, citing Alexander Hosie, *Manchuria, Its People, Resources, and Recent History* (London: Methuen, 1904), 157.

65. Jackson, *Splendid Slippers*, 57, citing Louise Crane, *China in Sign and Symbol* (Shanghai: Kelly and Walsh, 1926).

66. Fu-ge, *Tingyu congtan*, 7: 156. Since this figure is lower than the usual proportion cited for women with bound feet, one wonders whether nonbanner women were not adopting Manchu norms in slowly rejecting the practice.

67. Banner women who wore wide sleeves were said to be following Han norms (DQHDSL 1114: 18a). The gradual broadening of the sleeves of Manchu women's clothing was lamented by the nineteenth-century writer De-suo-ying in his collection, *Caozhu yi chuan* (cited in Liu, *Baqi zidi*, 85–86). This trend is readily apparent when one compares eighteenth- and nineteenth-century women's gowns. See the illustrations in Garrett, *Chinese Clothing*, 56–57, and John Vollmer, *Decoding Dragons: Status Garments in Ch'ing Dynasty China* (Eugene: University of Oregon Museum of Art, 1983), 24–31.

68. John Scarth, *Twelve Years in China* (Edinburgh: T. Constable, 1860; reprint, Wilmington, Del.: Scholarly Resources, 1972), 41.

69. Cf. the description of a Han woman accompanying pl. 25 in Alexander, *Views of Eighteenth-Century China*: "Great care is taken in ornamenting the head: the hair, after being smoothed with oil and closely twisted, is brought to the crown of the head, and fastened with bodkins of gold and silver."

70. Thomson provided detailed photos and descriptions of the Manchu woman's coiffure and recommended it to European readers. See Fig. 15. In much of his work Thomson showed himself very sensitive to the ethnic and regional nuances of hair and clothing in China.

71. "Pigtail" was a nineteenth-century slang word meaning "a Chinese person."

72. Another peculiarity of the Manchu female coiffure was the long side-locks some women wore that swept down from the ears and curved partly across the cheeks.

73. "Manzhou jiufeng" was the language used by the Qianlong emperor (DQHDSL 1114: 15a). There was also a special headdress, called a *dianzi* in Chinese, a wire-framed cap heavily decorated with feathers and strings of pearls all around the head that dangled to the eyebrows in front and to the shoulders in back. Fu-ge refers to a classical Chinese precedent, but it would seem that Mongol women's headdress was a closer simile (*Tingyu congtan*, 6: 148). See the photograph (showing the upper part of a "tian-ze") in Garrett, *Chinese Clothing*, 56.

74. Excerpted with permission from "The Eating Crabs Youth Book," trans. Mark C. Elliott, in Susan Mann and Yu-yin Cheng, eds., *Under Confucian Eyes: Texts on Gender in Confucian Society* (Berkeley and Los Angeles: University of California Press, forthcoming). Copyright © 2001 The Regents of the University of California Press.

75. Lai Huimin and Xu Siling, "Qingdai qiren funü caichanquan zhi qianxi," *Jindai Zhongguo funüshi yanjiu* 4 (August 1996), 3–33.

76. See the comments by Zhang Juling, *Qingdai Manzu zuojia wenxue gailun* (Beijing: Zhongyang minzu xueyuan chubanshe, 1990), 110–16. Zhang's observations, which are primarily anecdotal, seem to apply mainly to upper-class Manchus in Beijing.

77. Though the comparatively "liberated" social and economic status of women in Inner Asia historically is well known, more work might enable us to say to what degree differences between women are differences of class or differences of ethnicity. See Wittfogel and Feng, *Liao*, 17, 199–202, and Sechin Jagchid and Paul Hyer, *Mongolia's Culture and Society* (Boulder, Colo.: Westview Press, 1979), 94–95.

78. Older Manchu women could be celebrated for their chastity, however. In 1736 the Qianlong emperor ordered thirty taels for the construction of a *paifang* ceremonial arch to honor the mother (surnamed Gūwalgiya) of Ningxia garrison general Alu (QLMaZPZZ 52, Alu, QL1.5.17). For an early reference to the need to promote "moral education," especially filiality and chastity, among bannermen and women, see the 1699 edict of the Kangxi emperor in *Shengzu shilu*, 191: 24a.

79. DQHD (1733) 114: 28a.

80. YZMaZPZZ 819, Cangseli, YZ7.5.15.

81. SYBQ YZ 1: 11b–12a (YZ1.7.16).

82. On the other hand, the edict concluded, women who, of their own will, wished not to remarry were also granted that option provided they could

provide enough testimonials from family members and company officers demonstrating their sincerity (*Shangyu qiwu yifu*, YZ5: 15b–17a [YZ5.9.17]). The regulation was apparently well known; the same edict (dated YZ5.8.24) is quoted in a case found in *Jōkōkitō—Yōseichō*, ed. Kanda Nobuo, Matsumura Jun, Okada Hidehiro, and Hosoya Yoshio (Tokyo: Tōyō Bunko Seminar on Manchu History, 1972), 26: 31–33.

83. For more on the problem of widows in the banners, see my article, "Manchu Widows and Ethnicity in Qing China," *Comparative Studies in Society and History* 41.1 (January 1999).

84. In practice this seems to have affected only the daughters of garrison generals and lieutenant generals (DQHDSL 1114, 14b). The contrast offered by the Chinese and Manchu terms for this practice (the one sophisticated, the other plain) is one instance of the way in which Manchu-language sources provide the historian a different perspective on matters in the Qing.

85. Wang Daocheng, "Cong Xue Pan song mei daixuan tanqi: Guanyu Qingdai de xiunü zhidu," *Beijing shiyuan* 3 (1985), 306–7.

86. Note that going to the capital "because he had to present his sister to the Ministry for selection" is one of the three reasons that Xue Pan, the profligate nephew of Jia Zheng in the great eighteenth-century novel of manners, *The Story of the Stone*, enumerates for having to go to the capital (Cao, *The Story of the Stone*, 1: 119).

87. DQHDSL 1114: 11b–12b.

88. This was the fate of Jia Zheng's eldest daughter, Yuanchun. First "chosen for her exception virtue and cleverness to be a Lady Secretary in the Imperial Palace," she was later "appointed Chief Secretary to the Empress and . . . an Imperial Concubine" (Cao, *The Story of the Stone*, 1: 81, 304).

89. DQHDSL 1114: 18b–19b. Young women from separate-register households in the banners were also exempted.

90. On *zhihun*, see Ding Yizhuang, "Directed Marriage and the Eight-Banner Household Registration System Among the Manchus," trans. Mark C. Elliott, *Saksaha* 1 (1996), 25–29. More on banner women generally may be found in her monograph, *Manzu de funü shenghuo yu hunyin zhidu yanjiu* (Beijing: Beijing daxue chubanshe, 1999).

91. The ban on intermarriage between banner women and Han civilian males is found in chapter 1 of *Hubu zeli* (cited in Han, *Beijing lishi renkou dili*, 303). On Qing marriage policies, see Ding Yizhuang, "Banner-Commoner Intermarriage in the Qing," paper presented at meeting of the Association of Asian Studies, Chicago, March 1997; and Ding, *Manzu de funü shenghuo*. On concubinage, see James Lee and Wang Feng, "Male Nuptiality and Male Fertility among the Qing Nobility: Polygyny or Serial Monogamy," in

Caroline Bledsoe, Susanna Lerner, and Jane Guyer, eds., *Fertility and the Male Life Cycle on the Eve of Fertility Decline* (Oxford: Oxford University Press, 1999).

92. *Shengzu shilu,* 115: 3a.

93. Implementing a policy of periodic rotation between the capital and the provincial garrisons (or between the garrisons only) would have necessitated endless transfers of troops between different locations. Banner families constantly crisscrossing the country would have presented a logistical nightmare, not to speak of the enormous costs that continuous large-scale personnel transfer would have imposed or the burden that would have been placed on the official military post system, which took responsibility for supplying bannermen on the road. Added to this must also be the obvious strains such a policy would have put on banner families constantly moving from one city to the next, as well as on the Chinese living along travel routes, always inconvenienced when caravans came through with their many horses and wagons. Such concerns were of no small importance to the Qing court. In a 1705 discussion with the Xi'an garrison general, the Kangxi emperor cautioned that "issuing edicts in peacetime about stationing Manchu troops on the borders not only causes widespread suspicion, but building houses and transferring soldiers disturbs the lives of bannermen and misleads the thinking of civilians" (KXMaZPZZ 355, Boji, KX41.5.21).

94. Reflected in the dominant scholarly view of the problem, which concludes that "Beijing remained the Bannermen's homeland and the center of the Banner society" (Wu, "Development and Decline," 74). As will be shown, this was only partially true.

95. Cf. the comment by a Youwei scribe who requested permission to bring along his nineteen-year-old son, a soldier in Beijing, to the garrison, which, he stressed, was "also a place where Manchu soldiers are stationed." See *Jōkōkitō—Kenryūchō 1,* ed. Kanda Nobuo, Matsumura Jun, Okada Hidehiro, and Hosoya Yoshio (Tokyo: Tōyō Bunko Seminar on Manchu History, 1983), no. 21, 18–20.

96. *Shengzu shilu,* 115: 3a–b. Emphasis added.

97. Note, however, the reference to a Shunzhi-period regulation compelling families of deceased bannermen from garrisons at Jiangning, Shanhaiguan, and the capital area to return to the capital (BQTZ 38: 715).

98. DQHD (1690) 82: 17b; DQHD (1733) 114: 27b; BQTZ 38: 715.

99. According to regulations, a list of candidates to replace a deceased company comrade was to be prepared by the company and presented within one month of the vacancy coming open (DQHD [1690] 81: 15a).

100. *Shengzu shilu,* 127: 4a.

101. Cf. BQTZ 38: 715.

102. Quoted in QLMaZPZZ 53, Alu, QL1.6.6.

103. Widows who had decided to remain at the garrison could later be recalled to live in the capital by their sons or grandsons (but not nephews) who were officers or soldiers in Beijing (*Jakūn gūsai kooli hacin* [1742], 12: 28b–29a). As explained below, however, nephews could request transfers to Beijing to look after elderly uncles and aunts.

104. The rule was that Beijing-based banner officers and regulars over fifty who had no grown men in the household could recall sons or grandsons in the provincial garrisons to the capital in order to look after them. If they had no sons or grandsons, then nephews in the garrisons could also be called on to return; brothers were not supposed to be repatriated to look after brothers. As with all requests for repatriation for family reasons, applications had to be reviewed by the clan head and the company captain before being approved (ibid. [1742], 12: 29a–b.

105. DQHD (1733) 114: 28a–b; the same is also cited in BQTZ 38: 716.

106. YZMaZPZZ 11, Cangdzai, YZ1.11.9; Cangšeo, YZ1.9.29.

107. One of the few exceptions to this trend I have come across was at the Ningxia garrison, which, as described in Chapter 3, was decimated by a powerful earthquake in 1739. Though the court quickly authorized the disbursement of emergency loans and initiated the building of a new Manchu city in a slightly different location, a significant number of Ningxia garrison families (all from the Manchu banners) indicated a strong preference to return to Beijing (QLMaZPZZ 91, Dulai, QL5.9.13). It is important to point out, however, that they had emigrated from Beijing to Ningxia only fifteen years before, and so likely retained family ties in the capital. Moreover, life in Ningxia was assuredly not as comfortable as life in Hangzhou or Nanjing, or even Xi'an. Their situation was thus somewhat different from that faced by most garrison bannermen.

108. YZMaZPZZ 11, Cangšeo, YZ1.9.29.

109. The edict concluded in the acerbic style for which the Yongzheng emperor is so well known: "Let the absolute unfeasibility of both of the above propositions be announced through the posting of an imperial edict so that ignoramuses might reflect and come to their senses. Do not send any more of these foolish memorials" (SYBQ YZ10: 15a–b [YZ10.7.1]). The emperor's objection was not wholly without basis, as the bodies of officials, Chinese and Manchu alike, who died in the course of duty were returned to the native home, where they were formally "received" and, in the case of certain heroes returning to Beijing, ceremoniously bestowed posthumous names (Fu-ge, *Tingyu congtan*, 11: 237–38).

110. Cf. KXMaZPZZ 317, Okson, KX54.10.29, where the term is *anggasi cuwan*. This practice was winked at by local officials, whose palms evidently did not go ungreased (YZMaZPZZ 4, Cangde, n.d.). When the practice of "returning to the banner" was ended, provincial officials were left with the problem of what to do with hundreds of idle boats (*Gaozong shilu*, 620: 15a–b).

111. Whether the idea of burial in one's native place reflects Chinese influence is an open question. It is doubtful that the same concept of "ancestral home" as found among the sedentary Han Chinese should have arisen among the Manchus, a seminomadic people upon whom Mongolian influence had long been strong. This would seem to be supported both by the old Jurchen practice of cremation (see below) and by the burial of various early Jurchen/Manchu leaders, including Nurhaci and Hong Taiji, in locations far from their birthplaces. On the other hand, as mentioned in Chapter 1, there does seem to have been a strong tendency toward geographic ascription among the early Manchus.

112. QLMaZPZZ 52, Arigūn, QL1.5.2.

113. QLMaZPZZ 52, edict of QL1.5.25. This edict does not appear in the *Shilu*.

114. QLMaZPZZ 52, edict of QL1.5.25. Italics indicate imperial emendations to the draft edict.

115. *Gaozong shilu*, 72: 16a–18a.

116. *Shengzu shilu*, 115: 3a–b.

117. Of course, some garrison bannermen did own property, but since this was done through the banner bureaucracy evidently it was regarded as exceptional. What the court no doubt wished to avoid was the same sort of private wrangling over property deals that plagued Manchu-Han relations in the outlying metropolitan area.

118. Whether sent from the capital to the provincial garrisons, to duty in pasture lands in the southern Mongolian steppe, or in military agricultural colonies established in the Northeast, eighteenth-century bannermen had the annoying habit of soon quitting the land and making their way back to the capital. They faced punishment if caught, but their plight apparently evoked enough sympathy from fellow bannermen that some could rely on the company not to report their return to highers-up in the banner system (*Gaozong shilu*, 397: 2a–5a). It is not clear, however, how they maintained a livelihood back in Beijing if they were there illegally.

119. This perhaps may have had something to do with the unusual shape of Manchu coffins (Ch *qicai*, lit., "banner coffins"), with their peaked lids and bottoms, which differed from the flat surfaces of Chinese coffins (Ch *guancai*).

See Zhao Zhan, *Manzu wenhua yu zongjiao yanjiu* (Shenyang: Liaoning minzu chubanshe, 1993), 293. It is unclear whether Chinese bannermen used Manchu- or Chinese-style coffins (or both).

120. QLMaZPZZ 52, Arigūn, QL1.5.2.

121. Tan, *Beiyou lu*, 357. Cremation was certainly the most convenient way to bring home the remains of those killed in battle.

122. Tie and Wang, *Shengjing huanggong*, 271, citing *Shizu shilu*, 2; Feng Erkang and Chang Jianhua, *Qingren shehui shenghuo* (Tianjin: Tianjin renmin chubanshe, 1990), 254. They point out that the Shunzhi emperor himself was buried (citing *Shengzu shilu*, 9: 14a). Tomb excavation near Liaoyang has shown that Nurhaci's brother, Šurhaci, was cremated (Tie and Wang, *Shengjing huanggong*, 282n), and contemporary seventeenth-century witnesses recorded that among the Jurchen it was customary that "on the day after death it [the body] is taken to a field and burned" (Yi Minwhan, *Jianzhou wenjian lu* [*Konchu mun'gyon rok*] [ca. 1619; reprint, Shenyang: Liaoning daxue lishixi, 1978], 44).

123. *Baqi zeli*, 10: 27a; Wu, *Yangjizhai conglu*, 25: 272. Excavations of the tomb of a daughter of Songgotu who died in 1675 revealed that the corpse had been cremated. See Su Tianjun, "Beijing xijiao Xiaoxitian Qingdai muzang fajue jianbao," *Wenwu* 147 (1963.1), 50–59; thanks to Lydia Thompson for this reference. After the unfortunate Urcen (son of the Manchu Christian Sunu) killed himself in prison, his body, in a coffin, was burned outside the city limits and his remains trampled in the mud. Guards had to be posted to keep out curious Chinese (Gaubil, *Correspondance de Pékin*, 159). Cremation seems not to be mentioned, however, in Xu Ke's early-twentieth-century compendium, *Qingbai leichao*, nor, oddly, is it remarked by Zheng Tianting in his observations on Manchu funeral customs in *Tanweiji*. A detailed description of Manchu funeral practices is found in Zhao Zhan, *Manzu wenhua yu zongjiao yanjiu*, 281–301.

124. QLMaZPZZ 52, Arigūn, QL1.5.2.

125. DQHD (1733) 114: 28a.

126. Eight Banner clan and company cemeteries were located around the perimeter of the city; it seems all have since been converted to agricultural or other use.

127. This strategy appears to have been most common among bannermen sent back to Beijing from Canton and Fuzhou. In the mid-1720s people from these garrisons (who at this time were all in the Chinese banners) were warned that if they were caught escaping back to the provinces they would be arrested and punished. The policy banning local cemeteries and forbidding unauthorized returns to the garrison was confirmed again and again by the Yongzheng

and Qianlong emperors in a string of edicts from the 1730s and 1740s (BQTZ 38: 715; DQHD [1733] 114: 27b–28a).

128. *Gaozong shilu*, 362: 14b–15a.

129. YZMaZPZZ 11, Cangšeo, YZ1.929.

130. YZMaZPZZ 11, Cangdzai, YZ1.11.9. A common Chinese custom, burning money as a sacrifice was practiced also among the Manchus from before the conquest. See, for example, MBRT 3, Taizu 72, 1084, where it accompanies the distinctly non-Chinese (for the period) rite of sacrificing two oxen.

131. This change is reflected in *Jakūn gūsai kooli hacin* (1742), 12: 25a–b (QLMaZPZZ 52, edict of QL1.5.25). Italics indicate imperial emendations to the draft edict.

132. *Jakūn gūsai kooli hacin*, 12: 26b–27a. These regulations are also listed in DQHDSL 1113.

133. This was based upon the precedent established by the Ningxia garrison disaster, mentioned above. One should be wary of ascribing the Manchu emphasis on service to parents to the influence of Confucian norms of filiality. While these were certainly familiar to all banner people, what we know of native Manchu customs suggests that the rules governing relationships with elders was even more strict than it was among the Han (Tan, *Beiyou lu*, 357).

134. Wu, *Yangjizhai conglu*, 25: 278.

135. QLMaZPZZ 12, Sailengga, QL12.8.25.

136. *Gaozong shilu*, 506: 2b–3a.

137. The total amount of land authorized for purchase was 5,719 *mu*—not an insignificant amount. Frontier garrisons, where land was cheaper and population less dense, got more (2190 *mu* were for the Suiyuan garrison alone). The major provincial garrisons each got between 150–250 *mu*. No grants were authorized for the Nanjing or Guangzhou garrisons (DQHDSL 1119, 11a–12a).

138. *Gaozong shilu*, 1143: 25b, cited in Ding, *Qingdai baqi zhufang*, 196.

139. A policy initiative of 1733 ordered the sons of garrison officers to proceed to the capital at age eighteen to "make some study so that they learn virtue, and make others soldiers so that they earn their keep" (edict of YZ11.3.1, quoted in YZMaZPZZ 220, Guntai, YZ11.12.14). A 1725 request by the Jiangning garrison general to retain his seventeen-year-old adopted son with him at the garrison indicates that even before it became a formal requirement, it was normally expected that mature sons would be sent to the capital for assignment (YZMaZPZZ 377, Yonggina, YZ3.2.29). An

elaboration of the original edict stressed that "the children of bannermen allowed to remain a long time at the [father's] provincial post not only become lazy and dissipated, immature and unaccomplished, but at the yamen they also interfere with local matters, harming the reputations of their fathers or elder brothers." The emperor added, however, that he would entertain requests for exceptions to this rule in cases where extenuating circumstances were felt to exist. Such requests soon began pouring in. See, for example, YZMaZPZZ 220, Guntai, YZ11.12.14; QLMaZPZZ 67, Zhang Zhengwen, QL2.10.1. My translation of the edict is based on a comparison of the Chinese version of the edict in SYBQ YZ 8: 29a–b (YZ10.12.24) with the Manchu version quoted in QLMaZPZZ 67, Zhang Zhengwen, QL2.10.1. The policy was abandoned ten years later, and fathers allowed to choose whether to keep sons with them or send them to Beijing (*Gaozong shilu*, 390: 27b–28a).

140. DQHDSL 1113: 4b–5a. This process seems to have begun earlier than 1730, in fact. Separate garrison companies of Chinese bannermen were already being created at the Guangzhou garrison in 1685 (Meng, "Baqi zhidu kaoshi," 93–98).

141. Apart from the edict cited in note 135, cf. comments such as "inner and outer are entirely the same" (*dorgi tulergi yooni emu adali*), in reference to a Xi'an garrison general's lament that, though physically far from the emperor, he would still exert himself on the emperor's behalf (YZMaZPZZ 479, Yansin, YZ2.1.26); or "the edict having come down to inner and outer soldiers to all study and practice the *Wu jing* and *Qi shu*" (*dorgi tulergi cooha ambasa. hafasa de hese wasimbufi. yooni u ging. ci šu be urebume tacikini*) (YZMaZPZZ 81, Fušen, YZ3.1.2).

142. QLMaZPZZ 49, Fusen, QL1.2.2.

*Chapter 7. Whither the Manchu Way?*

1. "Manly virtue" (Ma *hahai erdemu*) was linked to skill at riding and at speaking Manchu, though it also seems to have comprehended a certain dignity and respectability—drunkenness, for example, was not in keeping with this quality (see below). In dismissing Ingjiyūn, a member of the imperial clan, from his post as guard, the Qianlong emperor cited his weak linguistic and equestrian skills, as well as a "disgusting" bowlegged walk, as evidence of a lack of *hahai erdemu* (YZMaZPZZ 264, edict of YZ13.10.6). At least three edicts of 1741 stressed "manly virtue," some in connection with riding, shooting, and hunting, others with the "Manchu customs of a bygone age" (Ma *nenehe forgon [i] manjusai tacin*) and with staying "sharp" (Ma *silin dacun*), strong, and healthy (QLMaZPZZ 101, Guwang lu, QL6.9.6; QLMaZPZZ 103, Coldo, QL6.11.8; *Gaozong shilu*, 143 12a–b). Keeping

in mind their common root (Manchu *haha*, Latin *vir*, "man"), the sense may not have been far from the Renaissance quality of *virtù*.

2. This assessment agrees with Fu Lehuan's view that court anxiety over "speaking Manchu, riding, and shooting" began under Hong Taiji (Fu, "Guanyu Qingdai Manzu de jige wenti," 444–47). The same point was first made by Ura Ren'ichi in a 1931 article, "Shinchō no kokusui hōzon seisaku ni tsuite," *Shigaku kenkyū* 1.1 (October), 114.

3. As already noted, the Jin was an obvious model for the Qing. The Liao, Jin, and Yuan histories appear to have been translated into Manchu at roughly the same time, between 1636 and 1644. The Shunzhi emperor ordered their publication in 1644 and they appeared two years later. See P. G. von Möllendorff, "Essay on Manchu Literature," *Journal of the North China Branch of the Royal Asiatic Society* 24 (1890), 30–31. In fact, it does not seem that Manchu translations of any dynastic histories other than these three were ever printed, or possibly even made. Dorgon later cited the *Jin shi* in cautioning against internecine feuding among the nobility (Wakeman, *The Great Enterprise*, 849).

4. *Jiu Manzhou dang*, vol. 10, 5295 (Chongde 1.11.13). Indeed, as the discussion of women's fashion in Chapter 6 shows, his prediction of widening sleeve widths was realized. As mentioned in the Introduction, this was the speech that the Qianlong emperor had engraved in stone for general edification. While much is often made of Qianlong's identification with his grandfather, the Kangxi emperor, there is reason to believe he was also very conscious of his great-great-grandfather, Hong Taiji. Three years before disseminating Hong Taiji's immortal warning, the Qianlong emperor erected a temple to commemorate the Qing victory in the First Jinchuan War (1747–49). In the inscription he noted that its name, *Shisheng si* ("Temple of true victory"), was the same as that of the temple founded by Hong Taiji in Mukden in 1638 (Waley-Cohen, "Commemorating War," 877–78). The Mukden temple was built to house a golden statue of the Mahākāla Buddha, supposedly originally cast for the Mongol emperor Khubilai, which was presented to Hong Taiji by the Chakhar Mongols in 1634. See Grupper, "The Imperial Manchu Cult," chap. 4, and Mark C. Elliott, "Turning a Phrase: Translation in the Early Qing Through a Temple Inscription of 1645," *Aetas Manjurica* 3 (1992), 17.

5. KXMaZPZZ, 351, Boji, KX 43.10.10.
6. YZMaZPZZ 527, Arigūn, YZ 13.4.2.
7. Hsiao, *Qingdai tongshi*, 22, cited in Wu, "The Development and Decline," 86.
8. Inaba Iwakichi, *Shinchō zenshi* (Tokyo, 1914); citation is from the

1914 Chinese translation, *Qingchao quanshi* (reprint, Taipei: Taiwan zhong-hua shuju, 1960) 2: 34; Spence, *The Search for Modern China*, 114.

9. Im, "Rise and Decline," 120.

10. "The Manchus may have those Manchu and Mongol ministers serving them with all their hearts and discretion, and those Kirin and So-lun generals fighting with expert horsemanship and archery" ("A Proposal to the T'ien Wang," in Michael, *The Taiping Rebellion*, 179).

11. *Shengzu shilu*, 112: 9a. According to one explanation, "slippers" referred to Chinese-style shoes. See Teng Shaozhen, *Qingdai baqi zidi* (Beijing: Zhongguo huaqiao chuban gongsi, 1989), 53.

12. *Shengzu shilu*, 192: 30a.

13. Ibid., 194: 12a–b.

14. GZMaZJ 5, Fusen, QL1.7.28, citing memorial of KX23.5.21.

15. YZMaZPZZ 506, Unaha, YZ3.10.3. *Eyembi* can also mean to "flow," "fall," or "sink."

16. YZMaZPZZ 434, Ilibu, YZ4.4.8. At least one other similar exhortation followed in the succeeding months (YZMaZPZZ 434, Ilibu, YZ4.10.4).

17. YZMaZPZZ 265, Fusen, YZ13.12.7; QLMaZPZZ 52, Bašinu, QL1.10.3; QLMaZPZZ 63, Bašinu, QL2.5.21.

18. QLMaZPZZ 52, Bašinu, QL1.10.3.

19. QLMaZPZZ 49, Fusen, QL1.2.2. Some of the horses from the Hangzhou garrison were stabled in Zhapu, where the weather was cooler. Until the mid 1700s, all provincial garrisons were required to procure their ponies in Mongolia, but these animals succumbed too easily to the southern Chinese climate. After 1753, local horses could be used instead (*Gaozong shilu*, 446: 2a–3a).

20. GZMaZJ 5, Fusen, QL1.7.18.

21. KXMaZPZZ 351, Boji, KX43.10.10.

22. YZMaZPZZ 110, Yansin, YZ4.10.2 and YZMaZPZZ 480, Yansin, YZ4.12.15. A powerful prince, Yansin's tenure at Xi'an was cut short when he was executed in connection with the factional politics taking place at the time.

23. YZMaZPZZ 165, Jalangga, YZ7.11.22. The statement that all men had complete equipment and were capable of using a bow of strength six are taken as confirmation that standards were reasonably high.

24. Judging from the number of memorials where references to this topic are found in the archives; for example, QLMaZPZZ 64, Cimbu, QL2.6.2; QLMaZPZZ 69, Cimbu, QL2.12.17; GZMaZJ 6, Coldo, QL5.R6.16.

25. QLMaZPZZ 61, Cimbu, QL2.4.7.

26. QLMaZPZZ 69, Cimbu, QL2.12.17. The meaning of *kemuni mudan*

*be dosobumbi,* which I have tentatively translated as "the men can still take it," is not entirely clear to me. The general's further remark that "the way of living of the Manchus has declined" (*Manjusa-i banjire doro eberefi*) should be understood to refer to a drop in their economic standard of living.

27. Ding's remark in this regard is pertinent: "As early as the Rebellion of the Three Feudatories banner had soldiers already failed to distinguish themselves in battle. Thus if on the different campaigns waged up through the Qianlong reign the strength of banner troops was not to be taken lightly, this was likely due to the court's ability to still call on the reserve forces of 'minority' troops [Chakhar, Sibe, Solon, Oirat] from the distant frontier regions" (Ding, *Qingdai baqi zhufang,* 161).

28. QLMaZPZZ 64, Cimbu, QL2.6.18. The general pitied them for the "certain hardship" that awaited them.

29. See the frontispiece. There were originally 260 such portraits, which hung in the galleries of the *Ziguang ge* ("Pavilion of Purple Splendor"), on the western side of the palace. Unfortunately, almost all have been lost. See Ka-bo Tsang, "Ji fenggong shu weiji," *Gugong wenwu yuekan* 93 (December 1990), 38–65, and "Portraits of Meritorious Officials: Eight Examples from the First Set Commissioned by the Qianlong Emperor," *Arts Asiatiques* 57 (1992), 69–88; Joanna Waley-Cohen, "Commemorating War," 891–96.

30. Wu, "Development and Decline," 85–86. See also Teng, *Qingdai baqi zidi,* 225–32, *passim,* where most references are to capital bannermen.

31. *Gaozong shilu,* 138: 7b–8b.

32. Ding, *Qingdai baqi zhufang,* 201.

33. SYBQ YZ1: 15b–16a (YZ1.10.3). The guards were given six months to shape up, and the situation seems to have improved for a few years, after which dissatisfaction with their laziness again surfaced (SYBQ YZ4: 67b–68a [YZ4.10.14]).

34. Teng, *Qingdai baqi zidi,* 225–26.

35. *Gaozong shilu,* 140: 18a–b.

36. Wu, *"Development and Decline,"* 86–87; *Gaozong shilu,* 143: 13b–14a; 408: 32b.

37. YZMaZPZZ 245, Mantai, YZ12.4.29.

38. SYBQ YZ2: 7b (YZ2.4.5).

39. Chen, *Langqian jiwen erbi,* 13: 560–61, "Taizu gongxing jiejian." The original version of this story, with a somewhat different moral, may be found in the *Manwen laodang.* There, Nurhaci ends by saying, "After getting this garment wet, wouldn't it be wrong to give it you as though new? Is it acceptable to give something once you've made it wet and unclean? My caring about things is only for the sake of all of you" (MBRT 1, Taizu 4).

40. Cf. Durand's comment that the emperor had to choose between Manchus "with talent but no virtue" and Han Chinese who "had virtue but no talent" (*Lettrés et pouvoirs*, 241).

41. *Shengzu shilu*, 165: 19b–20b.

42. YZMaZPZZ14, Famin, YZ1.2.10.

43. YZMaZPZZ 2, Yentai, YZ1.5.9. With a few flourishes of the vermilion brush, this memorial was transformed into an edict, included in SYBQ YZ1: 7b (YZ1.5.6). The discrepancy in dates may have resulted from an error in transcription or translation. Curiously, where the Chinese edict mentions only "strands of many pearls" the Manchu original specifies "Buddhist rosaries" (*erihe*), which evidently were used simply as jewelry.

44. YZMaZPZZ 13, Wanggūri, YZ1.8.4.

45. SYBQ YZ1: 16a (YZ1.10.7).   46. *Gaozong shilu*, 356: 6b–7b.

47. Ibid., 366: 13b–14a.   48. Ibid., 141: 12b.

49. SYBQ YZ1: 3a–4b (KX61.12.11).

50. YZMaZPZZ 13, Sunju, YZ1.8.7.

51. YZMaZPZZ 12, Ulibu, YZ1.9.20. Such a ban was in force at least by 1764 ([*Qinding*] *Baqi zeli* [1764], 10: 22a).

52. YZMaZPZZ 15, Bootai, YZ1.9.26. To solve this problem, he wrote: "At one of the training grounds a public school should be established for them. Someone from the army who possess pure ways, can speak and read Manchu, and knows how to shoot and ride should be chosen to head it and teach these young men."

53. SYBQ YZ5: 17a–b (YZ5.4.13). More, though not all, of the Chinese version of this remarkable edict is translated in Wu, "Development and Decline," 106–7.

54. These themes are well explored in Colin Mackerras, *The Rise of the Peking Opera, 1770–1870: Social Aspects of the Theatre in Manchu China* (Oxford: Oxford University Press, 1972), 212–18 ff.

55. This restriction was relaxed in the second half of the nineteenth century, when a theater open to both sexes was opened in the Shishahai district north of the palace (Andrea Goldman, personal communication, June 1998).

56. Mackerras, *The Rise of the Peking Opera*, 211. It seems this ban remained effective for at least a century. It did not at first apply, however, to the informal theater-restaurants known as *zashuaguan*.

57. *Shengzu shilu*, 44: 8a–9b. This edict is translated in Chapter 8.

58. YZMaZPZZ 13, Wanggūri, YZ1.8.4; *Gaozong shilu*, 77: 1b–2a. Mackerras says the first ban came in 1724 (*The Rise of the Peking Opera*, 213). The edict he cites is in *Shizong shilu*, 18: 4a–5a, and also in SYBQ YZ2: 7a (YZ2.4.5).

59. [*Qinding*] *Baqi zeli* (1764), 10: 23a. To avoid trouble, some theaters apparently posted signs requesting bannermen in the audience to remove their insignia of office before sitting down (Andrea Goldman, personal communication, June 1998).

60. Mackerras, *The Rise of the Peking Opera*, 213.

61. Teng, *Qingdai Baqi zidi*, 259–64; indeed, two of the most famous *dan* actors in the *jingqiang* companies of the middle Qianlong period were Manchu bannermen, and by the late 1800s members of the imperial lineage were becoming actors (Mackerras, *The Rise of the Peking Opera*, 90, 167).

62. YZMaZPZZ 11, Delgin, YZ1.8.14. Examples of measures announced against gambling may be found in SYBQ YZ6: 19b–20a (YZ6.6.4).

63. Zhang and Guo, *Qing ruguanqian*, 470–72.

64. Teng, *Qingdai baqi zidi*, 257; [*Qinding*] *Zhongshu zhengkao*, 15: 115a.

65. See, for example, SYBQ YZ4: 57b–58b (YZ4.6.13).

66. KXMaZPZZ 469, Siju, KX47.8.29.

67. YZMaZPZZ 111, Sibe, YZ4.4.10; YZMaZPZZ 184, Sibe, YZ8.6.2.

68. YZMaZPZZ 1221, Sumurji, YZ7.R7.24.

69. YZMaZPZZ 507, Unaha, YZ6.1.11. The "killing of cows" presumably referred to the illicit slaughtering of livestock belonging to local Chinese in order to provide meat for carnivorous Manchus. Because it removed cash from circulation, hoarding copper implements was blamed for inflationary tendencies; see the edicts in *Shangyu qiwu yifu*, YZ4: 20a–21b.

70. One of the few examples I have found is in *Jingkou baqi zhi*, 2: 10b.

71. Miyazaki Ichisada, "Shinchō ni okeru kokugo mondai no ichimen," *Tōhōshi ronsō* 1 (July 1947), 41, 55.

72. "If language, a cultural trait, holds a group of people together, the disintegration of the group is foretold when its members give up their native tongue. This was what happened with the Manchus" (Huang, *Autocracy at Work*, 167).

73. "The subject at which I was worst was Manchu: I only learnt one word in all the years I studied it. This was *yili* (arise), the reply I had to make when my Manchu ministers knelt before me and said a set phrase of greeting in the language" (Aisin-Gioro Puyi, *From Emperor to Citizen*, 56–57). The Manchu verb in question here is *ilimbi*, "to get up." *Ili* is the imperative form.

74. Anthony D. Smith, "The Origins of Nations," *Ethnic and Racial Studies* 12.3 (July 1989), 344–45.

75. Some initial steps in this direction may be seen in the article by Pamela Kyle Crossley and Evelyn S. Rawski, "A Profile of the Manchu Language."

76. For the initial working out of some practical rules in 1653, see *Shizu shilu*, 71: 8a–9a and 72: 9a–10a; for details on the whole process, see Miyazaki, "Shinchō ni okeru kokugo mondai no ichimen."

77. Crossley and Rawski, "A Profile of the Manchu Language," 70; see also Elliott, "The Manchu-Language Archives of the Qing Dynasty."

78. See Giovanni Stary, "A New Subdivision of Manchu Literature: Some Proposals," *Central Asiatic Journal* 31.3–4 (1987), 287–96; Martin Gimm, "Manchu Translations of Chinese Novels and Short Stories: An Attempt at an Inventory," *Asia Major*, n.s., 1 (1987), 77–114.

79. YZMaZPZZ 187, Kirsa, YZ8.1.24. Both Mongolian and Manchu are Altaic languages, and the Manchu alphabet is almost identical to the Mongolian, from which it was borrowed.

80. Cf. Jonathan Spence's comment, "What more admirable in 1675 than to be a Manchu bondservant with a classical Chinese education?" (*Ts'ao Yin*, x).

81. Elman, "Changes in Confucian Civil Service Examinations," 116. The most famous example of someone whose advancement in the bureaucracy owed to his failure to pass the Manchu examination is probably that of the poet and essayist Yuan Mei (1716–98) (ECCP 955).

82. In the 1670s Verbiest was one of the first to learn Manchu; two of his juniors, Gerbillon and Bouvet, were said to be capable enough after eight months of study to explain Euclidian geometry to the Kangxi emperor in Manchu. See Erich Hauer, "Why the Sinologue Should Study Manchu," *Journal of the North China Branch of the Royal Asiatic Society* 61 (1930), 156. The eighteenth-century French Jesuit Amiot believed that "five or six years of study would be enough for someone diligent to put himself in a position where he could read with profit all the books written in Manchu" ("cinq ou six années d'étude suffiraient à un homme appliqué pour se mettre en état de lire avec profit tous les livres écrits en mantchou"). Quoted in L. Langlès, "Alphabet Tartare-Mantchou," introduction to Joseph Marie Amiot, *Dictionnaire Tartare-Mantchou François*, 2nd ed. (Paris, 1789), xi. The Kangxi emperor's wish that the Jesuits should apply themselves to the study of Manchu may have owed to his own personal preference for speaking Manchu over Chinese. See Pierre Joseph d'Orléans, *History of the Two Tartar Conquerors of China* (Hakluyt Society, 1854; reprint, New York: Burt Franklin, 1971), 96. That Manchu lent itself to more concrete expression than Chinese was the belief of Father Gaubil. In 1754, faced with accusations against the Jesuit community in Beijing, Gaubil met with a minister and potential ally to whom he summarized the charges in Manchu, "to avoid the equivocations of the Chinese language" ("pour éviter les équivoques de la langue chinoise") (*Correspondance de Pékin,*

783). With respect to Manchu translations of Chinese texts, much the same point was made more recently by Joseph Fletcher, who wrote that one advantage of Manchu was that the "ambiguities of Chinese cannot be carried over into Manchu," because each element of Chinese syntax and the meaning of each Chinese character was made explicit in the process of translation. See Fletcher, review of Walter Simon and Howard G. H. Nelson, *Manchu Books in London: A Union Catalogue*, *Harvard Journal of Asiatic Studies* 41.2 (December 1981), 656.

83. On the latter two, see Wakeman, *The Great Enterprise*, 875–76. More details on Manchu in the early years of the dynasty may be found in Hanson Chase, "The Status of the Manchu Language in the Early Ch'ing" (Ph.D. diss., University of Washington, 1979).

84. Cf. *Shizu shilu*, 19: 22a–b, on the need to train more young Manchus in Chinese; ibid., 43: 16b–17a, on the need to train Chinese *jinshi* in Manchu to avoid the need for translation; ibid., 96: 7b–8a, on the inability of Manchu officials to read Chinese characters.

85. *Shengzu shilu*, 35: 5b–6a.

86. Cf. also the excellent discussion of this problem in Crossley, "Manchu Education."

87. Cf., for instance, *Shizu shilu*, 136: 9a–b. The whole history of eligibility of bannermen to sit for the provincial and metropolitan examinations is of course wound up in this problem. See Chapter 4.

88. Ibid., 84: 5b–6a. It seems that this ban was upheld until the foundation of banner schools for the imperial clan in 1723, where Chinese was part of the curriculum (Huang, *Autocracy at Work*, 174).

89. YZMaZPZZ 252, Hesing, YZ12.6.25. See below for more on Hesing's proposals.

90. Relying on BQTZ, Teng arrives at the same conclusion (*Qingdai baqi zidi*, 57). Fragmentary data (probably from 1728) giving the name, age, experience, and language competency of eight Manchu midlevel officials show all but one to have been literate in Manchu; none were noted as knowing any Chinese (GZMaZJ 4, n.m., n.d).

91. KXMaZPZZ 241, Yentai, KX44.12.1.

92. YZMaZPZZ 3, Dzengšeo, YZ1.4.16. The 1749 replacement of a Manchu candidate who could not read Chinese with one who could indicates that this recommendation was adopted (Teng, *Qingdai baqi zidi*, 60). Note, however, that the proponents of a 1656 initiative to remove from office Manchus illiterate in Chinese were rewarded with stiff punishments (*Shizu shilu*, 96: 7b–8a).

93. *Shizong shilu*, 13: 13a–b.

94. YZMaZPZZ 79, Yandene, YZ3.1.12.

95. YZMaZPZZ 81, Fušen, YZ3.1.12.

96. YZMaZPZZ 239, Fuming, YZ12.6.1. Writing toward the end of the Yongzheng reign, du Halde remarked that as the older generation gradually died off, the language, too, died, as younger people in the banners picked up Chinese more easily. But he also affirmed that Manchu continued to be spoken regularly at court. See du Halde, *Description . . . de la Chine*, 77, "Remarques sur la langue des Tartares Mantcheoux."

97. YZMaZPZZ 479, Yansin, YZ5.3.15. Ever the pedant, the emperor responded with some advice on how to learn Chinese by memorizing just a few characters every day.

98. SYBQ YZ6: 2a–b (YZ6.1.29).

99. SYBQ YZ11: 7b–8a (YZ11.11.27).

100. SYBQ YZ11: 10a–b (YZ11.12.29).

101. *Gaozong shilu*, 366: 11a–b and 443: 28b–29a.

102. *Gaozong shilu*, 620: 2b–3a.

103. YZMaZPZZ 283, Maitu, n.d. On internal evidence I date this item to the 1720s.

104. YZMaZPZZ 252, Hesing, YZ12.6.25.

105. The original reads: "suwe sidan-i juse be inenggideri saikan urebume tucibu. erde oci bithe hūlabu. inenggi dulin oci bithe arabu. yamjishūn oci beri tatabu. gabtabu. Manju gisun gisurebu. ume nikarabure" (KXMaZPZZ 469, Siju, KX47.8.29).

106. For an early exception (1723), see *Shizong shilu*,19: 34b.

107. YZMaZPZZ 377, Yonggina, YZ3.2.29.

108. YZMaZPZZ 111, Sibe, YZ4.4.10.

109. YZMaZPZZ 165, Jalangga, YZ7.11.22.

110. SYBQ YZ12: 8a–b (YZ12.12.6). Though the references in this edict are to garrisons in the military cordon, a direct appeal to garrison generals and its inclusion in monographs from the provincial garrisons suggests its message was intended for all garrison bannermen (cf. *Jingkou baqi zhi*, 2: 9b–10a).

111. QLMaZPZZ 52, Bašinu, QL1.10.3.

112. YZMaZPZZ 54, Yūnsy, YZ2.4.5.

113. YZMaZPZZ 252, Hesing, YZ12.6.25. This estimation of the linguistic situation should be taken at face value, I think, since it was written just two weeks after Hesing arrived to take up his duties as Kaifeng military commandant, and it is very unlikely that he had anything to hide.

114. YZMaZPZZ 32, Sunju, YZ1.10.24.

115. Teng, *Qingdai baqi zidi*, 86–93; Lei Fangsheng, "Jingzhou qixue de shimo ji qi tedian" *Minzu yanjiu* (1984.3), 57.

116. GZMaZJ 5, Fusen, QL1.7.18.

117. QLMaZPZZ 52, Bašinu, QL1.10.3.

118. QLMaZPZZ 50 *shang*, Sioi Yuwan Meng [Xu-yuan-meng], QL1.4.26. In contrast to the majority of memorials received during the early Qianlong reign, which were passed to the Interim Council for deliberation, the young emperor did not hesitate to approve this proposal. He returned to this same policy a year or so later, and, somewhat surprisingly, reversed his earlier decision to eliminate the Manchu requirement on the grounds that for Manchus knowing the Manchu language should be taken for granted (*Gaozong shilu*, 43: 8a–9b). At around the same time, he also resisted moves to make knowledge of Chinese required for the promotion of Manchus in the civil bureaucracy, since to do so would end with "everyone abandoning their old studies and learning only Chinese writing" (ibid., 68: 7a).

119. Huang, *Autocracy at Work*, 167. Neither of the citations in Huang's original footnote to this statement would seem to offer corroboration of such an estimate. In his 1947 article, Miyazaki also wrote that Manchu remained in common use through the Yongzheng reign ("Kokugo mondai," 53).

120. See Teng, *Qingdai baqi zidi*, 188–95. Two Manchu scholars who have worked extensively with the Qing Manchu archives date the decline of Manchu from the Qianlong reign, noting that the number of Manchu documents decreases markedly during the Daoguang reign (1821–49). See Tong Yonggong and Guan Jialu, "Lun Manwen de shiyong ji qi lishi zuoyong" (unpublished paper, 1990), 11.

121. Gaubil, *Correspondance de Pékin*, 188; L. Aimé-Martin, ed., *Lettres édifiantes et curieuses concernant l'Asie* (Paris, 1838–43), 4: 707. Cf. also du Halde, writing in the 1730s (and in the present tense): "From the time that the Tartar family now ruling has occupied the throne of China, the language of the Manchu Tartars, as well as Chinese, is spoken at court" ("Depuis que la famille Tartare maintenant régnante, occupe le trône de la Chine, on parle à la cour la langue des Tartares Mantcheoux, de même que la Chinoise"). See Jean-Baptiste du Halde, *Description . . . de la Chine et de la Tartarie Chinoise* (Paris, 1735), 77, "Remarques sur la langue des Tartares Mantcheoux."

122. On the *Ode*, see Elliott, "The Limits of Tartary."

123. See, for instance, 1750 references to officials of the Board of Works, San-he and Zhong-fo-bao, in *Gaozong shilu*, 355: 7a–b.

124. Cf. the 1749 complaint by a Chinese official that the Imperial Household Department and the Eight Banner yamen in Beijing wrote all their communications to provincial governors, Manchu and Han alike, in Manchu (*Gaozong shilu*, 359: 6b–7b).

125. QSG 477: 13009, in reference to Manchu bannermen at Chengdu.

In her field work in provincial garrison communities in the 1980s and 1990s, Ding Yizhuang has found that, among themselves, these people continue to use Beijing-style Mandarin to this day. With local Han Chinese, however, they use the local dialect. Ding Yizhuang, personal communication, November 1996; also Ding, "Contemporary Manchu Ethnic Consciousness as Indicated by Oral Records and Archives" (paper presented at the UCLA Center for Chinese Studies, Los Angeles, May 1999).

126. See Guan Jixin and Meng Xianren, "Manzu yu Shenyang yu, Beijing yu," *Manzu yanjiu* (1987.1), 73–81. There was even a special dialect for the Peking suburbs; a partial word list is given in Jin Qizong, *Beijing jiaoqu de Manzu*, 35–39. Beijing's hybrid language is also discussed in Elliott, "The Eating Crabs Youth Book."

## Chapter 8. Saving the Banner System

1. The essays are all found in chapter 35 of the *Imperial Collection*, titled "Eight Banner Livelihood" (*baqi shengji*), collated with other essays on financial policy. References to individual essays are given in the notes below.

2. I have not attempted here to provide a complete description of all aspects of the Eight Banner economy, an enormous and enormously complex subject. Even to adequately present the intricacies of just one area of economic activity—for instance, the problem of banner landholdings and estates—would require a separate full-length study. Regarding this and other aspects of banner finances, I have tried to present only as much information as necessary to illuminate their place in the larger institutional crisis in the banners.

3. Recent estimates of total annual state revenue during the Qing period hover between sixty and eighty million taels. See James Lee, *The Political Economy of China's Southwestern Frontier, 1350 to 1850* (Cambridge: Harvard University Asia Center, forthcoming), table 1.6; R. Bin Wong and Pierre-Etienne Will, *Nourish the People: The State Civilian Granary System in China, 1650–1850* (Ann Arbor: University of Michigan, 1991), 494. Traditional estimates of state expenditures, on the other hand, have consistently been pegged at between twenty-seven and thirty-eight million taels annually. See Chen Feng, *Qingdai junfei yanjiu*, 205; Lee, *The Political Economy of China's Southwestern Frontier*, table 1.1, note e). Scholars are apt to cite particular items as proportions of either revenue or expenditure. The widely differing results of doing so, however, are considerably lessened if one accepts Lee's revised estimate of between fifty-six and sixty-six million taels in average annual expenditures (almost twice traditional figures), in which case military expenditures account for roughly one-half of annual expenditures (or, alternatively, are equivalent to one-half or less of annual revenues).

4. *Shizu shilu*, 136: 21a–22b. This was an unusually high wartime figure.

5. Lee, *The Political Economy of China's Southwestern Frontier*, table 1.1.

6. Chen Feng, *Qingdai junfei yanjiu*, 194–99.

7. Funds to pay military expenditures came directly from the land tax (Ch *diding*). This was true both for the provinces, who were authorized to pay the expenses of the local military infrastructure (i.e., the maintenance of Eight Banner and Green Standard Army garrisons) directly from tax revenues, and for the capital and the Northeast, where soldiers were paid by the Board of Revenue from tax revenues forwarded from the provinces. When land tax revenues were insufficient, funds could be transferred between provinces and money from other tax sources (e.g., salt, customs) used to meet the military's budgetary demands. Details are set forth in Chen, *Qingdai junfei yanjiu*, chap. 4.

8. Ibid., 201.

9. *Ding* population figures for this year (cited earlier) make clear that about 47 percent of capital bannermen were registered in the top three banners. The lower five banners were, on average, about two-thirds as large as any of the top three banners. Assuming a steady per-capita ratio of resource distribution, each of the other two top banners had expenditures similar to those of the Plain Yellow Banner, or about 900,000 taels, while each of the lower five banners spent one-third less, or about 600,000 taels, yielding a total of 5,800,000 taels for all eight banners. To this need to be added costs for the Northeast garrisons, which already approached 1,000,000 taels in the late seventeenth century.

10. Chen, *Qingdai junfei yanjiu*, 221–22.

11. Figured using rough totals of six hundred thousand soldiers in the Green Standard and two hundred thousand soldiers in the Eight Banners (Luo, *Lüyingbing zhi*, 62).

12. Šuhede [Shu-he-de], "Baqi kaiken biandi shu," HJW 35: 3a.

13. Fan Xian, "Baqi tunzhong shu," HJW 35: 4a.

14. Liang Shizheng, "Baqi tunzhong shu," HJW 35: 4b.

15. Hešeo [He-shou], "Fuyuan chanchou xinken shu," HJW 35: 5b.

16. Zhang Ruogui, "Qing fa baqi zhufang gesheng shu," HJW 35: 7b.

17. *Shizu shilu*, 104: 10b–11a.

18. For example, the essays by Šuhede, Fan, and Liang, already cited, plus He-qi-zhong, "Genben siji shu" (HJW 1a–1b), and Sun Jiagan, "Kouwai zhubing shu" (HJW 8a–9a).

19. See *Shuangchengpu tuntian jilue*, ed. Li Shutian (Changchun: Jilin wenshi chubanshe, 1990).

20. Wang, *Shiqu yuji*, 197–98.

21. *Shengzu shilu*, 149: 3b; 150: 14a.

22. Wu, "Development and Decline," 101–3. See also Appendix A.

23. Šuhede, "Baqi kaiken biandi shu," HJW 35: 3b.

24. Hosoya, "Hakki beikyoku kō," 201–2.

25. *Shengzu shilu*, 44: 8a–9b. Mongol bannermen were also often faulted for excessive contributions to Tibetan Buddhist temples.

26. YZMaZPZZ 49, Foron, YZ2.3.26. One thousand copper cash was supposed to equal one silver tael.

27. *Shizong shilu*, 25: 3b–4a, cited in Hosoya, "Hakki beikyoku kō," 185. Hosoya notes these bannerman profiteers, but reserves the larger role for Chinese merchants. See also *Gaozong shilu*, 97: 13b.

28. Hosoya, "Hakki beikyoku kō," 182–83.

29. YZMaZPZZ 49, Foron, YZ2.3.26. For other reports of fiscal irregularities in the banner garrisons, see *Gaozong shilu*, 401: 8a–9b.

30. Li, "Baqi shengji," 92–93; Wu, "Development and Decline," 123–28; Huang, *Autocracy at Work*, 178–80. One scholar has called this "the last dream of the well-field system." See Wu Hui, *Jingtianzhi kaosu* (Beijing: Nongye chubanshe, 1985), 228.

31. Wu, "Development and Decline," 115–16. Another eleven thousand or so *yangyubing* posts were added in 1753, but the total then remained stable (*Gaozong shilu*, 438: 4a–b; DQHDSL 1121).

32. Wang, *Shiqu yuji*, 195–96.

33. Li, "Baqi shengji wenti," 92. Owners had good incentive to respond promptly. Land that had been sold within the last ten years was bought back at the original sale price; transactions over ten years old were redeemed at a 10 percent discount off the original price. Land that had been bought more than fifty years earlier was redeemed at half the sale price. See Wei, *Qingdai de qidi*, 3: 1543.

34. See the documents in ibid., 3: 1543–76.

35. *Shengzu shilu*, 149: 3b–4a; 150: 14a–b.

36. Ibid., 150: 14b–15a. Cf. also SYBQ YZ1: 17b. No money was ever deducted from banner salaries to cover repayment (*Gaozong shilu*, 78: 10a).

37. Wu, "Development and Decline," 119–21; Wang, *Shiqu yuji*, 197–98.

38. In 1742 the Qianlong emperor dispensed over one million taels of "making-ends-meet money" (Ch *zisheng yin*) to capital bannermen. The sudden influx of so much silver into the city drove the value of coins up 2 percent (*Gaozong shilu*, 164: 29a–b).

39. The earliest reports of homelessness among bannermen came in the 1690s, at which time the source of the problem was tied not to overpopulation but to wealthy official households "buying up the property of ten poor families to build their houses." At least seven thousand households were reportedly

reduced to paying rent and living in hardship. The solution proposed at the time was to construct sixteen thousand extra houses for homeless bannermen in the suburbs at a projected cost of more than three hundred thousand taels (*Shengzu shilu*, 167: 3b–4a). By the early eighteenth century, however, many bannermen were again tenants. A 1723 memorial analyzed the problem of bannermen who, despite the millions of taels that had been spent to pay up their debts, continued to live extravagantly and who, to satisfy creditors, had to sell or mortgage their houses and land. The solution put forth was simply to outlaw the sale or mortgage of property. The only exceptions would be allowed in cases where money was needed to pay for weddings and for parents' funerals, where loans would be made at a rate no higher than 2 percent. Anyone violating these rules was threatened with punishment, as was his superior officer (YZMaZPZZ 14, Dzengšeo, YZ1.2.8). One drawback with regulating rents, though it does not appear to have been brought up at the time, was that it would limit banner income from this source. Such income could be substantial: the Bordered Red Banner reported 1,186 taels received in rent from residential and commercial properties in the capital (*Jōkōkitō—Kenryūchō* 1, no. 19, 14–17). Rents ranged between eight *fen* and one and a half taels per room.

40. YZMaZPZZ 23, Mampi, n.d.

41. YZMaZPZZ 239, Boošan, YZ12.10.5.

42. YZMaZPZZ 11, Darma, YZ1.9.24.

43. YZMaZPZZ 49, Foron, YZ2.3.26.

44. Wei Qingyuan, "Qingdai Yongzheng shiqi 'shengxi yinliang' zhidu de zhengdun he zhengce yanbian," in *Ming-Qing shi bianxi* (Beijing: Zhongguo shehui kexue chubanshe, 1989), 188. See the discussion of the emperor's fiscal policies in Zelin, *The Magistrate's Tael*, 281; and Helen Dunstan, *Conflicting Counsels to Confuse the Age: A Documentary Study of Political Economy in Qing China, 1644–1840* (Ann Arbor: The University of Michigan Center for Chinese Studies, 1996), 152–53. The origins of the system can be traced to the early Kangxi reign, when money from the imperial purse was lent to Mukden imperial household department officials, who were simultaneously authorized to invest it in lucrative copper or salt operations. Any interest earned was returned to the emperor's coffers after a commission had been pocketed. This type of operation resembled any number of investment ventures involving Imperial Household money, whether for official or private speculation. Such dealings were not at all unusual in the seventeenth century; cf. the schemes devised by Li Xu and Cao Yin in Spence, *Ts'ao Yin*, 99–103.

45. Such as pensions, travel funds, and gifts to cover wedding and funeral costs. See Chapter 4.

46. Wei, "Qingdai Yongzheng shiqi 'shengxi yinliang' zhidu," 188.

47. Ibid., 195.

48. BQTZ 26, 502. I have found very little information about the operation of the investment funds program in the capital. Most of the money seems to have gone directly into buying land (Hešeo, "Fu yuanchan chou xinken shu," HJW 35: 5a–7b).

49. Xi'an: QLMaZPZZ 69, Cimbu, QL2.12.17b; Nanjing: YZMaZPZZ 511, Unaha, YZ10.10.2; Hangzhou: YZMaZPZZ 526, Arigūn, YZ10.3.19b; Jingzhou: YZMaZPZZ 210, Guntai, YZ10.5.13a; Ningxia: QLMaZPZZ 77, Alu, QL3.12.9; Youwei: *Jōkōkitō—Yōseichō*, docs. 19, 29, and 53; Tianjin: QLMaZPZZ 61, Ayangga, QL2.4.28, and QLHaZPZZ 7, QL7.3.22; Kaifeng: YZMaZPZZ 245, Hesing, YZ12.8.6; Tongguan: QLMaZPZZ 69, Cimbu, QL2.12.17b; Zhapu: YZMaZPZZ 167, Fusen, YZ7.R7.27. Additional grants were later made to Qingzhou (six thousand taels in 1733), Liangzhou (fifteen thousand taels, probably in 1738), and Zhuanglang (eight thousand taels in 1738) (Qingzhou: YZMaZPZZ 530, Arigūn, YZ13.1.27; Ningxia: QLMaZPZZ 77, Alu, QL3.12.9; Liangzhou: QLMaZPZZ 83, Uhetu, QL4.9.16 and QL5.12.17; Zhuanglang: QLMaZPZZ 81, Serguleng, QL4.7.8). Unless otherwise noted, the information that follows on investment funds is all taken from these documents.

50. *Jōkōkitō—Yōseichō*, doc. 19. The earliest such statements I found in the archives were from 1732.

51. Wei says that half of all investments were of this kind ("Qingdai Yongzheng shiqi 'shengxi yinliang' zhidu," 218).

52. During the Yongzheng reign, a rate of 2 percent monthly interest was already considered "relatively high" (ibid., 213).

53. Im, "Rise and Decline," 132 (for the Guangzhou garrison).

54. Wei, "Qingdai Yongzheng shiqi 'shengxi yinliang' zhidu," 209.

55. YZMaZPZZ 57, Ashai, QL1.12.16.

56. QLMaZPZZ 61, Ayangga, QL2.4.28. These figures, since they come from archival originals, should probably be accepted over the figure of ten thousand recorded in BQTZ 26, 502.

57. YZMaZPZZ 210, Guntai, YZ10.5.13.

58. SYBQ YZ10: 6b–7b (YZ10.5.7).

59. YZMaZPZZ 245, Hesing, YZ12.8.6. One of the more outrageous plans for use of investment fund money was that put forward by the Zhuanglang garrison in Gansu, where of the eight thousand taels given to the garrison to earn interest, lieutenant general Serguleng proposed to use fifty-six hundred taels for discount-rate loans to be made directly to bannermen who already owed money at higher rates, offering them a chance to consolidate their debts. When this was nixed by the Liangzhou general, Serguleng went ahead and

disposed of fourteen hundred taels as loans to bannermen needing new horses and gave an additional twelve hundred taels to each of the garrison's eight regiment colonels for opening "shops" run on the same basis as those in Kaifeng, and lending at the rather steep rate of 2.5 percent (QLMaZPZZ 81, Serguleng, QL4.7.8; Uhetu, QL4.7.21).

60. Wei Qingyuan, "Qingdai Qianlong shiqi 'shengxi yinliang' zhidu de shuaibai he 'shouche,'" in *Ming-Qing shi bianxi*, 236.

61. Ibid., 243–52.

62. Ibid., 239.

63. See Dunstan, *Conflicting Counsels*, 195–96 (text 4.e), who explains (169) that this had much to do with the common view that there was a fixed amount of wealth in the world.

64. QLMaZPZZ 61, Ayangga, QL2.4.28.

65. See, for instance, Zhongguo diyi lishi dang'anguan, "Daoguang chu chouyi baqi shengji shiliao," *Lishi dang'an* (1994.2), 3–12.

66. David Strand, *Rickshaw Beijing: City People and Politics in the 1920's* (Berkeley and Los Angeles: University of California Press, 1989), 13, 31.

67. Lao She, *Beneath the Red Banner*, 14.

68. The following account relies in part on Hosoya Yoshio, "Hakki shin-chō kōkōsatsu no seiritsu to sono haikei," *Shūkan tōyōgaku* (1963), 18–32; and Fu Kedong, "Baqi huji zhidu chutan," *Minzu yanjiu* (1983.6), 34–43.

69. These were roughly paralleled by the Yuan "auxiliary households," known as *tiehu* (Hsiao, *The Military Establishment of the Yuan Dynasty*, 19).

70. These English terms are my own. As far as I am aware, no accepted terminology for the translation of the household categories described here yet exists.

71. Fu Lehuan, "Guanyu Qingdai Manzu de jige wenti," 402; Hosoya Yoshio, "Shinchō chūki no hakki kosekihō no henkaku—kaiko o chūshin ni shite," *Shūkan tōyōgaku* 15 (May 1966), 51–53.

72. SYBQ YZ6: 17a (YZ6.4.28).

73. SYBQ YZ11: 5a (YZ11.4.29). This practice continued in the Yong-zheng reign. Hosoya appears to believe that before the Yongzheng reforms all entailed households were by definition indistinguishable from detached households ("Shinchō chūki no hakki kosekihō no henkaku," 54).

74. *Yuxing qiwu zouyi*, YZ2: 13b. A case from 1725 illustrates this well. In that year a petition was received by the widow of a Manchu soldier named Merge, a member of the Bordered Blue Banner garrisoned at Xi'an who had gone off to fight in Tibet. As his widow noted simply, "he did not come back." In accordance with the provision made by the Kangxi emperor for the support of such households, the post should have gone to a son. Since there was no son

of age, the post went instead to a young man, Barsai, who was the son of a household bondservant. Now, however, a company officer was trying to strip the post from the household altogether. Merge's widow begged the court to intervene and recognize the legitimacy of the earlier substitution. Citing precedents from the Kangxi era, the court restored the post to the household (YZMaZPZZ 434, Ilibu, YZ3.7.21).

75. Hosoya, "Hakki shinchō kōkōsatsu," 26.

76. That is to say, after the second half of the Yongzheng reign, the term *linghu* came on a par with *zhenghu* in terms of its connotation of primary social status in the Eight Banners. Fu's statement that "*zhenghu* and *linghu* belonged to the top rank of bannermen in the Eight Banners" should be understood with this in mind (Fu Kedong, "Baqi huji zhidu," 36).

77. SYBQ YZ7: 22b–23a (YZ7.6.4).

78. For example, separate-register bannermen could sometimes be appointed to vacancies in the Green Standard Army and were even, it seems, eligible for lower officer rank in the Chinese banners (Fu, "Baqi huji zhidu," 40). The category of entailed banner household was maintained after the reforms for servile households newly being made semi-independent. A memorial of 1734 suggests that separate-register households were referred to informally as the "old Chinese" (Ma *fe Nikan*) while entailed households were "entered Chinese" (Ma *dosika Nikan*) (YZMaZPZZ 238, Fusen, YZ12.8.2). Differences between separate-register and regular Manchu bannermen were still being discussed in 1753, when it was decided that separate-register bannermen found guilty of crimes should be treated as Han civilians (*Gaozong shilu*, 437: 11a–b).

79. Hosoya, "Hakki shinchō kōkōsatsu," 24.

80. Though not in every instance, it seems. In recommending a general increase in the number of Manchu and Mongol troops stationed at five important garrisons near Beijing (Baoding, Gubeikou, Xifengkou, Lengkou, Dushikou), one memorialist complained of irregularities such as "Chinese adopted sons calling themselves 'separate households' and wrongly filling in positions" that should go to "good, regular ones" (YZMaZPZZ 163, Yūnsy, YZ2.4.5).

81. GZMaZJ 5, Uhetu, QL5.12.17. The general asked that lower wedding and funeral subsidies be approved for them, and no subsidies if they had no actual military record.

82. QLMaZPZZ 67, Alu, QL2.10.14. I have extrapolated this total from the partial figures given in the memorial.

83. *Gaozong shilu*, 303: 15b–16a, cited in Wang, "Qingdai baqizhong de Man-Han minzu chengfen wenti," 56.

84. YZMaZPZZ 238, Fusen, YZ12.8.2. The Hangzhou census registers were compiled in 1727 and went back three generations.

85. QLMaZPZZ 85, Fusen, QL4.12.8.

86. The original reads: "meni meni hahai erdemu be taciha. ujiha juse. dangse faksalaha ursei dorgide beri hūsun mangga. yafagan de sain ningge gemu Manju beye adali umai ilgaburakū" (YZMaZPZZ 238, Fusen, YZ12.8.2). For *Manju beye*, see also QLMaZPZZ 67, Alu, QLZ.10.14.

87. The shift from *ding* to *hu* as the basic "accounting" unit in the Eight Banners is regarded as one of the more important steps in the bureaucratization of the banner system (Hosoya, "Hakki shinchō kōkōsatsu," 18).

88. Ibid., 18, 30, and Hosoya, "Shinchō chūki no hakki kosekihō no henkaku," 61–62; Fu, "Baqi huji zhidu," 42; Liu Xiaomeng, "Baqi hujizhong de qixiaren zhu mingcheng kaoshi," *Shehui kexue jikan* 50.3 (1987), 63.

89. *Yuxing qiwu zouyi* YZ2: 11b–13b. Part of this item is cited by Hosoya, but mistakenly attributed to the companion collection of documents, *Shangyu qiwu yifu* (Hosoya, "Hakki shinchō kōkōsatsu," 30).

90. Genealogies began to be received by the court as early as 1725 (SYBQ YZ3: 37a–b [YZ3.9.13]), and many have been preserved in the First Historical Archives, e.g., *Baqi dutong yamen dang*, no. 189, "Gulu šanggiyan-i Manju gūsai bithe. Dorgi yamun-i jakūn gūsai jy šu bithe weilere guwan de unggihe. Mini gūsai fere jalan alibuha nirui da sekiyen Manju Nikan hergen aramciha dangse" (Written report from the Manchu Plain White Banner. Sent to the Eight Banners monograph editing office in the Grand Secretariat. Papers written up in Manchu and Chinese on the origins of the companies in the first *jalan* of my banner), which is noted as having arrived at the palace April 27, 1734 (YZ12.3.24).

91. Examples of the two types are preserved in many library and archival collections, and many remain in private hands today. See Nicholas Poppe, Leon Hurvitz, and Hidehiro Okada, eds., *Catalogue of the Manchu-Mongol Section of the Tōyō Bunko* (Tokyo: Tōyō Bunko, 1964), entries 399–416; Huang Runhua and Qu Liusheng, *Quanguo Manwen tushu ziliao lianhe mulu* (Beijing: Shumu wenxian chubanshe, 1991), entries 924–34; Li Teh Ch'i, *Union Catalogue of Manchu Books in the National Library of Peiping and the Library of the National Palace Museum* (Beijing: National Library of Peiping and the Library of the National Palace Museum, 1933), entries 981.2–81.4; see also following notes.

92. *Baqi Manzhou shizu tongpu/Jakūn gūsai Manjusai mukūn hala be uheri ejehe bithe.* The original preface ordering the collection is dated January 13, 1736 (YZ13.12.1).

93. BQTZ 238: 5359. Unfortunately, I have not been able to find any extant copies of this work.

94. Li Lin, *Manzu jiapu xuanbian* (Shenyang: Liaoning renmin chu-

banshe, 1988), 5. This is a very important collection of some twenty of the 250 privately kept genealogies collected by the author and his research team during the 1980s. By 1990 this number had risen to over 400 (Li Lin, personal communication, September 1990). On other extant genealogies, see also Li, *Manzu zongpu yanjiu*; Li Lin et al., *Benxixian Manzu jiapu yanjiu* (Shenyang: Liaoning minzu chubanshe, 1988); and the note on the 1746 Niohuru clan genealogy in Lu Hua, "'Niu-gu-lu shi jia pu' yanjiu," *Manzu yanjiu* (1986.2), 81–84. It is to be expected that more and more of these sources will continue to emerge.

95. Li Jutan, "Manzu jiapu xiaoyi," *Manzu yanjiu* (1987.2), 64; Li, *Manzu jiapu xuanbian*, ix.

96. SYBQ YZ1: 15a–b (YZ1.9.27).

97. Li, *Manzu jiapu xuanbian*, 180, "Bai shi yuanliu zupu"; 416, "Wu shi jiapu."

98. KXMaZPZZ 7, Bodi, n.d. This memorial was included with twenty-four others in a packet dated KX42–56 (1703–17). The emperor's rescript read: "Very important report. [Let the] banner officials discuss and memorialize." This would support Hosoya's hypothesis that genealogical material was being kept by banner companies long before the Yongzheng reign, his assumption being the logical one that in order for the passage to have been traceable at the time of the reforms in the late 1720s and 1730s, records of some sort must have been kept that could have served as evidence of household origin as well as of company type. As Hosoya notes, after being expanded, genealogies went from being private to public records and were included in the *qifenzhi* section of the *Baqi tongzhi* (Hosoya Yoshio, "Shinchō ni okeru hakki seido no suii, *Tōyō gakuhō* 51.1, 9.

99. Li, *Manzu jiapu xuanbian*, iv.

100. The family tree shown in Li (said to be from the clan genealogy) is misleading, as it fails to indicate the splitting in 1655 of the original company concerned (BQTZ 8: 140–41). The line of inheritance shown (Alanju—Bulanju—Burkan [Bu-er-kan]—Tantai—Tuli—Cile—Junghai—Haijungga) may have been influenced by the honorary title of second-class *qiduyu*, which was passed in this line (BQTZ 93: 2139).

101. BQMST 8: 6b–7b (Donggo clan, "Age Bayan").

102. Taking the comparison one step further, it is clear that the information provided here was the basis for the accounts of Age Bayan and his descendants included in the biographical section of BQTZ 162: 4031 ("Alanju"). A similar difference between company and clan genealogies is observed in other cases, too. Compare, for example, the separate accounts of two branches of the Šumuru clan that provided hereditary captains of the

Fifth and Seventh companies in the second *jalan* of the Manchu Plain Yellow Banner, two in BQTZ (4: 51 and 146), and one in BQMST (6). Here the biographical texts in BQTZ appear to have been composed independently of the clan biography in BQMST, perhaps because of the unusual fame of the members of this family, who certainly had biographies stored in the Dynastic History Office. More background on the family can be found under "Yangguri efu" in ECCP 898–99.

103. The functions of the *jarguci* (a title borrowed directly from Mongolian) combined judicial with military command responsibilities (Zhang and Guo, *Qing ruguanqian*, 564–67). On the background of this position and its place in Yuan rule, see Elizabeth Endacott-West, *Mongolian Rule in China: Local Administration in the Yuan Dynasty* (Cambridge: Harvard Council on East Asian Studies, 1989).

104. QLMaZPZZ 67, Alu, QL2.10.14. Alu announced he was sending Fuju to Beijing for further cross-examination.

105. In a note on the language aptitudes of Chinese captives in the Eight Banner system, a seventeenth-century memoir explains, "all of them learn to speak Manchu [*Manyu*] fluently, so that you cannot distinguish them from the Jurchens. But when they get older, their native accents gradually come out and even though they can handle Manchu, ninety-nine times out of one hundred their accents sound coarse" (Liu, *Guangyang zaji*, 1: 32). This may be the first use of the abbreviation "Manyu," the modern Chinese word for the Manchu language. As mentioned earlier, the language was usually called *Qingyu* (or *guoyu*) in the Qing.

106. YZMaZPZZ 163, Batu, YZ7.9.11. Adoption in the Eight Banners is another area awaiting careful study.

107. This introduces another factor for the decline in linguistic skills among bannermen. Recalling that one-half of Hangzhou's Manchu bannermen could not speak Manchu well, one wonders whether they were the same one-half who were separate-register, adoptive, and entailed bannermen. The same question may be raised with regard to the simultaneous report that "among Chinese bannermen, fewer than one in ten can even mumble a few words in Manchu" (QLMaZPZZ 52, Bašinu, QL1.10.3).

108. *Gaozong shilu*, 506: 2b–6a, partially cited in Hosoya, "Shinchō chūki no hakki kosekihō no henkaku," 61.

109. Based on archival reports of the number of separate-register households created in the Plain and Bordered Red banners (about eight hundred in each), Fu estimates the total number of households reduced to separate-register standing at "not less than 10,000," of which more than 6,000 were (former) Chinese bannermen ("Baqi huji zhidu," 38, 42). These estimates

are naturally very rough, but they do seem to be supported by other reports, such as that from Hangzhou, where of 1,700 soldiers demoted to separate-register status, 900 were from the Chinese banners (QLMaZPZZ 85, Fusen, QL4.12.8).

110. There is also evidence that the birth rate among Chinese bannermen was higher (perhaps by as much as four times) than that of Manchu bannermen. See Ding, "Qianlong chao zhufang Hanjun chuqi qianyi," *Qingshi yanjiu tongxun* (1990.3), 12; and Ding, *Qingdai baqi zhufang*, 181–82.

111. Three memorials found in YZMaZPZZ 60, all dated YZ2.2.24, from Marsa (on the Manchu banner), Cimbu (on the Mongol banner), and Lu Siyūn [Lu Xun] (on the Chinese banner).

112. Fu-ge, *Tingyu congtan*, 3: 53.

113. *Shengzu shilu*, 131: 2ab–21a.

114. Ibid., 118: 4a–b.

115. Ura, "Kangun ni tsuite," 832–33, citing an edict of 1686 in *Donghualu*, Kangxi 40.

116. "Nian Gengyao buguo yi Hanjun zhi zi" (SYBQ YZ3: 27b [YZ3.6.9]), which, of course, he was—of the Bordered Yellow Banner. He was married to a sister of the emperor.

117. SYBQ YZ7: 31b–32a (YZ7.R7.25). The emperor gave them six months to at least memorize their resumés or he would reject their promotions. The little-lamented Nian Gengyao was almost flippant in admitting his poor knowledge of Manchu to Hangzhou lieutenant general Fusen when he showed up to assume, briefly, duties as Hangzhou garrison general in 1725. Two days after Nian's arrival, Fusen went to the general's yamen to read him the short, ominous edict formally entrusting him with the post: "The province of Zhejiang is very important. The position of garrison general is also very important. Your master has shown you great favor by thus using you. Ask heaven if you have not betrayed your lord's trust." When Fusen finished reading, Nian at first said nothing. Then, getting up, he laughed in Fusen's face, saying, "I don't understand spoken Manchu very well. Write it down and give it to me. Then I'll send a memorial." One can imagine the impression this made on the suspicious emperor. In his rescript he wrote, "What a miserable, damnable wretch! Now there is nothing else for me to do" (YZMaZPZZ 80, Fusen, YZ3.7.6).

118. SYBQ YZ9: 8a (YZ9.11.20). These included the descendants of Shang Kexi, Geng Jingzhong, Shi Tingzhu, Tong Yangxing, and others.

119. Cereng later became governor-general of Guangdong and Guangxi, and of Sichuan, before becoming actively involved in military campaigns (ECCP 220).

120. QLHaZPZZ 5, Cereng, QL5.8.29. In his rescript the emperor applauded, "Now this is the way to get things done!"

121. Sun Jiagan, "Hanjun shengji shu," HJW 35: 9a–b. Sun, a *jinshi* of 1713, served in numerous important positions in the central and provincial bureaucracy during his forty-year career. His knowledge of banner affairs may have owed to his experience as governor-general of Zhili, which exposed him to the flagrant abuse of Han civilians by bannermen and estate overseers (QSLZ 15: 1084–92).

122. Zheng, *Tanweiji*, 58.

123. Wang Shizhen, *Chibei outan* (1700; reprint, Beijing: Zhonghua shuju, 1982), 3: 57, "Hanjun Hanren."

124. Jin, *Qijun zhi*, 1a. Jin himself belonged to the Chinese Plain Red Banner.

125. *Gaozong shilu*, 748: 30a, cited in Ding, *Qingdai baqi zhufang*, 216.

126. Ibid., 164: 32b–34a, cited in Ura, "Kangun ni tsuite," 842, and Wu, "Development and Decline," 147.

127. Ding, *Qingdai baqi zhufang*, 161.

128. Ura, "Kangun ni tsuite," 843.

129. Wu, "Development and Decline," 149.

130. Hard statistics on preference between these options are virtually nonexistent. One reference (for the Jingkou garrison) says that about one-third of banner-leavers chose to register as civilians in the local *bao-jia*. The rest presumably became Green Standard soldiers (Elliott, "Bannerman and Townsman," 46). Apparently Chinese bannermen transferred to the Chinese army received 33 percent higher pay than Green Standard regulars (Wu, "Development and Decline," 150, citing an unnamed source).

131. *Gaozong shilu*, 459: 17a–17b, cited in Ding, *Qingdai baqi zhufang*, 185–86. I have been guided in this account of the expulsion of the Chinese bannermen by the excellent work by Ding Yizhuang and Liu Xiaomeng on the topic. See especially Ding, "Qianlong chao zhufang Hanjun chuqi qianyi."

132. KXMaZPZZ 355, Boji, KX41.5.21. One might also recall that in 1733 the addition of fifteen hundred troops at Xi'an required that a number of that garrison's permanent residents be moved to make room. It was decided to move three thousand Chinese bannermen to separate quarters in a new compound outside the southeast corner of the Manchu city (YZMaZPZZ 1068, Cimbu, YZ11.5.6).

133. The term is Wu Wei-ping's ("Development and Decline," 147).

134. See, for instance, *Gaozong shilu*, 469: 4b.

135. See the summaries in *Gaozong shilu*, 667: 18a–b, and 680: 19a–20b, cited in Ding, *Qingdai baqi zhufang*, 186–89.

136. Wu, "Development and Decline," 149.

137. Ura, "Kangun ni tsuite," 843.

138. For instance, on the grounds that both were the "hereditary servants of the dynasty" (Ch *benchao shipu*) in 1753 the emperor pledged to include Mongols together with Manchus under preferences for finding them positions in the provincial bureaucracy (*Gaozong shilu*, 443: 7b–9a).

139. See, for example, Song-yun, *Emu tanggū orin sakda-i gisun sarkiyan*, 360, 362, 394–95, 445, 449.

140. The original reads: "bing ni tong shi qiren, bu ke ouda" (routine Board of Punishments memorial, "*hunyin jianqing*" 184, Agūi, QL60.6.15). My thanks to Blaine Gaustad for bringing this item to my attention.

141. *Gaozong shilu*, 1434: 3b–5a, cited in Wang, "Guanyu Manzu xingchengzhong," 11.

## Conclusion. *Manchu Identity and Manchu Rule in China*

1. The story does not end there. The executioner complied with A-li-ma's request to dispatch him inside the city walls, but when his sword came down on A-li-ma's neck, it could not cut through the iron-hard muscle. A stronger swordsman had to be found. See Zhao-lian, *Xiaoting zalu*, "A-li-ma," 234–35.

2. I address this issue in "The Manchus as Ethnographic Subject in Qing *Biji* Writings" (paper presented at the conference Empire and Beyond: Historical China from the Ming to the Republic, Center for Chinese Studies, University of California, Berkeley, December 1997).

3. The idea that the Qing needed to strike a balance between Manchu and Chinese interests is certainly not new, but usually it is conceived of as a specific political problem of the early Qing that was resolved by the Yong-zheng emperor, who defanged the Manchu aristocracy. There is some truth to this view. What I am suggesting, however, is that this was more than a simple balancing of political interests and that the problem was endemic to Qing rule, since the preservation of difference between the Manchus and the rest of the population was an essential element of the Qing strategy.

4. I do not wholly exclude the possibility that the dynasty could have survived the fall of the banner system. But had the Eight Banners been disbanded and its people reclassified as *min* and forced to earn a living like the Han Chinese, the imperial house, too, would have had to remove all traces of "Manchus" and "Manchuness" from government structures and from itself in order to make its way as an ethnically nondescript (i.e., native) dynasty. It

might be argued that this was the direction things were moving anyway, and that it was only a matter of time before the Aisin Gioro remade themselves as Han. However, this would have necessitated the invention of a wholly new pedigree, and even a new name, for the imperial clan—projects not very likely to succeed. It is precisely here that one can see very clearly the way in which the fate of the ruling house was entwined with the fate of Manchus generally. Therefore, while I admit the theoretical possibility of total Manchu reinvention, given the short period of time within which such a reinvention would actually have needed to take place, I believe it is fair to say that, practically speaking, the court absolutely had to find a way to sustain the banners or it would indeed have faced delegitimation and collapse.

5. ECCP 748–49.

6. By "normative" I mean the specific group of court-promoted skills and attributes designated as part of the *fe doro*. By "performative" I mean the whole range of practices and privileges that were part of life in the banners and which distinguished its members from the surrounding Han population (which was by no means the same at every banner garrison).

7. Thus, since the Sibe and Daur were never fully integrated into the Eight Banner structure but always remained separate within the larger banner system, they achieved independent ethnic status at this time. The Solon and Chakhar were absorbed into the Mongol ethnic group.

8. Shen Qiyuan, "Nishi wuce," HJW 35: 13a.

9. G. Carter Bentley, "Ethnicity and Practice," *Comparative Studies in Society and History* 29.1 (January 1987), 26.

10. Ibid., 48. Bourdieu defines *habitus* as "systems of durable, transposable dispositions . . . structures [that function] as principles which generate and organize practices and representations that can be objectively adapted to their outcomes without presupposing a conscious aiming at ends or an express mastery of the operations necessary in order to attain them." From Pierre Bourdieu, *The Logic of Practice*, trans. Richard Nice (Stanford, Calif.: Stanford University Press, 1990), 53.

11. Pierre Bourdieu, *Outline of a Theory of Practice*, trans. Richard Nice (Cambridge: Cambridge University Press, 1977), 82. One is reminded here of Eriksen's point that ethnic concepts are important in investigating "the relationship between culture, identity, and social organization" (*Ethnicity and Nationalism*, 162).

12. Linda Colley, *Britons: Forging the Nation, 1707–1837* (New Haven, Conn.: Yale University Press, 1992), 11–54 ff.

13. Norman Itzkowitz, *Ottoman Empire and Islamic Tradition* (Chicago: University of Chicago Press, 1972).

14. See C. Matthew Snipp, "Some Observations About Racial Boundaries and the Experiences of American Indians," *Ethnic and Racial Studies* 20.4 (October 1997), 667–89.

15. Shen Yuan and Mao Biyang, "Rhyme in Manchu Court Poetry of the Qing," trans. Mark C. Elliott, *Saksaha* 4 (1999), 25–26.

16. The nature of Manchu imperialism and colonialism is also the subject of several essays in the *International History Review* 20.2 (June 1998), to which the interested reader is referred.

17. Fletcher, "Turco-Mongolian Monarchic Tradition," 240–41; cf. also David Morgan, *The Mongols* (Cambridge, Mass.: Basil Blackwell, 1986), 38–39.

18. The convoluted process by which Manchuria became integrated into Chinese national territory is discussed in Elliott, "The Limits of Tartary."

19. As in the following passage from a memorial of 1759: "Respectfully reflecting [on matters]: before the distantly radiating virtue and power of my sacred lord, the western marches have been pacified and the steppes, mountains, and rivers of the Dzungar Mongols have been unified with the territory of China" ("gingguleme gūnici enduringge ejen erdemu horon goro selgiyebuhe de erei onggolo wargi jase be necihiyeme toktobufi jun gar monggo tala. alin bira de dulimbai gurun-i nirugan dangse de uherilebuhe") (QLMaZPZZ 308, Seksen, QL24.8.4).

20. "War and empire, then, were the means by which the union between Scotland and the rest of Great Britain was made real" (Colley, *Britons*, 132–33).

21. Cf. Dru Gladney's statement that the People's Republic of China is a "new Chinese empire built on top of the old" (*Muslim Chinese*, 299). Of course, this leaves aside the question of how "Chinese" the old empire was.

22. See Fitzgerald, *Awakening China*, 182.

23. Sun Yat-sen, *The Teachings of Sun Yat-sen: Selections from His Writings* (London: Sylvan Press, 1945), 33–34.

24. Colin Mackerras, *China's Minority Cultures: Identities and Integration Since 1912* (Melbourne: Longman, 1995), 10.

25. "Zhou Enlai lun Manzu," in *Xinjiang Manzu* (Urumci: n.p., n.d.), 1.

26. See Mark C. Elliott, "Eighteenth-Century Ideas of 'China' and the 'Unified Polyethnic State'" (paper prepared for the Southern California China Colloquium Seminar, From Late Imperial to Modern Chinese History: Views from the Eighteenth Century, UCLA Center for Chinese Studies, Los Angeles, November 1998).

27. Chiang Kai-shek, *China's Destiny*, 2nd ed. (Kingsport, Tenn.: Roy Publishers, 1947), 50.

28. It is, I think, in this sense that Ping-ti Ho uses the term "Chinese" in

writing that Manchus and Chinese in the late nineteenth century were "all 'Chinese' in the same boat" ("In Defense of Sinicization," 149).

*Appendix A*

   1.  These figures come principally from two articles by An Shuangcheng, "Shun-Kang-Yong sanchao baqi ding'e qianxi," *Lishi dang'an* (1983.2), 100–3, and "Shunzhi chao baqi nanding Manwen dang'an xuanyi," *Manxue yanjiu* 1 (1992), 415–21.

# CHINESE CHARACTER GLOSSARY

age suo　阿哥所
baishi　白事
bantu　版圖
bao-jia　保甲
bao-yi　包衣
bao-yi zuoling　包衣佐領
baqi　八旗
baqi dutong yamen　八旗都統衙門
baqi Hanjun　八旗漢軍
baqi Manzhou　八旗滿洲
baqi Menggu　八旗蒙古
baqi shengji wenti　八旗生計問題
baqi zhidu　八旗制度
baqi zhufang　八旗駐防
bashi wu　八十五
beideng ji　背燈祭
beifen yongzi　輩份用字
"benchao shipu"　本朝世僕
biantong　變通
biji　筆記
bing　兵
"bing ni tong shi qiren, bu ke ouda"　并你同是旗人不可毆打
bingxiang　兵餉
bingxiang magan　兵餉馬乾
bi-tie-shi　筆帖士
bu　部
bu　步
"bu fen Man Han, dan wen qi min"　不分滿漢但問旗民
bubian　不便

bujun ying　步軍營
buzhang　部長
chao ji　朝祭
Chaoxian laigui rending　朝鮮來歸人丁
chen　臣
chengshouyu　城守尉
chi huangxiang　吃皇餉
chi jian　敕建
chu kou　出口
cunzhang　村長
Da Ming　大明
Da Qing　大清
dan　旦
dangpu　當鋪, 當舖
dao　道
daotiao　刀條
daoyang ge　稻秧歌
daren　大人
daxie　大寫
dazi　達子, 韃子
dazi xiang　達子香
dianzhihua　典制化
dianzi　鈿子
diding　地丁
ding　丁
Dongbei　東北
dou　斗
duibo　堆撥
duifang　碓房
duizi　堆子

duo qing　躱情
Duo-er-gun　多爾滾
duo-luo bei-le　多羅貝勒
dutang　都堂
dutong　都統
E-bi-long　鄂必隆
fang　坊
fangshouyu　防守尉
fanyi kaoshi　翻譯考試
fen　分
fengqi　風氣
Fengtian　奉天
fengtu ruanruo　風土軟弱
fengyin　奉銀
fu　府
fu-bing　府兵
fudutong　副都統
Gao-li bao-yi　高麗包衣
"ge qiyuan zidi"　各旗員子弟
gong　公
gongku　公庫
gongtinghua　宮廷化
guan　官
Guan di　關帝
guancai　棺材
guanling　管領
guanting　官廳
gui qi　歸旗
guo　國
"guochu bianli"　國初編立
guojia　國家
"guojia zhi genben"　國家之根本
guoshiguan　國史館
guoyu　國語
gu-shan e-zhen　固山額真
Han gao　漢稿
han　汗
Hanhua　漢化
Hanjun　漢軍
Hanren　漢人
haonu　豪奴
hongshi　紅事

hou Jin guo　后金國
hu　戶
hu　斛
hua　華
huangdi　皇帝
huaxia　華夏
hujun ying　護軍營
huoqi ying　火器營
hutong　胡同
huxiaren　戶下人
"iminzoku tōchi"　異民族統治
ji mashen shi　祭馬神室
jia　家
jiaji　家祭
jiakou miliang　家口米兩
jian　間
jiangjun　將軍
jianmin　賤民
jianrui ying　尖銳營
jiapu　家譜
jiaren　家人
jiashu　家屬
jiazitou　架子頭
jifu zhufang　畿輔駐防
jin　斤
jingqiang　京腔
jingshi　京師
jinlübaqi　禁旅八旗
jinshi　進士
jiu Han bing　舊漢兵
jiu Manzhou　舊滿洲
jiu qing　九卿
jue-luo　覺羅
jun　軍
junfu　軍府
junzi　君子
juren　舉人
kaihu　開戶
kouliang　口糧
laigui　來歸
laitou　來投
lang　狼

li　力
li　里
liangbatou　兩把頭
Liangshan bo　梁山泊
Lifanyuan　理藩院
lin　吝
linghu　另户
lingji dang'an hu　另記檔案户
lingshiwei　領仕衛
lishi tongpan　理事同判
lishi tongzhi　理事同知
liu　流
liushi qi　六十七
lütoupai　綠頭牌
lüying bing　綠營兵
lufu　錄復
man　蠻
Man-cheng　滿城
Man-Han guanyuan　滿漢官員
"Man Han yijia"　滿漢一家
Man-que　滿缺
Man-ying　滿營
Manyu　滿語
Manzhou　滿洲
"Manzhou jianpu zhi dao"　滿洲簡樸之道
"Manzhou jinshen zhi yi tu"　滿洲進身之一途
"Manzhou jiufeng"　滿洲舊風
*Manzhou shizu daquan*　《滿洲氏族大全》
"Manzhou suxi"　滿洲素習
Manzhou zuoling　滿洲佐領
manzi　蠻子
Manzi cheng　蠻子城
Manzu　滿族
*Manzu bao*　《滿族報》
Manzu tongbao lianyi hui　滿族同胞聯誼會
Mashen miao　馬神廟
mati xie　馬蹄鞋
mei-le zhang-jing　梅勒章京

meng-an mou-ke　猛案謀克
miaotanghua　廟堂化
minren　民人
minzu da jiating　民族大家庭
minzu da tuanjie　民族大團結
mu　畝
Mulan weichang　木蘭圍場
Nai-nai miao　奶奶廟
nanhai　南海
nei　內
nei zuoling　內佐領
neiwufu　內務府
Niang-niang miao　娘娘廟
niu-lu　牛彔
Nüzhen　女真
nucai　奴才
nuli　奴隸
nupu　奴僕
paifang　牌坊
qi　旗
qi miao　旗廟
qian　錢
qianfeng ying　前鋒營
qicai　旗材
qiduyu　騎都尉
qifenzhi　旗分志
qigu　旗鼓
qigu zuoling　旗鼓佐領
Qing gao　清稿
Qingwen　清文
Qingyu　清語
qinjun ying　親軍營
qinwang　親王
qiren　旗人
qitou　旗頭
qiu xian　秋獮
qiuzhang　酋長
qixinlang　起心郎
qiyuan　旗員
qizu　旗族
Rehe　熱河
ri　日

"ruji zhi you"　入籍之由
saiwai　塞外
shang san qi　上三旗
shen gan　神桿
shengchi rifan　生齒日繁
Shengjing　盛京
*Shengjing fu*　《盛京賦》
shengxi yin　生息銀
shengyuan　生員
shi　石
shi lu　食錄
shi　諡
shi, nong, gong, shang　士農工商
shishu　史書
shizu　氏族
shouchong　首崇
shui-dai　水帶
*Shuihuzhuan*　《水滸傳》
suì　歲
suishuzhuan　穗書篆
suiyi xing　隨意性
tai　台
tai qi　台旗
Taizu　太祖
tang dan　堂單
tangzi　堂子
taoren an　逃人案
teming　特命
tianxia　天下
"tianxia wanshi fashi"　天下萬世法式
tiaoshen　跳神
tiben　題本
tiehu　貼戶
tiemaozi wang　鐵帽子王
tonghua　同化
tongshi　通事
tongyi duominzu guojia　統一多民族國家
touchong　投充
tu　徒
tuntian　屯田

Wanshou gong　萬壽宮
"wei jiaoyang Manzhou zhi dao"　未教養滿洲之道
wei-suo　衛所
wen-hua　文化
"wo guojia yong bing"　我國家用兵
"wo Manzhou chunpu zhi feng"　我滿洲純樸之風
wu xing　五行
wuya　烏鴉
xi ji　夕祭
xia wu qi　下五旗
xiang　晌
xiang　餉
xiangmi　餉米
xiansan　閑散
xiaoqixiao　驍騎校
xiaoren　小人
Xibozu　錫伯族
xin　心
xin Manzhou　新滿洲
"xin shangjin zhi ren"　心尚進之人
Xing gong miao　行宮廟
xingliang　行糧
xin-zhe-ku　辛者庫
xique　喜鵲
xiucai　秀才
xiunü　秀女
xiyuan　戲園
xuan qing　玄青
yanglian yin　養廉銀
yangyubing　養育兵
yangzi　養子
yeji　野祭
yemiao　謁廟
yi　翼
yideng zhenguo jiangjun　一等鎮國將軍
yi-di　夷狄
"yi Han zhi Han"　以漢治漢
"yi yi zhi yi"　以夷治夷

yin     胤
yin-wu zhang-jing     印務章京
yishi     一視
yizitou     一字頭
yun     允
zashuaguan     雜耍館
zhang     丈
zhang-jing     章京
zhen     朕
zhengfu     征服
zhenghu     正戶
zhengjunhu     正軍戶
zhengshen qiren     正身旗人
zhihun     指婚
zhisheng zhufang     直省駐防
Zhongguo ren     中國人
zhonghua     中華
zhonghua minzu     中華民族
zhongyuan     中原

zhu     主
zhuangtou     庄頭
zhufang baqi     駐防八旗
zhufang zuoling     駐防佐領
zhupi zouzhe     硃批奏摺
zidishu     子弟書
zisheng yin     滋生銀
zongdu     總督
zongguan     總管
zongrenfu     宗人府
zongshi     宗室
zouzhe     奏摺
zulei     族類
*Zuo zhuan*     《佐傳》
zuodui     座碓
zuoliang     座糧
zuqun zhuquan     族群主權
zuzhang     族長

# REFERENCES

## Archival Sources

Unless otherwise noted, all numbers in the notes following an unpublished archival source refer to a packet number (*bao*). While a packet may contain many items, for documents that have been less thoroughly sorted (which includes the majority of Manchu materials), this is usually the most specific means of noting their provenance, as there are no codes or numbers for individual items. For this reason, particular information is given concerning the author and date. For example, a note reading "KXMaZPZZ 355, Boji, KX41.5.21" refers to packet 355 of the Manchu memorials of the Kangxi reign, in which can be found the memorial written by Boji dated the forty-first year of Kangxi, fifth month, twenty-first day. Abbreviations for frequently cited sources are listed here and in the Notes. Packet numbers are obtained by consulting archivists' catalogues, for which reference numbers have been provided.

*Baqi dutong yamen dang* (Eight Banner command archives). Catalogue no. 544/23-2, First Historical Archives, Beijing.

*Gongzhong Manwen zajian* (Miscellaneous court items in Manchu). Catalogue no. 324/4-49, First Historical Archives, Beijing.

*Gongzhong Manwen zadang* (Miscellaneous court archives in Manchu). Catalogue no. 323/4-48, First Historical Archives, Beijing.

*Guangxu-Xuantong-Minguo hukouce* (Household registers from the Guangxu, Xuantong, and Republican periods). "Xianghongqi Manzhou er jia-la, Bin-liang zuoling." Archives in the Chinese Academy of Social Sciences Library, Beijing.

GZMaZJ. See *Gongzhong Manwen zajian.*

*Huangchao bingzhi* (Monograph on the dynasty's soldiers). Draft materials from the Dynastic History Office (*guoshiguan*). National Palace Museum Archives, Taipei.

*Huangchao wuzhi dachen nianbiao/zhisheng zhufang jiangjun (fudutong) dachen nianbiao* (Chronological tables of officials in the military bureaucracy of the [Qing] dynasty/Chronological tables of garrison generals [lieutenant generals] in the Zhili and provincial garrisons). Draft materials from the Bureau of Dynastic History. National Palace Museum Archives, Taipei.

*Huke shishu* (Routine memorial copy-books, Board of Revenue). First Historical Archives, Beijing.

*Kangxi chao Manwen zhupi zouzhe* (Palace memorials in Manchu from the Kangxi reign). Catalogue no. 508/4-92, First Historical Archives, Beijing.

KXMaZPZZ. See *Kangxi chao Manwen zhupi zouzhe.*

*Qianlong chao Hanwen zhupi zouzhe* (Palace memorials in Chinese from the Qianlong reign). Catalogue no. 555/4-94, First Historical Archives, Beijing.

*Qianlong chao Manwen zhupi zouzhe* (Palace memorials in Manchu from the Qianlong reign). Catalogue nos. 158/4-19-2 through 4-19-12, First Historical Archives, Beijing.

*Qiansanchao tiben* (Routine memorials from the first three reigns). Catalogue no. 295/2-148, First Historical Archives, Beijing.

QLMaZPZZ. See *Qianlong chao Manwen zhupi zouzhe.*

*Yongzheng chao Manwen zhupi zouzhe* (Palace memorials in Manchu from the Yongzheng reign). Catalogue no. 505/4-89, First Historical Archives, Beijing.

YZMaZPZZ. See *Yongzheng chao Manwen zhupi zouzhe.*

## Published Sources

Abe Takeo. "Hakki Manshū niru no kenkyū" (Research on the *niru* of the Manchu Eight Banners). *Tōhō gakuhō* 20 (March 1951), 1–134.

Aimé-Martin, L., ed. *Lettres édifiantes et curieuses concernant l'Asie.* 4 vols. Paris, 1838–43.

Aisin-Gioro Puyi. *From Emperor to Citizen: The Autobiography of Aisin-Gioro Pu Yi.* 2 vols. Beijing: Foreign Languages Press, 1964.

Aisin-Gioro Ulasicun [Wu-la-xi-chun]. "Cong yuyan lunzheng Nüzhen Manzhou zhi zucheng" (Debating the Jurchen "Manchus" tribal name on a linguistic basis). In *Aixinjueluo shi sandai Manxue lunji* (Beijing: Yuanfang chubanshe, 1996), 381–88.

Alexander, William, and George Henry Mason. *Views of Eighteenth Century China: Costumes, History, Customs.* 1804–5. Reprint, London: Studio Editions, 1988.

Allsen, Thomas. "The Rise of the Mongolian Empire and Mongolian Rule in North China." In Denis Twitchett and Herbert Franke, eds., *The Cambridge History of China,* vol. 6, *Alien Regimes and Border States, 907–1368* (Cambridge: Cambridge University Press, 1994), 321–413.

An Shuangcheng. "Shun-Kang-Yong sanchao baqi ding'e qianxi" (Brief analysis of the number of military-age men in the Eight Banners in the Shunzhi, Kangxi, and Yongzheng reigns). *Lishi dang'an* 1983.2, 100–3.

———. "Shunzhi chao baqi nanding Manwen dang'an xuanyi" (Selected translations from Manchu documents on the number of able-bodied males in the Eight Banners in the Shunzhi reign). *Manxue yanjiu* 1 (1992), 413–30.

Anderson, Benedict. *Imagined Communities*. 2nd ed. New York: Verso Books, 1991.

Aritaka Iwao. "Gen-Shin nichō no tai Kan seisaku sōi no yūrai" (The origins of the differences in the policies toward the Han during the Yuan and Qing dynasties). *Shichō* 4.1 (March 1943), 16–32.

*Baqi Manzhou shizu tongpu/Jakūn gūsai Manjusai mukūn hala be uheri ejehe bithe* (Comprehensive genealogy of the Eight Banner Manchu clans). 80 *juan*. Comp. and ed. Ortai et al. 1744. Reprint of Chinese version, Shenyang: Liaoshen shushe, 1989.

*Baqi tongzhi chuji/Jakūn gūsai tung jy i sucungga weilehe bithe* (Comprehensive history of the Eight Banners, first collection). 250 + 3 *juan*. Ed. Ortai et al. 1739. 8-vol. reprint of Chinese version, Changchun: Dongbei shifan daxue, 1985.

[*Qinding*] *Baqi tongzhi* (Comprehensive history of the Eight Banners, imperially ordained). 342 + 12 juan. 1796; reprinted in [*Qinding*] *Siku quanshu* (Shanghai: Shanghai guji chubanshe), vols. 664–71.

*Baqi zeli/Jakūn gūsai kooli hacin* (Institutes and regulations of the Eight Banners). Manchu editions of 1742 (ed. Ortai et al.), 12 *juan*, and 1764 (ed. Laiboo et al., eds.); Chinese editions of 1754 (ed. Laiboo et al.), 1764 ("*qinding*") (ed. Laiboo et al.), and 1776 (ed. Fulungga et al.).

Bardet, Jean-Pierre, and Jacques Dupaquier. *Histoire des populations de l'Europe*. Paris: Fayard, 1997.

Barth, Fredrik, ed. *Ethnic Groups and Boundaries*. Oslo: Universitetsforlaget, 1969.

Bartlett, Beatrice S. "Books of Revelations: The Importance of the Manchu Language Archival Record Books for Research on Ch'ing History." *Late Imperial China* 6.2 (December 1985), 25–36.

———. "Ch'ing Palace Memorials in the Archives of the National Palace Museum." *National Palace Museum Bulletin* 13.6 (January–February 1979).

———. *Monarchs and Ministers: The Grand Council in Mid-Ch'ing China, 1723–1820*. Berkeley and Los Angeles: University of California Press, 1991.

Basilov, Vladimir N. "Chosen by the Spirits." In Marjorie Mandelstam Balzer, ed., *Shamanic Worlds: Rituals and Lore of Siberia and Central Asia* (Armonk, N.Y.: M. E. Sharpe, 1997), 3–48.

Batusis, Mark C. *The Late Byzantine Army*. Philadelphia: University of Pennsylvania Press, 1992.

Beattie, Hilary. "The Alternative to Resistance: The Case of T'ung-cheng, Anhwei." In Jonathan D. Spence and John E. Wills, Jr., eds., *From Ming to Ch'ing* (New Haven, Conn.: Yale University Press, 1979), 241–76.

————. *Land and Lineage in China: A Study of T'ung-cheng County, Anhwei, in the Ming and Ch'ing Dynasties*. Cambridge: Cambridge University Press, 1979.

Bentley, G. Carter. "Ethnicity and Practice." *Comparative Studies in Society and History* 29.1 (January 1987), 24–55.

Bo Yang. *The Ugly Chinaman and the Crisis of Chinese Culture*. Trans. and ed. Don J. Cohn and Jing Qing. Sydney: Allen and Unwin, 1992.

Bodde, Derk, and Clarence Morris, eds. *Law in Imperial China*. Philadelphia: University of Pennsylvania Press, 1967.

Bodian, Miriam. "'Men of the Nation': The Shaping of *Converso* Identity in Early Modern Europe." *Past and Present* 143 (May 1994), 48–76.

Bol, Peter K. "Seeking Common Ground: Han Literati under Jurchen Rule." *Harvard Journal of Asiatic Studies* 47.2 (December 1987), 461–538.

Bourdieu, Pierre. *The Logic of Practice*. Trans. Richard Nice. Stanford, Calif.: Stanford University Press, 1990.

————. *Outline of a Theory of Practice*. Trans. Richard Nice. Cambridge: Cambridge University Press, 1977.

Bouvet, Joachim. *Histoire de l'Empereur de la Chine*. The Hague, 1699.

BQMST. See *Baqi Manzhou shizu tongpu*.

BQTZ. See *Baqi tongzhi chuji*.

Brown, Melissa J. "On Becoming Chinese." In Brown, ed., *Negotiating Ethnicities in China and Taiwan* (Berkeley, Calif.: Institute of East Asian Studies, 1996), 37–74.

Brunnert, H. S., and V. V. Hagelstrom. *Present-Day Political Organization of China*. Trans. A. Beltchenko and E. E. Moran. Shanghai: Kelly and Walsh, 1911.

Burns, Thomas S. *Barbarians Within the Gates of Rome*. Bloomington: Indiana University Press, 1994.

Cao Xueqin. *The Story of the Stone*. Vol. 1, *The Golden Days*. Trans. David Hawkes. Harmondsworth, England: Penguin Books, 1973.

Ch'en Chieh-hsien [Chen Jiexian]. *Qingshi zabi* (Random notes on Qing history). 8 vols. Taipei: Xuehai chubanshe, 1977–85.

Chan, Hok-lam. "The Chien-wen, Yung-lo, Hung-hsi, and Hsüan-te reigns, 1399–1435." In Frederick W. Mote and Denis Twitchett, eds., *The Cambridge History of China*, vol. 7, *The Ming Dynasty, 1368–1644, Part I* (Cambridge: Cambridge University Press, 1988), 182–304.

———. *Legitimation in Imperial China: Discussions Under the Jurchen-Chin Dynasty (1115–1234)*. Seattle: University of Washington Press, 1984.

Chang, Sen-dou. "The Morphology of Walled Capitals." In G. William Skinner, ed., *The City in Late Imperial China* (Stanford, Calif.: Stanford University Press, 1977), 75–100.

Chao Ch'i-na [Zhao Qina]. "Qingchu baqi Hanjun yanjiu" (A study of the Chinese banners in the early Qing). *Gugong wenxian* 4.2 (March 1973), 55–65.

Chartier, Roger. *On the Edge of the Cliff*. Baltimore: Johns Hopkins University Press, 1996.

Chase, Hanson. "The Status of the Manchu Language in the Early Ch'ing." Ph.D. diss., University of Washington, 1979.

Chen Feng. *Qingdai junfei yanjiu* (A study of Qing military expenses). Wuhan: Wuhan daxue chubanshe, 1992.

Chen Jiahua. "Baqi bingxiang de shixi" (Tentative analysis of bannerman grain allotments). *Minzu yanjiu* 1985.5, 63–71.

Chen Jiahua, and Fu Kedong. "Baqi Hanjun kaolüe" (Short study of the Chinese Eight Banners). *Minzu yanjiu* 1981.5, 17–30.

Chen Kangqi. *Langqian jiwen chubi/erbi/sanbi* (Miscellaneous notes of a retired official, 1/2/3). 1880. Reprint, Beijing: Zhonghua shuju, 1984.

———. *Langqian jiwen sibi* (Miscellaneous notes of a retired official, 4). 1886. Reprint, Beijing: Zhonghua shuju, 1990.

Chiang Kai-shek. *China's Destiny*. 2nd ed. Kingsport, Tenn.: Roy Publishers, 1947.

Chow, Kai-wing. *The Rise of Confucian Ritualism in Late Imperial China: Ethics, Classics, and Lineage Discourse*. Stanford, Calif.: Stanford University Press, 1994.

Chu, Raymond, and William Saywell. *Career Patterns in the Ch'ing Dynasty*. Ann Arbor: University of Michigan Center for Chinese Studies, 1984.

Chuang Chi-fa [Zhuang Jifa]. "Cong shumu mingzi kan Qingdai Manzu de Hanhua" (Looking at the sinification of the Manchus through number names). In *Qingshi suibi* (Taipei: Boyang wenhua Enterprises, 1996), 73–85.

———. "Lang Shining 'shi jun quan' mingming youlai" (The source of the names for Lang Shining's "Ten Champion Dogs"). In Zhuang, *Qingshi shiyi* (Taipei: Xuesheng shuju, 1992), 144–48.

———. "Manzhou mingming kao—shuzi mingming de youlai" (A study of Manchu naming: The source of number names). In Zhuang, *Qingshi shiyi* (Taipei: Xuesheng shuju, 1992), 140–41.

———. "Qingdai gongzhongdang de shiliao jiazhi" (The historical value of the Qing palace memorials). In *Qingdai shiliao lunshu* (Taipei: Wenshizhe chubanshe, 1970), 2: 1–34.

Cohen, Paul. *Discovering History in China: American Historical Writings on the Recent Chinese Past.* New York: Columbia University Press, 1984.

*Collected Institutes of the Qing.* See *Da Qing huidian.*

Colley, Linda. *Britons: Forging the Nation, 1707–1837.* New Haven, Conn.: Yale University Press, 1992.

Comaroff, John. "Of Totemism and Ethnicity: Consciousness, Practice and the Signs of Inequality." *Ethnos* 52.3–4 (1987), 301–23.

*Comprehensive Genealogy of Eight Banner Manchu Clans.* See *Baqi Manzhou shizu tongpu.*

*Comprehensive History of the Eight Banners.* See *Baqi tongzhi.*

Constable, Nicole. *Christian Souls and Chinese Spirits: A Hakka Community in Hong Kong.* Berkeley and Los Angeles: University of California Press, 1994.

Cranmer-Byng, J. L. *An Embassy to China: Being the Journal Kept by Lord Macartney During His Embassy to the Emperor Ch'ien-lung, 1793–94.* Hamden, Conn.: Archon Books, 1963.

Crossley, Pamela Kyle. "An Introduction to the Qing Foundation Myth." *Late Imperial China* 6.2 (December 1985), 13–24.

———. "Manchu Education." In Benjamin Elman and Alexander Woodside, eds., *Education and Society in Late Imperial China, 1600–1900* (Berkeley and Los Angeles: University of California Press, 1994), 340–78.

———. *The Manchus.* Oxford, and Cambridge, Mass.: Blackwell Publishers, 1997.

———. "*Manzhou yuanliu kao* and the Formalization of the Manchu Heritage." *Journal of Asian Studies* 46.4 (November 1987), 761–90.

———. *Orphan Warriors: Three Manchu Generations and the End of the Qing World.* Princeton, N.J.: Princeton University Press, 1990.

———. "The Qianlong Retrospect on the Chinese-Martial (*Hanjun*) Banners." *Late Imperial China* 10.1 (June 1989), 63–107.

———. "The Rulerships of China." *American Historical Review* 97.5 (December 1992), 1468–83.

———. "Thinking About Ethnicity in Early Modern China." *Late Imperial China* 11.1 (June 1990), 1–35.

———. "The Tong in Two Worlds: Cultural Identities in Liaodong and

Nurgan During the 13th–17th centuries." *Ch'ing-shih wen-t'i* 4.9 (June 1983), 21–46.

Crossley, Pamela Kyle, and Evelyn Rawski. "A Profile of the Manchu Language in Ch'ing History." *Harvard Journal of Asiatic Studies* 53.1 (June 1993), 63–102.

Dabringhaus, Sabine. *Das Qing-Imperium als Vision und Wirklichkeit: Tibet in Laufbahn und Schriften des Song Yun (1752–1835)*. Stuttgart: Franz Steiner Verlag, 1994.

*Dantuxian zhi* (Gazetteer of Dantu County). 60 + 4 *juan*. Ed. Shen Baozhen, Lu Yaodou et al. 1877.

D'Anville, Joseph Marie. *Carte générale de la Tartarie Chinoise*. The Hague, 1737.

*Da Qing huidian* (The collected institutes of the Qing dynasty). Editions of 1690 (162 *juan*), 1733 (250 *juan*), and 1763 (100 *juan*).

*Da Qing huidian shili* (The collected institutes and precedents of the Qing dynasty). 1,220 *juan*. Guangxu edition (1899).

*Da Qing huidian tu* (Illustrations for the collected institutes of the Qing). 132 *juan*. 1818.

*Da Qing lichao shilu* (The veritable records of the Qing dynasty). Compiled by reign. Printed Tokyo, 1937. Reprint, Taipei: Huawen, 1964. (Shunzhi reign = *Shizu shilu*; Kangxi reign = *Shengzu shilu*; Yongzheng reign = *Shizong shilu*; Qianlong reign = *Gaozong shilu*).

*Da Qing quan shu/Daicing gurun-i yooni bithe* (Complete book of the Great Qing dynasty). 14 *ce*. Comp. Shen Qiliang. Beijing, 1683.

*Da Qing zhongshu beilan* (A survey of the military apparatus of the Qing dynasty). 6 *ce*. 1774.

Davis, R. H. C. *The Normans and Their Myth*. London: Thames and Hudson, 1976.

Davis, Richard L. "Historiography as Politics and Yang Wei-chen's 'Polemic on Legitimate Succession.'" *T'oung Pao* 59 (1983), 33–72.

Dennys, N. B., comp. *The Treaty Ports of China and Japan*. London: Trübner, 1867. Reprint, San Francisco: Chinese Materials Center, 1977.

Di Cosmo, Nicola. "Manchu Shamanic Ceremonies at the Qing Court." In Joseph McDermott, ed., *State and Court Ritual in China* (Cambridge: Cambridge University Press, 1999), 352–98.

Dikötter, Frank. *The Discourse of Race in Modern China*. Stanford, Calif.: Stanford University Press, 1992.

———. Introduction to Dikötter, ed., *The Construction of Racial Identities in China and Japan* (Honolulu: University of Hawaii Press, 1997), 1–11.

———. "Racial Discourse in China: Continuities and Permutations." In

Dikötter, ed., *The Construction of Racial Identities in China and Japan* (Honolulu: University of Hawaii Press, 1997), 12–33.

Ding Yizhuang. "Banner-Commoner Intermarriage in the Qing." Paper delivered at meeting of the Association for Asian Studies, Chicago, March 1997.

——. "Contemporary Manchu Ethnic Consciousness as Indicated by Oral Records and Archives." Paper presented at the UCLA Center for Chinese Studies, Los Angeles, May 1999.

——. "Directed Marriage and the Eight-Banner Household Registration System Among the Manchus." Trans. Mark Elliott. *Saksaha* 1 (1996), 25–29.

——. *Manzu de funü shenghuo yu hunyin zhidu yanjiu* (Research on life and marriage patterns of Manchu women). Beijing: Beijing daxue chubanshe, 1999.

——. "Qianlong chao zhufang Hanjun chuqi qianyi" (Brief discussion on the expulsion of the garrison Chinese bannermen during the Qianlong reign). *Qingshi yanjiu tongxun* 1990.3, 11–17.

——. *Qingdai baqi zhufang zhidu yanjiu* (Research on the Qing Eight Banner garrison system). Tianjin: Tianjin guji chubanshe, 1992.

——. "Qingdai de Man-han tonghun" (Manchu-Han intermarriage in the Qing). Unpublished paper, March 1997.

——. "Qingdai lishi tongzhi kaolüe" (A short study of the Qing civil commissioner). In *Qingzhu Wang Zhonghan xiansheng bashi shouchen xueshu lunwenji* (Shenyang: Liaoning daxue chubanshe, 1993), 263–74.

Dong Wanlun. "*Dongbeishi gangyao* zhong de Manyu yunyong" (The use of Manchu in the "Outline of the History of the Northeast"). *Manyu yanjiu* 1989.1, 51–61.

d'Orléans, Pierre Joseph. *History of the Two Tartar Conquerors of China.* Hakluyt Society, 1854. Reprint, New York: Burt Franklin, 1971.

DQHD. See *Da Qing huidian*

DQHDSL. See *Da Qing huidian shili.*

*Draft History of the Qing.* See *Qingshi gao.*

Dray-Novey, Alison. "Spatial Order and Police in Imperial Beijing." *Journal of Asian Studies* 52.4 (November 1993), 885–922.

Dreyer, June Teufel. *China's Forty Millions: Minority Nationalities and National Integration in the People's Republic of China.* Cambridge: Harvard University Press, 1976.

Du Jiaji. "Qingdai baqi lingshu wenti kaocha" (Investigation into Qing banner membership). *Minzu yanjiu* 1987.5, 83–92.

——. "Qingdai tianhuabing zhi liuchuan, fangzhi ji qi dui huangzu renkou zhi yingxiang chutan" (A preliminary discussion of the spread and prevention of smallpox in the Qing and its effect on population). In Li Zhongqing [James Lee] and Guo Songyi, eds., *Qingdai huangzu renkou xingwei he shehui huanjing* (Demographic behavior and social environment of the Qing imperial lineage) (Beijing: Beijing University Press, 1994), 154–69.

Duara, Prasenjit. "Bifurcating Linear History: Nation and Historians in China and India." *positions* 1.3 (1993), 779–804.

———. *Culture, Power, and the State.* Stanford, Calif.: Stanford University Press, 1988.

———. *Rescuing History from the Nation: Questioning Narratives of Modern China.* Chicago: University of Chicago Press, 1995.

du Halde, Jean-Baptiste. *Description géographique, historique, chronologique, politique . . . de l'empire de la Chine et de la Tartarie Chinoise.* Paris, 1735.

Dunstan, Helen. *Conflicting Counsels to Confuse the Age: A Documentary Study of Political Economy in Qing China, 1644–1840.* Ann Arbor: The University of Michigan Center for Chinese Studies, 1996.

———. "'Orders Go Forth in the Morning and Are Changed by Nightfall': A Monetary Policy Cycle in Qing China, November 1744–June 1745." *T'oung Pao* 82 (1996), 66–136.

Durand, Pierre-Henri. *Lettrés et pouvoirs: Un procès littéraire dans la Chine impériale.* Paris: Ecole des hautes études en sciences sociales, 1992.

Dzeng-šeo. See Zeng-shou.

Eberhard, Wolfram. *China's Minorities: Yesterday and Today.* Belmont, Calif.: Wadsworth Publishing, 1982.

Ebrey, Patricia. "Surnames and Han Chinese Identity." In Melissa J. Brown, ed., *Negotiating Ethnicities in China and Taiwan* (Berkeley, Calif.: Institute for East Asian Studies, 1996), 19–36.

ECCP. See Hummel, *Eminent Chinese of the Ch'ing Period.*

Eliade, Mircea. *Shamanism: Archaic Techniques of Ecstasy.* Princeton, N.J.: Princeton University Press, 1964.

Eller, Jack David. "Ethnicity, Culture, and 'the Past.'" *Michigan Quarterly Review* 36.4 (Fall 1997), 552–600. Reprinted in Eller, *From Culture to Ethnicity to Conflict* (Ann Arbor: University of Michigan Press, 1999), 7–48.

Elliott, Mark C. "Bannerman and Townsman: Ethnic Tension in Nineteenth-Century Jiangnan." *Late Imperial China* 11.1 (June 1990), 36–74.

———. "Chūgoku no dai'ichi rekishi tōankanzō naikaku to kyūchū Manbun tōan no gaijutsu" (An outline of the Manchu holdings of the Grand

Secretariat and Imperial Palace archives at the First Historical Archives, Beijing). *Tōhōgaku* 85 (January 1993), 147–57.

———. "Eighteenth-Century Ideas of 'China' and the 'Unified Polyethnic State.'" Paper prepared for the Southern California China Colloquium Seminar, From Late Imperial to Modern Chinese History: Views from the Eighteenth Century. UCLA Center for Chinese Studies, Los Angeles, November 1998.

———. The Limits of Tartary: Manchuria in Imperial and National Geographies." *Journal of Asian Studies* 59.3 (August 2000), 603–46.

———. "The Manchu-Language Archives of the Qing Dynasty and the Origins of the Palace Memorial System." *Late Imperial China*, forthcoming.

———. "Manchu (Re)Definitions of the Nation in the Early Qing." *Indiana East Asian Working Papers Series on Language and Politics in Modern China* 7 (January 1996), 46–78.

———. "The Manchus as Ethnographic Subject in Qing *Biji* Writings." Paper presented at the conference Empire and Beyond: Historical China from the Ming to the Republic, Center for Chinese Studies, University of California, Berkeley, December 1997.

———. "Manchu Widows and Ethnicity in Qing China." *Comparative Studies in Society and History* 41.1 (January 1999), 33–71.

———. "Resident Aliens: The Manchu Experience in China, 1644–1760." Ph.D. diss., University of California, Berkeley, 1993.

———. "Turning a Phrase: Translation in the Early Qing Through a Temple Inscription of 1645." *Aetas Manjurica* 3 (1992), 12–41.

———. "Vocabulary Notes from the Manchu Archives 2: On the *Booi*." *Saksaha* 3 (1998), 18–21.

———, trans. "The Eating Crabs Youth Book." In Susan Mann and Yu-yin Cheng, eds., *Under Confucian Eyes: Texts on Gender in Confucian Society* (Berkeley and Los Angeles: University of California Press). Forthcoming.

Elman, Benjamin A. "Changes in Confucian Civil Service Examinations from the Ming to the Ch'ing Dynasty." In Elman and Alexander Woodside, eds., *Education and Society in Late Imperial China, 1600–1900* (Berkeley and Los Angeles: University of California Press, 1994), 111–49.

———. *A Cultural History of Civil Examinations in Late Imperial China.* Berkeley and Los Angeles: University of California Press, 1999.

Endacott-West, Elizabeth. *Mongolian Rule in China: Local Administration in the Yuan Dynasty.* Cambridge: Harvard Council on East Asian Studies, 1989.

———. "The Yüan Government and Society." In Herbert Franke and Denis Twitchett, eds., *The Cambridge History of China*, vol. 6, *Alien Regimes and Border States, 907–1368* (Cambridge: Cambridge University Press, 1994), 587–615.

Eriksen, Thomas Hylland. *Ethnicity and Nationalism: Anthropological Perspectives*. London: Pluto Press, 1993.

E-rong-an, ed. *E-er-tai nianpu* (The life chronology of Ortai). ca. 1748. Reprint, Beijing: Zhonghua shuju, 1993.

Fairbank, John K. "Varieties of the Chinese Military Experience." Introduction to Frank A. Kierman and John K. Fairbank, eds., *Chinese Ways in Warfare* (Cambridge: Harvard University Press, 1974), 1–26.

Fairbank, John K., and Edwin O. Reischauer. *China: Tradition and Transformation*. Boston: Houghton Mifflin, 1978.

Fan Wenlan. *Zhongguo jindaishi* (A history of modern China). Beijing: Renmin chubanshe, 1947.

Fang Chaoying. "A Technique for Estimating the Numerical Strength of the Early Manchu Military Forces." *Harvard Journal of Asiatic Studies* 13.1–2 (June 1950), 192–215.

Farquhar, David M. "Emperor as Bodhisattva in the Governance of the Ch'ing Empire." *Harvard Journal of Asiatic Studies* 38.1 (June 1978), 5–34.

———. "Mongolian Versus Chinese Elements in the Early Manchu State." *Ch'ing-shih wen-t'i* 2.6 (June 1971), 11–23.

———. "The Origins of the Manchus' Mongolian Policy." In John K. Fairbank, ed., *The Chinese World Order* (Cambridge: Harvard University Press, 1968), 198–205.

Fa-shi-shan [Faššan]. *Taolu zalu* (Miscellaneous records of Tao's cottage). 6 *juan*. 1817. Reprint, Beijing: Zhonghua shuju, 1959; 2nd ed., 1984.

Feng Erkang. *Yongzheng zhuan* (A biography of the Yongzheng emperor). Beijing: Renmin chubanshe, 1985.

Feng Erkang, and Chang Jianhua. *Qingren shehui shenghuo* (Social life of people in the Qing). Tianjin: Tianjin renmin chubanshe, 1990.

Feng Jiasheng. "Manzhou mingcheng zhi zhongzhong tuice" (Various hypotheses on the name Manchu). *Dongfang zazhi* 30.17 (1 September 1933), 61–74.

Feng Jicai. *The Three-Inch Golden Lotus*. Trans. David Wakefield. Honolulu: University of Hawaii Press, 1994.

Feuchtwang, Stephan. "School-Temple and City God." In G. William Skinner, ed., *The City in Late Imperial China* (Stanford, Calif.: Stanford University Press, 1977), 581–608.

Feuerwerker, Albert. *State and Society in Eighteenth-Century China: The Ch'ing Empire in Its Glory*. Ann Arbor: The University of Michigan Center for Chinese Studies, 1976.

Fitzgerald, John. *Awakening China: Politics, Culture, and Class in the Nationalist Revolution.* Stanford, Calif.: Stanford University Press, 1996.

Fletcher, Joseph F. "The Mongols: Ecological and Social Perspectives." *Harvard Journal of Asiatic Studies* 46.1 (June 1986), 11–50.

————. Review of Walter Simon and Howard G. H. Nelson, *Manchu Books in London: A Union Catalogue. Harvard Journal of Asiatic Studies* 41.2 (December 1981), 653–56.

————. "Turco-Mongolian Monarchic Tradition in the Ottoman Empire." In Joseph F. Fletcher, *Studies on Chinese and Islamic Inner Asia,* ed. Beatrice Forbes Manz (Aldershot, England: Variorum Reprints, 1995), chap. 7.

Forêt, Philippe. *Mapping Chengde: The Qing Landscape Enterprise.* Honolulu: University of Hawaii Press. Forthcoming.

Franke, Herbert. "The Chin." In Herbert Franke and Denis Twitchett, eds., *The Cambridge History of China,* vol. 6, *Alien Regimes and Border States, 907–1368* (Cambridge: Cambridge University Press, 1994), 215–320.

————. "The Role of the State as a Structural Element in Polyethnic Societies." In Stuart N. Schram, ed., *Foundations and Limits of State Power in China* (London and Hong Kong: European Science Foundation, 1987), 87–112.

Fu Kedong. "Baqi guanbing baru lüying kaoxi" (Examination of Eight Banner officers and soldiers transferred to the Green Standard Army). In *Ming-Qing dang'an yu lishi yanjiu* (Ming-Qing archives and historical research), (Beijing: Zhonghua shuju, 1988), 2, 713–724.

————. "Baqi huji zhidu chutan" (Preliminary discussion of the Eight Banners household registration system). *Minzu yanjiu* 1983.6, 34–43.

Fu Kedong, and Chen Jiahua. "Baqi zhiduzhong de Man-Meng-Han guanxi" (Manchu-Mongol-Han relations in the Eight Banner system). *Minzu yanjiu* 1980.6, 30–32.

Fu Lehuan. "Guanyu Qingdai Manzu de jige wenti" (A few questions concerning Manchus in the Qing). 1957. Reprinted in Fu, *Liaoshi congkao* (Collected studies on Liao History) (Beijing: Zhonghua shuju, 1984), 396–449.

Fu Tongqin. "Qingdai de tangzi" (The Qing *tangse*). In *Ming-Qingshi guoji xueshu taolunhui lunwenji* (Tianjin: Tianjin renmin chubanshe, 1982), 269–85.

Fu Yuguang, and Meng Huiying. *Manzu samanjiao yanjiu* (Studies of Manchu shamanism). Beijing: Beijing daxue chubanshe, 1991.

Fu-ge. *Tingyu congtan* (Talks collected while listening to the rain). 12 *juan.* ca. 1860. Reprint, Beijing: Zhonghua shuju, 1959; 2nd ed., 1984.

*Gaozong shilu.* See *Da Qing lichao shilu.*

Garrett, Valery M. *Chinese Clothing: An Illustrated Guide.* Oxford: Oxford University Press, 1994.

Gaubatz, Piper Rae. *Beyond the Great Wall: Urban Form and Transformation on the Chinese Frontier.* Stanford, Calif.: Stanford University Press, 1996.

Gaubil, Antoine, S.J. *Correspondance de Pékin, 1722–1759.* Geneva: Librairie Droz, 1970.

Gimm, Martin. "Manchu Translations of Chinese Novels and Short Stories: An Attempt at an Inventory." *Asia Major*, n.s., 1 (1987), 77–114.

Gladney, Dru. *Muslim Chinese.* Cambridge: Harvard Council on East Asian Studies, 1991.

*Gongzhongdang Qianlong chao zouzhe* (Secret palace memorials of the Qianlong reign). 75 vols. Taipei: National Palace Museum, 1982–88.

Grousset, René. *Empire of the Steppes.* New Brunswick, N.J.: Rutgers University Press, 1970.

Grupper, Samuel. "The Manchu Imperial Cult of the Early Ch'ing Dynasty: Texts and Studies on the Tantric Sanctuary of Mahakala at Mukden." Ph.D. diss., Indiana University, 1979.

———. "Manchu Patronage and Tibetan Buddhism During the First Half of the Ch'ing Dynasty." *Journal of the Tibet Society* 4 (1989), 47–75.

Guan Dedong, and Zhou Zhongming. *Zidishu congchao* (Collected scripts of *zidishu*). Shanghai: Shanghai guji chubanshe, 1984.

Guan Jixin, and Meng Xianren. "Manzu yu Shenyang yu, Beijing yu" (The Manchus and Shenyang and Beijing speech). *Manzu yanjiu* 1987.1, 73–81.

Guan Jixin, ed. *Zhongguo Manzu* (China's Manchus). Beijing: Zhongyang minzu xueyuan chubanshe, 1993.

Guan Xiaolian. "Zai lun zouzhe qiyuan ji qi tedian" (Reconsidering the origins and peculiarities of the palace memorial). Paper delivered at the Second Conference on the Ming-Qing Archives and Historical Research, Beijing, October 1995.

*Guangdong tongzhi* (Comprehensive gazetteer of Guangdong). 334 + 1 *juan*. Ed. Chen Changqi et al. 1864.

Guo Chengkang. "Qingchu Menggu baqi kaoshi" (Examination and explanation of the Mongol Eight Banners in the early Qing). *Minzu yanjiu* 1986.3, 51–58.

Guo Songyi. "Qing zongshi de dengji jiegou ji jingji diwei" (Stratification, structure, and economic status among the Qing imperial lineage). In Li Zhongqing [James Lee] and Guo Songyi, eds., *Qingdai huangzu renkou xingwei he shehui huanjing* (Demographic behavior and social environment of the Qing imperial lineage) (Beijing: Bejing University Press, 1994), 116–33.

Guo Songyi, Li Xinda, and Li Shangying, eds. *Qingchao dianzhi* (The institutions and systems of the Qing dynasty). Changchun: Jilin wenshi chubanshe, 1993.

Guy, R. Kent. *The Emperor's Four Treasuries: Scholars and the State in the Late Ch'ien-lung Era*. Cambridge: Harvard Council on East Asian Studies, 1987.

———. "Imperial Powers and the Appointment of Provincial Governors in Ch'ing China, 1700–1900." In Frederick P. Brandauer and Chun-chieh Huang, eds., *Imperial Rulership and Cultural Change in Traditional China* (Seattle: University of Washington Press, 1994), 248–80.

GZD/QL. See *Gongzhongdang Qianlong chao zouzhe*.

GZMaZJ. See *Gongzhong Manwen zajian* under Archival Sources.

Han Guanghui. *Beijing lishi renkou dili* (The historical demography and geography of Beijing). Beijing: Beijing University Press, 1996.

———. "Qingdai jingshi baqi rending de zengzhang yu dili qianyi" (Eight Banner *ding* population increase and movement in Beijing in the Qing). *Lishi dili* 6 (1988), 197–208.

*Hangzhou baqi zhufangying zhilüe* (Draft gazetteer of the Hangzhou Eight Banner garrison). 25 *juan*. Ed. Zhang Dachang et al. Preface of 1894.

Harrell, Stevan. "Civilizing Projects and Reactions to Them." Introduction to Stevan Harrell, ed., *Cultural Encounters on China's Ethnic Frontiers* (Seattle: University of Washington Press, 1995), 3–36.

Hashimoto, Mantarō. "The Altaicization of Northern Chinese," in J. McCoy and T. Light, eds., *Contributions to Sino-Tibetan Studies* (Leiden: E. J. Brill, 1986), 76–97.

———, ed. *Kanminzoku to Chūgoku shakai* (The Han people and Chinese society). Tokyo: Yamakawa shuppansha, 1983.

Hauer, Erich. *Handwörterbuch der Mandschusprache*. 3 vols. Wiesbaden: Otto Harrassowitz, 1952–55.

———. "Das Mandschurische Kaiserhaus, sein Name, seine Herkunft und sein Stammbaum." *Mitteilungen des Seminars Für Orientalische Sprachen (Ostasiatische Studien)* 29 (1926).

———. "Why the Sinologue Should Study Manchu." *Journal of the North China Branch of the Royal Asiatic Society* 61 (1930), 156–64.

Heiberg, Marianne. *The Making of the Basque Nation*. Cambridge: Cambridge University Press, 1989.

Hershatter, Gail, Emily Honig, Jonathan N. Lipman, and Randall Stross, eds. *Remapping China: Fissures in Historical Terrain.* Stanford, Calif.: Stanford University Press, 1996.

Hevia, James L. "A Multitude of Lords: Qing Court Ritual and the Macartney Embassy of 1793." *Late Imperial China* 10.2 (December 1989), 72–105.

———. *Cherishing Men from Afar.* Durham, N.C.: Duke University Press, 1995.

HJW. See *Huangchao jingshi wenbian.*

Ho, Ping-ti. "In Defense of Sinicization: A Rebuttal of Evelyn Rawski's 'Reenvisioning the Qing.'" *Journal of Asian Studies* 57.1 (February 1998), 123–55.

———. "The Significance of the Ch'ing Period in Chinese History." *Journal of Asian Studies* 26.2 (February 1967), 189–95.

———. *Studies on the Population of China.* Cambridge: Harvard University Press, 1959.

Hobsbawm, Eric J. *Nations and Nationalism Since 1780: Programme, Myth, and Reality.* Cambridge: Cambridge University Press, 1990.

Hobsbawm, Eric J., and Terence Ranger. *The Invention of Tradition.* Cambridge: Cambridge University Press, 1992.

Hommel, Rudolf P. *China at Work.* New York: John Day, 1937.

Hosoya Yoshio. "Hakki beikyoku kō—Shinchō chūki no hakki keizai o megutte" (Study of the Eight Banners grain office: The economy of the Eight Banners in the mid-Qing). *Shūkan tōyōgaku* 31 (June 1974), 181–208.

———. "The Han Chinese Generals Who Collaborated with Hou-Chin Kuo." *Acta Asiatica* 53 (1988), 39–61.

———. "Hakki shinchō kōkōsatsu no seiritsu to sono haikei" (The establishment of Eight Banner household registers and its background). *Shūkan tōyōgaku* (1963), 18–32.

———. "Hakki tsūshi shokyū 'kibunshi' hensan to sono haikei—Yōseichō sakuryō kaikaku no ittan" (The compilation of the *qifenzhi* section of the *Baqi tongzhi chuji* and its background: part of the Yongzheng reforms of the *niru*). *Tōhōgaku* 36 (September 1968), 1–17.

———. "Manju gurun to 'Manshūkoku'" (Manju gurun and "Manchukuo"). In Hamashita Takeshi, ed., *Rekishi no naka no chiiki* (Regions in history), vol. 8 of Shibata Michio, ed., *Sekaishi e no toi* (Tokyo: Iwanami shoten, 1990), 105–35.

———. "Qingchao baqi zhidu de 'gūsa' he 'qi'" (*Gūsa* and *qi* in the Qing banner system). *Manxue yanjiu* 2 (1994), 47–51.

———. "Shinchō chūki no hakki kosekihō no henkaku—kaiko o chūshin ni shite" (Mid-Qing changes in the Eight Banner household registration laws: The *kaihu*). *Shūkan tōyōgaku* 15 (May 1966): 51–63.

———. "Shinchō ni okeru hakki keizai no ichi danmen—hōkyō seido no seiritsu o megutte" (A cross-section of the economy of the Eight Banners during the Qing: The establishment of the grain-stipend system). *Ichikan kōgyō kōtō senmon gakkō kenkyū kiyō* 7 (1972), 43–65.

———. "Shinchō ni okeru hakki seido no suii" (Shifts in the character of the Qing Eight Banner system). *Tōyō gakuhō* 51.1 (June 1968), 1–43.

Hosoya Yoshio, and Wang Yulang. "Kaifū hakki chūbō no kōei—shingai kakumeigo no kijin seikatsu no hitokoma" (The descendants of Kaifeng Eight Banners garrison—a look at bannerman life after the Xinhai Revolution). *Tōhō* 143 (February 1993), 6–11.

Hou, Ching-lang, and Michèle Pirazzoli. "Les chasses d'automne de l'empereur Qianlong à Mulan." *T'oung Pao* 55.1–3 (1979), 13–50.

Hou Renzhi. *Beijing lishi dituji* (Collected historical maps of Beijing). Beijing: Beijing chubanshe, 1985.

Howell, David. "Ainu Ethnicity and the Boundaries of the Early Modern Japanese State." *Past and Present* 142 (February 1994), 69–93.

Hsiao, Ch'i-ch'ing. *The Military Establishment of the Yuan Dynasty.* Cambridge: Harvard Council on East Asian Studies, 1978.

Hsiao I-shan [Xiao Yishan]. *Qingdai tongshi* (General history of the Qing period). 5 vols. Taipei: Taiwan shangwu yinshuguan, 1962–63; rev. ed. 1980. Reprint, Beijing: Zhonghua shuju, 1986.

Hsü, Immanuel C. Y. *The Rise of Modern China.* 3rd ed. New York: Oxford University Press, 1983.

Hu Jianzhong. "Qingdai wuqi zhuangbei yu zhizao" (Military provisioning and manufacture in the Qing). In Zhu Jiajin, ed., *Qingdai gongshi qiushi* (Searching for the facts on Qing palace history) (Beijing: Zijincheng chubanshe, 1992), 255–81.

Hua Li. "Cong qiren biancha baojia kan Qing wangchao 'qi-min fenzhi' zhengce de bianhua" (Changes in the Qing policy of separate rule for bannermen and civilians as seen in the enrollment of bannermen in the *bao-jia* system). *Minzu yanjiu* 1988.5, 97–106.

Huang Liuhong. *A Complete Book Concerning Happiness and Benevolence.* Trans. Djang Chu. Tucson: University of Arizona Press, 1984.

Huang, Pei. *Autocracy at Work: A Study of the Yung-cheng Period, 1723–1735.* Bloomington: Indiana University Press, 1974.

———. "New Light on the Origins of the Manchus." *Harvard Journal of Asiatic Studies* 50.1 (1990), 239–82.

Huang Runhua, and Qu Liusheng. *Quanguo Manwen tushu ziliao lianhe mulu*

(National union catalogue of Manchu-language library holdings). Beijing: Shumu wenxian chubanshe, 1991.

*Huangchao jingshi wenbian* (Collected writings on statecraft in our august dynasty). 120 *juan*. Ed. He Changling. 1826. Reprint, Beijing: Saoye shanfang, 1896.

*Huangchao wenxian tongkao* (General history and examination of Qing institutions and documents). 300 *juan*. 1785. 2-vol. reprint, Taipei: Taiwan Commercial Press, 1987.

*Hubei tongzhi* (Comprehensive gazetteer of Hubei). 100 + 5 *juan*. Ed. Wu Xiongguang, Bai-ling, Tong-xing, Tai-fei-in et al. 1803.

Huc, Régis-Evariste, and Joseph Gabet. *Travels in Tartary, Thibet, and China, 1844–1846*. Trans. William Hazlitt. New York: Harper and Brothers, 1928.

Hucker, Charles. *A Dictionary of Official Titles in Imperial China*. Stanford, Calif.: Stanford University Press, 1985.

———. *The Ming Dynasty: Its Origins and Evolving Institutions*. Ann Arbor: The University of Michigan Press, 1978.

Hummel, Arthur W., ed. *Eminent Chinese of the Ch'ing Period*. 2 vols. Washington, D.C.: U.S. Government Printing Office, 1943–44.

Humphrey, Caroline. "Shamanic Practices and the State in Northern Asia." In Nicholas Thomas and Caroline Humphrey, eds., *Shamanism, History, and the State* (Ann Arbor: University of Michigan Press, 1995), 191–228.

Humphrey, Caroline, with Urgunge Onon. *Shamans and Elders: Experience, Knowledge, and Power Among the Daur Mongols*. Oxford: Oxford University Press, 1996.

Im, Kaye Soon. "On Manchu-Chinese Relations at the End of the Qing: A Legal Case of Manchu Soldiers Beating a Chinese District Magistrate at the Jingzhou Garrison in 1899." Unpublished paper, March 1999.

———. "The Rise and Decline of the Eight Banner Garrisons in the Ch'ing Period (1644–1911): A Study of the Kuang-chou, Hang-chou, and Ching-chou Garrisons." Ph.D. diss., University of Illinois, 1981.

*Imperial Collection of Statecraft Writings*. See *Huangchao jingshi wenbian*.

Inaba Iwakichi. "Manshū minzoku ni kansuru ryōhōmen no kansatsu" (An examination of the Manchu nation from both perspectives). *Tōa keizai kenkyū* 13.4 (October 1929), 1–30; 14.2 (April 1930), 15–37.

———. *Shinchō zenshi* (Complete history of the Qing). Tokyo: Waseda University Press, 1914; Chinese trans. of 1914, *Qingchao quanshi*. Reprint, Taipei: Zhonghua shuju, 1960.

Ishibashi Hideo. "Jušen shokō" (A short study of the word Jurchen). In *Mikami Tsugio hakushi kijū kinen ronbunshū: rekishi hen* (Tokyo: Heibonsha, 1985), 163–75.

————. "Shinchō nyūkango Manju no koshō o megutte" (On the post-conquest use of the label "Manju"). In Ishibashi, ed., *Shindai Chūgoku no sho mondai* (Tokyo: Yamakawa shuppansha, 1996), 19–36.

————. "Shinsho no shakai—sono jōkyū mondai o megutte" (Early Qing society—the residence question). In *Orui Noboru hakushi kijū kinen shigaku ronbunshū* (Historical essays collected in honor of Dr. Orui Noboru) (Tokyo: Yamakawa shuppansha, 1962), 247–62.

————. "Shinsho no tai Kanjin seisaku—toku ni Taiso no Ryōtō shinshutsu jidai o chūshin toshite" (Early Qing policies toward Han Chinese— the period of Taizu's advance into Liaodong). *Shisō* 2 (October 1961), 1–17.

Ishibashi Takao. "Booi in the Ch'ing Dynasty." *Bulletin of the Institute of China Border Area Studies* 18 (October 1987), 197–208.

————. "Shinchō no 'honyaku kakyō' o megutte" (Concerning the Qing translation examinations). *Rekishi to chiri* 393 (May 1988), 1–17.

Itzkowitz, Norman. *Ottoman Empire and Islamic Tradition*. Chicago: University of Chicago Press, 1972.

Jackson, Beverly. *Splendid Slippers*. Berkeley, Calif.: Ten Speed Press, 1998.

Jagchid, Sechin, and Charles Bawden. "Notes on Hunting of Some Nomadic Peoples of Central Asia." In *Die Jagd bei den Altaischen Volken* (*Asiatische Forschungen* series no. 26) (Wiesbaden: Otto Harrassowitz, 1968), 90–102.

Jagchid, Sechin, and Paul Hyer. *Mongolia's Culture and Society*. Boulder, Colo.: Westview Press, 1979.

*Jakūn gūsai kooli hacin*. See *Baqi zeli*.

Janhunen, Juha. Review of *The Manchus*, by Pamela Kyle Crossley. *Studia Orientalia* 82 (1997), 288–89.

Jiang Xiangshun. *Shenmi de qinggong saman jisi* (Shamanic sacrifices in the mysterious Qing palace). Shenyang: Liaoning renmin chubanshe, 1995.

*Jiangningfu zhi* (Gazetteer of Jiangning prefecture, newly edited). 56 *juan*. Ed. Lu Yanzhao. 1880.

Jin Dechun. *Qijun zhi* (Monograph on the banner armies). 1 *juan*. ca. 1720. In Jin Yufu, ed., *Liaohai congshu* (Fengtian: 1933–36; reprint, Shenyang: Liaoshen shushe, 1985), 4: 2603–5.

Jin Qizong. *Beijing jiaoqu de Manzu* (Manchus in the suburbs of Beijing). Hohhot: Nei Menggu daxue, 1989.

*Jingkou baqi zhi* (Gazetteer of the Jingkou Eight Banners). 2 *juan*. Ed. Zhong-rui, Chun-yuan et al. 1879.

*Jingzhoufuzhi* (Gazetteer of Jingzhou prefecture). 80 + 1 *juan*. Ed. Gu Jiaheng, Ni Wenwei, et al. 1880.

*Jingzhou zhufang baqi zhi* (Gazetter of the Jingzhou garrison Eight Banners). Ed. Xi-yuan et al. 1879.

*Jiu Manzhou dang* (The old Manchu archives). 10 vols. Taipei: National Palace Museum, 1969.

*Jōkōkitō—Kenryūchō 1* (Archives of the Bordered Red Banner, Qianlong reign, 1). Ed. Kanda Nobuo, Matsumura Jun, Okada Hidehiro, and Hosoya Yoshio. Tokyo: Tōyō Bunko Seminar on Manchu History, 1983.

*Jōkōkitō—Yōseichō* (Archives of the Bordered Red Banner, Yongzheng reign). Ed. Kanda Nobuo, Matsumura Jun, Okada Hidehiro, and Hosoya Yoshio. Tokyo: Tōyō Bunko Seminar on Manchu History, 1972.

Just, Roger. "Triumph of the Ethnos." In Elizabeth Tonkin et al., eds., *History and Ethnicity* (London: Routledge, 1989), 71–88.

Kahn, Harold. *Monarchy in the Emperor's Eyes: Image and Reality in the Ch'ien-lung Reign.* Cambridge: Harvard University Press, 1971.

Kanda Nobuo. "Manshū minzoku no suibō" (The decline of the Manchus). In Niida Noboru, ed., *Kindai Chūgoku kenkyū* (Research on modern China) (Tokyo: Kōgakusha, 1948), 271–96.

———. "Manzhou guohao kao" (A study of the Manchu dynastic name). *Gugong wenxian* 3.1 (1971), 43–49.

———. "Shinsho no kangun bushō Seki Teishū ni tsuite" (Shi Tingzhu, *Hanjun* general in the early Qing). *Sundai shigaku* 66 (1986), 1–20.

Kanda Nobuo, et al., eds. *Hakki tsūshi retsuden sakuin* (Index to the Biographical Sections of *Pa-ch'i t'ung-chih*). Tokyo: Tōyō Bunko Manbun Rōtō kenkyūkai, 1965.

*Kangxi chao Hanwen zhupi zouzhe huibian* (The collected Chinese-language secret palace memorials of the Kangxi reign). 8 vols. Comp. First Historical Archives of China. Chief ed. Guo Zhulan. Beijing: Dang'an chubanshe, 1984–85.

*Kangxi chao Manwen zhupi zouzhe quanyi* (Complete translation of the Manchu palace memorials of the Kangxi reign). Comp. First Historical Archives of China. Chief eds. Guan Xiaolian, Qu Liusheng. Beijing: Zhongguo shehui kexue chubanshe, 1996.

Kessler, Lawrence D. "Ethnic Composition of Provincial Leadership During the Ch'ing Dynasty." *Journal of Asian Studies* 28 (May 1969), 489–511.

———. *K'ang-hsi and the Consolidation of Ch'ing Rule, 1661–1684.* Chicago: The University of Chicago Press, 1976.

Khaldūn, Ibn. *The Muqaddimah: An Introduction to History.* Trans. Franz Rosenthal. Princeton, N.J.: Princeton University Press Bollingen Series, 1967.

Kitamura Hironao. "Shinchō ni okeru seiji to shakai (1)—nyūkan mae ni

okeru hakki no kanjin mondai" (Politics and society in the Qing (1)—the
Eight Banners and Han Chinese before the conquest). *Tōyōshi kenkyū*
10.4 (January 1949), 60–69.

Kitayama Yasuo. "Shindai no chūbō hakki ni tsuite" (On the Qing Eight
Banner garrisons). In *Haneda hakushi shōjū kinen tōyōshi ronsō*
(Collected essays on East Asian history dedicated to Dr. Haneda [Tōru])
(Kyōto: Tōyōshi kenkyūkai, 1950), 489–503.

Kleeman, Terry F. *Great Perfection: Religion and Ethnicity in a Chinese
Millennial Kingdom.* Honolulu: University of Hawaii Press, 1998.

Ko, Dorothy. "The Emperor and His Women: Three Views of Footbinding,
Ethnicity, and Empire." In Chuimei Ho and Cheri A. Jones, eds., *Life in
the Imperial Court of Qing Dynasty China: Proceedings of the Denver
Museum of Natural History* 3.15 (November 1998), 37–48.

———. *Teachers of the Inner Chambers: Women and Culture in Seventeenth-
Century China.* Stanford, Calif.: Stanford University Press, 1994.

Kuan Tung-kuei [Guan Donggui]. "Manzu ruguanqian de wenhua fazhan dui
tamen houlai hanhua de yingxiang" (The influence of preconquest cultural
development among the Manchus on their later sinification). *Bulletin of
the Institute of History and Philology, Academia Sinica* 40 (October
1968), 255–79.

Kuhn, Philip A. *Soulstealers: The Chinese Sorcery Scare of 1768.* Cambridge:
Harvard University Press, 1990.

Kutcher, Norman. "The Death of the Xiaoxian Empress: Bureaucratic
Betrayals and the Crises of Eighteenth-Century Chinese Rule." *Journal
of Asian Studies* 56.3 (August 1997), 708–25.

———. *Mourning in Late Imperial China: Filial Piety and the State.*
Cambridge: Cambridge University Press, 1999.

KXHaZZH. See *Kangxi chao Hanwen zhupi zouzhe huibian.*

KXMaZPZZ. See *Kangxi chao Manwen zhupi zouzhe* under Archival
Sources.

*Kyū Manshūtō tensō kyūnen* (The old Manchu archives: the ninth year of
Tiancong). 2 vols. Ed. and trans. Kanda Nobuo et al. Tokyo: Tōyō Bunko,
1972.

Lai Huimin. "Qingdai huangzu de fengjue yu renguan yanjiu" (Nobility and
office among the Qing imperial lineage). In Li Zhongqing [James Lee] and
Guo Songyi, eds., *Qingdai huangzu renkou xingwei he shehui huanjing*
(Demographic behavior and social environment of the Qing imperial
lineage) (Beijing: Bejing University Press, 1994), 134–53.

———. *Tianhuang guizhou: Qing huangzu de jieceng jiegou you jingji
shenghuo* (The Qing imperial lineage: Its hierarchical structure and

economic life). Taipei: Institute of Modern History, Academia Sinica, 1997.

Lai Huimin, and Xu Siling. "Qingdai qiren funü caichanquan zhi qianxi" (A brief analysis of bannerwomen's property rights in the Qing). *Jindai Zhongguo funüshi yanjiu* 4 (August 1996), 3–33.

Laitinen, Kauko. *Chinese Nationalism in the Late Qing Dynasty: Zhang Binglin as an Anti-Manchu Propagandist*. London: Curzon Press, 1990.

Langlès, L. "Alphabet Tartare-Mantchou." Introduction to Joseph Marie Amiot, *Dictionnaire Tartare-Mantchou François*. 2nd ed. Paris, 1789.

Langlois, John D., Jr. *China Under Mongol Rule*. Princeton, N.J.: Princeton University Press, 1981.

———. "Chinese Culturalism and the Yüan Analogy: Seventeenth-Century Perspectives." *Harvard Journal of Asiatic Studies* 40 (1980), 355–98.

Lao She. *Zhenghongqi xia* (Under the Plain Red Banner). In *Lao She wenji* (Beijing: Renmin chubanshe, 1984), 7: 179–306. English ed.: *Beneath the Red Banner*. Trans. Don Cohn. Beijing: Panda Books, 1982.

Lattimore, Owen. *High Tartary*. New York: Little, Brown, 1930. Reprint, 1994, New York: Kodansha America.

———. *Studies in Frontier History*. London: Oxford University Press, 1962.

Lavely, William, and R. Bin Wong. "Revising the Malthusian Narrative: The Comparative Study of Population Dynamics in Late Imperial China." *Journal of Asian Studies* 57.3 (August 1998), 714–48.

Lay, G. Tradescant. "A Brief Account of the Mantchou Tartars at Chapu." *Chinese Repository* 11.8 (August 1842), 425–34.

Le Bohec, Yann. *The Imperial Roman Army*. New York: Hippocrene Books, 1995.

Lee, James. *The Political Economy of China's Southwestern Frontier, 1350 to 1850*. Cambridge: Harvard University Asia Center, forthcoming.

———. "Zhongguo lishi renkou zhidu: Qingdai renkou xingwei ji qi yiyi" ("The Chinese Demographic System: Recent Research and Implications"). In James Lee [Li Zhongqing] and Guo Songyi, eds., *Qingdai huangzu renkou xingwei he shehui huanjing* (Demographic behavior and social environment of the Qing imperial lineage) (Beijing: Bejing University Press, 1994), 1–17.

Lee, James, and Cameron Campbell. *Fate and Fortune*. Cambridge: Cambridge University Press, 1997.

Lee, James, and Wang Feng. "Male Nuptiality and Male Fertility among the Qing Nobility: Polygyny or Serial Monogamy." In Caroline Bledsoe, Susanna Lerner, and Jane Guyer, eds., *Fertility and the Male Life Cycle on the Eve of Fertility Decline*. Oxford: Oxford University Press, 1999.

Lee, Robert H. G. *The Manchurian Frontier in Ch'ing History*. Cambridge: Harvard University Press, 1970.

Legge, James, trans. *The Chinese Classics*. 5 vols. Oxford: Oxford University Press.

Lei Fangsheng. "Jingzhou qixue de shimo ji qi tedian" (The banner school at Jingzhou). *Minzu yanjiu* 1984.3, 57–59.

Leong, Sow-theng. *Migration and Ethnicity in Chinese History: Hakkas, Pengmin, and Their Neighbors*. Ed. Tim Wright. Stanford, Calif.: Stanford University Press, 1997.

Levenson, Joseph R. *Confucian China and Its Modern Fate: A Trilogy*. Berkeley and Los Angeles: University of California Press, 1968.

Li Fengmin, *Shengjing baqi fangwei zhi mi* (The riddle of the Eight Banner placement at Shengjing). Shenyang: Dongbei daxue chubanshe, 1998.

Li Hsüeh-chih [Li Xuezhi]. "Manzhou minzu jisi tianshen bi ji shen'gan de shiliao yu qiyin" (The sources and origins of the mandatory use of the spirit-pole in Manchu sacrifices to heaven). *Manzu wenhua* 2 (1982), 5–6.

Li Hua. "Kangxi dui Hanzu shidaifu de zhengce" (Kangxi's policies toward the Han literati). In Zuo Buqing, ed., *Kang-Yong-Qian sandi pingyi* (Critical biographies of the Kangxi, Yongzheng, and Qianlong emperors) (Beijing: Zijincheng chubanshe, 1986), 62–87.

Li Jutan. "Manzu jiapu xiaoyi" (A short discussion of Manchu genealogies). *Manzu yanjiu* 1987.2, 64.

Li, Lillian, and Alison Dray-Novey. "Protecting Beijing's Food Security in the Qing Dynasty: State, Market, and Police." *Journal of Asian Studies* 58.4 (November 1999), 992–1032.

Li Lin. *Manzu jiapu xuanbian* (A selected collection of Manchu genealogies). Shenyang: Liaoning renmin chubanshe, 1988.

———. *Manzu zongpu yanjiu* (Studies of Manchu genealogies). Shenyang: Liaoshen shushe, 1992.

Li Lin, Hou Jinbang, Pu Mingfan, and Gao Zuopeng. *Benxixian Manzu jiapu yanjiu* (Research into Manchu genealogies from Benxi county). Shenyang: Liaoning minzu chubanshe, 1988.

Li Qiao. "Baqi shengji wenti shulüe" (Synopsis of economic difficulties in the Eight Banners). *Lishi dang'an* 1985.1, 91–97, 47.

Li Shutian, ed. *Shuangchengpu tuntian jilue* (Brief history of the Shuang-chengpu military colony). Changchun: Jilin wenshi chubanshe, 1990.

Li Teh-ch'i. *Union Catalogue of Manchu Books in the National Library of Peiping and the Library of the National Palace Museum*. Beijing: National Library of Peiping and the Library of the National Palace Museum, 1933.

Li Xinda. "Guanyu Manzhou qizhi he Hanjun qizhi de shijian wenti" (On the problem of chronology in the formation of the Manchu and Chinese banners). In *Qingshi luncong* (Beijing, 1982), 4: 216–23.

Li Xun, and Xue Hong, eds. *Qingdai quanshi* (A complete history of the Qing). Vol. 1. Shenyang: Liaoning renmin chubanshe, 1991.

Li Yanguang, and Guan Jie. *Manzu tongshi* (A comprehensive history of the Manchus). Shenyang: Liaoning minzu chubanshe, 1991.

Liang Zhangju. *Langji congtan, Langji xutan, Langji santan* (Collected talks of Langji). 25 *juan*. 3 vols. 1846–57. Reprint, Beijing: Zhonghua shuju, 1981.

Lin Enxian. *Qingchao zai Xinjiang de Han-Hui geli zhengce* (Qing policies for separating Han and Hui in Xinjiang). Taipei: Taiwan Commercial Press, 1988.

Lipman, Jonathan. *Familiar Strangers: A History of Muslims in Northwest China*. Seattle: University of Washington Press, 1997.

Liu Chia-chü [Liu Jiaju]. The Creation of the Chinese Banners in the Early Ch'ing." *Chinese Studies in History* 14.4 (Summer 1981), 47–75.

———. *Qingchao chuqi de baqi quandi* (Encirclement by the Eight Banners in the early Qing). Taipei: Wenshizhe chubanshe, 1964.

Liu Guiteng. "Samanjiao yu Manzhou tiaoshen yinyue de liubian" (Shamanism and the evolution of music of Manchu shamanic ritual). *Manxue yanjiu* 1 (1992), 239–53.

Liu Shizhe. "Manzu 'qishe' qianshu" (Notes on riding and shooting among the Manchus). *Minzu yanjiu* 1982.5, 48–57, 40.

Liu Xianting. *Guangyang zaji* (Random jottings by Guangyang). 5 *juan*. ca. 1695. Reprint, Beijing: Zhonghua shuju, 1957; 2nd ed., 1985.

Liu Xiaomeng. "Baqi hujizhong de qixiaren zhu mingcheng kaoshi" (Examination of the various names of Eight Banner household categories for people in the banners). *Shehui kexue jikan* 50.3 (1987), 63–68.

———. *Baqi zidi* (The people of the Eight Banners). Fuzhou: Fujian renmin chubanshe, 1996.

———. "Ku-tu-le kao" (Study of the *kutule*). *Manyu yanjiu* 1987.2, 121–28.

———. *Manzu de buluo yu guojia* (The Manchu tribe and nation). Changchun: Jilin wenshi chubanshe, 1995.

Liu Xiaomeng, and Ding Yizhuang. *Samanjiao yu dongbei minzu* (Shamanism and the peoples of the Northeast). Changchun: Jilin jiaoyu chubanshe, 1990.

Liu Ziyang. *Qingdai difang guanzhi kao* (Study of the system of local administration in the Qing). Beijing: Zijincheng chubanshe, 1988.

Lu Hua. "'Niu-gu-lu shi jia pu' yanjiu" (Research on the "Niohuru clan genealogy"). *Manzu yanjiu* 1986.2, 81–84.

Luo Ergang [Lo Erh-kang]. *Lüyingbing zhi* (Monograph on the Green
    Standard Army). 1945; 2nd ed., Beijing: Zhonghua shuju, 1984.

Luo Guanzhong, attr. *Three Kingdoms*. Trans. Moss Roberts. Berkeley and
    Los Angeles: University of California Press, 1991.

Luo Yunzhi. *Qingdai Mu-lan weichang de tantao* (Investigations into the Qing
    imperial hunting reserve). Taipei: Wenshizhe chubanshe, 1989.

Ma Feng-ch'en. "Manchu-Chinese Social and Economic Conflicts in Early
    Ch'ing." In *Chinese Social History: Translations of Selected Studies*,
    ed. E-tu Zen Sun and John DeFrancis (Washington, D.C.: ACLS, 1956),
    333–51.

Ma Xiedi. "Guangzhou Manzu fangwen ji" (Notes on a visit to Canton's
    Manchus). *Manzu yanjiu* 1988.2, 36–41.

———. "Qingdai Mancheng kao" (Study of Manchu cities in the Qing).
    *Manzu yanjiu* 1990.1, 29–34.

Mackerras, Colin. *China's Minorities: Integration and Modernization in the
    Twentieth Century*. Hong Kong: Oxford University Press, 1994.

———. *China's Minority Cultures: Identities and Integration Since 1912*.
    Melbourne: Longman, 1995.

———. *The Rise of the Peking Opera, 1770–1870: Social Aspects of the
    Theatre in Manchu China*. Oxford: Oxford University Press, 1972.

*Manbun rōtō/Tongki fuka sindaha hergen i dangse* (The secret chronicles of
    the Manchu dynasty, 1607–37). 7 vols. Trans. and annot. Kanda Nobuo
    et al. Tokyo: Tōyō Bunko, 1955–63.

*Manchu Rites for Sacrifices to the Spirits and to Heaven*. See *Manzhou jishen
    jitian dianli*.

Mann, Susan. *Precious Records: Women in China's Long Eighteenth Century*.
    Stanford, Calif.: Stanford University Press, 1997.

*Manwen laodang*. See *Manbun rōtō*.

*Manzhou shilu/Manju-i yargiyan kooli* (The Manchu veritable records). Taipei:
    Huawen shuju, 1969.

[*Qinding*] *Manzhou jishen jitian dianli* (Manchu Rites for Sacrifices to the
    Spirits and to Heaven). 1781. In Jin Yufu, ed., *Liaohai congshu* (Fengtian:
    1933–36; reprint, Shenyang: Liaoshen shushe, 1985), 5: 2097–3192.

*Manzhou yuanliu kao Manjusai da sekiyen-i Kimcin* (Researches of Manchu
    origins). 1783. Reprint, Agūi [A-gui] et al., ed. Shenyang: Liaoning minzu
    chubanshe, 1988.

*Manzu jianshi* (A concise history of the Manchus). Beijing: Zhonghua shuju,
    1979. Reprint, 1986.

*Manzu shehui lishi diaocha* (A social-historical investigation of the Manchus).
    Shenyang: Liaoning renmin chubanshe, 1985.

Margalit, Avishai. "The Other Israel." *New York Review of Books* 45.9 (28 May 1998), 30–35.

Matsumura Jun. "On the Founding Legend of the Ch'ing Dynasty." *Acta Asiatica* 53 (1988), 1–23.

———. "The Founding Legend of the Qing Reconsidered." *Memoirs of the Research Department of the Tōyō Bunko* 55 (1997), 41–60.

Matthew, D. J. A. *The Norman Conquest.* New York: Schocken Books, 1966.

MBRT. See *Manbun rōtō.*

Mckhann, Charles. "The Nationalities Question." In Stevan Harrell, ed., *Cultural Encounters on China's Ethnic Frontiers* (Seattle: University of Washington Press, 1995), 40–46.

Meadows, Thomas Taylor. *The Chinese and Their Rebellions.* London: 1856. Reprint, Stanford, Calif.: Academic Reprints, n.d.

Meng Sen. "Baqi zhidu kaoshi" (Investigation of the Eight Banners System). *Bulletin of the Institute of History and Philology, Academia Sinica* 6.3 (1936), 343–412. Citations are from edition in *Ming-Qingshi lunzhu jikan* (Beijing: Zhonghua shuju, 1959), 218–310.

———. *Qingdai shi* (History of the Qing period). Taipei: Zhengzhong shuju, 1960.

Meng Zhaoxin. "Baqi nupu fendang kaihu wenti" (The question of *booi* becoming *kaihu*). *Qingshi yanjiu tongxun* 1984.2, 3–7.

Michael, Franz. *The Origin of Manchu Rule in China.* Baltimore: Johns Hopkins University Press, 1942.

———, ed. *The Taiping Rebellion: History and Documents.* 3 vols. Seattle: University of Washington Press, 1971.

Millward, James. *Beyond the Pass: Economy, Ethnicity, and Empire in Qing Xinjiang.* Stanford, Calif.: Stanford University Press, 1998.

———. "New Perspectives on the Qing Frontier." In Gail Hershatter et al., eds., *Remapping China: Fissures in Historical Terrain* (Stanford, Calif.: Stanford University Press, 1995), 113–29.

Millward, James, Ruth Dunnell, Mark C. Elliott, and Philippe Forêt, eds. *A Realm in Microcosm: The Manchu Palace at Chengde, Tibetan Buddhism, and the High Qing Empire.* Manuscript in preparation.

Mitamura Taisuke. *Shinchō zenshi no kenkyū* (A Study of the Qing dynasty in the Manchu period). Kyoto: Tōyōshi kenkyūkai, 1965.

Miyazaki Ichisada. *China's Examination Hell: The Civil Service Examinations of Imperial China.* Trans. Conrad Schirokauer. New Haven, Conn.: Yale University Press, 1981.

———. "Shinchō ni okeru kokugo mondai no ichimen" (A look at the question of the national language during the Qing). *Tōhōshi ronsō* 1 (July 1947), 1–56.

———. *Yōseitei, Chūgoku no dokusai kunshu* (Yongzheng, China's autocratic monarch). Tokyo: Iwanami shoten, 1950.

Mo Dongyin. *Manzushi luncong* (Collected essays on the history of the Manchus). Beijing: Renmin chubanshe, 1958.

Möllendorff, P. G. von. "Essay on Manchu Literature." *Journal of the North China Branch of the Royal Asiatic Society* 24 (1890).

———. *A Manchu Grammar, with Analysed Texts*. Shanghai: American Presbyterian Mission Press, 1892.

Momose Hiromu. "Shinchō no iminzoku tōchi ni okeru zaisei keizai seisaku" (Fiscal and economic policies under Qing alien rule). *Tōa kenkyūjo hō* 20 (February 1943), 1–116.

Montell, Gösta. *As Ethnographer in China and Mongolia, 1929–1932*. Stockholm: The Sino-Swedish Expedition, 1945.

Morgan, David. *The Mongols*. Cambridge, Mass.: Basil Blackwell, 1986.

Mote, Frederick W. "The Ch'eng-hua and Hung-chih reigns, 1465–1505." In Frederick W. Mote and Denis Twitchett, eds., *The Cambridge History of China*, vol. 7, *The Ming Dynasty, 1368–1644, Part I* (Cambridge: Cambridge University Press, 1988), 343–402.

———. "The Transformation of Nanking, 1350–1400." In G. William Skinner, ed., *The City in Late Imperial China* (Stanford, Calif.: Stanford University Press, 1977), 101–54.

Muramatsu Yūji. "Shin no naimufu sōen" (The Qing imperial household department estates). *Keizaigaku kenkyū* 12 (March 1968), 1–119.

Naitō Torajirō. *Zōho Manshū shashinchō* (Enlarged photographic album of Manchuria). Kyoto: Kobayashi shashin seibansho, 1935.

Nakayama Hachirō. "Hakki engen shishaku" (Attempt at an interpretation of the origins of the Eight Banners). *Jinbun kenkyū* 10.10 (September 1959), 74–95.

Naquin, Susan. *Peking Temples and City Life, 1400–1900*. Berkeley and Los Angeles: University of California Press, 2000.

Naquin, Susan, and Evelyn S. Rawski. *Chinese Society in the Eighteenth Century*. New Haven, Conn.: Yale University Press, 1987.

Narakino Shimesu. "Shindai buin daijin Man-Kan heiyō no jissai ni tsuite" (On the actual practice of equal appointment of Manchus and Han to Qing central administrative offices). *Gumma daigaku kyōikugakubu kiyō/jinbun shakaigaku* 16 (1967), 43–56. Reprinted in *Chūgoku kankei ronsetsu shiryō* 8.3 (1967), 93–101.

———. "Shindai jūyō shokukan Man-Kan hiritsu no hendō" (The shift in the ratio of Manchus and Han in important posts during the Qing). Reprinted in *Chūgoku kankei ronsetsu shiryō* 10.3 (1968), 83–94.

———. Shindai Man-Kan kanryō no shio ni tsuite" (Routes to office for Manchus and Han in the Qing). In *Kamada hakushi kanreki kinen rekishigaku ronsō* (Historical studies presented to Dr. Kamada [Shigeo] on his sixtieth birthday) (Tokyo: 1969), 288–98.

———. "Shindai Mankō Kanhaku no sai kentō" (A new look at the "favor-the-Manchus, deprive-the-Han" policies in the Qing). *Rekishi kyōiku* 12.9 (September 1964), 51–59.

———. "Shindai tokubu Man-Kan hiritsu no hendō ni tsuite" (On the shift of the ratio of Manchu to Han governors-general). *Gunma daigaku kyōikugakubu kiyō—jinbun shakaigaku* 14 (1965), 217–36. Reprinted in *Chūgoku kankei ronsetsu shiryō* 3.3 (1965), 551–60.

*Nihon ni okeru Chūō Ajia kankei kenkyū bunken mokuroku*. Tokyo: Centre for East Asian Cultural Studies, 1988.

*Nikan hergen i ubaliyambuha Manju gisun i buleku bithe/Yin Han-Qing wenjian* (A Manchu dictionary translated into Chinese writing). Comp. Mingdo. Beijing, 1735.

Norman, Jerry. *A Concise Manchu-English Lexicon*. Seattle: University of Washington Press, 1977.

Nowak, Margaret, and Stephen Durrant. *The Tale of the Nišan Shamaness: A Manchu Folk Epic*. Seattle: University of Washington Press, 1977.

Numata Tomoo, et al., eds. *Iminzoku no Shina tōji shi* (The history of alien rule over China). Tokyo: Kodansha, 1944.

Okada Hidehiro. *Kōkitei no tegami* (The letters of the Kangxi emperor). Tokyo: Chūō kōronsha, 1979.

———. "Mandarin, a Language of the Manchus: How Altaic?" *Aetas Manjurica* 3 (1992): 165–87.

———. "The Mongolian Literary Tradition in Early Manchu Culture." In Ch'en Chieh-hsien, ed., *Proceedings of the 35th Permanent International Altaistic Conference* (Taipei: Center for Chinese Studies Materials and United Daily News Cultural Foundation, 1993), 377–85.

———. "Seifuku ōchō to hiseifuku bunka: hakki, Pekin kanwa, shiteisho" (Dynasties of conquest and the culture of the conquered: The Eight Banners, "Mandarin," and *zidishu*). *Shirukurōdo* [*Silkroad*] 6.2–3 (February–March 1980), 16–20.

———. "The Yüan Seal in Manchu Hands: The Source of the Ch'ing Legitimacy." Paper presented at Thirty-third Permanent International Altaistic Conference, Budapest, 1990.

Old Manchu Archives. See under *Manbun rōtō*.

Oshibuchi Hajime. "Man-Mō minzoku no bunka keitai to Shina tōchi keitai" (Cultural patterns of the Manchus and Mongols and their forms of rule in China). *Nihon shogaku shinkō i'inkai kenkyū hōkoku* 11 (March 1941), 166–77.

———. "Shinsho hakki seido no seiritsu ni tsuite" (Concerning the foundation of the Eight Banners system in the early Qing). *Shigaku zasshi* 50.7 (July 1939), 132.

Otagi Hajime. *Chūgoku no jōkaku toshi* (The walled cities of China). Tokyo: Chūō kōronsha, 1991.

Ōtani Toshio. "Shinchō gunsei no oboegaki—hakki, rokueisei no keizaiteki kihan o chūshin toshite" (Notes on the Qing military system: The economic base of the Eight Banners and the Green Standard Army). *Tōyōshi kenkyū* 33.1 (January 1974), 110–19.

Oxnam, Robert. *Ruling from Horseback: Manchu Politics in the Oboi Regency, 1661–1669.* Chicago: University of Chicago Press, 1975.

Pang, Tatiana A. "Russian and Manchu Sources on Russian-Chinese Relations." Paper delivered at International Symposium on Non-Chinese Sources for Late Imperial Chinese History, Santa Barbara, California, March 1998.

Pang, Tatiana A., and Giovanni Stary. *New Light on Manchu Historiography and Literature.* Wiesbaden: Harrassowitz Verlag, 1998.

Parker, E. H. *China, Her History, Diplomacy, and Commerce.* London, 1901.

Peng Yuxin. "Qing wangchao pianchong Manqi de yiguan zhengce ji qi xiaoji houguo" (The consistent tilt in Qing dynasty policy favoring the Manchus and its negative consequences). *Qingshi luncong* (1992), 32–35.

Perdue, Peter. "Military Mobilization in Seventeenth- and Eighteenth-Century China." *Modern Asian Studies* 30.4 (October 1996), 757–93.

Petech, Luciano. *China and Tibet in the Early Eighteenth century,* 2nd ed. Leiden: E. J. Brill, 1972.

Polachek, James. *The Inner Opium War.* Cambridge: Harvard Council on East Asian Studies, 1992.

Polo, Marco. *The Travels.* Trans. Ronald Latham. Harmondsworth, England: Penguin, 1958.

Poppe, Nicholas, Leon Hurvitz, and Hidehiro Okada, eds. *Catalogue of the Manchu-Mongol Section of the Tōyō Bunko.* Tokyo: Tōyō Bunko, 1964.

Qian Shifu. *Qingdai zhiguan nianbiao* (Chronological tables of official posts in the Qing period). 4 vols. Beijing: Zhonghua shuju, 1980.

[*Qinding*] *Baqi tongzhi.* See under *Baqi tongzhi.*

[*Qinding*] *Baqi zeli.* See under *Baqi zeli.*

*Qingbai leichao* (Miscellaneous historical comments on the Qing). 12 *ce.* Ed. Xu Ke. 1917. Reprint, Beijing: Zhonghua shuju, 1984.

*Qingchu neiguoshiyuan Manwen dang'an yibian* (Translated compilation of Manchu archives of the early Qing inner historical office). 3 vols. Trans. and comp. First Historical Archives. Beijing: Guangming ribao chubanshe, 1989.

*Qingdai dang'an shiliao congbian* (Collection of historical materials from the Qing archives). 14 vols. Comp. and ed. First Historical Archives of China. Beijing: Zhonghua shuju, 1978–90.

*Qingdai de qidi* (Banner land in the Qing). 3 vols. Comp. Institute for Qing History, Archives Department, Research Seminar on the Chinese Political System of People's University. Chief ed. Wei Qingyuan. Beijing: Zhonghua shuju, 1989.

*Qingdai renwu zhuangao* (Draft biographies of Qing figures). Ser. 1. 5 vols. Beijing: Zhonghua shuju, 1985–88.

*Qingshi gao* (Draft history of the Qing). 529 *juan.* 48 vols. Chief ed., Zhao Erxun. 1928. Reprint, Beijing: Zhonghua shuju, 1976–77.

*Qingshi liezhuan* (Qing History Biographies). 80 *juan.* 1928. Beijing: Zhonghua shuju, 1987.

*Qingshi ziliao* (Materials for Qing history). 7 vols. Comp. Chinese Academy of Social Sciences, Institute of History, Qing History Research Department. Beijing: Zhonghua shuju, 1981–89.

*Qingwen zonghui* (General Manchu vocabulary). Beijing, 1897.

*Qingzhoufu zhi* (Comprehensive gazetteer of Qingzhou). 64 *juan.* Ed. Mao Yongbo and Liu Yaochun. 1859.

QLHaZPZZ. See *Qianlong chao Hanwen zhupi zouzhe* under Archival Sources.

QLMaZPZZ. See *Qianlong chao Manwen zhupi zouzhe* under Archival Sources.

QNMDY. See *Qingchu neiguoshiyuan Manwen dang'an yibian.*

QSCTB. See *Qian sanchao tiben* under Archival Sources.

QSG. See *Qingshi gao.*

QSLZ. See *Qingshi liezhuan.*

Rawski, Evelyn S. "Ch'ing Imperial Marriage and Problems of Rulership." In Rubie S. Watson and Patricia B. Ebrey, eds., *Marriage and Inequality in Chinese Society* (Berkeley and Los Angeles: University of California Press, 1991), 170–203.

———. *The Last Emperors: A Social History of Qing Imperial Institutions.* Berkeley and Los Angeles: University of California Press, 1998.

———. "Reenvisioning the Qing: The Significance of the Qing Period in Chinese History." *Journal of Asian Studies* 55.4 (November 1996), 829–50.

*Records of Talks by One Hundred Twenty Elders.* See under Song-yun.

Renan, Ernest. "What Is a Nation?" Trans. Martin Thom. In Homi Bhabha, *Nation and Narration* (London: Routledge, 1990), 8–22.

Riasanovsky, Nicholas V. *A History of Russia*, 4th ed. New York: Oxford University Press, 1984.

Rigger, Shelley. "Voices of Manchu Identity, 1635–1935." In Stevan Harrell, ed., *Cultural Encounters on China's Ethnic Frontiers* (Seattle: University of Washington Press, 1995), 186–214.

Ripa, Matteo, S.J. *Memoirs of Father Ripa.* Trans. Fortunato Prandi. London: John Murray, 1844.

Roth, Gertraude. "The Manchu-Chinese Relationship, 1618–1636." In Jonathan D. Spence and John E. Wills, eds., *From Ming to Ch'ing: Conquest, Region, and Continuity in Seventeenth-Century China* (New Haven, Conn.: Yale University Press, 1979), 4–38.

Roth-Li, Gertraude. "The Rise of the Early Manchu State: A Portrait Drawn from Manchu Sources to 1636." Ph.D. diss., Harvard University, 1976.

Scarth, John. *Twelve Years in China.* Edinburgh: T. Constable, 1860. Reprint, Wilmington, Del.: Scholarly Resources, 1972.

Schama, Simon. *Landscape and Memory.* New York: Vintage Books, 1995.

*Shaanxi tongzhi* (Comprehensive gazetteer of Shaanxi). 100 + 1 *juan.* Ed. Jalangga, Liu Yuyi, Shen Qingya et al. 1735.

Shang Hongkui. *Ming-Qingshi lunzhu heji* (Collected writings on Ming and Qing history). Beijing: Beijing daxue chubanshe, 1988.

Shang Hongkui, Liu Jingxian, Ji Yonghai, Xu Kai, comp. *Qingshi Manyu cidian* (Manchu lexicon for Qing history). Shanghai: Shanghai guji chubanshe, 1990.

*Shangyu baqi/Dergi hese jakūn gūsade wasimbuhangge* (Edicts to the Eight Banners). 10 *ce.* 1735.

*Shangyu qiwu yifu/Dergi hesei wasimbuha gūsai baita be dahūme gisurefi wesimbuhengge* (Discussions in memorials on banner affairs). 1735. 2-vol. reprint, Taipei: Xuesheng shuju, 1976.

Shen Yuan, and Mao Biyang. "Rhyme in Manchu Court Poetry of the Qing." Trans. Mark C. Elliott. *Saksaha* 4 (1999), 25–26.

*Shengzu shilu.* See *Da Qing lichao shilu.*

Shirokogoroff, S. M. *Ethnological and Linguistical Aspects of the Ural-Altaic Hypothesis.* Beiping: Commercial Press, 1931. Reprinted from *Tsing Hua Journal* 6.

————. *Psychomental Complex of the Northern Tungus*. London: Routledge and Kegan Paul, 1935.

*Shizong shilu*. See *Da Qing lichao shilu*.

*Shizu shilu*. See *Da Qing lichao shilu*.

*Shuntianfu zhi* (Gazetteer of Shuntian prefecture). 130 *juan*. Ed. Zhou Jiamei, Liao Quansun, et al. 1886. Reprint, Beijing: Beijing guji chubanshe, 1987.

*Sichuan tongzhi* (Comprehensive gazetteer of Sichuan). 47 + 1 *juan*. Ed. Huang Tinggui, Xian-de, Gao Weixin et al. 1736.

Sinor, Denis. *Introduction to Manchu Studies*. American Council of Learned Societies, 1963.

SJY. See Zeng-shou, *Suijun jixing yizhu*.

Skinner, G. William. "Urban Social Structure in Ch'ing China." In G. William Skinner, ed., *The City In Late Imperial China* (Stanford, Calif.: Stanford University Press, 1977): 521–54.

Smith, Anthony D. "Chosen Peoples: Why Ethnic Groups Survive." *Ethnic and Racial Studies* 15.3 (July 1992), 436–56.

————. "Ethnic Election and Cultural Identity." *Ethnic Studies* 10 (1993), 1–25.

————. "Ethnic Myths and Ethnic Revivals." *Archives Européennes de Sociologie* 25.2 (1984), 283–305.

————. "Nationalism and the Historians." In Anthony D. Smith, ed., *Ethnicity and Nationalism* (Leiden: E. J. Brill, 1992), 58–80.

————. "The Origins of Nations." *Ethnic and Racial Studies* 12.3 (July 1989), 344–45.

Snipp, C. Matthew. "Some Observations About Racial Boundaries and the Experiences of American Indians." *Ethnic and Racial Studies* 20.4 (October 1997), 667–89.

Solonin, K. Y., ed. *The Bretschneider Albums: Nineteenth-Century Paintings of Life in China*. Reading, England: Garnet Publishing, 1995.

Song-yun. *Emu tanggū orin sakda-i gisun sarkiyan* (Records of talks by one hundred twenty elders). 8 chaps. Ed. and trans. Giovanni Stary. *Asiatische Forschungen* series no. 83. Wiesbaden: Otto Harrassowitz, 1983.

Spence, Jonathan D. *The Search for Modern China*. New York: Norton, 1990.

————. *Ts'ao Yin and the K'ang-hsi Emperor: Bondservant and Master*. New Haven, Conn.: Yale University Press, 1966.

Spence, Jonathan D., and John E. Wills, eds. *From Ming to Ch'ing: Conquest, Region, and Continuity in Seventeenth-Century China*. New Haven, Conn.: Yale University Press, 1979.

Spicer, Edward H. "Persistent Cultural Systems." *Science* 19 (November 1971), 795–800.

Stary, Giovanni. "The Manchu Emperor 'Abahai': Analysis of an Historiographic Mistake." *Central Asiatic Journal* 28.3–4 (1984), 296–99.

———. *Manchu Studies: An International Bibliography.* 3 vols. Wiesbaden: Kommissionsverlag Otto Harrassowitz, 1990

———. "The Meaning of the Word 'Manchu': A New Solution to an Old Problem." *Central Asiatic Journal* 34.1–2 (1990).

———. "A New Subdivision of Manchu Literature: Some Proposals." *Central Asiatic Journal* 31.3–4 (1987), 287–96.

———. "Versuch eines Index des mandschurischen Pantheon." In Giovanni Stary, ed., *Shamanica Manchurica Collecta* 5 (Wiesbaden: Harrassowitz Verlag, 1998), 115–39.

Stary, Giovanni, et al. *On the Tracks of Manchu Culture.* Wiesbaden: Otto Harrassowitz, 1995.

Staunton, Sir George. *An Historical Account of the Embassy to the Emperor of China.* London, 1797.

STFZ. See *Shuntianfu zhi.*

Strand, David. *Rickshaw Beijing: City People and Politics in the 1920's.* Berkeley and Los Angeles: University of California Press, 1989.

Su Qin. "Qing lü zhong qiren 'fanzui mian faqian' kaoshi" (Examination of the 'excuse criminals from exile' provision for bannermen in Qing law). *Qingshi luncong* (1992), 75–87.

Su Tianjun. "Beijing xijiao Xiaoxitian Qingdai muzang fajue jianbao" (Brief report on the excavation of a Qing tomb at Xiaoxitian in the Beijing suburbs). *Wenwu* 147 1963.1, 50–59.

*Suiyuancheng zhufang zhi* (Gazetteer of the Suiyuan gazetteer). Ed. Tong Jingren. 1917. Reprint, Hohhot: 1984.

Sun Wenliang, Li Zhiting, and Qiu Lianmei. *Ming-Qing zhanzheng shilue* (Historical sketch of warfare between the Ming and the Qing). Shenyang: Liaoning renmin chubanshe, 1986.

Sun Yat-sen. *The Three Principles.* Shanghai: North China Daily News and Herald, 1927.

———. *The Teachings of Sun Yat-sen: Selections from His Writings.* London: Sylvan Press, 1945.

Sutō Yoshiyuki. "Shinchō ni okeru Manshū chūbō no tokushūsei ni kansuru ichi kōsatsu" (An examination of the particular nature of banner garrisons in Manchuria during the Qing). *Tōhō gakuhō* (Tokyo) 11.1 (March 1940), 176–203.

Swart, Paula, and Barry Till. "Nurhachi and Abahai: Their Palace and Mausolea—The Manchu Adoption and Adaptation of Chinese Architecture." *Arts of Asia* (May–June 1988), 149–67.

SYBQ. See *Shangyu baqi.*

Tan Qian. *Beiyou lu* (Record of northern travels). Ca. 1660. Reprint, Beijing: Zhonghua shuju, 1960.

Tao, Jing-shen. *The Jurchen in Twelfth-Century China: A Study in Sinicization.* Seattle: University of Washington Press, 1976.

Teng Shaozhen. *Qingdai baqi xianguan* (Wise Eight Banner officials of the Qing period). Beijing: Zhongguo shehui kexue chubanshe, 1992.

———. *Qingdai baqi zidi* (People of the Eight Banners in the Qing period). Beijing: Zhongguo huaqiao chuban gongsi, 1989.

Thomson, John. *Illustrations of China and Its People.* 4 vols. London: Sampson Low, Marston, Low, and Searle, 1873–74.

Tie Yuqin, and Wang Peihuan, eds. *Shengjing huanggong* (The Mukden imperial palace). Beijing: Zijincheng chubanshe, 1987.

Tillman, Hoyt Cleveland. "An Overview of Chin History and Institutions." In Tillman and Stephen West, eds., *China Under Jurchen Rule* (Binghamton: State University of New York Press, 1995), 23–38.

———. "Proto-Nationalism in Twelfth-Century China? The Case of Ch'en Liang." *Harvard Journal of Asiatic Studies* 39.2 (December 1979), 403–28.

Toda Shigeki. "Kakuto ara jō kōsei no sobyō" (The plan of fortifications at Hetu Ala). In *Yamashita sensei kanreki kinen tōyōshi ronbunshū* (Collected essays on East Asian history celebrating the sixtieth birthday of Prof. Yamashita [Taizō]) (Tokyo: 1938), 655–95.

Tong Jingren. *Huhehaote Manzu jianshi* (A brief history of the Manchus of Hohhot). Hohhot: Huhehaote shi minzu shiwu weiyuanhui, 1987.

Tong Yonggong, and Guan Jialu. "Lun Manwen de shiyong ji qi lishi zuoyong" (On the use and historical importance of the Manchu language). Liaoning Provincial Archives, unpublished paper, 1990.

Torbert, Preston M. *The Ch'ing Imperial Household Department: A Study of Its Organization and Principal Functions.* Cambridge: Harvard University Press, 1976.

*The Travels and Controversies of Friar Domingo Navarrete, 1618–1686.* 2 vols. Ed. J. S. Cummins, Hakluyt Society. Cambridge: Cambridge University Press, 1962.

Tsang, Ka-bo [Zeng Jia-bao]. "Ji fenggong shu weiji" (Recording ample merit, describing great achievements) *Gugong wenwu yuekan* 93 (December 1990), 38–65.

———. "Portraits of Meritorious Officials: Eight Examples from the First Set Commissioned by the Qianlong Emperor." *Arts Asiatiques* 57 (1992), 69–88.

Tsintsius, V. I. *Sravnitel'nyi slovar' Tunguso-Man'chzhurskikh iazykov.* 2 vols. Leningrad: Nauka, 1975.

Tulli, Antonella. "Due esempi di zidishu sino-mancesi." *Aetas Manjurica* 3 (1992), 290–391.

Twitchett, Denis, and Hans-Peter Tietze. "The Liao." In Herbert Franke and Denis Twitchett, eds., *The Cambridge History of China,* vol. 6, *Alien Regimes and Border States, 907–1368* (Cambridge: Cambridge University Press, 1994), 43–153.

Ura Ren'ichi. "Kangun (ujen cooha) ni tsuite" (On the Chinese banners [*ujen cooha*]). In *Kuwabara hakushi kanreki kinen tōyōshi ronsō* (Essays on East Asian history presented to Dr. Kuwabara [Jitsuzō] on his sixtieth birthday) (Kyoto, 1931), 815–49.

———. "Shinchō ni okeru kimin kankei no ichi kōsatsu" (Relations between bannermen and civilians in the Qing). *Shigaku zasshi* 49.7 (July 1939), 917–18.

———. "Shinchō no Kanjin tōchi no sho shūsō" (Various elements in the Qing control of the Han people). In vol. 1 of Ura, ed., *Tōyō kinseishi* (The modern history of East Asia) (Tokyo: Heibonsha, 1939), 5–112.

———. Shinchō no kokusui hōzon seisaku ni tsuite" (Qing policies for preserving the national essence). *Shigaku kenkyū* 1.1 (October 1931), 101–39.

———. Shoseidojō ni arawaretaru Shinchō no kanjin tōgyōsaku ni tsuite" (Qing policies for controlling Han Chinese as evidenced in various institutions). *Shigaku zasshi* 2.1 (July 1930), 61–83; 3 (April 1931), 59–78.

Uspensky, Vladimir. *Prince Yunli (1697–1738), Manchu Statesman and Tibetan Buddhist.* Tokyo: Institute for the Study of Languages and Cultures of Asia and Africa, 1997.

*Veritable Records.* See *Da Qing lichao shilu.*

Vollmer, John. *Decoding Dragons: Status Garments in Ch'ing Dynasty China.* Eugene: University of Oregon Museum of Art, 1983.

Wadley, Stephen. "The Mixed-Language Verses from the Manchu Dynasty in China." Indiana University Research Institute for Inner Asian Studies. *Papers on Inner Asia* 16 (1991), 60–112.

Wakeman, Frederic, Jr. *The Great Enterprise: The Manchu Reconstruction of Imperial Order in Seventeenth-Century China.* 2 vols. Berkeley and Los Angeles: University of California Press, 1985.

———. *Strangers at the Gate.* Berkeley and Los Angeles: University of California Press, 1966.

Waldron, Arthur. *The Great Wall of China.* Cambridge: Cambridge University Press, 1990.

Waley-Cohen, Joanna. "Commemorating War in Eighteenth-Century China." *Modern Asian Studies* 30.4 (October 1996), 869–99.

———. *Exile in Mid-Qing China*. New Haven, Conn.: Yale University Press, 1991.

Walker, David. *The Normans in Britain*. Oxford: Blackwell, 1995.

Wang Daocheng. "Cong Xue Pan song mei daixuan tanqi: Guanyu Qingdai de xiunü zhidu" (Let's begin by talking about the story of Xue Pan sending his sister to be selected: On the Qing xiunü system). *Beijing shiyuan* 3 (1985), 303–16.

Wang Qingyun. *Shiqu yuji* (Superfluous records of the imperial court). 6 *juan*. 1850. Reprint, Beijing: Beijing guji chubanshe, 1985.

Wang Shizhen. *Chibei outan* (Random talks north of the pond). 29 *juan*. 1700. 2-vol. reprint, Beijing: Zhonghua shuju, 1982; 2nd printing, 1984.

Wang Songling. "Lüelun Qingdai fengxiang zhidu de tedian" (Brief discussion of the special traits of the Qing system of salary and grain payments). *Qingshi yanjiu tongxun* 1987.1, 1–5.

Wang, Xiangyun. "Tibetan Buddhism at the Court of Qing: The Life and Work of lCang-sKya Rol-pa'i-rdo-rje (1717–1786)." Ph.D. diss., Harvard University, 1995.

Wang Zhonghan. "Guanyu Manzu xingchengzhong de jige wenti" (Some problems in the formation of the Manchu nationality). In Wang Zhonghan ed., *Manzushi yanjiu ji* (Beijing: Zhongguo shehuikexue chubanshe, 1988), 1–16.

———. "Qingdai baqizhong de Man-Han minzu chengfen wenti" (The question of the proportion of Manchus and Han in the Eight Banners). In Wang Zhonghan, *Qingshi xukao* (Taipei: Huashi chubanshe, 1993), 43–79.

———. *Qingshi xinkao* (New studies on the Qing). Shenyang: Liaoning daxue chubanshe, 1990.

———. *Qingshi zakao* (Miscellaneous studies on Qing history). Beijing: Renmin chubanshe, 1957.

Watt, John R. "The Yamen and Urban Administration." In G. William Skinner, ed., *The City in Late Imperial China* (Stanford, Calif.: Stanford University Press, 1977), 353–90.

Wei Qingyuan. "Qingdai Kangxi shiqi 'shengxi yinliang' zhidu de chuchuang he yunyong" (The foundation and use of the "interest-bearing silver" system in the Kangxi period). In *Ming-Qing shi bianxi* (Analyses of Ming-Qing history) (Beijing: Zhongguo shehui kexue chubanshe, 1989), 166–85.

———. "Qingdai Qianlong shiqi 'shengxi yinliang' zhidu de shuaibai he 'shouche'" (The decline and "gathering in" of the "interest-bearing silver" system in the Qianlong period). In *Ming-Qing shi bianxi* (Analyses of Ming-Qing history) (Beijing: Zhongguo shehui kexue chubanshe, 1989), 229–56.

———. "Qingdai Yongzheng shiqi 'shengxi yinliang' zhidu de zhengdun he zhengce yanbian" (The reorganization and policy evolution within the "interest-bearing silver" system in the Yongzheng period). In *Ming-Qing shi bianxi* (Analyses of Ming-Qing history) (Beijing: Zhongguo shehui kexue chubanshe, 1989), 186–228.

Wei Qingyuan, Wu Qiyan, and Lu Su. *Qingdai nubei zhidu* (The slave system in the Qing). Beijing: Zhongguo renmin daxue chubanshe, 1982.

Wei Yuan. *Shengwu ji* (Record of military glories). 14 *juan*. 2 vols. 1846. Reprint, Beijing: Zhonghua shuju, 1984.

Wilkinson, Endymion. *Chinese History: A Manual*. Cambridge: Harvard University Asia Center, 1998.

Wittfogel, Karl, and Feng Chia-sheng. *History of Chinese Society: Liao, 907–1125*. Philadelphia: American Philosophical Society, 1949.

Wong, R. Bin, and Pierre-Etienne Will. *Nourish the People: The State Civilian Granary System in China, 1650–1850*. Ann Arbor: The University of Michigan Center for Chinese Studies, 1991.

Wright, Mary Clabaugh. *The Last Stand of Chinese Conservatism: The T'ung-chih Restoration, 1862–1874*. Stanford, Calif.: Stanford University Press, 1957.

Wu, Ben. "Ritual Music in the Court and Rulership of the Qing Dynasty (1644–1911)." Ph.D. diss., University of Pittsburgh, 1998.

Wu Changyuan. *Chenyuan shilue* (Description of Beijing and environs). 16 *juan*. 1788. Reprint, Beijing: Beijing guji chubanshe, 1981.

Wu Hui. *Jingtianzhi kaosu* (Inquiry into the well-field system). Beijing: Nongye chubanshe, 1985.

Wu Wei-p'ing. "The Development and Decline of the Eight Banners." Ph.D. diss., University of Pennsylvania, 1970.

Wu Yuanfeng. "Qingdai neige Manwen dang'an shulüe" (Outline of the Manchu archives of the Qing grand secretariat). *Manxue yanjiu* 2 (1994), 274–85.

Wu Yuanfeng, and Zhao Zhiqiang. "Xibo zu xiqian gaishu" (Description of the westward migration of the Sibe). *Minzu yanjiu* 1980.2, 22–29.

Wu Zhengge. *Manzu shisu yu Qinggong yushan* (Culinary habits of the Manchus and cooking in the Qing imperial palace). Shenyang: Liaoning kexue jishu chubanshe, 1988.

Wu Zhenyu. *Yangjizhai conglu* (Notes from the Yangji studio). 26 + 10 *juan*. Preface dated 1896. Reprint, Hangzhou: Zhejiang guji chubanshe, 1985.

Wu Zhijian. "Qingdai qianqi Manzhou benwei zhengce de niding yu tiao-zheng" (The formation and adjustment of the Manchus-first policy in the early Qing). *Guoli Taiwan shifan dazue lishixuebao* 22 (June 1994), 85–117.

*Xi'an fuzhi* (Gazetteer of Xi'an prefecture). 80 + 1 *juan*. Ed. Le-er-jin, Bi Ran, Shu-qi-shen et al. 1779.

Xiao Fu and Tu Changsheng, eds. *Xibozu jianshi* (A short history of the Sibe nationality). Beijing: Minzu chubanshe, 1986.

*Xibozu dang'an shiliao* (Historical materials on the Sibe). 2 vols. First Historical Archives, Shenyang: Liaoning minzu chubanshe, 1989.

Xie Guozhen. *Mingqing zhi ji dangshe yundong kao* (Study of partisan movements in the Ming and Qing). Beijing: Zhonghua shuju, 1982.

*Xinjiang Manzu* (The Manchus of Xinjiang). Urumqi: n.p., n.d.

Yamamoto Mamoru. "Manshūgo *nikan* no igi" (The meaning of *nikan* in Manchu). *Shirin* 20.3 (July 1935), 163–67.

Yan Chongnian. "Manzhou guizu yu saman wenhua" (The Manchu aristocracy and shamanic culture). *Manxue yanjiu* 2 (1995), 119–39.

———. *Nu-er-ha-chi zhuan* (A biography of Nurhaci). Beijing: Beijing chubanshe, 1983.

Yang Lien-sheng. "Historical Notes on the Chinese World Order." In John K. Fairbank, ed., *The Chinese World Order* (Cambridge: Harvard University Press, 1968), 20–33.

Yang Qiqiao. *Yongzhengdi ji qi mizhe zhidu yanjiu* (Study of the Yongzheng emperor and his secret memorial system). Rev. ed., Hong Kong: Sanlian shudian, 1985.

Yang Xuechen. "Lüelun Qingdai Man-Han guanxi de fazhan he bianhua" (Brief discussion of the development and changes in the relationship between Manchus and Han in the Qing). *Minzu yanjiu* 1981.6, 16–26.

———, and Zhou Yuanlian. *Qingdai baqi wanggong guizu xingshuai shi* (The rise and fall of the Eight Banner nobility in the Qing). Shenyang: Liaoning renmin chubanshe, 1986.

Yang Yang. *Mingdai Liaodong dusi* (The Liaodong *dusi* in the Ming). Zhengzhou: Zhongzhou guji chubanshe, 1988.

Yang Yang, Yuan Lükun, and Fu Langyun. *Mingdai Nu-er-gan dusi ji qi weisuo yanjiu* (Studies on the *dusi* and *weisuo* of Ming Nurgan). Zhengzhou: Zhongzhou shuhuashe, 1982.

Yao Lingxi, ed. *Caifei lu* (Record of gathered fragrance). Tianjin: Tianjin shidai gongsi, 1936.

Yao Nianci. "Huang Taiji dujia lianghuangqi kaobian" (An inquiry into Hong Taiji's seizing sole control of the two yellow banners). In Wang Zhonghan, ed., *Manxue Chaoxianxue lunji* (Beijing: Zhongguo chengshi chubanshe, 1995), 75–98.

———. "Manzu baqizhi guojia chutan" (Preliminary discussion of the Manchus' Eight-banner state). Ph.D. diss., Central Minorities Institute, Beijing, 1991.

Yao Ts'ung-wu [Yao Congwu]. "Nüzhen hanhua de fenxi" (An analysis of the sinification of the Jurchen). *Dalu zazhi* 6.3. Collected in *Dalu zazhi shixue congshu* 1.5, 278–89.

Yao Yuanzhi. *Zhuyeting zaji* (Miscellaneous jottings of the willow-leaf pavilion). 8 *juan*. 1893. Reprint, Beijing: Zhonghua shuju, 1982.

Yelvington, Kevin. "Ethnicity as Practice? A Comment on Bentley." *Comparative Studies in Society and History* 33.1 (January 1991), 158–75.

Yi Minwhan. *Jianzhou wenjian lu* (*Konchu mun'gyon rok*) (Record of things heard and seen in Jianzhou). Ca. 1619. Reprint, Shenyang: Liaoning daxue lishixi, 1978.

*Yong-Qian liangchao xianghongqidang* (Bordered Red Banner archives from the Yongzheng and Qianlong reigns). Trans. Guan Jialu and Tong Yonggong. Shenyang: Liaoning renmin chubanshe, 1987.

*Yongzheng chao Hanwen zhupi zouzhe huibian* (Collected Chinese-language palace memorials of the Yongzheng reign). 33 vols. Beijing: First Historical Archives and Jiangsu guji chubanshe, 1989–91.

*Yongzhengchao qijuzhu ce* (Diaries of activity and repose from the Yongzheng reign). 5 vols. Beijing: Zhonghua shuju, 1993.

Yu Minzhong, ed. *Rixia jiuwen kao* (Examination of the history of Beijing). 160 *juan*. 1788. 4-vol. reprint, Beijing: Beijing guji chubanshe, 1958.

*Yuxing qiwu zouyi/Hesei yabubuha hacilame wesimbuhe gūsai baita* (Memorials in response to edicts on banner affairs). 1735. 2-vol. reprint, Taipei: Xuesheng shuju, 1976.

*Yuzhi zengding Qingwen jian/Han-i araha nonggime toktobuha manju gisun-i bulekū bithe* (Revised and enlarged dictionary of the Manchu language, imperially ordained). 32 + 4 *juan*. 1771.

YZHaZZH. See *Yongzheng chao Hanwen zhupi zouzhe huibian.*

YZMaPZZZ. See *Yongzheng chao Manwen zhupi zouzhe* under Archival Sources.

Zelin, Madeleine. *The Magistrate's Tael: Rationalizing Fiscal Reform in Eighteenth-Century Ch'ing China.* Berkeley and Los Angeles: University of California Press, 1984.

Zeng-shou [Dzengšeo]. *Beye i cooha bade yabuha babe ejehe bithe/Suijun jixing yizhu* (A record of my military exploits). Ed. and trans. Ji Yonghai. Beijing: Zhongyang minzu xueyuan chubanshe, 1987.

Zhang Bofeng, comp. *Qingdai gedi jiangjun dutong dachen deng nianbiao* (Chronological tables of garrison generals, banner commanders, and important officials of all regions in the Qing period). Beijing: Zhonghua shuju, 1977.

Zhang Boquan. "Lun Jindai meng-an mo-ke zhidu de xingcheng, fazhan ji qi pohuai de yuanyin" (Discussion of the formation of the *meng-an mo-ke* system during the Jin dynasty, its development, and the reasons for its collapse). In *Liao-Jin shi lunwen ji* (Shenyang: Liaoning renmin chubanshe, 1985), 343–71.

Zhang Boquan, et al. *Jinshi lungao.* Changchun: Jilin wenshi chubanshe, 1986.

Zhang Jinfan, and Guo Chengkang. *Qing ruguanqian guojia falü zhidu shi* (History of the Qing national legal system before the conquest). Shenyang: Liaoning renmin chubanshe, 1988.

Zhang Jinfan. *Qingchao fazhi shi* (A history of the legal system in the Qing dynasty). Beijing: Falü chubanshe, 1994.

Zhang Juling. *Qingdai Manzu zuojia wenxue gailun* (A sketch of Manchu authors and literature in the Qing). Beijing: Zhongyang minzu xueyuan chubanshe, 1990.

Zhang Qiyun, ed. *Qingshi* (The history of the Qing). 10 vols. Taipei: Guofang yanjiuyuan, 1961.

Zhang Yuxing, ed. *Qingdai dongbei liuren shixuanzhu* (Selected poems of Qing exiles to the Northeast). Shenyang: Liaoshen chubanshe, 1988.

Zhao Yi. *Yanpu zaji* (Miscellaneous notes exposed on the eaves). 6 *juan.* 1829. Reprint, Beijing: Zhonghua shuju, 1982.

Zhao Yuntian. *Qingdai Menggu zhengjiao zhidu* (The military and religious systems of Mongolia in the Qing period). Beijing: Zhonghua shuju, 1989.

Zhao Zhan. *Manzu wenhua yu zongjiao yanjiu* (Studies in Manchu culture and religion). Shenyang: Liaoning minzu chubanshe, 1993.

Zhao Zhizhong. "*Ni-shan saman* yu zongjiao" (The Nišan Shamaness and religion). In Wang Zhonghan, ed., *Manxue Chaoxianxue lunji* (Beijing: Zhongguo chengshi chubanshe, 1995), 174–98.

Zhao-lian. *Xiaoting zalu/xulu* (Miscellaneous notes from the whistling pavilion). 10 *juan.* 1814–26. Reprint, Taipei: Hongwenguan chubanshe, 1986.

*Zhejiang tongzhi* (Comprehensive gazetteer of Zhejiang). 280 + 3 *juan.* Ed. Shen Yiji et al. 1735.

Zheng Qin. *Qingdai sifa shenpan zhidu yanjiu* (Study of the legal and judicial system in the Qing). Changsha: Hunan jiaoyu chubanshe, 1988.

Zheng Tianting. *Tanweiji* (Arcane explorations). Beijing: Zhonghua shuju, 1980.

Zhen-jun. *Tianchi ouwen* (Random notes on the capital). 10 *juan*. Postface
   dated 1894. Reprint, Beijing: Beijing guji chubanshe, 1982.
*Zhongguo diyi lishi dang'anguan* (First Historical Archives of China). "Dao-
   guang chu chouyi baqi shengji shiliao" (Historical materials dealing with
   Eight Banner livelihood in the early Daoguang reign). *Lishi dang'an*
   1994.2, 3–12.
———. "Yongzheng monian bofang zhufang guanbing xiangxu shiliao"
   (Historical materials on the salaries paid to soldiers and officers at the
   garrisons in the late Yongzheng reign). *Lishi dang'an* 1986.3, 13–16.
———. *Zhongguo diyi lishi dang'anguan guancang dang'an gaishu*
   (Introduction to the archival holdings of the First Historical Archives).
   Beijing: Dang'an chubanshe, 1985.
*Zhongshu zhengkao* (Administrative treatise of the military apparatus). 4 *ce*.
   Ed. Mingju and Zhu Zhibi. 1672.
[*Qinding*] *Zhongshu zhengkao* (Administrative treatise of the military
   apparatus, imperially ordained). 15 *juan*. 1785.
Zhu Delan. "Qingchu qianjielingshi Zhongguo chuan haishang maoyi zhi
   yanjiu" (Maritime commerce by Chinese ships during the early Qing
   coastal blockade). In *Zhongguo haiyang fazhan shi* (Taipei: Academic
   Sinica, 1986), 2: 105–60.
Zito, Angela, and Tani E. Barlow. *Body, Subject, and Power in China*. Chicago:
   University of Chicago Press, 1994.

# INDEX

In this index an "f" after a number indicates a separate reference on the next page, and an "ff" indicates separate references on the next two pages. A continuous discussion over two or more pages is indicated by a span of page numbers. Page numbers in italics refer to figure captions or tables.

*Aba*, 57, 184, *185*
"Absorption Theory," 27, 29
Accompanying-in-death, 229
Acculturation (assimilation; Ch *tonghua*), 27f: later Manchus seen as assimilated, 16, 31, 353; the Manchus not disappearing as a group, 12, 304, 353; and the Manchu Way, 276–84, 289, 295, 342; pace as increasing in eighteenth century, 255, 299, 342; as usual answer to Manchu question, 3, 386n96; Yongzheng emperor on, 349, 351. *See also* Ethnic identity; Manchu language; Sinicization
Adjutant (*yin-wu zhang-jing; janggin*), 187, 422n126
Adopted children, 323f, 331, 333, 494n74
Agūda, 276
Agūi, 205
*Aha*, 51, 82ff, 438n151. *See also* Slaves
Aisin Gioro, 46, 52, 65, 79, 238, 502n4
Akdun, 205
Akina (Insy), 469n51
Alexander, William, 442n18
A-li-ma, 344–45, 501n1
"Altaic School," 28, 31–32
Alu, 156–59, 434n108, 472n78
*Amba janggin* ("great general"), 125f
*Amban* (state counselor), 62
Amin, 99
Amiot, Joseph Marie, 485n82

*Aniya aliha gūsa. See* Banner Inspectorate
Anhui, 154
An Lushan, 91
Archery, 179–80; bannermen test-takers having to prove their skills in, 204–5; bow strength, 179, 441n18; contests in, 179, 441n17; decline in, 278, 282, 283–84; Hangzhou improvement in, 280; and the Manchu Way, 8, 276, 347, 441n27; shooting from horseback, 180, *181*, 377n24
Arigūn, 261f, 264, 266, 431n77
Armor, 177. *See also* Equipment
Arsai (Cui Zhilu), 245, 469n51
Artillery and Musketry Division (*huoqi ying; tuwa agūrai kūwaran*), 81
Assimilation. *See* Acculturation
Audience system, 163f

Baigiyei, 151
Bandi, 157ff, 435n110
Banishment, 200
Banner commander (*dutong; gūsa ejen; gūsa be kadalara amban*): in banner administration, 138; in banner command structure, 135–36; in capital Eight Banners, *365*; in expeditionary garrisons, 126; as garrison commander, 96, 413n30; in political structure, 62
Banner elevation (*tai qi; gūsa doobumbi*), 86

decline of, 290–99, 352; documents in, 20, 291, 301, 346, 374n4, 383n69, 437n128, 488n120; and ethnicity, 68–71; in examinations, 204; glorified, 301; imperial efforts to encourage study of, 11; Jesuits learning, 292, 485n82; Jurchens as speaking, 68, 295–96; in Manchu Way, 8, 276f, 290, 296, 299–304, 377n23; and Mongolian language, 485n79; as more precise than Chinese, 485n82; and names, 243; as "national language," 291, 301; ; as never disappearing altogether, 291, 301, 487n96, 488n119; nuances of, 169; as a security language, 291; in use at court, 488n21; word for emperor, 397n77; word for general, 422n126; as written language, 70

Manchu question, 3, 12, 25, 31, 346, 355–61

Manchuria (*Dongbei*; "Northeast") 56, 63, 93, 125, 131, 263: banner population in, 117; civil commissioner in, 226; in early seventeenth century, 49; Eight Banners garrisons in, 94, 122, 195, 308; *gurun* in, 67; Han Chinese forbidden to migrate to, 67–68; as home to all bannermen, 256, 258; hunting in, 183f; land system in, 62; life in China contrasted with that in, 131–32; in Manchu memory, 458n46; Manchu population in, 43; mapping of, 68; in new Chinese nation-state, 357, 359; as place name, 391n9; in Qing empire, 357

*Manchu Rites for Sacrifices to the Spirits and to Heaven*, 238, 240f

Manchus: acculturation and assimilation into Chinese society, 3, 12, 16, 25–32, 255, 270, 352, 386n96, 503n28; in banner administration, 136; as "barbarians" to Han Chinese, 21, 22–25, 264, 356; bias against Han Chinese, 78, 167ff, 211, 338; British view of, 208; career advantages enjoyed by, 201–207, 215; characteristic customs and practices of, 8, 207, 224, 231, 234–55, 287–88, 313, 322, 346, 377n23; as compared to Mongols, 68f; competing views of, 20–26; culture of dependency among, 207, 284; as descendants of Qing bannermen, 43; diaspora of, 124,

255–71, 275; diet, 287; duty to family, 165–67; after fall of Qing dynasty, 387n98; fear of among Han Chinese, 128; fear of ethnic bias against as phobia of, 170, 233; gulf between Han and, 170, 207–209, 349; Han Chinese outnumbering, 3, 207; under Hong Taiji, 63–72; honor of, 166–68, 171, 218, 253, 280n47; idea of home for, 256–71; image of, 159, 176, 207–208, 322; intermarriage with Han Chinese, 254–55; literacy among, 293–94, 301, 489n92; the Manchu-Han family, 212–16, 226, 336, 359; "Manchuness" of, 168, 234–55, 276, 290, 352–53; meaning of "Manchu," 71–72, 402n116; as "men in stirrups," 300; mentality of, 215; military prowess of, 1, 205, 277, 358; Ming dynasty overthrown by, 1–2; as minority group in China today, 42–43, 488n125; myths of origins of, 42–47, 65; name adopted, 63, 71–72; names of, 241–46; neo-Confucianism sponsored by, 3f, 13, 28; new narratives of, 32–35; never appointed as magistrates, 219; origins of, 39–88; origins of name of, 47; as part of "Chinese people," 361; poor eyesight claimed by, 205; population growth of, 43, 363–64; posts reserved for, 133, 201–203, 226, 335; as protectors of the Chinese, 99, 228f; as "people of the banners" (*qiren*), 13f, 133, 208; as *qizu*, 15; as Other, 32, 234f, 270, 345; relations with Han Chinese, 3, 78, 167–70, 210–33, 349–50; relations with Mongols, 358; rights passed on to other, 331f; as sailors, 182; separate prisons for, 198; shamanism of, 235–41; sinicization of, 25–26, 276–77ff; smallpox vulnerability of, 400n108; softening of, 10–12, 279, 282; solidarity among, 164–67, 276, 356; special relationship with emperor, 164, 214; synthesis with Han Chinese, 29–30; "Tartar" origins of, 24; victimized by Han merchants, 222, 315, 460n60; women's place among, 246–55, 352. *See also* Eight Banners; Jurchens; Manchu identity; Qing dynasty

*Manchu Veritable Records (Manju-i*